Select Original Descriptive Documents on

The History of Santal Parganas, Bhagalpur and Monghyr (1770-1947)

Select Original Descriptive Documents on

The History of Santal Parganas, Bhagalpur and Monghyr (1770-1947)

Based on a Research-Project Report of Indian council of Historical Research (ICHR), New Delhi

Editor

Dr. Surendra Jha (Retd.)

Former Head,
University Department of History
S.K.M. University Dumka
(Jharkhand)

PATHAK PUBLISHER AND DISTRIBUTORS
New Delhi (INDIA)

Select Original Descriptive Documents on the History of Santal Parganas, Bhagalpur and Monghyr (1770-1947)

Editor : Dr. Surendra Jha

ISBN : 978-93-91952-97-6

Price : 4500/-

First Edition: 2024

Published by :
PATHAK PUBLISHER AND DISTRIBUTORS
E-6/33c & 34, Ground Floor, Sangam Vihar
New Delhi-110080
E-mail: pathakppd@gmail.com

In Association with :
RESEARCH INDIA PRESS

Typographic Design by: G. R. Sharma

Printed in India

Contents

3	William Harwood, Collector of Rajmahal.	Hon'ble Warren Hastings, Esq. President and Gentleman of the Committee of Circuit at Cossimbuzar.	10th Aug. ,1772	32-33
4	Warren Hastings, Samuel Middleton P. M. Dacres (Philip Milner Dacres) J. Graham. James Lawrell. Cossimbuzar (Cassimbazar)	Mr. William Harwood Collector of Rajmahal	24th Aug. . 1772	33-34
5	Samuel Middleton John Bathoe. Alexander Higginson. Moorshedbad	Mr. William Harwood Collector of Rajmahal and Boglepore	8th Sep. 1772,	34
6	Warren Hastings, Samuel Middleton P. M. Dacres (Philip Milner Dacres) J. Graham. James Lawrell. Cossimbuzar	Mr. William Harwood Collector of Rajmahal	13th Sep. ,1772	34-35
7	J. Stewart,Secretary, Fort William, Rajmahal	Mr. William Harwood Collector of Rajmahal	10th Oct. ,1772	35-36
8	Warren Hastings Fort William	Mr. William Harwood Collector of Rajmaul (Rajmahal)	13th Oct. 1772	36
9	Warren Hastings. P. M. Dacres. H. Goodwin. J. Graham George Vansittart Fort William,	Mr. James Barton, Collector of Rajemehall (Rajmahal)& Boglepore (Bhagalpur).	22nd Oct. 1773.	37-38
10	Warren Hastings, W. Aldersey. P. M. Dacres ,H. Goodwin J. Graham. George Vansittart. Fort William	James Barton, Collectorof Rajmehal	29th Oct. 1773	38-39

Chapter III
From Bhagalpur Collectorate Records (now kept in Bihar state Archives, Patna). Letters regarding Brooke, Browne and Cleveland Systems

16.	C. Chapman, Acting Collector, Bhagalpur	Captain James Browne, Commanding the Light Infantry.	11 April 1778 (Roshan-Baksh)	80-81
17.	James Barton ,	Warren Hastings, Calcutta,Revenue Proceeding 5 May, 1778	30 Apr. , 1778,	81-84
18.	Augustus Cleveland, Collector, Bhagalpur	Warren Hasting, Governor-General, Bhagalpur	13Jan. 1780	84-87

Records related to Cleveland system genesis and deterioration

19.	Augustus Cleveland, Begleypore	William Hosea, Chief Secretary Provincial Council at Murshiabad	3 Apr., 1780	87-88
20.	Cleveland	Warren Hastings,	1Jul. ,1780.	88-89
21	Augustus Cleveland, Collector, Bhagalpur	Governor – General and Council,	19Sep. 1780	89-91
22	Augustus Cleveland, Collector, Bhagalpur	Governor General and Council,	Ammar 19 Feb. 1781	91-92
23	Augustus Cleveland Collector, Bhagalpur	David Anderson, President and Committee of Revenue, Fort William,	6 Apr. ,1781	93
24	(Revenue Department, Original Consultations,		22 Aug. 1781	94
25	Augustus Cleveland, Collector, Bhagalpur	The Board of Revenue,	23 July,1782	94-95
26 26 A	Augustus Cleveland Collector, Bhagalpur Reply of the letter	The Board of Revenue, Fort William.	9 Aug., 1782	95-96
27	Augustus Cleveland, Collector, Bhagalpur	William Brooke, Chief of Purnea	23 Aug., 1782	99-97
28	C. Chapman, Collector, Bhagalpur,	William Taylor, Resident at Beerbhoom,	2 Jan. 1784	97-99
29	C. Chapman, Collector, Bhagalpur,	David Anderson, President Committee of Revenue,	3 Jan. 1784	99-100

30	C. Chapman, Collector, Bhagalpur,	Thomas Graham, President and members of the committee of revenue of grain, Fort William,	28th Jan. 1784.	100-102
31	C. Chapman, Collector, Bhagalpur	David Anderson, President Committee of Revenue,	31 Jan., 1784.	102-103
32	C. Chapman, Collector, Bhagalpur,	Warren Hastings and Council of Revenue, Fort William,	31 Jan. 1784.	103-105
33	C. Chapman, Acting Collector, Bhagalpur	Captain James Browne, Commanding the Light Infantry.	20 Jul. , 1784	106-107
34	C. Chapman, Acting Collector, Bhagalpur	Samauel Charters, Acting President of Committee of Revenue at Fort William	10Aug. 1784	108-109
35	C. Chapman, Acting Collector, Bhagalpur	Samauel Charters, Acting President of Committee of Revenue at Fort William	14 Sept. 1784	110
36	C. Chapman, Collector, Bhagalpur	David Anderson, President, Committee of Revenue at Fort William John Shore, President,	20 Nov. 1784	110
37	C. Chapman, Collector, Bhagalpur	Acting President, Committee of Revenue	28 Dec. 1784,	111-112
38	Roop Narain Deos Petition to governor sent	at Fort William,		112
39	C. Chapman, Collector, Bhagalpur,	Warren Hasting and Council of Revenue, Fort William	December 1784.	113-114
40	J. Fombelle, Acting Collector, Bhagalpur	Charles Butler, Secretary to the Board of Revenue Calcutta,	20 July –	115-120

Chapter IV

Chapter V
Judicial Records

32	Henry St. George Tucker, Sub-Secretary to Government in the Judicial Department.	J. Fombelle, Magistrate of Bhagulpur. 1	11thNov. 1796	238-239
33	J. Fombelle, Magistrate of Bhagulpur.	MajorHutchinson, Regualating Officer of the Invaild Establishment. 1	1st Feb. 1797	239-240
34	J. Fombelle, Judge-Magistrate of Bhagulpur.	G. H. Barlow, Secretary to Government.	27thFeb. 1797	240-241
35	G……. ., Assistant Regulating Officer of the Invaild Establishments at Bhagalpur,	John Fombelle, Judge Magistrate of Bhagulpur. 1	2ndMar. 1797	242
36	J. Fombelle, Judge-Magistrate of Bhagulpur.	Captain Shaw, Commanding the Crops of Hill Rangers at Bhagaplur.	4thApril, 1797.	242-243
37	Henry St. George Tucker, Sub-Secretary to Government in the Judicial Department.	John Fombelle, Magistrate of Bhagulpur.	7thApril, 1797	243-244
38	John Fombelle, Judge Magistrate of Bhagulpur	George Dickinson, Collector of Bhagalpur	11thMay, 1797	244
39	John Fombelle, Magistrate of Bhagulpur	Richard Ahmuty, Register to the Court of Circuit of Murshidabad Division. 1	13thMay, 1797	245-246
40	John Fombelle, Judge Magistrate of Bhagulpur	George Dickinson, Collector of Bhagalpur. 3	18thSep. 1797	246
41	George Dickinson, Collector of Bhagalpur.	John Fombelle, Judge-Magistrate of Bhagulpur.	19thSep, 1797	247
42	John Fombelle, Magistrate of Bhagulpur.	Henry St. George Tucker, Sub Secretary to Government in the Judicial Department.	27th Sep, 1797. Ranisarbeshwan	247-249

53	T. SHAW, Major Commanding, H. Sangers, Bhagalpur,	John Fombelle, …… Judge and Magistrate.)	22 Apr. 1801	277-278
54	J. Wintle, Magistrate of Bhagalpur,	G. Dowdeswell, Secretary to Government in the Judicial Department. 4.	5thMar. 1803	279-282
55	J. Wintle, Magistrate of Bhagalpur,	G. Dowdeswell, Secretary to Government in the Judicial Department. 1	5thApril, 1803.	282-283
56	G. Dowdeswell, Secretary to Government in the Judicial Department	J. Wintle, Magistrate of Bhagalpur. 2	11thApril, 1803	283-284
57	T. Shaw, Major of Hill Rangers Bhagalpur,	James Wintle, Magistrate of Zillah Bhagalpur	21thApril1803,	284-285
58	J. Wintle, Magistrate of Bhagalpur,	G. Dowdeswell, Secretary to Government in the Judicial Department. 4	10th May, 1803.	285-287
59	Acting magistrate of Beerbhum,	J. Wintle, Magistrate of Bhagalpur.	16thJune, 1803.	288-289
60	T. Shaw, Major Commanding, Hill Rangers, Bhagalpur,	James Wintle, Magistrate of Zillah Bhagalpur	11 July, 1803,	288-289
61	T. Shaw, Major Commanding Hill Rangers, Bhagalpur,	James Wintle, Maglistrate Zillah of Bhagalpur.	12 July 1803,	289-290
62	……. . (Illegible), Fort William	James Wintle, Magistrate of Zillah Bhagalpur.	15 July1803,	290-292

63	W. Spending, Acting Magistrate, Zillah Beerbhoom, Fouzdaree Adwlat,	George Dodeswell, Secretary to Government in the Judicial Department.	15 July1803,	292-293
64	G. Dowdeswell, Secretary to Government in the Judicial Department,	J. Wintle, Magistrate of Bhagalpur. 1.	21stJuly, 1803.	294-296
65	J. Wintle, Magistrate of Bhagalpur,	G. Dowdeswell, Secretary to Government in the Judicial Department. 1	27thJuly, 1803.	296-302
66	J. Wintle, Magistrate of Bhagalpur,	G. Dowdeswell, Secretary to Government in the Judicial Department. 1	1stAug. 1803.	302-303
67	J. Wintle, Magistrate of Bhagalpur,	G. Dowdeswell, Secretary to Government in the Judicial Department. 2	2nd Aug., 1803.	303-306
68	G. Dowdeswell, Secretary to Government in the Judicial Department	J. Wintle, Magistrate of Bhagalpur. 2	11th Aug, 1803.	306
69	J. Wintle, Magistrate of Bhagalpur,	J. Lumsden, Secretary to Government in the Judicial Department. 1.	15thAug., 1803.	307-312
70	G. Dowdeswell, Chief Secretary to Government	J. Wintle, Magistrate of Bhagalpur. 2	22nd Sept., 1803	312
71	J. Wintle, Magistrate of Bhagalpur,	T. H. Ernst, Magistrate of Beerbhoom. 2.	13th Oct., 1803	313
72	J. Wintle, Magistrate of Bhagalpur,	H. Pary, Acting Magistrate of Beerbhoom. 1.	12th Nov., 1803	313-314
73	J. Wintle, Magistrate of Bhagalpur,	J. Miller, Magistrate of Ramghur. 2	12thNov., 1803.	314-315

87	T. Shaw Major, Commanding HillRangers, Bhagalpur	J. Wintle, Magistrate of Bhagalpur	8 Nov., 1804	334-335
88	C. R. Blunt Magistrate of Beerbhum,	G. Dowdeswell, Secretary to Government in the Judicial Department. 3	29thNov., 1804	336
89.	J. Wintle, Magistrate of Bhagalpur.	G. Dowdeswell, Secretary to Government in the Judicial Department.	31stDec., 1804, Calcutta	336-338
90	J. Wintle, Magistrate of Bhagalpur,	G. Dowdeswell, Secretary to Government in the Judicial Department.	15th Jan., 1805	338-339
91	J. D. Erstine, Acting, Collector, Zillah Bhagulpur	Thomas Graham, Acting President and Members of the Board of Revenue, Fort William,	16 Jan. 1805.	339-340
92	J. D. Erstine, Acting, Collector, Zillah Bhagulpur	Charles Buller, Secretary to the Board of Revenue, Fort William,	24th Jan. 1805	340-341
93	F. Hamilton, Acting Collector, Zilla Bhagalpur,	Charles Buller, Secreatary to the Board of Revenue,	6 Feb. 1805	341-342
94	Translation of the Deposition of Meer Feyuz Ally, Darogah of Rajmahal taken on the oath		8th Feb. 1805	342-347
95	Extract from a letter from, Dr. Francis Buchanan dated the 1st February 1805.			347-348

Chapter VI
Revenue Records

15	" Translation of an Arzee from Roopnarain Deo Sarbarahkar of Tuppa Da-khilcoonj the zemindary of Sheo Prasad Chowdry insance.			380
16	F. Hamilton, Collector, Bhagalpur,	Charles Buller, Secreatary to the Board of Revenue, Fort William.	3rd March. 1806	381
16 A	F. Hamilton, Collector, Bhagalpur,	Charles Buller, Secreatary to the Board of Revenue, Fort William.	13thMar. 1806	382
17	" Translate of a Darkhast for the Khod Bandobust in perpetuity of Kismat Pergannah Conkjol, Zillah Rajmahal by the proprietor Emam Baksh Chaudry from 1213 Bengal style dated 28th of Phagun 1212 B. S.			383
18	"Translate of the engage-ment entered into by Emam Baksh Chaudhry referred to in the Collec-tor's letter to the Board of Revenue dated the 13th of march 1806.			383-384
19	F. Hamilton, Collector, Bhagalpur,	Charles Buller, Secreatary to the Board of Revenue, Fort William.	14th Mar. 1806	384-385
20	F. Hamilton, Collector, Bhagalpur,	Charles Buller, Secreatary to the Board of Revenue, Fort William.	15thMar. 1806	385
21	F. Hamilton, Collector, Bhagalpur, William.	Charles Buller, Secreatary to the Board of Revenue, Fort William	6thMar., 1807	386

22	" Translation of an Arzee presented by Hira Ram Chaudhry Zemindar of Tuppah Chumpanagar.			386-387
23	F. Hamilton, Collector, Bhagalpur,	R. Thackeray Secretary to the Board of Revenue, Fort William. "I beg leave to acknowledge the receipt of your letter of the 14th current, and to submit a statement of the Malikanah due to Hira of the 25th of November last amounting to Sicca Rupees 257-3.	27th April 1807	387-388
24	"Translate of An Arzee presented by Bishnath Singh zemindar of Talookah Ummerpore= (Amarpur Banka), perganah Chye, and Tuppah Havelly Bhaudans, pergannah Furkeah (Pharkia), through his Vakil Peyare Lall.			388
25	Hamilton, Collector, Bhagalpur.	R. Thacker, Secretary to the Board of Revenue, Fort William	7th May1807	389
26	J. P. Ward, Acting Collector, Bhagalpur,	James Pattle, Acting President and Members of the Board of Revenue Lower Provinces, Fort William.	14thSept. 1822	389-392
27	V. T. Taylor, Collector of Bhagalpur,	The Commissioner of Bhagalpur,	23rd Mar. 1876.	393

Chapter VII
Davis Report and Browni's Plan

Chapter VIII
Sultanabad & Ambar Records

Chapter IX

8	R. I. R. CHANDSON Collr, of Beerbhoom. Soory,	Colonel Burney Commg. 56 N. I. Soory.	Sept. 12, 1855	468
9	R. I. RICHARDSON Collr, of Beerbhoom. Soory,	Colnel Burney Commg. 56 N. I. . Sorry	Sept. 13, 1855	468-469
10	R. L . RICHARDSON Collector of Beerbhoom. Sooree,	Colonel Burney Commanding at Sooree.	Sept. 21st/55	469-470
11	R. I. RICHARDSON Collr. Of Beerbhoom Soory	Magistrate Beerb-hoom	Sept. 28th /55.	470-471
12	R. I. RICHARDSON Collr, of Beerbhoom	Colonel Burney Soory,	Sept. 28th, 1855	471-472
13	R. I. RICHARDSON Collr, of Beerbhoom,	Col. Burney, Commanding at Soriy.	Sept. 28th /55.	472
14	R. I. RICHARDSON Collr, of Beerbhom Soory	Colonel Burney Commanding at Soory	Sept. 29th /55	472-473
14 (A)	R. I. RICHARDSON	Colonel Burney	Sept. 29th /55	473-474
15	R. I. RICHARDSON Collr, of Beerbhom Soory	Colonel, Commanding at Soory	Oct12th, 1855	475
15 A	Commissioners of Nuddea	The magistrate of Bhagalpur	15 Aug. 1855	476

Extracts from Some Important Letters Issued by the Commissioner, Special Commissioner and Other Officers Deputed in Connection with Santal Rebellion August 15 September 26, 1855

16	A. C. Bidwell spl. Commissions	V. Grey secretary to the govt. to Bengal	23 August 1855	477
17	J. M. Elliot offi. Commander	Collector of Beerbhum	23rd August 1855	478
18	J. M. Elliot offi. Commander	Collector of Beerbhum	28 August 1855	478-479

19	J. R. WANES	The Collector of Beerbhoom	5th Sept. 1855.	480-481
20	H. W. B. Gordon, Commander	The Magistrate of Monghyr,		481-482
21	J. R . Ward Commissioner on Special Duty	The Collector of Soory (Birbhum)	9thSept. 1855	482-484
22	No. 80 (Camp: Raneegunge, 10th sept, 1855) B. PAROTT CAPTAIN Major of Brigade	Directive		484
23	No. 134 Commer's Office, Burdwan Dn. Burdwan,	The offg. Collector of Beerbhoom	27th Sept. 1855	484
24	R. I. Richaroson Collector of Birbhum	Brigadier Bird	Sept. 13th1855	485
25	The Magistrate of Beerbhoom	The commissioner Burdwan	24THSEP., 1855	486-488
26	R. I. Richardson Collector of Birbhoom	J. R . Ward Commissioner Ranigang		488
27	Richardson	J. R. Ward spl. Commission	27th Oct, 1855	489-490
28	R. Thompson	Major General Lloyd	6th Dec. 1855	491
29	R. Thompson	Honble A. Eden Koomerabad	8th Dec. 1855	492
30	Robert I Richardson	Brigadier Bird Commanding in the Beerbhoom and Bancoorah District Sooree,	Dec. 9th 1855.	492-493
31	Rivers Thompson	W. Grey Esqr. Secy. To the Governmentof Bengal. Fort William.	11th Dec., 1855	493-495
32	Frances Lowth, Esqr. Session Judge of Beerbhoom.	RIVERS THOMPSON Offg . Magistrate Zillah Beerbhoom	19th Dec., 1855	495-497

33	R. I. RICHARDSON Collector Sooree	W. Grey . Esqr. Secretary to the Govt. of Bengal.	31 Ist Dec., 1855	497-499
34	Mr. A. R. Thompson Dy Commissioner.	H. Stainforth Esq. Commissioner	Doomkah 13th Feb. 1856.	499-500
35	No. 85 Mr. A. R. Thompson Dy Comm.	H. Stainforth Esq. Commissioner,	Doomkah 20th Feb. 1856.	501-507
36	No. 175 Mr. A. Rivers Thompson.	The Secretary to the Govt. Of Bengal.	Nya Doom-kah 26th Feb, 1856	507-509
37	No. 178 Sd. Rivers Thompson Dy. Com.	The session Judge of Beerbhoom.	Naya Doom-kah 27th Mar. 1856	510
38	278. From Mr. Thompson	Govt & Ooduy Money & Neha Bhola and others	27 march 1856	510-511
39	A. R. Thomson Dy. Com-missionr Dumka	H. Stainforth Commissioner	27th March 1856	511-513
40	No. 220 Sd. A. R. Thomson. Dy. com.	The Secretary to the Government of Bengal . Fort William	Naya Doomka 7 Apr. 1856	513-541
41	No. 247 Sd. Rivers Thompson Dy. Com. (S. P) List of Prison-ers who fled from Dumka Jail	B. Wood Esq. R. E. Ronald Esq. Assistant commis-sioner.	Nya Doom-kah 14th Apr. 1856	515-518
42	No. 256 Sd. A. R. Thomson Dy. Com	The magistrate of the Midnapoor	Nya Doom-kah 19 Apr. 1856	518-519
43	No. 62 sd. E. f. Lantour offg. collr. Collector's office Bhagalpur	J. Pontet Esquire, Superintendent of Damin Koh Bhagalpur	20 oct . 1854 Bhaugal-pore	519-520
44	No. 29 Sd. Et . Lautour Collector. Bhag	G. J Browne Esquire. Commissioner of Revenue Bhagal-pore.	7th may1855.	520

45	Sd. E. F. Lantour Collector Collector'Office, Bhagalpore	James Pontent Esquire Superintendent of Daminkoh, Bhagalpore,	30th Apr. 1855	521
46	Sd. E. F. Lantour Collector	G. F. Brown Esquire Commissioner of Revenue Bhagalpore		521-522

Post-Hul

Report to be submitted quarterly by all the assistant commissioner on the subject noted below.

47	Sd. R. E . Ronald Deoghar Asst Commissioner's office		2nd October 1857	522-523

No. 3

Report to be submitted quarterly by the entire assistant commissioner's office dumka on the subject noted below.

48	Sd/ Ni. G Baraddon Assist Commissioner.		27. 12. 1857	523-524

No. 96

Report to be submitted quarter ly all the assistant Commissioners on the subjects noted below:-

49	Sd. N. G. Braddon. Asst. Commissioner		1 July 1858	524-526

No. 218

Report to be submitted quarterly by all the assistant Commissioner,s office dumka on the subjects noted

50	E. N. G. Braddon. Assistant commissioner Deoghar	Brown Wood Esq. Assistant Commissioner Raj Mahal	camp Sarath July 30th 1858.	526-588

Chapter X

Chapter XI – Chotanagpur Records

Chapter XII

Chapter XIII – List of Freedom Fighters

Chapter XIV – The list of Martyrs -

Acknowledgements

First and foremost, I must acknowledge the debt of Indian Council of Historical Research (ICHR) 35, Feroze Shah Road, New Delhi. The ICHR granted a Research Project (No. F-1-29/2007-ICHR (SIA-III) RP entitled "The collection, preservation and annotated edition of records related to Santal Parganas (1757-1947)." I am grateful to ICHR. This book is based on the Report of the Project Submitted to ICHR.

I am grateful to late Dr. P.K.Datta, of Department of History, Patna University Patna, who was the son of late Dr. Kalikinkar Datta, the celebrated historian of Bihar. Late Dr. P.K.Datta had, in his possesion, the Old Zamindari Records of Bihar (Two volumes) edited by Dr. K.K.Datta. These records are still unpublished. Late Dr. P.K.Datta made available the Xeroxed copy of relevant documents to me, which have been included in this book. I shall ever remain grateful to him.

I am grateful to Sri Bijay Kumar Modak, of Howrah who made me available many rare documents and books which helped me much.

I am also grateful to the staff of different Archives and Record-rooms who co-operated with me.

I must express my thanks to my family members-my wife Smt. Ranju Jha, my sons, Pranav and Pratyush, my daughters Praveena and Priyanka and sons-in-law Sri Pawan kumar Mishra and Sri Samarjeet Jha.

I thank Prof. Rajeev Mishra of A.N. Inter College, Dumka and Mrs. Banani Ganguly who typed and computed the manuscript.

Lastly, I must thank Suman Kumar Pathak of Pathak Publishers & Distributors, New Delhi who kindly agreed to publish the book.

Introduction

This book is the fruit of a Research Project of Indian Council of Historical Research, (ICHR) 35, Feroze Shah Road New Delhi (vide letter no F. 1-29/2007-ICHR (GIA-III) RP dated-30.9.2008).

The Project had been granted for the collection, annotation and editing of British (Original) Documents related to Santal Parganas (1757-1947). This region was a part of Bhagalpur and Monghyr region. I have collected a few important documents, letters, correspondences etc. related to this region. Now, I want to present it in public gaze so that researchers may get and study these documents easily without taking trouble to go the Record Room and Archives. The documents have been collected from West Bengal Archives Kolkata, Bihar State Archives, Patna and Bhagalpur Record Room as well as from personal labour. In these documents, I have also included some important documents collected by late Dr. Kalikinkar Datta. His collection of Zamindari Records of Bihar (in Two volumes) is still unpublished. Due to the grace of his son, late Dr. P.K. Datta, I could get a xeroxed typed copy of the documents related to this region. Those records have been included in this book.

Besides many original letters and correspondences, of early CompanyRaj have also been collected which may give a clear picture of anarchy, mis-governance and diplomacy of early Company rulers. I think these documents will be very helpful for the research-scholars.

The Santal Hul and its related documents have been collected from West Bengal State Archives, Kolkata, Bihar State Archives, Patna, Record Rooms of Bhagalpur district and Santal Parganas district as well as from Chotanagpur records. Enquiry report of Bidwell as well as Santal Civil rules have also been included.

Besides all these, I have given an almost exhaustive list of 77 martyrs of 1942 movement and an exhaustive list of freedom fighters and early revolutionaries of Santal Pargans in this collection. Hence, I think that this book will come as handy for many researchers who are interested in modern history of this region.

For the sake of convenience of readers, the book has been divided into fourteen chapters. The first chapter includes Old Zamindari Records of Kharagpur, Sultanabad (Maheshpur Raj) Ambar (Pakur Raj), Giddhaur, Kankjol and Kahalgaon. The second chapter includes early correspondences of company rulers from Decemeber 1771 to Feburuary 1774. It includes in all twenty original letters. The third chapter includes letters related to genesis, development and deterioration of Brooke, Browne and Cleveland systems. It includeds fifty one letters as well as other documents. These documents clearly show that the Cleveland system was not an act of philanthropy but the tactics of colonial control. Fourth chapter includes documents regarding. Estate of Sultanabad and Invalid Estates collected from Bihar State Archives Patna. The land and land control given to the loyal retired soldiers was known as Invalid Estates. The fifth chapter includes judicial records and letters. The chapter incorporates one hundred and one letters. The chapter sixth contains the letters related to Revenue Department from June 1805 to March 1876. It includes twenty seven letters.

The seventh chapter includes Davis Report (1860) which was the result of an enquiry set up by Commissioner of Bhagalpur on the Ghatwali Mahals of Zila Bhagalpur. This chapter also includes Browne's plan for regulating, Invalid Establishments.

The Eighth chapter includes the records related to the Zamindari of Sultanahad (Maheshpur Raj) and Ambar (Pakur). The Ninth chapter contains original records about the Santal

Insurrection of 1855-56. It includes altogether sixty letters and documents.

The tenth chapter includes Bidwell's Enquiry Report on the Santal Hul. A.C. Bidwell was the Special Commissioner for the suppression of the Santal Hul. He had submitted his Enquiry Report on the causes of the Santal Hul. This is an important document for researchers. It also includes Santal Civil rules for non- regulation administrative system for the Santals. It is a compendium of Santal Civil Laws (traditions and customs) which got the legal sanctity in Santal Parganas.

The Eleventh chapter includes Chotanagpur Records regarding the Santal Hul. It contains Nine letters. The twelfth chapter includes W.W.Hunter's Statistical Account of Bengal (Santal Parganas). It also includes R. Carstairs (Dy. Commissioner Santal Parganas) typical comments on the settlement operations in Santal Parganas.

The thirteenth chapter includes the list of freedom fighters of Santal Pargans. It includes the list of early revolutionaries, participants of Non-co-operation Movement, Civil Disobedience movements as well as Quit India Movement.

The fourteenth and the last chapter contains the names of seventy seven martyrs in Quit India Movement in Santal Parganans. The names, address and a shrot biographical information has also been given.

I hope that this collection of different types of original documents will be useful for all who want to delve deep into the history of this region commonly known as Anga (Bhagalpur, Monghyr and Santal Paragans).

For Montgomery Martins Edition of the Official Survey of Bhagalpur.

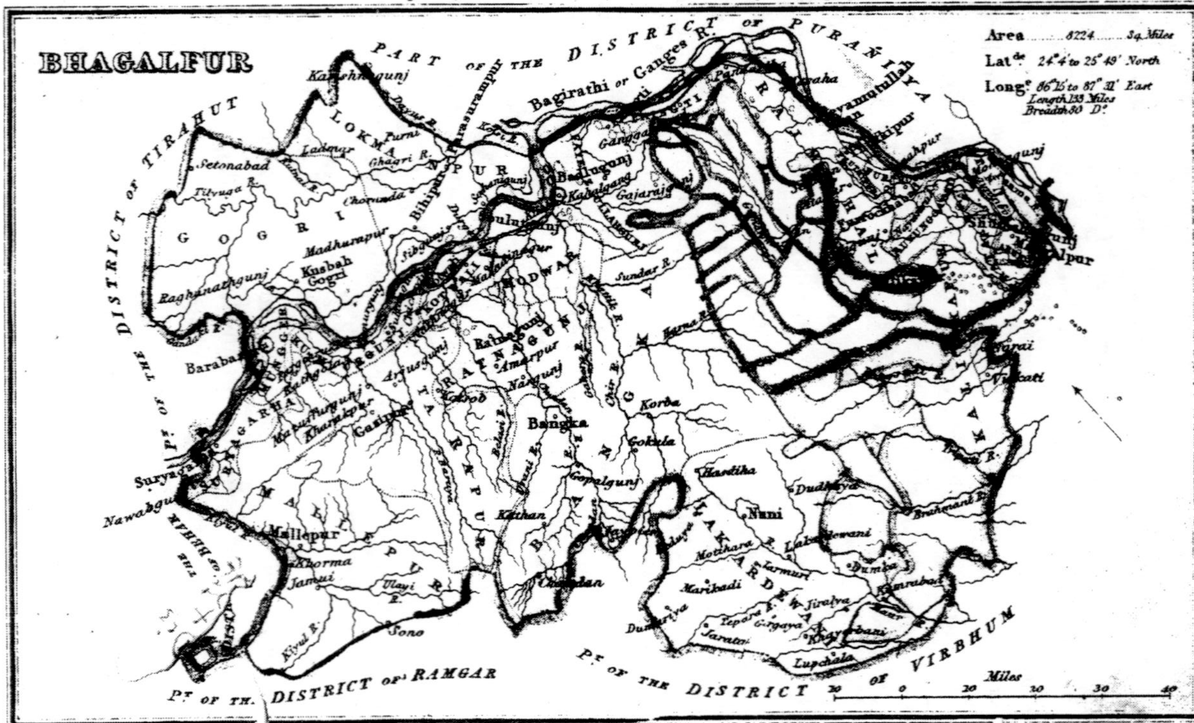

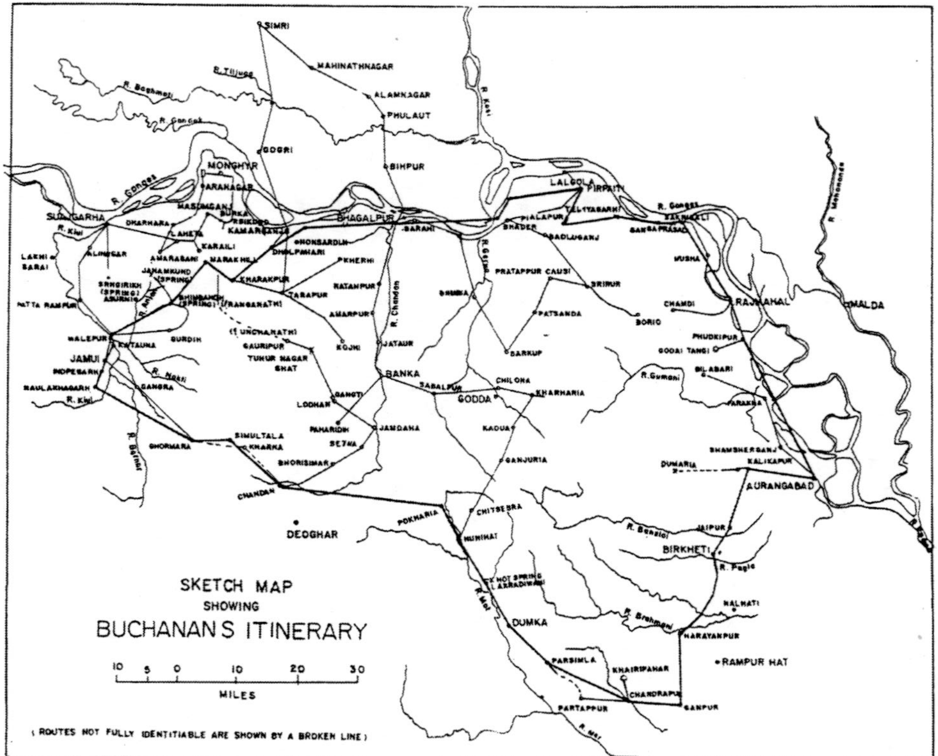
SKETCH MAP
SHOWING
BUCHANAN'S ITINERARY
10 5 0 10 20 30
MILES
(ROUTES NOT FULLY IDENTITIABLE ARE SHOWN BY A BROKEN LINE)
SIMRI
MAHINATHNAGAR
ALAMNAGAR
PHULAUT
GOGRI
BIHPUR
MONGHYR
BHAGALPUR
LALGOLA
PIRPAITI
R. Ganges
R. Kosi
R. Baghmati
R. Tilljuga
SURAJGARHA
JAMUI
BANKA
GODDA
RAJMAHAL
MALDA
R. Mahananda
DEOGHAR
DUMKA
BIRKHETI
AURANGABAD
RAMPUR HAT
CHITSEBRA
POKHARIA
KHARHARIA
CHILONA
SABALPUR
JAMDAHA
GANJURIA
BARKUP
PATSANDA
BORIO
CHAMDI
MUSHA
SRIPUR
CHANDAN
GHORMARA
SIMULTALA
KHARKA
SHORISIMAR
LODHAN
PAHARIDIH
SETHA
KOJHI
JATAUR
AMARPUR
RATANPUR
PKHERHI
TARAPUR
KHARAKPUR
BHIMBANDH
MALEPUR
KATAUNA
GURDIH
GAURIPUR
TUHUR NAGAR GHAT
PARSIMLA
KHAIRIPAHAR
CHANDRAPUR
GANPUR
PARTAPPUR
NARAYANPUR
NALHATI
JAIPUR
DUMARIA
KALIKAPUR
SHAMSHERGANJ
PARAKHA
BILABARI
PHUDKIPUR
GODAI TANGI
R. Gumani
R. Chandan
R. Mor
R. Brahmani
R. Bansloi
R. Pagla
R. Kiul
R. Barnar
R. Nagri
NUNIHAT
KADUA
BADLUGANJ
PRATAPPUR CAUSI
LAKHI SARAI
NATTA RAMPUR
GANGRA
MAHESHPUR

1

Zamindari Records

Old Zamindari Records of the Kharagpur Raj

The area of the Kharagpur Raj in Monghyr sub-division extended from the hills of Rajsahi Zamindari to those of the Monghyr and from the banks of the Ganges to the confines of Birbhum[1]. It was originally ruled by the Khetauris whose chiefs were supplanted in the 16th century by three Rajput brothers, namely Dandu Rai, Basudeo Rai and Menhar Rai. The fourth king in descent of Dandu Rai's family was Toral Mal, who embraced Islam and was recongnised by Jahangir as the Raja of Kharagpur. Muzaffar Ali, the eighth in descent, became the Raja of Kharagpur in A. D 1733-34 A. D. . He incurred the displeasure of Nawab Mir Qasim in A. D 1761-62, who removed him from the Raj of Kharagpur and made him a prisoner. On the downfall of Mir Qasim he secured his release from the prison, but was not reinstated in the management of his Zamindari. Mir Jafar after his restoration to Nawab Ship in 1763, despatched Mir Haidar Ali from Murshidabad to look after its Management. Mir Muhammed Kazin Khan, brother of Mir Jafar, and then Deputy Governor of Bihar persuaded Richard Barwell, Chief of Patna, to issue a Parwanah restoring Muzaffar Ali to his zamindari. As Muzaffar Ali was then seriously ill, he sent his son, Kuar Fazal Ali, to Patna to express his gratitude to Barwell for his favour. Barwell treated him well, gave Him a khelat and sent him back to Kharagpur with Abu Talib, the faujdar of that place[3]. But in 1767-68. Abu Talib poisoned the mind of Barwell against the Kharagpur Raja. Abu Talib even plundered the Raja's palace; the Raja went with his family to Jagannath Deo, the Ghatwal of Tappa Chanduary," for the safety of his life and honour"[5]. The Raja sent his son Kunwar Fazle Ali to Abu Tabib with a request to "safeguard his honour and life[6]. But Abu Tabib imprisoned him and sent him to Patna.

Muzaffar Ali then sent Bhola Nath, his mutasaddie,to Murshidabad to complain against Abu Tabib and to secure the Nawab,s favour for him. Bholanath secured an order from the Nawab for the release of Fazle Ali. But Shitab Rai, the Deputy Governor of Bihar, did not pay heed to it. Bhola Nath procured a second order for the release of Fazli Ali. At this Shitab Rai summoned Abu Taleb to submit an explanation, whereupon the latter poisoned himself to death. Fattulah was then sent to Kharagpur to manage the Estate. Shitab Rai took Fazli Ali to Murshidabad. But before starting for Calcutta, he, in consulation with Muhammad Reza Khan, Muzaffar Jang, Naib Nazim of Bengal, set Fazli ali at liberty. As the climate of Murshidabad did not suit Fazal Ali, he returned to Kharagpur with his mutasaddie leaving behind his Diwan Chuni Ram at Murshidabad as his representative. Chuni Ram pleaded ably before the Nawab for Muzaffar Ali, and it was decided that Muzaffar Ali would be restored to his Zamindari if some reliable person stood surety for his good Conduct-Chuni Ram presented Hyder Ali to stand as surety.

But at this time the Nawab received a letter from Fatullah in which the latter accused Jai Narain, Ghatwl of Khesar, and Bhola Nath, mutasaddie of Muzaffar Ali of murdering Pran Dutt, the Qanungo. The Nawab forwarded this letter to Shitab Rai,who in turn, sent it to Chuni Ram[7] Chuni Ram pointed out that it was a false and and malicious charge "due to the enmity the ghatwals, have always been after bringing disgrace and dishonour on the Raja and besides this Bhole Nath had been deposed from his post long time ago and this unholy murder had never been committed at Raja's instigation"[8].

But this replay did not satisfy Rai, who appointed Mir Hyder Ali Manager of the Kharagpur estate and Sent him to Kharagpur to take charge of this new Post asking an European subaltern, clerk to Accompany him with two companies of troops. Soon after their arrival at Kharagpur they were told by Bando Deo Ghatwal and two Rajput Ghatwals and Mukhim Ali, that Muzaffar Ali was instigating his Son Fazle Ali to rise in revolt against the Company's government. At this Company's troops marched against Fazle Ali, who on hearing of it fled towards the jungle and thus avoided capture. but Clerk captured Muzaffar Ali and sent him to Patna where he was put in prison in A. D 1770. At Patna, Muzaffar Ali pleaded his innocence and Petitioned to the authorities for restoration of his Zemindari to him. After investigation the charges Against Muzaffar Ali were found to be baseless and he was released from prison and being asked to remain at Patna, a sum of rupees two a day being sanctioned for his maintanace.

Nothing was immediately done with regard to his petition for restoration. But when in A. D 1773-74 Captain Brooke came to village Jamdaha in the Kharagpur estate to punish the rebellious Ghatwal chief Jagannath Deo, he sent for Fazle Ali. On hearing from him, the whole story about about Muzaffar Ali's deposition and imprisonment Captain Brook was convinced of the latter's innocence and when Warren Hasting came to Patna A. D (1773), he persuaded the governor-General to restore the Kharagpur estate to Muzaffar Ali, who thereafter was asked to proceed Kharagpur. But on returns, Muzaffar Ali died soon after this at Monghyr A. D (1772-73).

Muzaffar Ali had nominated his second son, Fazle Ali as his successor and Thomas Law, President of the Provincial Council of Revenue at Patna, offered a khilat to Fazle Ali in A. D 1773. But Fazle Ali died prematuelly in A. D 1775-76. After managing the estate for about two and a half year. Hastings recongnised Qadir Ali, posthumous son of Fazle Alli, as the Raja of Kharagpur and Chuni Ram was appointed manager of the estate. . A sanad was issued on 1 may,1781 enjoining upon Qadir Ali proper discharge of administrative function and collection of revenue.

Qadir Ali managed administration of the Estate efficiently and remitted revenue to Government regularly. when the Decennial Settlement was introduced Qadir Ali requested the government to settle the estate with him for ten years at increased revenue of rupees 16,000. The Government complied with his request. With the introduction of the Permanent Settlement in A. D 1793 the Zamindari of Kharagpur was settled with Qadir Ali. After Qadir Ali, Iqbal Ali khan governed the estate from 1820-1827. for his faithful services to the Company's Government during the first Anglo- 10 Burmese war Lord Amherst conferred on him the tittle of Maharajah. After Iqbal Ali's death in A. D 1234 fasle without any male issue, his brother Rahamat Ali Khan succeeded him. In A. D 1839 Rahamat Ali fell into arrears of revenue and his property, expect Haveli Kharagpur was sold on 19 January 1840. A portion of it was purchased by Raja Bidyanand Singh of Purnea. In 1845 the remaining portion of the estate was purchased by the Maharajah of Darbhanga.

For further information, see the book of Dr. Surendra Jha "Readings in regional history of Bihar and Jharkhand – the Sarkar of Monghyr (1556-1765)" Janki Prakashan, Patna 2004.

Notes and References

1. Proceeding of the Board of Revenue, 16 November, 1789,O. C. No. 9.
2. K. P. Mitra,"History of the Kharagpur Raj". English translation in Bengal Past and present.
3. Ibid.
4. Buchanan, An Account of the District Bhagalpur, p. 518.
5. Bengal: past and present, 1953. p. 55.
6. Bengal: past and present, 1953,p. 56.
7. Ibid.

8. Ibid.
9. Proceedings of the Board of Revenue, 7 january 1.790 pol. 83, no. 38
10. Bengal :past and present, 1953,pp. 60-61.

2

Zamindari Records of the Sultanabad Estate

Paragana Sultanabad in Sarkar Odambar (now in the Pakur sub-division of the District of Santal Paraganas) was bounded;on the north by the Rajmahal Hills; on the east by Murshidabad; on the north by Paragana Ambar; and on the south by Birbhum. It formed part of the Rajsahi Division till A. D. 1780, when it was incorporated into the Bhagalpur District by its Collector Augustus Cleveland. Banku Singh a Rajput from Gorakhpur, was the Founder of the Zamindar family of Sultanabad in A. D 1315-16. He had a brother named Danku Singh or Anku, who acquired Paragana Handu (Hand we) situated west of Sultanabad and east of the Kharagpur Raj[1]. After presenting handsome Nazarana to the Nawab of Bengal, Banku Singh obtained the tittle of Raja.

On the death of Banku Singh after years, his son,Gandharba Singh succeeded him, and the latter was succeeded by his son Hansraj Singh. On the death of Hansraj Singh the Zamindari was held by his son Doman Singh, whose son, Golel Singh Succeeded him. Golel Singh, whose son, Darbar Singh had two sons, named Kishan Singh and Kasusal Singh and a daughter named Ramani, who was married to Zamindar of Godda. After the death of Darbar Singh Kishan Singh succeeded the zamindari but he died without any Issue and so his younger brother Kaushal singh got the zamindari. On the death of Kaushal Singh in A. D. 1728-29,Ratan Singh became the Raja. Ratan Singh died in A. D 1753-54 without any issue and was succeeded by his son

1754-58. Garjan Singh died without any issue. Garjan Singh's widow Sarbeswari succeeded him. The East India Company's government made a settlement of the Sultanabad Zamindari with Rani Sarbeswari in A. D. 1789.

Rani Sarbeswari had administrative ability and employed the Mal Paharias for some works in the estate[2]. But she was dispossessed of the Zamindari by the company's government in A. D 1783 on suspicions of instigating the Pahariahs to commit some depradations in the plains and for failure to maintain peace. She was brought to Bhagalpur kept here in restraint till her death in A. D. 1807 by getting a monthly pension of Rupees 100, which was reduced to Rupees 50,the forfeited Paragana was let out in farm to Braj Nath Singh Izaradar for five years (1191-1195) Bengali year = A. D (1784-1789)[2].

Rani Sarbeswari's petition to the Board of Revenue in A. D 1789 for restoration of her zemindari to herself was not favourably considered. But on 24 August, 1792, the Governor- General- in-council issued orders for restoration of the Sultanabad Zamindari to a member of the old family and settled late Garjan Singh's relaticve Mokum Singh for the remaining eight years of the decennial settlement at an annual juma. of rupees 12,722 and odd. Mokum Singh died in A. D. 1803 and was succeeded by his widow Maheshwari Devi and then by his sister Janki kumari Devi, Rajput of Gorakhpur till 1888. Her husband, Gopal Singh, a Rajput of Gorakhpur, was awarded the title of Raja in A. D 1872 and of Maharaja in A. D 1875. Wood wrote in his Report,dated 31 August 1874, "Raja Gopal Chandra Sinha is a man of enlightened views and a liberal promoter of school;s and charitable dispensaries, construction of roads, and has lately taken on himself the repayment of some RS, 42,000 (forty two thousand rupees) beings the value of 19500 maunds of rice advanced to the raiyats of Paragana Sultanabad by Government during the recent scarcity in that Paragana".

Four years before her death in A. D 1888, Janki Kumari made over the property to her youngest son, Indra Narayan Singh, on whose death in A. D 1892, the estate passed on to his minor sons, Jogendra Narayan Singh, Debendra Narayan Singh with their mother Rani Radha Peary Devi, as their guardian.

Notes & References

1. Report Of Browne. Wood, Deputy Commissioner of Santal Paraganas, 31 August, 1874. It is mentioned in this Report that paragana Sultanabad comprised an area of 293 squre miles. The Raja and his sons held Zamindaries and pattanies in Murshidabad, Birbhum, Burdwan and Maldah as well.
2. The Raja of Kharagpur granted to Rani Sarbeswari a Ghatwali tenure consisting of thirtyeight villages.
3. Journal of the Bihar ResearchSociety,March,1956,p. 22.
4. Mokum singh was son of Ramani, Who was daughter of Darbar Singh.

Collected from old Zamindari Records Vol (ii) edited by Dr. K. K. Datta (unpublished).

3

Zamindari Records of the Ambar Paragana and the Pakur Raj

The Pakur Raj, situated in Ambar Paragana of the Mughal Empire had its headquarters at Pakur, a sub-divisionl town[1] in the District OF Santal Paragana which was created in 1855 after the Santal Insurrection of that year.

The origin of this Raj family can be traced to the period of the great Mughal Emperor, Akbar. To avoid the ravages of recurring pestilence at Lucknow and its neighbourhoods a large number of Kanyakubja Brahmins of that area migrated eastwards and settled at some localities near Kharagpur, now in the Monghyr District, Panchkote in the old Manbhum District, and in part of the present district of Santal Paragana. One of them named Sulakshan Tewary managed to get Jagir from the Mughal Emperor extending over Pakur and some neighbouring places. Sulakshan Tewary got a house constructed at Mohanpur in an adjacent hilly area and he was a man of religious temperament. His Diwan, Malik efficiently managed the administration of the Jagir. Guided by one Satyajit Roy, who was an accomplished man with skill in archery, the local ryots at first resisted realisation of rents by the Jagirdar. But they were soon pacified and agreed to pay rents from which the due amount of imperial tribute was remitted to Delhi.

The non-hilly tracts of Santal Paragana were included within Sarkar (Audambar) Odamber or Tanda comprising the Paragana of Sultanabad (in the possession of the Mahespur Raj), Ambar (in the possession of the Pakur Raj), and Kankjole) (a part of the Rajmahal sub-division) and certain other portions of Rajmahal. Sakar Odambar stretched from the southern boundary of Sakar Purnea, "Southwards across the Ganga, all along the right bank of that river down to the city of Murshidabad on the one hand, thoughtout nearly the whole of the Birbhum district on the other. How far it may have penetrated into the hilly country on thewest. It is impossible to determine, but probably some, at least, of the paragana, now no longer traceable, represent territory claimed as assessed (on paper) in these hills though not actually conquered"[1]. But Ambar is not mentioned in Ain-i-Akbari and probably it was not a paragana when this book was written. Major James Rennel locates it as Awmore in his Map which came out in A. D. 1779. Portions of modern Pakur and Rajmahal subdivision were included within the mahals or paraganas of Ambar, Kankjole, and Sultanabad. Hamilton Buchanam, who surveyed the Bhagalpur District in A. D. 1810-11 A. D., has left some accounts of these paraganas. But the same time a study of the boundary of Sarkar Mungher (mod. Monghyr), as given in the Ain-i-Akbari would show thar Sarkar Odamber ran far down southwards into the jungle tracts now in the Santal Paragana, but it is not possible "to fix any definite boundaries in that direction. Probably the Muhammadens did not more than make occasional raids into this wild and difficult country[2]............ .

After the death of Sulakhan in A. D1545, his son, Gopal Tewary, inherited the zamindari. Tradition affirms that Raja Man Singh, during his expedition against Pratapaditya, the powerful raja of Jessore who defied Mughal authority[3], received some assistance from Gopal Tewary's son,Prithvipal.

Highly appreciating the services of Prithvipal, Man Singh took him to Delhi with the consent of his father, who entertained Man Singh by his hospitality in his palace. Man Singh presented Prithvipal before the Mughal Emperor by praising his military ability. In recognition of the bravery and services of Prithvipal, the Emperor invested him with the title of Raja Shahi, which becomes hereditary to his family. Prithvipal, before leaving Delhi for Pakur, got some valuable presents on it from the Emperor. It is mentioned in late Shri Digambar Chakaravorty's Manuscript of history of the Pakur Raj family, which he wrote with much care and industry, that among other valuable things Prithvipal received from the Emperor the following eleven varieties of presents :- (1) A yellow flag called Jarda Nishan, (2) Punja of the Emperor, (3) one Urais,(4) two Shamans, (5) one Danka (drum),(6) one D. Khukhri, (7) On Murchal, (8) One Armour, (9) one Sword, (10) on Buckler, and (11) on a Katari. The yellow flag became the special badge of the Ambar Rajas.

Accoring to some, the Zamindari of the Tewary family was known as Ambar Paragana because there were many mango groves in this area. But there is another view that it was the gift of Man Singh, who was the Raja of Ambar. The latter view seems to be more plausible.

Gopal Tewary died, soon after Prithvipal's return to Ambar from Delhi. Prithvipal then succeeded to gaddi of Ambar and occupied it till his death in A. D 1579/80. He was succeeded by his son Kirtichandra Sahi. After Kitichandra Sahi's death in A. D 1620, no account of any kind of the Ambar Raj family for about hundred years is known. But there is no doubt that the raj continued to be held by the Tewary family. After this period of about one century, a sciom of Tewary family named Prabal occupied the gaddi of the Ambar Raj. Prabal died without any male issue in A. D. 1719 and succeeded by his nephew Bhupati Sahi.

The repeated Maratha inroads into Bengal and Bihar between A. D. 1742 and A. D. 1751 entailed immense sufferings on the people of Ambar as it was, like other areas, devastated by the invaders of which we get a graphic description in a contemporary Bengali work entitled " Maharastra Purana" by Gangaram and in several other contemporary works and records.

In utter confusion and panic caused by the Maratha ravages, the local people sometimes took shelter at secluded places in the neighbouring jungle areas, when the ghatwals, who guarded the ghats or the passes of the hills, gave them warning by beat of drums. Babu digambar Chakravory, who visited these jungle areas, writes:-

"All the inlets and outlets of these wild regions were very narrow with deep jungle on both sides and the paikes were so tortuous and unsafe being constantly crossed by hill strems that it was practically a task of great difficulty to proceed on the way without some guide hired to point it out. These passes were called Ghatees and guards called Ghatwalls were kept, at the entrance with a grant of Jagir lands which they enjoyed rent free. These guards fully armed used to keep watch day and night at mouth of the openings on a large tree, his house being situated near, hid within deep jungles. These Ghatwals, at the time when Brahmotter lands were resumed, took settlement of their Ghatwali tenures from the Government as Sikimi Taluks of the Zamindar. The rent assessed for the Ghatwali Jagirs is now paid through the Zamindar to the Government. All the Ghatwals had such drum made of Bronze, called Jajharghani Dunka and whenever the Ghatwals had noticed that the Maharatta plunderers had arrived they used to beat the drum with a peculiar note and other taking up the alarm of danger beat by their own drums and thus within a very short time all the people were apprised of the coming danger. A great confusion then ensured and all the people with their life and ptoperty which could be moved about retreated to the strong fortresses and impenetrable jungles."

The repeated Maratha invasions badly affected the economic condition of the people and this was further aggravated in one year at that time after there was also failure of monsoon rains. The Ambar raj was also hard hit by these and could not remit amout of revenue due from it to the Murshidabad darbar. To realise all arrear dues from the Ambar raja the Nawab of Murshidabad sent to his place a body of troops whose rations were to be supplied by the Raja. On his inability to meet Nawab's exorbitant demands Bhupati Sahi was taken to Murshidabad as a prisoner. His father-in-law, Anantaram, accompanied him there. All that Bhupati Sahi submitted to prove his inability to clear off all demands of Nawab in view of the difficulities after the ravages of the Marathas was of no avail.

The Nawab released Bhupati Sahi only after his father- in-law prayed to the Nawab for granting him the Zamindari of Ambar and by promising to clear off all the arrear dues by promising to clear off all the arrear dues. Bhupati Sahi did not return to Ambar, but spent the rest of his life as a recluse. To fulfil his promise to the Nawab, Anantram extorted money forcibly from the local people even by obtaining military help from the Nawab. This made him very unpopular. Anantaram died childless in about A. D 1754, his two daughters named Gauri and Parvati having predeceased him.

Anantaram's second wife Chandantayi then took[4] charge of administrstion of Ambar. Being an intelligent and pious lady she managed the affairs of the estate with tact and ability and earned much popularity among the people. It was during her time that the capital of Ambaṛ Raj was shifted from Mohanpur to Pakur and the family idol Madan Mohan was also brought there.

Rani Chandanmay in had no issue and so she adopted a nephew of Bhupati Sahi, named Ayodhya Ram, as her son and nominated him as her successor before she died about A. D. 1765.

The Ambar Estate had then to pay revenue to Rani Bhavani of Natore, whose zamindari extended over a wide area.

Due to the administrative evils during Clive's dual Government, general insecurity in the country and bad effects of the famine of A. D. 1770 revenue collection was very much impeded. So Ayodhya Ram failed to remit the stipulated revenue to the Natore Zamindar. For this he was taken to Natore almost as a captive, accompanied by his family priest Ananda Chakravorty. Soon he could conciliate the Rani of Natore and his Zamindari was restored to him, on his promising to pay the arrear dues as soon as possible. Ayodhya Ram died probably in A. D. 1780 and the next heir to the Zamindari was his son Baidyanath Sahi. In the year 1780 paragana Ambar, like paragana Sultanabad, was incorporated into the District of Bhagalpur at the suggestion of its collector Augustus Cleveland.

Baidyanath Sahi died in A. D. 1791. Of his sons, Devi Prasad Sahi and Prithvichandra Sahi, the former became the Raja. But he died childless and Prithvichandra Sahi then ascended the Gaddi of Ambar. Prithvichandra Sahi's period of administration was brilliant from various points of view. Vigorously active in matters of administration, he was also an accomplished scholar with profound knowledge of Sanskrit, Bengali and Urdu. Hamiltion Buchanan, who met him at Pakur on 13th December, 1810, during his survey of the Bhagalpur District, writes in his Journal. "He is a stout, sensible and obliging man, who not only visited me, a civility that very few deign to show, but invited me to visit him. His house is decent, and is gradually enlarging ". In his Report of the survey of the district of Bhagalpur Buchanan observes. "He is good- looking middle –aged prudent man, exceedingly civil, and his house more respectsble than that of the Raja of Kharagpur, althought his other expenses are moderate".

Prithvichandra Sahi was the author of a highly valuable literary work, entitled "Gouri Mangal". It contains plenty of details regarding social life and religious practices of the people in those areas. Prithvichandra was a deeply religious man, well-versed in Agama Shastras. He visited occasionally important places of pilgrimage at Deoghar, Tarapith near Rampourhat in the Birbhum district and at Bakreshwar near Sainthia in the Birbhum district. There are also to his credit works of public utility, such as establishment of (Sanskrit) tols and pathsalas (primary schools), excavation of tanks, etc. . Many scholars enjoyed his patronage and his hospitality and charity.

Prithvichandra Sahi died in A. D 1835 and his son Ramchandra Sahi succeeded to the gaddi of Ambar pargana. Ramchandra had a second wife named Kshemasundari. They had a daughter named Tarangini Devi. Raja Ramchandra Sahi was taken to Bhagalpur for medical treatment and died there in 1252 B. S. A. D (1846).

After this, Ramchandra Sahi's minor son became the proprietor of the Ambar Raj but he left world in 1850. He was the last representative of the Sahi family of Pakur.

Soon after Rani Kshemasundari Devi's daughter, Tarangini Devi was married to Gopilal Pande, eldest son of Sukhlal Pande, an inhabitant of village Kamalakund in the Bhagalpur district. Rani Kshemasundari was a pious lady of charitable disposition, whose kindness and generosity were extened to the poor and the needy and she promptly redressed the grievances of her tenants.

The people of Ambar paragana were very much harassed by the Santal Insurrection of 1855-57, a detailed description about which is given in a book written by late Digambar Chakraborty of Pakur early in the present century.

Gopilal Pande improved the condition of the Ambar zamindari in various ways. He established the Pakur Raj High school in 1859, only about two year after the establishment of the University of Calcutta, and also a girls' School at a site in front of the palace of the Pakur Raj. It was from the Pakur Raj School that Digambar Chakravorty, nephew of Rani Kshemasundari and only son of Panchanan, passed the Entrance Examination. He has left some manuscript notes on the history of the Pakur Raj and also detailed account of the Santal Insurrection.

Trangini devi had three sons, named Traesh Chandra, Sitesh Chandra and Kulesh Chandra and a daughter named Trigun Devi. She expired some time after the birth of her daughter. Gopilal Pande died at the age of 40 during the life-time of Rani Kshemasundari.

Rani Kshemasundari died at Nainsuk, near Dhulian, on the bank of the Bhagirathi at an advanced age in 1895. Gopilal Pande had three sons- the first Taresh Chandra, second Sitesh Chandra and third Kulesh Chandra. His second son Sitesh Chandra Pande succeeded the Rani in A. D. 1895. The two others had died before the Rani, Taresh Chandra leaving two sons – Satyendra and Pratapendra. The Government Conferred the title of Raja on Sitesh Chandra "in recognition of his liberality and charity. "

Raja Sitesh Chandra composed several songs in praise of Goddess Kail, Durga and Tara, Which were printed in a booklet, entitled ' Shakti Sangeet' at the New Calcutta Press, No. 3 Beadon Square, Calcutta. He left this world in A. D 1900 leaving his son Kumar Kalidas Pande (then only seven year old) and two daughters, Shailangini and Puspangini. Shailangini had excellent literary taste and there were some writings to her credit. Kumar Kalidas Pande was exceptionally intelligent and had a special taste for mathematics. He passed the Entrance Examination at the age of thirteen securing First Position in the Calcutta University. He passed F. A. Examination from the T. N. J. (now T. N. B.) College, Bhagalpur, and B. A. Examination from the Patna College. He was married to Jyotirmaye Devi. Rani Jyotirmayr Devi became a graduate and was a highly cultured lady; some years back she was Deputy Health Minister of the Bihar Government. Her death, a few years back, has been a great loss for the Pakur Estate. It was minly due to her generosity that kumar Kalidas Pande Memorial college was recently established at Pakur.

Notes & References

1. John Beames, "Notes on Akabar's Subahs, with reference to the "Ain- i Akbari"", Journal of the Royal Asiatic Socity'(1896).
2. Journal of the Asiatic Socity of Bengal,(1885,part1/p-172)
3. Nestland's Reports on the District of Jessore (1870). Its second edition, revised and corrected, was printed at the Bengal Secretariat Press in 1874.

4. It has been mentioned by Shrijut Ramendra Sundar Trivedi Dr. D. C Sen and Dr. Sukumar Sen. Some year back,(DR. K. K. Datta) I got a manuscript – Copy of it, (by Dr. K. K. Datta) belonging to the author himself, in a family at my native village Jhikarhaty, situated about three miles south-east of Pakur. At my request the Asiatic Society, Calcutta, has published this volume after getting it carefully edited by late Dr. Bimal Behari Majumdar. I have donated the manuscript to the Asiatic Society, Calcutta.

4

Zamindari Records of Giddhaur Estate

"Pergunah Gidhaur is a fine estate, but a considerable portion of it is situated in the district of Ramgar, and it is not mentioned in the Ayeen Akbery of Mr. Gladwin, unless it may be the Gundhor of Sircar Behar. The whole of what is contained in this district is situated in the division of Mallepur. Accroding to the family traditions, Raja Vikram Singha, a Chandel Rajput, was first Zemindar of Gidhaur. He originally resided at Agauri near Vijaynagar; but in a dream he was desired by Baidhyanath to go to Gihaur, and occupy the land, which was then waste, and the God gave him at the same time permission to take all the offering made at his temple. When he arose, the people obseeved on his forehead a mark of ashes; and, on being how the mark came, he told them his dream. Such an evident manifestation of divine favour encouraged all his kinsmen to follow him, and in a few days they set our for Dilli, to offer their services, which were accepted. Soon after, the Rajput informed the king of his dream, and obtained permission to go and occupy the country. The grant is said to have been dated in the Fusli year 473. (A. D. 1066) but that must, I presume, be a mistake, as the Fusil year, I believe, is a Muhammedan institution; and the Muhammedan king did not come to Dilli until long after that period (1205-1210). By this grant he obtained a right to Pergunah Gidhaur, Mahal Chakai a part of Ramgar. Pergunah Bishazari in the district of Behar, Pergunah Chandan Bhuka that will be afterwards mentioned ;

and Mahals Devghar and Sarma, and Perguna Tiyar, all in the district of Virbhum. The Raja, taking with him some troops, came into the country, which was then occupied by small hordes of thieves of the Dosad and Choyar tribes. I have already given an account of the Dosads. Choyar or archer is a name often given to the Bhungiyas. These he reduced, and possessed the country, until the year 504 (A. D. 1097). He was succeeded in regular descent as follows.

Singha Dev to 556 (A. D. 1149).
Dev Singha to 602 (A. D. 1195)
Ramnarayan to 668 (A. D. 1261)
Raj Singha to 704(A. D. 1297).
Darpanarayan to 748(A. D. 1341).
Rajmal to 798 (A. D. 1391)
Bariyar Singha to 844 (A. D. 1437).
Puranmal to 896 (A. D. 1489).

This person built the present temple of Baidyanath. Eight generations by the account are made occupy 392 years, which seems highly improbable, and reasonable allowance for their lives would brings the time of the first Zemindar within the muhammedan Period. Puranmal had two sons, and divided his estate between them. I shall first follow the succession of Hari Singh, the eldest, in regular descent from father to son.

Hari Singha enjoyed his share until 922 (A. D. 1515).
Devi Singha to 954 (A. D. 1547)
Kesari Singha to 979 (A. D. 1572)
Pahar Singha to 1015 (A. D. 1608)
Dolan Singh to 1060(A. D. 1653)
Krishna Singha to 1116 (A. D. 1709)
Padma Singha to 1124(A. D. 1717)
Syam Singha to 1150 (A. D. 1743)
Amar Singha to 1183(A. D. 1776).

This Raja had wars with Asuduzzuman and Alinuki, the Dewans of Virbhum. These wars were continued with various success from the 1171 to the 1177 (A. D. 1764- 1770), but in the year following the Moslem prevailed, and took entirely Devghar, Sarma, Tiyur, and Rohini. The 2/3 of the offerings of Devghar, which the family had hitherto enjoyed, were now also lost. Amar Singha made many complaints the remainder of this share of the estate, went to Calcutta with his Kinsman Darpa and complained to Mr. Meyers, who sent letters to the respective Collectors directing them to enquires who were the real proprietors of the lands. The answers were favorable to the claims of the family ; but all the lands had been sold for the arrears of revenue, except Devghar, which had been kept in the hands of government, and the income applied to discharge the arrears of revenue which the produce of the sale had not completed. The Raja has not yet given up hopes of being able to recover this.

Raja Gopal Singh, when I saw him, was 49 years of age, a fat heavy man, but very civil. His brothers, sons and kinsmen are very good looking men, and seem to be treated by the head of the family with great kindness. He can read only the Nagri character, and attened to accounts and the letters on business alone, neither understanding nor caring for the poets, the only author in the Hindi dialect. His native agents praise him as an excellent manager; but a Maronite Aleppo, who manges part of the estates for a woman thatfirms the rents, and who seems to be a very intelligent man, assures me, that he was in debt to every one who will lend him money, and extremely necessitious, which is followed by rapacity towards his tenatry. He lives part of the year in the share of his estate, that is in Ramgar, and part at Jamuyi in this district, but his houses are mean. His equipage however is numerous, and showy, and he lavishes large sums on dancers. "

The Gidhur Estate

Gidhaur was bounded by the plains of Bihar on the west, by Kharagpur on the north, by Kharagpur and Birbhum on the east, and by Kharadia on the South[1]. the Gidhaur Zamindari consisted of six paraganas, namely Gidhaur including mahal Chakai which was a part of Ramghur, Bishazari in zila Bihar, Chandan, Bhuka, Rohini including Deoghur and Bithaur. In his account of the District of Bhagalpure, Hamilton Buchanan gives the following account of Gidhaur Zamindari [2].

The British Government granted the title of Raja to Jaimangal Singh, descendant of Gopal Singh in recognition of his services during the Santal Insurrection of 1855-57 and in A. D 1861 he received an estate yielding a rental of Rs. 3,000 a year " to be head rent-free during his life-time in acknowledgement of the services he rendered during the mutiny in[3] 1857". He was granted the title of Maharaja in AA. D 1865 and the title of Maharaja Bahadur was made hereditary in the family in AA. D 1877 on assumption of the tittle of the Empress of India by Her Majesty Queen Victoria.

Notes and References

1. James Browne, India Tracts. p. 2.
2. Buchanan, An Account of the District of Bhagalpur, PP. 536-539.
3. L. S. S. O 'Malley, Bengal District gazetteers (Monoghyr),1909, p. 203.

5

Zamindari Records of the Tappa Manihari

Tappa Mahihari is situated in the north of the Godda Sub-division of the districts of Santal Pargana. When in A.D 1600 Raja Man Singh was marching to Bengal to punish a rebel chief Sobha Singh, he received help from Rup Karan, commandant of a local Nat paharia named Dariyar Singh, on whom Akbar had conferred the Zamindari of Manihari and who lived in Manjhwe valley where he built a fort called Lakragarh. Offer of help to Man Singh by Rupkaran offended his master[1]. Even then Rupkaran advanced to Bengal with Man Singh to render his services to him. As a reward for this, Man Singh granted to Rupkaran the mansab jagir, free of rent and in perpetuity, five paraganas, viz: Dursarf (in Purnea), Jamuni and Akbarnagar (in Rajmahal), Manjhwe and Kanjaila comprising the valley in the hills of the mountaineers. He also got Tappa Manihari, a part of the paragana of Bhagalpur as zamindari with the tittle of Raja. After the death of Sujan Singh, a member of that family, fiteenth in deçency, in (A.D.) 1780, His son Gajraj Singh succeeded him at the age of thirty-six. Though he had a brother, he got the whole estate and the monthly pension granted to Sujan Singh by Cleveland [2]. In A. D 1792, during the time of Gajraj Singh, Decennial Settlement was made of Tappa Manihari at Jama of Rs. 8,192. When Gajraj Singh became insane his property was managed by the Court of Wards from A. D 1804 till his death in A. D1834. After that his two sons, Raja Bhagwan Singh and Kumar Chandan Singh succeeded him[3].

Notes and References

1. Buchnan, An Account of the District of Bhagalpur, pp. 482-83. Mcpherson, Final Report on the Santal Paragana Settlement. p. 18.
2. Buchanan An Account of the Districts of Bhagalpur, pp. 482-83
3. L. S. S. O' Malley, Bihar District Gazetteers (Santal Parganas revised in 1938). pp. 393-4.

6

Zamindari Records of the Kankjol

Kanjol was the oldest and largest of the Rajmahal estates. It is mentioned in the Ain-i-Akbari as one of the divisions of sarkar Odambar. Buchanan narrates its early history[1]. : "It originally belonged to two brothers, Ganesham (Ghaneshyam)and Mahesh Das, who were Rarhi Brahmans. Ganesham being deprived of his share went to Delhi, became a Mohammedan and obtained a grant of the whole estate with many other in the vicinity of Rajmahal, where he returned and took up his residence being known as Abdulla. In A. D 1809 the estate was held by Abdulla's descendants in the fourth gereration and one- fourth by a lady purchaser called Rahtun Nessa. The grant to Abdulla must have been made about 1700 when Auranzeb was emperor, and the Rarhi Brahmans may have held it for centuries earlier"[2].

Notes & References

1. Buchnan, An Account of the District of Bhagalpur,(1870-1871) pp. 554-56.

2. Mcpherson, H. Final Report on the Santal Paragana Settlement. p. 23.

7

Zamindari Records of the Kahalgaon (Colgong)

About the family owning the zamindari of Kahalgaon Buchanan writes:-

"The Pergunah may be divided into two shares, Kahalgaon proper, subdivided into two several Tappas, about the name and extent of which no two authorities are agreed,and Tappa Madhuban. Kahalgaon seems originally to have belonged to a family of Brahmans of the Saryuriya division of the tribe of Kanoj. Who possessed it for five generations,and took the humble title of Chaudhuri[1]. Their names were Loknath, Narottam, Ramanath, Dinanath and Kripanath, the last person at various times and for different reasons,alienated by sale all that remained to the family, for several alienations of another kind had previously taken place. A branch of the family, now represented by Maniram, of whose possessions, I have above given account,received these as an appandage, holding them of the elder branch as Vassals(Melk); and several other persons obtained similar favours; but all these were liberated from their vassalage by the settlement of Lord Cornwallis. The greatest alienations, however, as usual, took place in favour of the Kanungoe or registrar of the Pergunah. This office was held for some time by a (Kayastha)family of seribes, which had divided into four branches. The head of one of these branches, named Giridhardas having become a Moslem,obtained the whole. His son Rahimullah left the office to Akel Muhammed, and they seem to have acquired a large share of the whole estate,probably from favour shown them as converts;but becoming extravagant, their lands have been sold.

To return to Kripanath, the last chief owner of Kahalgaon he left six sons. The eledest son, Parasnath,has purchased a part of the estate, in the name of his nephew, the eldest of the three sons of his second brother Gangaram, who is dead,but has left a son. The foruth son Matuk is alive, and has three sons. The fifth son is Padmanath, who in the wreck of the family has betaken himself to the proper duties of his sacred dignity,and has very considerable progress in science,but is burthened with two sons. The youngest brother, Bholanath, is dead,but has left three sons. So that on the wretched fragments of the estates there are 15 males to be supported; for, as the natives suppose, being very unfortunate, the Gods found no difficulty in procuring the souls of miserable sinners good enough to occupy the unhappy lot of decayed gentlemen.

This portion of Kahalgaon is now divided, in the public records, into 48 lots, many belonging to sundry partners,and several united into one person's property. One of the lots is the immediate property of the company, and is managed by an agent of the Collectors. None of the other properties are remarkable, and I find as usual some persons considered as the real owners of the lands, whose names do not appear in the public records. This division of the Perguna is much better cultivated than the other, which seems to be owing to the rate of rent being higher. I reckon, that of the 4,44,400 bighas which it may contain,about 1,45,500,or about 32 percent is occupied ; whereas the very utmost which I can allow for Madhuban is 25 percent.

Collected from "Bengal-Past and present" Journal Vol. 80,1961 pp. 01-15

By. Surendra Jha

OOO

Chapter II

William Harwood Correspondence

(1)

From,

J. Alexander
J. Graham.
Moorshedabad (Murshidabad)
Dated 23rd December, 1771

To,

Mr. William Harwood,
Supervisor of Rajmehal (Rajmahal)

Sir,

The Hon'ble the President of Council having thought proper to come to certain Regulations on the subject of the Coin of the country, establishing thereby the rates of its future currency, we now transmit you a copy of their orders to us on this subject under date the 6th of August last which we direct you will publish thought your District, and enforce the observance of them with all your authority and influence.... . us at what rate the siccas of the 11th June have hitherto been received in the collections of the present year's Revenue from the farmers and Riots(raiyats).

Notice is hereby given that the trade in the article of salt will pursuant to the orders of the Hon'ble the Court of Directors undergo a new and general regulation which will take place in the month of September next, with the produce of the salt works which will then begin to be manufactured for the ensuing season. All person as well Europeans as Native are therefore apprized that any advances made or imposed upon the Zemindars, farmers or Molungees (3) with a view to establish any claim or preference to the next year's produce of salt will be deemed collusive and invalid and are consequently to be forfeited.

Ist Regulation

That the farms shall be settled for the fixed term of five years to commence from the Ist of this Bysaac 1179 or the 10th April, 1772.

2nd That the farms shall consist of entire Pergunnahs (4), provided they do not exceed the annual amount of one lack of Rupees in which case they shall be divided into such equal portions as shall reduce the amount of each considerably below that sum unless the acknowledged responsibility and good character of the farmer shall support his pretensions to rent the whole Pergunnah and shall all villages or portions of land which have been hitherto left in separate farms shall be annexed to the Pergunnahs to which they originally belong.

3rd That the President with a Committee the Board will go on a Circuit through the Province to form the Bundibust (5) or settlement at the Sidder Cutcherry each District.

4th That the settlement of the Districs of Hougly (Hugli), Hidgerlee (Hijli), Calcutta Pergunnahs Burdwan, Midnapore, Berbhom(Birbhum), Bissenpore and PUcheet (Pachet shall be determined by the remaining members of the Board.

5th That a fixed zemindarry Dewan shall be chosen and nominated by the Board who shall be joined with the Collector in the superintendence of the revenue, that he shall keep separate accounts of the collections according to the established form of the country, countersign all orders circulated in the Mofussil (6), all receipts granted to the Farmers, and all invoices, and accounts transmitted to the Sudder.

6th That the Collector shall not use his own private seal in the execution of the business but that a general seal be struck with a proper inscription in the names of the Company as Dewan of the Provinces that one be lodged with each Collectors, to be by him affixed to all public deeds and orders where the Custom of the country and Rules of the business render it necessary and wherever this seal is affixed the Collectors shall attest it with his name.

7th That neither the Collector nor Dewan shall send sepoys, peons,or any other persons with authority into the Sudder belonging to the farmers excepting only on such occasions as shall indispensably require it for the maintenance of the peace or the immediate execution of Justice, in which the authority of the farmer shall be insufficient that on such occasions a warrant under the public seal and signed by the Collector shall be given in writing to the officer employed and be recorded in the Judicial proceedings with the reasons for issuing it but that no person be summoned on ordinary occasions except by a Tullub Chitty (7) to the farmer or order requiring him to produce the person summoned in a certain space of time.

8th The farmer shall on no account demand more from the Kists (8) than the ancient aboaba (abwabs) and what is stipulated in the pattah (10) and in the kewar pattah and that for every instance such extortion the farmer on

Conviction shall be compelled to pay back the sum which he shall have so taken from the riot (ryot), besides a penalty equal to the same amount to the Sircar and for a repetition of a notorious instance of his oppression on his riots the farmers lease shall be annulled.

9th That the farmers payment to Government shall in like manner be ascertained and established and no demand be made upon them above what shall be expressed in the Dowel (11) or Rent Roll delivered them with their lease.

10th that no new Matouts or assessment under the name of Mangun, Bauree, Gundee, Sood or any other aboab or tax shall be imposed upon the riots and that those articles of aboab which are of late establishment shall be carefully scrutinized and at the discretion of the Committee abolished if they are found in their nature to be oppressive or pernicious.

11th That all nozzers (12) and salamees (13) which are usually presented at the first interview as marks of subjection and respect be Collectors, as to the Zemindars, Farmers and their Officers.

12th That the old Farmers shall settle his accounts with such of the riots as are forthcoming in the presence of the new Farmers, or his Agents and the Ballances which shall be proved shall be on account of the new Farmer.

13th That a Mohrir or Writer of accounts shall be appointed on the part of the Government to every Farm, who shall take an account of all the receipts of the rents with the Farmer and transmit the same monthly to the collector at the Sudder Cutcherry of the province but without any authority to interfere in the collections.

14th That no peshkar(14).... . other servant of whatever denomination of the Collector or relation or dependent of any such servant be allowed to Farm land, nor directly or indirectly to hold s concern in any farm, nor to be security for any farmer, that the Collector be strictly enjoined to prevent such practise and that if it shall be discovered that any one under a false name or any kind of collusion, hath found means to evade this order he shall be subject to a heavy fine proportionate to the amount of the Farm and the Farm shall be relet or made khas (Government property), neither shall any European directly or indirectly be permitted to rent lands in any part of the country.

15th That none of the officers or servants employed in the collections,shall lend money to the zemindars, taaluckdars (Talukdars), Farmers, Riots or any other person whatever, within the District of which he shall have charge that in like manner the zemindars, Talookdars, Shiekdars (Shiqders)(15), of the Government be forbid to lend money to the riots, and for the cultivation of the country no more than 2 percent per mensem must be taken on Taccabee (16) advanced the Riots and the payment received not in kind but in money.

16th And to relieve the farmer from the necessity of borrowing money for the payment of his kists or instalment, that the kisbundee for the ensuing leases be so regulated as that the kist may be made payable at the usual period of the harvest proportionate to the estimated quantity and value of the crops and as local circumstances shall direct.

17th That all zemindary Chokees (17) shall be abolished and none kept but such as immediately depend on the Government under the Putchtera (18). Backshbunder (19) and Shahbunder (20), subject to such regulations as shall be hereafter established. "

OOO

(2)

From,

Your Most Obed. Hum'ble Servants
William Hastings
Samuel Middleton
P. M. Dacres (Philip Milner Dacres)
J. Alexander
J. Graham.
Cossimbuzar (Cassimbazar) (23)
Dated 3 August, 1772

To,
Mr. William Harwood
Collector of Rajmahal.

As we judge it expedient to carry into immediate execution, within the Districts subject to our control, the orders of the Company, respecting the suppression of the Zemindarry Ghaut-(Ghats)(21), you are required upon Receipt of this to cause Publication to be made at the Sudder Cutcherry and other convenient places in your District; That all such Zemindarry Ghauts within your Limits are totally suppressed and the Duties hitherto levied at them under you're the name of Radary Ghaut hassell (22), Cotbara, Mangun, Etraufee & Co. from this time abolished and you are forthwith to withdraw the officers now employed in the collection of the ..... at such Ghauts or Chokies.

To prevent any mis (understanding) of our intention we think it proper to add that it is the express Order of the Hon'ble Company that no customs on Goods passing by water shall be levied but at the established custom Houses of the Shawbunder, Buksbunder and Pachooterah and that all Ghauts or Chokies belonging to the Zemindars which have been erected on the Banks of the river for collecting arbitrary imposts on Boats passing and replacing shall be abolished and of the Loss of Revenue Sustained by this suppression you are to send us an Account. This order is not to affect the Duties which are levied at the Ghauts, Ganges and inland chokies, but they are to continue on the same footing as formerly.

N. B. - These letters reveal the earliest attempts of the Britishers for administrative organisation.

Surendra Jha

OOO

(3)

From,

William Harwood,
Collector of Rajmahal.
Dated 10th August, 1772

To,

Hon'ble Warren Hasting, Esq. .
President and Gentleman of the Committee of Circuit at Cossimbuzar.

Hon'ble,

Sirs,

I have received your orders of the 3rd instant for the abolition of the zemindary Chokies which have been published and enforced.

I must beg leave to acquaint this Hon'ble Committee, that exclusive of the Gully, Mungun,Etraffee and Imposts usually exacted at the interior zemindary Chokies there is an original duty collected here (which is collected nowhere else of the black merchants on the silk and white piece-goods purchased at the provinces), for which it has been ever customary to issue the Rowannahs (24) of this place which are given under the public seal of this at Syer (25) Pachouter; I am therefore to beg the. . of your orders whether these Rowannahs are to be issued here or the merchants to pay duties else where and if the chokey of this place to be entirely removed in like manner with common zemindarry chokies.

OOO

(4)

From,

William Hastings,
Samuel Middleton
P. M. Dacres (Philip Milner Dacres)
J. Graham.
James Lawrell.
Cossimbuzar (Cassimbazar)
Dated 24th August, 1772

To,

Mr. William Harwood
Collector of Rajmahal
Sir,

In answer to yours of the 10th instant we are to inform you, that as form your representation the duties collected at the Syer Pachuttra in Rajmahal seem to be different from those collected at the zemindary chokies we intend that they shall be an especial subject of consideration for the Committee when they proceed to the Settlement of that District. In the meantime it is our desire that you continue levying those duties till our final determination upon them, of which you shall be properly acquainted and instructed accordingly.

OOO

(5)

From,

Samuel Middleton
John Bathoe.
Alexander Higginson.
Moorshedbad
8th September, 1772

To,

Mr. William Harwood
Collector of Rajmahal and Boglepore

Sir,

In consequenc of orders from the Hon'ble the president and Council we have now to acquaint you that the Board of Revenue at this place has been this day dissolved. We are therefore to direct you to transmit your accounts from the first of his month to the Hon'ble the President and Controlling Committee of Revenue at Fort William with whom in future your correspondence is to be held, you will please to conserve likewise that the accounts of your District to the thirty first ultimo are to (be) addressed to the Chief and Council of Revenue at Moorshedabad as usual.

OOO

(6)

From,

William Hastings,
Samuel Middleton
P. M. Dacres (Philip Milner Dacres)

J. Graham.
James Lawrell.
Cossimbuzar
dated 13th September, 1772

To,

Mr. William Harwood
Collector of Rajmahal
Sir,

Having finished the business we had in charge of the City Messrs. Dacres,Lawrell and Graham, three of the members of this Committee, will continue the Circuit of the Districts for the purpose of effecting the settlements, which have not yet been concluded and establishing the general Regulations adopted by the Hon'ble the president and Council. We are therefore to advise you that they will proceed from hence in a few days, and to direct that you be prepared with every necessary material and information against their arrival to facilitate the completion of those measures in your District.

OOO

(7)

From,

J. Stewart,
Secretary,
Fort William
Dated 10th October, 1772

To,

Mr. William Harwood
Collector of Rajmahal
Sir,

I am directed by the Hon'ble the President and Council to signify their orders to you, that you immediately make enquiry into all struggling Europeans who may either reside or are only passengers in your district and that you stop all such till you receive further orders and also that you return an account to the Board of such as are provided with proper certificates or passports from the Foreign Companies without molesting them further, till the pleasure of the Board regarding them is known.

OOO

(8)

From,

Warren Hastings
Fort William
13th October, 1772
To,
Mr. William Harwood
Collector of Rajmaul(Rajmahal)
Sir,

This serves to advise you that we have this day formed ourselves into a new Board of Revenue consisting of the whole members of our Council for conducting the business of that Department at the Presidency and we have in consequence to direct that you do regulate yourself accordingly in your future correspondence observing always to address us as President and Council of Revenue at Fort William whereon the business of the Revenue may be concerned.

(Ed.) Harwood's Crrespondence revealing the initial attempts for creating administrative machinery makes a fascinating reading and gives us a peep into Colonial motives.

Surendra Jha

OOO

(9)

From,

Warren Hastings.
P. M. Dacres.
H. Goodwin.
J. Graham
George Vansittart
From William,
Dated 22nd October, 1773.

To,

Mr. James Barton,
Collector of Rajemehall(Rajmahal) & Boglepore(Bhagalpur).

Sir,

As the crops of Light Infantry are entirely employed in reducing to subjection the large extent of mountainous country lying between Mongheer, Boglepur and Beerbhoom and are therefore unable to spare any parties for the protection of the low country in the district of Rajemahal, we have empowered the Farmer to raise and entertain for the following establishment of Burgundasses viz. Three Companies-each consisting of-

1 Jemadar @ 12 Rupees P. m 12
4 Daffadrs @ 6rupees p. m. ...24
64 Burgundasses @ 4 Rupees p. m. 192 – 228 per -month.

The amount for three Companies will be Rs. 684/- per month, which sum is to be disbursed By Rajah Davy Singh and charged in the Rajemehal(Treasury Account from the lst of Cartic (26) (month of Kartik).

The farmer of Rajemahall has petitioned us for a further deduction on account of Sayr Maroocha & Co. - In part of this claim we find he is justly entitled to a consideration on account of the suspension of the Road Duties on Grain and we have therefore determined to allow him a deduction of Five thousand rupees per annum on this account so long as the suspension shall be continued.

The Balance of his Jumma Wassil Bakee for last year will by the allowance of Five Thousand Rupees about mentioned be reduced to Rupees 27,0077-6-0 which difference will be adjusted in his present year's Revenue by the Superintendent of the Khalsa.

Davy Sing the security for the farmer of Rajmehall having applied to us on the part of the Farmer and himself to pay his rents at the Khalsa, we have complied with his request and have in consequence to direct you to consider his rents as separated from your Collectorship. You will however still continue to transmit us the Challans (27) of remittances, monthly treasury accounts and account current Kistbundee as usual.

We have further to acquaint you that we have appointed Bahadoor Sing Paishcar (Peshkar) to Dewan of Rajemehall in the Room of Ramchund Goopt, and we have directed him in case any of the present Moharries belonging to the Cutcherry are unfit for their Employments to recommend to you such others as he can confide in.

○○○

(10)

From,

William Hastings,
W. Aldersey.
P. M. Dacres
H. Goodwin
J. Graham.
George Vansittart.
Fort William
Dated 29th October, 1773

To,

James Barton,

Collector of Rajmehal

Sir,

We desire you will in future transmit all your accounts according to the Bengall months and adjust those for the past months of the present year in the manner that will be pointed out by our Accomptant (Accountant).

OOO

(11)

From,

Thomas Lane"

Patna the Ist November, 1773

To,

Mr. James Barton,

Collector of Boglepore

Sir,

Pursuant to the Directions of the Honble the Council of Revenue, We have ordered Mr. Bright to deliver over to your charge the Pergunnahs of Havely Monghyr, Cawrickpore(=Kharagpur), and Cudgera, with all papers there to relative. We think it will be more in from that these Pergunnahs should be separated from the Behar collections from the Commencement of the present year and have accordingly directed that the collections made since that period shall also be remitted to you. Mr. Wordsworth is appointed an assistant under you.

Enclosed we send you an Account, but we do not suppose the collections from Monghyr will equal the sum at which it is rated.

You have also an account of the balances of former years, which if collected you will please to remit to us.

OOO

(12)

From,

William Hastings,
Rt. Barker
W. Aldersey.
P. M. Dacres
James Lawrell
H. Goodwin
J. Graham.
George Vansittart.
Fort William
Dated 22nd November, 1773

To,

Mr. James Barton,
Collector of Rajmehal and Bogglepore

Sir,

We desire that you will procure and transmit to us as early as possible an exact list of every European, not a convenated servant of the Company residing within your districts with an account of their Employments etc. conformable to the plan enclosed for your rotation.

ooo

(13)

From,

Warren Hastings
George Vansittart
23rd November, 1773
Fort William,

To,

Mr. Jams Barton,

Collector of Rajemahll etc.

Sir,

We have now to advise you that we have thought proper to put the collectorship of Rajemahall etc. under the management of a Council which have formed at Moorshedabad of which Mr. Middleton is appointed Chief.

We have in consequence to direct you to deliver over the charge whenever you shall have rendered your accounts and received orders to this effect from the Council about mentioned after which you will proceed to your station at Moorshedabad and direct your assistant to return to Presidency.

OOO

(13)

From– (Reply)

To,

Mr. James Barton.

Collector of Rejemahal. Bohlepore (Bhagalpur) and Monghur (Monghyr).

Sir,

Agreeable to the appointment of the Hon' ble the President and Council we have this day assembled and taken upon us the charge of the several

Districts committed to our management in consequene thereof your authority as Collector is abolished (29) and we desire you will transmit to us the seal of your office and the accounts of your collectorship made up to the end of Augun by the 15th of Poos. together with every in-formation in your power relative to the collections: you will also be pleased to send to us immediately the wakeels(=Pleaders,Ed) of the different farmers with their papers and accounts : in the meantime you will correspond with us in the same manner as your did with the superior council of Revenue at Calcutta by this we mean that your authority over the collections is to cease from the unddane (=Aghan month, Ed) till the 15th of poos (=Paushmonth, Ed)when the charge of Department will devolve to us.

Moorshedabad,
The 14th December, 1773

ooo

(14)

From–Fort William
To

The Provincial Councils of Revenue
Gentlemen,

Such warrants of the Naib Nizam for the execution of the sentences of the Nizamut Adaulut (Nizamat Adalat, Ed.)on prisoners in the districts under your authority as Your Chief may receive from the Hon"ble the president, you will cause to be carried into execution by the officers of the Court, and conform to the orders which may from time to time accompany them.

Fort william,
The 8th February, 1774

ooo

(15)

From–Fort William
To

The Provincial Council of Revenue
Gentleman.

Having determined that in future the established duty of 2 ½ (=2.5) percent at the government's custom Houses shall be collected upon grain as upon other merchandize we have directed the Board of Customs to issue the necessary orders for this purpose to the collectors.

We desire you will furnish us with an account of the revenue received from the collection of rahydarry (=road- tax, Ed.) duties at the Inland Chokeys(=Police posts, Ed.) in the years 1177 and 1178 (= Bangla Samnat) in the several districts under your charge and also an account of what was received from the collections in Hauts and gunges (=rural market and marke places, Ed). In the account of rahydarry duties you will, if possible, distinguish the amount levied upon grain and the amount levied upon other articles. If you transmit us the accounts of the gross collections. It will further be necessary that the charges should be specified so as to exhibit the net revenue and you will be careful not to include in these accounts the Revenue arising from the river Chokeys which have since been abolished, and for which deductions have been allowed to the renters.

Extract from the proceedings of the Council or Revenue held at Fort William the 17th May, 1774

"That every person who shall forcibly detain or sell any man, woman, or child as a slave. Without a cabawla or deed attested in the usal manner by the caujee (Kazi) of the place where the slave was purchased by the proprietor who shall decoy away or steal any children from their families or places of abode, shall be punished as the law to which he is amenable shall direct. That from the Ist day of July 1774 answering to the 21st of Rabbee ussany(= Rabicrop) or the 11th Assar bengal style (Assar= Asadh month), no person shall be allowed to buy or sell a slave grant any cabwla

after that date for the sale of any slave whatever, shall be dismissed from his employed, and such cabawla shall be invaild. "

ooo

(16)

From,

The Governor & Council of Revenue
Fort William
dated 12th July, 1774

To,

The Provincial Council Revenue.
Gentlemen,

In consequence of a reference made to us by the Provincial Council of Revenue at Dacca. We have lately had under our consideration the subject of the rights of masters over the offspring of their slaves is in general usage. In those districts where slavery in general usage any way Revenue, which we are informed is the case in the frontier part of Bengal, we must desire you particularly to advise us what is the usage and every circumstance connected with it, and we shall then given such directions as we may judge to be necessary, but considering the Reference in the meantime in the light of a general proposition, we are of opinion that the right of the master to the children of the slaves already their property, cannot legally be taken from them in the first generation, but we think that this right cannot and ought not to extend further, and direct that you do make publication accordingly.

(Ed.) Encouragement and efforts for legitimising the slave trade of children by the Company

Surendra Jha

OOO

(17)

From,

The Council of Revenue at Fort William

Dated 20th August, 1774 at Patna

To,

The Provincial Council

"Having resolved that the provision of the Ophium on account of the Company in the District of Monghyr shall be managed from the commencement of the new year's advances by the Chief and Provincial Council of Murdhedabad (Mursidabad Ed) to whose authority that District is in all other Respects amenable. we have instructed these Gentleman to correspond which you are taken proper measures for receiving the charge of that business which you are accordingly hereby directed to deliver over to them. "

ooo

(18)

From,

A Council of Revenue at Fort William

Dated 23rd at Murshidabad

August 1774

To,

The Provincial Council

We have received your letters of the 15th. We cannot but acquiesce in the property and justness of your representation relative to the provision of the opium (opium) on account of the Company in the district of Monghyr and we have therefore sent direction to the Chief and Council of Patna to put it under your management from the commencement of the new year's advances.

You will accordingly correspond with the gentlemen at Patna and taken the proper measures for receiving the charge from them.

OOO

(19)

From–Fort William
To,
Mr. James Barton.
Sir

In order to secure the collections of Mongheer, Boglepore and Rajmahal, to prevent the Embarrassment of accounts and completions of the renters of the former arising from the separation lately made of the major parts of that District from the Province of Bihar and its annexation of Bengal, and to form the line of the general terrain district on the side which lies contiguous to Mongheer, Bogulepore and Rajmahal.

We have thought proper to appoint you to the immediate supenntendence of these Districts in which capacity you are to act under our instruction and correspond with us. You would accordingly proceed thither with all convenient expedition and receive charge of your trust from the gentleman of the Provincial Council of Moorshedabad who have received our orders to that effect. In the execution of the objects above mentioned, you are in general to conform to the regulations and subsequent instructions by which the business in conducted at the Provincial Council so far as these will apply to the particular station to which you are appointed. When the peculiar state of the districts or the present situation of the business in any respect requires a deviation there from or our further orders for your conduct, you will not fail to make the necessary representation to us obtaining the same. Copies of the aforesaid regulations and subsequent instructions are accordingly endorsed for your guidance.

We enclose you also copy of a letter from the Provincial Council of Moorshedabad relative to the Provision of Opium on account of the Company together with the orders which we issued in consequence to Patna and Moorshebad (Murshidabad); as this trust will likewise for the same reason now devolve upon you, we have directed the Gentleman of Moorshedabad to transmit to you whatever correspondence they may have had with the gentlemen at Patna on the subject and his correspondence you will prosecute as you may see necessary so as to carry our orders into Execution.

ooo

(20)

From,

Bengal past and present vol-13 part I, 1954

To,

Captain Brooke's report laid by the President before the Board of Revenue.

(Vide, Revenue Board of the whole Council, Original Consultation.)

Dated 6th Sep. No. 32)

An account of the expedition against the rebellious zemindars of the jungle terry and against the robbers residing in the mountains of Mudwan (Madhuban) Barkope and Pertsundar (Patsunda), by Robert Brooke, Captain commanding the corps of light infantry.

To illustrate the account of the expedition some little information against whom it took place, may be necessary, as also the nature and situation of the country.

The Head Zemindar of the Jungleterry was called Juggernaut Deo (=Jagannath Deo). In the time of Cossim Ally Cawn(=Mirqasim), he was under the Raja of Currickpore (kharagpur in Munger dit) but upon the rajah being taken prisoner for his crimes and carried to Patna, he became, in a manner, independent and the country being full of thick woods and difficult passes and little revenue having been ever got from it, it was hardly thought of by government, till Juggernaut Deo taking advantages of this, entered into compact with the hill robbers of T(f) atteria (5) and granted out his lands to those who would take them on military tenure, by which means he got a number of armed men together and began to plunder the countries of Mungher, Colgong and Bogglepore. On this small detachments were sent against him at different times but always meeting with great loss and never remaining long enough to do anything but overrun the country which did little mischief to the people who could so easily conceal themselves and their effects in the woods, Jaggernaut Deo was encouraged to proceed in his robbery and rebellion. However to render himself as secure as possible, he rented(?) the little district of Tiur in the Jugleterry (=JungleTerai) of Beerbhoom and erected a fort there unknown by Government to which place he carried the plunder, he took from the open country of Mongher etc. until he had a convenient opportunity of disposing of it in Beerbhoom (Birbhum). In the same manner he plundered again in the Beerbhoom side and carried it to the district of Mongher. At last the Collector of Mongher went with a detachment into his country and after much negotiation prevailed on him to agree to pay a revenue of about Rs. 7000/-, but not having guarantee, hostages or any other security, the Collector was sooner returned to Mongher than he renewed his robberies and carried his depredations to the very skrit of Colgong, so that the whole country near the Jungle terry was depopulated and the Collector again taking the field with a small detachment in hopes of awing him to obedience was obliged to return, after having been fired upon. In the same manner the Hill Manjhis of Mudwan and Barkop acquiring strength and by slow degrees drew away the gutwars from the passes leading from the mountains to the low country and laid it waste even to Rajmahal, rendering the great road from Bengal to Bihar almost impassable to travellers by their murders and robberies and they had at last the imprudence to come down and shoot their arrows at the guard of the battalion, stationed at Nagisenbagh (Nageswarbagh). In this situation were affairs in this part of the country when the Hon'ble Governor in Council ordered Capt. Brooke with the force of Light Infantry to march and subdue them, directing him when he had struck terror by his attacks to use every conciliatory method in his power to bring the wild inhabitants of the country to relish a regular mode of life and make their thoughts turn from war to cultivation.

Captain Brooke's force having formed upon a plan approved of by General Barker. Ist of March, 1773 took the field from Patna, six weeks from the time the sepoys began to be enlisted and immediately attacked by those hill people who had been most troublesome to the low country. At first Captain Brooke made two attacks with about 60 picked men to inspire the rest of the battalion with emulation and confidence and successfully answered that end. He was interrupted in his operations and obliged to cross the Ganges to prevent Purnia from being plundered by the Sennasies (Sanyasis) which he executed by taking post with his small party beyond the city until the arrival of the corps by forced maerhes. When he pursued the enemy and was near cutting off their retreat, (bu) by an unforeseen accident they escaped, with the loss of a few of their strugglers, whom he took prisoners. The Light Infantry without halting retired to their station again immediately marched against the hill robbers, attacked them with success and **from thence by stratagem**, got through the passes into Juggernaut Deo's country without loss and marched through the woods driving the enemy from every place with little trouble till they had arrived at Tior(6)(Tiur) in and about which the enemy had principally collected their force and that of the hill-robbers, their allies. On viewing this place it was found that it could not be taken without artillery excepting by risking the loss of a number of men. The fort was situated in as small plain surrounded by thick woods and the Light infantry. Had flanking parties out. The enemy having lined the woods, one of their parries all at once attacked the place without orders. Captain Brooke was astonished, he sent a party up to bring them away. The party instead of doing so joined the rest and he was obliged to go up himself and bring them off with the killed and wounded he could find. The enemy immediately got spirit upon this and growing bolder than usual were drawn into an ambuscade when they suffered considerably and the crops encamped upon the plain for four days to show the enemy. It was not the parties being repulsed that made them march away which they were obliged to do to open a communication with Patna and Mongher. They effected this by securing the pass of Charky (?) and at least after great hardships sustained surrounded by woods full of the enemy, the artillery arrived safe and the fort was taken next day and razed to the ground. After this the country soon submitted and Juggernaut Deo was obliged to abandon it entirely From this business the Light Infantry proceeded once more to secure the hills and after many successful expeditions through them reduced them to the necessity of offering to submit to the directions of the Govt.

The whole of this service was completed in a little more than a year after the raising of the Light Infantry Corps, but not without great fatigue to officers and men.

Imagine Europeans particularly in this climate, not being able to carry house, tents or bedding in the hills **and obliged to be going perpetually backwards and forward to seize the opportunity for surprising the mountaineers who could not be brought under subjection but by stratagem and to put any stratagem into execution** required the utmost expeditious and fatiguing marches when water and provisions were extremely difficult to be got, particularly water, for even that laid up in the villages could not be drunk by the Sepoys, as the hill people are of no cast(e). It now became Captain Brooke's duty to carry into execution the second part of the instructions he had received from govt. For this purpose he had all along treated the prisoners with the most particular care; he even hired women to attend the women and children who were confined, letting no man have access to them belonging to the camp. Through the means of his people pleased with a treatment so different from that which they must have expected from the former custom of govt. when those who were taken were impaled alive or put upon work as slaves of life, we now began to treat with the mountaineers with success and to get their families released, and some few agreed to come down, erect habitations below and cultivate the waste lands. To them Captain Brooke was particularly attentive. So they found their advantage in the change of residence, while those who continued obstinate found themselves exposed to repeated attacks and therefore lived in perpetual dread of losing everything that could be dear to them. At last by degrees he got the whole of the hill-people to come down from Oduwanalla(7) (=Udhwa Nala)along the chain of mountains to beyond Barkop, an extent of 120 coss; the number of villages erected below in 12 months amounted to 283 and for a long time past, not a single inhabitant or passenger has been robbed.

The Government step by step directing Capt. Brooke, he was enabled to abolish the military tenures in the Jungle terry of Juggernaut Deo disarm the men who used to their depredation to near Colgong and Mongher, and to secure the frontier upon the old establishment. Besides the revenue was increased to Rs. 3000/- this year and as this was done in time of confusion and trouble it any be expected it will soon rise to a very considerable amount.

It is worthy of remark that although the incursion of the hill-people, has been from time immemorial dreadful to the low country. I have always obliged govt. for the protection its inhabitants to be at great and particular expense in keeping up large bodies of troops for this end. Yet that no attempt made until the present govt. to bring the mountaineers under subjection, and in the maps of Bengal, the interior parts of the Rajmahal chain are termed unknown it does not appear to have entered the thoughts of any during the Mughal govt. to attempt even an entrance into the country. The reason for this is obvious. their military enterprises are always conducted with great parade and executed by the cavalry and though many instances occur in the history of Hindustan in which ambition has fixed the mind of most men to daring undertakings in the open fields : yet their disposition never led any of them to wish for the conduct of an expedition where activity and discipline must supply the place of number and where the chief must sustain the fatigues of long marches on foot participate in all the distress and set an example of labour and patience to all the followers.

Since the establishment of British power in the provinces, frequent expeditions have been set on foot against the mountaineers of these parts, but these have only been temporary, designed for surprise or to intimidate in instances of great and notorious provocation and they have ever proved successful, when skilfully conducted ; that is to say, either the rebellious chiefs have fallen into the hands of the conqueror or their forces have been defeated and put to flight and the country ravaged. But we thought these successes have impressed the terror of the English power, yet it has never produced any other advantage. On the country, every example of rigour has served to animate the hatred of these people against our. govt. The fugitive chiefs have recovered their strength, the instant our forces have abandoned their country or other have succeeded them with the same hostile principles. Those among their chiefs who, from whatever motives have afforded their assistance to our troops, have fallen an immediate sacrifice to their ill judged attachment and the same scans of rebellion, invasion and devastation have been renewed. The different issue of the late undertaking may be obviously accounted for, by an application to the different principles on which it was formed and conducted – not by a precipitate, desultory and destructive war but by the steady prosecution of a concerted plan of conquest, by treating the prisoners taken of the enemy with kindness and inviting them to share in the blessings of peace and civilization when conquered. The continued adherence to such maxims must infallibly secure the advantage we have acquired ; the fidelity of the common people will be ensured by their interests and the presence of a military force will awe their chiefs into submission who alone could have an inducement in their ambition to dissociate them from us. Nothing seems wanting to perfect the system of govt. thus far so happily introduced into these savage and wild regions but to fix the boundary of Jungle terry district, by including in it such parts as from their natural state are incapable of civil control and effecting a junction of it with the commands of Capt. Camac and Capt. Crawford.

OOO

8

Chapter III
From Bhagalpur Collectorate Records, Now Kept in Bihar State Archives, Patna

1. Letter

From,
Warren Hastings

To,
Mr. James Barton
Dated 20 September,1774
Sir,

In order to secure the collections of Monghaar,(= Monghyr) Boglepore (=Bhagalpur) and Rajemahal, to prevent the Embarrasment of accounts and competions of the renters of the former arising from the separation lately made of the major parts of that District from the Province of Bihar and its annexation to Bengal, and to from the line of the Jungleterai district on the side which lies contiguous to Mongheer, Bogulepore and Rajmahal.

We have thought proper to appoint you to this immediate superintendence of these Districts in which capacity you are to act under our instructions and correspond with us. You would accordingly proceed thither with all convenient expedition and receive charge of your turst from the gentlemen of the Provincial

Council of Moorshedabad who have received our orders to that effect.

In the execution of the objects above mentioned,you are in general to conform to the regulations and subsequent instructions by which the business is conducted at the Provincial councils so far as these will apply to the particular station to which you are appointed. When the peculiar state of the districts or the present situation of the business in any respect requires a deviation there from or our further orders for your conduct,you will not fail to make the necessary representation to us for obtaining the same. Copies of the aforesaid regulations and subsequent instructions are accordingly endorsed for your guidance.

We enclose you also copy of a letter from the Provincial Council of Moorshedabad relative to the provision of Ophlum (opium)on account of the company together with the orders which we issued in consequence to Patna and Moorshedabad; as this trust will likewise for the same reasons now devolve upon you, we have directed the Gentlemen of Moorshedabad to transmit to you whatever correspondence they may have had with the gentlemen at Patna on the subject and this correspondence you will prosecute as you may see necessary so as to carry our orders into Execution.

OOO

2. Letter

From, WarrenHastings, W. Aldersay,P. M. Dacres
James Lawrell,Fort William
Dated 4 October, 1774
To,
James Barton

"We have this day directed Captain James Browne who has the command of the jungle Terry Lands bordering on the Districts superintended by you to correspond and settle with you the boundary of his District adjoining. It is not our intention that the whole correspondence shown be annexed to the Jungleterry but such part of it only as from their situation amongst the woods and Mountains cannot, with convenience, be managed by a civil Collector but require the continual Aid and Neighbourhood of a Military force to keep them in subjection. This, therefore must be the general principile on which the outline of the District is to be formed, and to render it less liable to dispute or confusion in the Accounts of the Collections we desire you will take an Account from the conogoes (kanunge) of the lands belonging to (Kharagpur) Curreukpore. Boglepore and Rajmahal, which are registered in the Books of Government under the Head of Jecoksum, and all places not included in this account we desire may be annexed to the Jungle Terry District, for the rest we must leave it to you both to settle the same of your respective jurisdiction in such a manner as shall be most conformable to the Ratas (=Raiyats) which we have given you, and which may be less liable to future misapprehension.

ooo

3. Letter

From,

Robert Palk, Simion Droz, E. Saw, E. Golding, Patna,

To,

James Barton

Dated 28 November, 1774

"We have received your letter of the 17th instant and enclosed send you a copy of an amount of the Junglettery to the Board. It doesnot appear from any paper in our office what collections have been made by the the Renters of Curruckpore from the severals

Mehals. These accounts can only be procured from the Conogoes Registers which particularize the payments of the inferior parts of the Pergunnah. No grant of the Jungleterry was connected with Havely Monghyr. "

ooo

4. Letter

From,
C. Chapman,
Collector, Bhagalpur
To,
Captain Robinson, Commanding the Battalion of Sepoys, dated 14 February, 1775.

"I have been favoured with your letter of this date enclosing copy of the order you have received from the supreme Council through the commander in Chief: the latter I have forwarded to Captain Browne and at the same wrote him fully on the subject in consequence of you representation to remain with your Battalion at this place till I receive an answer from captain Browne, as that Gentleman will be least able to represent the necessity he can make of the situation of the enemy.

ooo

5. Letter

From,
C. Chapman from Bhagalpur
To,
Captain James Browne
Dated 14 February, 1775.

"In Mr. Barton's absence I forwarded your letter of 10th instant to Captain Robinson, and at the same time represented to that Gentleman the necessity of stationing a few companies from his Batalion at Baggoreah (=Bagoria near Banka). As the enquiries regarding that part of the Curruckpore Pergunah (is) less to the company.

Captain Robison is arrived here with 6 compaines for that purpose, but he has since received order (copy of which I enclose) from the Surpreme Council through the commander in chief directing him to proced to the Presidency, leaving one company only in the garrison of Monghyr. As Captain Robinson is under march, he informs me that he cannot with any propriety detach any part of his Battalion, but for the present consents to march to Baggoreah. Provided there is an absolute necessity for it, which being properly represent will indemnify him for acting contrary to the absolute order he has received; and he intends therefore, remaining at this place till I hear further from you. He has also strongly represented to me that he believes nothing but the immediate want of troops to do the duty at Fort William could have induced the Commander in Chief to leave So small a force in the garrison Monghyr. The 3rd Brigade is now on the march for Dinapur and Likewise the 3rd &4th Battalions of sepoys under the command of Lt. Colonel waiting for the Monghyr station.

(Ed.) These records inform us about the grave law and order problem in Jungle-Teari due to the revolt of the Paharias and the Ghatwals led by Jagannath Deo. Captain Brooke's Report is more revealing, describing the difficult geographical situation and fierce resistance of the hill-Men. This led to the emergence a dual policy of Carrot and Stick. The Britishers Segregated the Paharias from the main current of the society and this led to the emergence of Non-Regulation system of Administration.

Surendra Jha

OOO

6. Letter

From
C. Chapman from Bhagalpur
To,
Captain Robinson
Dated 20 February, 1775.

"The farmer of Curreckpore has represented to me that a large of Jaggernath Deo's adherents have burnt several villages in thanah Cuckwarah (near Bankatown)and commited many depredations in that part of the Curreckpore Pergunah contiguous to Baggoreah, which has alarmed the inhabitants of all the neighbouring villages to so great a degree. That he is fearful that the country will be entirely deserted unless a detaochment of sepoys is sent there to protect them. He also represents that numbers of the Ryots (raiyatsor ryots) have already and on continually running away. I have, therefore, to request that you will be pleased to send a detachment to Baggoreah as soon as possible, which I have not the least doubt will effectually prevent the enemies again entering into either the Bhagalpur or Curreckpore Pergunah and I flatter myself this step will also remove every apprehension which at present the inhabitants seem possesed of, and by that means encourage them to return to their respective villages.

As I have not received an answer to the letter which I wrote on the 14th instant to Captain Browne, I take the liberty of strongly recommending that a part of your Battalion remain at this place till I receive further advice from that gentle, man, as he will, most probably, have occasion for a reinforcement the intelligencence I daily receive giving me any reason to suppose enemy are very troublesome.

P. S. : The names of the villages which have been burnt are as follows :- Curherreah, Icronah, Choonteah,(in Shambhunganj block) Aumespore, (Amarpur in Banka Disrict) Mysondey, (near Sulanjanj)Jumdahaw(near Deoghar).

ooo

7. Letter

From

C. Chapman from Bhagalpur

To,

Captain Robinson

Dated 20 February, 1775

"Enclosed I transmit you a perwana to the different". Zamindari, Tahsildars of the Bhagalpur and Curreckpore Pergunahs, which ontains an order for them to supply the officer commandings the detachment from your Battalion with every necessary he may be in want of on his paying for the same, and I must request when the services on which the officer is sent, are concluded that the Perwaannah may be returned to me. "

ooo

8. Letter

From,

C. Chapman from Bhagalpur

To,

CaptainJames Browne

Dated 20 February, 1775

"Nothing having received a reply to the letter which I did myself the pleasure of writing to you under date the 14th instant, I am apprehensive it has not been delivered to you. Enclosed, therefore, I transmit a duplicate of it.

I think it necessary to inform you the farmer of Curreckpore (Kharagpur) has represented to me that a large body of Juggernath Deo's adherents have burnt several villages in Thannah Cuckwara, (=Kakwara). And commited many depredations in that part of Curreckpore Pergunnah contiguous to Baggoreah, in consequence of which, Captain Robinson on, my application, has this day has sent three companies of his Battalion to Baggureah which I hope will effectually prevent the enemies again retiring into either the Bhagalpur or Curreckpore Pergunnahs.

As the intelligence I daily receive gives me every reason to suppose the enemy troublesome. I have strongly recommended to Captain Robinson that a part of this Battalion remain at this place, As you may probably have occasion for a reinforcement, and he has been pleased to acquire in it till I received further advice from you. "

OOO

9. Letter

From,

C. Chapman,

To,

Captain Robinson,
Dated 21 February, 1775

"Enclosed I have the pleasure to transmit you extract of a letter which I this day received from Captain Browne. As I imagine there is already sufficient force at Baggoresh to defend both the Bhagalpur and Curruckpore Pergunnah from the enemy and captain Browne has no occasion for your assistance. I cannot think of requesting you to detain the remaining part of your Battalion at this place any longer, but at the same time beg leave to acquaint you that I apprehend it to be absolutely necessary. A small force should still remain at Baggoresh till the fears of the Inhabitants are subsided, and they have been prevailed upon to return to their habitations, as the disturbances committed in that part of the country are fully confirmed.

I beg leave Sir to return my thanks for the ready acquie sence you have been pleased to pay my representation, and I am of opinion your stay here has been attended with very essential services to the country as the inhabitants are **so extremely timid at the least alarm** of an enemy, that I am well assured had you not compiled with my requisitions in remaining here, most part of them would have fled to the other side of the river. "

OOO

10. Warren Hasting ' Sanad to Roop Narain Deo,
Dated the 24th May, 1776

Sanad to Roop Narin Deo, the Zemindar of Khargpur in the District of Monghyr in the Soobah of Behar for the Parganas of Pairna (sic), & Besee and the Dhees of Darindeh Sakhware .... Mahals – Registered by order of the Governor gernal (in) council at Fort William the 5th June, 1776.

Rev. Deptt. (sd.) R. Summer, Secretary.
seal

(East India) Company Madarul Maham Sipeh Salar Diwan of the Provinces of Bengal, Bihar and Orissa devoted servant of Emperor Shah Alam Ghazi, 14th year (of the reign).

Know ye motasadies mohimat present and future, and the chowdries and Qanungos of Jungleteri Mahals appertaining to Kharakpur under Siercar Monghyr in the Province of Bihar.

Wheras parganas Chandwa and Passai and villages Danrasakhware, etc. ; have become less cultivated due to disorders and disturbances hence with a view to the (proper) cultivation of the said Parganas an annual jama at sonat rupees five thousand for the Fasli year 1184 without any abatement on account of calamities inclusive of land revenue (mal), sayer (imposts other than land revenue), nazrana, mehmani (i. e. guest charges), and other expenses except russom Zemindary, nacar (i. e. subsistence allowance), Ghatwary salary for the retainers, jagirgrants, and given in charity, barhmotar, bhatotar,shivotar,birt, ayma and amlak(millicks), etc.' and from 1185 Fasli (an annual jama) at sonat rupees seven thousand two hundred and ninety one, being the original assessement .... (7291) and enhancement madde thereon, without any abatement on account of calamities in accordance with the aforesaid terms is fixed in perpetuity as the jama year after year. The zemindari of the said Parganas is made over to Roop narain Deo Rai after the deposition of his father Jagannath Deo Rai. The said person (Roop Narain Deo Rai) shall look after the cultivation of the said pargana with a sense of security and pay into the Government treasury the land revenue regularly. Not a fraction more shall be demanded over and above the fixed istimari ancd mokurari jama (as above). He should exert his best so that rents may increase and the tenantry may cultivate (lands) better than before. Thieves, robbers, pick-pockets should not be allowed to live within the limits of his zeminderi,God forbid, should misdeeds like murder, affray, theft, robbery,burglary and dacoity,etc. occur within the said Parganas, he shall be held the responsible. When summoned, he shall appear before the Presence(Huzzoor) escorted by his retainers who hold jagir grants and the Sirdars and their men. He shall be careful of his boundaries and discharge his duties with devotion and Zeal. Be it known that the above named should be recognised as the zemindar of the aforesaid parganas and due services should be rendered to him. This is strictly enjoined. Dated, the 24th May,1776 A. d. agreeable to 5th Rubi-oos-sani of the 17th year of the reign agreeable to 24th Jeth, 1183 Bengali year. The End.

Endorsements

Parganas Chandwa,Passai, and village Danrasakhware, etc. of mahalat Jungleterry appertaining to Kharakpur in Sircar Monghyr in the Province of Bihar have become less cultivated due to disturbances hence with a view to the proper cultivation of the said parganas an annual jama in sonat rupees five thousandfor 1134 Fasli including land –revenue (mal), sayer,nazrana, mihmani and other expenses except russokm Zemindary, nankar,ghatwari, the salary of retainers and grants to jagirdars, charity lands, brahmotar, shivotar, birt,ayma, amlak, etc. and from 1185 Fasli at sonat rupees seven thousand two hundred and ninety one, being the original assessment and the enhancement, without any abatement on account of calamities according to the aforesaid terms is fixed in perpetuity as the annual jama and the Zemindari of the aforesaid Parganas is made over to Roop Narain Deo Rai after deposing Jagannath Deo Rai.

.... particulars of mahals inclusive of villages.

Pargana Chandwa .... 1 mahal durobusht.

Pargana Passai .... 1 mahal durobusht.

Pargana Satyari .... 1 mahal durobusht.

Pargana Danrasakware villages
(including Sarhi) .... 1 mahal durobusht.

Villages Gorda (forming
Ancient lease). ... 1 mahal

Villages from pargana Amlomtia. ... 1 mahal

1 mahal

Villages from pargana Hendwooa
(ba mojia mamula kadim kharij
jama baa mal khahad amad). . 1 mahal

From pargana Hazartaki one mouza
Kharij jama(ba mojib mamule
Hala sarhe mahal khahad

Amad)...... 1 mahal
Jama for the year 1184 Fasli From the year 1185 Fasli
for less cultivation fixed at annually rupees seven
Rs. 5,000.... thousand two hundred
and ninety –one fixed in
perpetutity.
Original assesement Enhancement
Rs- 5,000. RS. 2,291.

ooo

11. Letter
SANAD by Captain James Brown,
Dated the 24th November, 1776
Seal of the East India Company.

Captain James Browne, Sirdar of Jungleteri, Gidhaur, Karakpur, Bhagalpur, Colgong, BIrbhoom and Kharagdiha on behalf of (East India) Company.

Know ye Motasaddis, mohimat present and future and Chowdhries and Qanungos of Jungleteri mahals appertaining to Kharakpur under Sircar Monghyr in the Province of Bihar.

Whereas Parganas Chandwa, Passai and village Danra Sakhware, etc. under Babu Roop Narain Deo Rai, son of Raja Jagannath Deo Rai become less cultivated due to disorders and disturbances hence with a view to the (proper) cultivation of the said parganas etc. a zeminderi sanad has been issued by the Supreme Council to the said Babu as per terms given below with an annual jama at sonat Rupees five thousand for 1184 Fasli inclusive of land-revenue (mal.) sayer fouzdari, nazrana, mehmani, and other expenses except russom Zemindary, nancar of Qanungos, russom ghatwari for the salary of retainers and jagir grants, lands given in charity, brahmotar, shivotar, debotar, bishenprit, ayma madadash, etc. has been fixed so that he may peacefully look after the cultivation of the said mahals and pay the aforesaid land–revenue (malguzari) to the treasury and (with annual jama) at sonat ruppes seven thousand two hundred and ninety-one from 1185 Fasli without abatement on account of calamities according to the aforesaid rules has been fixed in perpetuity. The said babu shall pay the jama as per Sanad of the Supreme Council. Be it known to the authorities that they shall not demand a fraction more than the annual amount fixed in perpetuity which should be maintained. This is strictly enjoined. Dated, the sixth Shawal, 18th year of the reign agreeable to 1184 Fasli. The End.

sd.) James Browne.

(Ed.)- Both the sanads are important. The sanads provide us with detailed information on the structure and land tax and other levies. Rusum Zamindari was particularly a bone of contention. Whoever may be Tehsildar, they had to pay 2% as the token of superiority to the zamindar

Surendra jha

ooo

12. Letter

From,

James Browne,

To,

Warren Hastings

Dated 29 July, 1777

"Having read with the greatest attention the 3rd paragraph of your letter of the 11th inst, which contains a remark on the inefficiency of military punishment towards bringing to obedience the mountaineers of Rajmahal and an injunction to lay before your board some plan for that end,I will do myself the pleasure of replying to each part separately.

Part 1st: That the mountaineers should not totally abstain from plunder in every part of the hills in consequence of the punishment inflicted in one of two particular quarters will not be matter of surprise, gentlemen, when I have the honour to inform you that the scene of their depredation extends from Nooney in Jungletery of Curruckpore to Furrokabad, 16 cos below Rajmahal. Both these places you will find the maps and that Following the skirts of the hills as closely as possible all the way, **the shortest distance is 65 coss**. (=130 miles) This immense space is filled by a multitude of people of different sized and mostly inhabited by these public robber. Each hill has a chief called Manjhi nor is there any general interest which seems to unite any great body of these that the inhabitants of one or at least two hills. They did in the years of the famine collect together in bands in 4 or 500 from different hills when they designed to carry their depredations very far with the plain country but this is the only instance I ever heard of. In general the chief and the people of one hill are without any connection with any others. The very nature of such a system shows at first sight that the punishment of one quarter must have little influence on the rest which are remotely situated but it has always been an effectual remedy for a time to the parts actually attacked and to the neighborhood for since the expeditions in February, March, April and May, no kinds of disturbance has happened for those hills which have suffered and in general indeed, these, I have advised you, are very distant from that quarter as the last for instance which was committed below Rajmahal, about 60 cos distant from the scene of our late operations. I am induced to trouble you with this detail in order to obviate the objections your Hon'ble Board to the (of) employing military force against these banditi. I do not however mean to infer from hence that military execution should be considered as the only means necessary to bring these people to entire order and obedience. I think on the contrary it cannot, unless we suppose it extended to the entire extirpation of them which is hardly practicable, that it certainly is occasionally a just and rational punishment for the horrid barbarities they some times commit and always produces a suspension of them for some months................................ I recommend.

Part 2.

To put on effectual stop to the depredations of those people, one or two things seem absolutely necessary, either to establish some species of government over them within the hills or to make their coming down to plunder so dangerous as I shall deter them from attempting it on if both these ends could be provided for at once, the security would be still greater, I therefore beg leave to submit the following proposal to your consideration and humbly request you will please to remember that at present I have very little local knowledge of that side of the country, the constant disturbance in the jungle terry districts having always kept me employed to the southward, if therefore from better information on the spot, I should hereafter have occasion to alter or reject anything which I now propose I hope I shall not be suspected of inconsistency.

Suggesting that the division of hills described on the name as Sultanabad lying immediately west of Radshai (Rajsahi) of which it is a dependency be directly put under my authority.

At present that country is an asylum for all men who having offended on my side are afraid of punishment and who finding immunity from shifting from one part of the hills to another defy all restraints, and those into whose hills they fly, being out of my jurisdiction entirely disregard my order, well knowing I can neither serve or injure them.

I propose the re establishment of the family that formerly had excursive jurisdiction over the hills.

To secure the second object, I mean the renderiung any attempt to plunder in the low country so dangerous as I shall discourage any of the mountaineers from making them, I beg leave to inform your Hon'ble Board of the state of the countries bordering on those hills.

Curruckpore and Beerbhoom

In these districts the whole of the lands from the hills every village, has its respective chokey, the mountaineers therefore can do little or no to them,of the state of that country I am as yet uniformed but I believe no injury is done least by the mountaineers.

The Zamindari of the Jungleterry district depending on these division extending from Barcope to Farruckabad along the skirt of the hills have very large tract of land inJagheer for keeping up a number of Chowkidars at the several passes leading from the hills. These are under the authority of these Zamindars and formerly stationed near so each other that the firing a matchlock at once alarmed the next and so on all along by which means the mountaineers were never able to come beyond their line of chokeys, but in time the zamindar neglecting these establishment, many of the chokies become deserted and the famine of 1769 and 1770 falling with extraordinary severity **upon those district such number of the people of all denominations perished that this chokey-bundi was almost entirely destroyed on the sides of Baugalepoor, Colgong and Rajemahal and opened the way for those ravages into the very heart of the plain country which they plundered** almost with impunity till Capt. Brooke was sent against them, After forcing them to take shelter in their hills, he placed considerable numbers of the chokeys above described. I have also established a great many, but many more are still vacant and thereby the grand end of a perfect chain of them with communication from one to another for the purpose of general alarms and defence is destroyed, I would therefore recommend.

1 That all the vacant gauts be immediately manned with a proper force but as the jaghir lands formerly applied to the support of those chowkies have now been waste for many years, and cannot, of course, afford any maintenance to them at all, the chowkidar must be retained in mothly pay at least for the present till the aforesaid jagirs can be reconstituted. This expense should be defrayed out of the jagirs and allowances of the zamindars as far they will go, after making suitable provision for the zamindars and this is the more reasonable, since they have suffered the Chowkidary jagir to go to ruin. They have taken care to keep their own in a state of cultivation, probably by those very hands which should have guarded the passes from the hills and protected the plain country. I say only probably, because as yet I have no opportunity of enquiring on the spot, a report whether a report which I have is trueor false.

Should these resources however prove insufficient to answer the expense of re-establishing the Chowkeybundy from Farruckabad to Barcope, I think it an object worth of the attention of Government till the Chowkidar Jaghirs can be restored to a state of cultivation, I even think it want be strict economy, as the valueable sudder land of Baugalpore, Colgong and Rajmahal, would be thereby secure from disturbance and their vcultivation and rents increased annually.

2nd :- As the zamindar of the part of this Jungleterry from Bakcope to Farruckabad have showed themselves, so underserving of trust in the management of Chowkibundy, I would advise that they be not future allowed to have any authority over them but that instead of them the following officers be appointed or the part of Government.

That to every dhee (Dih=village) of these jungleterry tappas there be a jamadar who shall be accountable for all the Chowkies stationed at the passes, leading from the hills into his dhee. He shall be answerable that the Chokidars are never absent from their posts and in case of the hill people, attempting to force their way through any of his Chowkeys, it shall not only be his duty to repel them but to ascertain from what hill or hills the attempt was made, that orders being thereupon sent for that purpose to person in authority within the hills the offenders may be brought to justice. The Chowkidars at his several Chokies shall bereport to him all intelligence and occurrences.

Over these tapadars I advise that there be two Sazawals appointed the authority of the one to extend from Barkope to Shahabad, of the other from Sacragully to Furruckabad. There is no occasion for any from Sacragully to Shahabad, as there are posts of sepoys all the way. The Tappadars respectively within their limits to be under the orders of the Sazawals in the same manner and for same ends as the Chowkidar are to the tappadars. Little points of regulation for the better management of the Chowkibundy, shall beat their discretion but no considerable alteration to be made without previously advising me through the officer commanding at Diggoy and waiting for my order, the Sazawals shall also receive weekly reports of the state of the Chowkies from the several tapnadars and make their to the officer at Diggoy accordingly, but extraordinary occurrence shall be immediately reported, the officers reports shall be made to me in the same manner.

I beg leave to submit the whole of this proposal to your consideration, gentleman, as what appears to me the most likely means of fulfilling the intent in of government by putting an end to all further troubles from the hill people and should it meet with your approbation, I will form and transmit you estimate of the lowest expense at which it can be done, at the same time that I endeavour to fix a general system of government within the hills.

I must once more observe that since I was appointed to command at that station, I have so much employed in settling the communications in the jungleterry that, I have never had leisure to pay personal attention to the regulation of the hills, but those troubles are now at an end and I trust that after succeeding in the most difficult part of my business, I shall not fail in the most easy especially of I am encouraged and supported by the Government to such regulations as I may make from time to time for forwarding what shall appear to me the public benefit.

As through knowlege of this cluster of hills with all its outlets and the communication between several parts of it is an object which has long been desired by Government, and which also make the mountaineers subjection by force, as their further conduct merit I beg leave to observe that a surveyor might be appointed to great advantage with me in October as from the situation, I shall be in the centre of the hills, I can send him with proper escorts in every road quit to the plains on all sides, may almost ascertain the name of every hill,the future consequences of which cannot fail to be highly beneficial.

I would have accompanied the proposal with estimate of the charges that will be incurred in re-establishing the Chowkeybundy but as I am yet ignorant of the number of Chowkidars requisite for that purpose, it is impossible to from the estimates till I return to my station when I will transmit. Them as soon as possible. "

(Ed.) This report is important for knowing the system of Browne and his motives.

Surendra Jha

OOO

13. Letter

From,

C. Chapman, Acting Collector, Bhagulpur

To,

Warren Hasting

Dated 6 November, 1777

" I have been honoured with your letter of the 31st October, informing me of the application made by Cawder Ally(=Qadir Ali) the son of Fezul Ally late Zemindar of Curruckpoor to be invested with the rights and immunities of the zemindary as held by his father, and that you wait until you hear from me whether there are any objections his claim before you propose to the Board, the passing the Sunned.

Mozaffer Alley the last Zemindar of Curruckpoor, after being some months in arrears secured and sent to Patna, dispossessed of his zemeendary and after as long confinement died the end 1773 a prisoner in the Cutwalley Mozaffer Alley left several sons Fuzul Alley the father of the claimant Cawder Alley one of the youngest but neither he nor any of his brothers ever enjoyed the inheritance. Should it be judge proper to restore to any of this family, their ancestral patrimony ? It will not with the Board to give a preference to the sons of Mozaffer Alley according to priority of birth, to the sons in general, or the descendant of Fuzul Alley in which last case, as he is an infant of two years old. Precautions while be necessary to guard against the imposition of Agents in respect to the Company's interest, as well as that infant Zemindar.

The troubles in Currucckpoor originated with Mozaffer Alley, so that he seems to have been very justly dispossessed. they are now kept up by the Ghautwalls, who hold their several possession by no other Rights than his Grants, and the influence of that family has been so great that the people of the Purgunnah sought from Mozaffer Alley during his confinement grants of lands and villages and conceiving the grant to be good, paid the full value for them. The sons have since his death, pursued the same practice. With such influence a question will arise whether to p. . any of this family again in the purgnnah will not be giving a Head to the Ghautwalls and encourage them to continue the disturbances.

The claim of Cawder Alley comprises ten purgunnahs in any division and a country of still greater extent under charge of Captain Browne multiplying the Zemindars to the number of purgunnah might prove a more effectual method of brining the district under good Government, than by giving the whole into one hand. If this method could secure to the public a proper revenue from that line country without the expense, which in now incurred. The adoption is to be wished but to make grants to Zemaindars without advantages resulting from then to Government is a measure which I should suppose Sir you would never adopt.

OOO

14. Proposals of Browne

Browne's Proposals

(Revenue Department Original Consulatations No. 24, dated 27 January, 1778)-

"Proposal for the Government of the Hill people and for the re-establishement of the Choukies in the low country at the foot of the hills, on a footing which render them useful to Govt.

It is about 15 years since the hill people had any Government among themselves of a general nature from the period of its dissolution, they have become and troublesome to the plain country which they were never before, and their ravages have been the more violent, as they were stimulated by hatered against the zamindars of the low country **for having cut off several of their chiefs by treachery.** Formerly the hills of each Tappa were under one manjhi, to whom the manjhies of all the separate hills were bound to show obedience, He was bound by a muchulka to the zamindars of the Tappah and had jagir lands in the plain country granted for the support of himself and family in a suitable manner. If any robbery happened he was obliged to trace it and bring the chief to justice. All the Chokies within the hill were Hill people, whose business was to prevent any bodies of people from the inners hills,passing throught their ghaut, towards the plain country – **while this mode prevailed, no robberies were committed the hill people were happy and quiet and the low country people were safe from depredation**. Every year at the festival of the Dasserah, the head manjhi of each Tappa brought the rest of the manjhis with him to his zamindar rendered his oath of allegiance to Govt. The other manjhls renewesd theirs to him and each of them having received a turban and been feasted in their custom any manner, returned to their respective duties.

But in time, the zemindars falling into contempt with these hill chiefs, they attempted to make themselves independent of them, the former not having force to compel them to obedience were obliged to have recourse to treachery and cut off several of them at a public feast. The other manjhis and hill people left their respective ghauts within the hills and commenced their depredations on the plain country which have continued with little intermission, ever since. **The zamindary Chawkies, however, lying between the hills and the cultivated parts of the country kept things within bounds till the year 1769, when the famine Swept away numbers of these chockeys and kept the plain country entirely exposed to the ravages of the mountaineers.**

When Capt. Brooke came into this quarter,the only information he could receive was from the people of the low country. They counducted him against the hills which were most trouble some. they were reduced and many of them inhabitants compelled to settle in the country. They even informed him of the former Chowkeybundy in the low country. But they never gave him the least information of there having ever been any Government among the hill people farther than that of Manjih over each hill. They represented the hill people in general terms as a set of robbers who always had been and would always be open wars with society in general.

From the troubles in the southern parts of the Jungleterry. I have been entirely prevented from coming over to this quarter for the purpose of setting the hills till the last month(in the meantime)the zamindary ghatwals of the low country chowkles taking advantage of the hill peoples fear of any milltary force, have carried them oppression them to the highest state of barbarity and produced the shocking effects of which so many complaints have been made.

When I arrived here last month my first search was for the means of establishing some internal Government of the hills,when for the first time was discovered the particulars above stated. They are all founded on undoubted fact,corroborated by the evidence of both hill chiefs still in existence,the miserably poors having lost their former professions in the low country. I have consulted many of the Manjhis who have come into me and they all agree in asserting that if their ancient form of Government is restored,an efficient end will be put to all the present regulations. That they will pay implicit obedience to the chiefs who shall be established out of the several families and that those chiefs will pay the same to the Government. I therefore,think it my duty to recommend the following method of settling the internal Government of the hills.

That the successors of the several Sardar Manjhis of the different tappas be restored to the authority and possessions held formerly by their predecessors. But instead of holding them from the zamindar that they shall hold them by Sanads granted in the name of Government.

That they shall give muchulkas to Government specifying the services they are to perfrom and the penalties in case of failure in the performance.

That the inferior manjhls shall give muchalkas specifying their duties and penalties in the same manners and moreover holding them to their Sardar Manjhi for all purpose specified in the sanad.

That all the transactions with the hill people shall be carried on through the Sardar Manjhis where by every abuse arising from the capacity of the low country Gautwals and others will be prevented.

That the annual oath of allegiance with ancient oaths and ceremonies attending it be renewed,as these barbarians seem to have great reverence for that institutions.

That if Manjhi of any of the hill refuse to acquiesce in this establishment,they shall be treated as enemies.

That hauts be established at proper places to forward the intercourse of the hill people with the low country. These regulations would I believe sufficienty ensure the peace of the hills.

The nature of Zamindar chokeys lying between the hills of cultivated lands has been fully explained in my address of the 29th July last. I have therefore only to observe in addition with that I find it will be necessary to pay the chowkeydars who may be stationed at the Ghauts, now lying waste for eight months, after which their jaghirs which they will have recultivated in that time with support them and I recommend that all those jaghirs be fixed to them by sanads in the name of Government to which they shall be bounded by muchulkas, for the services there in specified. It appears but prudent to keep up those chokes,besides the internal Government of the hills,as the removal of them may be too great a trust to repose at once in the hill people.

By the enclosed estimate it will appear to you gentlemen that the expense of zamindari which I before thought would occur is omitted, as I find there is the Jagirdari establishment people for those duties. The sazawals and barqandzes are therefore the only people who will be in charge to Government, as the money advanced for re-esthablishing the chowkles, in fact, a loan to the zamindars,upon which too interest may be taken if you please to order to the burqandazes are set of people pechtier to this country are so very useful that I dare say keeping them will meet with your approbation. They are people of the low country who having learnt the language of the hills people are employed in transactions with them and so entire is their faith in these burcundazes that in time of great hostility they can go safely in the hills and any manjhi who is in arms will come down and submit on their assurance of his safety. The use which I propose making of them is to prevent any abuse towards the hill people by the officers of the zamindar on government,for which end I shall leave them in charge of the sarders manjhi to forward every complaint to me that it may be immediately attended to and the evil redressed as soon as it exists. The very nature of their employment shows the necessity of their being entirely free every authority and dependence but that of Government.

So considerable is the sum of money to be lent for re-establishing the Manihari and other Chowkles with those already due from the zamindars that I am induced to propose it with reluctance. However as the security is so good it will probably meet with your approbation and I dare say end of protecting the country in case necessity should call away the battalion to another quarter,will appear important to you gentlemen eapeclally as after all the money is not an expence but a loan. If you however, should make an use of the hill chowkles without the zamindary ones, the loans may be avoided,I will not however venture to recommend it till they are more civilized and fond in your determinate ideas of government than they are at present.

I have nothing to add to the proposal but my hope that it will meet with your approbation and that whatever be your determination I may be honoured with it as soon as possible for the entire establishment of those hills will take up sometime and not above three or four months remain to do it in, besides the visitation and settlement of Ammar and Sultanabad.

This may be said upon the subject that the expense of these chowkles is ultimately that of the country in general.

(Ed.) This document gives a very detailed information regarding the system of Browne, the predecessor of Cleveland System.

Surendra jha

ooo

15. Letter

From,

C. Chapman, Acting Collector, Bhagulpur

To,

Captain James Browne,
Commanding the Light Infantry.
This dated 13 March, 1778

On an agreement made with the Ackberpoor zemeendars and he neither then or since has pretended any other right, nor have you assigned any other reason for the extraordinary support you give him not only in what he first usurped but in further acts of violence, after the complaints were referred to you.

Here the matter rested and I waited for the agreement which was to put Saujan Sing's right out of doubt. When our next letter of the 6th December denied that any agreement existed between this disputing parties so that the foul play and the gross imposition of Soujan Sing and your fourjar was evident. Yet instead of restoring to the suffering party the profits which had arisen from the usurpation you propose to subject them to litigious investigation by Ameens. In this state of the business I can not agree to your proposal, and subject the people who have already suffered to the expense and delay which must attend your first proposal. But I assent to your next proposal that you strick off the jumma of those lands as a sum for which I am to be accountable. For Iwill agree to make good any loss that may arise to your collection from jagheer lands which form no part of your settlement.

ooo

16. Letter

From,

C. Chapman, Acting Collector, Bhagalpur

To,

Captain James Browne,

Commanding the Light Infantry.

Dated 11 April, 1778 (Roshan Baksh)

"I have received your letter of the 31ST March to Mr. Barton on the subject of Rajah Roshum Bucks'(Roshan Basksh) dispute with the inhabitants of Bhagalpur.

As you have thought it expedient to address the Hon'ble Governor General in Council in consequence you have doubtless informed them of the occasion of the dispute, as well as of (the) disturbance committed at the Rajah's Instigation. It now rests with the Board therefore to issue such orders as they may think necessary and until the receipt of them every step that might have been taken on our part to bring the matter to a decision must be suspended. This being the can I honour only to make a few remarks (the) which I must beg your attention.

In the following passage of your letter now before me speaking of the disturbance you say "however, natural, for those denied any other means of redress "I must confess myself at a loss to make out what it is you allude to and as this is a matter whichever shall probaply have to answer for to our superiors. I must request an explanation as you have no doubt some meaning in what you advance. Allow me to remark at the same time that positive assertions leave no room for misinterpretation, where as much mischief may be done by an indirect insinuation.

I must further observe to you Sir that the late disturbance at Bussuntpoor appears to me (to) be the consequence of your sending for the Zeminders, Vakeel and obliging them to execute Machulkas. First step which has naturally made the people entertain an idea of no lawful authority and Roshum Bucks having seen a Military force of great use, in Soujan Singh's dispute with the Ackberpoor Zemeendars, thought he might as well try the same method, particulary on the troops to exercise such atrocious act of violence.

But my astonishment at every thing else must cease when I see the order of the Honourable the Governor General and Council evaded or set at nought. How far your conduct in sending for the Conkjole Zemeendars Vakeels and obliging them to execute a machulk for producing some people to you within a certain number of days can be considered as consonant with the instructions you received under date the 3rd October last the power that issued them will be the best to Judge. "

○○○

17. Letter

From,

James Barton,

To,

Warren Hastings, Calcutta,

Dated 30 April, 1778

Revenue Proceeding 5 May, 1778

"I have been honoured with your letter of the 10th march, enclosing two regulations formed by Capt. Browne which you direct me to carry in to execution.

The first being an order for the zamindars of my division bordering on the hills to make registers of the inhabitants of every villages and to expel such as have not a visible method of living, shall have my best endeavour to carry with execution but I beg the Board to advert to me circumstances for similar order (So far as relates to the register) having been given some years ago and which I believe is yet unexecuted in every part of the province. For the Zamindar will not put themselves me charge of a sherista for the purpose of keeping a register of the inhabitant unless Govt. make it a point of it and for this end as the settlement of the year is making, I would recommend that a clause be inserted in the Kabulyats binding them to the performance of this article.

The second regulation prohibiting all but the hill people and Chowkidari pykes from carrying bows or arrows in general to the inhabitantas of my division. The hills and Chowkies all lying within Capt. Browne's district and as I apprehend the carrying this regulation into force may be attended with fatal consequence to the inhabitants of the low country and the public interests, I am confident you will not be displeased at my remark if they point out ill effects which may be expected from carrying the plan into execution.

The mountaineers now make their attacks on the villages of the low country in large bodies, through fear of metting with resistance from a people armed in the same manner as themselves, but should the villages as proposed by Capt. Browne be deprived of the only means of defence their circumstance will afford them to procure and the mountaineers are at the same time left armed, small parties of these free booters will come upon a defenceless people who will have no alternative but must fly on the first alarm and leave their property to be sacked.

I assure myself that when the Board consider these circumstances, they will settle the order, as the only end proposed by it is to prevent the people of the low country from assuming the appearance and robbing in the name of the mountaineers for nature has marked appearance of this people so peculiarey that it is impossible to mistake them for any other race.

From the accommodation made with Jagernath Deo in 1776, I had reason to expect the countries could no longer be subject to this assaults, but since the period of that accommodation the southern part of my division of Curruckpore has never been long free from the attacks of those men who Capt. Browne among the trouble makers represented as the active and dangerous of Jagernath Deo's adherents and as they were granted to the principal, they were bound as well as them to live peaceably and protect the country from assaults, that being the term by which they hold the gautwally grant. But at the time these adherents of Jagernath have enjoyed the advantage of restored grants on their supposed submission to Govt. troops have been required to guard their country against their practices.

The attacks of the mountaineers have lately been carried to an excess never known before, and within a few weeks Capt. Browne received from me account of 44 villages plundered many of them learnt and the inhabitants obliged to fly for safety with their cattle to the opposite side of the river, when they should have been employed in cultivating the land I am now compelled to lay their representation before the Board Capt. Browne confidently asserting that the time of these ravages in the best disposition towards Govt,. and that the losses proceeded from dacoits for whose petty robberies Capt. Browne said the zamindars are accountable.

To show on what good grounds Capt. Browne forms his opinion of the peaceable disposition of the mountaineers and thence arguing that the losses must have proceeded from Dacoits. He says the hostility of the mountaineers were excited by violences exercised upon them by the people of Munnihari and then resement marked with such accurancy as to spare in the same villages the property of those who had not offended them. They could not therefore be persons who had molested my division from whose inhabitants they experienced in evil but in the following village Capt. Browne allows the mountaineers did make irruptions into Colgong which lies in my division and is the part that offended most.

Against the opinion of Capt. Browne, founded on such contradictory circumstance, is the testimony

Of the inhabitants of the suffering country supported by a position ....

Capt. Browne considess the mountaineers never descended from their hills but to submit to him having been found in the possession of a hill manjhi.

The first line of the Jungletrry comprised the chain of hills running from Farruckbad to Noony, the lands lying at the foot of these hills (in which are the chowkies to prevent the incursion by the mountaineers and a part of Kurruckpore. This division has since been much enlarged and takes in a country of great extent and in the trouble excited by Jagernaut Deo Capt. Browne's force was found inadequate to the service it was engaged in and a reinforcement of six Brigade Company sent to this assiatance which force was still unequal to operation of so great extent and the protection of my frontier. For Jagernath Deo dividing his men into small parts plundered many villages, while other make a composition with him, giving an annual tribute of part they might have the quiet possession of the remainder.

In the five Tappas of Begulpore and Colgong which lie along the foot of the hill an extensive grants for the protection of the country against the mountainers and I submit to the Board the necessity of having these Tappas annexed to my district that the Chaukies purposely maintained for the defence of my district, may be under my authority and the jagirdar made responsible to me for the losses sustained from the incursions of the mountainners made through the jagir lands.

ooo

18. Letter

From,
Augustus Cleveland, Collector, Bhagalpur

To,
Warren Hastings, Governor-General,Bhagalpur
Dated 13 January, 1780

"I have the pleasure to inform the Hon'ble Board that success which had hitherto attended my endeavours, to regulate the chouki boundary and the means I hope used to bring down the Hill chief, have succeeded as much beyond my own expectation as the good effect already from them have equally astonished and satisfied the minds of the low country inhabitants.

The Ghauts and Chowkies of the northern range of hills existing from Saucargally of Shahabad and none entirely completed. the western rang from Shahabad to within to cop of Jumness is also and led the remainder of this range to the southward at the back of Sultanabad and running down close upon the Birbhum boundary being very much the troublesome and uncivilized part of the whole country as soon as I prevail on the Hill Chief and Ghautwals to come in and submit to me.

The eastern range from Sakarigally to Mohabatpur near upon a parallel with Furruckabad and closed upon the boundary of Ammar is also as far depends upon me properly adjusted. This I cannot say entirely to my satisfaction and some depredations which lately been committed near Donnapur for the high road between Suoty and Furrackabad and other places in that neighbourhood, the proprietors of which I have traced to the Ammar Hills. The then circumstances confirm me in an idea suggested by several of the Hills Chiefs themselves when I gave them the a feast last April at Rajmahal, Viz; that unless the whole range of Hills are put under my authority and the same system of governing them adopted throughout all the pains I am taking to put them in my own districts on a proper footing (particulary those to the southward of the eastern and western ranges, the one joining with Ammar and the other running close upon the back of Sultanabad) will be in vain. I am myself thoroughly convinced that all the inhabitants of the hills may in a short time be induced to submit ... as a proof of which..., within these nine months I have had the more flattering experience of the good effects to be expected from the system I have adopted – no less than than forty-seven Hill Chiefs and their adherents having voluntarily submitted to me and taken an oath of allegiance to Government during that time and I make no Doubt of the same system continues to be adopted. There is not a Chief in that vast extent of country who will not gladly renounce his hitherto precarious and desperate way of life for the ease and comforts he will enjoy in being obedient to and under the protection of a mild and regular Government.

I must do those who have submitted the justice to say – and I call all the inhabitants of this country in general to witness – that the hill people have not many years been so quiet as they have been for those last eight or nine months except as I before mentioned near the boundary of Ammar on the northern ranges and western ranges as far as I have settled them have in fact been on disturbances.

Should the honourable Board approve my endeavour to reconcile the minds of these people to a civilized Government and to make them useful members of the community which my success hither to flatters me with the hope of provided I have such support and assistance as may appear necessary. I shall be happy to dedicate a portion of my time to a service of so much importance to the country in general and to those parts in particular which I can easily do without neglecting the other advocations of my office. But I humbly beg leave to represent before I can attempt to settle everything on a permanent and lasting footing – I must request that the Pargans Ammar and Sultanabad may be put under my authority (they have never yet been farily put to the test – how far .... upon good terms with us. we have till lately ever considered as enemies and they have been treated accordingly. It is but consonant with our principles of justice and humanity to every means in our power to avoid a state of warfare. Why should they be denied to these unfortunate people, as they are immediately connected with the country in questions from a continuation of the same ranges of hills (inhabited by the same run of peoples running through them that it should be almost in vain to attempt making Regulation in the one that could not be enforced in the other and the Raja of Ammar who was in close connection with hill people being lately deceased which has occasioned dissensions the Pargana- the season of the year also considered – these cannot be a non-favourable opportunity that present for completing the Regulation of the Hills in these districts.

When I have completed the arrangements I have already undertaken I will lay the whole of my proceedings before the honourable Board and give them any information that comes to my knowledge.

In the meantime, I shall wait in an anxious expectation for your further order respecting Ammar and Sultanabad and for any districts you may think proper to honour me with.

❍❍❍

19. Letter

From,

Augustus Cleveland,

To,

William Hosea, Bogleypore
Dated of 3 April, 1780
Chief Secretary Provincial Council at Murshiabad,
Gentleman,

I have had the honour to receiveyour letter of the 26th uttimo and am much obliged to you for ready compliance with my wishes aparting, Murror Sing.

The circumstances to criminate him although of general nature – will I make no doubt be sufficiently proved to you by the Rany Sarbeswary or her agents – at all events however his conduct appears to me so very exceptionable and is attended with so many inconveniences and obstruction to the arrangements, I am making throughout the hills that I am unable to proceed whilst he is permitted to remain at large. if, therefore, on his apprehension you will be pleased to deliver him over to my charge, I will take upon me to answer for consequence attending his confinement and in the meantime you will, have the most favourable opportunity of informing your-selves of the general censure of his conduct in your own division. I have thought it necessary to address the Honourable Governor- General and Council.

OOO

20. Letter

From,

Cleveland

To,

Warren Hasting's
Dated 1 July, 1780

"I have had honour to receive your letter of the 23rd June informing me of your general sentiments on the subject of establishing regulations for the inhabitants of hill under my authority and directing me to let you know what will be the best method of carrying the plan you propose into execution.

In my address of the 21st April I estimated the members of hills at at about four hundred and proposed an allowance to every chief as the Hon Board however consider the expense of carrying my plan into execution too great – and as the hills of each tappah are under the authority of one or more chief maanjeejs and their deputees – to whom the manjys of the separate hills are bound to show obedience I beg leave to submit to your determination the propriety of giving handsome allowances to their chief and their deputies and none at all to the inferior manjiys or of giving a triflings pension to the whole indiscriminately.

The expense of the former I estimate as follows

26 chiefs @ 10/ per month. . 260/-

58 deputies @ rs 5/- per month. . 290

per mensem. . 550 and of the latter 3 rs. p. m. to 400 manjhis is rs. 1200/- the difference of their two estimates is not only considerable, but I am of opinion the first deserves a preference on many amounts as when the chief of the tappas are ever heartily attached to government. the inferior manjys will not imagine presume to do anything which may endanger the forfeiture of their chief's stipend whichever plan you may think proper to determine upon, I will upon the receipts of your order assemble the chiefs together and receive from them muchulkas binding themselves to be responsible for the peace and good order of their respective districts- in return with your approbation I will give each chief sanad specifying the sum to be paid to him, the services to be expected from him and the consequences on failure of his engagements – all which shall be drawn up in the strongest terms and the greatest attention paid to the due observance of them.

(Ed.) This letter is the original proposal which gradually evolved as the system of Augustus Cleveland.

Surendra Jha

ooo

21. Letter

From,

Augustus Cleveland, Collector, Bhagalpur

To,

Governor – General and Council,

Dated 19 September, 1780

"In consequence of your approbation of my proposal of giving allowances to the Hill Chief of the Tuppas and their deputies leaving it to me to carry your plan into execution in the best manners I am able and limiting the expense, to Rs 550/- per month, as signified in your letter of the 22nd August. Immediately summoned all the Chief and deputies of the several Districts under my authority and informed them that in consequence of the disposition they had for sometime past shown to remain on good terms with their neighbours in the low country and of the confidence they had placed in Government by giving themselves up to my protection and authority, they had been pleased to grant pension to the Chiefs and deputies as encouragements for their further good behaviour, but that in consideration of this indulgence they were to bind themselves in most forcible manner under pain of their severest penalty and suspension of their allowances to be answerable for their good order, and management of their respective Districts.

To this the Chiefs and deputies of the several tappas to the northward readily assented ; but those to the southward, which lie contiguous to the Perganas of Ammar and Sultanabad,absolutely refused to accept any allowances, on the terms prescribed alleging as reason that they could not be answerable for, the conduct of their neighbours and as they, have so often since the commencement of my arrangement has given proofs of their refractory disposition, without expressing the smallest inclination to surrender themselves of Government, they could now become every day more increased against my division and would plunder and destroy the villages in it with redoubled fury. Their motives for, and view in this I understand would be to compel the chiefs under my authority to resume their allegiance which they miss easily be induced to do rather than become accountable for disturbances which it would not be in my power to assist them in preventing and as they have an idea, that as long as any part of division remains unsettled chastisement would be either entirely suspended or more equally divided whereas, if otherwise the whole blame would inevitably fall upon them in case of disturbances.

I have already taken up so much of the Honourable Board's attention with my representation respecting the necessity of annexing the pergana of Ammar and Sultanabad to my collectorship that it is with the greatest reluctance I am once more induced to address you on the subject. But as I am convinced nothing but proper encouragement is wanting to bring the hill people in those two parganas, in the same peaceable state that I have with no much success brought those two in my own districts and as I am also confirmed in my opinion that even if similar arrangements take places in both divisions, there will still be disturbances and confusion near the boundaries of them. I should be wanting in my duty did I not humbly entrust the Honourable Board to take these circumstances into consideration.

I have been further induced to say this much on the subject in consequence of the very flattering apporobation amy plans in general, had the honour to meet with from Leiutenant general Sir I Coote, K. B. , in several conversation I had with him on his way both up and down the country and as my proposal for raising a corps of archers as represented in my address of the 21st April was particularly approved by him, I take the liberty of recalling your attention to this circumstance also; being persuaded of the good effects it will have in bringing the Hill inhabitants to a speedy state of civilization, - add to which the great service they may be of military operation at a future period."

OOO

22. Letter

From,

Augustus Cleveland, Collector, Bhagalpur

To,

Governor – General and Council,

Dated Ammar 19 February, 1781

"In consequence of your order under date the 19th December last I have the honour to inform you that I have entertained the number of Hill people mentioned in my proposal of the 21st April and so well pleased are these mountaineers with the service proposed to them that my only difficulty now is to frame excuses for not entertaining more the prescribed number.

I shall do myself, the honour of laying a full account of my proceedings and negotiations before you as soon as I can possibly connect them together. In the meantime, I have the satisfaction to observe that my success has exceeded my most sanguine expectations, and I flatter myself there will not again be any cause of complaints from the people of the low country on account of the insurrections or depredations of the mountaineers as long as a proper attention is paid to the regulations which have been lately adopted.

Uptill my arrival at this neighbourhood I had been given to understand that the Ammar and Sultanabad Paraganas comprehended all the inhabited Hills to the Southward, I now find however there are several in Balputteh one of the Jangleterry Paraganas in Beerbhoom and adjoining Sultanabad into the Southwest. This circumstance was first made known to me by some of the Hill Chief's in it sending me a petition to be included in the Pension list and to offer as many of their people as I chose to enlist in the corps or Archers.

As the parganna of Balputteh(=Belpatta near Dumka) is not under my authority I have thought it necessary to wait your order before I give any decisive answer to the Hill Chiefs.

Should you therefore think proper to direct that the pargannah be placed under my authority which would certainly make the jurisdiction arrangement without having the pargannah annexed to my Collectorship –Whichever you think expedient to dertermine upon ; my utmost endeavours shall be exterted for the public service in the execution of which it shall be my study to merit you approbation.

(Ed.) The request of Cleveland to transfer Sultanabad and Ambar of Bhagalpur

Surendra Jha

ooo

23. Letter

From,

Augustus Cleveland, Collector, Bhagalpur

To,

David Anderson, President and Committee of Revenue,
Fort William,
Dated 6 April, 1781

Gentlemen,

In my letter of the 3rd March I had the honour to inform you of my having appointed a Sezawal in the pargannahs of Sulanabad and Ammar at the joint request of the Radshy zemindar and of the Ryots in general to assist the former in the recovery of the just balance and the latter in the final settlement of their annual account.

I have now the honour to inform ou that the Radshy Zemindar's Gomasta has absconded from the Pargannahs without setting the account for the year 1187 under pretence of there being considerable balance still due to him whereas my Sezawal and the Ryots positively assert they have paid more than ought in justice to have been demanded of them according to the customary rates of the Pargannahs. I have therefore thought it necessary to depute my assistant Dr. Cockerells into the Moffosil not only to ascertain the amount of collection and the state of the Pargannahs but to encourage the Ryots in their cultivation by assurances of every protection and support which it may be in my power to afford them. "

ooo

24. Letter

(Revenue Department, Original Consultations, dated 22 August, 1781. No. 30)

"Ordered that the Account Settlement be sent to the Accountant General to the Revenue Department.

Answered as follows:-

Proposed establishment for the Capt. Of Hill Archers under the collector of Bhagalpur.

1. Sepoy Sevbadar. 40/-

1 Do havildar. . . . 16/-

1 Do Nailk @ 10/- 20

1 Doctor. . . . 15/-

1. Mohrir n10/-

1 Head Jamadar – Jourat the man who first entertained in the Company's service. . . . 80\-

15 jamadar @ 12/ ... 180/-

15 Naib @ 6/-. . 90/-

400 Archers @ 4/-. . 1,600/-

Per month Rs. 1,991/-

Bhagalpur, 31 July, 1781.

Augustus Cleveland, Collector"

ooo

25. Letter

From,

Augustus Cleveland, Collector, Bhagalpur

To,

The Board of Revenue,
Dated 23 July, 1782

"I take the liberty of enclosing you copy of a letter I have this day written to the chief of Purnea on the subject of a Boundary which has long been in dispute between the zemindars of Colgong and Durrumpore and as I see no prospect of bringing it to a decision without your Interference, I beg leave to suggest the propriety of an European Gentleman being deputed by you, or that the chief of Purnea and myself may be directed to send our Assistants for their purpose. "

ooo

26. Letter

From,

Augustus Cleveland, Collector, Bhagalpur

To,

The Board of Revenue,Fort William.
Dated 9 August, 1782

"Conformable to the Hon'ble Board's order transmitted in your of the 23rd March, I am taking measures to keep the Bagulpore Province khas during the ensuing year- And although it is not in my power at present to ascertain exactly what the amount of the collections may be, yet I have the pleasure to assure you, there will certainly be an increase on the present years Jumma. For the sake of regularity, therefore, I herewith do myself the honour to transmit for your approbation an account (torn) Bundoobust and husbundy (=Hastbandi) of the Baglepoor Province for the ensuing year, by which you will perceive (torn) have estimated the increase at Rupees 10,583-7-7. And I beg leave to assure you no attention shall be wanting on my part to realise the Revenue with punctuality."

OOO

26 (a). Letter (Replay of the above letter)

Sir,

We have received your letter of the 9th instant with an account Bundooust and kistbundy of the District of Bogelpore for the Beyhar year 1190 with, we entirely approve of and request you will transmit us a Persian copy of it.

We are, etc. . "

OOO

27. Letter

From,

Augustas Cleveland, Collector, Bhagalpur

To,

William Brooke, Chief of Purnea.

Dated 23 August, 1782

"I have been favoured with your letter of the 16th instant, I wish it was in my power to give you any hopes of the Disputes between the Zemindars of Durrumpore and Colgong being ear a conclusion, but after my acquiescence to the proposal contained in your letter of the 1st may, being again disappointed by the unwarrantable delays of the Durrumpore people, I confer I have given over all hopes of ever seeing the Disputes brought to a decision, until one or both of our Assistants or an English Gentleman is sent with full power to enquire into it and decide upon the spot. And I take the liberty of urging to you the propriety of addressing the committee on thesubject, to that effect.

In order to convince you that the delay in setting this Business must be entirely attributed to the Durrumpore people, Sacka Chund Tiarry, the Colgong zemindar's Gomastah immediately on the receipt of my order dated the 3rd May to settle the matter by arbitrators appointed four Arbitratrs on his part- Viz. Jaydass of Seermutpore, Oado Bughu of Ditto, Hazarry Mendul of Sutchmypore and Bekarey Mundul of Muddoopure- Borung. The two latter formerly inhabitants of Chuck Delowary. These four men Sacka Chund produced to Kirpa Naut Roy and Balchund. They immediately wrote down their names and promised that four should be appointed in the part of Durrumpore- after waiting fifteen days without any steps being taken by the Durrumpore people Sucka Chund was obliged to leave the place – as he found nothing was likely to be done and his Business called him to other parts of his Purgunnah. Previous to his departure however, he mentioned four Inhabitants of Durrumpore to Kirpa Naut Roy- Vizly. - Seeboo Matou of Gobrahey, Lutchou Roy of Busgudda, Juggunno of Chutteah, Golah and Annadey Roy of Dito and Declared.

Ordered that if they would not appoint people to act with him, that he would abide by any Decision those four would make an oath. But this also was rejected and the business of course remains in statusquo.

With respect to the sale of the grain, I think it ought to be disposed of immediately. I have, therefore sent orders to Shiek Mahomed to act in conjuction with any person you think proper to send in the disposal of it, directing him to receive the other – declaring at the same time, that both Sum are to remain deposit in our Cutcherries until the dispute be settled, when the whole will be accounted for to the proper owner. Flatter myself you will deem this equitable and will give orders accordingly. "

ooo

28. Letter

From,

C. Chapman, Collector, Bhagalpur,

To,

William Taylor, Resident at Beerbhoom,

Dated 2 January, 1784

"Under address to you dated the 3rd instant, I had the honour to acquaint you of my having required the assistance of 40 of the sebundy corps from Lieutenant Fredreck Wilson for the purpose of acting in conjunction with expedition against **Budhoo Khan Mehajee and Phauzdfar of Fatackpurrah**. In that letter I expressed to you my hope of speedy success in putting a stop to the growth of those seeds of insurrection which is spreading into wide Rebellion. I have now the satisfaction to inform you that I was not too sanguine in my expectation from In reply to your last letter I beg leave to aquaniit you that the march of the 19th Regiment into the neighbourhood of true(Tiur) has already been attended with every good consequence which could have been effected in so short a time. It is true that Roopnarain Deo has contrived to evade the utmost effort of the commanding contrived to evade the utmost effort of the commanding officer to gain posseeeion of his person. But such has been the caution observed, and such the subordination of the sepoys, that the ryots of the different villages inspired with confidence at their habitations and little farms being free from every kind of molestation are for the most part already returned to their occupation. and dwellings. The body of the Ghatwalls (a few particular adherents of Roopnarain Deo only expected) have already or are now making their Bundobust with their immediate superior the Rajah of Curruckpore, and for the presence of the regiment is immediately required for little more than to prevent Roopnarain Deo's secret partizans taking advantage of the district being entirely left without any force in the neighbourhood. I beg leave to suggest the expediency of the circumstance of the victinity of the 19th regiment being availed of by you for the purpose of reducing Bissen Das as well as other Ghatwalls who may be in a similar disposition, as also that of demolishing their forts. A measure on which the future perfect tranqutility of the whole jungleterry after the return of the troops into cantonments so materials depends that it should seem, the board would most readily acqiuiesce in such as applications from you to take advantage of the victinity of the troops to the possession of those refractory Ghatwalls.

(Ed.) - The system of Cleveland and the honeymoon of the Company soon fell on the rocks. These Documents reveal the fact vividly

Surendra Jha

OOO

29. Letter

From,

C. Chapman,

Collector, Bhagalpur,

To,

David Anderson, president committee of revenue,

Dated 3 January, 1784

"Agreeable with the 8th articles of the sebundy regulation transmitted in your letter of the 25th of August last, I have the honour to inform you that I have thus made a requisition of lieutenancy Frederick Wilson for a detachment of the sebundy corps to act in conjunction with 3 companies of hill rangers against Budhoo khan Mehajee and Phouzdar of Fatackpore to the east of Jamonie and a that a Subadar with 40 Sebundy Sepoys accompanied by 150 Hill Rangers will march tomorrow on this service.

It is with the utmost concern that I find myself immediately on the departure of Mr. Cleveland under the necessity of having recourse to Military Force in the Hill. But the frequent murders and repeated robberies committed immediately under the guidance and direction of the said Budhoo within these few weeks past, as well as the circumstance of his being in league with Roopnarain Deo, **force me withhold to that lenity which Mr. Cleveland from the hope that he might be brought to a proper sense of his duty to Government had for a considerable time prior to his leaving Bhagalpur shown towards him.** The Hill Sezawall and commandant of the Hill Corps are gone with the detachment and I have every reason to hope that the end of the expedition will shortly be accomplished by the sseizure of Budhoo and the principal ringleader of banditti who infested the borders of the pergunnah of Sultanabad and brought ill reputation on their neighbours the people of the surrounding Hill. "

OOO

30. Letter

From,

C. Chapman, Collector, Bhagalpur,

To,

Thomas Graham, President and members of the committee of revenue of grain, Fort William, dated 28th January 1784.)

"I have the honour to acknowledge the receipt of your letter of the 22nd instant, requiring information of the quantity of grain produced in the district under my charge, as also what balance might remain in store of the produce of former years. In reply to which I beg leave to inform you that orders have been issued for the purpose of obtaining particular accounts of the produce of the kharrif and budway (=Bhado) harvest from the several pergunnah which shall be transmitted to you as soon as they be all received and properly arranged; unless you should prefer having the report of the producer of the approaching ruby harvest (=Rabbi) included with it in which every thing cannot be transmitted sooner than the month of April. But with respect to my store of grain there is none that I can learn in any part of the district or at least if there be, it is such small quantity as not to be noticed.

In consequence of the Honourable the Governor General and Council's approbation of Mr. Cleveland's proposal for the establishment of Golsha(=Grain Gola) through these districts, and of your leaving the affixing of them at different stations in your letter of the 10th November to his direction, I beg leave to acquaint you that Golsha are erected for containing 20,000 maunds of the dimensions at different places as follows-:

- Golah at Aurangabad for mounds-: 1500
- Ditto at Rajmahal for Ditto-: 2500
- Ditto at Surrygully for Ditto-: 500
- Ditto at Gangaparshad for Ditto-: 2000
- Ditto at Colgong for Ditto-: 2500
- Ditto at Bhagalpur for Ditto-: 3500
- Ditto at Jehanguira
  Suntanganj for Ditto-: 2000
- Ditto at Monghyr for Ditto-: 3500
- Ditto at Sooragegerry(A…forDitto-: 2000

Maunds 20000

Mr. Hestley was written to be on the 13th November for the purpose of procouring the above quantity of rice in consequence of his requisition, remittance have been made for the purchase of it. As yet 2000 mounds only are received, but I trust that the remainder will shortly be delivered to the agent as Caragola deputed from hence form the purpose of receiving it and sending it off from thence to the different golsha.

Twenty one thousand eight hundred sicca rupees was sent on the 28th December to Mr. Hatley for the purpose of purchasing the grain and as it is your direction together with orders of Government that my correspondence on the subject by confidence to your committee. I must beg the favour of your information whether I am to open an account with you for the advance made for the above purpose as well as the charges incidental to the carrying into execution the plan for the establishment of golsha through these districts".

ooo

31. Letter

From,

C. Chapman,
Collector, Bhagalpur,

To,

David Anderson,
President Committee of Revenue,
Dated 31 January, 1784

The activity of this new raised corps. Upon the first – entering of the detachment in the circle of Hill attached to and under the control of Budhoo and his immediate connections. It was found that the number of men on his service were not sufficient to guard the different ghauts in such a manner, as to ensure the seizure of Budhoo and the principal insurgents. I, therefore, ordered another company of Hill Rangers to reinforce the detachment, and by the time they had joined. Budhoo had been so closely pursued that with the assistance of this reinforcement he was shortly taken prisoner with forty three of his adherents; who were brought into Bhagalpur this morning under confinement, and I have the pleasure to add that one man only of the Rangers received any wound which happened from the accidental discharge of one of their own carbines. Five of the prisoners being children. I have only confined them to the limits of the Hill cantonments. The remainder are thrown into chains until they shall have been adjudged by a Council of the Hill Chief agreeable to the admirable institution wisely adopted by the honourable Board. I have summoned the chiefs to Bhagalpur for this purpose and shall apprise your Committee and the honourable the Governor-General and Council of their presidency. "

OOO

32. Letter

From,

C. Chapman, Collector, Bhagalpur,

To,

Warren Hasting and Council of Revenue,

Fort William,

Dated 31 January, 1784

"Serveral robberies and depredations having been committed by Budhoo Khan Mahajee, and Phauzdar of Fatackparra on the borders of Jammoney during Mr. Cleveland's illness which just at his departure began to threaten wider rebellion in the Hills. I thought it necessary to take the most speedy method for giving an affectual check to the growing spirits of insurrection. It was with the utmost reluctance than at the immediate departure of MR. Cleveland. I should be reduced to disagreeable alternative of sending a Military force into the Hills or suffering your subjects in the Low Countries to be exposed to the cruelties of a few yet uncivilized Hill Chiefs. But the circumstances if Budhoo's having entered into league with Roopnarain Deo between **whom the ceremony exchanging Turbans had passed, urged me to be deceive** I therefore on the 3rd instant ordered a detachment of 3rd compaines of the Hill Rangers commanded by the Commandant, supported by the 40 of the Sebundy Crops, to proceed under the direction of Hill Sezawal against Budhoo and his adherents. But upon finding that this force was insufficient to ensure the seizure of the ringleader without length of time and much bloodshed, I ordered an additional company of Rangers a close and harassing pursuit of many days. The Rangers so completely encircled Budhoo's party that having possession of the different ghauts, they made prisoners of Budhoo with his family whom together with other captives amounting in all to 43, the detachments brought inprisoners to Bhagalpur this morning. Five of the prisoners being children I have given the liberty of the Hill cantonments too. The remainder are kept in chains until they shall have been tried by Court of their own chiefs whom I have summoned to Bhagalpur for this purpose. When they be convened and shall have adjudged the delinquents, I will do myself the honour of transmitting to you their proceedings. But I cannot quit this subject, without intruding a few words on you in favour of the officers and men sent on this expedition whose activity and conduct deserve every encouragement, Employed against the very inhabitants of their own country they have shown the utmost alacrity in making prisoners those few who to the disreputation of what had already acknowledged our Government until continued to make inroads of the low countries whilst they observed the utmost lenity to the unhappy families of those taken or slain in arms. Several Hill villages were unavoidably burnt and many of the enemy killed. But I have pleasure to inform you that only one man of the rangers received any wound which happened by the accidental discharge of one of their own carbines. The wound was slight and the man is recovering from it.

I have also the honour to inform you that I have in consequence of a representation from the commanding officer of the 19th regiment, that one complete Battalion will, now that the Fort of Ture(=Ture =Trikut Hill near Deoghar) is effectually destroyed and razed to the ground, be sufficient for the duty required in late Ghatwally Zamindary of Roopnarain Deo requested Captain

Pringle that he will keep one Battalion only in the field and order the remainder into the Cantonments at Monghyr.

The very loyal conduct and ready acquiescence of Jusman Sing the hereditary dewan in Roopnarain Deo's family and proprietor of the Fort Ture came upon me to solicit your notice and protection of him.

He long ago exerted his utmost to convince Roopnarayan Deo of the impropriety of his conduct, and to turn from the road of Rebellion unto the paths of loyalty and submission, but to no purpose, and from the moment that he found Roopnarain absolutely bent on pushing in opposition to Government,he withdrew himself from his infancy. He met Captain Pringle on the first summons and without hesitation delivered up that Fort to destruction which he held possession with the sufferance of Government. Since which he has distinguished himself by his activity in supplying the Camp with grain.

Roopnarain Deo is not taken neither do I suppose that it will be possible for the detachment to make him prisoner. But the prinicipal ghautwalls are come in and have submitted, the inhabitants returned to their habitation, cultivate their lands, and Roopnarain with a very few remaining followers remain fugitives in the jungles and the reserve of the 5 companies who continued in the field will be absolutely requisite until the Rubby harvest by off the ground.

(Ed.) Buddhu Khan Fauzdar is a remarkable character who defied the rule of the Company, not on any personal grievance, but he refused to accept its suzerainty

Surendra Jha

OOO

33. Letter

From,

C. Chapman, Acting Collector, Bhagalpur

To,

Captain James Browne,
Commanding the Light Infantry.
Dated 20 July, 1784

I have had the pleasure to receive your letter enclosing a petition presented to you by Neelmony and Luckinaut the zeminders of Akberpoor, in which they complain of having been dispossessed of their lands, and that the farm was given to Ruttun Chund, and their offer to pay an equal revenue rejected and further, that my predecessor established them in their zemindary on their former complaints against Rutton Chund.

Permit me in reply to the first part of the Zemindar's complaint having been dispossessed of their lands to represent, that they have not otherwise been dispossessed of them than by the farmer of the collection of the dues of Government in them, having been let to the person who offered the most advantageous terms; all their rights as Zemindars remaining to them in full force. The second part of the complaint that the farm was given to Rutton Chand and their offer to pay an annual revenue, rejected I must declare .... . is totally void of foundation and that it was not till the person who acted as the agent of these Zemeendars, refused to give any increase upon the jumma that I closed with the offers of Ruttun Chund. In the year 1189 Ruttun Chund having rented the whole Zillah of Rajmahal given an increase upon the jumma of this zemeendary of sd rs. -500-. The next year 1190 the farm remained with Nilmony and Luckinaut without any further increase, but this year Ruttun Chund consented to pay Sc-Rs. 500 more, and it has been chiefly owing to a competitin between Ruttun Chund and zemeendars of Rajmahal that the revenue has increased for some years past. To that last part of the representation stating that my predecessor established Nilmony and Luchinaut in their Zemindary on their former complaints against Rutton Chund, I can say nothing, as no traces of any complaints appear on the records, all of which I have perused with attention it was from the encomiums that I founding the public letters from my predecessor to your Board, on the managements of Ruttun Chund and the exactitude with which he paid his kists that I was induced to attend to the proposal which he made so on after my taking charge of the Collectorship.

I hope that I have stated will be sufficient to satisfy you that the complaints made by the Zemeendars of Akberpur is not well-founded. I have reason however, to believe that the cause of their dissatisfaction does not proceed from the circumstances stated in the complaint made to you, but to a dispute between them and=(Brahmottar) burmuter lands. The zemeendars asserting that they have held it rent free from time immemorial, the farmer on the other hand, proving that the late Collectior had resumed it,and that it had paid revenue from the beginning of the Bengal year 1188 to the present time. This matter had been lately brought before me, and I was taking measureto ascertain the truth when I received your letter. If you should think proper to direct the Zemeendars to attend me, I will take care that they receive the redress in this, and every other grievance to which may justly be entitled"

P. S I have given the same who brought your letter a duplicate of this.

ooo

34. Letter

From,

C. Chapman,
Acting Collector, Bhagulpur

To,

Samauel Charters,
Acting President of Committee of Revenue at Fort William
Dated 10 August, 1784

" I am concerned to inform you of an affray which has happened between the people of the Zemeendars of Betea Gopaulpoor in Rajmahal and those of Lutchmen Narain Canoongoe(Qanungo) of Moorshidabad. The enclosed translation of an Aurzee for the Zemeendars of Beeatea Gopaulpoor will inform you of all the particulars which have as yet come to my knowledge. I have taken step to prevent the dispute going any further and directed every inquiry to be made that may tend to elucidate the matter which I shall do myself the honour to lay before you. In the meantime I hope you will give such orders as may be necessary respecting the persons concerned in the dispute not under my authority."

"Translation of an Arzee from LallSunder and Kissen Persaud Roy Zemeendars of Bettea Gopaulpur in Rajmahal.

ooo

35. Letter

From,

C. Chapman, Acting Collector, Bhagalpur

To,

Samauel Charters,
Acting President of Committee of Revenue at Fort William
Dated 14 September, 1784

The Gunge Chowdallah belonging to the purgunnah Bettea Gopaulpoor dependant on Akburnaugur has from time immemorial belonged to our Zemeendary. To the south of the said Gunge, at the distance of one coss and half is the boundary of the villages Chaundpoor part of the said purgunnah and within it are some bigas of land belonging to Mohashai Luchme Narain Canoongoe, on which he had established a haut called Suckerbarry whether he carried goods for sale. Last year part of this land was carried away by the river and some remained, to this he forcibly obliged the import of our Gunge to repair and carried Boats of goods to be to be sold on pour boundaries and collected the duties of them. The people of our Gunge objecting thereto, he raised a disturbance and having got together an hundred Burcundages established a Tannah (=Thana)and forocibly collected and carried of the duties of the above mentioned Gunge. In consequence of this violence we placed some Burkundazes for the protection of the riots, and Beoparies frequenting the Gunga. On 30th Savan in the evening these disturbers 3170-or three quarter of an anna on **the revenues and on the jumma of <u>Furkea</u> for Sonat Rupees 2033. 4- which amounts to anna on the revenue.** The pergunnah Bhagalpur and Monghyr, I beg leave to propose, may remain khas for the reason (of) assigned by my predecessor in his letter to the committee dated the 22nd August last. Bangalpoor (Bhagalpur) I except till produce an increase of about st. Rupees 2500- and Monoghyr about St. Rupees 1100- from some lands being now brought into cultivation which have been waste for several former years. Cultivation chiefly producing rice, having suffered in a greater degree than the other purgunnahs as well from the drought of the last season as from the depredations of Roop Narain Deo. I propose, may be left under the management of Raja Cauder Alley, the Zemeendar, on the terms he held it last year. I do not find that any increase could be expected from the Bazar of Monghyr.

The total amount of the proposed increase in the revenue of the province of Bhagalpur of the year 1192 Fusslee is sonat rupees 10714-8-0 as per settlement enclosed.

OOO

36. Letter

From,

C. Chapman,

Collector, Bhagulpur

To,

David Anderson,

President, Committee of Revenue at Fort William

This dated 20 November, 1784

"I have the honour to receive your commands dated the 11th of October on the 16th following enclosing two papers presented to you said to be executed by Bowanny Chawdrain and her naibs; and directing me to endeavour to ascertain if the paper had been executed by her and with her consent; and to publish an advertisement at Baugalpoor and Rajmahal mentioning that Bowanny Chawdrain had disposed of her zemeendaryy of Sultangunge to Munshey Ahmud Zumain Khan and had petitioned for a Sunnud of confirmation ; and directing any who might have objections hereto to lay them before me within one month after the date of the advertisement.

In obedience thereto I have made every inquiry in my power respecting the papers having been signed by Bowanny Chowdrain and with her consent, but as she has been at Calcutta for this year past, I cannot absolutely ascertain the acts through from the representation made to me. I have no reason to doubt their being such and having published the advertisement conformally to the aforementioned instructions. The enclosed petition No. 1 and accompanying papers Nos. 2 and 3 were presented to me upon which I beg leave to refer to you superior judgement to decide. "

ooo

37. Letter

From,

C. Chapman,

Collector, Bhagulpur

To,

John Shore,

President, Acting President, Committee of Revenue at Fort William,

Dated 28 December, 1784,

"I had the honour to receive your commands dated the 11th of October on the 16th following enclosing two papers presented to you, said to be executed by Bowanny Chaudrain and and her Nabis directing me to endeavour to ascertain if the papers had been executed by her and with her consent, and to publish an advertisement at Bhagalpur and Rajmahal mentioning that Bowanny Chaudrain in had dispossed of her zemeendary of Sultangage to Munshey Ahmad Zamanu Khan and had petitioned for Sunned of confirmation and directing any who might have objections thereto lay them before me within one month after the date of the advertisment. In obedience thereto I have made every enquiry in my power respecting the papers having been signed by Bowanny Chaudrain and with her consent, but as she had been at Calcutta for this year past, I cannot absolutely ascertain the facts, though from the representations made to me,. I have no reason to doubt their being such, and having published the advertisment confermably to the aforementioned instructions, a petition copy of which I have the honour to enclose marked No. 1 was presented to me by Juggun Augustee claiming the Zemeendary of Sultangunge in consequence of a deed of Bowanny Chaudrain dated the 12th of Bhadon 1182 Bengal still also enclosed under no. 2 with the dispositions of the withnesses called in proof thereof under no. 3, and a paper containing an account of the discent of the said Juggun Augustee from the eldestt daughter of Gobind

Ram Chaudry, grandfather to the late Cossenaut Chaudhry, husband to Bowanny Chaudrain no. 4 upon which your superior judgements will decide and favour me with the necessary order for disposing Zemeendary in question. "

(Ed.) These Documents give us the idea of the Zamindars of Rajmahal and the Britishers.

ooo

38. Letter

To,

The Nabab Governor General
Bahadur.

The peition of Roopnarain Deo, zemindar of the purgunnah Chondwa Pussay in the jungleterry dependant on Curruckpoor, Sircar Monghyr, Subah Behar.

After compliments agreeable to the order of the collector, I am attending at Bhagalpur, who has made known to me your favourable disposition towards me, and of its being your pleasure that I should proceed to Calcutta. I obedience to your commands I was prepared to set out, when I received the news of the death of my grand-mother, whose funeral rites conformable to the custom of the Hindu I have no person at my house who can administer, I am therefore, under great distress to proceed on the journey ; moreover as zemindary is very inconsiderable the expense of so long a journey will be greatly burdensome to one of my poverty neither can I, a savage inhabitant of the jungle who never saw a great Darbar, and am inacquainted with the form of respect think myself qualified to appear in your presence but neverthaless I wait pleasure."

ooo

39. Letter

From,

C. Chapman, Collector, Bhagalpur,

To,

Warren Hasting and Council of Revenue,

Fort William

Dated December 1784

"When I had the honour to take charge of this collectorship in the month of February last, I found one battalion from the regiment of sepoys stationed at Monghyr, in pursuit of Roopnarain Deo a Ghautwall of the Jungleterry, whom your honourable board had ordered to be dispossessed of his lands for his refractory and disobedient behaviour and about whom and his father Jagernanth Deo many representations have been made to you from captain Brooke and Browne, and Mr. Barton and Cleveland. it was not long after, on the commanding officer finding that nothing more could be effected with one battalion, than barely giving protection to the country, that the other battalion was also required to join him and with his force the fugitive was pursued from retreat to retreat until the hot season was far advanced without and probability of apprehending him and a certain prospect of his ravages recommending as soon as the rains should begin and the troops be obliged to go into Cantonment. During all this time Roopnarain Deo made continual applications to me through different people to solicit his pardon, and the restoration of his lands, for which he engaged to pay the Revenue stipulated in the Sunnad granted by the Honourable Board at the intercession of Major Browne and promised for the future to behave himself in an orderly and peaceable manner. As I considered the regiment was kept in the field at a great expense incurred for Batta and other extra charges, & from the experience which also residence in the Hills had given me that Chiefs of this description were seldom as ever taken. I was at length induced to promise that if he would give me a proof of the sincerity of his profession by remaining perfectly quiet during the whole season of the rains, I would recall the regiment and become his intercessor that I find myself able to assure you that he has not deceived me, and that by the conduct I pursued I have saved the company, a considerable sum of money, the troops a disagreeable service, and eventually the lives of number of poor homeless people. I, therefore, most humbly implore the honourable Board to grant the request which for the reason above mentioned I am induced to make for a pardon being granted to Roopnarain Deo; which I am also further held to urge, as whatever may be recovered from his district allowing for the expenses of collection at the rate of about 150 rupees per month will become an addition to the resources of Government, and I think I may venture to pledge myself that the amount of Sicca rupees 7291/-specified in the Sunned formerly granted to him, copy of which I have the honour to enclose will be paid with punctuality. Raja Cauder Ali (Qadir Ali)the zamindar of Curreckpore to whom the Ghautwally was given on its being taken away from Roopnarain Deo having declared himself unable to manage it and never as, I believe, having received any advantage from the gift, I shall not deem it necessary to make him any deduction in his rent.

Should it not please the honourable Board to grant my request, it will be necessary for the regiment to march from Mongayr with the Hill rangers From hence, and if it be determined to apprehend Roopnarain Deo, parties from Manjor Crawford's regiment of light infantry should be directed to occupy the passes leading into Beerboom ; Chaikye (=Chakai)and Currickdeah,(=Kharagdiha) and I should recommend to the Commanding officer going from hence to divide his force in to parties consisting of no more than two companies. Each against one of which no body of them is in Roopnarain Deo,s power to bring into the field can stand, by which means he may be pursued by different routes, his attention distracted and possibly surrounded and taken.

I have the honour to be with the greatest respect".

(Ed.) Roop Narain Deo's petition for pardon. It also reveals the strength of Roop Narain Deo's followers.

Surendra Jha

OOO

40. Letter

From,

J. Fombelle,
Acting Collector, Bhagalpur

To,

Charles Butler, Secretary to the Board of Revenue Calcutta,
Dated 20 July -

"On the 7th of March last that late collecter addressed your Board relative to considerable tracts of land held rent free by several persons to whom they were granted for the purpose of maintaining the Chowkie's leading to the hills and recommended that the lands should be attached and the grants resumed.

1. Amongst the orders of the Board to the late Collector remaining unanswered, I find a letter from your Secretary, dated the 24th of march, last, in reply to the above reference calling for a particular and detailed statement of all the lands of the above descriptions and a copy and translation of one of the grants together with such further information as the late collector might be able to obtain.

2. Had Mr. Dickinson been aware of the many points of serious importance involved in the measure recommended by him I am persuaded that he would not have made, the reference he did in that having previously consulted the Magistrate as to the expediency

or inexpediency of totally annihilating a system very intimately connected with the peace and welfare to District. Had not I been ignotant of such a reference having been made till after Dr. Dickson,s decease, I should not have been thus long in submitting my sentiments on the occasion which I now take the liberty of doing in the united capacities held by me.

3. The Hills in this District are inhabited by a distinct and uncivilized race of people differing entirely in manners customs and religion, from the inhabitants of adjacent country and who, as far can be traced, were never subjected to the authority of the native Government. These people for a long time subsisted by plunder, and their incursions to which they were externed, and rendered all communications difficult and dangerous. The salutary and successful manners adopted by this Government to induce them to relinquish their predatory habits and to submit to the authority of the British administration are so so well-known and their good effect has been so generally felt that it is unnecessary to trouble your Board with a recapitulation of them.

4. Amongst the measures adopted by the native Government to repress the incursions of the Hill people, grants of land were assigned to persons denominated Ghatwalls rent free on condition of their entertaining a certain number of Pykes and Burkandazes for the above express purpose; these lands were situated immediately at the foot of the Hills and encompassed them in all sides; and this system of Police is so remote, that I cannot trace, the period of its commencement.

5. In the year 1780 the inhabitants of the Hills were estimated at one hundred thousand. naturally, mild and inoffensive they must have been impelled by

provocations and temptations of no ordinary nature to have been induced to have recourse to predatory habits for subsistence. Absence of grain in the Hills and the oppressive inimical conduct of the surrounding Zemindars are the reasons which I have heard assigned for their acting in the manner they did. Thus actuated by the double impulse of hunger and revenge having (as I have reason to belive) no other tie on their obedience to the gahtwally Choukies. Rushing like a torrent from their Hills with one accord their chowkies could have opposed but feeble and inefficient barrier to their ravaging the adjacent country; nor were they brought to a tough state of submission and obedience until harressed by a continual warfare carried on against them by government for several years, They listened to the conciliatory offers held out to them by the late Mr. Augustus Cleveland then Collector of the District. Previous, however, to this happy event Captain (late Lieutenant Colonel) James Browne, who commanded a corps of light infantry stationed in the district had so far, checked their predatory spirt as to be able to prevail on several of the Ghatwals and their respective establishments (who had field from the District together with a great proportion of the rest of the inhabitants) to return to their Jaghirs and resume their former duties. To these men Captain Browne granted sannads by the authority of Governor-general and Council, restoring and confirming their former tenures on the conditions attached to them. By degress all the Ghatwals and their dependents returned and were re-established by sannads granted to them by Captain Browne and successive executive officers having the management of the Districts; by whome vacancies have been also filled up as they occurred to the present period. I have the honour of submitting to you a copy of one of the Sannads Signed by Captain James Browne dated the 30th January, 1778. It grants to Mohan Sirder Ghatwal, and five pykes, one hundred and fiftyone bighas of land rent free, on condition of their preventing the incursions of the Hill people.

6. Dickinson states that the duties originally composed on the Ghatwals are no longer performed by or required of them and that the establishments which were once maintained are no longer in existence.

7. I so far agree with Mr. Dickinson, as to admit that the services of the Ghatwals have seldom required for long series of years. The humane and liberal policy adopted by Government has had the happy effect of keeping the Hill people (with a few triflying exceptions) in a state of good order and obedience during these last twenty years ; and I doubt not, will continue to do so, But as the restorations of the Ghatwally Establishments was one of the measures restored to by Government, It surely ought to be considered as entitled to some have in their success. As well might arguments be urged, against the necessity of the continuance of any branch of police that may have attained its objects, without reflecting That all institutions of this nature are equally meant to prevent the commission of crimes as to bring them to light when committed, so far from the services of them Ghatwalls never being required, I can assure your Board that I have more than once had occasion to have recourse to them ; a circumstance with which Mr. Dickinson must have been unacquainted.

8. Mr. Dickinson's source of reformation must have been equally defected with regard to the Ghatowally establishment being no longer in existence. That they may not be regularly lept up to the extent specified in

the Ghatwall's Sannads, I am inclined to believe ; but I have at the same time, the means of knowing that a very considerable proportion of these establishment is actually in existence and effective in preserving the peace of the district.

9. It is calculated that the resumption of these lands would yield a clear profit to Government of Rs. 25,000/- per annum. . Independent of other ill effects to be expected from the measure, I am really much inclined to think that calculation would turn out a delusive one. The lands are situated immediately at the foot of the Hills liable to the continual depredations of Hogs, Deer, Elephants, and other animals, which in such wild parts of the country are destructive leave to the husband man. the air must in general be unwholesome ; and the Jagheers must be mostly at considerable distance from any mart at which the cultivators can dispose of their harvest. This district is so far from having recovered the fatal diminution in its population by famine and emigration and immense tracts of land possessing every advantage are lying waste and want of hands to cultivate, were the ghatowally jaghirs to be assessed in common with all other Malguzary land, the disadvantages which I have mentioned would naturally induce the present occupants to quit their little productive tenures and to settle upon other uncultivated spots with which this district abounds, possessing a happier Climate and promising a more abundant return to their labour. Nor would a disappointment in this expected-addition source of revenue be the only evil resulting from the desertion of the Jaghirs; for so quick is Vegetation in this country that they would soon be covered with jungle and rendered impenetrable but to wild and destructive animals and to the Hill people themselves, thereby

... additional obstacles to a free communication with the hills, should it ever be here- after necessary to have recourse to coercive measures against their inhabitants and increasing the hunts and retreats of the disaffected.

10. I am aware of only circumstances which would at present justify the resumption of the Ghatwally jagheers; and that is to induce the hill people to quit their hills and settle in the plains. Could a measure of such importance be effected it would prove a source of wealth to Government and of confirmed security for future ages to this and surrounding districts against all further depredations ; whist it would be forwarding the cause of humanity by introducingJ amongst this rude and numerous race all the arts and blessings of civilized life. To the accomplishment of it, however, serious and almost unsurmountable obstacles are opposed - The independent spirit of the hill people, their attachment to their hills, the difficutly in reconciling the jarring sects amongst whom they would be settled and ensuring harmony between them, and the unceasing perseverance which would be principal ones. Events at present unseemly hereafter occur to render it unpracticable; but until that shall be the case I venture to offer it, as humble opinion that the uncertain prospect of a trifling addition to the resources of the Estate would not under existing circumstances warrant any alteration whatever in system of Police that for more than 20 years has been productive of such important benefits as well to the country at large as to the hill people themselves and of which the due exercise of that system in all its parts promises to ensure a long and happy continuance."

Sd/J. Fombelle

OOO

41. Browne's plan

For Adinistration of the Jungle Tarai.

'I will now beg leave to offer my opinion as to what I think the best method of government these countries, so as to render them a security, instead of a very considerable danger to these provinces, and as the end of my writing this sketch, is to convey truth and information, not to sacrifice to prejudice, I shall proceed to it without any regard to the suggestions of the votaries of professional distinction, who from sympathy may be apt to conclude, that I am influenced to prefer this plan by the necessity it, induces for keeping up military command here:- I shall with equal freedom propose a diminution of the present revenue, which will of course be approved, if I shew that, upon the whole, such a measure will be an advantages to Government, or rejected, if I fail to produce sufficient arguments to that end.

I shall lay it down as the basis of this plan, that the Rajahs of the mountains and jungles extending from the Mahrattah boundary south, to the plain countries of Midnapoor, Burdwn, Bietboom, (Birbhum)Bauglepoor, Monghier, and Bahar, north, are the natural and proper defenders of the honourable Company's provinces against the Mahrattahs on that side; and that those provinces would be safer through the affection and feudal services of these petty chiefs, supported by a small regular force, than with almost any force that could be spared for protecting this frontier in time of general warfare, if those chieftains, instead of attachment, should feel the sentiments of resentment and disaffection towards us.

I shall just beg leave to call to mind that all the passes leading from the Mahrattah territories into Bengal and Bihar, are within our own boundary, and that they are possessed by the Rajahs of the respective limits through which they pass: behind is a second line of Chokeydary gautwallies constituting the Jungle Terry almost all the inhabitants are armed, and hold lands of their respective chiefs on the feudal tenure, the chiefs were formerly bound by the same ties to the state, a slight tribute and the protection of the frontier against all invasions from the south :- The Government of Hindostan though these people were the natural defence of the frontiers, and of course that it was necessary by every means to attach them to the State, and to make their private interests coincide with that of the public; left dissatisfied with a government from which they felt more evil than good, they should invite, rather than oppose, the entrance of an enemy into the provinces:- I doubt not, that this political reflection had as much weight in preventing the native Governors of Bengal from attempting to levy a heavier tribute from thesecountries, as any deficiency of troops fit for such a service:- their conduct was certainly judicious – that an armed peasantry, if attached to the state, may do infinite injury to an invader, however formidable, in a country naturally strong. We need look no further for a striking proof, than the instance of the opposition given by the peasants of Poland, to a victorious army, led on by Charles the XIIth, of Sweden – had those peasants been disgusted with the state, and expected a change of masters, there is scarcely room for a doubt, that they would have conducted the very army, which, in other circumstances they opposed, nor could any body of regular forces stationed there, have compensated for, or counterbalanced their disaffection; for an invading army is seldom deficient of force, but almost always in point of intelligence, and it behoves the state liable to invasion, to take care they do not obtain it from any defection of their own people :- I will not, however, take up your time, sir, either general reasonings upon principals too clear to be disputed ; but proceed at once to apply them to the case for which this is written; I mean the State of this frontier within and without. Within, we have by military force and operations imposed a tribute much higher than ever had been paid before; but take all these countries throughout, I believe you will find, Sir, this increased tribute does not amount to eight annas per man, of those, who have thereby been alienated from the state ; and what are these people, not wretched, spiritless, unarmed bengales, inhabiting a plain centrical country, neither formidable by character or situation ; but an armed people, martial, proud, and independent, and constituting, by their situation, the only barrier we posses against that enemy, from whom more than from all other, the state may suffer greatest loss in its wealth and population.

The increased tribute has reduced the Zemindars from easy to straitened circumstances, and many of the younger branches of their familes, to be without any support; in such circumstances, need I say, that the whole body of the people are dissatisfied – Let no stress be laid on their paying their revenues ; the oppression of your troops, and the great attention of your officer on these services, to render their Government and themselves popular, and agreeable to these savage and martial chiefs, have hitherto effected this ; but these people have as yet had no temptations from without; you have but just to be at war with the Mahrattahs, and have as yet experience no necessity for removing to other places, those bands which hitherto have held together this crazy fabric ; let but that happen before some measures are taken to prevent the consequences and I doubt not, that a scene of universal confusion will ensue: nor do I think any addition of force which could be spared, would avail to keep out an invasion from the south, while the whole body of the people are dissatisfied with our Government :- A man from a superficial view, might suppose everything very solid and well compounded ; but I have an opportunity of seeing behind the curtain and can assert, that it is by no means so. With respect to the outside of this frontier, Maharashtra districts are divided from ours, generally speaking, by an ideal line ; the Zamindars on both sides are in many places closely connected ; a negotiation through that medium, might be set on foot by the Maharashtra Government in a few days. If they offered powerful borders, while our borders, generally dissatisfied, are also impoverished, and by not united to the State, do you think, sir, they would have virtue enough to resist the temptation, or indeed would it be any virtue to do so? The answer I fear is plain and negative : a body of Mahrattahs thus introduced into the heart of the Province of Bengal, would in six hours inflict greater loss than the revenues of all these frontier countries put together, amount to in a year and whenever they should be compelled to fly from your troops, (which would not be very suddenly) their old allies our borders, would find means of getting them as safely back as they advanced ; for as I said before, an army would not suffice to guard all these passes without the aid affections of our own borders; and with them, a very little force would do a great deal. It has been before observed, in opposition to idea of substituting regular troops to these feudatories that none but the natives of these countries could exist. In those unwholesome mountains jungles, through which the passes immediately lead; and I beg leave to call it to mind, as an argument of the utmost importance: for the reality of the fact I appeal to all the surgeons and officers who have been on these services. - In 1774, when Captain James Crawford was employed in reducing the frontier Zamindaries of Pachete, he fixed some posts near the passes leading from the Baugmoory Hills, and though they were weekly relieved, yet such was the devastation made in his battalion by keeping up those posts, that at one time he had near three hundred men sick. The urgent necessity of affairs, compel led him to support this measure though the consequences were so fatal in spite of every precaution he could use, which were such indeed, as would not have entered into the imagination of almost any person but him, who was one of the first public and private character I ever knew; I hope, Sir, you will excuse this small tribute to the merit of one of the dearest friends I ever had, whose memory I shall ever hold sacred, and the loss of whom, both to the public and myself, as it is irreparable? I shall never cease to lament.

These being the evils attending the present mode of. Government established in these countries,the remedies I beg leave to offer to Your consideration are as follows :

That the tribute now levied upon these countries be reduced to such a sum as the Zemindar shall cheerfully and voluntarily agree to pay, binding themselves by mutual fidelity and feudal services ;- a most sacred oath to be annually renewed, to fidelity and feudal services; each **Zemindar having one of his children or nearest kindred always residing with the commanding officer of the division to which he belongs** ; as a further security and mark of obedience – This plan to be made general thought the Mountains of Midnapoor Pachete, Naikpoor, Ramgur, and Pelamow; as also throughtout the Jungle Terry of Berbhoom, Curruckdea, Guidore, and Curruckpoor. I am not well acquainted with the amount of the revenues of any of these districts, excepting those which have been under my authority; but I conjecture, that this deduction (by which many thousand of armed men would be secured to the service of the state, to which they now only want an opportunity to shew their enmity) would not amount be above one lac of rupees per annum; a sum which, I said before, is not equal to the loss which would be suffered in six hours by an incursion of Mahrattahs.

II. That the waste lands in all these countries, which are not hereditary property, be given in Jaghier, to worn-out Sepoys in the service, who shall be encouraged and agree to settle there with their families, on the tenure of feudal service.

III. That to remedy the scarcity of money, the Zemindars be allowed to pay in part of their rents in such articles produced in their districts, as are not of perishable nature (such as iron and damman) at fixed prices; these goods to be carried at their expense to the Cutcherry of the division, and to be disposed of by contract, for the company, or otherwise as may be directed – **The cultivation of opium may be attempted, where the soil will admit of and grain and other provisions, army be received on the say terms, and lodged in magazines for the use of the**

troops, these and the neighbouring quarters, the old stock being annually disposed of.

IV. That with respect to the administration of Justice the Zemindary courts be allowed the power of adjusting all little matters either civil or criminal, subject however to appeal, in the former cases to the Commander, and in the latter, to the Fiujdary court of the district; but that no considerable case be congnizable by the zemindars; but refered solely to the Commander of the districts, who, in civil cases, will decide according to his instructions from the board, and in all criminal ones, will lay them before the Faujdaar Adowlat.

V. That as a force on the part of Government is absolutely requisite to support these feudal troops, if attacked from without, and by superior authority to control and keep them from all disputes and violence from within. I beg leave to recommend, that the whole of this frontier be divided into three military commands, viz.

One to include all the frontier of Midnapoor, vix.

Mhurbunge Burraboom and Singbook Manboom Dolboom

The second, all they of Pasheit, (=Panchet)

Tomer and Pateoom, and the Jungle terry lying behind it, viZ. of Pateoom Bierboom Curruckdea, Chackye and Curruckpoor. The third, all that of Nagpoor, Ramgur and Palamow, viz. Nagpoor Burwah Palamow Toory Sheergauty Rampur

In order to give that degree of weight to the three officers commanding at these stations, and that unity of authority which is absolutely requisite such countries, for the ends of intelligence and action, without which, nothing essential can be effected by them, I recommend it as absolutely necessary, they each do collect the tribute from the Zemindars of his division, and appropriate, and account for it, in part of the disbursements of his corps. - There is certainly no necessity for civil servants being employed in such trifling collections, it occasions, and a division of authority highly detrimental to the service, besides an immense increase of expense ; for one civil collector, to be equal to they of three or four military ones put together; and surely as to expediency; and officer, if his common sense, can manage the account of fifty or sixty or sixty thousand rupees, as well as if he had been bred up in counting horse all his life.

These three commands to be independent of each other; but to keep up constant communication and intelligence, and co-operate together for the general good, in case of public emergency, when their forces might be obliged to join, the eldest officer would of course command; I propose the independence, because each must be the best judge of what is proper in his own district; but were those three commands nature of man, be for interfering in every thing, and of course would often do so, where he had but little knowledge of the subject.

As the easy terms to tribute will render all compulsion to pay it unnecessary, the only posts required, will be against foregin enemies ; I can on this point only speak of the districts under my authority, which can be entered from the south, by way of Ramgur and Pacheit, or from the Bahar province to the west and north-west; the true scene of action is the Jungle and passes, but the troops destined for it should be stationed near them, and secured from insult.

The fort at Chackey, fully answer every such and with respect to that pass.

That of Curruckdea, is too remote from the pass of that name, and I therefore advise the... one at a small expenses near Gommah. These two will affect every defence and communication requisite towards Bahar.

Towards Ramgur, I would recommend to repair the fort of Doomchanuse, which is within two cose of Corumma, the grand pass from ramgur to Curruckdea.

Towards Pacheit, I would propose repairing the fort of Deopoor,(south of Serampoor) which is within four cross of the Toondey pass, leading from Pacheit to Curruckdea.

These two forts would also keep open the communication with Bihar by way of Curruckdea, in case the main body of the Jungle Terry commands should march to assist that of Ramgur or Pacheit.

Breastworks of stones and coarse chunam, which could be made here, might at a small expenses be erected across the Principal passes, with strong gates ; and some of the many old cannon lying about in different places, might be mounted, and added to the strength of these breastworks, with little or no expenses; which would render the access next to impossible, when we were supported with the grand essentials, the affections and interest of the natives.

This is the plan, I beg permission to offer consideration, and it is, as I elsewhwere said, an improvement, not an abrogation of the ancient Government ; the feudal soldiery are not only preserved, but supported by the troops of government, who at the same time will much more effectually answer the end of control over these Jungal Chiefs, than their former feudal lords possibly could.

A small reduction of revenue takes places, but it is to secure the affections and services, and render yourselves safe from the enmity of thousand of your own unarmed subject, situated between you and your most formidable enemy: it is an act worthy of the dignity and wisdom a great political state as this is, and cannot become upon any better ground than the short sighted scheme ways and means, which never look beyond the present hour.

I know nothing that I can add to this sketch, but my earnest wish, that it may in any degree answer your intention and expectation : as to the successful execution of the plan, I feel an entire confidence, that nothing is requisting for ensuring that, but the sanction and approbation of that state, for whose service it was formed.

ooo

42. Letter

From,

C. Chapman,

Collector, Bhagalpur

To,

William Couper,

President and Members of the Board of Revenue

This dated 6 June, 1785

"I have received your sub-Secretary's letter of the 26th May enclosing copies of the petition of the zemindar of Akbarpoor and Muuckrarean.

I beg leave to inform you that previous to my appointment to the charge of this station the greater part of the Rajmahal district was let to Rutton Chund the present farmer for three or 1190, 1191 and 1192. I received the Committee's orders to make the statements of 1191, when the agent for the Zemindary of Akbarpoor, and for the other zemindaries not included in Rutton Chund's lease applied to me for a decrease in their rent to the amount of four or five thousand rupees which they, at length, brought down to three thousand after which no further proposal was made to me. In the meantime Rutton Chund offered to take the remaining part of the district at an increased rent of two thousand rupees for the year 1191, and three thousand for the year 1192. Being very anxious that the revenue should not fall off immediately on my taking charge of the Collectorship, I recommended the offer of Rutton Chund to the Committee which they were pleased to accept and to approve the settlement I had made in their letter to me of the 27th of September 1784.

N. B :- I have directed the most particular inquiry to be made into that part of the zemindars complaint stating the farmers collecting a new tax of an anna in each rupee on the last year's revenue and if I find it will be put, an effectual step to it to be refunded to his assertion, That the farmer is ruining the country, I can assure the complaint is without foundation, being fully convinced that it is in an empowering state.

As Rutton Chund has fulfilled his engagement with the utmost punctuallity for which and for his attention to the improvement of the country he has been repeatedly recommended to the Committee by my predecessor in office. I humbly presume to hope that he may not be deprived of his farm till his lease shall be out which will be at end of the present year 1192, after which (of) the zemindars should propose equitable terms for farming their zemindary to them-selves, I shall be happy to recommend them to the acceptanceof the Committee.

As it appears several years since the Gola Behrau claimed by Abdee Narain has been annexed to Conkjole, I must request time to inquire in to the particulars but with respect to the request to be allowed to pay the revenue of Hurreepoor and four villages at the Khalsa, I have only to observe that the same objection applies to it as to that made by Neelmunny and Luckynauth. The whole revenue of the villages is only sicca rupees 359. 8".

OOO

43. Letter

From,

C. Chapman, Collector, Bhagalpur

To,

Samuel Charters,

President and Members of the Board of Revenue

Dated 18 June, 1785

"I have received your sub-Secretary's letter of the 3rd instant enclosing a copy of a petition of Bullabhy Khaunt Zemindar of the purgunnah Koorhund in reply to which I beg leave to represent the term of this purgunnah was granted to Rutton Chund in the time of my predecessor for the years 1190,1191,1192 at sicca rupees 8701 perannum, and that in 1187 the year in which the zemindar represents the farms was first given to Rutton Chund the revenue stood at Rupees 4916-15-16.

So it will appear from this statement that Rutton Chund at the time of his entering into his engagements agreed to a very considerable increase which he has punctually paid. I cannot conceive it to the intention of Gont. To deprive him, or other farmers of their leases who have behaved well till the term of them shall be expired ; which seems to be the opinion of some of the Zemindaars who have delivered in their petitions at the Presidency but that when lands are to be let, the Zemindars on offering an equitable rent should be indulged with the preference. I humbly request the Committee will be pleased to favour me with their sentiments on this particular to which I will non-Scrpulously conform.

All Rutton Chund engagements will be out at the end of the present year 1192 for which as the faith of government has been pledged to him, and as a considerable accession of revenue has been acquired through him. At the same time that he has behaved with great moderation in the country, I beg permission to recommend his continuance."

OOO

44. Letter

From,

R. Adair, Rajmahal,

To,

William Cowper, President and Members of the Board of Revenue

This dated ....

"I beg leave to transmit to you the petition (of) some Ryotts of this zealah complaining against Poorun Singh the Zemindar of

Chuck Delowry and to request you would be pleased to authorise me to summon him before me in order to enquire into and redress the grievance stated which I have reason to believe really exists.

I also beg leave to mention to you Gentlemen, that this Mehal situated chiefly (with) in my district made in the year 1783 a part of the Rajmahal jumma, and to submit it to your judgement whether the replacing it on that footing would not prove to the comfort and security of Ryotts by furnishing them with a station at a moderate distance where upon such occasions their complaints might be heard and redressed.

As a further argument for re-annexing the Mahal Chuck Deloway to this district I may add that disputes often occur between Poorun Sing and Roshun Bucksh Zemindar more than once urged tham to prepare for, and almost to commit hostilities, which dispute might either be finally transmitted or kept in due subjections, was Poorun Sing as well as the other zemindar under my authority.

ooo

45. Arzee of Byge Naut Baijnath zemindar

From,

R. A., Collector, Rajmahal

To, John Shore, President of the Khalsa, dated 11 February, 1788.

" I am just favoured with your letter of the 15th December 1787 forwarding an Arzee from Byge Naut zemindar of Bagumabad no. 2376 for my inquiry and report. In reply I am to inform you that 6 annas of the purgunnah above mentioned appeared to have been sold by auction, for a balance of Revenue in the year 1191 and that, that proportion of it was purchased by Rutton Chund, who has to this time held possession of it by the tenure of a Sunnud granted to him by the chief of Morshedabad. In the last General Revenue Regulations the purgunnah was annexed to this collectorship and Byge Naut complained to me as he has set forth nearly in the terms in which he has since represented his case to you. As I was unacquainted with the circumstance complained of I wrote to Mr. Dason from whose district the mahal was a sepration enclosing him a copy of the Arzee, and Sunnud granted to the purchaser and requested to know if the sale was considered valid and if Rutton Chund was recognized as zemindar, and beg leave to enclose to you an extract of his reply and further to inform you that the purgunnah is at present in the state in which I receive charge of it from that Gentleman.

The more material point of the Arzee relates to circumstances which happened some years before the Mahal was annexed to this Collectorship and of which I have no official knowledge, and as the parties concerned in the transaction are beyond the limits of my authority I have no means of ascertaining the truth of the representation. "

46. Letter

From,

R. A., Collector, Bhagalpur

To,

John Shore,

President and Members of the Board of Revenue,

Dated 1st April, 1789

"Accompanying I have the honour to transmit you statements in abstract and detail (of) made out from the zemindary papers of Rajemahal which were procured in obedience of your order date 5th May, 1788 and to the following effect that in order to supply the deficient information in respect to the resources of the several zemindaries. I should call upon the zemindars by purwannas requiring the attendance of the Sheristadars of their respective Cutcherries with their Muffussil Accounts Settlement and Collections as far back as their Dufter could furnish them and report their answer, as well as how far I might conceive the materials so produced authentic or otherwise. The answer of the zemindars to my purwannas were sent you under date 17th july 1788, which not deeming satisfactory you were pleased to direct by your letter of the (no date mentioned) a measurement to be made of their lands unless the papers demanded were produced.

The preparations made to survey their lands in conformity to these instructions had, after some farther delay, effect on the zemindars to produce the materials from which the enclosed statements are extracted, and which they desire to have considered as furnishing a complete Hustabood of Rajemahal, including the jumma Kuurch or account of receipts, and expenditures for the purpose of exhibiting the profit, loss under which they at present respectively hold their Zemindaries; and to serve as a guide to Government in fixing the jumma for the usual term under the proposed ten years settlement, of which intended measure they seem by some means or other to have been early apprised.

With respect to the authenticity of these materials you must be sensible that under your prohibitory orders regarding local scrutinies into the affairs of a zemindary I am must at a loss for any determinated ground on which to form an opinion and destitute of the means of ascertaining by proofs whether the accounts are fabricated or not, and that the only guide I have in judging is the probablilty or otherwise which appears on the face of the papers themselves compared with my own general experience and observation of the circumstances of the zemindars and their zemindaries.

Thus situated I am fearful my respect will prove less decisive than you may expect. But on a subject which concerns a measure of much present and future importance as a settlement for ten years, it is necessary you should not be misled by a greater reliance on asserted facts than they may really deserve, nor myself brought under responsibility for imputed information, the truth of which I had it not in my power to grain an adequate knowledge.

After these presatory observations which I trust will meet with due consideration I proceed to offer you such remarks, as upon full deliberation have occurred to me the nature of the enclosed accounts. The sets No. 1 & relate to the year 1191 and 1192 but as they include only two Mahals they cannot be of much use. These are made out from papers the further back. . of any that have been produced by the Zemindars. The set No. 3 for the year 1193 contains 40 Mahals and the set no. 4 comprehend the Zeelah complete for the year 1194. To each set of accounts is annxeed an abstract exhibiting at one view comparative statement of the receipts of each zemindar with the surplus or deficiency of his income to his expenditure.

Under the heads Assul, Abwob and Sewoy in the detailed accounts you will find the produce of the original ground rent, taxes and duties both ancient and modern particularized in their several denominations, the total of these heads comprehend the whole of the Mofussil collections and profits, and the adjoining column the amount stated to have been borrowed by the zemindars to make good their engagements. The Head khuch contains the Zemindary disbursements and their private expenses,and the balance if any. . the sums remaining in their hands at the end of the year.

In the abstract accounts, the sums stated to have been borrowed are omitted, for the purpose of more readily showing the ability, or otherwise of the zemindars to fulfil their engagements with government according to the documents they have produced, and which appears with column entitled surplus and deficiency.

These accounts could they be depended on might be serviceable in determining the future jumma, but although as was before mentioned I have not the means of proving them false, yet I cannot believe them true and there is no appearance of a sudden decrease in cultivation to account for the deficiency they exhibit and it cannot have been of long standing or the zemindars must have been ruined and their credit ceased with those from whom they would be supposed to have raised loan. It is only three years ago that the man who held the whole zillah in farm gave a voluntary increase of the jumma and would willingly have renewed his engagements at the expiration of this lease. The profits, which induced him to make the offer, fell into the hands of the zemindars who in return for the indulgence of government in reinstating them either have injured the Zeelah by their mismanagement or trusting to the obscurity in which they think the affairs of the Mofussil are led to all but themselves bring forward a deception as to its produce and expenses of collection. If the latter be their aim it must be confessed they have taken it with some judgement, for with every advantage that can be had in investigating the truth of these papers and the actual produce of their zemindaries, some particulars of each would still be liable to concealment. Their own private expenses and the real disbursements to be variety of zemindary servants they employ can be known only to themselves and the artifice of granting Pattahs at a low rate to serve a temporary purpose long experience with Mofussil mode of imposition has enabled them to practise with effects the bringing to Account Salammies and (Salami)other Petty advantages may have with a view to give an appearance of eandour and possibility to the whole but admitting the account receipt to be faithful, stated the disbursements I must still conclude otherwise for the reason already given, that three years ago the farmers found profit his (in) engagements and there has been no apparent difference in the state of the country since to account for such a deficiency as in now stated by the Zemindars, but on the contrary I am of opinion that it would rather bear an increase ought to be to particularise the proportion of it on each Mahal and to state specifically my reasons for fixing it I could only answer for the documents now submitted joint to such general observations as I have also communicated to you and you will easily judge whether such materials would be adequate to the purpose or not.

I am to believe however not withstanding they pretend deficiency, that the zemindars would willingly engage for a renewal of their lease on the jumma of former years except in the different Mahals formerly reported to you either for one year or more and that under the latter mode they might be induced to consent to an increase though, at present, I have no assurance of obtaining any not having thought myself at liberty to mention the subject to them. "

(Ed.) These letters relate to the relations of the East India Company and the Zamindars of Rajmahal region.

Surendra Jha

OOO

47. Letter

From,

A. Seton,

Collector, Bhagalpur

To,

John Shore,

President and Members of the Board of Revenue,

Fort William

This dated 9 November, 1789

"On the 5th instant I had the honour of informing you that, lest a longer delay in making the settlement should prove injurious to the cultivation, I intended forth-with receiving conditional engagements from the Zeminders for that of their respective lands subject of courses as is expressed in my acceptance to your revision and correction of the several purgunnahs comprising this Zillah the circumstance of Curruckpur were such as to press for immediate attention and arrangements. **This immense purgunnah which extends from the Hills of Sultanabad to those of Monghyr and from the bank of the Ganges to the confines of Birbhom, is at present the property of Rajah Cawder Alii,** a minor, the management of whose affairs has been conducted by a person called **Chuny Laul** since the year 1760 when he was appointed Peshkaur by the late Mr. Cleveland, Collector of this district. I made it my first business to ascertain whether this man had acquitted himself himself properly of his trust, and whether the Rajah and his mother, were satisfied with his conduct. The result of my enquiries was advantageous to Chunny Laul and the Dowager Ranny assured me in writing that he was an old servant of the family, and that she wished him to be continued, in the management of her son's affairs. To satisfy myself however that the ranees approbation was voluntary. I desired that my Dewan might have a conference with her, to give her an opportunity of explaining without restraint whatever she might have to say relative to her son or his concerns and, in particular to ascertain whether ther were any relation of her late husband, whom she wished to have charge of the young zamindar's education or affairs. This conference accordingly took place and it the Ranee confirmed the contents of her letter, Viz. : that Chunny Laul was an old and confidential servant of the family, and that she wished him to be continued in office Adding that neither she nor thelate Rajah had any near relations alive.

Under these circumstances. I would recommend the continuance of Chunny Laul or rather his appointment in capacity of surburrahkar, as decribed in the 9th Article of the resolution contained in the letter of the 20th May from the Governor-General in Council to your Board which exactly applies to the case in question, but for the reason already submitted to you conceiving that the safety of the current revenue might be endangered by a longer delay in making some conditional arrangements, I called upon the Rajah to deliver in a Durkhawast for the Mal or land revenue of the purgunnah on account of the current fusselly year 1197 and as it was evident that the terms would be dictated by Chunny laul, I told him that I expected his signature to be affixed to it, and should cinsider him as responsible for the measure.

The Jummah of last year was rupees 48301-10-3 sunnaut but from papers and accounts which I procured since my arrival I had reason to believe that it could as a large increase, nor has the event deceived my expectation. you will perceive by the accompanying copy and translation of the Durkhaust that after deducting sunnaut rupees 1575-6-11 account the Ganges, Bazar and hauts (at) contains a net increase of sunnaut rupees 16,000 on the land revenue only. You will also be pleased to observe that the principal relative to the sort of rupees laid down in the 7th Article of the resolution of the 18th September last, has been literally adhered to the sannaut rupees being in the first instance converted into Siccas and an option left with the Zemindar either to pay his kists in Siccas or in Sannauts at the same rate of batta (2 per cent) in which they are now converted into Siccas. In fixing upon this as the local rate of Batta, I have been guided by the reports of the bankers. whether it be exact medium or not, I cannot presume to say but it is at least equitable and impartial in this that it is adopted as the reciprocal rate in each calculation. It is indeed probable that from the scarcity of Siccas the Zamindar will generally avail himself of the option of paying in saunnauts.

Notwithstanding the favourable character, I heard of Chunny Laul, I thought it necessary to take some precautions for securing to the Rajah the profits of some considerable jagheers specified in a sunnud granted to him by the Governor-General in Council on the 1st April, 1781. I accordingly stipulated that a person should be appointed on the part of Government to superintend the jagheers, and that to secure a faithful appropriation of the amount one of the two following modes of payment should be adopted viz. : either that the Zemindar and a joint receipt from him and his mother taken in return in duplicate, one to be transmitted to Bhagalpur, and the other to remain with the Tehsealdar of the Jagheer as a voucher; or that the amount should be at one remitted to this place, and paid here to a person appointed by the Rajah and Ranee, whose joint receipt should be taken in return,exclusive of which I desired the Ranee to write me a separate letter on receiving each payment of these two modes, the ranee prefers the first. It rests with you to determine which shall be adopted. I further informed her that in order to watch over her son's interest, she might appoint a confidential servant to remain with the Tehseeldar, have access to his accounts and, as far as representations went,check his conduct. Exclusive of desire to prevent any embezzlements of the usufruct of the Jagheer, I had an other view in stipulating that a person should be stationed in the purgunnah on the part of Government,viz: to correspond with me occasionally on the state of the country, and procure authentic information respecting its internal parts, without creating jealousy or wearing an appearance of vexatious investigation with a view to future resumption, which as far as relates to rent free lands specified in the sunnud, I took upon me to declare was not the intention of Government.

Such Gentlemen, are the arrangements which I have thought it necessary to adopt with respect to Curruckpur when amended and modified by your superior wisdom. I trust they will effectually secure the attainment of the ends for they have been adopted. "

(Ed) This letter throws useful light on the working of native estates in the area. It also informs us on the hitherto unknown aspect of the history of Kharagepur Raj.

Surendra Jha

OOO

48. Translation of the proposal of Rajah Cawdir Ali Zemindar of pergunnah Curruckpur for the settlement …… in 1197 Fuslee.

In the year 1196, the Jummah of the said Mehauls was sunaut rupees 48301-10-3 on deducting from that amount, the jummah of the ganges, Bazars =(Small mandis & markets), and Hauts, viz. : Rs. 1575-6-2 now become a huzzooree collection there remains the sum of sunnaut Rs. 46,726-4-. . to which I hereby agree to add an increase of Rs. 16000 sunnaut amounting together to Rs. 62726-4-1/2 sunnnaut, or Rs. 61,446-8 Moorshidabad Siccas, on deducting the Batta at 2 percent, viz. : Rs. 1279-12-2. I engage to pay this jummah in Sicca rupees or in the event of my being unable to pay the same in Sicca rupees when the kists become due, I engage to pay the value there of in full weight sunnauts, at the above specified Battah of 2 percent, and exclusive therof to pay the secretary's Russom of 2 percent. Miscellaneous it bring understood that my Nankar Moffussil Akhraiat are not included in the lands paying the above jumah.

4th November, 1789

Rajah cauder Ali. Chunney Laul Peshkar.

Translation of the reply of Rajah Cawder Ali. Zamindar of Curruckpoor, to a question put to him by the Collector of Bhagalpur relative to the rate of Battah at which his jumah was to be converted into sicca Rupees.

From-collector Bhagalpur

OOO

49. Letter

From-collector Bhagalpur

To,

Thomas Law, Collector of Bihar

I have received your question to this effect. " The revenue of your zamindary has heither to been paid in Patna Sunnaut rupees. In the event of your engagement for the present year being made out in sicca rupees, what rate of Battah do you require? It being understood that, if at the time of payment you cannot procure sicca the amount shall be again converted into sunnauts, at that rate ". My reply is this. It is true my Cabliat has nitherto been made out in Patna Sunnauts, sicca rupees are not current in this Zillah. If my engagement be now made out in sicca, I request that the amount may be calculated from sunnauts into sicca at Batta of 2 ½ percent, and should I be unable to procure sicca I then request that the amount may be calculated back into sunnauts at the same batta of 2 ½ percent."

ooo

50. Letter

From,

A. Seton,Collector, Bhagalpur

To,

John Shore,Presenting and member of the Board of Revenue,
Dated 26 November, 1789.

"On the14th instant I had the honour of communicating to you the substance of the Shroff's reports respecting the relative value of sicca and sunnaut rupees at Bhagalpur. I now have the pleasure of replying to that part of your letter of the 5th instant which directs me to ascertain and report the rates at which sunnaut rupees are collected by the Zamindars from the ryots.

Previous to the receipt of that letter,I had called upon three of the principal zamindsrs of this Zillah, viz. those of Phurkea, Chey and Curruckpur to report the required rates of Battah in their repective purgunnahs and now have the honour to transmit enclosed attested copies of their replies, together with translation. By these appears that in curruckpoor the average Batta on all rupees but Patna sunnauts,was 3.1/8percent. That in Chey, there was no Batta,and that in Phurkea there in Mofussil even the payments are no rupees tendered but sunnauts. As from the option which both the sudder and Mofussil Malguzars' now have, of paying either in sicca or (at affixed and equiltable Batta)in sunnauts, the zamindars can have no interest in concealing the former rates. I know no reason why the present statements should not be correct I must say the report of the zamindar of Curruckpoor seems most probable as it corresponds to the nearest with the information which I have received from other quarters. The currency of the latter and the circumstance of the engagements between the Zamindars and under-renters being invariably made out in that kind of rupee has hither to given it a superioity which more than counterbalanced its intrinsic want of value and option of paying the revenue to the sudder Malguzaurs either in Sunnauts or in siccas at a paid and equitable Batta, not having been perfectly understood in the Mofussil, the Shroffs naturally found their advantages in buying up, at Certain periods,sunnauts which of course occasioned a scarcity of them in the Mofussil at the very time when they were most wanted. In consequence of this, payments of revenue were frequently tendered to the zamindars and farmers in different sorts of sicca rupees which as it was contrary to the letter of the engagements of the under-renters, and as there was no fixed rate of Batta between the stipulated and the tendered species of rupee, threw the under-renters and ryotts but too much into the power of the Zamindars Shroffs and others who had money in command. From this short outline of the cause and nature of the abuse it is scarcely necessary to add, that the effect of the 10th Paragraph of the resolutions of this Lordship in council under date the 8th September last(a copy of which I enclose to save you the trouble of a reference)and the binding the Sudder Malguzaurs to extend the option to the under-renters and Ryotts will henceforth restore the sicca rupees to a greater degree of currency and operate as an effectual check on those who aim at drawing advantages from the poverty of the Mofussll Malguzaurs."

Jama Transmitted by Cleveland

Mr. Cleveland,Collector of the district - Rs. 49317-5-14
Deduct as the usual Inaum of the said
Rajah Mozaffer All. Rs. 15815-11-11
Remainder being the amount-settlement
Of the year 1188 F. S. . . Rs. 34101-10-3

Particulars of the above

Jummah of Purgunnah Curruckpur	Rs. 30213- 2- 3
Deduct Inaumats purgunnah Cudjerah,(=Kajra) being an ultamgah (=altange). .	6300-0-0
Deduct Havelly Curruckpur account:-	
"Sehehenock" or table expenses. .	Rs. 6200-0-0
"Afzoon "Gunge. . . .	150-0-0
"Cumbur Gunge. . . .	61-0-0
"Russoome zemindary. .	3022-11-11
"Allowances of the Canoongoes of Purgunnah Hindoa (Handwe). .	82-2-0-0
	15815-11-11
Remainder being the net Jummah of Purgunnah Curruckpur. .	14397-6-0
Jummah of Ichanguirah and Musdey Separated from Sircar Monghyr. .	2401-0-0
Jummah of Purgunnah Sunghole. .	179-1-5
" " Dhurrerah. .	1709-14-0

" " Ghor Ghaut and Suckora. .	120-0-0
	4409-15-15
Total exclusive of the zemindary -	4409-15-15

Jummah of the Jungleterry Mahals
Separted from the Purgunnah of Gordah-

Gordah Amlooa, Mutea ...	669-9-3
Chundoo Pussay ...	7291-0-0
Register in the Cumroutha ...	Rs 161-1-0

Khalsah this

Ist day of Jumah of Bahurmanpoor, dependant May 1780 on Bhagalpur exclusive of the

Signed/- zemindary.	Rs. 2754 – 3- 3
Dencan "of Chundun ...	1317-12-0
to R. D. "of Hundua ...	2818-0-0
"Sehera Mohara ... 282-10-10 Total ...	Rs. 34101-10-3

Dated on the 1st April 1781 corresponding with the 22nd of Cheyt 1188 F. S. and answering to the 6th of Rabiul Sany in the 23rd of the regin.

Zanted order of the

A true translation.

Honourable Governor-

General in Council, Signed - A. Seton,

Fort William, the Collector. "

1st May, 1781

Revenue Deptt.

Signed. T. Bangh
Seceretary

ooo

51. Letter

From,

A. Seton,

Collector, Bhagulpur

To,

John Shore,

President and Members of the Board of Revenue,

This dated 13 December 1789,

"On the 29th ultimo I had honour of replying to your letter of the 16th of that month, when I sub-mitted to you the principal amount upon which I ascertained the amount of the Gunga Bazar and Hauts in Curruckpoor and transmitted a copy and translation of the Sunned granted by the Governor- General -in -council during the admistration of Mr. Hasting, to Rajah Cawder Ali, zamindar of that Purgunnah. I mentioned at the same time two instances of inaccuracy in point of date in the copy in question, which I observed, I had found amongst the records of this office. I now do my honour to enclose another copy of that instrument which though a literal transcript of the original sunnud in the possession of the Rajah corresponds exactly with that which has been already transmitted and contains the very same in the accuracies with respect to dates, viz. (that though in the body of thesunnud its date is said to be Secretary to the Governor-general in Council and that in that the preparer of reports it is called the 1st May). That both in the body of the instruments and in the Secretary's attestation the year is said to be one thousand seven hundred and eightyone. Whereas in the attestation of the preparer of the reports it is called one thousand seven hundred and eighty. The present copy being the exact counter-part of the last and only transmitted for the sake of regulary I think It unnecessary to swell your records with another copy if the translation.

On reperusing that part of your letter of the 16th which relates to the appointment of a person to superintend the Rajah's jagheer, it appears to me that your approbation of that measure is rather conditional than absolute. You are pleased to observe, that your approval of it as it appears to have been done in concert with the Ranny. I think it therefore my duty to mention that though the appointment in question had for its object the introduction of correctness into the management of the Rajah's affair, and though it evidently gave a degree of a consequence to the Runny, and rendered her independent of Cunny Laul, the surburrahkar, yet she may rather be said to have acquiesced in the measure than to have desired it. As the rajah is an orphan, and a young man of family and of large property, it was such of my wish, that his estate should be so managed as to provide his minority a fund for the improvement of his country when we become of age. With this view I recommended to the Ranny the appointment of some honest and intelligent person unconnected with the officer of the Malguzari lands for the sole purpose of attendency to the private concerns of her son. She however did not seem sensible of the necessity of the measures and rather consented to it from a deference to my recommendation, than from a conviction of its expediency. I deem it my duty to state these circumstances to you and have only to add that no person is yet appointed in quality of manager of the jagheers, and that nor shall be appointed until honoured by the receipt of your further order. As the appointment it is take places, has not the safety or improvement of the public revenue, but merely the advantage of an individual for its object the expense of it will of course be defrayed from the income of the jagheer.

ooo

Chapter-IV

From Bihar State Archives Patna (K. K. Datta), Patna. Collection from Judicial Records of Bhagalpur District

01. Extract of the letter of Collector Bhagalpur
    Dated 7th February 1791. **Sultanabad** (Maheshpur Raj)

The Circumstances of this dispossession of **Ranny Sarbessary** as far as they could be **traced were reported to the Board of Revenue under date 24th May, 1789** and their decision thereon was signified in a letter under date the ... copies of all which documents are herewith enclosed for the Board's further determination on the same subject.

OOO

02. Extract of a letter from the Board of Revenue,
    Dated 18th March, 1791. Sultanabad

The collector having omitted to furnish the information required in our letter of 19th January last whether Rany Sarbessary has any children or if there be any near relations of her deceased husband. We must again require the same.

OOO

03. Copy of the letter of Collector Bhagalpur
    Dated 30th March, 1791. **Sultanabad**

Gentlemen.

Under date the 19th instant you are pleased to observe that the collector had omitted to furnish information required respecting the **Ranny Sarbessary** and that you therefore again call upon him to report whether the said Ranny has any children or if there be any near relations of her deceased husband.

I have now the honor to inform you that the Ranny was long since called upon to answer those question herself, which neglecting to do the same were addressed to her in a Purwannah of which document she in writing acknowledged the receipt under her seal, but to this honor no further answer from her has been received. I can therefore, at present, only transmit you, the result of the best enquiries I have been able to make elsewhere, by which it appears that the Ranny has no child of her own but that there is some probability of her having after the death of her husband been induced to adopt one although who it was she did adopt is not with certainty known as no such person ever appeared here that that with respect to her husband's relations it is believed there are only very distant ones of any to be found.

The instant I receive more satisfactory intelligence on this subject which can only be procured from the Ranny herself it shall be communicated to the Board.

OOO

04. Extract of the letter of Collector Bhagalpur

Dated 12th May, 1791. **Sultanabad**

I have received your letter of the 27th ultimo requiring a furher rectified Bengal settlement for 1797 B.S. as well as a separate account settlement for ten years that I should **summon Mockum Singh and Jebun Singh** in order to report their Qualifications to manage the Zamindary of Sultanabad, if restored by Government to the family of Ranny Surbessary, and that I should report the result of my advertisements for farming the Mozah Hurrypore and the Hissa Imaum Bucksh of Conkjole Pergunnah in Rajmahal.

3. I have had Mockum Singh before me and from Personal examination and general charge I have no doubt of his being found capable of managing the business of the Sultanabad Zemindarry, if it should be restored to the family of the Ranny Sarbessary.

He seems about forty years of age, and an intelligent man, and as he is immediate Heir to the Zemindarry, I did not hesitate to receive his Derkaust for nine years at the past years Jumma, which was formed on an Investigation of the mofussil accounts in the preceding year when an increase of Rupees 4,5000 was obtained from the then farmer, I hope I have not been irregular in submitting Mockum Singh's proposals in whatever light they may be considered (previous to the restoration of the Zemindarry, as my only motive is to enable the Board to determine the Settlement of the remaining Mehals of the Bengal division should they think proper so close with Mockum Singh there as manager Heir or Farmer Jeban Singh is a minor of ten years of age more removed in relationship, incapable of managing for the Ranny or for himself, were he even the immediate successor. Proposal of Mockum Singh for the Hbood Bundoobust Settlement of Pergunnah Sultanabad Chuckla Akbarnugur offering to engage for aJumma of Sac. Rs 11,45,027 for a term of Nine years, or from the year 1798 to the year 1206 Bengal style exclusive of Akrajout Purganauty Dehatty, and Mamobyu and also of Moshaira Zemindary should this my Durkaust be acceptable, I will pay my Revenue as Tufseel Jumna of each of the above mentioned nine years.

(Particulars)

Jumma of 1798 (as it was in 1797 exclusive of the sayer
Rs 12,722 percent 3.)

(SD) Mockum Singh.

ooo

5. Letter

From,

Mr. G. Dickinson,
Collector of Bhagalpur,

To,

Mr. Henry Lodge,
Judge-Magistrate of Bhagalpur. 2
Dated 5th July,1793

The Hill People in whose behalf I addressed you on the 2nd instant having been now detained five days which is directly contrary to the Treaty entered into with to our superiors to admit the charge should you, often having had before you the papers required in your letter of the 1 (which I shall give directions to be prepared as soon as possible) refuse your sanction indeed, I would most readily suffer, the loss myself rather than they should any longer remain under a tree exposed to the inclemencies of the weather or be in any degree the cause of interrupting that peace which has for so many years remained undisturbed.

OOO

6. Letter

From,

Mr. Henry Lodge,
Magistrate of Bhagalpur,

To,

G. H. Barlow, Sub-Secretary to Government.
Dated 7th July, 1793

In consequence of your letter of the 10th instant from the Nizamat Department, I am to request you will lay before his Lordship in Council the accompanying **statement for repairing**

the Jails at this station calculated so as to answer every purpose until a Brick one may be erected on a supposition that eighteen months, if not two years, must elapse before it can be finished and in state to admit of prisoners being confined therein with a degree of attention to their health.

If it meets his Lordship's approbation, I request the necessary order may be issued to the Collector for supplying me with the amount.

Estimated expenses to repair the jails, etc. at Bhagalpur.

The large Jail in which The whole of this Jail is in upwards of 400 ruinous state. The umbers prisoners are confined, and thatch so destroyed as not consists of two very large only to expose the prisoners to straw buildings, a Guard the inclemency of the weather Room and a separate but to render it really dangerous detached place with a while the mud wall surrounding large shed under the area of the jail being destroyed.

There is only one wall and no drain to carry off the filth neither is there any separate places as an hospital for the sick. To put this into repair so that no further expense any become necessary to Government (ere a Brick Jail can be Completed) and to erect an hospital make two more wells, a drain, and for repairing the mud walls, I conceive no less a sum than two thousand five hundred Rupees requisite. Rs. 2,500.

This being in a tolerable state of repair requires an additional well, a drain mending the choppers, and mud wall, for which the sum of three hundred and fifty Rupees may suffice. Sicca Rs. 350.

In fact there is (now only) the remains of a few huts bearing that name which the prisoners in many places renders it insecure dress their victuals.

The small jail in which about 250 prisoners are confined consist of one large straw building, a Guard room and shed.

The Dewanny Jail........................ .

A building for the confinement of Debtors and other in arrears of revenue to government, as the number in all probability will not be very considerable can I conceive be erected with every convenience and safety for a thousand rupees –Sicca Rupees 1,000

And for the further sum of seven hundred rupees a habitation for the law officers and Amlah of the Courts of Circuit may be erected.

There being no place of present in which they can be accommodated at, nor any place to be hired even for the purpose.

Sicca Rupees. .	700
Sicca Rupees. .	1,000
Sicca Rupees. .	350
Sicca Rupees. .	2,500
Total Rupees.	4,550

OOO

7. Letter

From,

J. Fombelle,

Judge-Magistrate of Bhagalpur

To,

James Stuart,

Deputy Register of the Nizamut Adawlut. 2

Dated 10th July, 1793

In conformity to the orders of the Nizamut Adawlut, communicated to me in your letter of the 25th ultimo, I beg leave to acquaint you, for their information that I have every Police Jurisdictions in the Zillah under my charge, as prescribed by **section XIII regulation XXII of 1793.**

OOO

8. Letter

From,

J. Hutchinson,
Regulating Officer Invalid
Establishments, Bhagalpur,

To,

Mr. H. Lodge,
Magistrate of Bhagalpur,
Dated September, 1793

I beg leave to acquaint you that in pursuance of a requisition of the late Collector at this place I undertook to reform and relieve as much as in my power the Invalid Tannah and accordingly commenced at Janghnirah and my progress there met with Mr. Grants' approbation and thanks.

During my stay at Janghnirah the several zemindars seemed exceedingly willing and satisfied that a small portion of the waste unproductive part of their lands which they could not cultivate had been given by Mr. Cleveland in Jagheer to the pensioners to clear. However I found that the zamindar of Curruckpore had charge of their zemindaries and had an agent or under-render – **a man called Kessee Isser who was to the last degree jealous, and inimical to the** old soldiers notwithstanding as per my reports, the peculiar hardships and distress of this Tannah, and the hidden cause which shunned the light I hope will soon be developed. This man had shut up one side of the villages so closely by cultivating a Bigah or two on the east flank and by establishing a Hazam **and Serry which he brought for the purpose from a place nearby called Constablegunge** (although there was abundance of waste lands beside so that he left no ingress or egress). With Mr. Grants authority and concordant to his general Perwannahs, I ordered an opening to be left that the Invalids Cattle or livestock might have a passage as well as themselves to go out and in, in consequence of which the said **Kessee Isser so soon as the Collectors set off for Calcutta, went to Curruckpore and fabricated a plausible complaint....** While it excited my wonder how he had got lands north of the Ganges, and these zemindars ceded to him or the collections of those zemindars and while I believed the zemindars who gave the unproductive lands were the true and actual proprietors of the soil, I could not reconcile how the youth Rajah, could oppress and alienated (sic) their rights and properties from them, while English Government were emancipating and restoring them all by every possible means to their just or hereditary rights and as I cannot conceive upon what tenure the lands in question can appertain to the Invalids of Janghirah while the zemindars give me grants for the lands and the Youths-Cawderrallies–People assume all authority so to do denying their right to what the zemindars would grant for the good of Institution immediately and ultimately for themselves or heirs and the country in general. I therefore with all due deference appeal on behalf of the Institution of your Judgement. Kessee Isser on hearing of my intention to appeal this matter came to me at Bhaugulpore to offer to relinquish the spot close to the Tannah which was the nuisance and oppression on terms as per P. S. Persian paper, but I could form no accommodation compatible with my duty to Government and the Institution and also to those poor zemindars who became involved a principal deeply concerned on their own behalf as well as the pensioners, on the part of whom I have the honor to submit the several papers of complaint by the Adjutant of Janghnirah... / also Bullabh Sein Canungoe of Janghnirah Parrassnath Sudder Canungoe, Assud Allie Aumeen and Hossin Beg Adjutant to prove my assertion.

ooo

9. Letter

From,

Mr. John Fombelle,
Magistrate of Bhagalpur

To,

John Harington,
Magistrate of Zillah Moorshedabad.
Dated 26th December, 1793

I have been favoured with your letter of the 21st instant, suggesting the expediency of sending to you **Duloolll Khorde; Gosena and Gorah,** who are represented to have been concerned in a robbery committed within your jurisdiction from Sultanabad, when they have been apprehended, to Moorshedabad, for the purpose of being tried with their accomplices before the Court of Circuit for that Division.

ooo

10. Letter

From,

Mr. G. Dickinson,
Collector of Bhagalpur,

To,

Mr. John Fombelle,
Judge-Magistrate of Bhagalpur
Dated 1st January, 1794

I have been honoured with your letter of yesterday's date and in reply beg leave to inform you that the services on which I am occasionally obliged to employ the Military Force belonging to this station are, Ist. To Escort the Treasure for the payment of the invalid Thannahs- 2ndly. To guard the different species of Rupees transmitted for recoinage to the Patna Mint and the produce remitted by the Assay master in return and 3dly. To accompany the Revenue collected in the Rajemahl Portion of the District to the Sudder Cutcherry at Bhaugulpore.

Exclusive of the above occasional services, I require and always have had a regular Guard at the Rajmahl Treasury and Cutcherry which should consist of more than can I fear be spared the party stationed there at present being only a Havildar Naick and six sepahis which are not in my opinion altogether sufficient. With respect to the seasons of the year when the Military are occasionally employed, I have to observe that those who are required in the Ist Instance above mentioned leave this with the Treasure on or about the Ist of April and Ist of October (the Periods fixed by the Regulations for he pay to be issued) and return as soon as the duty upon which they are sent is performed which of course must depend greatly upon circumstances.

It is also a matter of great uncertainty when I may have occasion to call for the services in the second instance as it (is) impossible for me to ascertain **in what species of Rupees the Revenue may be paid but** with respect to the duties required from them as stated in the 3rd I am obliged to apply to the Commanding Officer monthly.

It is only on one other occasion that I think myself authorized to employ them which is when I am making a Tour through my district on the public service when I may require a small Guard for the protection of my Baggage and etc.

I have only farther to add that tho' I have found the crops attached to the station fully sufficient for such other Revenue Duties as I have had occasion to employ them upon, I think it my Duty to remark that for the Sudder Treasury and Khazanchee's House. The late Govern-General (sensible of the necessity of the measure) was pleased at my Predecessor's request to order a Zemmadar's party from the Garrison at Monghyr.

1. Vol. no. 413

2. The enclosures are not printed
3. Vol. No. 417

ooo

11. Letter

From,

Mr. John Fombelle,
Judge-Magistrate of Bhagulpur,

To,

John Shore,
Government-General in Council
Dated 2nd April, 1794

I had the Honor to receive on the 21st ultimo your Sub-Secretary's letter, dated the 21st of February authorizing me to insert the amount of the hill Establishment in my account, an calling upon me to ascertain and report whether it is still necessary to keep up so large an Establishment for the Hills.

2. I beg leave to observe that the Establishment of the Hill Sezawul and that of the Burkundauzes for the hills are perfectly distinct. The former was allowed soon after the In habitants of the Hills were induced to demean themselves peaceably and leave off their predatory way of life. **The salary to the Sezawul Abdool Russool Khan, is Rs. 101 per mensem,** which, considering the importance of his office and the Zeal and Ability with which he has performed the Duties of it for a great number of years, he being the only person who has yet held the appointment, I cannot consider more than he deserves; **he is allowed a Naib, two Mohrirs, and seven Burkundauzes at the Sudder amounting to Rupees 48 and a Naib, a Mohair, and two Burkundauzes in Tuppah Munneharry in Pergunnah Talka Jumuee in Curruckpore in Pergunnah Bailputta and Hourawa likewise**

in Curruckpore and in Pergunnah Ambar and Sutanabad, making in all five small Establishments amounting to Rs. 17-8 per month each. He is also allowed **seven Bundwasys or Interpreters,** who understand both the Language of the Hill people and that spoken in the Plains at two rupees per month each. As I have reason to believe that these several small Establishment are not more than sufficient to enable the Sezawul to execute the Trust reposed in him, I hope they will be continued

3. With Regard to the Establishment of Burkundauzes which comprises remainder of the sum granted by government, I find upon Enquiry that it was allowed many years since in consequence of large Bodies of the Hill People coming down and committing every sort of Violence and Depredation. These Burkundauzes with an Exception to one Jemautdar and twenty Burkundauzes stationed at Bhagalpur for the purpose of sending into the Hill as Business might require, were stationed in the five most central sic situations in the Hills in order to prevent further outrages and the Event has justified the Measure as I do not find that any Incursions or Robberies of any consequence have since occurred. On a reference to the Records of my Office**, I observe that the hills are about four hundred in Number and I am well informed that they are peopled by** many Thousand of Inhabitants, although no correct computation can be made of them as they are totally ignorant of the art of writing I wish, I could add, that the meritorious Exertions of the late Mr. Cleveland had succeeded so far as to have induced such a numerous race of people to mix in any material degree with the Mass of the Inhabitants of the Plains or to introduce amongst themselves the useful arts of civilized life; whether owing to their natural Indolence, their love of Liberty and to their Prejudices or to a want of Encouragement from the Neighbouring zemindars I known not, but certain it is that neither of those important Ends has yet been attained as therefore their peaceable conduct is in a great Measure owing to the humane

policy of Government in allowing Pensions to their Chiefs and to the Check that is kept over them, I cannot yet venture to propose that the five Establishment comprehending the charge of the thirteen Tuppahs in the Hills should be discontinued; but, as the services of the Jemautdar and Burkundauzes stationed at Bhaugalpore for the purpose of transmitting occasional orders into the Hills can be easily dispensed **with I will with your permission discontinue them from the end of this month which will occasion a Diminution of the Establishment for the Hills of one hundred rupees per month viz.** I Jemautdar at twenty and 20 Burkundauzes at four Rupees per mensem.

I have the Honor to be Sir.

ooo

12. Extract of the letter of Collector Bhagalpur

Dated 10th April, 1794. **Sultanabad.**

The accompanying answer from the Ranny Sarbessary, I trust will be satisfactory to the Board on the subject of her deceased husband's heirs and relations.

Question to the Ranny Sarbessary.

Did your late husband Gurjun Singh leave any children, or are there any near relations of the deceased. If there are any what are their names and the degress of relationship let the answer be given in writing under your seal.......

Answer

There are no children of my late husnband but there are his relations by name Baboo Mockum Singh the son of his father's brother or his first cousin, and Baboo Jebun Singh, another his first cousin.

The seal of Ranny Serbessary.

(Ed.) These records reveal the working of the Maheshpur Estate.

They also throw light on the rebellious activities of Rani Sarbeshwari

Surendra Jha

OOO

13. Letter

From,

J. Hutchinson, Esqr, Superintending Officer,
Invalid Institution, Bhagalpur

To,

Mr. John Fombelle, Esqr, Superintending Officer,
Judge-Magistrate of Bhagalpur,
Dated 25th April, 1794

It was not my intention to have troubled you with any remarks, relative to the complains of the several disputants near Kirhee were I not pressed to forward a Petition representing that in the late Ammeens measurement he has included the Public Tannah Dagger and Jagheer roads which is counteracting my plans and the usages of the Institution altho' he was cautioned to the contrary by my orders. If a proper high road and roads such as I have directed in all the Tanahs were to run thro' the Jagheers of individuals to their loss some of them would have little or no land to cultivate, the businesses the spots of waste lands being retained under various partner in the center of the Jagheers and circumjacent and adjoining, was long since settled and forbidden. In Behar I was under the **disagreeable necessity of prosecuting two native Gentlemen, who from jealousy persecuted the old soldiers,** by destroying their roads and the facts and damages appeared so evident and so clearly against them. On the evidence adduced, and the maxim or principle, that neither road, Mosque, Mutt nor Gaest, can be Jagheer, that the defendants deprecated punishment, and offered a thousand rupees damages, which Mr. Seton having admitted he paid me the amount, which was disbursed for the use and embellishment of Tannah Mabarrachabad. I pray you excuse for mentioning a matter digressing from the present point in question. I mean it as an example how a body of poor people might suffer, not being allowed regress and ingress to their portions of land.

Mr. D' Amurgues being taken sick in the execution of his duty and some new Tannahs requiring establishment is the cause why **Tannah Kerhee**(kheri) has not been regulated, when that takes places proper roads, will as usual be traced out, and I imagine will be equal to a twentieth or sixteenth part of the whole.

I some time since mentioned an objection to the Aumean, as a person who had been Moonsey to Tannah Sitanabad, in which great derangement had taken place from the inability of the Aumeen and neglect to Duty and Inexperience of the said Moonsey who had absconded from that Tannah. Whenever I Regulate a Tannah the leaving proper thoroughfare in the first precaution, and I beg leave to submit to your attention, what must be the confusion and discard amongst the old Veterans were their land to be portioned off in squares, or along divisions, and they left to dispute whose Jagheers the roads should be made through. I have ever endeavoured to prevent any encroachment on the Jagheer roads, and flatter myself that the Aumeens perversely counteracting my arrangements, will not become a precedent after my having the honor to submit an explanation of the case to yourself.

I have the pleasure to send a Petition relative to the purports of this letter and am.

Sir

Your most obedient humble servants.

ooo

14. Letter

From,

J. Hutchinson, Esqr, Superintending Officer,
Invalid Institution, Bhagalpur

To,

Mr. John Fombelle, Esqr. . ,
Judge-Magistrate of Bhagalpur,
Dated 3rd July, 1794

I have the Honor to acknowledge rect (receipt) of your letters relative to **a complaint made against some officers on the Seopay Invalid Establishment belonging to Tannah Mungulpore.** I beg permission to acquaint you that the complaint is of five years standing having been laid against the whole Tannah heretoforce, altho' it should more properly be, **against Messrs, Adair, Seton and Grant former Collectors (who me thinks would have redressed Kissun Kunt had he been right).**

He is the principal malcontent against Mr. Adair for having in the compliance with the old regulations of the Institution, and the orders of Government, established a Tannah on the waste lands of the Zemindaries of Mungulpore, previous to the promulgation on the intent of the soil, on certain conditions.

Mr. Grant being at Rajmahal in 1792 and not having time to go on the spot while I was at Mungulpore he made a requisition that I would Enquire again into the reiterated obstinate complaints of Kissen Kunt, which having complied with, have the Honor to annex the proceeding thereon to which I am ready to make oath.

On the appointment of Messrs. Dickinson and Lodge, Daostoor Moffick (the old complaint)was revived, and on my going to Mungulpore **I found there had been another attempt by his 6 Anna Hissadar to eject the Pensioners, which I was not acquainted with, and it seems the Commandant harassed with the business,** sent up a Subadar who signed as agreement in the me of the whole Tannah which was fabricated by the **famous Treasurer Soorup Chund** it seems, and this has occasioned great confusion.

Having put the Subadar in arrest and held a court of General enquiry into his Conduct, it appears evidently to have been an infamous transaction indeed, and I have annexed a copy of the court of Enquiry, which was on oath and which will speak for itself and the Subadar is ready to make Oath, that the substance of the paper he put his mark to, is not as was represented to him however that be, the paper in every state, is totally Invalid.

Las January, on my return from Mungulpore to Rajemhal I called **Sam Roy the** ten anna Hissadar and told him, as he had often confessed to me, and must be conscious that his complaint and conduct was merely at the instance of Kissun Kunt, he had better appoint me (as he had by far the greatest portion of land given in Jagheer) to be umpire and remeasure all the lands and I would defray the expenses or pay 300 Rs. to that end. He consented and gave me a written agreement, and next day went before Mr. Dickinson Collector, and declared that Invalids never had Encroached. This was in January last. However in a couple of days he told me, the other parties would not agree, a and of course he must recede from his agreement with me. Let me entreat you, Sir to read with attention the annexed copy of letter to my Enquiry from Mr. Grant, addressed to William Cooper, Esqr; President of the Board of Revenue, which especially after his (MrGrant's) experience tantamount to a full clear unequivocal decision in favour of the defendats, who have been harassed for these five years past by complaints of Kissun Kunt no one of which I believe he ever could establish. As to the fresh auxiliary Zemindar **Soorup Chund Junr,** as it is the first I have heard of him, it occurs to me he enters the list to make matters appear more formidable. I beg leave to Refer for all the Persian documents, to the Commans of defendants to support their cause and be adduced evidence, being public records and have also the Honor to submit the Mungulpore

Tannah Book containing an account of particulars of the land and the incumbents, thereon this book is a new form, taken from the pension records, and was lodged in the Magistrates and collectors public office, until the new regulations when the Books were delivered to.

OOO

15. Letter

From,

Mr. John Fombelle, Esqr. . ,
Judge-Magistrate,

To,

G. H. Barlow, Sub-secretary to the Governor- General in Council in the Judicial Department

Dated 17th July, 1794

I have been honoured with the Receipt of your letter of the 20th Ultimo, which arrived here on the 8th Instant, requiring Information relative to the armed Establishments and Detachments of regular Troops employed under me.

2. My letter to the Governor General in Council of the 11th January last, in answer to Circular letter from the Secretary to the Government of the 29th December, contained the most material part of the Information now required ; I nevertheless recapitulate the Purport that Letter, adding such further remarks as have occurred to me on the Occasion.

3. Only thirty Burkundosses and twenty Peons are allowed for guarding the Jails and for Fouzdarry Processes Considering the Number of Prisoners, confined at the station, (between five and six hundred), that almost the whole of them are daily out either for the Purpose of purchasing the neceaaaries of life or of repairing

the public Roads and that they are all liable to be called upon by the Superintending officer of the Invalid Tannahs to assist in cleaning any new Tannahs that may be established, I cannot but think that the Establishment of Burkundosses for taking care of the Prisoners and guarding the Jails is too small and accordingly take the Liberty of submitting to Government whether a small addition may not be authorized till the number of Prisoners is reduced : Independent of the above mentioned Establishment twenty Peons are allowed Dewaury Purpose, which with the Peons attached to the Cutwaly, (Kotwah)comprise " the whole of the Burkundosses, Pykes and other armed Establishment which I am allowed to entertain for guarding the Jails or the public money, or Records under my charge."

4. The order contained in the Second Paragraph of your letter regarding " Detachments of regular" Troops" I humbly conceive not to be applicable to Station. The Military Force in this District consist the Crops of the Hill rangers and the Garrison of Monghier (Monghyr). The services on which the former is employed are fully stated in the accompanying Copy of a letter from the Commanding officer, already before Government ; independent of which small Detachments are occasionally required to escort Prisoners to the Presidency, to attend Executions at a Distance from the Sudder Station, and on various other occasions which it is impossible to define. This Corps has been so lately new-modelled, that Government will deem it advisable to withdraw the whole or any Part of it from the District, when the purpose for which it was originally raised is considered: Viz. , of not only conciliating the affections of a numerous severity but of keeping them in awe by a Corps raised from amongst themselves, and which in case of necessity, is much better calculated to act with vigor and Dispatch in the wild mountainous Parts inhabited by their Countrymen than Brigade Troops : and the Corps has been now so long habituated to obedience and Discipline that I Should hope their Fidelity might be depended upon; Atho' I do not

know that Government have actually bound themselves by any Engagement either with the Corps, or with the Hill Chiefs and Manjhees, not to send the former to any Part of the Company's Possessions they might think proper, I have not doubt but that the Corps considered that they wereraised for the express Purpose of serving in this District only, a nd as the Circumstancesof their never having been employed elsewhere during the Number of years since they were first embodied cannot but confirm this Idea in their minds I have no Doubt but that Government will deem themselves bound by Justice as well as policy to let them look upon this as their Home station, altho' I have no Doubt but that the corps would readily and cheerfully proceed on any casual service out of the District should it ever be found necessary to employ them on it.

5. I understand that a jemadars Guard is allowed from the Garrison of Monghyr for the Protection of the Collector's Treasury; but no part of the Garrison is employed under me.

ooo

16. Letter

From,

Owen O. Neale, Esqr. ,

To,

Mr. John Fombelle, Esqr. . ,
Judge-Magistrate of Bhagalpur
Dated 5th September, 1794

I have had the Honour of Receiving your letter on service the 14th inst. Conformable to the order of Government I beg leave to acquaint you I arrived in the Earl of Sandwich Charless Dean Esqr. Comdr. In the year "77 and my Occupation since has been agent to two General O. M. Gerorge Templer Esqr. Elephant

Contractor and quitted the Post General I commenced Mercht. And am now in the employ of **John Glass Esqr.** Conducting his **Indigo business at** Colgong. There is no other European here about but myself. Doctor Glass has Mr. Campagnola an Italian (sic) in his service at Pealpore. I have the permission of Mr. Hasting & Lord Cornwallis to reside in this country and hope I have not abused Either.

OOO

17. Letter

From,

B. Campagnola, Esqr. ,

To,

Mr. John Fombelle, Esqr. . ,
Judge-Magistrate of Bhagalpur
Dated 5th September, 1794

In obedience to your orders to furnish you a memorandum of my place of abode which is Pealapore, my present Employment the Indigo Manufacture, and the period of time, for which I have resided in India, it is for the space of eleven years.

I have at present no European in my Employ.

I shall also communicate to you or the Executive officer in your District Information similar to the above on the 31st of December of each year.

OOO

18. Letter

From,

Mr. G. Dickinson,
Collector of Bhagalpur,

To,

Mr. John Fombelle,
Judge-Magistrate of Bhagalpur
Dated 30 October, 1794

I yesterday received a notification from your Registrar that Rajah Cauder Ally, Zamindar of Carruckpore had instituted a suit against the Hon'ble Company on several counts as per a petition annexe. And a consequent requisition to furnish the Vakeel on the part of Government with the necessary instructions to enable him to defend the said suit and to command him to appear in Court for the purpose on the 13th November, 1794, at nine o'clock in the forenoon.

In reply, I think it my duty to state to you two points in objection to the above requisition in both of which, however, I shall be guided by your decision viz. Firstly **I have no confidence either in the ability or exertion of the Government Vakeel consequently** to entrust to him the pleading of any cause of importance in which the Hon'ble Company are concerned would in my opinion be giving up the point at once. I object therefore to his being employed in the cause.

Secondly admitting the several counts stated by Kadir Ally to be founded, I do not think myself bound to defend the suit until he has made good all balances due from him to Government, and those exceed the sum for which he prosecutes, in fact. I am inclined to believe that the suit would not have been instituted, but to gain time, for however speedy your decision, Sir, might be, **Kadir Ally does not mean to abide by it, without appeal if unfavourable to him** and he well knows that I cannot, should it be the reverse.

OOO

19. Letter

From,

Mr. John Fombelle,
Judge of Bhagalpur,

To,

Mr. George Dickinson,
Collector of Bhagalpur
Dated 5 November, 1794

I have been favoured with your letter of the 30th ultimo relative to the suit instituted against the Company by the **Zemindar of Curruckpore.**

2. In answer to your first objection to defending the suit in question. I beg leave to observe, that although Toffiel Ally, the Pleader on the part of Government, does not appear to be either a man of talents or capable of much exertion, I should conceive that he would find little or no difficulty in attending to such instructions as you might have to give him regarding the suit in question, the decision upon which, I conclude, will principally rest on within documents. Should you, however, still object to employing him in the said suit, you will be pleased to communicate to me your objections at large to his defending it, together with the grounds of them, when I shall be enabled to judge of the expediency of postponing the examination of the cause until a reference is made to the Government General in Council on the subject.

3. With regard to your second objection, I can only observe that you as well as myself, have the regulations for your guidance in all cases that can possibly occur and that as I am bound by duty to receive and enquire into all complaints not proscribed by any existing regulation, I do not consider myself at liberty to give your second objection any weight.

4. I beg to be favoured with an early answer to this letter and am Sir.

OOO

20. Letter

(Regarding Sultanabad)

From,

Mr. G. Dickinson,
Collector of Bhagalpur,

To,

Mr. John Fombelle,
Judge-Magistrate of Bhagalpur
Dated 12th January, 1795

I have been favoured with your letter of the 18th November and 9th ultimo, and in reply to the question contained in the former thereof beg leave to inform you that in order have been received by7 me within this year and a half conferring upon Mocum Singh, Zemindar of Sultanabad the Title of rajah or vesting him with any authority whatever in the Hills in the neighbourhood of that Pergunnah - in short that no correspondence has been held by Government with me which in any respect relates to that proprietor. I enclose authenticated copies of the correspondence held by my predecessor on the subject of the Settlement of the Mahaul as required in the 2nd Para. Of your letter and I have pleasure to be Sir.

ooo

21. Letter

(Regarding Handwe and RoopNarain Deo)

From,

Mr. John Fombelle,
Judge-Magistrate of Bhagulpur
Dated 15th January, 1795
To,
Mr. William Douglas,

Judge of the Murshidabad Court of Circuit. 1.

Accompanying I have the honor of submitting to you a Calendar of Prisoners committed to Prison or held of Bail-at this station, drawn out in the prescribed form, together with the Hinduvee and Persian proceedings appertaining thereto to which I beg leave to add the following remarks:-

No. 39

Notwithstanding the full acknowledgement of this prisoner of having perjured himself, I must confess that I am inclined, in some measure, to give credit to his original information, as the man appeared rather to act under the impulse of fear when he retracted his former evidence in the presence of Roopnarain Deo, his master, I hope to be pardoned for expressing a hope that you will admit the expediency of not prosecuting the enquiry so far as to subject Roopnarain's Zamindarry (which) is in the vicinity of the Hills' the inhabitants of which have only of late years been subjected to obedience. This Zemindar and his ancestors, from their ferocity of manners and contumacious conduct, have more than once caused much blood to be shed, and I have some reason to think that Roopnarain and his people are not yet sufficiently divested of their ferocity and prejudices to be treated with hardships. He and his predecessors have repeatedly, I am told, refused obeying the summons of the executive officer in this district, and the last time that Roopnarain came down to Bhaugulpoor (**now near eleven years**) on a summons from the Cutcherry, backed by the deputation of an intelligent and considerable armed force. After this, it is with pleasure I mention, that he made no hesitation in complying with my summons, and came to Bhagalpur with only a few common attendants. As such an instance of confidence and obedience ought to be encouraged, and as I am in hopes that the serious admonition which I gave him against assuming any improper and unsure authority, and the treatment which he experienced, will have the good effect of continuing him in a state of obedience. I shall be happy if you concur in the opinion which I have taken the liberty to express.

OOO

22. Letter

From,

Capt. J. Hutchinson,
Superintending Officer of the Invalid Thana
Establishment, Bhagalpur,

To,

Lieutenant Colonel P. Murray,
Adjutant -General.
Dated 29th January, 1795

I have had the honor to receive the general publication of the 40th and 41st articles of the Invalids Jagheerdars Regulations and to avoid being prolix as my first reports were deemed, shall hereto annexed, briefly explain the several points required.

(Enclosure)

I or the foregoing purpose (and after the Widows were paid) the Surplus went toward them, the following allowances were only drawn, for the great variety of Demands viz.

For Baughulpour Disbursed by Capt. H... .... 995 3 0
For Tirhoot. . Disbursed by Capt. H... .... 343 11 3
For Bihar. . Disbursed by Lt. Greene...........650 4 0
For Shahabad ...only 3ml. and a 80. . Disbursed by Lt. Carsuthers.......
For Sarun... See annexed letter.
Disbursed by Lt. Carsuthers.........

Sicca Rupees Sicca 1,933 11 3

Zellah Baugalpore Upon the high Road

Cut thro the Rocks of **Jurampore near Rajah Mahal** 1

Pyallahpore, Colgong and Bersio. . ... 3. .

Gour and Capgong and Bersio 2

Augurpore 1

Chipervon Himutpore and Nowagurry. . ... 3 ...

Derrarah Allenugur and Rampore .... 3 ...

Zellah Tirhoot 8

J. HUTCHINSON
Supg. Officer I. i

BAUGHULPORE:
25th January, 1795

(Ed.) Hutchinson Papers are Vital for tracing the history of Invalid Thanas

Surendra Jha

OOO

23. Letter

From,
Mr. John Fombelle,
Judge-Magistrate of Bhagalpur

To,
Sir John Shore,
Governor-General in Council 1.
Dated 23rd February, 1795

On the 31st of March, last I had the Honor of submitting to you a petition from the **Zemindar of Curruckpore**, praying to be permitted to appoint a Vakeel to undertake the Management of all suits in which he might be engaged in the Dewany Adawlut of this Zillah, and I, at the same time, added, that as the Zemindar's objections to the Pleaders who had been appointed by Government appeared to me to be in general well founded, I should shortly take the Liberty of laying before you a **Report of the Merits and Demerits of the respective Pleaders.**

2. The Hope that practise and the study of the Regulations, as well as a view to their own immediate interest, would in time have rendered the Native Pleaders more competent to the Stations they filled, and, in some Degree, have compensated for the want of a liberal Education and have obviated the necessity of their being removed; and the constant Routine of official duty, have hitherto induced me to postpone the perform of an unpleasant Task. As, however, a long period has now elapsed without my perceiving any change for the better, I should feel myself deficient were I any longer to delay submitting to you my promised Reports.

3. Section V, **Regulation VII, 1793 prescribes, that the pleaders are to selected from amongst the student in the Mahomedan College at Calcutta and the Hindoo college at Benares;** but that if these college shall not furnish a sufficient number of Pleaders, other Men of good character and liberal Education are to be admitted. A though the Regulations admit of pleadings being held, and Documents delivered, in any of the Native languages, it is inferable from the section above quoted, **that every Pleader should have a competent knowledge of the Persian Language,** as, without it, no person could be considered qualified for the office, all Sannuds, Deeds of sale, Caboleats etc. , etc,. being for the most part written in that language. From the Reports which I have now the Honor of submitting, the Sudder Dewany Adawlut will perceive that only two of the Vakeels set up any Pretensions of Qualifications requisite for their office. **Tofeil Ally**, the **Pleader on the part of the Company and Subbur Oollah** – but my report will shew, that the first is totally

incompetent to the important Trust of defending suits instituted by or against Government, and that the latter does not possess a single Requisite for the office he holds. I have taken the Liberty of proposing that Tofeil Ally may have the option of continuing to act as one of the authorized Vakeels until a person of abilities can be found to succeed him as such, should he not prove himself equal to his situation before that time, and that **Mussaheb Khan and Golaum Shurreeff** may also be permitted to remain for the present. This proposition, however, is submitted conditionally because, if the Sudder Dewany Adawlut can replace hem with persons possessing superior Qualifications, their Removal would be a desirable Event; but such is the Dearth of abilities amongst the Inhabitants of this District, that I despair of being able to find successors to them better qualified than themselves. The remainder of the Mahomedan Vakeels, the Court will observe, have never read any Book of Mahomedan Vakeels, the Court will observe, have never read any Book of Mahomedan Law and are otherwise disqualified for their situation.

4. With Regard to the Vakeels of the Hindoo Persuasion, I cannot but think, as Persian Documents and Voucher, which a due attention to the Interests of their Constituents require they should be able to read and understand, are constantly **put into their hands that a knowledge of that Language is as necessary a Qualification for a Hindu as for a Mahomedan Vakeel**, although from the nature of the Hindu Education, a less Degree of Proficiency in it might be expected. Non of the present Hindu Vakeels have ever read any Book of Hindu Law, and their knowledge of the Persian Language amounts to little more than an almost unintelligible smattering, I have ventured to recommend that **Jugul Kishore, Nund Kishore, and Gopaul Surmah,** may remain for the present, but beg to be understood as having done so under the same condition as is expressed relative to Tofeil Ally, etc.

5. Sixteen Vakeels were originally allotted to the Dewany Adawlut of this District, eight of each persuasion. From an observation of fourteen Months, I am of opinion, that such a number is more than sufficient and, in support of it, beg leave to mention, that my Report of Causes undecided on the 31st of December, last (which will be shortly submitted to your court) exhibits no more than 220 of that Description 26 of which number are under reference to arbitration and of all these by far the greatest proportion are of very trivial amounts, I therefore like the liberty of recommending that the number of Vakeels be reduced to twelve, six of each persuasion.

6. I also beg leave to recommend the **Hoolaubbur Hossain**, whom I have reason to believe a Man ofTalents and Education, may be appointed to the office of Pleader on the Part of Government in Lieu of Tofeil Ally and that **Neamut Ullah**, who has been proposed by the **Zemindar of Curruckpoor in Consequence of the Licence** contained in Mr. Register Barlow's Letter of the 5th Of June last, and who, on Examination, appears well qualified for the office, may be appointed one of the Established Vakeels; I further request Permission to propose **Ruttun Loll** as one of the Hindu Vakeels, he has acted several years as a Vakeel, appears active and intelligent, and reads Persian with tolerable facility. Should not the Court fill up the places of these I have proposed should remain (which I earnestly hope they will the Vakeels will be as follows:-

Mahomedans	Hindoos
Hoolzubbur Hossain	Jugul Kishore.
Tofeil Ally	Nund Kishore
Mussaheb Khan	Gopaul Surmah
Golaum Shurreeff.	
Neamut Ullah.	

1. There will still be a Deficiency of one Mahomesan and two Hindu Vakeels which I hope Government will be pleased

to fill up by a selection from the students of any of the established College, otherwise, the Vacancies must remain until I succeed in my Endeavours to find Persons properly qualified for being appointed thereto.

2. I have only to add that, although I have applied for Hoolzubbur Hossain I am not ignorant that he is already employed as one of the established Vakeels of the Sudder Dewany Adawlut, I trust however that the court will not disapprove of my having presumed to propoe him, as it will be easy for them to find a substitute for him in Calcutta, whilst I should be at aloss whom to recommend in Lieu of him to fill up the Place at present held by Tofeil Ally. The appointment will, at the same time, promote the interest of Government and be of personal advantage to Hoolzubbur Hossain.

I have the Honor to be with great Respect etc.

ooo

Chapter V

Judicial Records

1. Letter

From,

Mr. John Fombelle,
Magistrate of Bhagalpur

To,

Mr. G. H. Barlow,
Sub-Secretary to Government in the Judicial Department. 1
Dated 26th February, 1795

Paragraph. I have been favoured with your letter of the 30th Ultimo communicating to me the orders of the Governor-General in Council relative to such of the Prisoners in Confinement in my jail as have been sent from other zillahs, and are not incapacitated from hard Labour from Age or Infirmity.

2. The Prisoners above mentioned were originally sent to this station from an Idea that they could be more usefully employed here than elsewhere in which Government were not mistaken, as the most frequented high road in the company's Territories runs immediately through it and for many Milies is within the ... of the Labour of the Convicts without the (use) of which it would soon be rendered impossible in many places, the Hilliness of the Country and the loose sandy nature of the soil, occasioning its being broken up by every heavy Fall of Rain. The convicts have been likewise frequently usefully employed in clearing Ground for invalid villages, and may still occasionally appropriate their labors to preparing Ground for new comers who may be hereafter admitted on the Establishment. It also deserve mention that when it is considered now much time is necessarily consumed in conveying Prisoners, shackled with Irons, to and from the places where they are destined to work and that having no instrument to

be active or industrious, even Severity or the Dread of punishment can scarcely compel them to make common Exertion. The Advantages derived from their Labors is trivial indeed when compared with the number.

2. From what I have above taken the liberty of mentioning the Board will perceive that I am desirous of keeping as many convicts at this station as they may be pleased to permit me, and as I trust that they will not disapprove my Reasons for so doing, I shall venture to detain two description of prisoners sent here from other Station when I am honoured with their further orders.

4. The number of Prisoners sent here from other Stations, on whom definite sentences have been passed is, is 146; of these one is to be released in 4 months, one in 6 months, one in 11 months and nine on giving Security for the future good Behavior. These I have taken upon myself to detain, as they are all of them likely to be soon released. I have also detained thirty three (33) of the number above mentioned, who are incapable of hard labor from age and infirmity. The remaining one hundred and one (101) shall be conveyed to Moorshedabad, as soon as the Magistrate of that City shall have informed me that he has prepared a proper Place for their accommodation.

5. The two remaining descriptions of Prisoners sent from other zillahs consist of,63 whose residents has never been received, (about whom I have separately addressed the Nizamaut Adawlut) and of 132 whose Trials have been referred to the Court of Circuit, but on whom no definite sentences have been yet received. I am in hopes from the considerations urged in the second Paragraph of this letter, that such of these Prisoners as may be hereafter sentenced to further and definite confinement will be permitted to remain here altogether until they have fulfilled their respective sentence. At all events as many of them will undoubtedly be released on a perusal of their Trials, and, as it is impossible at present to say on whom this Lot may fall, I conclude that, under these circumstances, Government will be unwilling to employ

them on a duty which may probably prove fatal to many of them, and that they will consequently allow of their remaining here at least till the definite orders of the Nizamaut Adawlut shall have separated the innocent from the Guilty.

6. Understanding that Government have accepted the Proposals of Messrs. Lambert & Ross for erecting the Jails at this station, and as, in consequence of the advanced state of the season, the Contractors must naturally be desirous of marking. . . . . . and laying, the Foundation as speedily as possible, I beg leave to submit the following observations, in order to enable the Governor General in Council finally to determine on the Extent of the Jails before the Building is commenced.

7. My own Prisoners under sentences (I mean to those apprehended in this District) amount to,

Men.	158
Women.	14
Total	172

Incapacitated for Labor, from age and infirmity, or the prisoners sent from the Zillahs on whom definite sentences have been passed, and who of course, will remain here.

Prisoners sent from other Zillahs whose original Trials have not been received	63
Prisoners sent from other Zillhas whose trials have been referred to the Court Of Circuit, on whom no definite Sentences have been yet received.	132
	195
Calculate that only one third of this number will be Released on a revisal of their Trials.	65
Remain to be accommodated in the Jail. . .	130
Total number to be accommodated in the jail. .	335

The words, marked nos. 5 and 6 in the plan are only
calculated to contain. Under sentences. 160
Balance. . . 175 Deduct, _ Women. . . . 14
Number of prisons under Sentences for whom ———
additional accommodation is required. 161
———

In the event of the two Description of Prisoners above mentioned remaining where they are. the Board will observe, from the above statement that two more wards or revisions similar to those marked no. 5 and 6 in the Plan, must be added to the jail intended to be erected.

Again should Government object to retaining the Prisoners alluded to in the preceding Paragraph at this Station, the Statement will stand thus. -

Prisoners apprehended in this district under Sentences. . 172
Deduct women, for whom separate accommodations 14
provided. —— 158

Incapacitated for hard labour,from age and Infirmity of 33 those prisoners sent from other stations on whom definite Sentences have been passed.

Incapacitated for hard Labor, from age and Infirmity 35
of the Prisoners sent from other Station whose cases
have not yet been finally decided on. ——
68

Total number to be accommoated
The wards marked no. 5 and 6 in the ——— 160
Calculated to contain only. ————
Numbers of Convicts for whom additional 56
Accommodation ——
will be received.

10. From the Preceding Statement, the Board will observe, that were if the Prisoners Whom I am desirous of detaining should be sent to Moorshedabad. , it will still be necessary to add another ward or revision of the same dimension as no. 5 or 6.

11. Whislt I had the honor of holding the appointment of Registrar to the Nizamut Adawlut, I recollect that it was suggested to remove such Prisoners as had been Convicated of any heinous crimes,and sentenced to Imprisonment for Life or for a considerable number of years, from the District where they had been apprehended to more distant Station not only for the purpose of preventing their forming schemes, from the ……………………………………for disturbing the peace of…………… Society…………………………….they must frequently have ………………………from their Proximity to such of their ……………………………………………as had not been apprehended but likewise that they might feel the full Weight of their punishment by (an Evil more particularly to be apprehended in the Eastern District and in the vicinity of Bawkergunge where it is known that the most dangers Gangs have been and possibly still are occasionally formed) being deprived of those comforts and indulgence which an easy communication with their families and connexious might put in the Power of many but which they aught to have forfeited by their Crimes, this point I believe has never yet been finally determined on the Event however of the Measure being hereafter adopted this Station in my humble opinion presents itself as the most elegible of any for removing Prisoners of this Description firstly from its centrical situation secondly from the useful manner in which the prisoners can be employed thirdly from the salubrity of the country which allows of their being capable of mire labor here than in most other jn plans and lastly from the advantages of having the corps of hill rangers without any additional expence to government for guards should these considerations induce government to and more prisoners to this station or should they think proper to determine

that those .... ready to be conveyed to Moorshedabad shall return here when the duty on which they are about to be employed shall have been finished the Honourable Board will be pleased to recollect that .... must be enlarged accordingly.

12. I humbly beg leave to recommend this subject of this address to the early consideration of the Governor –General in council in order that no unnecessary delay may prevent the contractor completing the jails within the period specified in their Engagements.

I have the Honor to be.

OOO

2. Letter

From,

J. Fombelle,

Judge-Magistrate of Bhagalpur.

To,

Sir John Shore,

Governor-General. 1

Dated 3rd March, 1795

I have the honour of informing you, that a Hill court was held this day for the trial of such prisoners as have been apprehended since the last meeting of the Hill Assembly. The following is list of the prisoners, to which I have annexed their respective crimes and the sentences passed on them.

No. Names Crime

Sentence 1 Singha...... plundering in Bailputtah ca. . . .

2years imprisonment ;

commuted to 39 stripes

2 Hejrah .... .. Ditto. ..... 20 Corahs

3 Daissah. ... .. Ditto. ..... 25 Corahs

4 Kutba. . . . .. Ditto. . . . . . 15 Corahs
5 Coosumha. . . . . Ditto. . . . . . 25 Corahs
• Singha Gheery. . . . . Ditto. . . . . . 39 Corahs
7. Soondra Gheery. . . . . . Ditto. . . . . . 30 Corahs
8. Jadhoo. . . . . . Ditto. . . . . . 20 Corahs
9 Agnah. . . . . . Ditto. . . . . . 15 Corahs
10 Ruggoos. . . . . . Ditto. . . . and also charged with To receive 100 Corahs and to murdering the mother in Law of be released.
11 Doolah, Purjah. . . . Charged with the murder of a per. Death Son at Rumserpoorah.
12. Samoo. . . . . . plundering in Bailputtah & ca. 20 Corahs

13 Buddoo. . . . Theft in Court Jale. . … To be confined one year and to
14 Bumgroo receive ten corahs each.
15 Boopa. . … Charged with the murder of his wife Postponed till the next meeting, the examination of further witnesses being necessary
16 Hudjoo. . … Manjee charged with poisoing Guya Acquitted.

Unless called upon for the rest, I shall only have occasion to trouble your Hon'ble Board with the enclosed copies and translates of the proceedings held on the trial of two of the prisoners : but, Ruggoah No. 10 and Doolah, Purjah No. 11 merely adding, that in conformity to the discretionary power you have been pleased to vest in me, I have committed the sentence passed on Singha, to a severe corporal punishment. Having no cause to disapprove of the sentences passed on the other prisoners, I shall confine my remarks to the two cases above mentioned.

OOO

3. Letter

From,

Thomas Brooke,
Magistrate of Beerbhum,

To,

Mr. John Fombelle,
Judge-Magistrate of Bhagalpur 1.
Dated 13th March, 1795

In consequence of the robberies committed by the hill people on the Inhabitants of the low lands in **this Zillah Gundrup Sing and Treboohun Singh two hill Rajahs who appear to have an extensive jurisdiction and a general authority over the Pahreahs being** accused as principal in these lawless depredations were repeatedly summoned to attend at this Cutcherry but as the court possessed no means of enforcing its process, it has only been within these few days that Treboobun Singh has been apprehended, and as it will be absolutely necessary to suggest to Government some plan for the future protection of the Inhabitants, I therefore previously seek the assistance of your information on a variety of points which come under discussion and have the pleasure to enclose you a copy of the **Examination Of Treboobun Sing** as also a list of Hills (which has been delivered to this Court **by Ojeen Singh** (a Hill rajah) stated, as dependencies on this Zillah and will beg your answer on the following points:-

1st. Whether the whole, or any part of the hill numbered in the list are considered a dependencies on Boglepore.

2nd. If they are, under what regulation they are managed.

3rd. If they have been separated from the Boglepore Zillah, at what time, and on what occasion.

4th Supposing the hills, or any number of them are under the Jurisdiction of this Court, I will beg to be favoured with a copy of the Regulations and the means that are made use of in Boglepore, in reducing the hill people to the control of the Jurisdiction of the Court, and to submission to the order of Government.

5th Under what regulations and restrictions are the Passes guarded, to whose charge are they committed, have they any allowance in money or in Land for their service, and by whom is the allowance granted.

As the motive for submitting these questions is the general protection of the Inhabitants of both Districts I trust any apology for the trouble I am giving you will be considered unnecessary.

OOO

4. Letter

From,

Mr. John Fombelle,
Judge-Magistrate of Bhagalpur,

To,

Mr. G. H. Barlow,
Sub-Secretary to Government in the Judicial Department. 2
Dated 19th March, 1795

Section III Regulation XXII 1793 prescribes, that Landholders and Farmers of Land are not in future to be considered responsible for robberies committed in their respective Estates or Farms, but in certain case: Section **XIII of the same Regulation directs, that all Pykes, Chokedars and other Descriptions of village watchmen are declared subject to the orders of the Police Darogahs.** This latter Section I presume, implies that all Landholders and Farmers are bound to entertain as any village Watchmen as their respective villages may require and their own circumstances will admit of, as it cannot be supposed that the Police Establishment are adequate to the Protection of an extensive District, without the occasional aid of such Watchmen, several landholders having lately refused to entertain the requisite number of Pasbauns etc. And some of them having even entirely withdrawn those who had been before employed as such I request that the Hon'ble Board will be pleased to inform me, whether I am authorized to require persons of the above Description to keep such a number of Pasbauns etc. as may have been here to fore entertained or I may deem necessary for the protection of their respective Villages and their circumstances will admit of and, in the event of their not attending to such orders Good whatever property may have been stolen, when there shall be Grounds for believing that a Robbery has been committed for the want of the necessary villages watchmen.

2. There is another point of which I beg to be Honored with the orders of the Governor General in Council. Several complaints have been made to me by persons desirous, as they stated of being released from slavery, and climbing their Freedom. In some cases of this nature I have been at loss how to act, not having been able to find in the office any order or Regulation that could regulate my conduct. I recollect that Government long since issued a Proclamation forbidding the exportation of Slaves from these Provinces under several penalties, but I do not remember any Order or Regulation abolishing the custom of buying or selling Slaves not intended for exportation. should there be any to this effect or at all relating to the subject, I request that I may be furnished with them. If not, that the Board will be Pleased to communicate to me such order on the Head for my future guidance, as they may think proper. The Mahomedan Law, I know, sanctions the Traffic in slaves and there is scarcely a native of any Respectability who does not entertain one or more, and I am persuaded that innumerable instances might be cited of the Descendants of slaves continuing in a state of slavery in the same family for several Generations.

ooo

5. Letter (Regarding Handwe)

From,

Mr. John Fombelle,
Judge-Magistrate of Bhagulpur,

To,

Sir John Shore,
Governor-General in Council 1.
Dated 31st March, 1795

It having been represented to me that some of the hill People in **Pergunnah Hindooa**, on the confines of Berbhoom, had been committing outrages on Beoparees and others passing through the Hills, I beg leave to inform you that I have deemed it necessary to depute Abdool Russool Khan the Hill Sezawul, to make the Circuit of the Hill in that pergunnah for the purpose of restoring peace and order, and of apprehending such of the Hill people as may have been guilty of the Disorders complained of.

2. having received a Letter from Magistrate of Beerbhoom (acopy of which is enclosed) stating that outrages had been committed by the Hill people **in pergunnah Bailputtah**, I have; for the reasons set forth in my answer (copy of which is enclosed) conditionally extended the duty of Abdool Russool Khan to the Circuit of the Hills in that Pergunnah likewise, and I have no doubt, from his activity and abilities, as well as from the influence he has with the Hill People that he will restore Order and tranquillity without meeting with any opposition. I have obtained an Escort from the Crops of Hill rangers consisting of a Havildar and twelve sepoys, to accompany him.

3. The Judicial and Revenue Jurisdiction of Pergunnah Bailputtah has hitherto appertained to the Beerbhum Zillah but, for reasons urged by Mr, Cleveland, it long since made subject to the Foujdary Authority of this District. It is now near two years since the Darogah of Bharoo in Beerbhoom had taken Mochull

as from the chiefs as of the Hills in that Pergunnah, rendering themselves amenable to the Foujdary authority of Beerbhoom. I have little doubt but that this was done by authority. But, as the measure appears to me pregnant with very serious evils to the Inhabitants of that part of the Country as well as (people) this District, and to Beoparies and others passing through the Hills, I shall take the liberty of submitting to your Hon'ble Board my sentiments on the subject so soon as I shall have received Mr. Brook's answer to my letter.

OOO

6. Letter

From,

Mr. John Fombelle,
Judge-Magistrate of Bhagulpur,(Belpatta)

To,

Thomas Brooke,
Magistrate of Beerbhoom 2.
Dated 31st March, 1795

1. On the 25th Instant I was favoured with yours of the 13th, relative to out rages committed by the Inhabitants of the Hills in Pergunnah Bailputtah, and requiring information on sundry points.
2. Previous to answering your querries, I beg leave to mention, that in consequence of the Representation of Mr. Cleveland,and in order to render the Jurisdiction of the Hills complete, the whole of Bailputtah was, many years since, made subject to the Foudary authority of this Zillah, I cannot trace any orders for doing away this arrangement, but I find from a Derkhaust of Abdool Russool Khan, the Hill Sezawal, as well as from two Perwannahs issued by my predecessor to

the Darogah of Thannah Bharoo, and to Tribohun Sing, ets. Chiefs and Gutwauls of Bailputtah, (copies of which are enclosed), that the Darogah above mentioned took Mochulkas from the Chiefs, etc in 1200 Fussily, rendering themselves amenable to the Fouzdary Jurisdiction of Beerbhoom, from which time I understand, they have considered themselves as no longer under the authority of this Zillah. Before that period, I am informed, that the Inhabitants of the Hills in Pergunnah Bailputtah demeared themselves peacefully and quietly, but, felling themselves forced from the authority to which they had so long submitted, they have, it appears of late, **evinced a disposition to return to their former predatory way of life**. The Hill People of Hindooa and Bailputtah are so intermixed, that the discoders reigning in the latter have been in some degree, communicated to the former. I have consequently deputed Abdool Russool Khan, the Hill Sezawal, to make the Circuit of the Hills in Hindooa, for the purpose of restoring Peace and Order, and of apprehending such of teh Hill Chiefs as may have been guilty of the Disorders complained of; and as I am persuaded that his activity and conciliatory Manners, as well as his influence with the Hill People, will render him the must effectual instrument in quelling the Distrubances in Bailputtah, I have extended his Duty to the Circuit of the Hill in that Pergunnah likewise, provided such a Measure meets with your approval, which, as the Restoration of Peace and Order in our mutual object, I am persuaded will be the case I have then desired the sezawal to wait on you, for the purpose of regulating his conduct by your Determination. Should no orders have been received from Government for removing Bailputtah from the Fouzdary authority of his District, he will of course, execute the orders I have given him, and which I have directed him to resubmit to your Inspection ; But should the contrary be the case and you should not deem yourself authorized to sanction the extension of the sezawal's tour to the Pergunnah of Bailputtah, I request that you will be pleased to favour me with an early communication of your sentiments and Determination, in order that I may be enabled to address the Governor- General in Council on the Subject, as I have no doubt, in my own mind of the Impolicy of working upon a system which has proved an invaluable blessing to the inhabitants in the neighbourhood of the Hills, as well as to the subject at large to the Hill people themselves.

3. The enclosed Persian Papers will give you that all the Information you require although I hope they will be useless to you, as I trust that both Government and yourself will concur in the opinion, that, containing Bailputtah under the Fouzdary authority of this Zillah, is the only effectual Mode of securing order and tranquillity into that Pergunnah, which, I am informed, **has been much depopulated by Emigrations since it has been considered as under the authority of Beerbohm.**

4. As it would not only since been an act of injustice to have rendered the Hill People subject to Laws to which they were a stranger and neither in a language which they did not understand, but might likewise have frustrated the exertions that were made to reduce them to obedience and civilization, Government were pleased to resolve, on adapting the existing system for their management, that all Hill People are accused of crimes not of a trivial nature, should be tried before an Assembly of their own Chief and m'hanjees, to be convened for that purpose, every half year or as often as occasion might arise, at the sudder station of Bahgalpoor ; and as, Tribobun Sing comes under the Description of those who are amenable to the Assembly aforesaid, and cannot, infact be tried before any of the Court without a Violation of the system adopted by Government with the concurrence of the Hill People, I

request that you will be pleased to send him to me, as well as any other Hill People who may have been apprehended, in order that they may take their trial before the assembly which will be held here in the month of May.

OOO

7. Letter

From,

Mr. John Fombelle,

Judge-Magistrate of Bhagulpur

To,

Henry St. George Tucker,

Assistant Sub-Secretary to Government in the Judicial Department 2.

Dated 20 April, 1795

1. I have received your letter of the 10th Instant informing me, that, in consequence of my Representation, the Governor-General in Council had been **pleased to separate the Foujdary Jurisdiction of Peregunnah Bailpttah from the Zillahof Beerbhoom and to annex it to the of Bhaugulpoor.** I shall again address Hon'ble Board on this subject so soon as the Result of the Hill Sezauul's Deputation shall have been communicated to me.

I also received, on the 19th Instant two further letters from you of the 16th Instant, the former acquainting me that you had transmitted Regulations 35,36 and 37 of 1795 (only 35 and 37 of which are yet received) and the Latter communicating the Board 's orders on my Reference of the 19th ultimo, Regulation 37 being received too late to be attended to in the abstract Registers for the past Month, I have only to inform you that the Rules therein laid down will be observed in those to be transmitted in future.

(Ed.) These documents reveal the working of Paharia Estates near Dumka. For a better grip on the Paharias, Cleveland got these areas transferred to the district Bhagalpur from the District of Birbhum

Surendra Jha

OOO

8. Letter

From,

Mr. John Fombelle,

Judge-Magistrate of Bhagulpur

To,

Mr. G. H. Barlow, Sub-Secretary to Government in the Judicial Department 1.

Dated 5th May,1795

1. In my letter of the Ist instant, I omitted to notice arzees which I received from the Hill sezawul previous to those already submitted to the Hon'ble Board, I now beg that you will be pleased to lay the enclosed translates of them before the Board, as the first contains additional reasons in support of the Proposition which I have taken the liberty of submitting to Government for establishing **a Police Tannah at Noony in Hindooa,** and as they both relate to subjects sufficiently interesting for the information of the Hon'ble Board.
2. The Sezawul 's suggestions regarding the Gautwauls nine in my original introductions to him and I shall adopt the necessary measures for guarding the Ghauts and Chokeesand for preventing future disturbances in Hindooa and Bailputtah, as well as for,tracing the cause and instigators of those that have already happened and which I firmly believe originated in the separation of the Foujdary Jurisdiction of Bailputtah

from this Zillah, and consequently from the operation of the judicious system which was established for the Management of the Hills.

3. On a reference to W. Brooke Publication in consequence of the Board's orders I observe that he has made over to this district the seven Kirhee Hills, which are represented to be situated in Pergunnah Noony, I shall therefore consider these Hills as under my authority, notwithstanding they appear to be situated neither in Bailputtah or Hindooa, until I am honoured with the Board's orders in the subject.

4. As there is no regular Dauk between this Bailputtah and as the Distance is considerable and the conveyance of letters, precious and uncertain I have taken upon myself to establish a Dawk for the purpose of keeping up regular and speedy (disposal). It shall be discontinued the Moment the Disturbances to the southward are at an end, which I hope will shortly be the case.

5. Be pleased to inform the Governor-General in Council, that I have just received a letter from the Sezawul, dated the 2nd instant, mentioning that **Gundroop Singh** one of the sirdars of the Bailputtah Hills, had come in and **delivered himself.**

Enclosure 1

List of hills with the names of the Proprietors and who may be considered dependent on the Zemindar of Beerbhoom

From 41m the Tribute they annually (pay).

Names of the Hills Names of the proprietors who Head Ryots called have he Title of Rajah. Mandees Who either have the management of Hills Under the	Rajahs of are the proprietors.
Dowgurreah	Treebhubun sing
Ram Mangee. Jilly	Ditto
Balloo. Burraroo	Ditto

Ditto Narsee Ditto DoorgahDiggee
GunteahCowporah Treebhubun sing
ManugoKenbudddia Ditto Singun Maut
Under charge of Treebhubum Lutchu
Sing's brother. Soondurrea Ditto Erra
Assunsool Ditto
DoorooBoogah Gundrup singRampoor Ditto
KutkooRussma Ditto Fraas Seemul
Gorjun Sing Puckedrrea
Ditto SingahPuckedrrea Ditto
DaiwahKutpucker Ditto
Harrew

Enclosure 2.

Translation of an arzee from Abdool Russool Khan Hill sezawul dated the 8th and receive the 16th of April 1795. I have already communicated to you my arrival at Hindooa. I now inform you of the situation of that Purgunnah, Evil minded people are **creating great disturbances on** the 14th of chiyte 1202 fussely at noon these people plundered Kuttenaul and other beoparies in their highway at Gybataun Khejoory of property to the amount specified in the Accompanying list given in by the Beioaries **Poorunder Sing** Zemindar of the purgunah abovementioned is quite a child whatever is done in the Purgunnah is done by **Roopchand** and **Anoopchund paishkars** of the said Zemindar. The established gauts and chokiest the pergunnah are in such confusion that the Gautwauls do not keep any watch or lookout, neither do they take care of the gauts and chokies. From the Misrepresentations of these paishkar the Gautswauls are made to believe that are solely subjects to the authority of the Zemindar without being amenable to the Tannadare or any other person. The Paishkars having subjected the Gautwauls to their authority employ them as they please. In they Gauts and chokies theft and robberies are committed. The Gauts and chokies theft and robberies are committed. The Gauts chokies in this pergunnah should be arranged and settled in such a manner as to put a stop to such a predatory conduct, **the management of them cannot be super intended by the Tannah of Banca as** they are three days distance from it and the country is wild and woody consequently, the Darogah cannot attend to them as he sought out. If it is your pleasure I will prepare an account of the number of Gautwauls Berkundauge Pykes and Dhobes as well as of the quantity of land assigned to them respectively whether cultivated or uncultivated Specifying the names of those persons who are present and I will further taking the necessary measures for the Causing the Gautwauls to attend to the service required of them as that the passage of the thieves may be stopped as well as for compelling them in concert with my naib to watch and guard the ghauts and passes whatever transaction may arise requiring to be inquired into in the adawlust may in the first instance be communicated to the **Banca Tannah** it will also be adviseable that the naib sezawul should send a monthly return of the Gautwauls to the Darogah of the tannah above mentioned.

This 8th of April, I have sent people towards thev Dhandpull Hills to enquire and search after they Thieves and shall proceed in the Thieves and shall proceed in they evening to Beerohoom.

Signed. Abdool Russol Khan
Hill Sezawul

(The list specifies property to the amount of no. 85-86)

(Ed.) – Abdul Rasool Khan the Naib Sazawal of Damini-i-koh, was mainly responsible for the deterioration of the system of Cleveland Fombell's correspondence makes it clear. In this letter, he writes about the Paharia Estates near Dumka.

Surendra Jha

OOO

9. Letter

Translation of an arzee from Hill Sazawal, dated the 11th and received the

16th of April, 1795. (Handwe)

I arrived at Bharas the morning and shall proceed this evening to Soory. Having seen the Gentlemen of that place, I shall communicate to you purpose of our conversation. (Recapitulates the substance of the preceding arzee). Throughtout of Bailputah to the confines of Hindooa the **Thieves are creating great disturbances**. Two or three hundred people of this description pervade the Jungles in both these pergunnah, and plunder every person they can get in their power. By your good fortune, on my return from Soory, all these disturbances will be settled.

(Signed Abdool Russool Khan,
Hill Sezawul.
A true translation.
Signed J. Fombelle.
Judge and Mogistrate.

10. Letter

From,

Mr. G. H. Barlow,
Sub-Secretary to Government in the Judicial Department.

To,

Mr. John Fombelle,
Judge-Magistrate of Bhagalpur 1.

Dated 15th May,1795.

I am directed to acknowledge the receipt of your letters of the Ist and 5th instant, and to inform you that the Governor General in council approves of the measures which you have pursued for the purpose of quelling the disturbances in pergunnah Hindooa and Bailputtah, and authorizes you to charge to the account of Government, the amount of the expense which may be incurred for the temporary Dawke established by you.

2. I am further directed to inform you that the Governor General in Council authorizes you to establish a Police Tannah at Noony in Pergunnah Hindooah with an Establishment of 83 Rupees per month, as recommended by you, and to disburse such sum as may be found absolutely necessary for the purpose of building a place for the accommodation of the Darogah and Police Officers.

3. The Governor General in Council has been further pleased to resolve that **Purgunnah Bailputtah and the seven Kurpie Hills** mentioned by you, be separated from the Zillah of Beerbhoom, and annexed to the Zillah to Bhaugalpore as recommended by you.

ooo

11. Letter

From-

Mr. John Fombelle,

Judge-Magistrate of Bhagalpur.

To,

Mr. G. H. Barlow, Sub-Secretary to Government in the Judicial Department 3.

Dated 26th May, 1795

I have the pleasure to acquaint you, for the information of the governor-General in Council, that Abdool Russool Khan, the Hill Sezawul has taken **six of the principal leaders of the hill marauders** who have long infested **Bailputtah and Hindooa** and the adjacent country; that there are only three Sirdars remaining who are not yet taken and that a Tannadary

Gautwauls, in the Sazawal's possession, has engaged to cause these three men to be delivered up in ten days.

2. The sirdars who have been taken, have given in a list of twelve places in which they have been in the habits of committing robberies, and have acknowledged the murder of one person. They added, that they were aided and abetted by Gautwauls and other in Beerbhoom who supported them, instigated them to act as they have done, and purchased the stolen property at whatever price they chose to give. Several of these persons, infinitely **more culpable than the uncivilized hill people**, who are two easily made the dupes and fools of designing men, have been already apprehended, and I hope, will meet with the punishment due to their crimes. The sazawal has further informed me, that he has good grounds for believing, that several Pykes' Gautwauls, Munduls, and Mocuddums at the foot of the hills in the Rajeshahy district have been likewise concerned in similar mal-practices. I have directed him to make the most particular enquiry on this head, and to endeavour to ascertain the names of the persons who have acted in this unwarrantable manner, in order that they may be apprehended and dealt with according to their deserts.

3. I am happy to add that Bailputtah and Hindooa are reported to me to be in a state of peace and quiet, and that I expect the Sezawul and his party back again in a very few days. The establishment of a **Police Tannah at Noony**, in Pergunnah Hindooa(which I took the liberty of recommending in my letter of the 1st instant)will effectually secure the tranquillity of those parts of this district ; the peace of which has of late so materially disturbed, and I humbly hope that Government will be pleased to give their sanction.

(Ed.) This Correspondence of Fombell reveals the situation in the Hilly areas in and around Dumka.

Surendra Jha

ooo

12. Letter (Regarding Handwe)

From,
Mr. John Fombelle,
Judge-Magistrate of Bhagalpur.

To,
Mr. G. H. Barlow,
Sub-Secretary to Government in the Judicial Department 1.
Dated 9th June, 1795

I have pleasure to acquaint you, for the information of the Governor-General in Council, that I have this day received a letter from Abdool Russool Khan, the hill Sazawal, dated the 7th instant, communicating to me agreeable intelligence, that peace and tranquillity were restored to those parts of Bailputtah and ca. which had of late been the scenes of the depredations of the hill people, that there was no likelihood (sic) of further disturbances, and that he only wanted my orders to return to Bhagulpore, as there was no occasion for him to remain where he was any longer than till the arrival of the Darogah, and Officers of the new Police Tannah which Government have been pleaded to authorize me to establish, who left this two days ago. I have accordingly instructed him to return immediately, together with the detachment with which he had been furnished from the corps of hill rangers, with an exception to a small party consisting of an officer and twelve sepoys, which I wished to remain where they were, with the Sezul's naib until the present favourable appearances, of transquility were fully confirmed and until the officers of the new Police Tannah had thoroughly entered on the the execution of their duty.

2. The prisoners in the Sazawal's possession are, **sixteen Sirdars of the predatory hill people of Kurhee and ca, six Sirdars apprehended in Bailputtah,** and ten who were delivered over to him by Mr. Brooke, for the trial of whom a meeting of the hill chiefs and Manjies has been summoned, the result of which, I

shall lose no time, in submitting for the consideration and orders of the Governor-General in Council. Besides these prisoners, the Sezawul has charge **of ten Gutwauls and ca, who are supposed to have been the principal, if not the sole because, of the late depredations,** and whose respective cause will be particularly enquired into on their arrival at Bhagulpore.

3. A few days ago the Sezawul informed me, that his party had separated for **the purpose of making a more effectual search after the Marauders,** that one party, under the command of Kudroo, (Pro British) Soubadar, had fallen in with a party of them, on the 30th ultimo, headed by Rehmutta, Sirdar, who not only refused to deliver themselves up, but actually discharged a shower of arrows at Kudroo's party not withstanding they were warned of the consequences, that, upon this attack, **Kudroo ordered twenty five shots to be fired at them which killed three men.** I was unwilling to communicate this circumstances of the Board until more particulars and the result of the skirmish had come to my knowledge, and I am now happy to add that the Sezawul has reported to me, that not only no bodies were found, **but that Rehmutta himself (who has been since taken)** had informed him that no one had fallen from the fire of our party. This being the case, I should not have now troubled in the hon'ble board on the subject had not Lieutenant Shaw acquainted me, that he had communicated the first part of it to the Adjutant General.

(Ed.) This Document is important giving the hitherto unknown information on the Sardari System of the Paharias.

Surendra Jha

OOO

13. Letter

From,

Mr. John Fombelle,

Judge-Magistrate of Bhagulpur.

To,

Mr. G. H. Barlow, Sub-Secretary to Government in the Judicial Department 1.

Dated 23rd June, 1795

I beg leave to acquaint you for the information of the Governor-General in Council that **Abdool Russool Khan, the Hill Sezawul, returned to Bhagulpore on the 18th instant with forty-three prisoner; ten Chokeydary Gautwauls** accused to entertaining hill people in their employ for the purpose of committing robberies, and receiving a share of the plunder from them; four Mundles accused of finding the hill Marauders in the necessaries of life, and thieves in making up the silver articles and ca. which they had stolen into ornaments, and otherwise concerned with them, and a servant of the two Gautwauls accused to carrying orders from his employers to the hill people to commit robberies and of bringing their share of the plunder for the hill.

2. The hill prisoners will be tried in two or three days by court composed of the hill chief and Manjees who are daily coming in for that purpose. I was some time ago, in doubts how far it would be just to subject the hill people of the **Kurhee or Kulhee hills (situated in Pergunnah Noony dependent on Beerbhoom)** to be tried by the court above mentioned, but those doubts are now removed as I understand that the inhabitants thereof speak the same language as the neighbouring hill people who have been long included in the Hill system, and with whom they closely connected by marriage and frequent intercourse.

3. Having examined the Ghautwauls and the other low-landers and these being grounds for believing that the charge against them are well founded that they are **inhabitants**

of Pergunnah Noony in Beerbhoom. My reasons for doing so are these. In the first place the **Marauders did not confine their depredations to Beerbhoom**, but **extended them to Bailputta,(** now annexed to this district) to several parts of Rajeshahy (in which Zillah one person was murdered by them) and I have reason to believe to Pergunnah Hindoos;(=Handwe) secondly although these **Gautwauls were not actually present when the robberies were committed, I think they should be considered as parties from having instigated and supported the perpetrators of them;** thirdly, the robberies having happened in three Zillahs, it appears (t)o immaterial in which of them the parties are tried; and lastly the principal evidences are in this district, and the prisoners can likewise be committed with the very persons whom they are accused of abetting and supporting. I shall communicate these reasons to the Magistrate of Beerbhoom, and, in the event of their not appearing satisfactory to him, the point will of course be submitted for the consideration and orders of the Governor-General-in-Council.

4. I am sorry to add, that the principal perpetrators of a murder and robbery in Bailputtah have contrived to elude every search that has been made for them ; I am in hope, however, that they will before long be discovered and brought to justice.

(Ed.) – This document throws light on the deteriorating law and order situation in Damin-i- Koh.

Surendra Jha

OOO

14. Letter

From,
Mr. John Fombelle,
Judge-Magistrate of Bhagulpur.

To,

Sir John Shore, Governor-General in Council 2.

Dated 29th June, 1795.

In my letter to Mr. Sub Secretary Barlow of the 23rd instant, I had the honour to inform you that the hillmen who had been brought to Bhaughulpore by Abdool Russol Khan the Hill Sezawul would be tried in two or three days by a court composed of they hill chiefs and manjhees who were daily coming in for that purpose.

2. I now beg leave to acquaint you that **two hundred and thirteen hill people viz. eleven sirdars nineteen, naibs and one hundred and eighty three majhees having their assembled they commenced trying** the prisoners on the 27th instant, continued their investigations on the 28th and completed them this day. The following is a list of the prisoners opposite to whose names I have inserted an abstract of their respective sentences. From this list your honourble that fourteen more prisoners have been brought since the date of my letter to Mr. Sub Secretary one of whom I am happy to add was the sirdar of the party that attacked and plundered the doomka Tannah on which occasion a man was

Murdered. The fourth paragraph of my letter above mentioned alluded to this robbery and murder's.

ooo

15. Letter

From,

Henry St. John Tucker,
Assistant Sub-Secretary to Government in the
Judicial Department

To,

J. Fombelle,
Judge-Magistrate of Bhagulpur.
Dated 3rd July, 1795

I am directed to acknowledge the receipt of your letter of the 23rd ultimo), and to inform you that the Governor-General in Council, for the reasons stated therein approves of your having committed the Gautwalls and other to take their trial at Bagulpore instead of sending them to Beerbhoom for that purpose.

ooo

16. Letter

From,

Lieutenant T. Shaw,
Commanding Officer the Hill Rangers

To,

J. Fombelle,
Judge-Magistrate of Bhagalpur.
Dated 16th July, 1795

Accompanying I have the honor to forward, a Petition from **Cudroo,** Hill Subadar,in behalf of his Detachment's right to the few prizes taken by it, while under his conduct and **Taze Mohamed**, Hindostanny Jummdar, during its service in Purgunnahs Hindooa and Bailputtah, which marched hence to those Purgunnahs on the 29th April, last, and which he could not prefer sooner, without leaving out of the list of articles subjoined to it such things, as were taken by Doukie Jummedar and party left in Hindooa.

I shall not presume to estimate the merits of the Petition, or to say that it establishes the right of the pettitioners to the articles they claim, (the value of which must be trifling and insignificant) but if any of the Hon'ble Company's Troops have a right to such things, as may be saved from the flames, when ordered to burn and destroy the lurking places of a Bandit, or to property found in any recess, or fastness carried by storm, I will venture to hope the rights of the Rangers, will be allowed to be good. I confidently trust their ready submission to the Civil power, in giving up all the things they had been for some time possessed of when called on by the Hill Sezawul, in consequence of orders, from the Judge and Magistrate so to do, and which from their little valuation (being hardly worth the trouble of carriage) they must have prided themselves in more as trophys, than from their intrinsic worth, will not be considered as any argument against their rights, their submission on this occasion was in my mind the more commendable. as I rather think, neither European Soldiers, nor Brigade Sepoys would have surrendered them to any person, but their officers, and the Ranger must now feel themselves, the more sorely aggrieved, having two precedents in their favour while acting under the orders of the late enlightened and humane Mr. Augustus Cleveland, whose memory and Regulations are to them equally Dear and Revered. On those two expeditions, which was to sieze or punish their Brothers, the Mountaineers, who were refractory and in arms, against the good order and peace of their neighbours in the Plains. **They obtained prizes that in their estimation were of considerable value –particularly at one time, they brought back several hundred heads of cattle**, all of which he desired them to keep as fair and honourable earned spoils. the service of the Rangers then was similar to the present, the value of the

Prizes however was widely different, as they formerly obtained property to some amount, whereas on the late service, which was as hazardous,and as long, what they saved from the flames or got from the chiefs **Rehmutta cave**, or lunhing place, were barely worth the trouble of bringing away.

I shall only beg leave to add more, that as the Sezawul Abdool Russool Khan has reported favourably of the good conduct of the detachment during the service, without accusing one individual, of marauding or plundering, there are good grounds for presuming, that the detachment did not wander from the line of their duty to take any thing which they were not fairly entitled to, and it may perhaps be allowed, that carrying off the arms and utensils of Depredators, which were attained in the pursuit of them, was as necessary to check their predatory incursions as destroying their habitations and haunts.

P. S. - With the petition I have the pleasure of sending a translation1 which, I pursume will be found to convey the letter and spirit of the orginal as far as consistent with the idioms of the two languages.

(Ed). The system of Cleveland put the Hill- Men against the Hill-men and there was a 'Drama' of trial by the Sardars. These Doucuments reveal the working of the Hill-Courts

Surendra Jha

ooo

17. Letter

From,

G. H. Barlow,

Sub-secretary to Governments in the Judicial

Department,

To,

J. Fombelle,
Magistrate of Bhagalpur.
Dated 27th July, 1795

Representations having been made to the Governor-General in Council that frequent attacks have lately been made by Dekoits between Sikrigully and Boglepore on the Boats of merchants navigating that part of the River, he desires you will take immediate measures for the apprehension of the offenders, offering rewards for the discovery and apprehension of them, taking such other steps for that purpose as you may think proper.

ooo

18. Letter (Regarding Sultanabad)

From,

J. Fombelle,
Judge-Magistrate of Bhagulpur.

To,

Sir John Shore,
Governor-General in Council. 2
Dated 28th July, 1795.

1. On the 6th of May, 1783 Government were pleased to determine" that in consequence of the facts which appeared to be established against **Ranny Serbessery Zemindar of Sultanabad**, of her being concerned in the Robberies committed by the Hill people of that Pergunnah, she should be totally dispossessed of her Zemindary and not permitted to reside in or near Sultanabad on any account whatever : The grounds of this determination are contained in enclosers no. 1. I know not, nor is it material to the present question, how the Zemindary was managed from the period above

mentioned to the 24 August, 1792, when the Governor-General in Council issued orders for restoring the Pergunnah to the Family of the former Zemindar and for making the Settlement accordingly with Mocun Sing, who as appears from the information given by the Ranny, is the son of her deceased husband's Father's Brother or his first Cousin. The settlement was made with him accordingly and he is still in possession of the zemindary. (Letter from Mr. Cleveland dated the February and 29th March, 1783.)

2. Enclourse No. 2 consists of a **dirkhaust from Abdool Russool Khan Hill Sezawul, representing that Mocum Sing** had summoned Haroo Coohur, Soonaye Coohur and Goondaye Coohur, Hill Sirdars of Coohur Hill in the Pergunnah of Sultanabad, for the purpose of confiring the title of Rajah on him, that the two former (the third being ill) accordingly attended on him, and having received twenty-five rupees, conferred the title of Rajah on him by putting the Tika on his Forehead, in consequence of which he was considered as Rajah throughtout all the Ghauts, Hills and Villages in Sultanabad. It also contains the examination of Haroo Coohur and Soonaye Coohur, from which it appears, that Mockum Sing used most invidious and unjustifiable means to induce these Men to deviate from their duty (indeed almost from their allegiance) by complying with his wishes, First by giving them money, then by, informing them that a perwannah had arrived from the Huzzoor, and lastly by intoxicating them before he could obtain his purpose. Enclosure No. 2 further contains the examination of Mockum Sing, in which he acknowledges, having summoned the Hill Chiefs in question, and having received the Tika from them, although he states that this ceremony was not meant to confer the title of rajah on him, but merely preparatory to his performing Poojah in the Hills, and he adds that he had

been styled Rajah from the time of being put in possession of the Zemindary.

3. From Enclosure No. 1, from an Investigation into Distrubances that have, at times, since happened, and from the result of the Enquiry into the cause of the Disorders that are only just now qulled in Bailputtah etc. there can be no doubt but that the Hill people (since they have been reduced to obedience) have seldom Committed depredations but at the Instigation of the Lowlanders. It is consequently incumbent on Government, particularly whilst the Hill people in their present uncivilised states, to present any Lowlander from gaining an ascendancy over such a numerous and rude race of Mountaineers, which may hereafter be employed in renewing those destructive disorders which so long harassed the country. The inviolable regard for authority entertained generally by the Hill people inhabiting the whole Range of Hills which those in Sultanabad form a Part, would have alone induced me to have given implicit credit to the Desposition of the two Chiefs, but had I been in doubt it would have been removed by the subsequent confirmation of the fact by some more respectable Hill people in as far as relates to Mockum Sing being styled Rajah from the period of the Tika Raj having been conferred on him by Haroo and Soonay, and by the information of several respectable inhabitants of this District that he did not assume the title of Rajah for some time after he obtained his Zemindary. If his intentions were so innocent as he pretends they were, why act in the underhand Manner he is represented to have done? He knew the fate of his immediate predecessor in the Zemindary and ought consequently to have been aware of the delicate Grounds on which he tread with regards to his Intercourse with the Hill People. I will not absolutely pretend to say that Mockum Sing had any further object views than the

gratification of personal vanity, as I have not yet heard of any ill consequence that have resulted from the circumstance in question, but considering the material depravity of Human nature (nowhere more consequence than are the native of his country), how eager Mankind in general are for the exercise of power when once within their grasp, and the dangerous use that might be made by a daring and active character of an influence and ascendancy over such a numerous and rude race as inhabit the Hills in these Districts, I cannot but think that the present case for the interference of Government, and that a proper check should to put to all the future attempts of a silmiar nature. The importance of it puts it beyond my own immediate congnizance, and I am in doubts how far it would be proper in me to turn it over to the Court of Circuit. I therefore take the Liberty of submitting it for consideration and orders of your Hon'ble Board although I, at the same time, venture to express a hope, that as no… had consequently leave us. . grounds his intentions are dubious, Mockum Sing may not suffer more from your displeasure than by being compelled to pay such time as you may think proper,and by being deprived of his title and assumed authority in the Hills in the most public manner, which with the permission of your Hon'ble, be done as soon as I can assemble the Hill People for that purpose. the annual Jummah of Sultanabad is about Rs 12,000-0-. The two Hill Chiefs themselves would have been more culpable than they are, had not they been purposely reduced to a state of Intoxication before they could be prevailed upon to what, when sober, they had reprimanded them very severely, and I shall be guided in my further conduct towards them by your orders.

4. With regards to Mockum Sing having generally assumed the title of rajah, and the ground, as he asserts, of his Father and uncle having been styled so before him, I shall submit this

circumstance for the orders of your Hon'ble Board without any further remark than that I cannot ascertain that he even had authority from any superior Power, entitled to bestow such a Distinction, for so doing.

5. I should apologize for having long delayed submitting these circumstances to your Hon'ble Board,and which would have been done earlier had not I waited some time for an answer to reference which I was obliged to make to the Collector on the subject, as well as for the arrival of some Hill People to corroborate the Despositions of their Bretheren.

I have the Honour to be with the greatest respect, etc.

OOO

19. Letter

From,

G. H. Barlow,
Registrar to the Nizamat Adalat,

To,

J. Fombelle,
Magistrate of Bhagulpur. 1
Dated 29th July, 1795

The object of the appointment of the Gutwauls and Darogahs of Police, in the Cities and Zillahs being chiefly to prevent robberies, murders and other enormities affecting the security of the lives and property of individuals, and representations having been made to the Court that the authority vested in these officers of taking congnizance of the complaints on which the Magistrate is empowered to decide, affords them an opportunity of interfering in all petty disputes and private differences between individuals, and is often perverted by them to the purpose of extortion, or oppression, without being productive of any adequate advantage to the people at large as in general the complaints are of a nature which must render it more advantageous for both parties that they should be dropped altogether or amicably adjusted, and where they are of a different description, the party injured if determined to prosecute them can always have recourse to the magistrate, the court wish for your opinion how far it would be expedient to deprive the Gutwauls and Darogahs of Police, in the Cities and Zillahs of the power of taking cognizance of or interfering in any shape whatever (expecting for the Magistrates) in any complaints theft excepted, on which the Magistrates are empowered to decide and to restrict their authority to receiving charges for theft, and for murder, robbery, or other enormities which the Magistrates are required to refer for trial to the Courts of Circuit.

(Ed.) This important Document throws much light on the working of an aboriginal estate like Maheshpur Raj. It is to he recalled here that the Zamindars claimed Rajput Status for them but the political Culture was that of an aboriginal estate.

OOO

20. Letter

From,
J. Fombelle,
Magistrate of Bhagalpur.

To,
G. H. Barlow, Sub-Secretary to Government
in the Judicial Department. 2
Dated 2nd August, 1795

I had yesterday the honor of receiving your letter of the 27th Ultimo communicating to me the orders of the Governor-General in Council in consequence of " Representation having been made to Government that frequent attacks had lately been made by

Dakoits between Sicrigully and Bhaugulpore on the Boats of Merchants navigating that part of the River. "

1. I am sorry that your letter does not contain any information on the following points : viz. the particular time when these attacks are represented to have been made, the names of the places at which they are said to have happened, the Description of the Boats so attacked, the names of the proprietors, and whether they were attacked from the water or the shore, as well as a list of the articles that may have been plundered, should any of the Boats have been actually robbed ; for, without these particulars, I fear it will be in vain to hope to trace and apprehend the offenders. I, nevertheless immediately on the receiving of your letter, sent orders to the fout police Darogahs within any reasonable Distance of the River between Aurungabad and Selimabad (the two Extremeties of the Districts) to make the most diligent search of the all persons of the description mentioned in your letter, threatening them with the severest displeasure of Government, should it be hereafter proved that they either have been or are negligent in the Discharge of their Duty, but holding out the prospect of handsome rewards, over and above those authorized by the Regulations, should they succeed in apprehending the persons in question. I have, at the same time, issued publication offering considerable rewards to whomsoever shall apprehend or cause to be apprehended any person or persons coming under the description of a Dakoit ; and I have further written to the Magistrate of Purnea to take the necessary measures for ascertaining whether the Darkoit did not come from his side of the river.

2. It is to be lamented that instead of preferring their complaints immediately to the Supreme Government, the sufferer did not give information at the first Cutchery they came to; for, had they done so, the offenders would probably have been taken; whereas the delay that has taken place, and the

want of the particulars I have recited will I fear, obviate the possibility of a discovery of them. I cannot, however, but entertain doubts either that the representations which have been made to Government are unfounded, or that, if attacked, the merchants were attacked by Boats which come for the express purpose from the Purnea side of the River, or that the attacks were made on the other side of the river altogether, and any circumstances of the kind really happened within my jurisdiction, and, had the Dakoits issued from this districts, I cannot but think that I should have heard of them through some other channel, if not through the regular one of the Darogahs : and I am the more confirmed in this Idea from having been informed by Captain Hutchinson, the superintending officer of the Invaild Tannahs who had been lately below Rajemahl, and has been several times of late a considerable way down the River, that he has not heard of any such attacks or robberies having happened, although several Invaild Tannahs are established in the vicinity of the river, and he receives constant. I shall not, however, on this account, be the less diligent in my endeavours to apprehend the persons who are supposed to have been guilty of the offences which have been communicated to me, as I am fully sensible of the dangerous tendency of giving evilminded people reasons to believe that wildness of many parts of this districts can enable them to plunder the community with impunity.

3. Presuming that Government will readily adopt any suggestion which may be submitted to them for the better protection of the community that may appear reasonable and expedient and the present occasion affording an opportunity of introducing the subject, I take the liberty of laying before them the following propositions, conceiving that the adoption of them would not only add materially to the security of the crowds of travellers continually passing through this district,

but would like wise tend more to prevent Robberies on the water, and at a smaller expense, than any other measure I can think of. There are four police Tannahs in this ddistrict in the vicinity of the great river, viz. at Aurungabad near Sooty, at Rajmahal, at Fyzoolah Gunga (or Buddle Gunge), at Sunkerpore Khadwar (or Gogah), and at Monghyr. Athough several of these places are at very considerable distance from each other Yet, considering the nature of the country, and as I have not yet had reasons to believe that they are inadequate to the purpose required of them, I shall not trouble the Board concerning them. I never the less deem it my duty to notice to the Hon'ble Board the great distance between Rajemahl and Fyzoolah Gunge, being no less than forty –four miles without any intermediate Tannah intervening and through the wildest, and most uncultivated parts of the districts should travellers or Boats be attacked in the Mid-way (by fat the wildest and most dangerous Part, being between Sicrigully and Gungapershaud), the complainants would have near two days journey to trable before they could reach the nearest tannah, a delay which would almost preclude the possibility of apprehending to offenders. It is unnesessary to point out to Government, that this district is the greatest thoroughfare in the Company's Provinces, that the concourse of people continually passing and repassing is immense, and that Boats of all description are hourly coming to in different parts of it. In order therefore to give the greater security to Merchants, travellers, and others, and to affored them speedy means of Redress in the event of their being attacked or robbed, I venture to propose that a police Tannah be established by the river side at Gangaprashaud, being about midway between Rajmahl and Fyzoola Gunga : and, the most effectually to prevent robberies on the water I would further recommend that there be attacked to the Tannah alight expeditious, boat, rowing six or Eight oars with a Jemadar and five Burkundauzes on Board, to be moving backwards and forwards, for a certain distance, during the whole night : but I would at the same time, recommend, that the Magistrate of Purnea be likewise authorized to entertain a Boat of the description and Force in order to co-operate with my people when occasion required, such Boat to be stationed sufficiently near, on the other side of the river to observe and make signals : I do not know whether the Magistrate of Purnea has a tannah in the vicinity of the river opposite to Gungapershaud, or nearly so, but, if he has not, I am persuaded that either removing or established one thereabout would be attended with much public Utility. Notwithstanding the precautions of Government, dacoit Boats must frequently make their way even higher than this through the innumerable Creeks and Nullahs that the periodical Rains open for them and, when this is the case, they may rob almost with impunity, so long as they keep to the river, as the officers of Government have no means of pursuing them. I understand that the late Mr. Cleveland had four river chokies established, viz at Rajmahl, Pointee, the Mouth of Bhaugulpore Nullah and Monghyr and that he succeeded in seizing several Dakoits at Dakoits Boats.

4. Should Government be pleased to adopt my suggestion, the expense would be as follows, independent of the first cost of the Tannah Cutchery & ca viz.

For the Tannah-

1 Darogah	30
1 Jemautdar	8
1Mohurriers and Akragunt	10
2 Burkundaujes	48
	96

For the water Chokeys –	
Brought forward	96
1 Jemautdar	8
5 Burkundaujes	20
1Manjee	5
1Goliah	4
8 Dandies	24
	61
	157

5. In the event of this proposition being approved, I have only further to submit to the consideration of the Governor-General in Council, how far it would be just to impose the expense attending it on the inhabitants of this district, as it would be incurred less for their own immediate protection than for that of the community at large.

(Ed.) This important document shows the difficult law and order situation and half hearted attempts to Contain it.

Surendra Jha

ooo

21. Letter

From,
Lt. T. Shaw,
Commanding the Hill Rangers,

To,

J. Fombelle,
Magistrate of Bhagalpur. 1
Dated 8th August, 1795

I have had the honor to receive your letter dated 6th August, 1795 accompanying an extract of your letter to the Governor-General in council under date 29th June, 1795, also an extract from the resolution of the Governor- General in Council in the Judicial Department under date the 24th July, 1795.

I beg leave to assure you that I feel much qualified by the handsome manner in which you were pleased to mention the services of the detachment of Hill Rangers while aiding the Hill Sezawul as well as on other occasions, and also that our mutual reports of the activity and good conduct of the party which accompanied the Sezawul has afforded so much satisfaction to the Governor-General in Council that the Board have been pleased to confer so honourable a mark of its approbation as a Donation of 300 Rupees to be distributed among that Party.

Herewith I beg leave to submit a plan for the distribution of the donation, as I conceive it will be most gratifying to the troops to receive their respective shares of it in money, for your approval, and shall be much obliged by any improvement which you may be so good as to point out, after which I shall be ready to attend you at any time most agreeable to you to inform the crops of the resolution of Council and to make the distribution to the Party which served, at Belpatta. As I however expect to be honoured with the Commander in Chiefs orders, accompanying a copy of the Resolution of the Governor-General in Council, it occurs to me there will be some propriety on deferring it a few days.

With regards to that part of the resolution of the Governor-General in council which directs the Arms and articles captured by the detachment during its expedition to be restored to the troops. I am sorry to confess that I cannot draw the same reference from it, as you have in the 4th paragraph of your letter of the 6th inst. Because in the first place, I humbly conceive that the decision of the Hon'ble Board as conveyed to you grants all the captors politioned fron tho' the time for the arms and articles being restored is not definite, secondly that this decision being expressly on the subject referred it may not be thought necessary to give you further orders on it (unless the form of office prescribe it) for I donot apprehend that the petition or reference contained any thing that will induce the Hon'ble Board to change its determination as already notified, and lastly, being persuaded that the arms against the good order and peace of the country, I confidently hope they will not be restored to such description of persons thi' I here the liberty to give my reason when my opinion does not entirely agree with yours, I shall nevertheless attend to your desire and defer communcicating that part of the resolution of the Hon'ble Board to the detachment.

OOO

22. Letter

From,

G. H. Barlow,

To,

J. Fombelle,

Magistrate of the Zillah of Bhagalpur. 1

Dated 18th September, 1795

I am directed by the Governor General in Council to acknowledge the receipt of your letter of the 5th instant, and to communicate to you the following Resolutions.

2. The Governor general in Council, for the reasons stated by you, entirely approves of your delivering over the Prisoners of their respective sirdars, on their engaging to produce them at the meeting of the Hill Chiefs who may be assembled for the purpose of trying them, and he further authorizes you to commute sentences of temporary imprisonment to corporal punishment with the reservation proposed by you, and this authority is to extend to any Persons who may hereafter be apprehended and convicted of having been concerned in the disorders in Hinduah and Bailputtah.

3. The Governor General in Council approves of your several propositions for extending to these Pergunnah the same system which has been established for the Governemnt of the Hills in Bhaugulpore, and he authorizes the payment of the monthly pensions recommended by you to the Sirdar,Naib and manjees in Baugulpore. He also approves of your propositions respectively to two Gautwauls in Pergunnah Noony, and authorizes you to dismiss Sunful and Sachund and to appoint two other persons properly qualifiled in their room. They are to be subject to your authority as Police Officers, and the Hill people who may be apprehended by them are to be at Baugulpore agreeably to the former resolution of the Board directing that Hinduah and Bailputtah be annexed to your jurisdiction. With respect to the lands appropriated to the maintenance of the Gautwauls you will hereafter be furnished with instructions, the Board of Revenue having been called upon to report on what terms these lands were originally by the Zemindar.

In reply to the last Paragraph of your letter I am directed by the Governor- General in Council to inform you, that although he is aware of the propriety of your motive, and has entire confidence that the trust which might be reposed in you would be faithfully exercised for the benefit of the Public Service, he deems it unadvisable on general principles, to deviate from the rules already prescribed regarding the Disbursements on account of the Hill Government.

OOO

23. Letter

From,

J. Fombelle,

Judge-Magistrate of Bhagalpur.

To,

Henry St. George Tucker,
Sub-Secretary to Government
In the Judicial Department.
Dated 30th March, 1796.

I request that you will be pleased to submit to the Governor-General in Council the enclosed copies of a letter written by me to the Magistrate of Birbhoom and of Mr. Brookes Answer.

2. As the Jagheers appropriated to the subsistence of the Ghautwauls of Chunderpoorah and Surrinda on the sole sources from which they derive their support, no salary whatever being paid to them, then appointments of the Persons whom I sent from hence to succeed Sanfuland Sachund would have been negatory were not the Ghautwauly Jagheers possessed by their predecessors annexed thereto: I therefore granted them a joint Sunnud, putting them exactly upon the same footing as their predecessors, with as exception to making their subject to my authority instead of that of the Magistrate of Beerbhoom. So, however, Mr. Brooke has not deemed himself warranted in giving these men the sanction of his authority for taking possession of their Jagheers without a previous reference to Government. I have recalled them to Bhaugulpore, where they will remain until I am honoured with the Hon'ble Board's orders on the subject.

3 Presuming that the papers which I have already submitted to Governement will have shown the expediency of keeping every necessary check upon the Borders of this and the Beerbhoom district, and consequently of continuing under proper regulations, the Ghautwauly establishments at the plans above mentioned, I shall not take up the time of the Hon'ble Board by adding anything on that head.

OOO

24. Letter

From,
Henry St. George Tucker,
Sub-Secretary to Government
in the Judicial Department,

To,
J. Fombelle,
Magistrate of Bhagulpur. 1
Dated 1st April, 1796.

I am directed to acknowledge the receipt of your letter of the 3rd ultimo with its enclosure, and to inform you that the Governor General in Council has been pleased to pass the following Resolutions thereon.

The Governor General in Council confirms the sentences passed by the Assembly of Hill Chiefs on the several prisoners whose trials are reported by you carried into execution, the sentence of imprisonment passed on the prisoner Singha being commuted to corporal punishment agreeably to the discretionary power vested in you for this purpose.

OOO

25. Letter

From,
Henry St. George Tucker,
Sub-Secretary to Government
in the Judicial Department,

To,
J. Fombelle,
Magistrate of Bhagalpur. 2
Dated 8th April, 1796.

I am directed by the Governor General in Council to acknowledge the receipt of your letter of the 30th ultimo, and to inform you that the Board of Revenue have been directed to attach the lands alluded to therein, the Revenues of which it is intended to appropriate to the charges of an establishment for the Police of the Hills instead of assigning the lands in Jagheer to Ghautwals.

As soon as the Board may report the amount of the assessment you will be furnished with the necessary information and instructions with respect to the Establishment to be entertained.

ooo

26. Letter

From,

J. Fombelle,
Magistrate of Bhagulpur.

To,

J. H. Harington,
Register to the Nizamat Adalat
Dated 22nd August, 1796.

I have been honoured with the receipt of the orders of the Nizamut Adwlut dated the 3rd and received the 14th instant,2 requiring me to transmit a detailed statement of my existing Fouzdary Establishment including such parts of the police Establishments as are defrayed by Government, and to report whether any and what reductions can be made therein without prejudice to the public service.

In obedience to the Hon'ble Courts, orders, I now make the report required of me.

Foujdary Establishment.

	Rs. as	
• Serishtadar	50 0	
• Persian Mohurrirs at 20 Rs. .	40 0	
• Bengal Mohurrirs at 15 Rs. .	30 0	
1. Daftary	5 0	
1 Bookbinder	5 0	
Pins, ink, paper and thread. .	20	0
1. Junautdar . .	20	0
1. Native record- keeper. .	30	0
20 Chprasses 4 Rs. each. .	80	0
Total.	280	0
1 shirdah	25	0
30 Burkundauzes at Rs. 3 each ...	90	0
1 Tubbub ...	20	0
1 Fazeenaburdar. . . .	4	0
1 Zellad.	4	0
1 Gorecound. . . .	4	0
Saks	427	0

I have little to observe, in addition to the remark contained in the accompanying copy of a letter to Mr. Sub-Secretary, Barlow, dated 31st October, on the subject of the above establishment. The remark are in general applied to the Dewany establishment, but, they are also in great measure applicable to the Foujdary Establishment, take the liberty of submitting them to the Hon'ble Court. The Seristadar and other Mohurrirs are old servants, their allowances appear to me to be moderate, and their number is not more than sufficient to perform the duties required of them, particulary when it is considered, that, as a considerable portion of this district is in Bengal, some of the Mohurrirs must be conversant in the Bengal languages acknowledge of which and of the Nagree Character and Hindoostany language are seldom or ever comprised in the same person. I am consesequently sorry that I cannot recommend any reduction in my Foujdary Establishemnt, on the contrary, I must beg leave service to call the attention of the Hon'ble Court to the inadequacy of the Burkundauzes allowed to take care of the prisoners, which I have already submitted to the consideration of the Governor-General in Council. No. 2 is a copy of my last representation on the subject, dated the 24th of February last, and No. 3 contains my objections to employing the corps of Hill rangers to take care of the prisoners in lieu of the Burkundauzes, as was proposed by the Hon'ble Board. further experience has confirmed those objections, and has fully conviced me that rangers are not individually equal to the task of executing the duties performed by the persons who at individually equal to the task of executing the duties performed by the persons who at present guard the prisoners independent of very few of them understanding the Hindoostany language, and of the discipline of the corps being very materially affected, should such a measure be ever adopted. It would not be understood to me that this corps is a useless burden to the Company on the contrary, the formation of it was part of almost judicious and successful system for conciliating the Hill people to our Governemnt and to a peaceable mode of life, and its being raised and stationed in this districts obviates the necessity of having a detachment of brigade troops employed in it, would otherwise be requisite, whilst it performs a number of useful important duties.

Cutwaly Establishment.

Rs. a

		Rs.	a
• Cutwaul		20	0
• Jamudar	.. ...	8	0

Mohurrir and Krajant. . .. 10 0

- Head pausbon and 11 Pausbauns. . 37 0

At Rs. 3 each

- Dholee 3 0
- Singharea 3 0

Saks 81 0

1. The above establishment appears to me as moderate as it will be, and not to admit of areduction.

Police Establishment defrayed by Government Police Tannah at Gungapurs land.

Rs. a		
1 Darogah	30	0
1 jamaudar	8	0
1 Mohurrir, Stationary and Cutcherry rent	10	0
12 Burkundauges at Rs. 4 each	48	0
Total	96	0

Guarboat attached to the above Tannah.

1 Jamaudar	8	0
5 Burkundauges at Rs. 4 each ...	20	0
1 Manjee	5	0
1 Goleeah	4	0
8 Dandies at Rs. 3 each. . ..	24	0
Saks	175	0

2. I find, on a reference to the Collector, that the above is the only police establishment within my jurisdiction, the expense of which is defrayed by Governemnt and I am not aware that any reduction can be made in it without detriment to the public service, on the contrary, Government

have been pleased to authorise me to build a much larger Guard Boat than the one at present employed, and to entertain eight additional Dandies as soon as it is ready. I beg leave, however, to refer you to the concluding part of enclosure no. 2, as I therein suggested the expediency of sebundy sepoys being played on Boat the Guard Boat, in lieu of Burkundauzes, in the event of my being permitted to raise a sebundy corps, being persuaded that from their discipline,and the superiority of their arms they would be much better calculated for the duty. So far from my being of opinion that any reduction can be effected under this head, I should have long since recommended the establishment of two more police tannahs, had I not been apprehensive that Government, in consideration of the trifling revenue collected from this district, would have been averse to incurring the expense, and had I not been persuaded that the inhabitants, were liable to bear any (increase) to the police tax already levied from them. The two plans I allude to are, **between the Tannah at Aurrungabad** (the Eastern Boundary of my District), **Rajmahal** and between the two former in 36 Miles, and between the two latter up wards of 30 miles, without any intermediate Tannah intervening. I have no tannah to the west of Monghyr. I hope for the Courts, pardon for obstructing this observation on their notice, and for adding, that the high road through this district,(Many part of which are wild and uncultivated, and favourable to the commission of crimes) is the greatest thoroughfare in the company's provinces.

1. Hill Establishment

1 Hill sezawul. . Rs. a

Establishemnt under Do. at the Sudder Station.

Rs	Annas		
1. Naib Sezawul.	15	0	
2Mohurrirs a Rs. 5 each. .	10	0	
7. Burkudauzes at Rs. 3 each. .	21	0	
Contingencies. . ..	1	8	
Total. .	148		8

Establishemnt under Do. in the neighbourhoos of the Hills.
In munneary.

1 Naib. . ..	7	8
2 Mohurrir	5	0
3 Burkundauzes at Rs. 2-8-0 each.	.5	0
	57	8
Brought forward Rs	166	0

Ditoo, in Talka, Jumay, Hindooah and etc. Rajemahl and Ambar Sultanbad, five establishemnt as above seven Bundwauries, or interpreters,in Munneary(=Mamihari), Mudwun (Mudhuban), Mudjooah(Maheshpur), Goordah(Godda), Rajmahl, Ambar and Sultanabad at Rs. 2 each.

0

Saks. . 250 0

3. The above establishment are entirely under, and are paid by the Hill Sezawul and considering the importance and extent of his duties, I am of opinion that they are not more than sufficient, and that they will not admit of any reduction without detriment to the public service.

Establishemnt at five passes in the Hills. (Ghats)
At Chokey near Putchaiteea in the Rajmahl Hills,

Rs. a			
1 Jmaudar	20	0	
23 Burkundauzes at Rs. 4 each	92	0	
1Mohurrir	5	0	
•		0	
at Chokey Coah parah in Do. as above		117	0
	234	0	

Rs. a			
Brought forward Rs. .	234	0	
at Chokey Pukercah, in the Sultanabad Hills as above	117"		
at Chokey Pukercah in Do. as above		117"	
at Chokey Deodhanr, in the Curruckpoor Hills, as above. .		117"	
Total		585 0	

6. I have little to add to what is contained in enclosure no. 4 being copy of a letter to the Governor- General in Council, dated 2nd April, 1794 on the subject of the Hill Establishemnt, in which I recommended the only reduction in it that I thought practicable, and which was accordingly effected. Till considerable **Bodies of the very numerous race of Hill people in these disricts are prevailed upon to quit their Hills and settle in the plains, and by adopting the arts and manners of the lowlanders in lieu of their present rude habits,** under the chuks so long since held over them proportionably unnecessary, events which do not yet seem likely soon to happen, I am persuaded that Governemnt will be sensible with such important benefits to the Community,and to the hill people themselves for such a series of years, and in all human probability, will long continue so. The salaries of the Jamaudars and Burkundauzes do not appear to me to admit of any

reduction, considering the nature of the duties on which they are employed, and the distance they are from their families.

ooo

27. Letter

From,

J. Fombelle,
Magistrate of Bhagulpur.

To,

Henry St. George Tucker,
Sub-Secretary to Government
in the Judicial Department. 1
Dated 30th August,1796.

Having made the enquiries relative to the Gautwauli Jagheers of **Chunderpoorah and Surrinda**, as promised in the third paragraph of my letter of the 30th ultimo, I now beg leave to submit to the Hon'ble Board the enclosed Dirkhaust, and translate, which has been presented to me on the part of Bloanaut Munder,(Bholnath Mandal) offering to form the Jagheers abovementioned for ten years at a Jumma, which from every information I have been able to obtain, is as much as they can well bear. Bolanaut did not come to himself, but both himself and his security are represented to me as being responsible men, a point which will, of course, be ascertained by the Collector who may make the settlement with Bolanaut, should his proposals be accepted. The person who presented the Dirkhaust has informed me, that Bolanaut is desirous of paying his revenue to the Collector of this district, provided the settlement is concluded with him. The Hon'ble Board will be pleased to determine this question as also, whether the Jagheers above mentioned are to be considered under the Judicial as well as the Magistrate authority of this station.

2. The Hon'ble Board will observe, that, after the First year the Jumma will fall short of my proposed police establishment

only Rs. 576 per annum, which deficiency I would recommend should be defrayed by Government (in the event of the Tannah being establishment), unless it should be ascertained that the inhabitans of that part of the country, subject to the payment of the police tax, are able to bear this addition to the present assessment, which I much doubt.

3. When the Hon'ble Board are pleased to determine on the points contained in this letter, permit me to request that you will submit to their notice the concluding paragraph of my address of the 30th ultimo.

(1) Enclosure

Dirkhaust of Bolanaut Munder, Inhabitant of Mouza **Comerdeha, Pergunnah Mohummudabad, Zillah Beerbhoom**.

About one Thousand, two Hundered, and sixty Bighas thirteen Biswaks, have at several times been allowed for the Jagheers of the Gautwauls if Chunderperah and Surrindaj in pergunnah Noney I request that the settlement may be made with me for the land abovementioned, and that it may be farmed to me for ten years on the following terms, viz; to pay aJumma of six Hundred and one rupees (Rs. 601) for the year 1203 b>L. ' and Jumma of nine Hundered rupees (rs. 900) from the Commencement of 1204 to the end hof 1212 B. L. , and I offer Deep Chaund Roy, an inhabitant of Rungong, pergunnah Mohummudabad, as security for the due performance of my engagements. I am hopeful that an auimiulnamah and pottah may be granted me on the above terms by the Huzzoor.

(Signed) BOLANAUT MUNDER

Inhabitant of Comerdeha a true translat

(Signed) J. FOMBELLE)

Magistrate.

ooo

28. Letter

From,

J. Fombelle,
Magistrate of Bhagulpur

To,

Henry St. George Tucker,
Sub-Secretary to Government in the Judicial Department. 1
Dated 22 October, 1796.

Section 2nd Regulation 34 of 1793 prohibits all persons from manufacturing spirituous liquors without a licence from Government. On receiving from the Collector a Register of the licenses granted from his office. , I instructed my police Darogahs to ascertain and report to me the names of all persons who manufactured and vended intoxicating liquors or drug within their respective jurisdictions, without due qualifications, that they might be dealt with according to the Regulations. Amongst others, the names of several persons in the vicinity of the hill were reported to me as coming under the penalties prescribed by Governement. On examining them, I found that they manufactured spirituous liquors solely for the hill people, and for the few inhabitants of the Gautwauly Jagheer, that some of them paid a very trifling Revenue to the hill Chiefs in whose Jagheers, that they were settled (for many of the Chiefs have almost from time immemorial, had small assignments of lands made of them by the neighbouring zemindars in order to conciliate their good will and prevent their incursions), and others to the Gautwauls, I have every reason to suppose that these men did not believe that they were subject, to the payment of the Tax, and so trifling must be their profits, and so necessary their establishment, that were if not for infringing a very important regulation, and for the apprehension that the indulgence migh be abused, I should be inclined to recommend that they might be continued on their former footing as it is, I shall take the liberty to submitting to the Hon'ble Board such propositions on the subject as my observation and enquiries induce me to think are expedient, I belive that has for ages been rooted in the whole race, or to impose such tax on intoxicating liquors in the neighbourhood of the hills as would either almost amount to a prohibition, or restricts the hill people in the use of their favourite, Beverage, would, I am persuaded, be equally impolitic as dangerous. Except the specie that goes into the hills through the medium of the pensions granted by Government and of the pay to the corps of hill Rangers, the inhabitants of the hills have no other pecuniary resources than what they derive from the sale of a variety of misshapen wooden articles which some of them occasionally bring down to the foot of the hills of dispose of. Money therefore is exceedingly scarce amogst them, and the liquror that they purchase must consequently be proportionably cheap, or the means of obtaining it would not be withn their power. Bout by for the greater number I understand barter Indian corn, and other grain that grows in the hills, in exchange of liquor at rates that they are able to pay, and as Governement would do Doubt, be aware of persons manufacturing and vending spirituous liquors without taking out licences. I take the liberty to recommend, that the Collector may be authorized to grant licence to such a number of persons in the vicinity of the hills as I may mention (and which it will be duty to take care shall be no more than is actually necessary) none of them to be liable to a higher tax than three rupees per Annum,(that sum being the greatest to the best of my Information, that has been vend liquor to any other person or persons than the hill people and the inhabitants of the Gautwauli Jagheers. As the licences will be only granted for one, year, should it be hereafter found that higher rates can belivied with safety, they amy be easily increased. in the meanwhile, as some time must lapse previous to the receipt of the Hon'ble Board's orders on this reference, and as the Collector is not authorized to grant licences at a lower rate then six annas per diem without the express permission of Government, I have taken upon myself to authorize the persons whom I have now examined (only nine in number, although I understand that there are a few more in the same predicament) to continue manufacturing and vending liquors as here fore until I am honoured with the Board's orders, that no cause of disconent may be occasione to the hill people.

The Gautwauly Jagheers being granted to the Gautwauls for particular services to be performed, and those held by some of the hill people being in a manner in the same footing, I see no necessiy for proposing any compensations to be made to them for debarring them for the future from deriving any advantage on the above account.

OOO

29. Letter

From,

Henry St. George Tucker,
Sub-Secretary to Government
in the Judicial Department.

To,

J. Fombelle,
Magistrate of Bhagulpur
Dated 28th October, 1796.

I am directed to acknowledge the receipt of your letter of the 22nd instant, and to inform you that the Governor-General in Council approves of your having granted a temporary authority for the manufacture and vend of spirituous liquors among the Hill people, but that previously to determining generally on your propositions, he has thought proper to order a reference to be made on the subject to the Board of Revenue.

OOO

30. Letter From,

J. B. Laing,
Assistant to the Collector of Bhagalpur

To,

J. Fombelle,
Magistrate of Bhagalpur
Dated 31st October, 1796.

In consequence of a letter received a day or two ago from Secretary to the Board of Revenue, enclosing copy of your address to the Sub-Secretary to the Governor-General, under date 30th August last, on the subject of the proposal of Bolanaut to Farm certain lands in Pergunnah Noney, (ca), I am desired by the Collector to request that you will order the above mentioned person, or his vakeel to attend at his Cutcherry.

ooo

31. Letter

From,

J. Fombelle,
Magistrate of Bhagalpur

To,

G. H. Barlow, Secretary to Government.
Dated 2nd November, 1796.

I request that you will do me the Honor to submit to the Governor-General in Council the enclosed copy and translate of a petition[2] which has been presented to me by **Phool Chund**, an inhabitant of this District, and Paishkar to Rajah Roshun Bukhs Zamindars of Mudwun(Madhuban). From the tenor of the petition, and from the purport of the Examination of Phool Chund, I had little Doubt but that the Europeans, denominated in the former as Serjeants, were Sharif's Officers, executing a writ of the Supreme Court. Having no precedent, or Order of Government, for my guidance, I confined myself to issuing a warrant to the Europeans, requiring them either to produce the authority under which they acted, or to appear before me for the purpose of answering to the charge that had been preferred against them. The warrant was served on **one of the Europeans in Purnea**, the Magistrate of which District, **Sundersland,** and previously apprehended him in Consequence of the Complaints which will be found in the accompanying petition although I have not yet received any Information from Mr. Graham on the subject. The answer of the European I now enclose.

4. I request that the Hon'ble Board will be pleased to furnish me with their Orders for my Guidance on all future occasions Court to be executed in this District, unless the person or persons serving the same shall previously produce or communicate to me their authority.

ooo

32. Letter

From,

Henry St. George Tucker,

Sub-Secretary to Government in the Judicial Department.

To,

J. Fombelle,

Magistrate of Bhagulpur. 1

Dated 11th November, 1796.

I am directed by the Governor-General in Council to acknowledge the receipt of your letter of the 2nd Instant2, and to inform you that you are not to obstruct or interfere with any any Sheriff's Officers charge with the execution of writs issued under the authority of the Supreme Court, and that should you in the present instance have confined or taken bail from any persons acting on the part of the Sheriff the Governor-General in Council desires you will immediately discharge them.

2. I am directed to apprize you as guidance to you on all similar occasions that may herafter occur, that the Supreme Court is empowered by the legislature to issue its process in any parts of the provinces of Bengal, Bihar and Orissa.

OOO

33. Letter

From,

J. Fombelle,

Magistrate of Bhagalpur.

To,

Major Hutchinson, Regulating Officer of the Invalid Establishment. 1

Dated 1st February, 1797

I have been favoured with your letter of the 25th ultimo, enclosing the petition of **Mohummud Asheek, Soubadar**, & ca. Invalids' of Tannah Mangulpoor, relative to some shocking murders committed on the persons of Emoum-ud-dien, Commandant, and his family, and to the plundering the property of the said Commandant at Mouza Gurhie Zillah Rajshaby: These atrocious acts (as appear from the petition) having been committed upwards of twelve Cross from Mungulpoor, and consequently, a little short of that distance from the boundary of my district, you must be sensible that it is out of power to do more than to instruct my Police Daroga to the eastward to exert themselves to discover and apprehend the perpetrators of them, and to transmit a copy of the petition to Mr. Cowell, the Acting magistrate of Zillah Moorsheddabad, (in which jurisdiction I believe Gurhie is situated) which I shall do today. It is scaroely necessary for me to point out you that the Magistrate of Murshidabad will require the Viva Voca evidence of the persons who have any knowledge of this melancholy business to enable him to proceed in it.

In order to enable my Darogas at Rajmahl and Aurungabad to search after the perpetrators of the acts above mentioned, I will be obliged to you give orders for their being furnished with descriptive lists of the property stolen.

ooo

34. Letter

From,

J. Fombelle,
Judge-Magistrate of Bhagalpur.

To,

G. H. Barlow, Secretary to Government.
Dated 27th February, 1797.

The Governor-General in Council was pleased to inform me, on the first of April 1796, that I should hereafter be furnished with instructions respecting the future trial of the Hill Prisoners by the Assembly of Hill Chiefs, **after ten months having** been elapsed without hearing any thing further on the subject and several prisoners having been a considerable time in confinement for trial, charge with crimes of a capital nature, I took upon myself to summon a meeting of the Hill Chiefs at this station early this month, for the purpose of trying the prisoners who had been committed since the last adjournment, as well from having found an idea that the promised instructions might possibly arrive before the court was held, as from a hope that even if they did not arrive in time, the period that had elapsed, the number of prisoners for trials, and the nature of their offences, would secure me from the displeasure of Government for no having waited for their instructions, particularly as their orders on this occasion did not prohibit me from summoning a Hill Court in the event of instructions not arriving in due time. A court was accordingly held on the 9th and 10th instant where the following prisoners were put upon their trial to whose names I have subjoined, the crimes with which they were charged and the sentences passed upon them respectively:-

Names	Crime	Sentence
1. Roopah, Purjah of Paoroo Hill	The murder of his wife	Death.
2. Daorkah Purjah of Chalgorah Hill	Ditto	Postponed for the examination of further witness.
3. Purbah, Purjah of Laitee Hill	Ditto	Postponed for the examination of further witness.
4. Mutt o, Manjee of Chooa Lallas Hill	For the murder of his wife	To be imprisoned three years, of pay thirty rupees to heirs of the deceased
5. Chkmdoo, Purjah Puckoreeah Hill	Of the Murder of Soondra his uncle	To receive 25 stripes with the Corah and to be released after having paid a fine of 26 to Jugtoo.
6. Soorajah Mhanjee of Cooch las Hill.	For having beaten The brother of Jawarh thereby occasioning of his death four months after wards.	To pay a fine of fifteen Rupees to Jumarh, the heir the deceased

OOO

35. Letter

From,

G……. . , Assistant Regulating Officer
of the Invaild Establishments at Bhagalpur,

To,

John Fombelle,
Magistrate of Bhagalpur. 1
Dated 2nd March, 1797

Kishen Mohum a prisoner confined in the Bhagulpore Jail and under the present charge of Abdol Ally Darogah, has represented to me, that he knows the persons, and residence of the people who lately robbed and murdered the commandant of the Invalid Village of Mungulpore, and has offered his service to apprehend them. He is the person who discovered the party who robbed and were supposed to have murdered Mr. Glass Bearers.

I beg leave to recommend you questioning the said Kishen Mohan on the subjects and of your taking such steps as may appear to you proper, for the apprehension of this terrible Gang of Murderers and Robbers.

ooo

36. Letter

From,

J. Fombelle,
Judge-Magistrate of Bhagalpur.

To,

Captain Shaw,
Commanding the Crops of Hill Rangers at Bhagalpur. 3
Dated 4th April, 1797.

Intening to depute the hill Sezawul, on Sunday next, to visit the several Ghauts and Chokies in this District, and having received repeated representations from the Magistrate of the Moorshedabad Zillah of several daring Atrocities having been lately committed by a desperate Gang, supposed to issue from the confines of this or the Beerbhoom District, it appears to me expedient that he should be accompanied by a small guard, which I will according be much obliged to you to furnish from the Corps under your Command ; the strength of it will, of course, rest with you ; but I conceive that there will not be occasion for more than twelve men, and an intelligent officer.

OOO

37. Letter

From,

Henry St. George Tucker,
Sub-Secretary to Government
in the Judicial Department.

To,

John Fombelle,
Magistrate of Bhagalpur. 4
Dated 7th April, 1797.

I am directed to acknowledge the receipt of your letter of the 27th February and to inform you that the Vice-President in Council on a consideration of the proceedings which accompanied it, has been pleased to pass the following Resolutions.

No. Roopah, Purjah of Pooroo Hill- Sentenced to suffer Death.

1. The Vice-President in Council has been pleased to resolve that the sentence of Death passed on the prisoner be confirmed and he directs that you have it carried into execution accordingly.

No. 4 Muttroo.

No 5. Chundoo

No. 6 Soorjab.

5. The Vice-President in Council approves of the sentences passed on the always Prisoners respectively, and he desires you will carry them into execution accordingly.

(Ed.) These Documents are important for revealing the working of Invalid Jagirdarias.

S. Jha

OOO

38. Letter

From,

John Fombelle,
Magistrate of Bhagalpur

To,

George Dickinson,
Collector of Bhagalpur
Dated 11th May, 1797.

I have now the pleasure of sending you two of the Hill people entitled to receive Pottahs for the manufacture of spirituous liquors; viz Gunga Naib, of Ayoodha Hill Tuppah, ... and Chundoo Naib Janee-Bit-hah, pergunnah Gurhee. When the remaining Hill people entitled to Pottahs come in they shall be immediately sent to you.

OOO

39. Letter

From,

John Fombelle,
Magistrate of Bhagalpur

To,

Richard Ahmuty,
Register to the Court of Circuit of
Murshidabad Division. 1
Dated 13th May, 1797

I have received the Court's circular orders of the 27th of March, relative to prisoners in my custody who are able to comply with the sentences of the Court of Circuit awarding fines against them on account of Deyut or on any other grounds,and in obedience thereto, beg leave to acquaint you, for the information of the court, that two prisoners of the above description are in confinement at this station of whom the following are the particulars, Vizs.

Hurdut- His crime, theft, sentence, to receive 25 stripes with the Tazeena, to be confined one year from the 29th of April, 1796, and to pay to Kishnoo, the prosecutor, the sum of twelve rupees, on account of the property stolen from him. This prisoner represents, that he has not the means of paying the fine awarded against him, unless he is permitted to proceed to Mouza Doomry, Zillah Ramghur, his place of abode: His reputed residence being at such a district I am unable to report upon his ability to discharge the fine; He certainly does not possess the means where he is.

Dhurrum- His crime, theft, sentence, the same – same as that passed on Hurdut and on the same Date.

This prisoner has been so ill for some time past, that I have been obliged to take his letter off : His representation is the same as that of Hurdut, except that he is an inhabitant of Pautjore, Pergunnah Chuckaye, Zillah Ramghur: My report on the first prisoner is applicable to this man also.

(Ed.) These letters reveal the working of judicial system during the period of Early Company Rule.

Surendra Jha

OOO

40. Letter

From,

John Fombelle,
Magistrate of Bhagalpur

To,

George Dickinson,
Collector of Bhagalpur. 3
Dated 18th September, 1797.

For many years past the hill people pergunnah Sultanabad have been accustomed to receive the annual sum of one hundered rupees from the Kurratch zemindary of that pergunnah, to enable them to celebrate the Dussarah. In consequence of having addressed you on this subject on the 13th of October 1795, and of my having referred to you the petitions of the Hill Sirdar, **Harro Coohur**, the sum abovementioned has I understand, been annually paid till this year, Haroo Sirdar, has now represented to me that you have refused either to make him this annual payment or to grant him an order on the pergunnah for it, and that, if it is not paid, as usual, he and his brethren will not be able to celebrate the approaching Dussarah, I request that you will be pleased to inform me whether this representation is correct, and, if so, Whether you persevere in your refusal to furnish the Hill people of Sultanabad with the sum in question that, in such event I may take upon myself to advance the money, and apply to the Governor-General in Council for definite orders on the subject.

OOO

41. Letter

From,

George Dickinson,
Collector of Bhagalpur.

To,

John Fombelle,
Judge-Magistrate of Bhagalpur. 1
Dated 19th September, 1797.

I have been favoured with your letter of yesterday's date and have the honour to inform you in reply that the representation made to you is perfectly correct and that I conceive it incumbent upon me to preserve in my refusal to grant the order on the proprietors of Sultanabad for Rs. 100 in question.

The example of my predecessor with respect to the issue of the order, and the hitherto ready compliance on the part of the proprietors of Sultanabad in making the payments may plead somewhat in excuse for my having hitherto been guilty of Error but the objections lately started by the said proprietors through their Vakeel having led me to enquire whether the claim could be made upom the foundation of any existing Engagements between them and Government and the negative appearing conceive that I should be guilty of the greatest impropriety in persisting in it.

(Ed.) Letters related to early judicial system of the Company.

Surendra Jha

❍❍❍

42. Letter

From,

John Fombelle,
Magistrate of Bhagalpur.

To,

Henry St. George Tucker,
Sub-Secretary to Government
in the Judicial Department. 1
Dated 27th September, 1797.
Ranisarbeshwari

In October, 1795 a petition was presented to me by **Haroo Coohur, the principal Sirdar of the hills in pergunnah Sultanabad** representing that it had been long customary for him to receive the annual sum of one hundred rupees from the collections of that pergunnah to enable him and his brethren to celebrate the Dussarhs poojah,, but that he had not been able to obtain this allowance either on that or the preceding year, and praying for redress: Copies of my letter to the Collector, on the occasion, and of his answer, appear in enclosure no. 1. The allowance was in consequence paid that year, as well as in 1796 without the necessity of a reference from me. Previous to the present Dussarh, Haroo Coohur complained to me that the Colector had refused to grant him the usual pergunnah : No. 2 contains copies of my letter to the Collectors in consequence, and of his answer, as well as translate of the Hill sezawul's Report in 1795 in the same subject, equally applicable to the present occasion. As the Collector has not been pleased to state the grounds of his objections to authorizing the disbursement in question it only remains for me to communicate to the Governor- General in Council such information as I have able to obtain on the subject in addition to what is contained in the Sezawul's report : The allowance in question has been paid from time immemorial; till the resumption of the zemindary of Sultanabad, in the time of Ranni Serbaiseree, in 1190 Fussily, it used to be paid by the zemindary of the pergunnah: but from that period to the present, perwannah has been annually granted on the collections for its being disbursed, with an exception to two or three years when the pergunnah was held Khas, on which occasions the money was advanced immediately from the treasury and to the year 1794. When Mocum Sing, the zemindar, himself celebrated the Dussarah in the Hills for which interference he was, at my representation, severely reprimanded : The source of my information is the Sezawul, and which I have no reason whatever to doubt: The custom must have originated at the time when the hill people were the terror of the country ; and its having obtained, without interruption, for such a series of years ought; in my opinion, to have induced the Collector to venture to make the disbursement in the present instance, applying to the Hon'ble Board for orders for the future: sanctioned as this payment appears to have been by immemorial custom and ' forming as it evidently does, a link in the chain of that system which has so long been pursued, with the happiest effects, with the hill people, I did not hesitate taking upon myself to make the disbursement immediately, the Collector refused to do it : Should the Hon'ble board be pleased to approve of what I have done, I hope for their permission to insert the charge in my accounts, and, at the same time, request to be honoured with their orders for my future guidance.

(Ed.) Letter related to the Zamindari of Sultanabad showing its customs and aboriginal connections.

Surendra Jha

OOO

43. Letter

From,

J. B. Laing, Acting,
Collector, Bhagalpur

To,

William Cowper,
President and Members of the Board of Revenue,
Dated 20 April, 1798,

"I have been honoured with your sub-secretary's letter of the 10th ultimo to the collector with its enclosures and agreeably to the orders contained there in have the honour to inform you that the progress made in the formation of the quinquennial register of the Bahar portion of this district has been from various cause confined to the year 1202,1203 and part of 1204 F. S. with the exception of purgunnah Chunduah and Passee, forming a portion of purgunnah Churruckpur the zemindar of Rajah Quadir Ali through whom the rents are paid, and which are held at affixed jummah under a Mocurrery Sunnud by Roop Narayan Deo who not withstanding the issue of repeated purwannahs has hitherto neglected to furnish the desired information which in attention appears to me deserving of severe punishment. Justice however induces me to observe that he has promised to prepare the paper required with as little delay as possible, that his Moharrir is now in attendance at this cutcherry, and that he has pleaded his Mocurrery tenure in excuse for his past misconduct. 2ndly, that though the register of intermediate mutations has not been kept up in the reqular form prescribed. Yet a particular account of them has of course been taken and will be regularly entered here-after. A misconstruction of the 48th regulation 1793 has occasioned this omission as I imagined that it was not to nor could correctly be made till the quinquennial register had been completed.

With respect to the Bengal portion of the district I am sorry to state to your Board that your orders have been badly and solemnly executed there owing to the Zemindars not one of whom had till within these very few days, transmitted documents sufficiently clear and explicit to enable me to proceed on. Various incorrect accounts have been delivered in but whether the proprietors have been actuated by obstinacy or, as they say, have really misunderstood the regulations, copies of which they, as well as the registrars have, I know not. I have, however, represented these circumstances to the Collector at Mungulpore and transmitted to him copy of the letter hereby acknowleged ; and I have no doubt but that, as soon as his business at that

Purgunnah shall be finished he will exert his utmost endeavours to enforce the commands of Government."

OOO

44. Letter

From,

John Fombelle,
Magistrate of Bhagalpur.

To,

Henry St. George Tucker,
Sub-Secretary to Government
in the Judicial Department. 1
Dated 19th May, 1798

I have received you letter of the 11th communicating to me the orders and sentiments of the acting Governor-General in Council on my address of the 5th instant.

1. I beg that you will assure the Hon'ble Board, that I did not propose the restriction, contained in my letter above mentioned in paying the pensions to the hill chiefs without sufficient grounds and due deliberation. The records, which have been carefully examined afford me no information on the subject but, I long since learnt from the aumlahs, who have ever since the arrangement for the hills was introduced, the following particulars, the accuracy of which I have no reason to doubt. For the first year in which pensions were allowed to the hill chiefs, they were permitted to come in to be paid at whatever distance of time they pleased. But, the late Mr. Cleveland (then Collector) finding that the irregularity in their attendance still continue after having been reconciled to their obedience to Government and to the arrangement that had been consequently adopted, thought it expedient ; from second year, to introduce the very rule which I submitted for the consideration of the Hon'ble Board in my letter of the 5th instant, that is, he

declared to them, that if they presented themselves to receive their pensions within three months they should invariably be regularly paid: but that, from that time, none of them should receive more than three months arrears at a time however long they might stay away. the same irregularity still continuing to a certain degree, all my predecessors enforced the rule above mentioned more or less as circumstances, in their opinon, required : Had I succeeded in finding any order of Government sanctioning the measure, I would not have troubled them on the subject, but, this not being the case: and, observing but little, if any, change in the customary irregularity of many of the hill pensioners in their attendance, I was desirous of obtaining the authority of the Hon'ble Board to give force and permanency to a rule which, however expedient it might have been, had never, to my knowledge, obtained their sanction, and which all my predecessors enforced at their discretion according to existing circumstances: If the introduction of the rule in question was deemed advisable so soon after the arrangement for the hills had taken place, it must be considered so now in a very superior degree, as the comforts and resources of the hill people at the former period bore no comparison with those which they now enjoy from a long continuance of peace and security, and from the circulation of specie throughout the hills through the medium of the pensioners and the hills corps; a conviction, therefore, of the safety as well as of the expediency of the measure induces me again to take the liberty of submitting it to the consideration of the Hon'ble Board, in the hope that they will be pleased to fix it as an established rule for the future, not to be deviated from without their express sanction. In the event of my proposition being adopted, no other conclusion can be formed, with regard to occasional absentees, than that mentioned in the second paragraph of my letter of the 5th instant. I beg to be honoured with an early answer.

ooo

45. Letter

Public Notification, Dated 5th February 1800, issued by J. Fombelle, Judge –Magistrate of Bhagalpur. 8

To-morrow, the 6th February, 1800 having been appointed by the Right Hon'ble the Governor-General in Council as a day of general thanks giving to Almighty God for the signal and important successes obtained by the naval and military forces of His Majesty and his Allies, and for the ultimate and happy establishment of the tranquillity and security of the British possessions in India, the ladies and gentlemen, and other Protestant inhabitants of this station are requested to give their attendance at the house of Mr. Dickinson, at eight O'clock in the morning of the said Sixth of February for the purpose of observing the same, in pursuance of the proclamation dated the 15th of January, 1800.

OOO

46. Letter

From,

J. Winter,
Sergeant Major of the Bhagalpur Hill Rangers,

To,

John Fombelle,
Judge-Magistrate of Bhagalpur
Dated 5th February, 1800

In Captain Shaw'absence, I beg leave to acknowledge the Receipt of your Notification and in obedience thereof, will attend at the place appointed tomorrow morning, also in compliance with your intimation, will direct the Ranger to Parade, provided with sight Cartridges, in the front of Mr. Dickson's Houses at the hour appointed. Thinking you would expect a written acknowledgement of the receipt of your letter, I humbly trust I shall not offend in taking upon me to answer it.

ooo

47. Letter

From,

George Dickinson,
Collector of Bhagalpur.

To,

John Fombelle,
Judge-Magistrate of Bhagalpur. 1
Dated 16th April, 1800.

1. Regulation VI of 1800 rendering it necessary that I should be furnished with your opinion on various points previous to the conclusion of the settlement of the Abkari Mahal for the year 1207 B. S. already commenced I think it my duty to lose no time in submitting to you and requesting the favour of your sentiments on the following particular and propositions.

2. Destillers having been always considered at liberty to relinquish their Licenses whenever they thought it proper so to do. The number of Licensed, I never thought it necessary to enquire into but it had been the practice immediately to destroy the Pottahs relinquished and if at other periods the same parties applied for new Licenses to issue such (or the payment in lieu of the stamp duties prescribed) for the remaining period of the year only, consequently every license expired with the Bengal or fasly year during which it had been issued. Those, therefore, which were rented in 1206 B. S. are no longer in force.

3. In the Rajmahal on Bengal portion of the District the Abkarry settlement of which is now under consideration the number of stalls worked under licenses has never at any period exceeded thirty or fallen below fourteen of which generally speaking six or eight have been worked in the Town of Rajmahal and the residue in the different village. The stamp duties paid by Abkars residing within the Town have been for every license Sa. 10 and the daily tax Sa. Rs. 0"12. 0 & by those in the villages Sa. Rs. -5 and sa. 0. 6. 0 per diem.

4. As far as I have been able to ascertain, the profits hither to derived by either class of the above manufacturers have never been great and must now in consequence of the period of vend being limited from sun rise to sun set instead of from day light till nine at night as was authorised by the old form License be considerably diminished, any further alteration in the system therefore does not appear to me necessary as however you may perhaps be of a different opinion and as it is requisite to determine upon the number of stalls to be licensed during the current year as well as of the places of vend I will state mine in the form of a proposal.

5. I propose then that the number of stalls licensed for the manufacture of spirituous Liquors in the Bengal or Rajemahl Division of the districts be limited to twenty four. That the daily tax paid to the same as at present viz. 12 annas per diem in the Town of Rajemahal and 6 annas in the villages –That the particular places be:-

In the town of Rajemahal not more than

Stalls

6

In Mouzah	Doulutpore	Pargannah	Amba	1
Do.	Kaleapore	Ditto	Do.	1

Kant	Downapore	Ditto	Downapore	2
Do.	Jusmuntpore	Ditto	Chuckunddeah	1
Do.	Byerbunnah	Ditto	Cassimnughur	1
Do.	Mumrespore	Ditto	Konkjol	2
Do.	Prawnparah	Ditto	Ditto	1
Do.	Pelaus gautehee	Ditto	Ditto	1
Do.	Serampore	Ditto	Ditto	1
Do	Chuck Chund	Ditto	Mungulpore	1
Do.	Ilehluparah	Ditto	Ditto	1
Do.	Neerunjinpore	Ditto	Sultanabad	1
Do.	Ballauak	Ditto	Ditto	1
Do.	Serampore	Ditto	Bahaddoorpore	1
Do.	Govindpore	Ditto	Duss Hazarree	1
Do.	Rampore	Ditto	Ditto	1
				24

That the Inscripition directed to be fixed up at the outer door on the shop Board be in the Bengal Character.

6. Hookmy Dookaun Shraub Bickree as I believe that very few of the Drug authorized to be manufactured and sold and none of those prohibited are consumed in this Districts I conceive that if a License applied for under the new Regulation, one shop liable to a tax of 4 annas per diem might be authorized in the Town of Rajemahl but I doubt whether ever, so small a demand will not be tantamount to a prohibition of sale, upon as supposition however that a License be taken out. I propose the following Inscription for his shop Board.

   Hookmy Dookaun Beckree Chutah Khyef.

6. With regard to the number of licenses to be issued for the sale of Toddy, or Taurry or the places where the vend should be permitted. I am not at present prepared to give an opinion but as the necessary stamps for such licenses have not yet been provided the delay can I presume be but of little importance.

The period prescribed for my annual visit to Rajemahal is very near at hand, on my arrival there I will enter upon the various necessary enquiries and submit to you the result. In the interim I presume it would be advisable aboslutely to prohibit the sale of toddy whether in its fermented state or otherwise except by the Pausees immediately under the trees.

(Ed.) This document tells us about the Excise Policy of the Company. This Excise duty was very comprehensive and meant for country liquors prepared from the juice of toddy trees.

Surendra Jha

OOO

48. Letter

From,

Thomas Pattle and Richard Rocke,

Judges of the Murshidabad Court of Circuit.

To,

John Fombelle,

Judge-Magistrate of Bhagalpur. 3

Dated 10th June, 1800.

The Nizamut Adawlut having been pleased to direct that we should call for your opinion on the expediency of extending to any jungle Mehal within your Zillah or Jurisdiction (if it contains any Mahals of that description) an arrangement proposed for regulating the Police of the Jungle Mahals in the Midnapore Districts, we transmit you the accompanying Copy of the Extract from the proceedings of Government of the 65 March and is ultimo and we desire you will with as little delay as possible give us your sentiments on the arrangement proposed specifying to what Mahals in your Zillah it may be made applicable or whether you would recommend any Modification of it or the adoption of any other measures which may appear to you better calculate to effect the object which Government had in view in their orders the Magistrate of Midnapore of the 6 March.

You will at the same time be pleased to report for our Information whether the proposed plan or any part of it may in your opinion be adopted with advantage to Government of the Country in Districts falling under the specific designation of Jungle Mahals.

1 (Enclosure no. 3.)

To,

H. S. T. G. TUCKER, ESQR. , SECRETARY OF THE GOVERNMENT IN THE REVENUE AND JUDICIAL DEPARTMENTS, FORT WILLIAM.

Sir,

I have the Honor to submit for the consideration of Government a copy of the rules which I have delivered to each of the Zemindars of the Jungle Mahals whom I have invested with the management of the police in their respective Zemindarries agreeably to the orders transmitted to me on the 6th ultimo.

1. The provision necessary to give effect to an arrangement of this kind with a set of men, whose habits of Life must occasion them much difficulty and embarrassment some months experience. Should my observation of the Conduct and proceedings of the Zemindars hereafter suggest any measures which may appear to me better calculated to to promote all the objects of their appointment I shall not fail to point them out, and if necessary submit draft of a Regulation for the Establishment of an efficient police in the Jungles.
2. In the meantime, I propose the rules herewith submitted be forwarded to the Magistrate of any other

Districts, in which there may be Jungle Zemindars that they may communicate their ideas on the subject and notice any variation which local circumstances may render advisable or expedient.

3. The plan must for the present be considered as experimental. If at this time I should attempt to frame a complete Regulation detailing all the Rules that I may conceive necessary for the guidance of these Zemindars in their capacity of police officers, I should run the risk of framing one which it would be expedient to alter or annual in the course of a very short time.

4. My Chiefs study in drawing out these. Rules have been to make them short, simple,easily understood and suitable to the ideas and capacities of those for whom they were framed. Since my arrival at this place I have had constant communication with the Jungle Zemindars who after their acquittal at the last sessions of the Court of Circuit, were detained at Midnapore by the directions of the Judge of Circuit.

5. I have found the Zemindars in general rude and illiterate wholly incapable,I am sure, of comprehending any Regulation but the simplest and easiest and not one of them such as I should consider qualified for the appointment of police Darogah.

6. These men however are looked up to with respect and veneration by their Ryots and are the only persons capable of managing their Estates and defending their vast territories from the depredations of the Choars and of one another.

7. Willing to enter into any engaments that may be required from them for the faithful performance of their duty as police Officers, every rule proposed by

me for their conduct has received their unanimous and most cheerful acquiescence and in fact I have inserted scarcely anything but what they suggested themselves, they seem to consider the employment of them in this capacity as proof of confidence of which they express the highest satisfaction and gratitude.

8. I must here take the liberty of explaining a circumstance which appears to have been misunderstood. No resumption of the Pyker Lands place or ever could take place consistently with the terms on which the Zemindars hold their Lands in any of the Jungle Mahals. The Revenue payable to Government from the Jungle Mahals instead of 9th/10th do amount in general to more than 1/9th or 1/10th of their produce.

9. As the resumption of the **Pykar lands** in the Jungles of Ranny's Estate appears to have been the principal, if not sole cause, of the disturbances which have so long prevailed there, it may reasonably be expected that the orders of Government to restore them will put an end to the disturbances as soon as they can be completely carried into effect.

10. In the 15th Instant I issued publications jointly with the Acting Collector inviting the Pykes who have long wandered about the country and many of whom have become Choars for want of any other of subsistence to come to Midnapore by the 20th of April in which case they are informed that a settlement will be concluded with them for the Pykar Lands in the Jungles upon the terms on which they formely held them, and that otherwise these Lands will be given up on the same conditions to other persons and never be restored to them.

11. I should suppose there will be no difficulty in finding as many men as may be required, able and willing to serve as Pykes, a great many who were formerly so employed in different parts of the district having been deprived of their Lands at the time of the **decennial settlement**.

12. The zemindars of the Jungle Mahal derive no immediate pecuniary benefit from the arrangement, they will on the contrary be subject to some expense since they are required to keep accounts and send intelligence in writing to perform which duty I shall contrive to render it as easy as possible, one Mohurir at least will be necessary to each Zemindar.

13. The Zemindarry of Roypore (Bengal) formerly belonged to Durjun Sing but was sold by sale auction in Burdwan in 1203 for the recovery of arrears of assessment and immediately afterwards made over by the purchaser to the Present proprietor. Durjun Sing considering himself aggrieved by sale of his Estate send the Collector in the Dewanny Adawlut of Burdwan to which Districts Roypore formerly belonged and the cause having against him in 1203 since which time he has done every thing in his power to prevent the purchaser from getting possession of his Estate. He negotiated with the Choar of Beerbhoom and other distant Zemindarries, invited them to assemble their force, join there to his Pytro, and lay waste the Zemindarry of Roypore. A Naib and 2 or 3 other persons employed by the purchaser in the Collections were put to death in 1205 and other Naib who was deputed to Roypore about six months ago suffered the same fate soon after his arrival. There is reason to believe that many of the Ryots are attached to Durjun Sing and have always been ready to assist him in opposing the purchaser though the latter does

not appear to have shown any inclination to oppress or deprive them of any advantages he found them in possession of Durjun Sing having been ascertained to be in arms Detachemnt of Sepoys was sent from hence to Ryopore several months ago and most of the Ryots having run way from their villages wherever several troops made their appearance they were supposed to be in league with Durjun sing and treated accordingly. Then Houses and Grain, indeed whole villages were burnt and plundered lives lost till at length the whole Zemindar was quite deserted and laid waste.

14. I am credibly informed that till within these very few weeks there was not to be found in the whole Estate a single Ryots and scarcely a Houses, not of course a spot of cultivated land. Previous to the breaking out of the disturbances this Zemindar equal to at least 5 or 6 times the sudder Jumma, a Company of Sepoys is still stationed and I propose by stationing guards on the borders of the Estate to protect the whole and endeavour to encourage the Ryots to return. The officer detached there informs me that a few Ryots have begun to rebuild their houses and that more are coming in every day.

15. As soon as the purchaser can get a sufficient number of Pykes to protect his Estate, I shall deliver a sunnud to him or his manager in the same manner as I have done to the other Zemindars.

16. If I should fail in .... To return, I shall recommend the Estate be put under the charge of one or more of the neighbouring Zemindars, who will probably be best able to afford the protection and encouragement necessary to induce the Ryots to come back and

cultivate their lands. I have spoken to the Zemindars on this subject and they expressed the utmost readiness to comply with my wishes the State of their own lands is such as to require all their attention.

17. The Zemindar of Poolcoosma is related to Durjun Sing after committing dreadful ravages in the estates contiguous to his own, he opposed the regular Troops sent against him for a considerable period and many lives are said to have been lost during the contest. On one occasion his People massacred Siateen Pykes belonging to the zemindars of Lolgur and Ramgur with whom he has long been at variance. The zemindary Poolcoosma was in the end entirely laid waste by the sepoy owing probably to the circumstance of his Pykes having become Choars, a great number of villages were destroyed, his own Houses or Fort plundered and burnt and many of his people killed. He was committed for trial, but acquitted at the late Jail delivery by the Court Circuit.

18. Though I cannot presume to express any opnion on the trial particularly as I have not seen it, yet his guilt appears to be a fact of such general notoriety that I am very much at a loss to account for there not having been sufficient evidence to convict him. I am fully convinced of his guilt both from the proceeding of the Magistrate and from the information I have received on making private enquiries into the affair (some of the Gentlemen still at Midnapore were in the Jungles during the opposition made by him to the troops and were present when he surrendered) I cannot but regret exceedingly this man has not been made a server… of to deter others from the acts which …. Committed.

19. Government will…unwilling that a person of such… should be entrusted with the charge in his Zemindary ye I known no…the Commission might be given.. .indeed without endangering the… of the Jungles. The Zemindar of Poolcoosma appears to have a large body of pykes under his immediate command, and is nearly formidable of all the Jungle Zemindars, as well as to Durjun Sing. Were any attempt therefore made to deprive the Poolcoosma Zeminbdar of his Zemindarry, or even to make him an exception to the General rule that has been adopted of giving the Jungle Zemindars the charge of the police, I conceive that it might have the effect of increasing the disturbances, of checking the Zeal and exertions of those who are best able to put a stop of them, and of setting some of the Zemindars at variance with the others. It must rest with Governemnt to determine which alternative it would be advisable to adopt, to pardon or connive at his past guilt and employ him or to set him aside and incur the hazard of all the mischief which is likely to ensue. I have allowed him to leave Midnapore where he was detained with the rest of the Zemindars and informed him that I should submit his case to Governemnt. Since his return home he has behaved with perfect propriety.

20. The Chief difficulty I find in the duy which I am endeavouring to execute arises from the state of the Zemindary of Beerbhoom. On this subject it is my intention to enter at some length in a separate address which shall be transmitted in a day or two.

21. There is a Jungle Zemindarry at the north-west extremity of this Districts called Chunta which till lately always belonged to the Districts. It appears to have been annexed to Beerbhoom because the whole of it lies

between the and Birbhum and Burdwan Zillah. But as I understand the Zemindar expressed to the Collector his desire that it might continue under Midnapore and his Vakeel lately spoken to me very urgently on the subject and as it is intended that the same plan should be carried into execution thought out the Jungles. Government may perhaps see no objection to it being reannexed to this Zillah at least till the arrangement may be compleely carried into effects particularly as from its situation I am aware of no material inconvenience that can come for such ameasure.

22. If the plan now carried into execution should succeed in any degree answering my expectation the Darogah now stationed in the Jungles in my opinion very shtorly be withdrawn entirely without danger. For the present, they will remain and the Zemindars be possessing a concurrent Jurisdiction with them will I hope acquire some knowledge of the Fouzdary Regulations.

23. It is my intention for the present to detain the Sepoys where they are stationed, I see no material objection to their remaining in the Jungles except in Beerbhoom which is remarkably unhealthy.

I am & Ec

(Signed) H. STRACHEY, Magistrate.

ZILLAH MIDNAPORE

The 9th April, 1800.

OOO

49. Letter

2 (Enclosure no. 4.)

Rules for the Jungle Zemindars in their Capacity of Police Officers.

1. The Zemindars shall recive sunnuds from the Magistrate vesting them with the police in their respective estates.
2. They shall not be deprived of their sunnuds except for misconduct proved to the satisfaction of the Governor-General in Council.
3. They will engage to keep up a certain establishment of pykes, the number to be determined by the Magistrate.
4. The pykes shall be numbered and a list of their names kept in the Office of the Magistrate. On the death or removal of any of them the Zemindar shall fill up the vacancies. They are to be armed in the same manner as they have been hitherto force and are not to change their arms without the sanction of the Magistrate.
5. The Pykes and all persons employed under the Zemindar as police Officers shall be subject to the orders of the Magistrate, punishment by him for misconduct whether by removing them from Office, depriving them of their Lands or otherwise according to the nature of the offence.
6. With regard to persons charged with Crimes or misdemeanours, the Zemindars are to observe the Rules prescribed in Regulation of 1793 for the conduct of the Police Darogah.
7. The Zemindar will be supplied with Copies of the said Regulation and they are expected to pay the utmost attention to it and as far as may be practicable make it the rule of their conduct as police Officers.

8. It shall be the duty of the Zemindar to send the nearest Police Darogah or to the Magistrate whichever may be most convenient to him, all persons charged with murder Robbery, or other heinous Crimes within 24 hours after the party accused may be apprehended.
8. The Zemindars may apprehend all Choars or othe plunderers of whatever description while committing a breach of the peace. In other cases no person shall be apprehended without a Complaint preferred in writing.
9. The Zemindars will be careful to take security from prosecutors and witnesses be appear before the Magistrate on acertain Day.
10. In complaints for petty assaults or abusive Language, the Zemindars may take Razeenamahs as the Darogahs are at present empowered to do, provided the parties shall deliver such Razeenamahs within 24 hours after the accused may have appeared at the Zemindars Cutcherry.
12. No Zemindar shall summon, other Ryots of another Zemindar.
13. The pykes of one Zemindar are not subject to the orders of another. But it is expected that all being servants to of the Sircar when occasion requires their Cooperation will jointly use their utmost endevours to pursue and apprehend Choars and other disturbers of the peace.
14. If the Choars should plunder and commit depredations in one Zemindary, the Zemindar is empowered to call upon the neighbouring Zemindars for assistance and in every such case I shall be the duy of the neighbouring Zemindar to assemble their whole force and if occasion require to attend in person and exert themselves to the utmost in restoring and preserving the peace by apprehending, expelling or destroying the Choar.

15. Any Zemindar or .... . 1 Officer may be convicted of ... wilful ... affording his utmost assistance on such ... will be liable to the forfeiture of his ... fine and imprisonment according to the ... of the Cae.

16. When the Magistrate is of opinion that a Crime of this Nature is proved against a Zemindar and that he has became subject to the penalty of forfeiting his Estate the proceeding shall be submitted to the Governor-General in Council for his final decision.

17. The Zemindars will transmit constant and Regular information to the Magistrate of all Occurrences relating to the police of their zemindaries.

18. They will send monthly accounts according to a form which shall be furnished them by the Magistrate.

19. All accouns, Letter & ets. shall be transmitted by the Zemindars in the Bengal language and all order is sent to the Zemindars by the Magistrate in the same Language.

20. The Zemindars enagaged to be responsible for the amount of all property robbed or stolen within their respective estates, the person robbed may recover the value in any Court of justice competent to take congnizance of the claim.

21. In Estates the proprietors of which shall be disqualified from age, sex or other cause the manager shall receive a Sunnud and perform the duties herein laid down for the Zemindar.

(Signed)

H. STRACHEY,

Magistrate.

ooo

50. Letter

From,

G. Dickinson,

Collector of Bhagalpur,

To,

John Fombelle,

Judge-Magistrate of Bhagalpur. 3

Dated 16th June, 1800.

In reply to the queries put to me in your letter of the 29th ultimo I have the honor to inform you, that the zemindars and Mockurryddars (Mokarridar)are bound by their Khabooleats(Qubuliat) as appears by the enclosed extract to keep the roads and bridges in repair but that particular of their engagements, was even previous to the abolition of the Sayen, I believe, always considered to mean no more than that they should take care to put them in a passable state during the dry season for the produce of their whole Estates would not be equal to rendering them what they ought to be, in a district which is so complete a thoroughfare as this is. Indeed in the arrangement of this Jummah the proportion of pyddwar (=crop-yield) allowed for Mofussil and other charge is scarcely equal to admit of their performance of the most losses, construction of the ferries and I am convinced that if they were interpreted more strictly and improvement was attempted it would be impossible to collect the Government Revenue.

In the Khauss Mahals the duties fall upon the Khauss Thesuldar (Tahsildar) and the expense eventually on Government, the gross collections being debited for the charge which is limited to as small a sum as possible. In fact a little Earth is thrown into holes which may have been made in the roads. Stakes are driven into the nullahs and water courses. These are covered with bamboos, straw etc. ; which constitute temporary bridge and I do not consider myself authorized to admit of anything more – if I did I should probably be forced to make the amount good from my own salary for my approbation or disapprobates of a charge is by no means final. With under renters I have had no concern, they and the Zemindars have always settled matters between themselves how I never enquired and cannot therefore inform you, but I scruple not be assert that it would be unjust to expect more from the Landholders than they annually perform, and in some instances I think it unjust to expect so much.

ooo

51. Letter

From,

G. Dickinson,
Collector of Bhagalpur,

To,

John Fombelle,
Judge-Magistrate of Bhagalpur. 2
Dated 5th July, 1800.

In continuation of the subject of my address of the 16th April last, I have now the pleasure of transmitting to you the result of my enquiries into the nature and extent of the trade in Toddy carried in Zillah Rajemalal with my opinion as to the means most likely to ensure the purpose intended by the 6th regulation of 1800 in as far as the increase of the public revenue may be effected without critically prohibiting all traffic in that article.

2. The Taur and the Kundjoor(=Khajur) are the only species of tree from which Toddy or taree is extracted, the season of the former commences about the 10th of March and ends about the 10th of June, that of the latter begins with the third week of December

and continues until the middle of march. One tree yield upon an average about **180 seers of juice in the season,**and as seers are sold by the Passees for one anna, the proceeds of one tree amount to Sa. Rs. 2. 13 per annum.

3. The number of Taur and Kudjoor trees growing in this Zillah is between 4,000 and 10,000, but the produce of 690 is more than equal to the consumption. It is usual however for the Passees to rest 690 in order to effect a regular supply from 690 because they find it very expedient to give each tree successively one year to rest after three years of production.

4. The above number of 690 taurs is rented by 48 Passees, 15 trees in actual produce being fully sufficient to engage the whole of one person's attention. The occupation is not only difficult but dangerous. The accidents which terminating amounts to 4 percent per annum at least a seventh of the employed are for some time incapable of profits should be considerable and as the season of manufacture lasts but six months the proceeds of that period should afford subsistence for the whole year.

5. Estimating the produce of 60 trees during the season at 180 seer each the quantity of Toddy produced in this Zillah will be 1,24,200 seers which at the common price of 4 seers for an anna will give Sa Rs. 1,940. 10 as the value of all the Toddy manufactured in this Zillah. From the above sum deduct the rent of 321 Taur trees at 4 annas, and of 635 Kudjoor trees at 2 ann each, or Sa Rs. 159. 10 and contingencies such as rope, knives and earthen pots called Lutnces Rs. 60. 0 and these will remain to be divided between 48 persons for their labour and danger during six months. Rs 1,721, nearly six rupees each per mensem during the season, or almost three rupees a month for the whole year.

6. It appears then that no increase of rent can be levied from the Passees without reducing their profits below what they ought to be to afford subsistence, or so far increasing the price of Toddy as effectually to prevent its use. Whether the prevention of its sale altogether as aliquor might not occur by increasing the consumption of spirits, an addition to the revenue their derived more than equal to that which the sale of Toddy can afford, is not a matter of present investigaion, so very little however does fermented Toddy appear to be an article necessary to convenience that no petition have been laid before me for removal of the restriction which I have imposed on its sale until the requisite measure of licences and ascertaining of places of vend shall have been accomplished.

7. Of the whole, quantity of Toddy produced in the Zillah one-half is purchased by the Pykars and retailed at an adventage of 50 percent provided they can dispose of the whole quantity, Rs. 9,705 which are laid out in the purchase will afford Rs. 485-2-6 in addition to the purchase money. Upon this excess, I propose a tax of 25 percent which I consider to be the utmost which can be laid on the articles with safety and I am the more inclined not to exceed that proportion, because I have found that inconsequence of the receipt increase of daily duty on the stills in Rajmehel, proposed by you and confirmed by the Board of revenue not more than a single Licence has been hitherto applied for the Abkars of the town.

8. Twenty –five percent upon Rs. 485-2-6 will amount exclusive of fracting to Sa. Rs. 121. 4 which I propose to raise in the following mode:-

	Rs.
By licences to 13 Pykars at 2 rupees each	26
By a monthly tax of 8 annas	78
	124

The above sum of 124 rupees deducted from 485-2-6 leaves Sa Rs. 361-2-6 to be divided between 13 persons on a capital of Rs. 970. 5 being about 35 percent or a percent proceed to each person of Rs. 27. 91 for six months house rent, risk, labour and interest of money.

9. I think that the following distribution of licences will answer every necessary purpose:-

The town of Rajemahal. . . .	Kutra. . . .	3
	Moynah Tullah. . . .	3
	Nawabi Bazar. .	1
Conkjole. . . .	. . Place. . . .	1
	Puranporrah. .	1
Murgulpore. .	. . . .	1
Dounapore. .	. . . .	1
Cossimgunge. .	. . . .	1
Gungapursaud	. . . .	1
	Total. . . .	13 shops

10 I think that will naturally tend to secure the small revenue drawn from Toddy to prohibit the sale of I in its fermented state by any other person than Pykars, and I am strongly of opinion that an increase of rate may with more facility be proposed and effected hereafter than at the present moment.

OOO

52. Letter

From,

J. Lumsden,

Registrar to the Nizamat Adawlut,

To,

John Fombelle,

Magistrate of Bhagalpur. 1

Dated 30th July, 1800.

I am directed by the Nizamat Adawlut to acknowledge the receipt of you letter of the 3rd Instant with the proceedings held before the Sirdars, Naibs, and Manjees of the hills in your district on the trial of Khoshaul Purja for Murder, and to transmit to you the enclosed Extract from their proceedings of the 16th Instant containing the sentence which was passed on the said Khoshaul Purja as required by Clause 4th, section 13th, Regulation Ist of 1796.

2. The Court however being of opinion from the Evidence adduced at the trial that the Prisoner was actuated by the Impulse of the Moment and had no previous malice against the deceased, his case was submitted under clause 5th, section 13th, regulation Ist of 1796 to the consideration of the Most Noble the Governor-General in Council, who has been pleased at their recommendation of committe the sentence of death passed on Khoushaulee Purjah to a sentence of punishment with thirty-nine stripes, imprisonment and hard labour for one year.

3. You are accordingly directed to cause this sentence to be carried into Execution after having called the Prisoner before you and made him acquainted with the sentence which has been passed upon him.

4. The court further directed that you will acquaint prisoners, as well as the Principal Hill Sirdars, Naibs, and Mangees, that they would have proposed that Khhoshaul should have been imprisoned for a longer period than one year, had they not been induced to shorten the term with a view of accommodating the sentence, as far as appeared to be consistent with the principle of justice, to the suggestion of his judges that he should not be deprived of the means of providing for the subsistence of his own wives and children, and of the wives and children of the deceased Kudra Purja.

(Ed.) This Document gives a vivid account of the mercantile attitude of the Company rulers, who were determined to collect as excise tax as much as extractable, leaving only the Subsistence level income to toddy traders

Surendra Jha

ooo

52 (a). Letter

From,

C. S. Maling,
Acting Magistrate of Bhagalpur,

To,

G. Dickinson,
Collector of Bhagalpur. 1
Dated 29th November, 1800.

I beg to enclose you copy of a representation which I have received from Emaum Buksh Choudry, Zemindar of Kismut Pergunnah Conkjole, stating his reasons for not acting conformably to section of Regulation of 22 of 1793, and requesting you will inform me whether his assertion is correct, and if so, that you will be pleased to make me acquainted with your sentiments on the subject.

OOO

52 (b). Letter

From,

G. Dickinson,
Collector of Bhagalpur,

To,

C. S. Maling,
Acting Magistrate of Bhagalpur,
Dated 3rd December, 1800.

In reply to your letter of the 29th ultimo received yesterday I have the Honour to inform you that Emaum Baksh Chowwdry's representation is perfectly correct his Estate, having been held Khauss for the last ten years.

That an Establishment of Pykes, Pausbauns, Chowkeydars etc, is in every Estate necessary for the enforcement of the Collections and the security of the Public Revenue is appoint I am by no means inclined to disputes on the contrary, the necessity is evident but how far the land-holders may now be considered bound to entertain such for the purpose of Police rests not with me to decide. it is true that in settled Mahals deduction from the estimated gross produce for Deehauttee and Pergunautte charge was on the conclusion of the Novennial settlement invariably allowed and that part of those charges were supposed to be incurred by the proprietors in the entertainment of the different classes of people alluded to, but I cannot find that in any one instance either their number or stations were ever particularized, nor do I myself understand or believe that the land-holders understood that they are bound themselves by their engagements either to the maintenance of a specific number or admitted that any portion of what they might find it convenient to entertain should be made subject to the orders of a Police Thannah Darogah as no Land-holder, however, could with decency or indeed without meriting punishment object to their performance of the duties required of the Pausbauns etc. by **section XIV, Reg, XXII of 1793.** The only grounds they can have for complaint is that they shall be forced to entertain a particular number at a later period and when the necessity does not exist because they found it convenient to do so at a former when it did.

In Estates held Khauss the case is different, so far at least as that Government without any even apparent breach of engagement may direct the entertainment in each, of any Establishment they deem necessary and of tendering them afterwards to the proprietors at a consequent reduced Jummah but it appears to me that without Government authority, neither the Collector nor the Magistrate can with any propriety presume to order therein the maintenance of any specific Establishment of whatever nature. For my own part, I have considered it my duty in such Estates to reduce the expenses as much as possible but I have not had the good fortune to succeed to the extent of my wishes. These charges uncommonly high in Emam Buksh's Portion of Konkjole, called for my particular notice and as the representation made to me of the duties performed by the outpaharees occasioned one to think that their services might be dispensed with without any injury to the public Revenue. I felt myself strongly urged to give the measure a trial.

Since these persons are considered necessary for the maintenance of the Police. , I beg that you will be pleased to inform me of the smallest number which may be entertained and of the places at which they may be established, in order that they be appointed and that I may be enabled to procure the sanction of Government to the disbursement through my immediate superiors, the Board of Revenue.

OOO

53. Letter

From,

T. SHAW,

Major Commanding, H. Sangers,Bhagalpur,

Dated 22 April, 1801,

To,

John Fombelle,...... Judge and Magistrate.)

"I had yesterday evening the honor to receive your letter of the 21st instant acknowledging the receipt of my letter of 20th which, if not impeded by the Hill sezawall, would have been delivered at Noon that day.

I shall be exteremely sorry if what I proposed in that letter,and which I did on mature consideration for the good of the service,would deprive Dumor Havilder of the appointment of Sirdar of Cowpall- to which as the sister's of the late Sirdar Harroo Cower, he was elected on the consulation of the Mand. aans or Chiefs of that Tappah as the legal successor during the minority of the Deceased(?) Grandson Gondeha – or, that my proposal should be inconsistent with the good management and good order of the inhabitants of that Tuppah. On these considerations as well as others which I shall, for the present, forbear to mention,as they may eventually from a future representation on the conduct of the Hill Sezawall Abdool Rasool Khawan to Durmoo,Ilament much of your having rescinded the Resolution, appointing Durmoo the Sirdar, as it must be attended with great vexation, to the Chiefs Mandjanns who elected him, as well as another delay to their obtaining the allowance for the Dusserah Poojah, which I understand has been deferred so long, beyond the usual period of payment as to interfere much with the happiness and comfort of the inhabitants,whose superstition is such, that the impute every affliction,and all casualties to they vengeance of their God Dewat, for not having observed that the appointment of Sirdar may be restored to Durmoo Havilder. I will grant him leave at once to proceed to the Hills, to observe the usual Poojah, and he may have a consulation of the chiefs, Whether he can consistently,and with the good of the service, hold both appointments, by having a Sirdar Naib _ all of which will, of course, be submitted to you for your approbation and confirmation, should his holding both the incompatible or country to your opinion of what,is right, he will then have to relinquish his appointment as Sirdar, or leave the Rangers, in which he has served nineteen years or more, in the latter case, he declared his conviction that the present Sezwal will endeavour to ruin him, and such apprehensions if not Glsmissed, whether well or ill founded must influence his choice.

(Ed:) These letters throw lights on the several deeds and misdeeds of Naib Sazawal.

OOO

54. Letter

From,

J. Wintle,

Magistrate of Bhagalpur,

To,

G. Dowdeswell,

Secretary to Government in the Judicial Department. 4.

Dated 5th March, 1803

Previous to the departure of my predecessor several Decrees were passed against Dhurrum Deo, Remjeet Singh, Mangun Singh & ca. persons at the suit of Roop Narain Deo, Zemindar of the Jungle Terry lands of Curruchpore for Balance of Revenue due on account of the lands held by them respectively in farm, but from some cause or other these Decrees were not enforced. The Vakeel of Juggernaut Deo therefore made application to this Court to carry the Decrees in question into execution, and the necessary orders to that effect were in consequence issued. The Peons entrusted with the executions against the Defendants, have returned, and depose that Dhurrum Deo and the above named persons have shut themselves up in an old mud fort belonging to Dhurrum Deo and have assembled together about 150 Men with matchlocks determined to resist any attempts to attach their property or to take their Persons into custody, and some of the Defendants have autually forcibly carried off some Property attached under the Courts orders. Considering Dhurrum Deo's to be the outrageous conduct, any being unwilling to create disturbance in the Jungle Terry Districts, if it could be avoided, I wrote a friendly Perwannah to him pointing out the impropriety of his conduct and the severe consequences it would bring upon him, and at the same time told him that the court would be very ready to hear, whatever grievances or objection he had to state personally, and as far as possible offered him redress. To this he sent an evasive answer, which indeed insinuated that my predecessor was afraid to carry his Decrees into execution apprehensive that by so, doing he might cause a disturbance in the Jungle Terry. As I could consider his conduct in no other light than a resistance of the Courts authority I summoned him to come in and answer to the resistance, and on his disobeying the summons I have issued the publication for that purpose directed by the 22nd and 25th sections 4th Regulation of 1793.

While this Business was going forward an application was made by the collector to cause the police Darogah of Banka to offer his Tehsildar (who holds Roopnarain Deo's lands in attached on account of his being in Balance) assistance and support agreeable to 9th section 7th Regulation of 1799 in reattaching some crops which Dhurrum Deo and the other Defendants had forcibly cut and carried off, though they were then under attachment for their Rents. The darogah agreeable to my orders proceeded with his Burkundasses and the Collectors' Tehsuldar to Dhurrum Deo's Residence but was unable to gain **admittance as he found a force with lighted Matches and Fire arms ready** to oppose him and was told that he would be fired upon if he made any attack. the other Defendant had joined him, thus setting both the court's and Collectors's authority at defiance. The Crops carried off had been lodged in the mud Fort.

Seeing no chance of enforcing the Decrees in question by the attachment of the Defendant's Property, a Precept has been sent to the Collectors to attach their Farms and collect the Profits until the amount of the Decrees are liquidated, but as they have already resisted his authority in the legal Discharge of his Duty, there can be no doubt that they will resist the present order of court, as they have an armed force in readiness to support them.

Not wishing to proceed to extremities, before I have laid the case before Government, I request you will do me the favour to submit this address to His Excellency the Most Noble the Governor General in Council for His Consideration and orders.

Dhurrum Deo is the person mentioned in Captn. J. Browne's descriptuion of the Jungle Terry Page 61.

From what I can learn Dhurrum Deo claims a right and wishes to share the Profits of the Estate with Roopnarain Deo, with whom the settlement was made. The former also holds several tracts of land without paying rent for the same, which the latter prosecuted him for and obtained from my Predecessor a Decree in his favour against which Dhurrum Deo never appealed th'o he now resists the execution of it, and it is entirely owing to the Deholding their just rents that Roopnarain Deo has fallen so much in Balance. Between these Persons and Roopnarain Deo their exists a great enmity so that the Co-operation of the latter will be readily afforded in any vigorous measures that it may be necessary to person.

His Excellency I doubt not will be fully of opinion, that it is neither consistent with the honor or justice of a powerful Government like the present to allow of the authority of the Courts of Justice being set at defiance by apetty Farmer in the heart of the Hon,ble Companys Possessions, who in fact by assembling an armed Force to oppose the execution of the Laws has erected the standard of Rebellion.

I therefore request His Excellency's sanction for persuing the undermentioned measues for the purpose of reducing Dhurrum Deo to obedience, as he is the head of the present refractory confederacy and by proceeding against him, the rest will submit of course, viz.

Ist. To issue a Proclamation requiring this Force to disperse and notifying that any person firing upon or resisting the Officers of Government will be treated Rebels. Also requiring Dhurrum Deo and the other Defendants to surrender themselves on or before a certain Day.

2nd- That in the event of disobedience to the above requisition the Magistrate dispatch a Military Force from the Crops of Hill Rangers to reduce them to obedience and support the authority of the Court and Collector and for that purpose, the Detachment be instructed to fire upon the Insurgents, if opposed.

3rd That Roopnarain Deo be called upon to afford his assistance in cutting off the retreat of the Insurgents.

4th. That the Gautwals under the Magistrate receive orders to the same effect.

The force under Dhurrum Deo and etc. doesnot at present consist of more than 200 Men and his Mud Fort is untenable (having been reconcitred). A Detachment of 150 Men from the Hill Rangers will be equal to the Task. I have no idea that Dhurruim Deo will attempt to withstand them, but rather take to the jungles. Most probably when he finds vigorous steps taken against him, he will surrender as he has every thing to loose and nothing to gain by the contest. He may then be proceeded against as the Regulations direct or Government may please to order. His present opposition arises from bad advice, and idea that the Court is unable to enforce its orders. It becomes necessary to convince him to the contrary, and that illegal opposition will always meet with an adequate punishment.

I request to be honoured with the Commands of His Excellency the Most Noble the Governor- General in Council on the subject of this address as early as possible.

And have the honor to be sir.

ooo

55. Letter

From,

J. Wintle,

Magistrate of Bhagalpur,

To,

G. Dowdeswell,

Secretary to Government in the Judicial Department. 1.

Dated 5th April, 1803.

I have the honor to address you on the 5th ultimo respecting the contumacious conduct of Dhurrum Deo, Runjeet Singh, Mangun Singh and ca. on which I have not yet honoured with the orders of Government.

As these persons have not only disobeyed the summons published agreeable to the Regulations mentioned in the ist Paragraph of my letter of the above mentioned Date, but also resisted the attachment of their Farms by the Collector under the Courts Precept, notified the attachment of their Farms by the Collector under the Courts Precept, notified in the 5th Paragraph of the said letter, it becomes absolutely necessary to act with energy against them in the manner proposed in my former address, otherwise it will be in vain to expect any obedience to be paid to the orders of the Courts of Justice in the Jungle terry part of the district. And as I am credibly informed that Dhurrum Deo is in correspondence and treaty with a Free-booter named. Nawaub Singh, who as the head of about 300 armed Men is infesting the Border of this and the Beerbhoom and Ramghar Districts, no time should be lost in acting against Dhurrum Deo and before they have time to unite wirth Nawaub Sing. The approach of the Rainy Season, if delayed till then, will prevent all vigorous operations. I therefore again beg leave to request that you will solicit the Commands of His Excellency the Most Noble the Governor-General in Council on the subject of my address of the 5th ultimo as speedily as possible.

OOO

56. Letter

From,

G. Dowdeswell,

Secretary to Government in the Judicial Department,

To,

J. Wintle,
Magistrate of Bhagalpur. 2
Dated 11th April, 1803.

I am directed to acknowledge the receipt of your letters of the 5th ultimo and the 5th instant, and to acquaint you that His Excellency the Most Noble the Governor- General in Council approves the measures which you propose to adopt in consequence of the 7th Paragraph of your letter. You are accordingly authorised to carry those measures into effect, previously consulting however with Major Shaw, the officer commanding the corps of Hill Rangers, respecting the strength of the Force which should be employed in reducing Dhurrum Deo and his adherents to obedience.

Should any probability exist of a stronger force being required for the above mentioned service than what can be conveniently furnished from the Corps of Hill rangers, you are desired to apply to the officer Commanding the Troops at Dinapore to have such a party of sepoys in readiness, as may eventually be required.

❍❍❍

57. Letter

From,

T. Shaw,
Major of Hill Rangers Bhagalpur,
Dated 21 April, 1803

To.

James Wintle,
Mangistrate of Zillah Bhagalpur

"I have this moment had the honor to receive your letter of yersterday's and in obedience to the desire contained in it, dispatch my Soobedar and Adjutant Beriar Sing, with a company augmented to 80 Rank and file to apprehend Dhurrun Deo, and his Adherents in resistance to the authority of Government at Durrumpoor, and at the same time,a Jamadar and 20 Rank. and File to act in subordination to Beriar Singh in apprehending Mangun Sing, whose general place of residence, I understand, is at Mundya (Morya in the Map) and on the road to Durrumpoor.

I shall particularly instruct the Soobadar to avoid, if possible, the dffusion of human blood in this the execution of self-defence,should the several persons mentioned in your letter being seized, whom you have desired to be apprehended.

From the information which I have been able to Obtain, I conclude the above mentioned Detachments will be fully adequate to the duty required of them, and I hope it will be effected without the loss of life.

I will instruct the Soobadar on the points contained in your letter, and have the pleasure to assure you, that I have full confidence on the peaceful Ryots and inhabititants of the country being perfectly safe from any molestation or injury in the conduct of the Rangers.

OOO

58. Letter

From,

J. Wintle,

Magistrate of Bhagalpur,

To,

G. Dowdeswell,

Secretary to Government in the Judicial Department. 4

Dated 10th May,1803.

In consequence of the authority Government of the 11th ultimo to send a Military Force against Dhurrum Deo, Mungun

Sing and etc. to reduce them to obedience[4], I consulted with Major Shaw commanding the Corps of Hill Rangers as to the Force necessary for that purpose, when after due consideration we were of opinion that 100 Rank and File were fully sufficient, but that with the view to prevent if possible any effusion of Blood, and these refractory Persons from making any preparation for defence, it would be adviseable to March the Detachment to Dhurrum as secretly as possible previous to issuing the Proclamation proposed in the 7th Pargraph of my letter under date the 5th March, last. A Detachment of 100 Men was accordingly sent off on the 17th ultimo at night. The Hill Sezawul was ordered to assemble 200 of the Gutwally Paykes, and after securing the Ghauts to proceed them to Dhurrumpore. The Zamindar Roopnarain Deo was instructed to send a hundred Pykes to Jumday to join the Detachment on the 18th at Night and to proceed with it to Dhurrum Deo's Mud Fort. He was also directed to send the remainder of his Pykes during the Night to surround the Mud Fort at a distance, and prevent the escape of the Male contents until the arrival of the Detachment which was directed to invest the Mud Fort at Day-break of the 19th and then to issue the Proclamation with which the Adjutant was charged requiring Dhurrum Deo to surrender immediately, and the other Persons in three Days. But owing to the distance from Bhagulpore (20 Coss) which took the Detachment 2 Nights to accomplish, **and the want of co-operation on the part of the Zemindar Roopnarain Deo,** the Enemy got previous intelligence of the approach of the Troops, and at 3 O'clock on the morning of the 19th evacuated the Mud Fort and made their escape to the Jungles. Altho' the Detachment reached Mud Fort at Day-break. A second Proclamation was therefore issued by me allowing a further period of ten Days for their surrender, at the expiration of which finding that none of the Malecontents availed themselves of it and that no intelligence could be obtained of the place of their retreat (for to search for them through the Jungle

Terry People, which was solicited in vain) I thought it prudent to recall the Detachment after securing such of their property as could be found which is but trifling. Considering the heat and unhealthiness of the season and in a Jungle country under all the circumstances of the Case, I hope his Excellency the Most Noble the Goveror- General in Council will approve of my having recalled the Troops.

The failure of the attempt to secure Dhurrum Deo and etc, was in agreat measure owing to the want of Co-operation on the part of the Zemindar Roopnarain Deo, for whose ignorance and wild manners however some allowance is to be made. On the same grounds I am enduced to recommend rather lenient measures in regard to those misled persons who have so foolishly shewn a disobedience to Government. I therefore only propose as punishment for their offences, that His Excellency will be pleased to authoroize the Zemindar to annul the Losses of their farms, which they have justly forfeited by their Misconduct. Dhurrum Deo (their Leader) has besides been fined by the Court in the Sum of 4000, Rupees for resisting its authority. These Punnishment will perhaps be sufficient to ensure their good behaviour in future.

OOO

59. Letter

From,

Acting magistrate of Beerbhum,

To,

J. Wintle,
Magistrate of Bhagalpur.
Dated 16th June,1803

'In continuation of the late acting Magistrate 's letter to you of the 14th February last regarding the depredations committed by Nawab Sing and Kripal Singh, I have now the pleasure to enclose you a publication issued by order of His Excellency the Most Noble the Governor- General in Council offering a reward of **300 rupees for Nawab Sing and 200 Rupees for Kirpal Sing**. I have to request you will take every step to give the same the utmost publicity and at the same time to issue strict orders to your police offcers and the different Landholders bordering on Tuppa Sarhut Deoghur cautionoing them to be careful that these men find no asylum within your jurisdiction (which) there is no doubt but that they will attempt in nay difficulty. I have deputed a Havildar and twelve Sepahees to assist the police officers in their apprehension and I will thank you to order yours in case of emergency to afford them every assistance.

ooo

60. Letter

From,

T. shaw,
Major Commanding,Hill Rangers, Bhagalpur,
Dated 11 July, 1803

To,

James Wintle
Magistrate of Zillah Bhagalpur

"Pursuant to your directions in your letter of the 7th instant,I sent an order to recall the party from the old fort of Durrumpoor, at the same time as I had ordered it, consisting of 1 Jamadar and 30 Rank and File with one Drummer, to remain there, in consequence of an application from Thakoor Roop Narain Deo who represented to me, that if such a party were not left, the Refractory Petty Chiefs who had so long triumphantly .... the authority of your court, and contumaciously done the collectors officers away with, would return, raise their adherents,prevent cultivation by intimidating the Ryots and plunder the country, which they might effectually do, without fear of opposition, and securely deposit their plunder in the extensive and thick Jungle. Where they are supposed to be now lurking. I wrote to Thakoor Roop Narain Deo to acquaint him of your instructions to withdraw the party,that he might take such measure as he thought proper to relieve the rangers and secure the old Fort at Durrumpoor, and recommended,should he consider their continuance absolutely necessary,to state the necessity in an application to you. I also wrote to the jamadar to deliver up his post to Roop Narain Deo's people and to remain a few days should the Thakoor require it.

Herewith I have the honour to forward copy of an application which I received this morning from Thakoor Roop Narain Deo and beg leave to offer my opinion that the party should continue at Dhoorumpur for the purposes set forth in it. Their Sirdars are not wanted by him, and they would be mischief, which any force however great,from the nature of the country, might not be able to remedy hereafter. I have the pleasure to add that the party now near three months at Durrumpore are very healthy. "

OOO

61. Letter

From,

T. Shaw,
Major Commanding Hill Rangers,Bhagalpur,
Dated 12 July, 1803

To,

James Wintle,
Maglistrate Zillah of Bhagalpur.

"As I do not pretend to determine whether a discretionary authority rests in me to leave the Party at Durrumpore,having given my opinion and reason to your that their remaining there for the pursuit is for the good of the service, while I am not bound with any in return but a repetition of your order. I have submitted our correspondence to Government,and requested to be honoured with the orders Excellency the most noble the Governor General in council thereon. I have also reported that the Party shall be recalled, and vacated Durrumpore the moment Thakur Roop Narain Deo's people may relieve it arder.......... . Effect are now given. "

ooo

62. Letter

From,

.... (Illegible),

Fort William, dated 15 July, 1803

To,

James Wintle,

Magistrate of Zillah Bhagalpur.

With a view to obviate the deteriment which must necessarily result to the efficiency and discipline of the regular corps of the army from being dispered in small detachments throughout the country. His Excellency the Most Noble the Governor General in Council considers it to be proper to direct that all Detachments employed for the purposes of the Police within the District under your charge should be ordered to return to Head quarters,as soon as they can be withdrawn without endangering the peace and security of the country.

2. His Excellency in Council however desirous of ascertaining your sentiments with regard to any measures which it may be expedient to adopt for securing the peace and tranquinity of the District in the event of the means with which you are already

furnished for securing that important object appearing to be insufficient in consequence of any regular Troops being withdrawn from the district directs me to desire that you will submit with the least possible delay your report and opinion on the following points.

First, Whether the Police Establishments at present entertained by Government are adequate to the local purposes for which they are required.

Second, In the event of your deeming an addition to the present police establishments to be indispensibly necessary,what addition you would propose to be made to them and in what manner you would recommend the expense to be defrayed.

1.) You will accompany your Report with whatever further Information you may possess, connected with the points now referred to you,or with the general security of your District.

4.) If any peculiar circumstances should require the continuance of any detachments now stationed at out –Posts in the District under your charge you will immediately report the same for the orders of Government. His Excellency **in Council at the same time relies on your precedence and discretion in not employing any regular Troops except in cases of real emergency,**which from the present state of the country are not likely to occur.

5.) His Excellency in Council has it in contemplation to place the sebundy corps throughout the Provinces or an improved establishment; and you will understand the intention of the Governnor General in Council to be rest the internal peace and good order of the British Possessions on the foundations of the just and benevolent system of Government established in the Provinces, and of a sufficient Police, the united operation of which, causes combined with the vicinity of considerable military force assembled at the several Cantonments and stations appears to the Governor General in Council to promise the maintanece of tranquility under any circumstances which may occur. Any Civil officer whose application to the Military Power shall interfere with the due execution of the proposed system will be required to furnish the most ample and satisfactory reasons for any deviation from the principles herein prescribed. "

OOO

63. Letter

From,

W. Spending,
Acting Magistrate, Zillah Beerbhoom, Fouzdaree Adwlat,
Dated the 15 July, 1803

To,

George Dodeswell,
Secretary to Government in the Judicial Department.

"On the 30th of May I had the honor to transmit to you for the information of his Excellency the Most Noble the Governor-General in Council, intelligence of the disturbances which had occurred in Tuppah Sarhut Deoghur,headed by Newaub Sing and KirpalSing, two Ghatwals of that place, and in compliance with His Excellency orders contained in your reply. I offered the rewards therein authorized and took every step I thought calculated to ensure their apprehension.

On the 6th instant,a design was formed by the Daroga in conjunction with the Millitary detachment to surprise these men in their retreat in the Jungles, in the excecuting which, a general action took place between them, **many of the insurgents are said to have been killed and wounded, seven Burkundazes were wouned on the Darogah, Nawaub Sing and his party retreated into the Jungles,** and the Darogah got possession of his house the strength of his party neither enabled him to retain his position purse (for) his advantage.

The state of the detachment at Soory had before rendered it necessary to the party at Deoghur from a Jemadar and 20 rank and file to a Havildar and 12, and the Darogah reports **that without a large reinforcement nothing further can be attempted with any prospect of success, the whole force at Soory not on duty are but 50 Rank** and file, and Deoghur being 15 days march from this, I cannot advise their being detached, neither do I believe the force would then be adequate, as Newaub do I believe the force **would then be adequate,as Newaub Sing has assembled some assisted by many of the Gautwals in this district, as well as in Ramghur and Bhagalpoor.**

Deoghur being nearer Bhagalpoor than this, it occurs to me that the measure best calculated to succed would be the affording the assistance of a Detachment from the Hill Rangers, and should the state of that Battalion admit of it, I would recommend a strong party under an intelligent Subadar being sent thereof at least 80 Rank and file.

Should this proposition meet with His Excellency's approbation, I would advise that the office in command should be placed solely under the orders of the Magistrate of this Zillah, that he should be empowered to issue parwanahs to the different Daroghas in this District as well as in Ramghur and Bhagalpure, that the Magistrates of those Districts should be apprised of his being detached, and of the power vested in him, and directed to afford him every assistance.

As to increasing the rewards which have been offered, I do not think, at present that it would be attended with must advantage, and I would recommend that they should remain as they are, till it is seen how the detachment succeeds.

The Hill Rangers I should think better calculated to act with effect than the regulars among the Jungles and Hill in that part of the country, and I trust if this step meets with His Excellency's approbation than these outrages will soon be put end to. "

ooo

64. Letter

From,

G. Dowdeswell,

Secretary to Government in the Judicial Department,

To,

J. Wintle,

Magistrate of Bhagalpur. 1.

Dated 21st July,1803

The Commandant of the Corps of Hill rangers at Bhagulpore having submitted to government his correspondence with you respecting the continuance of Detachment at Durrumpore, I am directed to inform you that under the circumstances stated by that officer. His excellency the Most Noble the Governor- General in Council has been pleased to approve Major Shaws proposition for continuing at present a party of the Hill Rangers at Durrumpore, for the purpose of preserving the peace of the Country against any incursions whch may be attempted by Dhurrum Deo, or the other refractory Talookdars of Roopnaraion Deo, the Zemindar of Chundapaswai.

1 (Enclosure no. 3.)

To,

George Dowdeswell Esqr. ,

Secretary to Government in the Judicial Department, Fort William

Sir,

On the 30th of May I had the honor to transmit to you for the information of His Excellency the Most Noble the Governor-General in Council intelligence of the disturbances which had occurred in **Tuppah Sarhut Deog**hur, headed **by Newaub**

singh and Kirpal Singh, two Gatwals of that place, and in compliance with His Excellency's orders contained in your reply, I offered the rewards therin authorized, and took every step, I thought calculated to ensure their apprehension.

On the 6th Instant, a desigh was formed by the Darogah in conjunction with the Military detachment to surprize these men in their retreat in the Jungles, in the executing which, a general action took place between them, many of the insurgents are said to have been killed and wounded, seven Burkundazes were wounded on the side of the Darogah, Newaub Sing and his party retreated into the Jungles, and the Darogah got possession of his house the strength of his party neither enabled him to retain his position nor pursue his advantages.

The state of the Detachment at Soory had before rendered it necessary to)reduce) the party at Deoghar from a Jemadar and 20 rank and file to a Havildar and 12, and the Darogah reports that without a large reinforcement nothing further can be attempted with any prospect of success, the whole force at Soory not on duty are but 50 Rank and file, and Deoghur being 15 days march from this, I cannot advise their being detached, neither do I believe the force would then be adequate, as Newaub Singh has assembled some hundred adherent, and is reported to be secretly assisted by many of the Gautwals in this district, as well as in Ramghur and Bahgalpoor.

Deoghur being nearer to Bagalpor than this, it occurs to we that the measure best calculated to succeed would be the affording the assistance of a Detachment from the Hill Rangers, and should the state of that Battalion admit of it, I would recommend a strong party under an intelligent Subadar being sent thereof at least 80 Ranks and file.

Should this proposition meet with his Excellency's approbation, I would advise that the office in command should be placed solely under the orders of the Magistrate of this Zillah, that he should be empowered to issue parwanahs to the different

Darogahs in this District as well as in Ramghur and Bhaglepure, that the Magistrate of those Districts should be apprised of his being detained, and of the power vested in him, and directed to affored him every assistance.

As to increasing the rewards which have been offered, I do not think, at present that it would be attended with much advantage, and I would recommend that they should remain as they are, till it is seen how the detachment succeeds.

The Hill Rangers I should think better calculated to act with effect than the regulars among the Jungles and Hills in that part of the country, and I trust if this step meets with His Excellency's approbation than these outrages will soon be put end to.

Zillah Beerbhoom Fouzdaree Adwalut,
The 15th July, 1803
I have the honor to the
(Signed) W. SPENDING Acting Magistrate

OOO

65. Letter

From,

J. Wintle,
Magistrate of Bhagalpur,

To,

G. Dowdeswell,
Secretary to Government in the Judicial Department. 1
Dated 27th July,1803.

I have the honor to acknowledge the receipt of your letter of the 21st Instant informing me that under the circumstances stated by the Commandant of Hill Rangers. His Excellency the Most Noble the Governor- General in Council has been pleased to approve of Major Shaws proposition for continuing at present a party of the hill Rangers at Dhurrumpore, for the purpose of preserving the peace of the Country against any incursions which may be attempted by Dhurrum Deo, or the orther refractory Talookdars of Roopnarayan Deo, the zemindar of Chundapassye.

I humbly conceive that the Commandants reference to Government ought to have been made through me agreeable to the established custom of the service, that I might had an opportunity of stating my sentiments also to His Excellency, instead of His orders being solicited on a partial representation, but as this was not the case and I am unacquainted with its contents, I am compelled to offer some Comments posteriorly, on what I cannot but consider an improper interference in the Duties of the Magistrate by the Commandant of the hill Rangers.

In consequence of the authority of Government a Detachment of 100 Men was sent **to Dhurrumpore on the 19th April**, last against Dhurrum Deo and the refractory Talookdars, the Hill Sezawal with 200 Gautwally Pykes afterwards joined them at that place, and the Zemindar Roopnarain Deo and ca. and preventing their escape. The latter, however, they effected through the negligence of the Zemindar and tho ' the whole Detachment remained at Dhurrumpore upwards of three weeks not the smallest intelligence could be obtained of them. The Hill Sezawal personally wanted on the zemindar desiring him to point out where the Fugitives were but it appeared very evident from his conduct that his object was to evade any interference, as he stated that he had sent five or six persons only in search, and that the continuance of the Detachment in the Mofussil had caused the ryats and ca. Inhabitants to desert, and would be of great injury to the Country. In fact so much was the zemindar alarmed that he sent off his Wife and Family with the greatest part of his Force to a strong hold near Puree, instead of employing the latter in the apprehension of the Fugitives, and was preparing himself to follow them. The Zemindar's Vakeel personally solicited me to recall the Detachment, and Major Shaw likewise represented the alarm the zemindar was under from the presence of the Troops, and advised their recall. Seeing there was no chance of apprehending Dhurrum Deo and from the want of co-operation on the part of the zemindar, who had throughout the Business observed the most supine and evasive Conduct, I consented to withdraw the Detachment, and directed Major Shaw to leave a Party of 30 to take care of the Grain, etc. found on Dhurrum Deo's premises until it was publicly sold by the Court in satisfaction of the Decresss passed against him. The sale took place on the 8th May,and I naturally supposed that the remaining Party had been withdrawn on delivering over the Grain to the Purchaser. But about two months after I accidently learnt that the Party were still at Dhurrumpore. On hearing this I applied to the Commandant (Major Shaw) to know if this was the case, who two days after personally informed me that he had kept them at the desire of the zemindar. I observed that there was now no occasion for their stay, and that I should send him an order to recall them. Not wishing to take any notice of his having kept the party out near two months beyond the time I had desired, merely on his own authority and without ant intimation to me of the Zemindars asserted application I merely sent him an order (vide accomapnyment) to withdraw it. In answer to this (vide) altho' he stated that he had issued the necessary instructions for the recall of the party, yet mentioned that he had recommended the Zemindar to apply to me for its continuance, and at the same time enclosed a copy the zemindars application to that effect. The Zemindar had the same Day made an application to me in the exact Words of that addressed to Major Shaw (vide Original & ca. Translate) but it being out stamp Paper as required by the Regulations, and otherwise irregular and inadmissible as will be presently shown, I did not issue any order on it, but simply repeated my Instructions of the 7th Instant to the Commandant to recall the Detachment (Vide D) considering that any explanation in reply to his letter be useless after the authority he had assumed, and the method he had used to counteract my first Order.

I must observe that it is rather extraodinary the Zemindar who has an armed Force at his Command of 7 or 8000 Matchlocks and full as much beloved and respected by the Inhabitants and Ryots of the Pergunnah as Dhurrum Deo & ca. who, were they all unanimous could not muster a force of more than half that number, should feel so sudden an alarm about their return when he did not interest himself in the smallest degree to secure them at the time, the Detachment was sent on his application, altho' it is notorious to every one (Major Shaw excepted) that he is not only at all times able to apprehend and secure them, but must have known & ca still does were they are secreted, on the contrary his greatest anxiety was to get the Detachment withdrawan and made application through his vakeel and Major Shaw to me for that purpose. But he has magically found out that the Detachment he so much dreaded is to be of wonderful service to him. These pretended alarms of Roopnarayan Deo & ca. the Commandant of the hill Rangers are on the very face of them evidently absurd, for it Dhurrum Deo's Party are so insignificant (which has been fully proved) as to be kept in awe by thirty Mountaineers, whom Major Shaw will not I presume pretend to say possess more courage than the People of the jungleterry it follows that the Zemindar with 7 or 800 armed Men can have nothing to fear from them while he is authorized to repel their attacks. If on the contrary he has grounds to fear their force, the present Detachment is insufficient to keep the Country in peace, but this is contrary to the fact fully established. His application (Vide Original) gives room for suspicion that the Commandant was the Instigater of it. The latter part clearly shows the zemindar has no ill will towards or fear of Dhurrum Deo & ca. it is equally surprizing that the Commandant of Hill Rangers who strongly interested himself in favour of the Zemindar to get the Detachment recalled and as I have reason to believe about that time wrote to the Commander-in-Chief that the corps of Hill Rangers were not calculated for such a service as then sent upon should now assert that they cannot be so well employed elsewhere.

I have strong grounds to believe it never was the Zemindar wish or intention to push the Business against Dhurrum Deo & Co. so far as it it has gone, and that his vakeel not only exceeded his instructions in soliciting the aid of Militry Force, but also misled the Court by stating Dhurrum Deo's Force far beyond the number, it consists of in fact a single man not hitherto made his appearance or faced even the 30 Mountaineers. This is more fully proved by the Zemindar's vakeel having purchased the whole of Dhurrum Deo's property sold at Public auction, with the avoiwed intent of giving it back to Dhurrum Deo.

But admitting that there was any ground for alarm from Dhurrum Deo's party which I trust I have shewn there is not any application from the zemindar for aid, is irregular and unadmissible and what he had no right to make as he had nothing to do with the Collections or Cutivation of the Lands either at the time he is said to have applied to Major Shaw, or at the present. The whole of the Estate is under attachment by the Collector, and any support required must be applied for by him to the Magistrate. But no such application has been made by him. As far Dhurrum Deo & Co. returning and impeding the Cultivation. I have to observe that there is none to impede the Crops have been sown some time ; and at the end of the Fussily year now nearly expired before the harvest can arrive the whole of (Dhurrum Deo's & Co.). Leasos will have been annulled by the collector agreeable to 7th Clause, 15th Section, 7th Regulation of 1799, in consequence of their failing in their engagements. If they afterwards resort to plunder which it is hardly to be supposed they will attempt after witnessing the late steps taken against them by Government, they will of course be proceeded against accordingly. But such a step the Zemindar has more than sufficient force to prevent aided by the Police, and if he is so supine as not to assist in defence of his just authority, I cannot see any possible necessity for Government to take any further trouble in His Family disputes, further than to preserve the Peace, which the Magistrate will adopt the necessary measures to do on any attempt to disturb it. The Commandant of Hill rangers has set forth the contumacy of these refractory petty, Chiefs towards the Courts of justice and collector as ground for his propositions. The latter can at all times legally punish such contumacy without the interference of the Commandant.

With the utmost respect towards His Excellency, I beg leave to submit for His consideration the serious ill consequences that must result from the Commandant of Hill Rangers or any other Person being authorized to carry on secret Correspondence with the Zemindaars, and to circumvent and act in opposition to the Orders issued by the Courts either Civil or Criminal. Such a measure must naturally tend to create doubt and uncertainly in the mind of the Magistrate as to the line of his Duty and cramp his exertions. It must more particulary tend to Weaken that obedience and respect in the natives to the Ordres of the Courts of justice (especially in the Natives of the Jungie Terry Who have never been over obedient) Which Government for so many year have been endeavouring to inculcate and must Confuse and prefiex the inhabitants, and make them unable to discover to Whom they are to look for redress of oppression or injustice, When they see an officer acting under the order of the Magistrate setting aside His instructions and publicly authorized to circumvent them. In short it must tend to Weaken that foundation upon which His Excellency wishes to rest the British Government in India as stated in the Chief secretary to the Government Letter of the 15th Instant.

But even if the necessity by Major Shaw had been made out, which I am fully of opinion there is not a shadow of Ground for, on principals of Policy, the continuance of the Detachment at Dhurrumpore is at this time very objectionable. It drives the misled Men (Dhurrum Deo & Co.) from their habitations shuts the Door against Repentance, and from necessity may compel them to join Nawab and Herpaul sing who have been plundering and ravaging the Beerbhoom District, and for whoseapprehension Government have advertised a large reward, and thus organize a formidable Band of Insurrection and Plunder in the heart of the Hon'ble Companys territories, at a time when the utmost exertions of Government may be required to cope with and repel a more formidable Enemy. I foresee much more Mischief likely to arise from the continuance of the Detachment at Dhurrumpore, than can possibly happen from its absence, and I therefore earnestly recommend that His Excellency may be pleased to instruct Major Shaw to withdraw !

I request you will submit this address to His Excellency the Most noble the Governor- General in Council, with my apologies for occupying so much of His time.

ooo

66. Letter

From,

J. Wintle,
Magistrate of Bhagalpur,

To,

G. Dowdeswell,
Secretary to Government in the Judicial Department. 1
Dated 1st August, 1803

I have honor to acknowledge the receipt of your letter of the 21st ultimo enclosing copy of a letter from the Acting Magistrate of Beerbhoom, and desiring I will report (after communicating on the subject with Major Shaw) whether a Detachment of Hill Rangers can be employed without inconvenience, and with a reasonable prospect of success, on the service suggested by the Acting Magistrate of Beerbhoom.

Herewith I have the honor to forward a copy of Major Shaw a reply to my letter by which His Excellency the Most Noble the Governor-General in Council will observe that as Detachment of the strength specified can be furnished without inconvenience. But unless there is probability of Nawaub Singh & ca. standing the attack of such a force (which I doubt) I think there will be little prospect of success at this season of the year, when the country is half covered with water, and the foliage of the Jungles in that part of the country so stick as to afford the insurgents a secure retreat against any search, and should the Detachment not immediately fall in with the robbers, the unhealthiness of the atmosphere in the Jungle Terry would soon render them sickly, and unfit for service. If the expedition is delayed until the breaking up of the rains, the Detachment may then march with every prospect of success and without any apprehension of those inconveniences which at the present season are likely to occur.

OOO

67. Letter

From,

J. Wintle,

Magistrate of Bhagalpur,

To,

G. Dowdeswell,

Secretary to Government in the Judicial Department. 2

Dated 2nd August, 1803

I have the honor to acknowledge the receipt of your letter of the 21st ultimo accompanied by a copy of a letter and enclosure from the Board of Revenue and informing me that His Excellency the Most Noble the Governor- general in Council desire I will furnish the Regulating officer of the Invalid Tannahs with thirty convicts accompanied by their proper proportion of guards to assist in the repair of the embankment in the Invalid Tannahjs & ca.

I request you will represent of His Excellency that the number of prisoners that should be employed in making the high road through this district, which is of the utmost importance to the public and particularly to the Hon'ble Company's Army, which all from time to time passes through the Districts, is already greatly diminished by the convicts allowed by Government as follows viz-

Major Shaw	20
D. Glass	30
Monghir Garrison	50
	110

And

That if an additional number of 30 is to be allowed to Captain Wilton, it will be attended with much greater inconvenience, than any benefit that can be derived from their labor in the Invalid Tannahs, scattered as the latter are over an extent of country of 80 milies where it is impossible for Captain Wilton to superintend them, and being removed from the control of the Magistrate little or no work would be done by them. It is evident that five times the number would not be sufficient for the purpose required by captain Wilton. I humbly conceive it never was the intention of Government that the Invalids should sit with their hands before them like gentlemen. It is surely their duty or that of their Ryots to repair any embankments that may be necessary about their respective Tannahs and lands, but I am sorry to say that instead of being of service to the State in clearing waste lands as was expected, they have hitherto, for want of proper management, I suppose, been an injury to it by enticing away the ryots from the revenue lands to carry on their cultivation while they themselves lead the most indolent lives. Should His Excellency not withstanding, think it proper to allow Captain Wilton the proposed number of convicts, I take the liberty to request that some of the neighbouring Magistrates may be directed to furnish me with 100 convicts, to enable me to and him the number ordered, as the regular Releases from the jail far exceed the Convictions, and in a short time the public works must be put stop to, if Government think it necessary to furnish different individuals with convicts.

I hope His Excellency will allow to recall to his recollection the number of roads about the town & ca., of Bhagulpore, that continually require repair. the extensive high road through the District my predecessor was instructed to make, and which I am carrying on. The necessity for clearing the passes of Sirccragully, Terriagully and Gungapersaid of the Jungle that confines, the road on each side in those places, particularly at Shahabad where the Hon'ble Company's treasure was plundered to the amount of 22,000 rupees and where most of the robberies and murders in this Zillah, are perpetrated in the utmost security, from the retreat and asylum those thick Jungles afford, and He will be convinced that these are objects of for more public importance, and utility than the one suggested by Captain Wilton and must require that can be spared. The latter improvements I am very desirous to carry into execution with a view to the further security of the Districts, and of travellers from robbery and murder, but if the Magistrate's hands are tied up by the convicts being taken out of his charge, the plan of improving and rendering the high road through the Districts safe and passable had better to abandoned. It has been completed to Colgong, and the prisoners are now clearing the Jungle in that neighbourhood and working on towards Pialapore clearing the Jungle near the road as they proceed.

I request you will submit this address to His Excellency the Most Noble the Governor-General in Council for his consideration and orders.

OOO

68. Letter

From,

G. Dowdeswell,

Secretary to Government in the Judicial Department,

To,

J. Wintle,

Magistrate of Bhagalpur. 2

Dated 11th August, 1803

I am directed to acknowledge the receipt of your letter of the is instant, and to acquaint you that His Excellency the Most Noble the Governor-General in Council on a consideration of the circumstances stated by you and Major Shaw, is of opinion that instead of employing a Detachment of Hill Rangers at present, with a view to the apprehension of Nawaub Sing, and other, it would be advisable to suspend that measure until the cold season, when the Detachment will be able to act with greater probability of success, and the least possible injury from sickness.

2. The foregoing remark will be communicated to the Magistrate of Beerbhoom with directions to consult with you the period of time most eligible for the march of the Detachment.

OOO

69. Letter

From,

J. Wintle,

Magistrate of Bhagalpur,

To,

J. Lumsden,

Secretary to Government in the Judicial Department. 1.

Dated 15th August, 1803

I have the honor o acknowledge the receipt to Government's order of the 15th ultimo respecting the employ to Detachments from the regular Corps for the purpose of Police, a nd the efficiency of the Police Establishment.

2. I have the pleasure to state that no Detachments from the regular Corps are at present employed in this Zillah, but deeming the present Police Establishment inadequate to the local duties of the District, I shall proceed to reply to the other points alluded to in your letter.

2. That the Police Establishment at present is insufficient, particulary for the protection of the borders of the Districts near the Ganges, and the numerous traders & ca. con. continually proceeding up and down the latter, I have not only experienced in the official discharge of my duty, but the fact has been supported and frequently represented to Government by my predecessor Mr. Fombell, and fully so in his letter of the 2nd September 800. Guard boats are undoubtedly necessary to accomplish that security it being a common practise for gangs of Dakoits to come across the river in boats from the eastern side and rob and plunder the country on the western shore, as well as boats proceeding up and down the river which they are enabled to do with the greatest facility, from there being no force to oppose them. In case of alarm they immediately take to their boats, and are presently out of the reach of the Police officers, I have lately seized a gang of 53 of this description. I am therefore decidedly of opinion that four

guards boats to be stationed at Rajamehal, Pointy, Bhagulpore and Monghyr are absolutely necessary for the full protection of the trade the country and the inhabitants on each side of the Ganges.

The expence of which is estimated as follows viz. -

1 Manjy-5

I Goliah-4

10 Dandies @ Rs-. 3 each -30

I Naik- 7

4- Sepoys @ Rs. 4 ans. 8 each -18

Total -Rs 64.

- Boats at Rs. 64 per mensem Deduct -256
- Establishment of the present guard 71

boat at Rajmehl ————————

Sa Rs. 185

4th. The Rajmehl guard boat is at present only furnished with Burkundazes, who are not the least calculated for such a duty. The guard boat is also a hired one, and unfit for such a service. They should be of the same kind and dimensions as those used at Dacca or Backergunge. The probable expense of getting four such made at Sylhet and transported to this station perhaps be about 150 Rupees each or Sa Rs. 600 for the four.

5th. A small Police Chowkey at Suffiabad is also absolutely necessary, that places being in a lonely stuation near the Curruckpore Hills but on the high road to Patna and where most travellers stop for rest, who are frequently robbed. The expence of which will be as follows viz. -

1 Jemantdar. .	8
4 Burkundazes. .	16
Saks.	24 per mensen

6th. To secure the peace and tranqulity of the District under any circumstances that may occur, I conceive some alterations in the Corps of Hill Rangers are necessary. At present it consists of too great a proportion of hill people to the Hindoostannies. The former the good Parade soldiers, want an example and stimulus to rise them into activity, and make them what soldiers is ought to be. They invariably fall asleep on guard, and are otherwise negligent when off the Parade, and from the greater part not understanding any but his own language, are totally unfit for sentinels at the Magistrate's cutcherry & ca. as they do not comprehend any orders given to them. Beyond the usual phrases of command consequently in case of sudden danger, they would afford little protection to the Magistrate or any other person about of the presence of their Commander. The due proportion I think to be about one- third Hindostannies to two-thirds of Hill People, by which they would be properly mixed, and at all times have companions to emulate, and to lead them to the proper discharge of their duty, and such a Corps would probably be equal at all times to the defence of the Districts, which I doubt its being at present. On this point however Major Shaw, the Commandant, will be better able to state the exact alterations are requisite.

7th In the event of probable attack from an enemy, such as the Mahrattas, for example I think the invalids of the different Tannahs (who are able) should be called upon to defend the Districts near their respective Tannahs, by Parading Mounting Guard & ca. And that the Regulating Officer of that establishment should be instructed to prepare list of such men as may be equal to that duty ; the number and description of private arms, weapons, & ca. they can muster both to protect the Rybts of the neighbouring villages and defend themselves. The Ghautwalls must of course be called upon to act with vigour at their respective stations.

8th With a view to defray the expence of the proposed additional Police Establishment, as well as generally to inform the system of Police, by throwing obstacles in the way of the commission of crimes I am of opinon that some restraint should to put on Bankers, Shroffs, Gold and Silversmiths and Braziers, who are well known to be the purchasers of stolen goods, such as jewels, ornammens, brass pots & ca. for the obtainment of which articles, robberies and thefts are most frequently committed and probably Dakoits and thieves are very often set on and aided by these descriptions of persons to carry on their depredations. There can be truth more clear than that there would be very little theft and robbery were there no receivers of stolen goods, and the axiom applies as much to this country as to Europe. The restraint I propose is similar to that on retailers of spirituous liquors viz,-

1st–That every Banker, shroffs Gold and Silversmiths and Brazier be obliged to take out a licence annually on stamped paper for the exercise of his profession or trade, under the seal and signature of the Magistrate. The respective stamps to be of the value! of Rs. 8, Rs. 6, Rs. 4 and Rs. 2

2nd–That each of the abovementioned persons enter into an obligation an give a responsible security, that they will on no account purchase jewels, ornaments of silver gold or brass or utensils of copper or brass, from any person whatever, but in the presence of the Police Cutwals, Darogahs, or the Munsiffs of the respective jurisdictions, under penalty of Rs. 200 Rs. 150, Rs. 100 or Rs. 50, for every time they may make such prohibited purchases.

3rd–That person of the said profession or trades, purchasing any of the articles above specified which may be proved to have been stolen, or from a person of bad character knowing him to be so shall be sentenced by the Magistrate to six months impresnment and hard labor on the public roads.

4th–That no person be allowed to exercise the profession or trade of Banker Shroff, Gold and Silversmith or Brazier in any town or village but those who take out the prescribed licence, excepting as journeymen or workmen to Licenced Bankers & ca.

5th–That Licenced Bankers & ca. be made answerable for the conduct of their journeymen, working in their shops only, and shall not allow the latter to work for them at their own houses under the penalty specified in Article 2nd.

6th–That any person exercising the trades or professions above specified on his own account without a licence or purchasing any of the articles above specified provided he is of the above trades or professions, or otherwise without previously notifying his intention to the Culwal, Darogah or Munsiff of the Division, and producing the purchaser before one of those Officers) shall pay a fine of Rs. 100, Rs. 75, Rs. 50 or Rs. 25, or in default of payment be committed to confinement and hard labor for six months.

7th–That any person melting down gold silver, copper or brass for another person without a licence, or without previously producing before the Cutwal, & ca. the person at whose request he proposes to melt down such gold silver & ca. be committed to (hard) labor and confinement for six months.

8th–That any person being desirous of disposing of jewels, gold, silver or brass ornaments, copper or brass utensils, to any other persons than the Licenced Traders & ca. give previously notice to the Police Cutwal, Darogah & ca. in failure of which to be fined or imprisoned at the discretion of the Magistrate to the amount or for the period above specified.

9th–That unlicenced persons to whom any of the above articles may be offered for sale, although they do not actually purchase them be required immediately to report the seller to the Police Cutwal, Darogah & ca. under pain of being fined for such negligence.

10th–That the Magistrate keep a Register of all licences granted, specifying the name of the person and place, where any of the above proffesions or trades are authorized to be carried on.

11th–That the Police Officers apprehend all persons acting in opposition to these rules and forward them to the Magistrate.

12th–That informers be allowed a moitve of all fines on convictions levied under these rules.

13th–That person licenced as above hang up aboard over their door, specifying their profesion or trade, and being so licenced.

14th–The above rules, tho' but roughly sketched will shew His Excellency the object I have in view. The rates of the licences may be increased or diminished as may appear adviseable.

15th–In conclusion I shall only add that I shall always be cautious in requiring the aid of regular troops, where I can possibly do without their services.

ooo

70. Letter

From,
G. Dowdeswell,
Chief Secretary to Government

To,
J. Wintle,
Magistrate of Bhagalpur. 2
Dated 22nd September,1803

His Excellency the Most Noble the Governor- General in Council having received information that the business of the public service has been considerably impeded from the delay and difficulty experienced in obtaining Mangies and dandies to conduct boats laden with public stores for the Upper Provinces, and from attempts made by persons of that description to desert they had engaged, I am directed to acquaint you that His Excellency in Council has been pleased to desire you will furnish the Officers in charge of boats employed on the public service with every assistance in obtaining Mangies and Dandies, and in providing for the faithful discharge of the duty which those persons may undertake to perform.

ooo

71. Letter

From,

J. Wintle,

Magistrate of Bhagalpur,

To,

T. H. Ernst,

Magistrate of Beerbhoom. 2.

Dated 13th October, 1803

On the 15th July last the Acting Magistrate of Beerbhoom recommended that Detachment of Hill Rangers should be employed under his orders, in reducing Nawaub Sing and Kirpaul sing to obedience but on account of the rains His Excellency in Council was pleased to direct on the 11th august, that the measure be suspended until the cold season. The rains being now at an end the roads dry and passable the detachment can march whenever you wish. I therefore request you will inform me when and to what place they are to march that the necessary orders may be issued to the Commandant of Hill Rangers.

OOO

72. Letter

From,

J. Wintle,

Magistrate of Bhagalpur,

To,

H. Pary,

Acting Magistrate of Beerbhoom. 1.

Dated 12th November, 1803

I beg leave to acknowledge the receipt of your letter of the 29th ultimo, with its enclosures. The letter does not contain any information that can be of use in furthering the object we have in view. Having consulted with Major Shaw I beg leave to inform you that Burriah Sing, Soobadar and Adjutant with 80 Rank & file of the Corps of Hill Rangers will march from hence on the 20th instant with direction to proceed to Sarhaut (Sarath) and place himself under your orders as suggested in the late Acting Magistrate of Beerbhoom's letter of the 15th July last, Major Shaw and myself are of opinion that independent of the Soobadars being empowered to issue Perwannahs to the different Darrogahs of Beerbhoom, Ramghur and Bhaugupore, the Magistrate of Ramghur and yourself should issue orders to the Darrogahs, Gutwalls, Zemindars & ca. adjacent to the place where the Officers are assembled to afford him every information in their power respecting the hounts and retreat of the latter, and every support in attacking and securing them, as well as in enabling the Detachment to obtain sufficient supplies of provision & ca.

We are also of opinion that if Soobadar should find it impossible to secure their persons, or bring them to action he should be empowered to destroy their habitations, seize whatever property of their he can find, delivering the latter to the charge of your Darrogah and otherwise to annoy and disperse them as much as he is able, with which view both yourself and the Magistrate of Ramghur should detach all the force that can possibly be spared from the other duties of your respective Zillah, to co-operate with the Bhagulpore Detachment. The Soobadar will of course report his arrival at Sarhaut to you, through the Darrogah of that place.

OOO

73. Letter

From,

J. Wintle,

Magistrate of Bhagalpur,

To,

J. Miller,
Magistrate of Ramghur. 2
Dated 12th November,1803.

I beg leave to enclose an extract of a letter from the late Acting Magistrate of Beerbhoom (whose suggestions have been approved by His Excellency in Council and to inform you that the Detachment of a Soobadar and 80 Rank and files will march from hence for Sarhaut on the 20th instant. I request you will have the goodness to issue orders to the Darrogahs, Gutwalls and Zemindars on the orders of your district to afford the Soobadar every information and assistance in their power in securing Nouwab Sing, Herpaul Sing and ca and to co-operate with him as far as possible, as well as to enable the Detachment to procure necessary supplies of provision & ca. in the event Perwannahs as the Soobadar may find it necessary to issue to them relating to the service on which he is detached.

ooo

74. Letter

From,

Lieutenant Colonel Shaw of the Bhagalpur Hill Rangers,

To,

J. Wintle,
Magistrate of Bhagalpur 1.
Dated 6th February, 1804.

Herewith I have the honor to forward for your information extracts from two reports of my adjutant from which it appears few of the Gautwalls co-operate with his party, and without the hearty co-operation of the Gautwals on the several Zillahs in which the Jungle Terry is situated, we can have little hope at seizing the Rebels, or of expelling them from their numerous lurking places in those extension Jungles, in which my accounts say they do not remain two days in the same place.

.... Roopnaran Deo's people and Bissundeo have been with the detachment at Rangers all the time it has been in the Jungles less and I am sorry to learn that on Tuesday last Gunderip Singh Roopnaraon Deo's maternal uncle was killed at the head of his party, while in pursuit at the outlaws, with the Rangers, which pursuit was continued for five coss, and two parties skirmishing all the time till the Rebels made their escape in to the Jungles, this not without to my shame and I hope as many as the Report says.

OOO

75. Letter

From,

J. Wintle,

Magistrate of Bhagalpur,

To,

J. Miller,

Magistrate of Ramgarh 2.

Dated 9th February, 1804.

I beg leave to transmit you copies of two letters from Lieutenant Colonel Shaw Commanding the Hill Rangers with copies of their enclosures, and to recommend to your consideration the necessity of a vigorous co-operation with the Magistrate of Beerbhoom and myself, for the purpose & seizing the insurgents Nawab Sing Kirpaul Singh & ca. it is very certain that these persons with their followers find protection and support in your District, and I cannot help thinking that if your Darrogah of Curruckdeah Khoda Buksh and the Gautwals, Zemindar & ca. of his Division did their duty, the Rebels might speedily be seized. All that is required of them is to point out the retreat of the rebels to the subadar of Hill Rangers, who has a force with him fully sufficient to seize the whole Gang, but unless he can get authentic information on this point, it is in vain the Detachment remaining in the Jungles. If this spirit of insubordination and plunder is not speedily crushed, it may spread widely in a short time, and hereafter not be so easily overcome. Allow me, therefore, request you to issue the most positive orders to the Darrogah Khoda Buksh, and the retreat of the rebels, which unless he is desirous of screening (which I suspect) he can find no difficulty in doing.

ooo

76. Letter

From,

Lt. Col. Shaw,

To,

J. Wintle,

Magistrate of Bhagalpur. 1.

Dated 23rd April.

Herewith I beg leave to forward extracts from reports of the address commanding the party at Roonay which came with his letter of the 20th instant and to which, I request your immediate attention as, I apprehend without more effective assistances from the Magistrates at Bhagulpore, Beerbhoom and Ramgur the services at the detachment will be negatory, while the evil which if has, so far in vain, endeavoured to correct, army has not even checked may, if suffered to exist much longer spread and extend thro the Jungle Terry in the three districts. I have no reason to think the officers who have commanded the rangers on this duty, have not exerted themselves to the utmost......

ooo

77. Letter

From,

J. Wintle,
Magistrate of Bhagalpur,

To,

J. Miller,
Magistrate of Ramghur. 1.
Dated 25th April, 1804.

I beg leave to forward a copy of a letter and enclosures received from the Commandant of Hill Rangers, and to suggest the necessity of your immediately sending a company of sepys to co-operate with the Hill Rangers, as well as taking into custody the Gautwals in your Zillah who are mentioned to have been aiding and assisting Nawab Sing & his Gang. The impunity with which he has hitherto been allowed to act in consequence of the apparent neglect and inattention of your Police Officers must give him & his Gang courage to persevere in their depredations, and to set the authority of Government at defiance, and unless such active measures are adopted as may lead to the apprehension or destruction of the Insurgents there is every reason to expect that their numbers will increase and that the evil will spread beyond the Jungle Terry.

OOO

78. Letter

From,

J. Miller,
Magistrate of Ramghur,

To,

J. Wintle,
Magistrate of Bhagalpur.
Dated 4th May,1804.

I have received your letter of the 25th ultimo 2 accompanying copy a letter addressed to you by Lieut. Colonel Shaw commanding the Hill Rangers with the Extracts of Reports therein alluded to respecting the assistance afforded to Nawab Singh and his adherents by some Ghautwals in Curruckdeah, and recommending my detaching a Military Force to Co-operate will the Hill rangers in their apprehension. With respect to some of the Ghatwals who are accused to assisting Nawab Singh and whose names are specified in the representation of the Jemehdhar, I beg to inform you that they **were apprehended by my Darogah some months ago, but rescued from the Police Officer by Nawab Singh** and his followers when on their way to the nearest Tannah in the Beerbhoom District, and who have since eluded every attempts for their reprehension, I therefore cannot discover on what grounds you attribute culpable neglizence on the part of my police Officers, I informed you in my letter of the 16 of February, of my having suspended the Darogah of Curruckdeah, and I beg leave to observe that there is no evidence forthcoming to establish the misconduct as described to him.

As the Ramghur Battalion is at present absent from the district it prevents my applying for a party to strengthen the Detachment of Hill Rangers in the Beerbhoom District, and as the Police Establishment of Curruckdeah only consist of a Darogah a Jemehdar and 6 Burkoündazes, It is not more than adequate to the extension of current duty. I think, therefore, the officer commanding the Detachment should be instructed to pursue and apprehend Nawab Singh his adherents and likewise such of the Ghautwals as he has good reason to suspect being concerned with Nawab Singh in the events of their taking refuge either in this or the Bhaugulpoor District, as it is observable that the officer states in his last representation that he cannot pursue offenders into another Districts without receiving orders for that purpose I have again enjoined the Jummehdhar in charge of the Thannah that on obtaining any certain intelligence of the offenders to lose no time in communicating it to the Officer Commanding the Detachment of Hill Rangers, and to Co-operate with them.

ooo

79. Letter

From,

J. Wintle,

Magistrate of Bhagalpur

To,

J. Sherburne,

Collector of Bhagalpur 3.

Dated 8th June,1804

I have received your letter of the 5th March last and 4th instant,and should long since have replied to the former had it not been mislaid and only just found and in consequence of search made on receipt of the latter.

By the orders of Government of the 23rd of December 1802 I was authorized to entertain an additional Tannah at Sacreegully in lieu of the Establishment of Dowrahs and Bazar Chowkeydars in Tuppah Mudhoobun the Escheated Jaghir of the late Roshun Buksh, and was informed that the Board of Revenue would be directed to discharge those Persons. The Magistrate's precept to you of the 29th May 1802 was prior to the abovementioned orders of Government consequently if any expense in Tuppah Mudhoobun has been subsequently incurred on this account the Magistrate has nothing to do with it.

Whether all the villages Viz, Beershey, Pialahpore, Sahaband, and Pointy form a part of the late Roshun Buksh's Jaghir I cannot say, but if they do the additional Tannah authorized is evidently inadequate to protect so great an extent of high Road as from Telliaghurree to Ghogah, more than half of which passes through a Jungly country almost entirely uninhabited, and where Chowkeydars are of course necessary to protect Travellers Merchants & ca. the allowances to such persons in the Behar part of this District are included in the Mofusil Serinjamy of each village, and they are not considered as immediately forming a part of the Police Establishemnt. If Beershye & ca. are distinct Talooks from the Jaghir of the late Roshun Buksh the Tulookdars must bear the expense, If Government has become the Proprietor, it must also bear the expense in that capacity.

OOO

80. Letter

From,

J. Wintle,

Magistrate of Bhagalpur.

To,

Captain D. Sloane,

Incharge of the Corps of Hill Rangers. 1.

Dated 14th July, 1804.

I am favored with your letter of the 7th Instant enclosing a Roll of Mountaineers entertained in the Corps of Hill Rangers fit to join and do duty.

On inspection of the Roll I observe the names of persons inserted as Manjees who are totally unknown as Men of respectability or possessing any influence with the Hill people,an objection appears also against some of the Hill mentioned, which are known to be almost entirely unihabited.

The custom adopted by the commandant of Hill Rangers for some time past choosing Recruits, and thereby changing the Manjees (who are under the authority of the Magistrate) at his pleasure I consider to be contrary, and totally destructive of the system formed by Mr. Cleveland and approved by Government, for ruling the Mountaineers. The allowances made to the Manjees in consideration of their furnishing a private for the Hill Corps for whom they were consideration as responsible, was intended as a link to connect the Principal Manjees and those who possessed most influence in the Hill with the State, and experience has proved the utility of that system but the innovation made by the commandant tends to destroy that system, to take the control out of the hands of the Magistrate and place it in his own, and totally to reverse the effect intended. It was never I presume in the contemplation of Government that every Man furnishing a private for the Hill Crops should be entitled to the allowances and consequence of a Manjee, and that the head, Men of most influence should be discharge, and deprived of their Pensions to make –room for Men of no sort of consequence, and who are totally unknown. The erection of a little Hut on an uncultivated Hill (which is all the claim many of the Persons put down as Manjees by the commandant possess) cannot entitle them to this advantages. The object Government had in view undoubtedly was that the privates for the Hill Corps should be furnished by the Sirdar Manjees possessing cultivated Hills and villages, and having the most influence and authority, in consideration of which they receive from Government a Monthly allowance. In this case the connection is natural and beneficial to both parties.

The Manjees & ca. have always been considered under the control and authority of the Magistrate, and it is presumable. He is the best qualified to point out what Manjees possesses most influence and authority and whose Hills are the best populated and most capable of furnishing Recruits. When the Commandant has occasion for new Men, he should apply to the Magistrate stating the number who will thereupon take the necessary measures to furnish such Men from such Hills and Manjees as he may judge proper, the choice of the Men for the Corps will of course rest with the commandant, but the Magistrate cannot consider himself authority to remove an old and respectable

Manjees, merely because the Commandant of Hill Rangers may choose to take a Recruit from a Man entirely unknown to him.

Under this explanation I am sorry I cannot insert the names of the Persons mentioned in your present list as Manjees in my Official Roll, so as to enable them to the Manjeeaut allowances. And I have to request that whenever you may have occasion in future for Recruits, you will make the necessary application to me, when I shall procure Men from the Hill Sirdars and send them for your selection.

I also request you will furnish me with a Persian list of all the Mountaineers at present in the Hill Corps, specifying the names of their Hills, and of the Manjees respectively.

ooo

81. Letter

From,

J. Wintle,

Magistrate of Bhagalpur.

To,

Captain D. Sloane,

Incharge of the Corps of Hill Rangers. 1.

Dated 21st July, 1804.

I am favored with your Letter of the 19th Instant, in reply to mine of the 14th Instant.

Permit me to observe " that the names of the Hills and Manjees being taken and registered from the accounts given by the recruits themselves, " is not sufficient authority to warrant an alternation in the original roll of Hills fixed by Mr. Cleveland's arrangement, and also the person inserted in your roll may be " regular established Maniees within their respective limits ", that circumstance can neither entitle them to furnish Recruits or give them a claim to the Bounty of Government. There are hundred of regular Manjees who have no kind of claim to either. The manner in which your second question is stated does not, I conceive, correspond with the real matter of fact. I have no reason to suppose that the Manjees possessing influence require the interposition of the Magistrate's authority to induce them to exert their influence in furnishing Recruits His notification of their being required would be sufficient.

Form your observation " that you apprehend Mr. Cleveland's System does not limit the furnishing of Recruits for the Rangers to a few particular Manjees, however well known, such individuals may be" it would appear I have not clearly Explained myself on that point. I did not mean to support such an inference, but only that His system confined the furnishing recruits to such Sirdar, Naibs and Manjees as were originally pensioned by him or more properly speaking to the Sirdar & ca. of the Hills selected, which by further investigation into the Records of my office appears to be number 557. Thee were selected out of many thousand Hills, and to the Sirdars & ca. of the only was the Bountry of Government granted, in consideration of which they agreed to submit themselves to the laws of the sate (except in Criminal Cases which are tried by their own assembly of Chiefs), to demean out themselves peaceably and quietly to cause their dependant & ca to do the some, to preserve the peace of the Hills, and to furnish Recruits for the rangers as a further chain of connection with the State. Agreeable to this system the Recruit is in a manner the consideration for the Bounty. But when the commanding Officer chooses a Recruit from a new Hill and Manjee, not specified in Mr. Cleveland's original Roll and thereby causes and old Sirdar to be dismissed, the system is reversed, and the Bounty becomes consideration for the Recruit. While the Commanding Officer confines his selection to the original 557 Hill no question can arise between, but when he deviates from that boundary as has recently been the case, it become, I conceive my duty to put a stop to it.

You observe that if Lieut. Colonel Shaw's mode of choosing Recruits be irregular, the irregularity appears to have existed from the period of that Officers appointment to the Command. In answer to which I must remark that the long existence of an irregularity can never be considered a sound argument for its continuance. I regret with you that the question should have arisen during Lieut. Colonel, Shaw's temporary absence but the roll which chiefly occasioned it, was transmitted to me after his Departure I do not recollect receiving more than one Roll From him which was shortly after my taking charge of the District, when I was not sufficiently acquainted with the Hill arrangement, to form an opinion of the probable consequence, however, I have no objection to let the question rest till his return.

I cannot see that my procuring Recruits from the Hill Manjees for your selection can be attended with the consequence mentioned in the 5th Paragraph of your Letter or that it has any thing to do with the duty or discipline of the Corps. I disclaim all intention of interference in that respect. Whether the Magistrate is or is not excluded from interference I cannot judge, as I am unable to discover among my Records the Minute of Council mentioned by you. But by the accompanying extract you will perceive that the Commanding Officer of Rangers can have no possible claim to the authority he has in some instance assumed. My requesting you to apply through me for recruits, was merely to provide against that innovation. If the Commanding Officer confines his choice of Recruits to the original 557 Hills (which are surely sufficient) all the Manjees of which receive the Manjeeaut allowances it amounts to the same thing. Should he not have a list of those Hills I shall be happy to furnish him with one, but I cannot consider it consistent with my Duty to sanction recruits from any other Hills that is, to entitle the Manjees of the latter to the Manjeeaut allowances.

I must again request you to furnish me with the list of hill rangers at present in the corps required in the concluding paragraph of my letter of the 14th Instant to enable me to correct my Offical Roll, as although I have regularly received lists of such Mountaineers as were enrolled in the Corps, They do not specify the names of the persons who have been removed, & ca. which has occasioned an arbitrary discharge of the Hill Manjees, and in some instance possibly an unjust one.

ooo

82. Extract of a Minute of His Excellency the Most Noble the Governor-General in Council dated the 26th July, 1804.

The Knowledge hitherto obtained in Europe respective certain branches of the natural History of the Continent of India and of the Indian Isles, is defective. notwithstanding the progress which has been made within the last twenty years in the prosecution of scientific enquiries connected with the manners, Produce, and antiquities of his part of Asia, any of the most common Quadrupeds and Birds of this country are either altogether unknown to the Naturalists of Europe, or have been imperfectly and inaccurately described.

The illustration and improvement of that important branch of the Natural History of India which embraces an object so extensive as the description of the principal part of the animal Kingdom, is worthy of the munificence and liberality of the English East India Company, and must necessarily prove an acceptable service to the world.

To facilitate and promote all enquiries which may be calculated enlarge the boundaries of general science, is a duty imposed on the British Government in India, by its present exalted situation, and the discharge of that duty is in a more especial manner required from us when any material addition can be made to the public stock of useful knowledge without involving considerable expense.

The Governor-General entertains a confident persuasion that with the facilities which we now possess for the collection of accurate information from every part of India, the Natural History of this quarter of the Globe may be greatly improved and extended, within a comparatively short period of time, without involving the necessity of any material charge on the public resources, but this desirable object will never be attained unless it shall be made the duty of some public officer properly qualified for this service, to collect information and to digest and publish the result of his researches.

Under these considerations the Governor-General has had it in contemplation for some time past to select a person conversant in natural History to be employed in the cultivation of that useful science in the Asiatic Possession of Great Britain.

The knowledge, the learning and the former habits of Doctor Francies Buchanan have rendered him perfectly competent to performance of this task, and the governor General accordingly proposes that Dr. Buchanan be directed to collect materials for a correct accounts of all the most remarkable Quadrupeds, and Birds in the Provinces subject to the British Government in India, and to extend his enquiries as circumstances shall admit to the other divisions of this great contient, and to the adjacent.

To facilitate the discharge of this duty, the Governor General has provided an establishment at Barrackpore, where the Quadrupeds and Birds, which may be collected for Dr. Buchanan will be kept until they shall have been described and drawn with that degree of attention to minute distinctions, which is essentially necessary for the purposes of the Natural Historian.

The Governor General proposes that circular orders be transmitted to the principal Civil and Military Officers at every fixed station under this Presidency, requiring them to instruct the Medical Gentlemen under their authority to Doctor Buchanan's letters, that the principal Civil and Military Officers be further directed to authorise their Medical Officers to solicit assistance and information from all Officers of Government under their persons employed in the service of Government, to afford to their Medical Officers the necessary assistance information which can be obtained from the most intelligent persons in the vicinity, respecting their Natural History and to furnish such aid as may be necessary for the conveyance of the animals to the Presidency.

The Governor General proposes that the Right Hon'ble the Governor in Council of Fort St. George the Hon'ble the Governor in Council of Bombay, and His Excellency the Governor of the British possessions on the Island of Ceylon, and the Lieutenant Governor of Prince of Wales Island, be requested to direct the proper Officers under those Government respectively, to correspond with Dr. Buchanan, and to afford every practicable assistance to Doctor Buchanan in the prosecution of his researches within the limits of their local authority and that similar orders be sent to Malacca and to Bencoolen.

With the view of facilitating Dr. Buchana's correspondence, it will be necessary that the post Master General should be ordered to receive and forward free from Postage all letters written by or addressed to Dr. Buchanan on the subject of his researches in the department of Natuaral History, and that the Governments of Forts St. George, Bombay, and Ceylon, be requested to issue similar orders to the Post Masters General at those settlements respectively. All letters written by or addressed to Dr. Buchanan on matters connected with the duty now committed to him must be superscripted on the Envelope with the name of the writer, and with the Words Natural History of India.

Resolution –Ordered that an Extract from the above Minute containing copies of Paragraphs 1 to 9 inclusive be sent to Revenue and Judicial Department and to the military Department, from whence the necessary orders are to be issued to the public officers employed under those Departments, requiring them to instruct the Medical Gentlemen under their authority to correspond with Doctor Buchanan on the subject of the Natural History of India, and to afford every practicable assistance to Dr. Buchanan, in the prosecution of his researches, within the limits of their local authority.

Ordered that Doctor Buchanan be furnished with a list of those Gentlemen employed under the orders of the Revenue and Judicial Department, and of the Military Department, who shall be instructed to correspond with doctor Buchanan.

OOO

83. Letter

From,

Secetary to Government Judicial ….

Council Chamber,

Dated 26 July 1804,

To,

John Miller,

Magistrate of the Zillah of Ramghur.

"I am directed to acknowledge the receipt of your letter of the 13th instant with its enclosures, and to acquaint you that His Execellency the most Noble the Governor General in Council on a opinion that the detachments of a Military force for the apprehension of Nawab Singh and his adherents should be postponed until after the expiration of the season of the rains as proposed by the Officer Commanding the Ramghur Battalion.

1. You are desired to communicate the sentiments of Government on the above points to Colonel Broughton. You will likewise consult with him the measures be adopted for the apprehension of the year. You will likewise of, Course communicate regularly the steps proposed to be taken for the attainment of that object to the Magistrate of Bhagalpur. "

OOO

84. (Enclosure 1.)

Translate of an Arzee from the Darogah of Rajmahal

On the 14th July, 1804 Captain (Lieutenant) Hume, who is proceeding from Fort William to the westward, with 30 or 40 Magazine Boats arrived at Rajmahal Ghaut. Without giving me any notice, he sent one of his Sepoys to Rajah Bazar to fetch Coolies and Dandies, when a quarrel arose in the said Bazar between the said Sepoy Joy Sing Serberacar & Goor Buksh of that place. In that quarrel and dispute the Cooly,Goor Buksh, bit the cheek of Sepoy with his teeth. Sir, the Gentle man hearing of this from his Sepoy, sent Sepoy and khalassies to seize the said Joy Sing and Goor Buksh and also sent orders to the Tannah to send a Burkendauz along with them. The Sepoys and khalassies accordingly bound the said Joy Sing & Goor Buksh and carried them before that Gentleman. About 2 hours after dark the said Gentleman sent his Sepoy to call me to him. I attended with my Omlah. He ordered me to enquire whether Goor Buksh bit the Sepoy's cheek, and tore his cloths, or not. Sir, from the declrations of the Royts it appeared, that in the quarrel the said Goor Buksh bit the Sepoy's cheek & also tore a small part of his cloth's. After which the said Gentleman took from the abovenamned a fine of Rs. 5 and gave it to his own Sepoy, and ordered his Sepoys and khalassies to tie up both persons to a Tucktee, and flog them with a Rattan. In consequence the Sepoys & khalassies tied the hands and feet of Joy Sing and Goor Buksh to a Tucktee in presence of the Gentleman and gave each 40 or more stripes with a Rattan, in such a manner that the blood came from their bodies, and they are unable to sit or stand. After which he ordered me to supply Coolies & ca. Sir, agreeable to the Gentleman's order whatever Coolies and other necessaries could be procured in concert with the Zermindars I furnished. This day's the 16th July, he departed for the westward. I think it necessary to inform you of these particulars.

Order of the Magistrate. the Darogah has acted very foolishly in allowing such an interference in his duty. when the Lieutenant sent to call him,and ordered him to investigate his cause, he ought to have told the Lieutenant, that this was the province of the Magistrate. In future he will be more careful to cause the necessary supplies to be furnished to Officers through himself, and that no violence be offered to any person. Neither the Lieutenant nor any other Gentleman has right to inflict punishment.

Dated 19th July, 1804

(Enclosure 2)

Translate of a representation from the Police Darogah of Rajmahal

Tuppaseeah Mohulladar of Rajah Bazar has given notice at the Tannah, that Goor Buksh, inhabitant of Rajah Bazar, whom Captain (Lieutt). Hume ordered his Khalassies to flog with aRattan, was ill from that date, & died this day. Two boys of the deceased who are of tender age, have not made any representation at the Tannah. In consequence of my being indisposed I could not proceed to the place where the corps was, but sent the Mohurir and Jamantdar there agreeable o the notice given by the Mohulladar Bhyer Lool, Mohurir & ca. ShaikBenuck jemantdar hold an inquest on the body in presence of the deceased neighbours, and brought it to the Tannah. The heirs have not made any complaint against ant person at the Tannah, I therefore, agreeable to the notice given by the Mohulladar inform you of the business, and send enclosed the Sooruthaul of the deceased corps brought by the Mohurir & Jemantdar from which you will learn the particulars.

Dated 16th August, 1804.

Sooruthaul of the corps of Goor Buksh of Rajah Bazar, who was about 45 years of age, and died on the 15h August 1804 taken in presence of Bawun Chauker, Tuppaseeah Mohulladar and six other persons, inhabitants of Rajah Bazar, who examined the body.

On the Back 25 marks of Rattan, which had dried up. Under the right arm a wound from which matter in length 2 finger, breadth 3 Barley- corns; depth Barley –corn. Under the right thigh one would from which matter issued in length 2 fingers, broad 2 Barley-corns, deep Barley –corn.

(Signed)

Bhyero Loll Mohurir & ca.

Order of the Magistrate. The Darogah will inform himself of the name of the kbalassies who flogged the deceased, and report it to the Magistrate and make enquiry among the neighbours of the deceased Goor Buksh, whether he died in consequence of the flogging received from the Khalassies or was previously ill. The Darogah being present as the time, will state his opinion, whether Goor Buksh died from that flogging, or from what other cause. He will report accordingly to the Magistrate.

Dated 20th August, 1804

(Enclosure 3)

Translate of the reply of the Darogah of Rajmahal

After repeating the substance of the above orders "Your Servant went himself and made enquiry of the neighbour of the deceased Gor Buksh. They replied that previous to the flogging Goor Buksh was not ill, and that from the date on which it took place he did not come out of his house. We think that the said Goor Buksh died from that beating. The son brothers of the deceased also declared that the deceased died in consequence of the beating. The deceased also while leaving said that the blow with the Buttend of the Musket received from the Sepoys at the time of seizing me, and the strips of the Rattan were such that my Liver pains me. Sir at the time the Khalassies beat Goor Buksh, one Khalassey only did not beat him that I can remember his name, and at the place where he was flogged, there were several Khalassies, Sepoys and a crowd of people, and at the dark of night, I therefore cannot say exactly who among the Khalassies beat the deceased Goor Buksh. I am unacquainted with their names, and was standing at a distance. The Captain (Lieutenant) asked the Khalassies whether the blood flowed from Goor Buksh's back, or not, Goor Buksh himself said with a loud voice in the flowed from Goor Buksh's back, or not, Goor Buksh himself said with a loud voice in the midst of the beating "there is no blood in my body to flow, it is dried up." Sir in my opinion it does not fully appear that the deceased died from the flogging, because the deceased did not die at that time, but after the expiration of 26 days he died at his own house. But the beating the deceased received was severe. I inform you of those particulars. "

Dated 1st September, 1804.

OOO

85. Letter

From,

J. Miller, Magistrate,

Zillah Ramghur,

Dated the 8 September, 1804

To,

Jame Wintle,

Magistrate Bhagalpur.

"I shall do myself the pleasure to inform you, conformably to the order contained in the enclosed letter from Mr. Secretary Dowdeswell, of the steps which may be adopted at the proper season for the apprehension of Nawab Singh and his adherents.

If you have received any recent accounts respecting Nawaub Singh Force, I will thank you to communicate them to me. "

OOO

86. Letter

From,

J. Miller,
Magistrate of Ramghur,

To,

J. Wintle,
Magistrate of Bhagalpur. 1.
Dated 24th October,1804.

Under the 8th ultimo I transmitted to you a copy of the orders of Government respecting Nawab Singh and his adherents, and have now the pleasure to enclose copy of an Arzee from the Police Darogah of Curruckdeah and request the favour of your informing me whether the Detachment of Hill rangers has been recalled from Sarut as mentioned by the Darogah, for should the disturbances in this quarter have been suppressed I conclude there will be no occasion for a party of sepoys being detached from the Ramghur Battalion.

OOO

87. Letter

From,

T. Shaw Major,
Commanding Hill Rangers, Bhagalpur,
Dated 8 November, 1804

To,

J. Wintle,
Magistrate of Bhagalpur.

"I have the honour to acknowledge your letter of the 8th instant, addressed to Capt. Sloane in charge of the Hill Rangers with its enclosurces, and to acquaint you in reply that a detachment will be in readiness to march to Sarhut whenever it may be called for; but I must at the same time observe that a party consisting of more than 40 or 50 men cannot be detached on this service, without materially interfering with the other duties required of the corps. From the tenor of the you have been pleased to transmit to me, I doubt not but this force will be deemed sufficient, if indeed any miltary force should be thought necessary, but I can clearly of opinion, that so long as Nawab Sing does not openly appear at the head of body of armed followers, but shelters, as hitherto, among the Hills and extensive Jungles, employing a military force with a view to seize his person, or that of any of his adherents, cannot be productive of any good but on the contrary to make his apprehension more difficult. From the Reports of the Native Officer, who commanded the detachment of Hill Rangers, lately called from that country, I have no doubt but Nawaub Sing has an understanding with most, if not all, the Ghatwalls and Zemindars in the neighbourhood. Their extreme unwillingness to afford any information or assistance to the detachment, by which it might have been enabled to come upon him, or to discover his haunts, clearly evinces this, and at the same time shows the employing sepoys to pursue fugitive individuals through Jungles of such extent and intricacy ; a service which can be successfully performed only by those whose local residence, and habits of life, have enabled them to acquire a thorough knowledge of the country.

Upon my view of the subject, from all the information I have received, I am fully persuaded that the most likely, if not the only practicable mode of apprehending Nawaub Sing and the delinquents connected with him will be, by obliging all the Ghatwalls in the vicinity of his haunts to exert their best endeavours for that purpose."

OOO

88. Letter

From,

C. R. Blunt Magistrate of Beerbhum,

To,

G. Dowdeswell,

Secretary to Government in the Judicial Department. 3.

Dated 29th November,1804.

I have been duly favoured with your letter and enclosure of the 22nd instant communicating the orders of His Excellency the most Noble the Governor-General in Council regarding Newaub Singh, and his adherents.

2nd- That the apprehension of Newaub Singh, and Kerpaul Sing, would greatly conduce to the peace of that part of my district in which they reside, and from a most beneficial example thought the Jungle Mehals, there can remain no doubt, as however his sirdars appear at present to be carrying on their depredations through the means of small bodies of dependants and have not since the rains, appeared at the head of any force too powerful for my Police Officers to oppose, I am of opinion that no necessity does at present exist for the detachment of a Military force.

OOO

89. Letter

From,

J. Wintle,

Magistrate of Bhagalpur.

To,

G. Dowdeswell,

Secretary to Government in the Judicial Department.

Dated 31st December, 1804, Calcutta.

I think it my duty to lay before His Excellency the most Noble the Governor-General in Council for his consideration the accompanying translation of representations made to me by the Police Darogah of Rajmahal. These would have been submitting earlier, but as I was coming to Calcutta, I was desirous of making some previous enquires of the Darogah Personally at Rajemahal as to the punishment inflicted on the deceased by order of Lieutenant Hume. As none of the relations of the deceased have preferred any charge against that Gentleman or his Khalassies, I do not wish to offer any observations on his conduct further than to state that I have been informed that Lieutenant Hume is deranged in his intellects, and had been so once before previous of his having charge of the Store Boats.

It may not however be irrelevant to state that frequent irregularities and improprieties are committed by Officer and other in charge of Magazine, Store and Troop Boats on their passage up the country in seizing Ryots from there ploughs, taking provisions without paying for them & ca. Frequent calls have been made on my Police Officers and myself to furnish two or three hundred Dandies at a time, which it has sometimes been impossible to comply with, from the number & frequency of store Boats which the exigency of the Public Service required to be pushed forward, and the skirts of the Bhaugulpore Districts bordering on the great River being out thinly peopled that part of the country has been almost stripped of inhabitants to forward this service. I have uniformly directed my Police Officers to give every possible assistance on such occasions, but when the Officers & ca. In charge of boats themselves interfere without applying to the regular authority, the exertions of the former are less liable to prove effectual, as the villagers are accustomed to take to flight on the approach of a Military force. Private Gentlemen never find the want of Dandies and Collies which is so frequently the complaint on the Public service, from which it would appear that there must be some mismanagement in hiring boats for the Public Service, for if the owners were properly paid and regular security taken for the full number of dandies, it is almost impossible so great a deficiency of Dandies could arise, from sickness and desertion as is frequently represented by persons in charge of Store & ca. Boats. As the regular and quick despatch of these boats is at all times of great importance to the state, particularly at the present period, His Excellency may perhaps deem it advisable to form some Rules for that purpose. And should the subject appear to Government as of such consideration such Regulations as have occurred to me to be conducive to that end.

OOO

90. Letter

From,

J. Wintle,
Magistrate of Bhagalpur,

To,

G. Dowdeswell,
Secretary to Government in the Judicial Department.
Dated 15th January, 1805.

I have the honor to acknowledge the receipt of your letter of the 3rd instant desiring me to state more particularly why I did not obtain the necessary information on the subject of Goor Buksh's decease and report the circumstances of the case at an earlier period.

I reply to which I beg leave to state for the information of Government that at the time I received that I previously had pointed out to the latter the impropriety of his conduct. I heard he had not only been insane some time previous to his having charge of the magazine boats, but his conduct at Bhaugulpore was so irregular and flighty and at Mongheer so evidently evinced marks of insanity, that Dr. Moore, the Surgeon of that station had I understood reported his situation. His conduct at Dinapore from private accounts received, also shewed him to be in a state of mental derangement. Under these circumstances, a nd no person coming forward to prosecute for the death of Goor Buksh, it appeared to me that no criminal proceedings could be immediately held against Lietutenant, Hume in his then state of mind. And that as I was shortly after coming to Calcutta, and wished to satisfy myself at Rajmahal by further enquiries of the Police Darogah I conceived a short delay in reporting the case to Government could be of no material consequence. On my arrival I found that I had omitted to bring copies of the Report, and was therefore obliged to write to the acting magistrate to forward them; the copying, transmission and translation of these papers necessarily created a further delay, and was the cause of my report being made so late necessarily created a further delay, and was the cause of my report being made so late.

I hope under this explanation that Government will not attribute to me any neglect of duty, or suppose me backward in administering justice to every description of the Hon'ble Company 's subject within my jurisdiction. The delay in reporting the case, if not strictly regular arose from a mistaken opinion. Had Lieutenant. Hume been in a state of sanity, I should have reported directly upon his conduct.

Due obedience will be paid to the orders, of Government contained in the 4th paragraph of your letter above mentioned on my previously obtaining from the Commissary of stores, some necessary information respecting the present mode of hiring store and other boats.

OOO

91. Letter

From,

J. D. Erstine,

Acting, Collector, Zillah Bhagulpur

To,

Thomas Graham,

Acting President and Members of the Board of Revenue,

Fort William,

This dated 16 January, 1805

"On a report from Mr. Dickinson under date the 6th of September 1799, Government was pleased to grant an abatement of revenue to the amount of 907-8-17 to Herpras Chaudry the zemindar of Luchimpoor on account of damage from the encroachment of the Ganges. I am now informed that on the opposite side a large tract of land to the extent of nearly 20,000 Beghas has been formed in consequence of this variation in the course of the river, and is now become fit for cultivation. Bishnath Sing the Zemindar to whose estate this land is contiguous has taken possession of it and claims it as his legal property, in consequence of which Government suffer the annual loss of the sum before mentioned as they are precluded by the decennial settlement from making any addition claim upon Bishnath Sing on account of this accession of land. I beg leave however leave, to submit to the consideration of the Board whether the proprietor of Luchhimipoor may not be able to substantiate a claim of this land or to portion of it according to the quantity he may have lost in which event Government will be entitled to recover from him the account of the jamma originally assessed upon his estate.

ооо

92. Letter

From,

J. D. Erstine,Acting, Collector, Zillah Bhagulpur

To,

Charles Buller, Secretary to the Board of Revenue, Fort William,

This dated 24 January, 1805

"I have the honour to acknowledge the receipt of Mr. sub-Secretary Thakerry's letter of the 15th instant with its enclosure and I beg leave to inform you, that the sum therein alluded to, was received from the proprietors of Lakheraj Land, on account of Rusoom Canoongoes, and that there is no other authority for refunding the account, than the Board's letter of the 8th June 1804, as stated by the auditor to have been already quoted by the Collector.

Though the Board in their letter do not expressly order any collections on the above account to be refunded yet as they declare it to their opinion that Government have no claim to the account formerly paid to the Sudder Canoongoes, by the proprietors of lakheraj Land, and directs that the demands on that account be discontinued, Mr. Sherburne appears to have considered this communication as sufficient authority for refunding the amount collected.

Previous to the receipt of the above orders, Mr. Sherburne had actually collected from different Lakherajdars and Mokarridars the sum of Rs. 1060-2 ans.

On account of Rusoom Canoongoes of which the sum of Rs. 370 has been refunded on the authority above mentioned. The balance Rs. 690-2 ans. remains in deposit in the Treasury respecting which, I beg the instruction of the Board."

93. Letter

From,

F. Hamilton, Acting Collector, Zilla Bhagalpur,

Dated 6 February, 1805

To,

Charles Buller, Secreatary to the Board of Revenue,

"I have the honour to acknowledge the receipt of your letter of 14th December, 1804 addressed the late acting Collector, on the subject of the resum of Kishen Datt's lands by the collector.

It appears by the records in this office that Mash Thakur uncle to Kishen Datta held the two villages of Hanee Chuk and Dewan Chuk, rent free till their resolution by the collector on the 3rd of December 1801 when after having investigated the claims of the deceased, and finding that they were just, the collector directed their relinquishment on the 8th of July, 1802.

On reference to the enclosed examinations taken before me, it will be observed that from the time of the late Mr. Cleveland, several investigations have been made on this subject the result of which proves that Kishen Datt's claims to hold these villages as their, to Mahesh Thakur rent free are just. The Collector in his Purwanna under date the 8th July, 1802 directing the relinquishment, states, that they are to be relinquished till the result of some future enquiry is known, I have not been able to discover among the records any enquiry on this Head.

On the 9th of may, 1804, the Collector issued a purwanna to the Tehsildar to attach these land again,assigning as a reason that they had been resumed by Mr. Cleveland, On reference however, to the records, and after making any investigation which I thought conducive to substantiate this point, I cannot discover that they ever were resumed by Mr. Cleveland.

I have presumed to direct the attachment to be taken off till the receipt of the Board's final orders.

A copy of the collector's letter under date the 23rd of March 1802 accompanies as ordered by the Board. "

ooo

94. Translate of the Deposition of Meer Feyuz Ally, Darogah of Rajmahal taken on the 8th February, 1805

On Saturday, , the 14th July, 1804, about 3 o'clock P. M. intelligence of the approach of Magazine Boats was received at the Thannah. On hearing this I assembled my own & the zemindary

Aumlah was ready in the Thannah to afford assistance. after this I heard a noise in the Bazar, when I had gone to my house to eat something, and in the interim a Haveldar arrived at the Thannah from Captain Hume, the Gentleman in charge of the Boats requiring Tauje Khawn, the Jemadar of the Thannah to send a Burkendauz with him in order to apprehend a person who had beat a sepoy belonging to the party & bit his cheek. In compliance with his desire the Jemadar sent Chumroo Burkendauz along with him, and when I returned to the Thannah told me these particulars. Chumroo having met the gentleman's sepoys & khalassies who had seized & bound two men named Goor Buksh & Joy Sing in about an hour returned to the Thannah informing me of their approach with the two men's arms fastened behind them, and who they had beat severely when I perceived them as the Burkendauz reported to me coming on the public road which leads by the Thannah.

After about an hour of the night the Captain, having brought his Boats to the Shore near Dewabghaut a sepoy with his bayonet fixed came to me saying it was his orders to bring the Darogah immediately. I therefore went I perceived Goor Buksh & Joy Sing siting on the river side with their arms bound surrounded with sepoys khalassies & other. The Gentleman called me on board his boats his boat & enquired the name of the judge. I replied I had Mr. J. Wintle is the Judge & Magistrate of Bhaugulpore the place is under his authority & I am a Darogah under him. He asked why I had not given him assistance, I replied received no orders nor had any sepoy is come to me to require it, that the sepoy who had got into the quarrel had gone to seize Dandies without informing me and that it appeared this dispute had arisen between him and the Serberakar of the Rajah Bazar. He ordered me to go on shore & enquire who had beat the sepoy. Being much alarmed I complied & coming on shore & asking the people standing about a man named Bhodic said that Goor Buksh in the tumult occasioned by the impress in the Bazar as the sepoy was beating him had bit the sepoys cheek. I informed Gentleman of his who directed me to fine the two men five Rupees as they remained bound, Nuthoo one of their relations gave the sum to me of which the Gentleman being informed ordered the sepoy who had been beat to take it, and said to me look how the man's Clothes are torn I perceived this to be the case in same degree about his neck but it did not appear who had done it. The Captain then directed his sepoys & khalassies to prepare the Tucktee (three Bamboos tied together him order to suspend a man previous to influcting punishment and to punish them) they obeyed & first tying up Goor Buksh very tight & fastening his feet, they commenced flogging observe if the blood issued from his back when Goor Buksh called out for mercy that there was no blood left to issue the gentleman then called for the cane to see whether or not it was broken & ordered the other man to be tied up, and Goor Buksh to be made to sit down & another dozen to Canes to be brought where they beat Joy Sing in the same manner after which the Gentleman observed that Goor Buksh had not got enough & told the people to beat him again which they did Goor Buksh said nothing but continued sobbing, when the Gentleman ordered them to be released, Their relations took them away on beds, the Captain then ordered me to furnish 20 Dandies & other things, that were requisite in which with the assistance from the Zemindars & ca. I complied as far as I was able:-

Question–What length of time elapsed from the commencement of the disturbance till assistance of a Chuprassey was required from you?

Answer–About a Ghuree.

Question–When the Gentleman ordered you to take five Rupees from Goor Buksh & Joy Sing what reply did you make?

Answer–I was afraid and said nothing.

Question–Since you had done nothing to offend the gentleman why did you not say that these men ought to be reported to the Magistrate who would punish them according to their guilt, that you had no authority to interfere in fining them to superintending their punishment?

Answer–When I went into the Gentleman's Bunglow he was angry & sent me on shore to make the enquiry. Having complied with his order as to the fine he again ordered me out of the Boat & I had no subsequent opportunity of speaking to him.

Question:- You were not in the Boat during the punishment at what distance did you perceive it ?

Answer:- Where the men were punished was about 10 or 12 Hauts from the Boats and about 5 or 6 Hauts from the place where I was standing.

Question:- What fault did Joy Sing commit that he was punished ?

Answer:- I heard nothing.

Question:- Where is Joy Sing at Present?

Answer- He has gone to Moorsedbad.

Question- When his punishment was inflicted where was the gentleman sitting within the Cabin or on the outside?

Answer- He was sitting in the Cabin with the Door open.

Question- Were there any lights where the punishment was inflicted?

Answer:- There were no lights, but the gentleman's khedmutgar came once with a lantern & see the back off GoorBuksh, and said the blood, was issuing from it.

Question- At what time did the khedmutgar bring the lantern & was Goor Buksh afterwards beat?

Answer- I do not exactly recollect but I fancy it was after the punishment was completed.

Question- When the man brought a light to see the mans back & made his report did the Gentleman send for Goor Buksh that he might himself observe his situation ?

Answer- He did not come near he only saw from his Boats.

Question- How was he able to observe the punishment from within the Boats ?

Answer- He was looking towards the place there were lights in the Boat & the punishment was inflicted at a short distance.

Question- Could you see the gentleman from the place where you were standing?

Answer- I could very plainly.

Question- Are you positive that Goor Buksh was silent the second flogging, that a light was brought & his condition examined before this took place?

Answer- I think I am correct in what I have said, but I have been very ill for three or four months & this business took place near eight months ago, I may possibly not be very Correct.

Question- Do you know the names of the people who beat the deceased?

Answer- Many people beat their names I do not know.

Question- From all the circumstances as they appeared to you from the conversation you had with Captain. Hume & from what passed in your hearing between the Gentleman & his people did you conceive him to be his perfect sense?

Answer- This I cannot positively say he could never however had been sane have acted in this manner. a Haveldar accompanying him came to the Thannah & said to me the gentleman s senses were disordered that he had attempted to shoot him he (Havoldar) with a pistol, but fortune protecting him it missed fire & that on arriving at Cawnpoor he should prepare a complaint & bring him to Court martial.

Question- Did the Haveldar say when this occurred?

Answer- He said it was previous to the arrival of the boats at Rajemahal.

Question- I did not see his opinion respecting the cause of the death of Goor Buksh?

Answer- I did not see him from the time of the beating to the day of his death, I was told that previous to his beating he was not ill but conducted the affairs of his family. I cannot say if the beating actually occasioned his death but his family told me it was the case.

Question- How many lashes did Goor Buksh receive & in what manner ?

Answer – I think upwards of 40 very severely but I did not remain in one place to be able to count them.

ooo

95. Extract from a letter from, Dr. Francis Buchanan dated the 1st February 1805

I am sorry, that my efforts for accomplishing the objects of the institution put under my charge have not been so successful as I could have wished. I have written a circular Letter to many of the Medical Officers on the Bengal Establishemnt, as will be seen by the accompany List, and among other request I have desired these Gentlemen to furnish me with a list of the guadoupees, that are to be found in the vicinity to where they are stationed. Although ample time has now elapsed since the circular letter has been transmitted Mr. Cooke & Sylhet,Mr. Macrx at Chittagong, Mr. Lawe at Moradabad Mr. Gardiner with this request. I am therefore afraid that without some additional inducement little assistance is to be expected from that quarter.

Resolutions-Ordered that an Extract from Dr. Buchanans Letter be transmitted to the Revenue and Judicial Department, to the secret Political and Foreign Department to the Department for the affairs of the ceded and conquered provinces and to the Military Department, from whence orders are to be issued to the public officers employed under those Department requiring them to repeat to the Medical Gentlemen under their authority the orders passed by His Excellency in Council on the 26th of July 1804 directing the Medical Gentlemen to correspond with Dr. Buchanan on the subject of the Natural History of India, and to afford every practicable assistance to Dr. Buchnan in the prosecution of his researches within the limits of their local authority.

(A true Extract)
THOSBROWEN,
Secretary to the Government
Judicial Department.

The 7th February 1805.

ooo

96. Translate of the Deposition of Taje Khawn Jamadar of the Thannah of Rajmahal taken on oath, the 8th February,1805 A. D.

Question- What you know respecting the death of Goor Buksh?

Answer- In the evening of the 14th July, 1804, a sepoy came to the Thannah from a store boat & said to me give a chaprassy a long with in order to apprehend a ryot who has entered into a dispute with a sepoy & behaved improperly I sent Chumro, a Burudauz of the Thannah with the sepoy. After about a Ghuree I perceived that the same sepoy having seized Goor Buksh, Joy Sing & Bhodic & tied their arms was carrying them away & that that Chumroo Burumndauz was along with him. After about a Ghuree of the night a sepoy with his bayonet fixed came to the Thannah & told Meer Feyuz Ally, the Darogah that the Captain called him. The Darogah & myself went to the Captain and perceived Goor Buksh & Joy Sing bound near the place Bhodic was also there, but he was not bound. The Captain called Meer Feyuz Ally, the Darogah on board his boat & ordered him to ascertain if these two people had bit his sepoys Cheek or not. The Darogah understood from Bhodoic that this was the case & also that they had torn his cloths. The Captain ordered the Darogah to fine both 5 Rupees & to give it to the sepoy. The Darogah mentioned this to Goor Buksh & Joy Sing, Nuthoo Sing, the brother of Jot Sing gave the 5 Rupees & in compliance with the Captains orders the Darogah gave hit to the Sepoy. The Darogah then said to the gentleman I will now take leave. The captain replied, remain to see these two men punished & then go. He then ordered the Tucktee (three bamboo prepared for the purpose of tying up a person previous to inflitcing punishment) to be prepared and directed the Khalassies to beat them. The Khalassies complied & first tied up Goor Buksh & punished him after which the Captain said take a lantern & observe if the blood flows from the back of this men or not. Goor Buksh replied there is no blood left in my body that it should flow from it when one man was fatigued with inflicting the punishment another relieved him 7 a Khedmutgar having brought alight & observed Goor Bukhs back said the blood flows from his back. At this period the Captain ordered his people to release this man & make him sit down & punish the other. The Khalassies according to this order tied up Joy Sing & flogged him when the Captain directed him to release & to punish the first man a second time. The Khalassies obeyed after which the Captain sent a man again with a light to observe if the blood issued from his back. The man came & looking at his back said that it was the case when by the Captains orders the Khalassies released him. The friends of the two men then took them away.

Question –Why was Joy Sing beat?

Answer- I do not know for what reason.

Question:- Did you hear what the Captain said?

Answer- The Captain was in the boat & I was shore near the boat.

Question – from the date of this in what state did Goor Buksh continue and at what distance of time did he die & what is your opinion respecting the cause of his death?

Answer- I was relieved at Rajemahl & came to Sicreegully, I am ignorant respecting the time & cause of his death.

Question:- From the conversation of the Captain with the people & with his own servants which you heard did you conceive him in possession of his intellects?

Answer- I could not observe from his conversation that he was out of his accompanied to sheet to the Thannah & told the Darogah that this Captain had attempted at shoot him but that the gun did not go off & that having arrived at Danapore he should seek redress. Of any thing else I am ignorant.

Question:- After Goor Buksh was beat in what state was he ?

Answer- He was senseless and said nothing.

(A true translate)
(Sd.) ILLEGIBLE

OOO

97. Translate of the Deposition of Nuthoo Sing on oath, the 8th February,1805

Question - What relation of yours was Goor Buksh? Relate all the particulars respecting him.

Answer- On the 14th July, 1804 about 3 o'clock p. m I was in the Cutcherry when Moorly, the son of Goor Buksh came to me & said that the sepoys having beatwen my father are taking him away I left the Cutcherry & saw 3 sepoys were taking away bound Goor Buksh & Joy Sing my elder brother. They carried both to the river side where the Captain Budgerow was, The gentleman said keep those men who have beat the sepoy & call the Darogah Meer Feyuz Ally went to the gentleman. I am ignorant what conversation took place in the boat when the Darogah came on shore & enquired of Bhodic. What Goor Buksh had done to the sepoy. He replied that Goor Buksh had bit him. The Darogah informed the Gentleman this, when the Gentleman ordered a fine of 5 Rs. To be taken from each which I paid to the Darogah. when the Gentleman ordered his khalassies to fix up Goor Buksh and him after doing this Joy Sing was also tied up & punished in the same manner. When Goor Buksh was again tied up and beat & then released. Then we took them up & conveyed them home & tried to recover Joy Sing got better but Goor Buksh in the course of a month died.

Question- In what state of health was Goor Buksh previous to this beating?

Answer- He was in good health & conducted his business.

Question- Subsequent to his illness in what state was, could he get up & sit down & eat & drink?

Answer-He remained on his bed he was unable to rise even for the offices of nature sometimes took a little Pegion soup or alittle (Mohanbhoog) adish composed a flower, sugar & Ghee?

Question-After the beating did Goor Buksh ever say any thing?

Answer He sometimes said my throat is closed. I can speak no more I am sitting when the sepoy came & beat me without cause.

(A true translate)
(Sd.) ILLEGIBLE

98. Translate of the evidence of Chumroo, Burkundauz taken on oath the 11th February, 1805

Question – Do you know any thing respecting the fate of Goor Buksh?

Answer- On the 14th July, 1804 A. D when about a Ghuree of the day remained a sepoy came to the Thannah of Rjemahal and said he was sent by Mr. Tlumi to get the assistance of Burkundauz from the Darogah in order to apprehend an inhabitant of Rajmahal who had a quarrel with a sepoy Taje Khawn. The Jemadar of the Thannah sent me along with him we set off together, I perceived on the road that the sepoys having bound Joy Sing & Goor Buksh were bringing them away & also that they were beating them. I went along with them to Dewanghaut where the Captains Budgerow was. The Gentleman asked me who I was I replied a Burkundauz of the Rajemahal Thannah. he then ordered me to call the Darofgah & sent his sentry along with me I went to the Thannah & carried the Darogah back with me to the Gentleman Budgerow where we arrived in the evening. The Darogah went on board the boat to the Gentleman & coming on shore the Capain directed him from his Budgerow to fine Joy Sing & Goor Buksh 5 Rupees. I did not see whether the Darogah exacted the fine or not The Captain ordered his Khalassies to tie then up & beat them. the Khalassies first bound Goor Buksh & beat him with a cane & then releasing him, tied up Joy Sing & beat him when, they again tied up Goor Buksh & flogged him a 2nd time. At the time the Captain told a servant to take a lantern & observe the state of the back of Goor Buksh who reported that the blood was remaining flow his back when he was released. I went the Darogah to the Thannah, I am ignorant in what manner or at what time the people took Joy Sing & Goor Buksh home.

Question – In what manner did the sepoys after seizing Goor Buksh & Joy Sing convey them away?

Answer- They tied their hand & put them under a guard.

Question – What sort of cane were they beat with & how many strokes did they receive?

Answer- A common cane such as used for a similar purpose in the Adawlut. When one was broken they took another. I cannot say how many were used it was night & a concourse of peple were assembled. I observed so far that two or three canes were broken in inflicting the punishment.

Question :-Did you see Goor Buksh after the punishment previous to his death ?

Answer- I did not.

OOO

99. Letter

From,

G. Dowdeswell,

Secretary to Government in the Judicial Department,

To,

William Armstrong,

Magistrate of Bhagalpur. 1.

Dated,28th February, 1805.

His Excellency the Most Noble the Governor- general in Council having had before him a letter from the magistrate dated the 20th instant, respecting the expense incurred in the erection of a Bridge at Berarny, I am directed to acqaint you that His Excellency in Council has been pleased to pass the account of the expense incurred for that purpose amounting to Sicca Rupees 26-12-3.

OOO

100. Letter

From,

G. Dowdeswell,

Secretary to Government in the Judicial Department,

To,

William Armstrong,

Magistrate of Bhagalpur.

Dated, 28th February, 1805.

His Excellency the Most Noble the Governor-General in Council observing from the report received from you respecting Europeans within your Jurisdiction, that T. R. Dent appear to have recently established himself in the interior of the Country without a local license for residing District of Bhagalpore, I am directed to desire you will require the above mentioned person to return to Calcutta, unless any particular circumstances should exist which may appear to you entitle him to reside any longer in your jurisdiction.

ooo

101. Letter

From,

C. Oldfield,

Judge of Bhagulpur Court of Circuit,

To,

William Armstrong,

Acting Magistrate of Bhagalpur.

Dated, 4th March, 1805.

As I find the faujdary Serishtadar, that no orders have been issued for the attendance of Mussamaut Maumn inhabitant of Masonee in pergunnah Kejra, and Mussamaut Chandreo inhabitant of the same place whose evidence has again been ordered to be taken by the Nizamut Adawlut, in the trial of Gunnesy. I have accordingly to desire you will immediately issue the necessary summons for their attendance with as little delay as possible.

I have also to request you will order a local enquiry to be made ascertain whether Gunnesy was seen by any of the neighbors at the house of Doodhee whilst the deceased Doomun was resident in it and further that you will cause witnesses to attend this Court, to prove the prisoner Gunnesy having admitted before the Magistrate that he passed a night at the house of Doodhee when Domun was there.

(Ed.) These proceedings of the Court throw sufficient light on the Judicial system and its mockery during the early rule of East India Company

Surendra Jha

ooo

Chapter–VI

1. Letter

From,

F. Hamilton,
Acting Collector,Zilla Bhagalpur,
Dated 3 June, 1805

To,

Charles Buller,
Secreatary to the Board of Revenue

"I am sorry to be under the necessity of pointing out an error which has been commited in executioning the Board's orders of the 23rd of August 1803 relative to the settlement of mauzah Pitasah with Roy Kirpanath the ostenslble proprietor of the lands heitherto improperly held rent free in that village, upon half of the Paydawar Jummah.

The business came before Mr. Erskine who signed and issued the Pottah and qabooliat in favour of Mir Bhuggoo. However a few days after Mr. Erskine discovered the above letter and in consequence of Mir Himmat Ali's laying claim to the land in question, he recalled the Pottah and directed him to substantiate his claim in a given time, here the business rested a very short time after I took charge of the office and while Himmat Ali was absent the same Pottah and qabuliat under Mr. Erskine's signature were brought before me to be again issued. After referring to Mr. Erskine's proceedings I enquired whether the new claimant

(Himmat Ali) had proved his right, and finding that he was not present, I did not hesitate to issue the Pottah Sometime ago referring to the records respecting holders of Lakhraj (=Rent free) Lands,I also discovered the Board's letter above noticed,and on my enquiring of the almah respecting this circumstance they said, that they never knew that such a letter was in the office. I therefore, request the Board's instruction whether the Pottah granted to Mir Bhugoo be continued or withdrawn,and an engagement with Roy Kirpa Nath be entered into agreeably to the instructions contained in the said letter. Thus have I been led into the commission of an error,which might have been prevented,had the amlah informed me of the circumstance respecting the discovery which Mr. Erskine made of the letter. It is probable that previous to Mr. Erskine's investigation they did not know of the existence of this letter but there can be no exuse for their with holding that knowledge from me afterwards, besides Mir Bhuggoo in his durkhast, copy of which accompanies, states, that the Pottah and Aumilnamah remained in the Shiristah to be copied. Jaimangal Sing acting Dewan says,that the papers were in his (Mir Bhuggoo's) possession for seven or eight days, and were then recalled by Mr. Erskine. The Record Keeper again says, that they never. Were in his possession at all; so that they Mir Bhuggoo took charge of the land, and made the collections without any authority at all.

Shunker Dutt head Monshi by whom a copy of all papers is taken, at the time of reading his darkhast was aware of these circumstances,but did not acquaint me of them, I have consequently suspended him till I am honoured with the orders of the Board. The late Dewan and the Monshi confess that Mr. Erskine, on discovering these circumstances,was very angry indeed, though they affect ignorance of the cause, and a person now in the office was present at the time Mr. Erskine read and explained the Board's letter, and directed the recall of the papers. "

OOO

2. Letter

From,

F. Hamilton,

Acting Collector, Zilla Bhagalpur,

Dated 17 June, 1805

To,

Charles Buller,

Secreatary to the Board of Revenue"

I have the honour to acquaint you for the information of the Board of Revenue that Chyte Sing, natural son of Bhawany Sing Subadar, deceased, proprietor of mauza Jool Govind is a minor.

Bhawany Sing first came into the district as an Invalid in 1786. He was three times married and has no surviving issue.

Averting to the 6th clause 11th Regulation 1793, I am of opinion that Chyte Sing be the legal proprietor of the estate. First, because he has no will or other writing authenticated by withnesses by which the Bakasht of the estate can be substantiated. Secondly, because Chhote Singh nephew of the deceased Bhawany Singh has ever been with him since his first settling in this thana in 1786. The warisnama which accompanies entitles Chyte Singh to the possession of the Sobadar's Jageer. But I donot think that it authorizes him to keep possession of the estate to the exclusive of Chyte Singh. On enquiry I found he is not generally looked upon as the legal heir and if it be the established Rule, which I understood it is, for the heir apparent to perform the funeral rites of a deceased Hindoo the nephew is certainly entitled to the possession of the estate as he performed them.

I request to be honoured with the Board's orders respecting the mode to be adopted to ascertain the age of the present possessor. Should he be deemed the heir at law. "

ooo

3. "Translation of the Arzee of Nund Lall Amin deputed by the Collector to ascertain and investigate the alluvial lands in possession of Bishnath Singh.

After ackowledgment the Purwannah sent by me, he states that agreeably to your orders I remeasured mauzah Quasimpoor, the next morning being Sunday. I went to Aquidatpoor for the same purpose, but how can I represent the misconduct of Durbari Lall's Amlah. Pheku Chawdhri with 14 persons came on the spot and forcibly snatched away the string from the Jerreebcuss nor would they suffer the lands to be measured, the chuprasi with me, exclaimed against it, but they said they would not attend to the orders of the Collector, as they had received directions from Durabari Lall not to suffer the lands before measured to be remeasured, and consequently they would not suffer it."

A true translation
Signed. Fred. Hamilton.
Collector. "

ooo

4. Letter

List of the Zemindars to whom advances have been made on account of Daur Baunds, and those who are expected to come forward for it.

Name of zem-indars	*Name of Estate.*	*Sudder Jumma*	*Amount advanced*	*Amount to be advanced*
The widow of Rooder	Khas Tuppa champa Nagar	1174.5	58.0.0	-
Sri Narain	Mauzah Nisf Umbaye	3746=701101	186.0.0	
Heera Ram	Khas Tuppa Champa-Nagar Rus-solpoor	4856	240.0.0	
Paras Nath	Ditto	2111-5-14	105-0	
Deep Chund	Khas Tuppa Chandipah	291.12.18.3	50.0	
Muniyar	Ditto	920.1.17	46.-	

Rehman Khan	Khas Tuppa Dakhilcoonje	1358.10.1.2	68.-	
Hitchoo Khan	Mauza Sham-suddinpur	9223.12.3	46	
Gokil Chund Tewary	Mauza Ma-huddipur	2957.7.16	147-8	
Rajah Quadir Ali	Pergunnah Kharagpur	59,986.15.13	----	3500
Sheo Dutt	Khas Tuppa Dakhilcoonje	3987.1.6	--	200
Manick Chund	Khas Tuppa Unwarahbad	1030.13.5.1		55
Colly Prasad	Mauzah Bhawnipur Dysree	915.9.8.2		45
Jeechoo and Tayjah	Mauzah Coonnuth -Birnodah	767.14.8		38
Sheblal Tewary	Mauzah Coindeh	1050.9.5.3		51
Munsa Ram	Basdeopoor	1379.14.6.1		66
Tillak Ram	Rampur	891.15.5		41
Bechoo Chaudhry	Khas Tuppa jethore	1243.3.2.3		62
Kishen Ram	Khas Tuppa Pooranahdace	2203.7.2.3		110
Khoda Buk-shsh	Mauzah Derowah	1212.4.41.1		60
Bussawan	Buzroog Derowah	1768.5.13.1		88
Chunni Mundur	Mauza Chaurah	1003.15.5		50
Benode Mudur	Mauza Baiju Dhee.	659.1		33

Total Sicca Rupees… 945. 8 4753

ooo

5. Letter

From,

F. Hamilton,
Acting Collector, Zilla Bhagalpur,
Dated 4 July, 1805

To,

Charles Buller,
Secreatary to the Board of Revenue

"The enclosed Arzee from Roop Narain Deo, zemindar of Chundwa Passaye contains a petition to have that part of Rajah Quadir Ali's Estate separated, from which he holds a sunnad under the signature of the Governor –General at a fixed Jumma, and which Jamma he himself pays into the company' Treasury and for which an abatement is made in the Rajah's Treasury and for which an abatement is made the Rajah's revenues. He wishes his own name to be registered and that the nominal interest of the Rajh in his zemindary be done away.

I think it necessary to acquaint you that on receipt of the petition, I addressed a Purwanah to the Rajah in consequence of which he attended himself, and produced a Sunnad under the same signature, in which those mahals which constitute Roopnarain's Estate are likewise included, but in this sannad dated 1178 F. S Roopnaan,s Sanad is not annualled, for this reason I have been induced o solicit the orders of the Board.

I beg leave to add, that though Roopnarain pays his revenues into my treasury, he pays them in Sonnat rupees and the difference between those and sicca is paid by Rajah Quadir Ali.

Roopnarain having frequently presented petitions to the same effects., Which my predecessors did not deem worthy of consideration, I could wish that the Board, in order to prevent a repetition of them, would declare the purgunnah of Chandwah passaye to form a part of the Raja's zemidary, for I am clearly of opinion, that he is not entitled to a separation as the time prescribed for the application in section 14th Regulation 1st 1101, has long since expired, Accompanying are the Sannad. "

(Ed.) This Arzee or petition of Roop Narain Deo, the Zamindar of Chandwa Passai explains many factors for his rebellion.

Surendra Jha

OOO

6. Letter

From,

F. Hamilton,
Acting Collector, Zilla Bhagalpur,
Dated 6 July, 1805

To,

Charles Buller,
Secreatary to the Board of Revenue

"I beg leave to acknowledge the receipt of your letter of the 12th ultimo, and to acquaint you, that Mauzah Pitash is now in the possession of Mir Bhuggoo,and the revenue of it are paid by him,on making this enquiry, Mr Himmat Ali came forward with the accompanying Durkhast (a translation of which also accompanies) claiming the Mauzah as his rent –free property and which I deem proper to submit to the Board with copies of his documents for their consideration and orders. I further beg leave to notice to the Board that in consequence of your letter of the 23rd of August 1803, Roy Kirpa Nath is also in attendance. I think the documents of Himmat[ll] are sufficient to establish his claim to the land, rent free nor can I trace a reason for any engagement being entered into with Mir Bhuggoo in opposition to the orders of the Board of the 23rd August 1803. "

"Abastract translation of a petition of Syed Himmat Ali aimahdar of mauzah Pitsah, presented to the Collector of Bhagalpur.

Mauzah Pitsah containing 359 blghas of rent free lands situated in Tuppa Berary Purgunah Colgong were conferred on my ancestors by a grant of Shah Jahan Badshah in the Hyri year 1033, of which 110 Bighas have been in my possession till the year 1209 Fussly, and 190 Bighas the Shares of my Maternal Grand father now under mortgage to whom I am the surviving heir. In the year 1209 F. S. Mr. Sherburne issued a proclamation for registering the Sannads in consequence of which, Syed Assad Ali my farther, deputed me for his business, I accordingly attended the Cutchery and got all my almah rent free grants registered, excepting seven documents relative to mauzah Pitsah, when I was taken sick with a fever and remained sometime very ill. On the 2nd of November 1802, another proclamation was issued by the Collector,noticing that the registry office would be closed at the end of the same month, and on the 9th issued a Dustak against my father to appear with his documents relative to Pitsah, on the following day I appeared at the Collector's Cutchehry with the documents but he would not register them but directs its attachment and dispossessed me. When Mr. Sherburne went to Rangpur Mr. Eskine arrived at Bhagalpur, the Amlah from wickedness got a durkhast from Mir. Bhuggoo(claiming this land as his Milk and offering to farm the same)presented to Mr. Erskine, and obtained orders to grant him a Pottah, on his being about four days in possession of the mauzah I was informed of circumstance,when I presented a petition to Mr. Erskine relative to my right begging him to release my land ; on considering the representation he directed the recall of the Pottah from Mir Bhuggoo, and attached the mauzah having had business at Moorshidabad where I went,on my return I found Mir Bhuggoo again in possession of the same Poattah. Mir Bhuggoo is not entited to a Bighas of the lands in question, how could he have obtained possession of the mauzah. Every document both original and copy I have in my possession,let them be seen,and my lands restored to me. Should the Board of Revenue not admit my claim,I will have recourse to a court of Justice for redress.

A true translation.
Signed /F. Hamilton'
Collector. "

OOO

7. Letter

From,

F. Hamilton,
Acting Collector, Zilla Bhagalpur,
Dated 29 July, 1805

To,

Charles Buller,
Secreatary to the Board of Revenue

"I have the honour to acknowledge the receipt of your letter of the 16th instant in attention to which I directed the attendance of Mir Bhuggoo, to whom the contents were duly explained. He refused giving any answer and said he has no documents. Copy of my proceedings together with a translation accompanies.

In the late Collector's report on this subject dated 15th June 1803, Mir Bhuggoo is not mentioned as a claimant-nay he writes that he (Mir Bhuggoo) had disposed of a share of that land viz. 50Beghas to which it does not appear, that he has the least right and the Amin who went to attach the lands,says,that Mir Bhuggoo was not in possession of a single Cuttha. How then ought any engagement to have been entered into with Mir Bhuggoo, considering the Regulations and the direct orders of the Board respecting Roy Kirpa Nath. It appears evident to me, that the Board Could never have looked upon Mir Bhuggoo as the occupant,and with due deference I presume to suggest the hardship under which Mir Himmat Ali will labor if compelled to have recourse to a Court of Justice, besides the great expense to establish his right to lands which have been in possession, and in that of his family for a series of years. I think possession might be given to Mir Hummat Ali and leave Mir Bhuggoo to prosecute his claim if he has any which I have good reason to believe he will not venture to do, in a court of justice.

I further beg leave to acquaint you, that Mir Himmat Ali has been engaged in procuring his documents from Patna and Morshidabad, and showed me a petition which he intended to give into the court against Government for dispossession,which he deferred on my saying I would enquire into the Circumstances."

Translation of a petition of Peyre Lall

In the year 1207 F. S. a proclamation was issued for the appearance of Mir Asaulat Ali, Malik and zamindar of mauzah Purrayah, in Pergunah Salimabad and muzah Alinagar in pergunah Soorajgurrah on the side of the river Keol(=Kiul),and another was issued in 1210, by the different Collectors,and now a third proclamation has been issued by you,but neither he nor any of his heirs have appeared within the given time to prove their title and right to the Malikanah in question, consequently it appears,that he has no heirs, and from the Canoongoe's reports it seems, that the proprietor has been absent more than 40 years, and as it is necessary to admit a Malik,without which the necessary advantage to Government and the management of the mauzahas cannot be well conducted. I am hopeful that my offer for the purchase of the Malikanah of the above mentioned mauzahs for sanot Rupees 201 be submitted for the approbation of the Board of Revenue and that I will pay the annual jumah of the mauzah of the mauzah as proprietor, viz. :

Sudder Jummah of Purrayah - 105-0-0
" of Alingar - 168-4-10"

A true translation.
Signed/ F. Hamilton,
Collector. "

OOO

8. Letter

From,
F. Hamilton,
Collector, Bhagalpur,
To,
Charles Buller,
Secretary to the Board of Revenue,
Fort William, dated 24 November, 1805.

"I have the honour to enclose a Durkhast presented by Raja Ali with an English Translation,and presume to intrude a few remarks on the subject, which to me appears, of some importance,is as much as the welfare of an individual is concered, who owes his everything to the British Government.

In a manuscript copy of the History of the Zamindars of Bhagalpur complied(compiled), I believe by Mr. Davis in Obedience to the orders of then President and Members of the Board of Revenue under date the 12th February 1787,and persevered among the records of this office,neither Roop Narain Deo nor any of his ancestors are specified as zemindars; nor any of his ancestors are specified as a zemindars; nor even a mention made of their name, and it strikes me,that had any claim on their fact then existed, it would have been brought forward, if not by others Certainly by themselves as the compilers say in the 5th paragraph of the address to the Board, accompanying the History that for the most part it is given on the credit of their traditional accounts alone, which he has no reason to disbelieve as on the many occasions he had of comparing them with those given by families whose relationship was very remote, and whose interests were opposite, he had observed little variation so late then as 1787. I think Roop Narain could not have been considered as a Zemindar. The history of Khargpur after mentioning the ancestors of the present Raja, decribes the estate given to them,which was restored to the present Rajah on the same terms as his ancestors held it and ... this estate is comprised Chundway Pussaye to which Roopnarain now lays claim as. separate zemindary belonging to himself and grounds this claim simply on his having, for some time past, paid his revenue. It could not be traced any where as yet another contemporary account of the Zamindars of Bhagalpur is a correspondence,dated September,1787 from the Collector of Bhagalpur to John Shore, President of the Board of Revenue. [(Ed.)—This is corroborated by Dr. K.K. Basu's article in Bengal past and present 1932] into the Collector's treasury. This is in some degree true, but how or by what authority he has done so is not to be discovered. His name does not appear on the Books of this office, receives no receipts, and he pays his revenues in Sonat Rupees, but the difference between the Sonat Rupees and Sicca Rupees is made good by the Rajas,to whom a receipt in full is given for the whole of the assessment in this zemindary in which Roop Narain pretends to hold a separate and district estate called Chundway Pussaye, and it is in direct opposition to the Regulations that any persons should pay his revenue directly into the Company's Treasury whose name is not registered on the Books of the Collector. His right to separation has not been acknoeledged by the Board,who referred him to the court of Justice for redress, and the period prescribed in Section 14th Regulation 1st of 1801 to prefer claims for separation has long since elapsed ;so that I cannot conceive on that account he is to be indulged in which he wishes while it militates against the existing Regulations of Government and operates to the immediate and future injury on another. In this district there is a dependant styled Ghautwal who for the preservation of Tarriai, Ghaut or passes receives from the principal Tehsildar of the place a certain tract of land some are temporarily some in perpetuity as a remark for this trouble. Roopnarain is one of share and holds a Ghaut from the Rajah's ancestors (subsequently confirmed by the Governor-General in Council) of some lands on which a fixed Jumma is assessed with this particular,excepting, Ruso Zamindary,Nankar Ghautwally. Roopnarain Deo some time ago refused payment of the Rusoome zemindary 2 annas. Rajah Quadir Ali complained in the Adawlat and gained his cause, which was appealed and the degree of the Zillah court confirmed. No force no coercion was used to carry the degree into execution,but it is very true that Fatah Jung Khan, Roopnarain's wakil, has spread a report that Rajah Quadir All sent along with my Perwanah 12 Burkundazes, 200 sepoys to enforce my orders. However, Roopnarain's original receipts of the Perwanah under his own signature is enclosed in which he says that one peon had delivered the Purwanah to him. Shortly after this, I was honoured with the Board's directions not to make any alteration in the mode which the revenues had been paid by Roopnarain Deo which I have certainly obeyed,though in so doing I receive revenues from a person whose name does not appear on my Books.

I humbly wish the Board would take these circumstance into their consideration, for if their orders are to be ultimately carried into execution, the loss in money as well as in dignity that the Rajah will suffer is almost serious, as all the Ghautwalls in this district are concerting among themselves the means to divert the Rajah of his right to their lands.

Some of Rajah Quadir Ali's Tahsildars are now in existence, who collected the revenues of Chunday Pussaye since the expiration of the Rajah's minority.

I entrasat the Board's pardon for trespassing to so much in their time, but I have thought it my duty to represent these circumstances for their consideration."

ooo

9. "Translation of a petition of Rajah Quadir All Zamindar of Mahalat Kharagpur

The Milkeat zemindary, Chowdrye, Canoongoee, and Moquddemury right attached to pergunnah Kharagpur, with the Russon zemindary of two annas in the Rupee,have been the right of my ancestors and in every pergunnah the officers Gomashtash,with the power of Chowdrye, Moquddemy, Canoogoee and Ghatwally were granted by Sannads of my ancestors. When my grandfather Rajah Mozaffar Ali incurred the displeasure of Nawab Quasim Ali khan, then Sobah of Azimabad and of his Naib Rajah Shetab Roy, every thing fall in confusion,so that I was plundered of all the papers,and documents relative to my zemindary,in consequence of which several Ghatwalls,who were nominated by my ancestors rebelled against me,on which account the Governor General in council deputed Captain Brooke and Browne to quell these disturbances and the Jungleterries of Kharagpur, Guidore, Bhaglpur, Colgong and Beerbhoom. My father Rajah Fazal Ali was called for by those gentlemen and under their directions quelled the disturbances of the Ghatwalls,and obtained a Sannad for the whole of the Jungleterry Pergunnah Chundwah Pussays agreeable to former usages, under the seal and signatures of those gentlemen, under the authority of the governor General which Sannad I hold. In the year 1183 Fussly, my father died and I was then but an infant,in consequence of which everything relating to my zemindary fell again in confusion. In the year 1184 Fussly,Jagarnath Deo obtained the farm of dehaut Jumdahale pergunnah Chundwa Pussaye, Suthearry. Dehaut Fitmoch in pergunnah Hindoah from Captain Browne for the annual Jummah of Scant Rupees 5000. After this in the year 1185 Fussly he gave in another durkhast for the Mokararry of several dehaut of pergunnah Goordah and pergunnah Amlomoteah,at an increase of Jummah of Rupees 7291. after deducting the two annas Russoome zamindary, and the Nankar Canongoe and obtained a Mocurrey Sannad (a copy of the

Kafeatnamah I have,of the manners in which this Mocurrery Bandobust was made). In the year 1188 F. S. the Governor General in Council, and the Gentleman of the Zillah investigated my right, and established me in my zemindary Moquddemy,and Cannogoe of the whole of the pergunnah Kharagpur,with the title of Rajah,as it stood with my ancestors,and in consequence of my having thus obtained my right and title. The balance due from the Jungleterry Ghautwalls for the preceding year 1187 F. S. were recovered from me by the Gentleman of this Zillah, which can be proved from the office of the Collector, inclusive of Chundawah Pussaye. The Gentleman of Zillah issued Parwannab to Roop Narain Deo and other Ghutwalls, together with the Malgoozars of the Mofussil,directing and requiring them respectively to pay also the Revenues to me,a copy of this I have,and I am confident,a copy of it is to be found in the office of the Collector. Roop Narain Deo consequently presented a Kabooleat to me under his signature(calling himself a Mootageer and Ghautwal) for the Mocurrey of the place in his possession,inclusive of the two annas zemindary Rusoome Khazanchi,and Betta Noctannah, and accordingly obtained a Pottah from me. In conformity to which he paid his revenue to me at Kharagpur and at times through Fatth Sing and Bukhtawar sing tehsildars on my part, and at Bhagalpur through my wakeel, those Challan and Wasil Baqui accounts under his 1190 F. S. **MR. Cleveland attached the whole of my zemindary on account of arrears due to** Government and on account of a debt due to captain Browne, and confined Choony Lall, my Peshkar, he then **sent Murdan Sing. Conjul Sing and Parashal Sing as aumeels**,and the cutchhery of Kharagpur was removed to Bhagalpur,and he appointed **Manick Chund** as Tehsilder and Bahadur Sing Sirishtadar,and recovered the revenues from the whole of my zemindars,as also from the Mustageers and Ghautwalls and from Chundwah Pussaye and received them at the Cutchery from Manik Chund, with whom my Amalahs also acted, to see the revenues duly accounted; these papers are also to be found in the office, and Bahadur Sirishtadar is yet alive and present. In the month of Jeth of the same year, the whole of the arrears and debt were recovered and realized, and Mr. Cleveland relinquished my zemindary, and directed the Aumalah he had deputed,to make over to me all papers and documents and accordingly I received them. These papers I also have by me. In the year 1191 F. S. Roop Narain Deo disobeyed my orders, and as I was too young, Mr. Cleveland authorized Chunni Lal my Peshkar arrived at the place, Roop Narain Deo made his escape and fled after this. Mr. Cleveland allowed my Peshkar a Milltary, and as Roop Narain Deo had fled, my peshkar made the Bandousts of Chunwah Pussaye and after a few days returned the Sepoys to their station and Mr. Celeveland gave me a Purwanah dispossessing Roop Narain Deo which Purwanah I have Sir. The pergunah Chundwa Pussaye is included in my Bandobust and Jammah, and was never alienated and several papers of Poattahs, from the council and Zillah, I possess,with the Nakhilahs to this effect. From the time of my ancestors to the time Brahmins,poors in the pergunahs of Chundwah Pussaye dehats as Burmooter, Sheboter, Fookraneh, Jagheerat and Inamat under our own grants and most probably the heirs of these Lakherajdars must have them yet, and must have had them registered in the office of the Collector some time in the year 1209 F. S. but the particulars of them were furnished to the Collector in the year 1189 F. S. . Further,my ancestors granted to the ancestors of Nawab Sing alias Nawab Khan the mauzah called Ungarroo, the Gopal Deo the son of Bhekum Deo, mauzah Tuppah Dhee,to Dharam Deo, mauzah Dhopin, and in the year 1181 F. S. my father Rajah Fuzel Ali granted to Nainsuk Manik Sing, Keul Sing, Jugesser Sing, the mauzah Bhoresour attached to pergunnah Dandah Sukwarrah upon a Sharrayee jammah of five rupees; these person must have the Sannads With them for the above grants. Nainsuk Dutt,and Herlal Dutt,and Herlal Dutt, who were my Gomashtahs at Chundwah Pussaye, though not there now, are yet alive,and no doubt,but that they must have some sannads of my ancestors in their possession. From the time of the fromer Rajah two Tehsildars were always employed in each pergunnah to prevent disputes among the aumils and Jagheedars viz. ; one for the collections of Mall Revenue, the other for the collection of Russoome zemindary and Nankar. In the time of my grandfather Rajah Mozaffer Ali, Mohammad Khan the father of Aziz Khan, and Abdul Rasool Khan(the present Hill sezawal) were tehsildars of the Pergunahs of Jungleterry portions,for many years and one of them, the latter is yet alive who if inquired of, will centainly explain of zemindary right to those parts of the Jungleterry now possessed by Roop Narain Deo, Gulah Roy, Shuchdaur tehsildar of two annas Russome zemindary and Nankar of the pergunnahs attached to the Jungleterry continued in the service for many years, his grandson Jawhir Mull, is now living, Datta Ram and Bishen Datt gomashtahs acting as Chowdries; Bengali Sing Moharrer of pergunnah Dandah Suckwarrah and Monorut Singh and Sheodutt Sing Ghautwals of Suckwarrah of the same place, Kishan Ram and Sohri Sing gomashtahs acting as Chowdries of pergannah Goordeh,Bhola and Conjmun gomashtan and acting as Chowdries of Perganah Amlomoteh. Rajah Purandur Sing the nephew of Sobah Sing deceased, and Anoop Chund the son of Gopi Chund, Motasuddy of the above Rajah. Boodum Sing Lall & sing, the brothers of the Rajah above mentioned Brijbhookun Sing Ghatwal of Saharah and Maharah; Bhikhari Sing Ghatwal of Cummerdeha, attached to Hendooah; Ruttun Chund Moharrir who was with my Peshkar Chunnilal. In the pergunahs attached to the Jungleterries, are persons well acquainted with all the affairs of my zemindary rights, and Dheer Sing Sirishtadar of the peshkar is yet living; I am confident,that all the papers relative to the collections of every description of Chundwan Pussaye must be in his Sirishtah. In the Year 1188 when the Mustagery bandobust of the mahal of Roopnarain Deo Ghautwal, was about to be made at the cutchery of Kharagpur, Several Ohededars of the place were continually present, from the beginning of the entering into a Bandobust to the time he received a Pottah and give in his Kabooleat for pergunnah Chundwah Pussaye, and are informed of all particulars. Sometime ago Roop Narain Deo objected to pay the Russoom Canongoe, upon which I complained against him to Mr. Fombelle, the then Judge of this district, and at the time of Mr. Wintle his successor, the claim was inquired into and from documents my right was proved, and I obtained a degree from the court for Sonat Rupees 1023 per annum. Roop Narain Deo appealed to the Morshidabad Court and the Court of appeal confirmed the decision of the Zillah court; these degrees I have. Now Fatah Jung Khan the Vakeel of Roop Narain Deo has falsely spread reports in Bhagalpur and in the Jungleterries, which are openly talked of that the Collector has authorized Rajah Quadar All by a Perwanah to receive Khazanah from Roop Narain Deo, but that the latter will not submit to it, but enter into war and create disturbances, so that many lives shall be lost. It is unknown how this report reached the Board of Revenue, or what good grounds the Board listened to them however the Board with a view to prevent those pretened disputes have directed that Roop Narain Deo should pay his Revenue into the Collector's Treasury in the same manner as former 1 however contrary to the established usages and the Regulations; for instance,why should Roop Narain Deo Ghatwal, alone, be exclusively allowed this privilege it will naturally be understood, that none of the Ghatwalls are to pay their revenues through me, and such a principle is already in agitation, by Bhole Ghatwall of Chattoreah(Katoria), Pyroo Sing Ghatwal of Mungraur, Odwant Sing Ghatwal of Peaurphair Ghatwalls attached to Kharagpur, my zemindary who have collected together,and are consulting in what manner to resist paying their Revenues to me heretofore;such serious evils are likely to take rise from the false reports of Fatah Khan, and as to Roop Narain Deo, he is by no means inclined, or has any thoughts of creating disturbances, and being an old being an old Ghatwal, he will not presume to do so. Before,when he once disobeyed my orders, some time in 1191 F. S. Mr. Celeveland deputed my Peshkar to dispossess him, he fled and would not make any resistance. Now that under the protection of the English Government I have obtained my age, and still continue under their aid. How can the Jungleterry Ghatwalls, presume to make resistance? Sir, should not Roop Narain Deo be directed to pay His Malagozary to me, the other Ghatwalls will also at the instigation of Fath Jung Khan, destist from paying their revenues to me and create disturbances, how then, and from what Estates,shall I be able to pay my Malgozary to the English Government, and as these, and all and are saying among themselves that the Collector, Judge and the Board of Revenue,from the report of Fatah Jung Khan, have determined,with the view prevent disturbances to issue such orders; now then, when the Rajah shall demand his revenues from us we also will proclaim the like, and the Board will issue the same orders respecting us also. Sir, should the Ghatwals, who are my servants, be indulged in such wickedness, and not pay me their Malgozary how shall I be able to pay the revenue of Government, and Mr. Cleveland were pleased to honour me with will be reduced to disgrace and dishonour,and from the respect and attachment of all description of person, to their known Justice, now will presume to resist their orders those who have attempted to do so, have already met with the punishment due to their conduct, and should Roop Narain Deo possess such thoughts, he certainly will feel the consequences. Roop Narain Deo has paid his Revenues to me from the year 1188 F. S. to 1197 F. S. but some time after the death of my Peshkar Cunny Lall,when I was very young. I could not manage my estates and officers found an opportunity and got his Revenues taken at the Collector's Cutcherry distinctly, and exclusively, but they are included my Jammah and Dakilah in full is given to me accordingly to the Bandobust. I am therefore,hopeful, that a Perwanah be issued to Roop Narain Deo directing him to pay his Revenues to me of Perganah Chundwah Pussaye and that I may accordingly to Bandobust, pay the full amount of my malgozary to you. "

A true translation.
Signed/ F. Hamilton,
Collector. "

OOO

10. "Translation of Perwannah issued by the Collector of Zillah Bhagalpur to Rajah Quadir Ali,Zemindar of Mahalat Kharagpur dated 31st August 1805 corresponding with the 17th of Bhadou 1212 Fusly

The Rajah of Kharagpur having presented a Darkhast to the following effect, the same was read setting forth, that Roop Narain Deo had presented a Darkhast for the purpose of separating parganahs Chundwa Pussaye attached to Kharagpur, my zemindary, which darkhast together with my answer and copies of my other documents relative to my zemindary were reported to the Board of Revenue. The Board of Revnue having made enquiries respecting the right of my zemindary, issued orders that parganah Chandwah Pussaye could not be separated from Kharagpur, my zemindary. As Pergannah Chundwan Pussaye,Suthehary and dehats Jamadahah and umlomoteach (Amlo-Motia), in Perganah Goordah from my zemindary, and in consequence of the above orders the separation could not be effected. I am hopeful that the revenues of the above-mentioned places will not be received at the chtchery from Roopnrain Deo and that a perwanah be issued to him,directing him to pay them to me at my Sudder cutchery in Kharagpur, and to attend to my orders as become a zemindar to issue; also that a Perwanah be issued to me directing me to receive the collections of the places in Question in conformity to my Sanad and Potah and pay them into the Treasury at Bhagalpur."

Sd. Rajah Quadir Ali. "

"As previous to the above representation, the Darkhast of Roop narain Deo for obtaining a separation from Kharagpur and Rajah Quadir Ali's objects hereto, has been submitted to the Board of Revenue, and the answer to that reference being received in a letter from Mr. Scretary Buller dated the 12th of July 1805 to the following effects, that Pergannah Chandwah Pussys could not be sparate from the zemindary of Rajah Quader Ali,and if he (Roop Narain) have any claim to a separation to refer the same to a court of justice. Agreeable to regulation 1st Section 14th of 1801, Roopnarain should have presented his darkhast for separation within the space of one year, which he never did. By what authority Roopnarain Deo pays his Revenues exclusively appears very extraordinary to the collectors, as from the records it does not appear that any separation ever took place; probably known the payment of the revenues exclusively was made in conformity to the orders of some former Collectors a further reference to the records, was therefore made but nothing could be found to that effects,again Roopnarain Deo pays his revenues in Sonat rupees and the batta, or difference, is taken from Raja Quader Ali,as being the zemindars of Kharagpur, and it is contrary to the usage of the country of revenue for lands that have not been legally separated or from persons whose names are not registered in the Books of the Collectors. It is, therefore, incumbent to give Pussaye to Rajah Quader Ali the Zemindar of Kharagpur, and you are, therefore, directed to receive them from Roopnarain, and forward the same to the Cutcherry to the Collector. Herein fail not. "

A true translation.
Signed/ F. Hamilton
Collector. "

(ED.) These Documents are important for re-constructing the history of Kharagpur Raj.

Surendra Jha

ooo

11. Kankjole

(Genealogical Account of part of the ConkJole)

Mahur-ul-Nissa who married Mahomed Akrum, by whom she had one daughter. Abdullah Chowdry had one son, Mahomed Afgun who had two daughters.

Baby Jaun who married Mahomed Nafir by whom she had one daughter. Hummer-Ul-Nissa who married Cauf.... Assum Cawn by whom she had one son, Mahomed Haffir and one daughter.

Wizier-ul-Nissa who married (thrice)tyre, who died without issue. Auneer-Ul-Nissa who married Meer Noor Ally by whom she has two sons and one daughter.

(Kankjole) zemindar

N. B:- Abdoolah choudry was succeeded in the zemindary by Mahomed Afzul was not succeeded by Mahomed Akrum, who was succeeded by Mahomed Naffer who was succeeded by Mahomed Tyre, on whose death the zemindary reverted to Hummer-ul-Nissa the present Zemindaar, who,with the consent of Mahomed Tyre's widow Wizier-Ul-Nissa, is now desirous of assigning over the zemindary to her Grandson Emaum Bucks.

OOO

12. Letter

From,

F. Hamilton,
Collector, Bhagalpur,
Dated 21 December, 1805

To,

Charles Buller,
Secreatary to the Board of Revenue, Fort William.

"I beg leave to submit for consideration and orders of the Board of Revenue the accompanying copy of an Arzee presented by Dirgbejoy sing the Zeminder of Talookah Pokerawah in pergunnah Surujgarha. This claim appers to me just, in every point of view the separations effected by Mr. Dickinson, being illegal and repugnant both to the letter and spirit of the Regulation and the proclamation of the Governor Gerneral in Council, was as such condemned by the Board of Renvenue. These circumstances have already been fully explained to the Board by Mr. Sherburne in his address of the 8th of May 1802, in consequence of which the Board were pleased to direct the re-annexation to the Zamindars of all the lands illegally separtated from their Estates, the court of Adalat has also confirmed the same on the 5th of last November, the case of Digbejoy Sing is exactly the same as that of Hire Ram and other. I have not however presumed to pas any orders until I receive the directions of the Board of refer you to Mr. Sherburne's address above quoted. "

OOO

13. Letter

From,

F. Hamilton,
Collector, Bhagalpur,
Dated 22 January, 1806

To,

Charles Buller,
Secreatary to the Board of Revenue, Fort William.

"I beg to submit for the consideration and orders of the Court, the accompanying copy and translate of an Arzee from the Sabarahkar of Tuppa Dakhilconj (Near Jagdishpur, Bhagalpur) and to request their authority to incur the expense therin mentioned for the repairs of the high roads. "

OOO

14. "Translation of an Arzee of Digbejoy Sing Zemindar of Talookah Pokerawah in Pergunnah Soorajgarha.

The whole of Talookah Pokerawah in my Milkeat, and the bandobust of it from former times has descended to me. When proclamations were issued for the Decennial Settlement, I obtained the Bandobust Settlement of its from Mr. James Grant upon the same terms as my ancestors held it, and accordingly received my Pottah and gave in my Kabooliat and I have paid my kists regularly every year.

On the 10th of November 1798 the orders of Council under date the 7th September 1789 were promulgated by Mr. Dickinson the then Collector relative to the perpetuity of the Decennial Settlement. After the expiration of the Decennial Settleement I petitioned to said Collector in conformity to a publication then issused and obtained a Perwanah to the tenor and effects of an umulnamah(Aminama) dated 26th of Magh 1206 F. s. for the continuation of my Talookah upon the usual footing in perpetuity, and in Assin 1207 F. S. after the Tauzi Account a perwanah was issued to me for the first Kist of that year, which I paid into the Collector's Treasury, a copy of which I have, In Katik the Collector deputed a sezawal and made it khass, and afterwards the then Dewan in collusion with the Mofussil Moquddums, who were no more than Sarbarhkars and had nothing to do with zamindary Bandobusts, called for them and without any enquiry into the Hustabood Accounts nor through the General mode of sending an Ameea(Amin) agreeably to the regulation, nor from any authority of the Board of Revenue entered into a Bandobust with them for five Mahals attached to my Talookah, upon reduced Jammah, for instance, Chuk Narsing, whose jammah in the Decennial Settlement stood Rs. 343-7-10 was engaged for Rupees 273-15- in perpetuity and the rest in the like manner, so that these differencse were added to the jammah of my remaining Mahals. The Collector was inclined to enter into engagements with me for these remaining mahauls, but in consideration of the Regulations, Proclamation, and Perwanah in perpetuity. I objected to it, because they always occasioned a loss and could never pay their fixed jammah. I nevertheless addressed him that in confotmity to his perwannah, the regulations (meaning Sections 3rd and 4th of Regulation I of 1793) and the Proclamations of Government my engagements could not be annulled, he would not, however, listen to me but insisted and wrote them down among the khood Bandobusty Mahauls, on these account a sezawal is sent every year to my Mahauls, and after collecting all he can during the year, for the balance, occasioned by actual loss, my estate advertised for sale every year, I have presented my grievances and the occasion of the losses, to the collectors, but I have never been heard finding my self helpless, I borrowed and sold my property and paid up the arrears for the sake of saving my zemindary. There are three Talookahs in pergannah Surajgarha, Pokerawah,Powy and Jujwarrah whose decennial bandobusts were upon the same terms and priciples and although the two latter Talookahas had Mocuddums no alterations or changes were made in them excepting in that of my Talookah. The said Collector did also violate the orders respecting the Decennial Settlements in the case of Hira Ram Chaudry Rooder Mohan, Sri Narain and Paras Nath, zamindars of tuppahs(=tappa) champanagar near Bhagalpur)and Rasoolpur by dispossessing them in 1207 Fussly, of several mahauls and entering into engagements for them with the Mocuddums,(=Mukaddam) without any authority from the Board of Revenue. In the year 1209 F. S. , they preferred their complaints to Mr. Sherburne who referred the circumstances to the Board of Revenue, with copies of their petitions, and the Sezawal's Sanad which after consideration and investigation, they were pleased to direct to be annulled, those mehauls that were illegally separated to be restored to the Zemindars in question agreeably to the Decennial Settlements copies of which orders will be found in the Collector's office, and they accordingly obtained their rights. Soon after this the Mocuddums complained in the Zillah Court, which suit was dismissed by the Court on the 5th of November 1805. Sir, as my case is exactly the same and of the same nature, I am hopeful that in conformity to Government's Proclamations the Perwannah of Mr. Dickinson, the regulations and the orders of the Board of Revenue dated 21st of May 1802, in the case of Hira Ram be also graciously extended towardsme, and that I may obtain justice. The reason why I did not set forth my grievances before, now, is, that I waited the result of the complaints of the Mocuddums against the Zemindars, and against the orders of the Board of Revenue in the Zillah Court, which only last month, was tried and dismissed.

15. "Translate of an Arzee from Roopnarain Deo Sarbarahkar of Tuppa Dakhilcoonj the zemindary of Sheo Prasad Chowdry.

A Perwanah has been issused by the Magistrate of the Zillah to Bolaki Lall Darogha of thana Ruttungunga,(=Ratanganj) calling upon all the zemindars, through whose zamindaries the high roads run, to repair them within their respective estates, and should any one refuse so to do, to report the same to the Magistrate Among others, I was called upon and a copy of the Magistrate's Perwannah was furnished to me, in consequence of this order through their respective zemindaries Sir, the expense for repairing the roads in the Estate of Sheo Prasad Choudry will be about 60 Rupees but I cannot incur it without orders, I therefore, inform you of the circumstances and request your orders".

A true translation.

OOO

16. Letter

From,

F. Hamilton, Collector,Bhagalpur,

Dated 3 March, 1806

To,

Charles Buller,

Secretary to the Board of Revenue, Fort William.

"I beg leave to acknowledge the receipt of your letter of the 28th ultimo and to acquaint your for the information of the Court, that Tuppa Dakhilcoonj was never before under Sarbarahkary management, I called upon the Sarbarahkar now managing the estate for an account of the expences for repairing the roads of former years; enclosed is a copy and translate of his answers.

"Translation of an Arzee from Roopnarain Deo sarbarahkar of Tuppa Dakhilcoonj the zemindary of Sheo Prasad Chowdry insance.

I have received your Perwannah relative to commending the repairs of the roads, and also to report the extent and expences incurred in the preceding years on account of repairing the roads, I have agreeably to the orders commenced repairing them, and for the estimate and account particulars of charges for repairs of past years, I called upon the Amla of the Zemindar, they replired that such charges were generally defrayed by the Zemindar himself, on which account those particular are not be found in the Serishtah, and added that for clearing jungles and filling up hollows the expences annually amounted from 30 to 35 Rupees, but the manner that the Magistrate now directs the road to be made,Viz" 22 cubits broad and slandng was never done before. Sir, I am now repariring the roads, when finished I will submit an account particular of the charges. "

Signed/Roop Narain Deo,
Sabarbhkar Dakhiloonj
A true translation.

ooo

16 (a). Letter

From,

F. Hamilton, Collector,Bhagalpur,

Dated 13 March, 1806

To,

Charles Buller,

Secreatary to the Board of Revenue, Fort William.

"I beg leave to acknowledge the receipt of your letter of the 11th ultimo, and to acquaint you for the information of the Board of Revenue, that I issued the usual advertisements for the Farm of Kismat pergannah Conkjool,(=kankjol= Rajmahal) and intimated the same to the proprietor, no tenders have however been made to me by any person to farm it. The proprietor, Imam Buksh, presented to me Darkhast, copy and translate of which are herewith transmitted, offering to enter into an agreement for an annual jammah of Sincca Rupees 11500 clear of all charges from 1216 B. S. . the Board will observe from the accompanying statement extracted from the records of my office that the net collections received by Government in the last twelve year,Viz: from 1200 to 1211 B. S. inclusive, amount to Sicca Rupees 1,22,358-8-7-2 which gives an annual average of Rupees 10196. 8. 11. 1 Contrasted with the amount collections for former years, I confess, I think the present offer advantageous to Government and equitable with respect to the proprietor nor have I any hope or expectation that a better one will be made. I have repeatedly tried to farm the Estate, but without success. I have consequently, in attention to the order contained in the last paragraph of your letter of the above date, concluded the settlement with him for Sicca rupees 11501 annually, subject however to the reversal of the Board. Should they not approve of it, enclosed is his Iqrarnamah withan English translate binding himself to stand by any orders with he may be favoured."

OOO

17. "Translate of a Darkhast for the Khod Bandobust in perpetuity of Kismat Pergannah Conkjol,Zillah Rajmahal by the proprietor Emam Baksh Chaudry from 1213 Bengal style dated 28th of Phagun 1212 B. S.

Kismat perganah Conkjol an account of its high jammah has been held khas from the time of the Decennial Settlement to the year 1212 B. S. and whatever revenues have been annually received are well known. I have now been called upon for the Bandobast of it although the assets are still deficient, Nevertheless, as it is my property, I agree to enter into a Bandobast in perpetuity for Kismat pergannah Conkjol inclusive of petty Talookdars attached to it, from the year 1213 B. S. for an annual jamamh of Sicca Rupees 11,501 exclusive of Dehauty and Pergunatty charges and all Gundah Mamooli charges, and I will receive from Government, from the treasury of the Collector, the Moshagara I have hitherto received and still an receiving monthly, whether the Mehal be under Bandobasty engagements with me or otherwise."

A true translation.

Signed /F. Hamilton Collector."

ooo

18. "Translate of the engagement entered into by Emam Baksh Chaudhry referred to in the Collector's letter to the Board of Revenue dated the 13th of march 1806.

I Emam Baksh Chaudhry zemindar of Kismat, Pergunnah Conkjol, Have entered into a Khood Bandobast for the Kismat aforesaid for an annual jummah of Sicca Rupees 11501, agreeably to a Darkhast and Qabooliat and have received and obtained a Pottah and Ammalnamah for the same to commence from the year 1213 B. S. and as this is to be reported to the Board of Revenue for their sanction and confirmation, I therefore of my own free will and consent declare and give in this writing, that if the Board of Revenue should confirm the settlement, well and good, if not, I will without any manner of objection return and make over the Pottah and Amalnamh to the Collector Dated 11th march, 1806.

A true translation.
Signed /F. Hamilton
Collector. "

OOO

19. Letter

From,

F. Hamilton,
Collector, Bhagalpur,
Dated 14 March, 1806

To,

Charles Buller,
Secreatary to the Board of Revenue, Fort William.

"I beg leave to acknowledge the receipt of your letter and enclosure of the 7th current, and to acquaint you for the information of the Board, that the property in question originally belonged to Mr. Chrles Trower,who sold it to Mr. John Hunter, from whom I purchased it by quick sale, Consequently I have no little deeds or conveyance in my possession, nor did Mr. Hunter, I suppose received any he purchased it. The premises are wellknown to be my property agreeably to the plans already furnished to the Board, Standing on eleven cottahs of lands, subject to the payment of rent to the zamindar, at the rate of one rupee per Begha, per annum, and is bounded on the north by the Collector's dwelling houses and by the high road to the South, and to the east and west by the Collector's pleasure grounds from which it is separated on each side by a Pucca Brick wall. "

20. Letter

From,

F. Hamilton, Collector, Bhagalpur, dated 15 March, 1806

To,

Charles Buller,

Secreatary to the Board of Revenue, Fort William.

"I beg leave to acquaint you for the information of the Board of Revenue, that Rahat –un –Nisah the Zemindar of Kismat Pergannah Conkjole has sold her portion of the zemindery together with the Moshara which she received from my treasury monthly of Sicca Rupees 108-14-6-1, to Salaumunt Roy, who is now in attendance at my cutchery to receive it, referring to Mr. Sherburne's 15 letter of the 6th of June, 1804 and the Board's orders thereon, under date the 19 th of the same month, directing that the Moshare mentioned in it, shall not be sold with the land belonging to Rahut –un- Nisa. I request the Board's instructions for my guidance. Salaumunt Roy holds a regular deed of Sale from Rahat –un –Nisa for the zemindary and the Moshara and I fear, should be deprived of the letter reference will be had to a court of Justice.

I cannot trace among the records whether Mr. Sher-burne made any reply to second paragraph of your letter of the 19 th June, 1804 here in alluded to, I can however add for the information of Board, that the Moshara received by Sayfullah Chaudhry, is now enjoyed by his son Ahmadullah Chaudhry.

ooo

21. Letter

From,
F. Hamilton, Collector,Bhagalpur,
Dated 6 March, 1807

To,

Charles Buller,
Secreatary to the Board of Revenue, Fort William.

"I beg leave to submit for the consideration and orders of the Board of Revenue, the accompanying copy and translate of a Petition presented to me by Hira Ram Chaudhry Zemindar of Tuppah Chumpanagar and have only to add for their information, that there are several degress of Moorshidabad Court of Appeal to the same effect as that given against Baudeh Khyrah, in other zemindaries, nor am I advised by the court to stay the execution of the degree in question.

ooo

22. "Translation of an Arzee presented by Hira Ram Chaudhry Zemindar of Tuppah Chumpanagar.

Madho Ram Ghosh complained against me in the adawlat for possession of Mauzah Baudeh Khyrah. The Zillah Court dismissed the suit, the plaintiff appealed to the Moorshidabad Court of Appeal, where the Zillah degree was reversed ; I have now appealed to he Sudder Diwany Adawlat under Regulation II of 1805, and have appointed Ram Bhajan Jha to procced thither and carry on the suit, now in conformity to the degree of the Moorshidabad court of appeal, the plaintiff has given a Darkhast to you to dispossess me and give him possession of Mauzah Baudeh Khyrah, and you have according isused the order. An ameen has been deputed to fix the jamma of Mauzah Habibpur in conformity to a degree of the Sudder Dewany Adawlat, and the orders of the Board, under Regulation I of 1793, but

Baudeh Khyrah which is situated in the same Tuppah and equally dependant on Champanagar is to be separated upon the jummah it bore in1207 Fussliy when that Bandobust was never approved of by the Board. If the degree of the Sudder Dewany Adawlat in the suit of Habibpur be admitted,the degree of the court appeal in separating Baudeh Khyrah is invalid and should the latter be admitted. As I have appealed to the sudder Dewany Adawlat in the suit of Baudeh Khyrah. I am ready to give security till that court has determined how the plaintiff can be put in possession. I am therefore, hopeful that the execution of the degree of the Moorshidabad court of Appeal may be stayed till the Sudder Dewany Adawlat have determined upon it, or that a copy of my arzee be submitted to the Board of Revenue.

A true translation.
Signed /F. Hamilton
Collector. "

OOO

23. Letter

From,
F. Hamilton, Collector,Bhagalpur,
Dated 27 April, 1807

To,

R. Thackeray Secreatary to the Board of Revenue, Fort William. " I beg leave to acknowledge the receipt of your letter of the 14th current, and to submit a statement of the Malikanah due to Hira of the 25th of November last amounting to Sicca Rupees 257-3.

I am sorry to observe in reply to the second paragraph of your last mentioned letter, that although I have made known to the other zemindars the sentiments of the annexing to their respective jammahs the amount produce of the Tarr, and Khajoor trees attached to their estates, none have to this period come forward with that view, but they now wish to have possession of the Mahals agreeably to the Regulations, though in their respective Pottahs, the exception thereof is made, as the Board will obseve from the accompanying copies of 21 arzees, received in consequence of my Perwanahs to them; there are all of the same tenor therefore a translate of one of them accompanies. "

OOO

24. "Translate of An Arzee presented by Bishnath Singh zemindar of Talookah Ummerpore (=Amarpur Banka), perganah Chye, and Tuppah Havelly Bhaudans, pergannah Furkeah (Pharkia), throught his Vakil Peyare Lall

I have received your Perwanah agreeable to the orders of the Board of Revenue dated the 25th of November, 1806 calling upon me to enter into settlements for the Tarr and Khajoor trees in my zemindary. Sir,in conformity to Section XI Regulation VI of 1800, Section XII Regulation XXXVI. The Paidawar of the Tarr and Khajoor trees are the right of the proprietor of the soil, and Government is to receive 25 percent on the amount of the Pottahs granted by the proprietors to the Passees. This usage exists in the Zillah of Tirhoot also; I am therefore, hopeful, that in conformity to those Regulations I may be permitted to have possesstion of them as I am not willing to include the amount of the paidawars of Tarr and Khajoor, with my jummah, as offered in your perwanah. I am confident, that from the justice of the Board of Revenue, I shall obtain my right,"

A true translation.
Signed /F. Hamilton
Collector. "

OOO

25. Letter

From,

Hamilton, Collector, Bhagalpur.

To,

R. Thacker,Secretary to the Board of Revenue,
Fort William
Dated 7 May, 1807

"I beg leave to submit copy of an arzee presented by **Sungram Sing (an infant of five years of age) the adopted son of Ranny Surbessery thro**. His vakeel Khemahjeet Roy, representing the death of the Ranny, Yesterday who received a pension of 50 Rupees per mensem from Government, from my Treasury, on the recommendation of the late Mr. Cleveland under the 29th of March 1783, for her support, during her life time, in consequence of her being dispossessed of her Zemindarry of Pargunnah Sooltanabad. The object of the petition is, a continuation of the pension in question to him, also during his life time. He is the son of one of the Ranny's distant relations, and his father Oochub Singh is yet alive, he also from his youth was supported by the deceased Ranny.

2. I request the Board's instructions whether her pension is to cease from this date or on the 31st of this month. "

ooo

26. Letter

From,

J. P. ward, Acting Collector, Bhagalpur,
Dated 14 September, 1822

To,

James Pattle,

Acting President and Members of the Board of Revenue Lower Provinces, Fort William.)

51) The Board of Commissioners under date the 26th of March called upon this office by discredition of Government for certain information regarding the Ghatwall Tenure in this District and requested the magistrade to furnish a similar report – The report from this office was submitted on the 21st of may following:-

52) There are three descriptions of Hill Tenures:

   1) Assignment of lands made by Government for the support of a police to protect the Hill passes.

   2) Assignment of lands made for the maintenance and support of the Hill Chiefs and their families.

   3) the "Daminkoh" or skirts of the Hills which the Hill Chiefs claim in proprietory right to as appending to their Hill possession.

53) The above lands are of great extent extending along the lease of the Hills from Monghyr to the borders of Beerbhum a distance of 160 miles.

54) The first descriptions were made over to the hill people in 1779 the first subjects to a trifling quiet rent payable to the Sircar through the Zamindar in whose estate the lands are situated and the latter is claimed as belonging to the hills.

55) The police, however, for which the lands were assigned is at present in consequence of the tranquil state of the country but partially kept up. The Zamindar of neighbouring estate taking advantage of this have been gradually encroaching on the Jagheers at present claim a right to the lands as being situated within their estates.

56) In consequence of their usurpation the lands have been mostly forsaken by the hill people and for want of Ryots to cultivate are now waste and evergrown with Jungle.

57) Unoccupied as the lands now are by the hill people by having driven away by the Zamindars and the zamindars from not being able to procure other Ryots to establish themselves there as cultivators; **a favourable opportunity now offers for Government to assert its right to the lands, they are extremely extensive and thus being reclaimed from their present state would add to the prosperity of the district and yield a very considerable Revenue-** of the right of Government to them I conceive there can be no question – the lands were originally set apart for the hill people who were to render service to the estate and it was expressly conditioned in the grants that in failure of those services being perform or if misconduct should be proved against the Jagheerda the lands are liable is not I believenecessary but if necessary it is not kept up the lands therefore might revent to Government and measures should be used to prevent their being encourached (encroached) by the Zamindar.

58) The information in regard to the relation in which the Ghatwalles are considered to stand to the Zamindar, I beg to refer your Board to my address to the Board of Commissioners dated the 21st may which contained all the information in the subject- that the records of this office affords- and which I was desired to supply a report on the same subject will be found in your office submitted about the same time by the Magistrate of this district at the request of the Central Board.

59) I conceive that it would be very descirable to have the lands surveyed – a line of boundary defined to separate them from the Zamindars estate which when completed, it might for consideration, in what manner it would be most advisable, to dispose of them- and the present uncertainty as to whom the right of property in the lands belongs (there being considerable debatable between the Government, the zamindars and the hill people) a considerable portion of the

district has been forsaken and left in an unproductive state, there are in some places on the borders of the zamindari estate some small spots here and there in cultivation but the greater proportion is a waste and jungle.

60) From the above statement which contains an abstract of the proceedings adopted in regard to bring on the rent Roll of Government the lands of the descriptions above explained the Board will observe that has been done and what remains to be done. The attention of the office is at present directed to make the settlements of resumed rent free lands and as the Board have desired that settlement should not be proposed without the fullest information of the produce and capabilities of the lands being previously acquired by personal survey of each spot. I must occupy some time before the Lakhraj part of the land can be completed, when that is done the enquiries into the other sources will remain to be command upon. It may not be unnecessary for me to state in this place great facility in the conduct of the enquiries now in progress would be acquired if one of the member of your Board to visit the District in they- season. If it would be the determination of your Board to make a tour of any of the Districts under your control you, would not perhaps find a district where your personal Superintendece would be attended with greater advantage **then might obviate** the necessity of reports and explanation being sent from this office, a duty that occupies the Collector no inconsiderable time and from the time that must elapse before order in any particular case referred can be obtained, occasion interruption as the office is engaged in enquiries which the result might lead to a considerable improvement of the land Revenue your Board may perhaps concur with me in opinion that it would be advisable the proceeding should be conducted under your personal superintendence".

ooo

27. Letter

From,

V. T. Taylor,
Collector of Bhagalpur,

To,

The Commissioner of Bhagalpur,
This dated 23 March, 1876.

1. "Referring to your office letter No. 3052R. dated 2nd February last I have the honour to forward here with records connected wih the Settlement of 11 Ghatwalle estates mentioned therein.

2. All the Ghatwalle estates mentioned in your letter under reply are situated within the zamindari estates belonging to Messrs. Gisborne& Co. From the records I cannot find out the exact time when they took possession of the Ghatwaly tenures, but it appears that they were in possession of these tenures before they were resumed by Government.

2. It does not appear that they presented any petition before for the release of those Ghatwallis.

3. A copy of W. Davies general report is herewith sent."

ooo

Chapter-VII

1. DAVIS GENERAL REPORT

Dated 20th September, 1860

Memorandum on the Ghatwalli Mahals of Zilla Bhagalpur

There has been some delay in submitting the report called for by the Commissioner in his letter no. 82 dated the 14th June last, in consequence of the necessity I was under, of awaiting the result of search set about by the Foujdaree and Collectorate record keepers for papers relating to these Mahals. This search was only recently brought to a close and has ended, I regret to say, unsatisfactorily.

A copy of a Roobkary of the Collector of Bhagalpur dated the 19th November 1813 (referred to as appendix No. 7 of the Privcy Council's decision) and an unattested copy of a Ghatwali register were the only two records found in the Collectorate. There were no papers in the Foujdaree Mahafez Khana among the records relating to Damin-Koh. Sherista a copy of register attested by MR. Edwards Lautour was discovered and sent to me by Commissioners. These together with unacurate copy of Mr. Sutherland's report dated the 8th June, 1819 complete the meagre list of records which have come under my examination.

Setting aside the register which are merely lists of Ghats, Ghatwally, etc. there remains the Roobkary and the English report to refer to for the purposes of this enquiry.

A copy of the first and extracts of all such portions of the letter as relate to this matter are attached to this memorandum for conveniences of reference. The Roobkary is a very important document and goes a great way towards the Settlement of the question under consideration if the matter contained in it is drawn as stated from records then existing in the collectorate. It will be observed however, that the only paper mentioned by name are two Sanads and a decision of the civil court. Separating and setting aside the information collected from these for the rest of the facts mentioned in the Roobkary we have the vague authority of the "Sherista", whatever that may be, if it is true, that Vernacular records existed and were available for reference in November 1813 their entire disappearance within a few years seems strange and unaccountable but that they had disappeared in 1817 or 1818 when Mr. Sutherland commenced his enquiry is clearly proved by the way he attends to them, for howwhere does it papers than the Sanads given to the Ghatwals and the register said to have been prepared by the Foujdaree Court in 1793 Referring to the latter he speaks of it as" apparently conforming with and made from documents existing " in the Collectors's office other incidental remarks Ceattered throughout report clearly show that he had not had access to any Vernacular records. Considering then, that the records in Sherista are not mentioned by name and that none were forthcoming within 5 year from the date Roobkary was written, it may be fairly questioned whether the register of 1793 except any other records were in existence and available at that period under all circumstances in no enquiry having any pretensions to strictness, would facts, said to rest on such vague and doubtful authority as is implied by the terms " Tukee Kastee" sheristah be admitted as satisfactorily established, while, however, expressing these doubts as regards our own estimation of the value of such evidence we cannot avoid seeing and admitting that this Zemindar as regards his claim and that we could not dispute its authority if it were pressed upon us in a court of justice.

The decennial preparatory settlement of the country was effected in 1790. Fresh arrangements confirm **that settlement in perpetuity were taken from the owners of the Zamindaries in which these Ghatwally Mehals are situated mostly in the year 1803** Mr. Sutherland commenced his enquiry in 1818. The interval between these two occurrences was not more than

16 years a period sufficiently short to allow of the reasonable presumption that most of the parties who had taken part in that important transaction were alive and capable if consulted of throwing some light on the history of these tenures and the mode in which they had been dealt with at the settlement. No Zamindar however, seem to have been examined on the point and in the few instances in which some appeared before Mr. Sutherland of their own accords, their object on coming forwards was to claim the Zamindaree perquisite of which they declared themselves to have been improperly dispossessed. Mr. Sutherland sums up the substance of all the information he collected during the course enquiry in paragraphs 146 and 147 of his report and on a careful review of the **whole I am inclined to think that the evidence in favour of the Zamindars preponderates**. The only paper mentioned in Mr. Sutherland's report which is at all opposed to this conclusion is an extract from a report of the Superintendent of Police dated 1811 wherein it is Stated that these lands were Separated from the Estates to which they belonged and a compensation was made to the Zamindar by a proportionate remission in the public revenues which Mr. Sutherland qualifies by the Cautious remarks" **if the Superintendent of Police writes on correct information".** Turning to the resumption records, I find matters equally unsatisfactory there. In the hope of coming across at least in some of the numerous suits disposed, of informations likely to be useful in this enquiry, I have undergone much wearsome labour in wading through this endless repetitions. The monotonous uniformity of the facts and arguments used throughout Strikes very forcibly and the careless nature of the enquiry and the absence of all research for date suitable to each separate class of case are apparent throughout. The tenures on Mudobun an estate known to have been purchased on account of Government after the Decennial settlement on its sale for arrears for revenue and its subsequent transfer to a private individual on

a reduced Jama are treated in the same manner as tenures in other estates which had undergone no change. Those in Belpatta and Sultanabad with Sunnads from the zamindars are not distinguished from Mehals the sanads for which were given by captain Browne and Mr. Cleveland. The formula used at the commencement is so closely adhered to, to the close of the country, **that had a set of Robkarys been lithographed with blank spaces left for names and dates to be filled up as each suit was brought up for decision most of these cases** have been disposed of equally as well without trouble in shorter time and at a smaller cost to Government. The one fact most strongly insisted upon and brought forward with unvarying regularity and in the same words in every proceeding is "that the said lands had not undergone a settlement up to that time for the settlement was effected in 1197 F. S. " While the said lands were set a part in 1181 F. S. " I was quite satisfied by my previous enquiry that there was no proof extending to show that these tenures even if set apart before the perpetual settlement, had they been wholly exempted from payment of Rent, but I do not find equally certain as to the date on which they were set apart. According to Mr. Sutherland, they had existed from time immemorial and **having gone to decay were reconstructed by Captain Browne and Mr. Cleveland between the year 1775 & 1788 A. D.** but nowhere could I find authority for their entire re-establishment in one year and that year 1181 F. S. . The records keeper suggest that 1181 F. S. was a clerical error for 1781 A. D. but it is difficult to believe that such en error could creep into every proceedings recorded as they were at different intervals and through several years, nor can it be reconciled with the facts of its appearance in the_proceedings of the special commissioners. From the following lists of Sanads prepared from Mr. Sutherland's report that the date of **Captain Browne's earliest Sanads is 1775** or 1182 F S. and that heand Mr. Cleveland continued from several years after to grant others, and it is proved beyond a doubt from the papers quoted in Mr". Sutherlend's report that these Mehals were not all "set apart in one and the same year

Given by Captain Browne
1775
1778

Given by Mr. Cleveland
1781
1782

Given by Captain Browne.
1787
1788

1790	Given by Mr Sadga
1797	Given by Mr. Fombelle.
1803	Given by Mr. Wintle
1812	Given by Mr. Sandford-
1815	Given by Mr. Parry.
1172	B. S. by Shooja Sinha, Zemindar of Jumoonee
1197	B. s. Imembux Zemindar of Kankdol
1202	B. S. Kadir Alli Zemindar of Kharukpore.

1203, 1219, 1220, 1222, 1224 and
25 6. . by Raheetwary, Zamindar of Sultanabad.

Having, as I think, shown that the records relating to these tenures existing in 1836 were identical with those we have now got that the sources of information available at that period were not superior to ours and that the facts most strongly insisted upon in the resumption proceedings is proved to be incorrect, the grounds for forming a judgment upon the question seems narrowed to a small compass, and of the discovery of fresh documents in the office of the Board of Revenue or elsewhere is thought to be hopeless and the decision must become to upon the evidence just reviewed, then there appears to me to be little cause for doubt or hesitation. The fact that these mehels were exempted from assessment at the settlement made in 1790 has clearly not been established. On the contrary there is a preponderance of evidence on the other side Showing that they were burthened with rent, the payment of which was levied by the Zemindars. It follows then according to the ruling of the Privy Council, that resumption in these cases was ordered upon insufficient grounds.

The conclusion I have come to above does not apply to the mehels in Pergena Jamoonee. The circumstances connected with which (as shown in the accompanying statement) are wholly different. Its application to the mehels in Parganah Madooban may also be open to question considering that that estate became the property of Government subsequent to the decennial settlement and was held khas for upwards of 12 years before it was made over to the ancestors of the present Zamindars.

W. R. Davies,
Deputy Collector,

Bhagalpore,
The 20 September, 1860

OOO

INVALID ESTABLISHMENT

"The board, having now before them the reports on the Invalid establishment in Bhagulpoor and Behar,required in the Resolution of the 13th August last, it becomes to enter into a consideration of that extention(extension) branch of the Invalid Establishment.

Exclusive of calls of justice and humanity to attend to the condition of the men already placed in the districts of Bhaugulpore and Behar, it is a pressing duty on government to put the establishment on such a footing as shall make it an acceptable and even desirable situation for future Invalids, because it is chiefly upon that establishment that our increasing Invalids can be provided for upon any moderate scale of expense,for it appears by letters from several of the collection, that the mode of providing for worn out soldiers which is the least burdensome of any that of granting them discharges from the service and double proportion of land must fall into disuse, as lands in quantity demanded and in the situations sought for by the Invalids,can no longer be obtained.

The uninterrupted continuance of Captain Hutchison for more than two years on the duty of inspection had enabled him to discover the most minute defects in the establishment, and his indefatigable assiduity and penetrating discernment have traced those defects to their source, and though it appears from his reports, that in the course of the last three years the situation of the Invalids has been much mended and relief applied in various case yet it is also manifest that there are such radical defects in the system, that nothing less than a general Reform and the establishment of a new code of Regulations can advance the institution to that degree of perfection and prosperity of which it is capable. At the same time that humanity to the Invalids calls for the interference of Government in their behalf, Justice to the Zemindars no less Demands that their rights as proprietors of land should be attended to It will therefore be necessary to devise other means of obtaining lands for the Invalids than those which have hitherto been had recourse to. The only possible mode of doing this consistently with the above principles that of purchase excepted, appears to be for Government to obtain the lands on aLease from the Landholders by private agreement fairly concluded. There cannot be doubt but as much land as may be required will be procurable by this method and the Tenure will be far more secure and valuable to the Invalids and their heirs and successors, for as it will be founded upon a bonafide private agreement the Courts of Justice will protect them and their Heirs in the quiet enjoyment of their lands and all their rights and privileges. The Zemindars in Bhaugulpoor and the Invalids settled in that District are in general at enmity with each other. The former consider the Invalids the usurpers of their property and harass them by every means in their power, and as the collector observes, would readily seize any opportunity that might offer of dispossessing them altogether, the same inimical dispositions will be transmitted to their posterity. The Invalids aware of the predicament in which they entertain of the security of their tenures have made frequent applications for sinnuds which however have never been issued to them. Nor does it appear how Government could formally and deliberately grant away the property of Individuals against their consent or without making them any compensations for it.

Upon the above grounds the following plan is submitted with Remarks annexed to such of the Articles as seem to require any explanation:

Browne's PLAN

It is thought advisable on the following ground to extend the Regulations to the Collecter ship of Shahabad, Tirhoot and Saran. The climate in and Saran. The climate in this district is remarkably healthy and they contain extensiveTracts of wasteland Which might be procured With little difficulty.

The Governor-General in Council sensible of the great importance of the Invaild Jageerdar and anxious to put it on such a footing as shall make it productive of the benefits originally expected from it, viz,: a comfortable Retreat for worn Native soldiers with ample subsistence for themselves during their lives and a decent provision for their families after their decease, and at the same time secure the rights of the Zemindars and thereby reconcile them to the institution and being satisfied from the Reports of the present inspecting officer Captain Huchinson and the Remark of the Collectors that those objects can only be obtained by a general Reform of the Establishment and the adoption of a new code of Regulations for the future management of it is resolved that all former Regulations relative to this institution be abolished and the following substituted:

That the Establishment of Invalids villages now confined to the Collectorship of Bhaugulpore and Bihar be extended to the Collectors of Shahabad, Tirhoot and Saran.

First: As soon as possible after the th Native officers,Sepoys and Sarcars be assembled at Monghere after the annual period of invaliding vizt.

The 31st of March a Calculation shall be made of the number of officers and

Privates expected to be transferred to the Jagheerdar establishmenton the Ist of

April in the ensuing year and also of the provided for in each collector-ship.

The calculation to be transmitted as soon as it is formed to the collectors of Revenue. The Collectors immediately upon the receipt of it to proceed to Secure (in the mode and upon the conditions of hereafter Specified) the required quanity of lands, so that the Lands expected to be wanted for the Invalids in each year may always be obtained, nearly one before hand. The collector to take particular care to select the most healthy spots that we can procure brought into culivation at a Small expense. The number of Invalids to be provided for in each district would be comparatively small and the quantity of land required for them would be obtained with proportionable facility. The number sent annually to each District would not in all probability be greater than might be conveniently settled in one villages, and consequently in many evils arising from the Tannahs being too extensive would be obviated.

Second: The conditions of hereafter Considerable advantages will arise from sending this early estimation to the Collectors of the number of Invalids to be transferred to their respective Districts. It will give them time to look out for the most convenient and Healthy situation to complete the necessary arrangements with the Proprietors to make the allotment of the lands for the different ranks and carried into execution the measures directed in the following article,which are conceived to be essential towards rendering the villages floursbing and productive. Every man will be put in possession of his assigned quota of ground immediately upon his arrive in the District without. trouble or expense, and his little property will be immediately applied to the purchase of stock instead of being dissipated during the long period which at present frequently elapses before the Invalids obtain complete possession of their assigned portions of Lands.

Third:- That when the Collector has met with a spot of waste land calculated for the purpose of establishing a Tanaah he makes aproposal to the Zemindars in writing to take a lease of it on the part of Government on the following terms:

1st :- The land to continue the property of the zemindar and **never to be separated from his Zemindary.**

2nd:- The Pottah to include the Julkier Bunker and Phulker or all Trees and the produce of their fisheries and pasture Land.

3rd: That the Invalids shall hold the Land free of Rent or any tax whatever during their lives, that after their death the land shall devolve to their heirs.

4th : That for the first five Years after the heirs of Invalids shall have come into the possession of land **they shall pay to the Zemindar a sum equal to one-tenth of the net produce of the Lands by way of Malikanah.**

5th That after the expiration of that period of five years the payment of one-tenth as Malikanah directed by the above Article shall **cease,and the collector assess theLands with a neat rent equal to two-thirdof the amount paid forLands of the same description in the District.** This rent not be liable to any variation and to be paid to the Zemindar.

6th: That if the original Granter shall die within seven years from the date of his being put in possession of his lands

his heirs shall continue to hold their rent free until the expiration of the said period of seven years, when the two preceding Articles are to have effects as there in prescribed.

7thThat if an Invaild shall die without heirs it shall be given to the option of a fresh man coming upon the Establishment to supply his place in the Tannah upon his agreeing to taken the lands upon the terms to which he would have succeeded to them had he been the heir of the deceased. If no fresh man will agree to take the lands upon these terms they shall return to the Zemindars who shall dispose of them in such manner as he may think proper.

8th:-That if an Invalid shall die and leave heirs who are not willing to receive the lands upon the foregoing terms or are incapable of cultivating them, they shall be allowed to dispose of their rights to some of the invalids belonging to the Tannah, the Purchasers becoming subject to all the contions in the articles regarding Heir.

9th If any invalid shall be idle and perverse, wholly neglecting the villages of his 'Jagheer after the second year it shall be forfeited and given to a fresh man.

10th If any heir to a Jagheer leave his portion unattended to twelve months after his claiming it, and bring ordered possession, it shall be deemed forfeited and shall be transferred to any other Invaild who will take it upon the same terms as he would have been entitled to hold it had been the heir of the deceased. In the event of Refusal the Jagheer is to revert to the Zemindar as provided for in the 7th Article.

11th That when the period arrives for assessing the Lands which have devolved to the Heirs or successors of Invalids such parts of them as could be cultivated and are not brought into cultivation shall be resumed and the zemindars shall be a liberty to grant Pottahs for them to whom soever he shall think proper unless the person who shall have omitted to cultivate them shall enter into Engagement to bring them into cultivation in the course of a year cultivating from the commencement of the year in which they became liable to the final assessment and in all future years to pay for them as cultivated Lands.

12th The Malcannah(=Malikana) and rent to which the lands are declared liable in the 4th and 5th Articles to be collected by the Collector and to be accounted for to the Zemindars by credit being given him for the amount in part of his stipulated annual payments to Government **no increase of Revenue to be levied from the zemindar during the Term of the Enggements** which may subsist between him and Government on account of the Rent or malconnah which may become payable to him from the Lands of the Invalids during the term of the said Engagements.

13th Wherever an Invaild or his heir or successor is put in possession of land the Regulating officer is to obtain from the zemindar through the Collector a separate Pottah for such person which is to express the terms on which he is to hold the land as specified in the preceding articles and when any Jagheer becomes liable to the permanment assessment the regulating officer shall obtain from the zemindar through the collector a Pottah in the name of the possessor specifying the amount of the Rent or assessment, the quanity of Land, the Boundaries there of and the terms the tenure as above defined.

14th The zemindars shall be allowed to station a mutsuddee in the Tannahs to take copies of the Account of the rent and malconnah that may be due to them and to inform them of every infringement of the terms under which the Invalids are to hold the Land specified in the agreement between them and Government.

15th Whenever all the Lands in a Tannah shall have become liable to the permanent Rent or assessment directed in the 5th article Government shall withdraw its interference and the tannah shall be considered upon the same footing as other villages in the zemindary, the Heirs and successors of the original Grantees continuing to hold their lands upon the terms specified in their Pottahs.

16th As long as the tannah remains under the charge of Regulating officer, Government to be responsible to the Zemindar for the payment of his Maliconnah and rent. When the officers of Government shall be withdrawn upon the arrival of the period specified in the Preceding Article the Zemindar to be at liberty to recover his rent from the heirs and successors of the Invalids in the same manner as form other Dependant,talookdars by the process laid down in the general regulations of the 20th July 1792.

17th If an Invaild or his heirs or successors shall die without heirs the jagheer or such part of it as may have been held by the deceased shall devolve to the zemindar who shall be at liberty to grant a Pottah for it to dispose of it to such person and upon such terms as he may think proper.

18th All differences between Government and the Zemindar and between the latter and the Invalids or their successors respecting the nature of the Invaild tenures to be decided in the Dewanny Audawlut.

19th : An agreement to be exchanged between the zemindars and government to the above effect and to be declared the Instruments to be referred to upon any dispute arising between Government and the Zemindar and between the latter and the Invalids on all points to which it relates.

Fourth: When a collector has procured a tract of land for the Establishment of a **Tannah he is to have the jungle-growing upon it cut down and removed** and to cause to be made such Embankments reservoirs or water courses as may be necessary for the culativation of the lands of the tannah (Tunnh). The making of these works to be entrusted to some help-ful cultoivators so as to ensure a proper supply of water to the different Jagheers. These works to be considered as belonging to the Tannah in General and the distribution of the water to be Invariably made under the direction of the head mutsuddee or other principal native officers stationed in the Tannah on the part of the Regulating officer,the original expense of these works to be defrayed by the public under the immediate direction of the collector and subject to the control of the Board of Revenue. The expense of the annual Repairs to be defrayed from the fund allotted for that and other purpose in the 40 articles of these Regulations.

Fifth: If the collectors shall here **of any Estate to be sold by** private sale and it shall contain a sufficient quantity of Waste land and shall be properly Situated for the Establishment of a Tannah or if any such Estate shall be ordered to put up to public sale, he shall inform Government in order that it may be purchased for the establishment of a Tannah if circumstances should render it advisable.

Talooks of a similar description of the zemindary as new tannah are established the old ones will gradually revert to the zemindars. were not some period to be fixed for upon the same footing as other dependant Talooks, they would, in a course of time become extremely numerous and besides the expense with which they would necessarily be attended, they might.

Sixth: That whenever Invalids shall be established upon Lands, the property of Government, they are to hold them of government upon the same terms as Invalids settled upon zemindary lands hold of the zemindars.

Seventh: That widows being heiresses to their husbands jagheers shall be allowed to forfeiture of their Jagheers, which after their death shall devolve to their heirs at law.

Eighth: That it be the duty of the regulating officer which the aid of his assistants to superintend the conduct of the Invalids in the several villages and settle all interal petty disputes between the Invalids and other inhabitants of the tannah in such manner as many appear to him equitable.

Ninth: Disputes or misconduct of magnitude to the prejudice of good order in which an invalid is the defendant or person complained against to be investigated by Court-martial, ordered and approved by the Regulating officer.

Tenth In case where a dispute shall arise between the invalids or other inhabitants of the Tanants regarding debts or other contracts concluded within the Tannahs or respecting any real or personal property being or lying within the limits of the Tannah the parties shall have the option of be productive of other object of Government cannot be to plant the country with Military colonies but to form for the Invalids during the levies and to let their descendants who must be numerous gradually blend with the mass of the people.

The measures suggested in this article are considered to be essential towards rendering the Tannah productive and flourishing.

It is conceived that the want of this aid from Government in the first instance (the expense attending which will be inconsiderable to the public) has been the chief cause of so many of the jagheers of the Invalids in the Boglpore District having remained entirely uncultivated and of a still greater number continuing so unproductive as to afford occupants but a scanty maintenance.

At present the Invalids instead of having their lands delivered over to them in a cleared state and fit for immediate cultivation are obliged at commence with cutting down jungle or throwing up embankment or digging reservoirs. To begin with works of so laborious a nature must be extremely disquieting to people who from infirmities and habits of life are little calculated for the evils of husbandry, on the other hand, if they employ people to perform these works, their hire absorbs the money which might be applied to the purchase of Bullocks and other stock for the purpose of cultivation.

But independent of these considerations the lands included in a Tannah can never be rendered productive to the occupants, unless all the jungle is cleared away at once, and the works necessary for preventing inundation and ensuring a some General plan so that the whole Tannah, army equally drive the benefit of them. It cannot be expected that any systematic measures of this nature will be perused by a number of Invalids independent of each other as far relates to the cultivation of their lands and differing in their habits and dispositions as wellas in the extent of their pecuniary ability.

The crops of an industrious man who has cleared his land will be eaten up by the wild animals that harbor in the Jungle upon the land of his neighbor which may be only partly cultivated or left waste altogether appointing arbitrators for the adjustment of their claims should both parties agree to this mode decision the regulating officer or his assistant is to see that arbitrators and an umpire to decide upon differences of opinion between the arbitators (unless the parties shall expressly agree to abide by the decision of the majority of the arbitratira)are fairly chosen and that the necessary arbitration Bonds are executed by the parties.

The Regulating officer shall confirm the award and pass a decision in conformity hereto unless be shall be clearly of opinion that the arbitrators have been guilty of gross corruption or partiality in either of which case he shall set aside the award or make such attraction in it as he may think equitable.

Eleventh: If either of the parties shall omit or refuse to appoint arbitrators, the Regulating officer shall pass such decision upon the claim as may appear to him equitable.

Twelfth: The Regulating officer shall be authorised to enforce his decision by causing the delivery of the property(provided it be or be within the limits of any of the Tannahs) to the party in whose favour the decision may be passed or if any sum of money shall be adjudged and the party against whom the decieion shall omit or refuse to satisfy the With respect to securing the lands from inundation and supplying them with water at the proper times, it is impossible for each invalid to make separate works of this nature for his own jagheerdar. Besides the impracticability of his furnishing the expense, the extent of ground which such works generally occupy would leave many but little land for cultivation. There rseervoirs in one jagheer would often be the ruin of the adjacent ones either by slopping the water from flowing into them, or by occasioning their being inundated.

The whole tannah may be rendered unproductive by the neglect of a few individuals or from their refusal or want of ability to contribute towards the expense of any works which the majority might be inclined undertake.

An Embankment properly constructed and kept in repair may secure a whole Tannah from inundation and in like manner are reservoir (which in the parts of the country in question in is formed by throwing up a maund of earth across low or sloping grows and a water course (which is a small aqueduct drawn from Rivers or nullahs to convey water into the Reservoirs) Judiciously made, may supply a whole Tannah with water and by making these works the general property of the Tannah and committing the distribution of the water to the several Jagheerdars to the public officers appointed to superintend the Tannah all disputes regarding water be precluded quantity of it for the cultivation of his lands.

Same by the public sale of any property he may possess within the Tannah.

Thirteenth: But it is to be understood that the Regulating officer is not to take cognizance of any complaint or claim where the cause of action shall have arisen or the property claimed shall be situated without the limits of the Tannahs. Such suits must be court lodged and decided upon in the court. By the adoption of these measures the Invalids instead of having the difficulties which they at present experience and encounter at the outset will be able to derive a comfortable subsistence from their Jagheers in the first or at furthest in the second year; and their lands will soon be as productive and be cultivated at as small expense as any other lands in the country.

Fourthteenth: The Regulating officer shall not sell any property lying without the limits of the Tannah in satisfaction of any decision that he may pass in cause which he is above authorized to determine, but if a decision shall be passed by the Regulating officer against any Invalid or Inhabitant of any of the tannah for any sum of money on a Bond or other contract or agreement which shall have been executed or made within the limits of the Tannahs and the person against whom the decision is passed shall not have property within the Limits of the tannah sufficient for the liquidation of it, but shall possess property without the limits of the tannah the Regulating officer shall send a copy of his decision to the judge of the District who after the time limited for appealing against the decision **shall have elapsed, shall cause it to be enforced by the sale of the property of the party against whom it may be passed in the same manner as if the amount had been decreed in his own court.**

Fifteenth:_The regulating officer is not to issue any process or to exercise any authority whatsoever beyond the limits of the Tannahs.

Sixteenth:_If any claims of a civil nature shall arise between the Invalids or other inhabitants of the Tannahs and either the Plaintiffs or both plainff and defendant shall be desirous or bring the same before the court of Justice in the District in the first instance instead of preferring it to the Regulating officer, they are permitted to bring the same before the court accordingly.

<u>**Seventeeth:**</u> If any Invaild shall be charged before the Regulating officer with murder, house breaking, robbery, theft, or other heinous crime, the Regulating Officer shall send the party accused to the Magistrate of the District who shall proceed against him in the same mannar as he is directed to do against other persons, charged before him with crimes or Offences and apprehended under his own warrant.

Eighteenth: An appeal to be made to the Dawanny Adawlut of the District from the decision passed by the Regulating officer in all causes for personal property where the sum of money or the value of the property claimed or decreed **shall exceed fifty Rupees and in all causes whatever** for real property lying within the Tannah provided that the petition of appeal shall be presented to the Judge within six weeks after the date of the decision of the Regulating Officer.

Nineteenth : If any Invalid or others inhabitants of a Tannah shall have a claim of a civil nature upon Land- holder or other person sending without the limits of the Tannahs or if any Land-holder or other person residing without the limits of the Tannahs shall have a claim of a similar nature upon an Invalid or other inhabitant of the Tannah or if any Invalid or inhabitant of the Tannans shall have a charge of a criminal nature to prefer against any person residing without the limits there of or if any person not being a resident of a Tannah shall have a charge of a similar nature to prefer against an Invalid or other inhabitant of a Tannnah, such suits or charges are to be considered as exclusively cognizable in the Civil or Criminal Court of the District.

Twentieth : To prevent the Invalids or their heirs being residents within the Tannans and possessing the whole or a part of their Jagheers, being harassed with Law suits and that they may be enabled to defend, Or prosecute suits in the Court of Justice without being obliged to attend in person or incurring trouble **or expense the regulating officer is empowered to instruct the native pleader or attorney for Government (an officer of which description is to be appointed attend** the several court of Justice) **to plead the cause of the Invalids free of cost in the following cases:**

First Where an Invalids or his heir above described has a claim of a civil or a charge of a criminal nature to prefer against any Landholder or other person residing without the limits of the Tannah, or a Criminal charge against any Invaild or inhabitant of the Tannah being of the nature of those specified in the 7th article of which the Regulating Officer is not empowered to take cognizance.

Second Where a claim of a civil nature is preferred against an Invalid or his heir aforesaid by a landholder or any other person who is not an Inhabitant of a Tannah.

Third : Where an invalid or his above –described shall prosecute another Invalids or –in habitant of the Tannah in the Court of Justice in the first instance (against the consent of the Defedant as authorized in the 16th article instead of bringing the claim before the Regulating officer.

Twenty-first The Regulating officer is prohibited ordering the attorney for Government to plead the suits of Invalids in the Following cases.

First To prevent the Invalids or their heirs abusing the above indulgence of having their suits pleaded by the Attorney for Government the Regulating Officer shall not instruct the Attorney to undertake suits or prosecutions of the nature which shall appear to him unjust orfrivolous not to defend any such claims that may be made against Invalids which shall appear to him well-founded. In such cases the Invalid is to be left to prosecute the claim or charge or to defend the suit in person or by Vakeel at his own cost.

Second: Where an Invalid or his heirs above –described shall be prosecuted for a criminal offence whether the prosecutor be or be not an in- habitant of the Tannah.

Third: Where an Invalid or his heirs aforesaid of a Tannah shall appeal from a decree of the Regulating Officer or his assistant.

Fourth: Where Invalids or their heirs shall agree to any suits in which they are parties being brought in the first instance before the Court of Justice as authorized in tho 16th article.

Twenty-second 22: The Process of the Civil and Criminal Courts of Judicature and of the Police officers is to be current and have force in the Invalid villages. In the same manner as in any villages and the invalids and all other inhabitants of the Tannahs are to pay due obedience thereto under pain of paying such fine or suffering such punishment as the court are authorised by the General Regulations for the administration of Justice to inflict on persons disobeying or resisting their process;

Twenty-third: All money-lending amongst the Invalid to be discouraged as much as possible and the 25th Article of the General Regulations for the admis-of Justice passed on the **23rd of November 1792** is to be fixed up in the cut cherry of every Tannah. The Regulating officer and his assistants are to conform to in settling claims for debt.

Twenty-fourth: That the jagheers whilst possessed by Invalids shall not for money borrowed by them nor after their decease be answerable for debts contracted by them but when the Jagheers fail to the heirs or successors of Invalids they will become answerable for debts contracted by such heirs and successors in the same manner as other lands held under similar Tenures.

The original proportion was Exactly double what are now proposed, and upon experiences have been found infinitely too large for the management of any of the Invalids on the Esiabliahment and beyond their means of Cultivation from which circumstances many inconveniences have occurred,parts or the Jagheers were of necessity thrown to a very considerable and impracticable distance from the villages where the Invalids were to reside for the cultivation.

In consequence was in detached spots and often in the midst of jungle and big grass speedily again spreading itself over the small portions which were cleared at a great expense and labour and furnishing cover for distructive animals.

Twenty fifth: That the portions of lands be as follows:A Subadar of Infantry and first Jamadar of Cavalry.... 100 Beghas.

A Jemadar of Infantry 2nd Jamadar of Cavalry and Serang ...50 Havildar or Infantry, lst Duffadar of Cavalry and Feudal " 30 Bighas Naik of Infantry.

2nd : Duffadar of Cavary and Cassop ... 25Bighas

Sepoy Trooper Lascar Drummer Trummeter end.

Twenty-sixth : That the Establishment of the villages and the distribution of the lands be made upon the spot by the collectors or his assistant in concert with the Regulating officer or his assistant and that the distribution of lands commence by allotting to the most infirm and lowest in rank their portions contiguous to the villages.

Twenty-seventh: That in allotting Invalids to a village there shall always be a proportion of commissioned non-comm-issioned officers and sepoys and that the number of men in each Tannah shall be regu1ated by the quantity of land which can be annexed to it, and where that quantity shall be very extensive that Toldha or divisions from the great Tannaha shall be made on different parts of it in which a proportion of all ranks shall be placed, the Tolahs-being still attached to the Tannah.

Twenty-eigth : That the Invalids shall retain his full pay for one year ater being put in possession of his land, and that afterwards the pay be as follows to continue for lifes. Subadar and is Jemadar of cavalry. . 18 Sica-Rupees permonth. _ Jemadar. Rs 12 Do 7. Permonth According to the present mode of payment invalids retains his full pay for three years; it is than reduced one"-third and in two years after another third the remaining third continuing for life. Among men unaccustomed to look forward the enjoyment of full pay for so long a time operated as a check upon Industry on the village, lands, the reduction

Sepoys and Trooper. 3-0 Drummer_Truppetnr on. 3-0 and Bhestic

Serang. .	. . 6–0
Tenudeb. .	. . 4-0
Cossop. .	. . 3-8

Lascar. . . . 2-12.

Havildar. . Ist Duffadr. . 4-8 Permonth

suffi-cient to afford the Invalids All the could not deny themselves any by applying a small portion of their monthly income to the expenses of cultivation,cultivators necessarily deprived of some of these comforts by the reduction of one-third they could still loss submit to add to their wants by expending a part 0f their reduction of another third left the pittance so small that not only nothing out of it could be spared but it was in itself unequal totheir substance hence those frequent instances of distress amongst the Invalids mentioned by Captain Hutchinson and the numerous objects of compassion. Amongst their widows and children.

The mode of any now propesed, will in a greater, degree guard them from the effect of such improvidence, for should example and exhortation failed in inducing them to direct their attention to their lands, their pay will at all times secure them from absolute want. With regard to the difference of expence which the alteration will produce, it is obvious that for invalids who shall here Subadhr.

Twentyninth: That this rate of pay to apply to the
invalids now on the Bhaugul-pore and Behar Establishments.
That the pay shall be issued every
Six months viz on the Ist of April
and Ist of October. .

Thirtieth : That the reduction in pay to commence immediately after one of the stated periods of inspection,so that though the allowance of the Invalid should fail half year to be reduced between those periods the full pay shall be continued till the end of the half year.

Thirty-first : That the several Invalids be required to be present at their respective villages at the two stated periods of Inspection any payment and that in fail-are thereof they be struck off the establishment after came on the Establishment there will be in the first three years be a very considerable saving and in the period of sevenyears there will be a saving from each Subadhr Rs. . 744. Jammadar. . 120 Havilder. . 108 Naick. . 48

Sepoy. . 56It is true that by extending this mode of payment those who having been five years on the Establishment have gone through the two first gradation of pay and are now on the most reduced portion a considerable increase of expense will arise but so miserable is the situation of some of the men of that description and so great their distresses that Government have in some instances been obliged to afford them pecuniary relief, beside, unlesis the relief Establishment for worn out soldier does actually furnish the means for a comfortable subsistence any money expended upon it is misapplied, and such an Establishment in point of policy becomes prejudicial for the right men suffering under the pressure of want must create many uncomfortable

Thirty-second : That a Regulating officer be appointed who shall have the general superintendence over the establishment in the five Districts.

Thirty-third- That two assistants be appointed to act under the instructions of the Regulating officer.

Thirty-fourth: That an al1owance of 200 sica rupees per month be given to the regulating officer and an allowance of 120 Rupees permonth to each of the assistants in addition to the pay and full Batta of their resp-ective Ranks and that both the Regulating Officer and the assistants be allowed the Tent money of their res-pective Ranks for the pur-pose of Supplying them-Selves with campequipage.

Thirty-fifth: That an allowance of 120 Rupees permonth be made to the Regulating Officer for writers,Moon-shees and stationery.

Thirtysixth: That the collection be allowed the sum of 50 Rupees per month for Moohshies lst and to transmit a contingent bill for any. personal expenses which he may occasionally incur/ either in visitûng the Thanahs or on any other accounts.

Thirty-seventh: That to each Tannah there be allowed a monshee at the monthly wages of a Sonaut Rupees.

Thrity-eight: That to the establishment in each district there be allowed an aumeen at the monthly wage of 30 Sonaut Rupees, and also an assistant of Vakeel who shall be native officer to attend at the cutch-erry. With the monthly allowance in addition to his pay of 10 Sonaut Rupees.

reflections in the minors of the native soldiers occasionally pass through the Invalid villages. The proportions now proposed are villages. The proportions now proposed are something below the lst reduced pay and considerably above the 2nd reduced or lowest pay. The allowance at present are to the collectors for Moonshies per month 209 Sica Rupees.

6. out of the latter sum were maintained a moonshy and a native Doctor and some other public servants about every villages but both Mr. Grant and Mr. Seton. Have lately reduced the expense of each village by striking off the native Doctors who were in general totally ignored and consequently useless. The saving arising from the above reduction has been thrown into a fund and applied to the great relief many distressed objectsamong the windows and children of deeceased invalids who if now deprived of that assistance would be again shown in the state of want and distress from which they have been extricated.

At present the allowance to the civil surgeon Sica-rupees 266-7-6 but as the Invalids are scattered over a large tract country they can receive very little assistance from the Surgeon by having a place to resort to in case of wounds breaking out a fresh or in obstinate disorders, medical relief may be administered to them.

Thirty-ninth: That the Regulating Officer be permitted to employ some person possessing a practical knowledge of survery to assist him in meaning off the several portions of lands to whom an allowance shall be made of 120 sonaut Rupees per month; with 50 Rupees per month for the provision and carriage of camp equipage.

Fortieth: Exclusive of the a foregoing fixed allowances, pecuniary aid will occasionally be required for the purpose of assisting the Invalids in making wells, writing drains, and other useful masks about the villagers and also for affording relief and support to widows and orphans left destitute by demise of their husbands and father before a sufficient portion of their Jagheer shall be brought into cultivation so as to yied them a maintenance and for those purpose a sum not exceeding 40 sica-Rupees per month may be drawn for each villages.

Forty-first:-That the money expended in the above purposes shall be drawn for monthly in a contingent Bill signed by the Collectors for their respective districts and the regulating officer jointly and that every three months the Collector and the Regulating Officer jointly shall render a detailed account of the appropriation and expenditure of the money drawn for to the Commander in Chief.

Forty-Second: That a hospital or Infirmary shall be built in each District at the Residence of the Judge for the reception of wounded, lame or such men who may occasionally require medical assistance and the civil surgeon of the district be allowed the sum of 250 Siea Rupees per month for attending it and supplying necessaries.

Forty-third: That the Bundowane or Prisoners condemned to labour be employed in assisting to build the Infirmary and that 30 of them be attached to it for the purpose of keeping it clear and that the whole of them he employed in occasional servicesin the Tannahs.

Fortyfourth: That on the first of every month Muster or the Invalids of the general Tannnahs shall be taken by the respective Monshies and a Roll signed by him and the senior native officer of the Tannnah in which shall be inserted the casualties of the preceding month with their dates and in which absentes shall be noticed, shall be transmitted to the Regulating officer,or if he be not in the District to the Assistent who may be present.

Fortyfifth: That the Collector of each District be furnished with a monthly Return of the men of every Rank on the Establishment in his district either by the Regulating Offieer or the assistant who may be in the district and that the Regulating Officer dotransmit to theCommender in chief monthly Return of all the men on the Establishment in the three Districts particularizing those of each districts.

fortysixth: That it be the duty of the Regulating officer or one of his assistants to see the pay issued at the stated periods. **Fortyseventh:**-That the Collector **be considered as the Pay Master to the Establishment** and that the pay be disbursed by his servants in the presence of the Regulating officer or one of his assistants who is to carry with him a Roll of the men in the several villages exhibiting the dates when they were actually put in possession of their portions of land, and the officers under whose inspection the pay shall be issued is to certify at the end of his Circuit to the commander in Chief that the just claims of the several men have been satisfied in his presence.

Fortyeight: That the Regulating Officer after pay has been issued at the stated periods shall make a General Return of all the men in the three district, specifying the villages they belong to, and in what class of pay, keeping those of each District separate and distinct. One copy to be sent to the Adjutant General for the Commander in Chief and one to the Military Auditor General.

Forty nine-That the heirs of the deceased men who may be claimants for portions of pay due to any Invalid dying in the intermediete periods of Muster shall attend the inspecting officer and be paid their dues at the time and in the same manner as ordered for the disbursement of pay at the respective villages, any claims not perfered at the 1st ensuing period of payment after the casualty has happened shall be deemed inadmissible.

Fiftieth:-That leave of absence be granted by the Regulating officer or one of his assistants and if an Invalid exceeds his time of furloughs although he should be present at the day of payment, apportion of his pay for the number of days he has exceeded his leave shall be stopped and carried to the account of Government if good and sufficient reason be not assigned to cause a mitigation of such severity.

Fiftyfirst:-That Annual Returns be transmitted by regulating officer to the Commander in chief of the quantity of land in cultivation.

Fifty second:-That the Regulating officer being the superintendent of the Establishment in the five Districts all Communications to the Commander in Chief relative to the Invalids shall proceed from him, as also all communications to the Collector, excepting in cases requiring their immediate interference on which occasions one of the assistants in the absence of the Regulating officer must be the channel to the Collector,and the Regulating officer may be fully informed of all occurrences in every part of the Establishment the assistant who may be in the district where they happen in immediately to make written Report of them to the Regulating officer and also transmit to him copies of all correspondence which he may find it necessary to carry on with the Collector on occasions of emergency.

Fiftythird : That all arzees from the Invalids intended for the consideration of the Collector be previously signed by the Regulating Officer or one of his assistants.

Fiftyfourth : That it be strongly recommended to the Invalids to collect some of their relations and dependants to assist in bringing their lands into cultivation,but that they be by no means prohibited or prevented from employing the Ryotts or laboures of the district upon such terms as they can procure them.

Fiftyfifth : That a portion of Ball ammunition, and a few stands of arms be given to some particular Tannahs where they happen to be much exposed to the devastation of wild beasts and that the Regulating officer do indent for those articles through the Military Board.

Fiftysixth :- That every Invalid when transferred to the Establishment shall receive Coat but that thereafter no clothing shall be served out to them from the Company.

Fiftyseventh :- That at the periods for transferring Invalids to the Jagheerdar Establisment which shall be on the 1st of April of every year the men so to be transferred shall have the choice of the five Districts.

Fiftyeighth :- In the absence of the Regulating officer the powers vested in him to be expercised by his assistants.

Fiftyninth :- That the men now on the Establishment be paid up to the 1st of April and that from that period these new Regulations commence.

The foregoing Regulations are applicable only to Tannahs that may be established in future. It may be advisable however,to bring the Tannahs already established in Bhogulpore and Behar under the present Regulations as far as may be practicable consistently with the terms on which Government have made over the lands to the persent occupants. Justice to the Zemindars requires that the nature of the Tenures of the Invalids should be defined, and either that some compensation should be granted to them for their lands or at all events that a period should be limited when the Jagheers are again to be annexed to their zemindarry and to pay them an equitable rent. It is equally necessary for the Invalids that these points should be adjusted as soon as possible by private agreement with the Zemindars,that their heirs and successors may at all times have this agreement to appeal to, and that they may be secured against any infringement of it by application to the Courts of Justice. Were the Zemindars to prosecute Government for the recovery of most of the lands which are held by the Invalids in Bhaghulpore (a measure which they might and no doubt will take some time or other unless they are now bound by specific agreement as proposed.) neither the Invalids nor Government would be able to make a very good defence.

By adjusting with the zemindars the terms on which the Invalids now settled in Bhaglepore and in (Bihar) are to hold their lands the above circumstances will be guarded against, all the Invalids' establishments will be under one uniform system,and the Right both of the Zemindars and the Invalids and their heirs and successors as founded upon the terms of the Deed will be equally under the protection of the Laws.

For the purpose it may be advisable to adopt the

First : To instruct the Collectors to end-evaour to counclude agreements with the Zemindars rendering all lands now held by Invalids in Bhoglepore and in Bahar(Bihar) (**excepting those Granted to the Invalids under the Regulations of February 1789)**subject to the articles of these Regulations.

Second : To remodel the Tannahahs in been granted to them in excess to that proportion excepting where Bhagulpore there can be little doubt but the landholders will readily acquire in this proportion as the lands now occupied will in a very short time be again annexed to their estates and the heirs and successors of the Invalids will be nearly upon the same footing as other Jungletoory.

Tallokdars holding of them. The heirs of the Invalids cannot object to these terms as by the original Regulations of 1781 it is declared that the lands and Bahar (Bihar) as far as relates to portions of Land and to fix for each Invalid now On the Establishment the quote Of land assigned for his Rank by the Twenty fifth article of these Regulations also to extend this Rule to the heirs and Successors of Invalids who have come into Possession of jagheers resuming from both been granted to them in excess to that proportion excepting where the occupants shall have brought into cultivation a larger quantity of land than is now fixed for man of their Ranks in which cases they are not be deprived of any part which is in actual Cultivation but to continue to possess the whole under the several conditions prescribed in the new Regulations shall upon the Death of the original Grantees be liable to the payment of reasonable rent.

Third : The Commandants now upon the Establishment to remain at the Same footing as at present.

Fourth : To declare that several articles for administering Justice in cases in which the Invalids or other Inhabitants of the Tannahs already established in Bhaglepore and (Bihar).

With respect to the Invalids who have accepted double portions of land under the orders of February 1789, no part of the present Regulations are applicable to their situation They are dispersed in different parts of the country receive no pay, are under no Military controls are entirely unconnected with the service. They are in fact Raytos of the Landholders in whose estates they are settled and are subject to the Jurisdiction of the country courts in the same manner as other individuals. It will be necessary however to secure them and their heirs in the possession of the lands which have been made over to them and to instruct the collectors to obtain Pottahs for them from the Zemindars granting the lands to them and their heirs as dependent Talooks,agreeably to the terms of the Regulations of the 18th February1789 and 24th December 1790.

Ordered

Ordered copies of the above be transmited to the several collectors for their information and guidance.

Ordered that such parts of the above regulations as have any connection with the Revenue Department be entered the Book standing orders."

(Proceedings,-Board of Revenue, Fort willam, 1 April, 1793)

(Ed.) These documents throw much light on the rules and regulations relating to Invalid Jagirs:

Surendra Jha

ooo

Chapter-VIII

Sultanabad and Amber Records

1.

From,

J. W. Sage, Collector,
Bhagalpur, Dated 15 March, 1821

To,

R. M. Tilghman,
Sub-Secretary to the Board of Commissioners
For the Province of Bihar and Benares, Camp- Monghyr.

"Amongst the postponed cases in my office I found one relating to the **Zemeendaree of Sooltanabad regarding** which the late Mr. Battye on the 28th of June 1819 directed a report should be made to the Board. That Gentleman's intentions however were not carried into execution & finding on examination that one material letter on the subject had been torn from out the letter book, I applied on the 23rd of last October for a copy which having had the honor to receive with your letter of the 5th December, I proceed to furnish my report: The Zemeendaree of Sooltanabad was the property of Gurjun Singh, husband of Ranny Serbesseeree and in consequence of some disturbances created by Certain Hill people, Mr. Cleveland on the 14th oF February 1783 reported his having detached a party of troops to seize the disaffected & in the 3rd paragraph of his letter that gentleman remarks strong suspicions exist of the Hill chiefs having been instignted to the revolt by Ranny Serbessery Zemeedar of Sooltanabad.

2 nd :- Mr. Cleveland having held investigations on the subject recommended on the 29th March 1783 to Government that the Ranny should be dispossessed of her Zemeendarry and not be permitted to reside at or near Sooltanabad. This measure

was sanctioned by Government on the 6th May 1783and a pension of 100 Rs. (reduced afterwards to 50/-) per month was allowed to her.

3rd It does not appear from the records of my office that any further correspondence took place till the 20th of February 1789. When a petition from Ranny Sarbesseree was forwarded by the Board of Revenue, Enclosure No. 1 to Mr. Collector Adair for report. On the 24th of May, Mr. Davies furnishes two reports (enclosures 2 & 3) and on the 21st of September 1790 Mr. Grant in his address, enclosure No. 4 to the Board remarks that Sooltanabad is the only land belonging to Government in this district.

4th on the 30th of March 1791 Mr. Davies informs the Board that the Ranny Serbessery had been called on to state whether she had any relations and on the 12th of April following, Mr. Grant transmits her answer (No. 4) in which she states that she had no children by her husband who on his death in 1177 B. S. left two relations (first cousins) named Mokum Singh and Jeebun Singh.

5th Mr. Grant in enclosure NO. 4 observes or to be let to the Zemeendar if the sufferings of the widow shall be considered to have sufficiently atoned for the crimes of Gurjun Sing. This is evidently erroneous for Gurjun Singh died 22 years pervious to the forfeiture of the Zemeendaree which at the time of its being forfeited was property and in possession of Ranny Serbesseeree, on whose conduct Mr. Cleveland reported in February 1783. This circumstance I mention to show that some of the reports in this case have not been correctly made.

6th On the Zemeendaree being forfeited, it was **let in farm to Gungagoviend Sing till** the year 1792- when Mokum Sing requested, he might be allowed to take charge of the Zemeendaree for eight years at an annual Jumme of Rs. 12722. 7. 3. His offer was accepted and the Tehseeldar on the part of Government was ordered to be withdrawn.

7th on the 24 th of August 1792 Government authorize the restoration of Sooltanabad to the family of the former Zemeendar and direct the settlement to (be)made with Mokum Sing allowing the continuation of the Ranny's pension for life.

8th It is clear that Government sanctioned the estate being restored to the family of the former Zemeendar, but why Mokum Sing should have been acknowledged as heir to Ranny Serbesseree, I cannot devine, for he was only a first cousin of her husband's (Gurjun Singh) and merely farmer of the Estate. Besides, Jeebun Sing, another first cousin to Gurjun Sing was alive and had as much right to a share as Mokum Sing, though I cannot admit the right of either.

9th Mokum Sing however, obtained an aumulnamah and procured by, what means I know not, for no authority exists in either my English, or Persian record office his name to be registered as Zemeendar of Sooltanabad. He died in 1803 when his widow Myheserre (for alth'o she is styled Ranee), has no right to assume that title was put into possession by the;late Mr. Sherburne.

10th :-The adopted son alluded to in Dr. Davies's letter of the 30th March 1791 (enclosure No. 10) named Sungram Sing has produced a tumleeknameh, granted to him by Ranny Serbesseeree six months previous to her death which, happened in June 1807. By this deed it appears that the Ranny bequeathed the whole of her property to him as her adopted son & to prove his having been adopted by her he also produces a Bawusta Vyanarth furnished by one of the pundits.

11th Sungram Singh however, it is to be observed did not produce these documents till 1819 – altho' he was allowed a pension of 10 Rs. Per month by Government out of the 50/- granted to Serbeeseree until he shall have attained an age which may enable him to procure a maintance for himself.

12th On consideration of all the circumstances of the case, it appears to me that the present occupant Myheseeree holds the Zemeendaree of Sooltanabad under an invalid tenure, the husband Mokum Sing never having been acknowledged by

Government as Zemeendar. That the estate is the actual property of Government whose rights ought to be asserted by a prosecution being immediately institute against her.

13th Her having been so long in possession is the only plea she can urge against a suit being commenced, for neither Mokum Sing nor herself has ever entered into regular engagements for the perpetual settlement of the Estate which consists of 30541 Beegahs exclusive of Lakheraj land, etc. , that allotted to Invalids, 28000 of which are in cultivation, although the revenue now paid amounts only to Rs. 12,722. 7. 3 per annum whereas it is capable of yielding on a moderate calculation, Rs. 20,000 per annum.

14th Copies of the correspondence on the subject together with the Persian proceedings are transmitted for the Board's inspection. The latter I beg may be returned, and I trust the Board will recommend to Government adopting the measures. I have proposed, otherwise a serious loss must accrue to Government, whose interests, was I to lose sight of, I should be highly to blame."

OOO

2.

From,

J. P. Ward,
Acting Collector Bhagalpur
Dated 9 April, 1822

To,

R. M. Tilghman.

"On the 26th of June 1807 the Board of Revenue on the recommendation of the Collector were pleased to continue to Sungram the adopted **son of Ranee Surbuserry**, a portion of the pension held by the late Ranee, Viz. , 10 Rs. Per mensem. The pension was to continue until the boy then five years of age should arrive at that age which might enable to obtain for himself a maintenance.

2nd. Sungram Singh having attended this month to receive his pension and having now arrived at the age of 21, I must obtain the sanction of the Board to a further continuance of his stipend before I shall consider myself authorized in paying it. I must at the same time add that the young man can neither read nor write and is, as far as I can judge, unable to obtain a livelihood by any profession. He has been kept in a Shameful state of ignorance perhaps with the view that that the pension might be continued to him in perpetuity. He is living with his mother whom I learn he supports from the Government pension. I have the honor to enclose for the Board's perusal copy of the reports of the Collectors which led to the grant of the pension to Sungram Singh and of the Board's orders in reply, and shall be glad to receive their orders in regard to the continuance of it, or otherwise. "

OOO

3.

From,

Monghyr,

Dated 19 September, 1780

To,

The Governor- General and Council, Fort William.

"Honourable Sir, and Sirs,

In consequence of your approbation of my proposal of giving allowances to the Hill Chiefs of the Tuppas and their deputies leaving it to me to carry for plan into execution in the best manner, I am able and limiting the expense, to Rs 550/- per month, as signified in your letter of the 22nd August, immediately all the chiefs and deputies of the several Districts under my authority and informed them that in consequence of the disposition they had, for sometime, shown to remain on good terms with their neighbours in the low country and of the confidence they had placed in Government by giving themselves up to my protection and authority, they had been pleased to grant pension to the chiefs and deputies as an encouragement for their future good behaviour, but that in consideration of this indulgence they were to bind themselves in the most forcible manner under pain of their severest penalty and suspension of their allowances to be answerable for their good order, and management of their respective Districts.

To this the Chiefs and Deputies of the several Tappas to the northward readily assented; but those to the southward which lie contiguous to the Pergannas of Ammar and Sultanabd absolutely refused to accept any, allowance, on the terms prescribed alleging as reason that they could not be answerable for the conduct of their neighbours as they have so often since the commencement of my arrangement has given proofs of their refractory disposition, without expressing the smallest inclination to surrender **themselves to Government they could now become every day more incensed again my division and would plunder and destroy the villages in it with redoubled fury.** Their motive for, and view in this I understand would be to compel the Chiefs under my authority to resume their allegiance, which they miss, easily be induced to do rather than become accountable for disturbances which it would not be in my power to assist them in preventing and as they have as idea, that as long as any part of division remains unsettled chastisement would be either entirely suspended or more equally divided, whereas, if otherwise the whole blame would inevitably fall upon them in case of disturbances

I have already taken up so much of the Honourable.

Boards's attention with my representation respecting he necessity of annexing the Perganna of Amar and Sultanabad to my collectorship that it is with the greatest reluctance I am once more induced to address you on the subject. But as I am convinced nothing but proper encouragement is wanting to bring the Hill people is those two perganas, in the same peaceable state that I have with so much success brought those two in my own district and as I am also confirmed in my opinion that even if similar arrangements take place in both division, there will still be disturbances and confusion near the boundaries of them. I should be wanting in my duty did I not humbly entreat the Honourable Board to take these circumstance into their consideration.

I have been further induced to say this much on the subject in consequence of the very flattering approbation my plans in general, and the honour to meet with from Lieutenant General, Sir Coot, K. B in several conversation I had with him on his way both up and down the country and as proposal for raising a corps of archers as represented in my addresss of the 21st April was particularly approved by him; I take the liberty of recalling your attention to this circumstance also; being persuaded of the good effects it will have in brining the Hill inhabitants to a speedy state of civilization–add to which the great service they may be of military operation at a future period."

OOO

4.

Deed of Gift By Rani Janki Kumari in 1295 B. S.

In 2nd March, 1295 B. S. (14th January, 1889) Rani Janki Kumari executed a registered deed of gifts in favour of her then surviving son. Kumar Indra Narayan for the major portion of Sultanabad reciting therein that Sultanabad is her Stridhan property and reserving certain minor properties. e. g (1) Mouza Lakshmipur created Patni by her in the name of her daughter Kamal Kumari for Rs. 125/-

2. Gift of 500 Bighas of land to the son-in-low of Kamal Kumari and her daughter.

It was further therein that Kumar Harendra Narayan while to management of the Estate minsappropriate large sum of moinies(money) and purchased many valuable furniture and ornaments which he can keep in the custody of his wife and children. The value of the ornaments and other valuable articles together with the monies misappropriated are sufficient for the better mode of living of his wife and children. . The value of the ornaments and other valuable article together with the monies misappropriated are sufficient for the better mode of living of his wife and children and it was through his mismanagement that the Estate has incurred so much debts.

ooo

5.

Suit(Suit) No. 61 of 1889

In 1889 Rani Janki Singh brought a suit for possesestion of the various Patni and Darpatni properties in Bengal which were alleged to have been acquired in the Benami of Naba Kumar Singh brother of Maharja Gopal Chandra Singh from the income of Sultanabad and which properties were then bequeshed by a will executed by Naba Kumar in favour of Harendra Narayan and were in the possesstion and enjoyment of Jatindra Narayan. Then suit No. 61of 1889 was compromised on 2-10-1890 between Jatindra Narayan and Rani Janki Kumari on the understanding that Bengal properties were to be released in her favour and in that compromise Jatindranath admitted that the will executed by Naba Kumar Singh in favour of Harendra Narayan is not a true one and that he believes that all the Bengal properties were acquired in the Benami of Naba kumar and that really those properties, being acquisted from the income of Sultanabad, belong to Rani Janki Kumari.

ooo

6.

Will of Janki Kumari in 1299 B. S.

On 17th April 1892 Rani Janki Kumari executed a will in favour of Indra Narayan divesting herself of her remaining property of the Sultanabad Raj and died in 1892. (1299).

OOO

SULTANABAD

7.

Wood's Reports

"About the year 722-23 two brothers **Banku Singh, the elder and Anku Singh the younger chattree** by caste came from Theri home in Lucknow, Aoudha, on visit to the relatives, **the then Raja of Kharagpore** and hearing of the disturbed state of the country immediately leased of the Kharagpore Raj applied for the aid of the Kharagpore Raja to enable them to take possession by force of arms of a portion of such disturbed tract of country which was the scence of constant strife between neighbouring chiefs each having small forts posted in various parts of the country and were already at enemity with one other. Collecting a band of upcountry men only being aided by Kharagpore Raja, the two brothers were successful in their raid and subjugated a considerable extent of country. Banku Singha the elder brother took possession of what is known called Pargana Sultanabad while younger Anku appropriated all the hill tract situated **south of the Banshloi river and north of the Brahmanee Node;** east of the Kharagpur Raj, Pargana Handua, west of Sultanabad.

Having firmly seated themselves in power, and successfully put down all opposition the two brothers presented a handsome

Nazarana to the then Nawab of Bengal and applied for title and obtained the title of Raja over the tracts of country each had appropriated to himself. Banku Singha thus became Raja and was founder of the Sultanabad Raj family. After enjoying the raj some years, Banku Singha died and was succeeded by his son Gandhrn Singh, On the death of the latter he was succeeded by his son, Hansraj Singha, who was succeeded by his son, Doman Singh, whose son Golel singh, succeeded him. Golel Singh was succeeded by his son. Durjan Singh, the latter by his son, Narbar Singh, who left three children, two sons Kisan Singh and Khoshal Singh and one daughter, SreematiRamanee. Kishan Singh died without issue and was succeeded by Khoshal Singh who died in 1135 B. s. leaving two sons Ratan Singha and Gurjan Singh. The former held the Raja Title 1160 and the latter 1165. Neither leaving issue, the widow of Gurjan Singha, Rani Sarbeshwary succeeded to the Sultanabad estate and it was held by her at the time the British Government assumed charge of Bengal and settlement was made with her in 1176 B. S. . Some fourteen years afterwards that is in 1190, in consequence of the Rani mismanaging the estate, It was taken out of her hand and managed through Government officials for 9 years, when in 1199 B. S. Makham Singh, being the son of his sister Shrimati Ramanee, was appointed Zaminder of Sultanabad and property vested to the family and in 1205 B. S. settlement was made with Makham Singh. He died in 1209 B. S. without male issue, but left one daughter Shreemati Rajmanee, who was married to Babu Dayal Singh of Kanhoopore in Zillah Murshidabad. Rani Maheshwari succeeded to estate on the death of her husband Makham Singha and held it up to the time of her death in 1237 B. S. When she was succeeded by her grandson, Raghnath Singha, the son her daughter Shreemati Rajamani by Babu Dayal Singh. Raghunath Singh dying while a minor, the estate, devolved on his sister Rani Janaki Kumari, in 1249 B. S. and is still held by her. In 1241 Rani Janki Kumari married BabuGopal Chandra Singh and had by him two Sons kumar

Harendra Narayan Singha and Kumar Indra Narayan Singha and one daughter, Shreemati Kamal Kumari, married to Babu Janaki Proshed Singha of Lakhimpur; both sons are also married and have children. Babu Gopal Chandra Singh was created a Raja Bahadur on the 18th July,1867, by His excellency the Viceroy and Governor General of India, Sir John Lawerence in consequence of his many of public liberality specially in connected with the recent famine in Bengal. Raja Gopal Chandra Singh Bahadur is the son of Manohar Singha of Zilla Gorakhpur in the N. W. Province and relative of the Maharaja of Bansee of that Zillah. Raja Gopal Chandra Singh is a man of enlightened view and a liberal promoter of schools and charitable Dispensaries, construction of roads and has latterly taken on himself the repayment of some Rs. 42,000/- fortytwo thousand rupees being the value of 19500 maunds of rice advanced to the rayats of Pargana Sultanabad by Government, during the recent scarcity in that Paragana. The Raja recovering such advances from his ryats by instalements hereafter.

Paragana Sultanabad comprises an area of 293 square miles. The Raja and his sons also hold zemindars and Pattanies in the adjoining districts of Birbhum, Murshidabad Maldah and Burdwan.

B. Wood.
Deputy Commissioner.
Settlement.

ooo

8.

From,

R. Carstairs,
Deputy Commissioner Santal Parganas

To,

The Commissioner of the Bhagalpur

Division and Santal Parganas,

Dated 1 Febuary, 1890

Pargana Sultanabad is a portion of the Pakur sub-division of this District and covers an area of 292/93 square miles, At last census, it was found to contain a population of 83,244 distributed among 483 villages. The population is doubtless considerably larger by this time as the country has been filling up. The whole of this composes the single estate of Sultanabad which has for about 500 years been in the family of the present proprietors. The heads of the family have been always known as chief or Rajas and in former times used to levy war and exercised a species of superior feudal right over the Pahariahs in the neighbouring hills at the end of last century were brought under the direct control of the Government by Mr. Cleveland. It is the ancient custom of the family that the Estate remains undivided, succession passes to a single heir. Petitioner Maharani Janki Kumari Debi was heir to the Estate, and her husband Gopal Chandra Singh was made a Maharaja by Government for his services. At his death, (One) four years since, his widow, who is still alive, remained in possession of the Estate. Her son Kumar Harendra Narayan Singh managed, and on his death last year her second son Kumar Indra Narain Singh succeeded to the management. She has recently made over the property to her son Kumar Indra Narayan Singh, he is now proprietor, and he is the petitioner whose application is now submitted for orders. "

OOO

9.

Copy of re-settlement Repors

By, Mr. Allenson in Survey and Settlement Operations in the District of Santal Parganas -1898-1907

"Sultanabad is another estate belonging to a lady situated in the same Surkar Odamber and not mentioned in the Ayeen

Akbery. In my account of the southern tribe of mountaineers, I have mentioned that two Rajputs named Anku and Banku, coming to this part of the country, the latter united himself to the highlanders while the former obtained Sultanabad. According to the family traditors he was succeeded in adirect line by Bara Ray, Hangs Ray, Kushal Darbar, Khosal, and Garjan Singh who was killed during a plundering expedition leaving no children. His widow Sarbeswary succeeded, but in the Bengalese year 1198

(A. D. 1782) having been accused of robbery, the family failing and having been convicted, she was confined for life and died in the year 1807. In the year 1792 Mr. Spake then Governor bestowed the estate on Mahkum Ray, son of Kalyan Sinha by Anupa Ray, a daughter of Darbar above mentioned. Mahukum dying without children was succeeded by his widow Maheswari, now about 36 years of age. She cannot read but it said to be attentive to business and to live in a decent manner.

Maheswary held till her death in 1830. Raghunath Sinha, her daughter's son next held for two years. On his death, his sister Janaki Kumari Devi became proprietor and held from 1832 to 1888. She married Gopal Chandra Sinha, Raja in 1875 and Maharaja in 1885. The Maharaja is referred to at page 8 of Mr. Bolton's note as the author of suggestions which were considered in framing the Settlement Regulation III of 1872. **He behaved very well during the agitation of 1871, as will appear from pafe 1 of the same report**. His widow made over the Zemindari of Sultanabad to her youngest son, Indra Narayan Sinha by deed of gift in 1888. She died in 1892, Indra Narayan Sinha died in 1895 and was succeeded by his four minor sons, Jogendra, Debendra, Jnanendra and Fanindra with their mother,Rani Radha Peari Debi as executrix and guardian During the present settlement operations, quarrel was in progress between the sons and their mother and the debts of the family has accumulated that there appeared to be little hope of saving it from ruin. The gross

income of their estate is about Rs- 1,85,000 /- but the debts amount to more than Rs- 16 lakhs. since settlement operations were completed, the estate were takn over in November 1907 by the court of Wards on the joint petition of the Rani and her sons. Negotiations are now in progress to raise a loan on moderate interest and there is some hope that with Court of Wards management this ancient family which has owned Sultanabad for at least 300 years will be set on its feet again. "

RECORDS

SULTANABAD

10.

(Report of J. A. Craven, Settlement Officer,
Santal Parganas, 1898.)

"In the early times Pargana Sultanabad was covered with dense forest. When the Aryans Invaded Bengal, the aborigines of the plains were driven into the forest and hills, some of them finding their way to this tract of country. Some years afterwards when the Mohammedans obtained supremacy many Hindu sought refuge here and founded villages. The aborigines owed no allegiance to Subedars of Bengal and this part of the country was inaccessible, no attempt was made to subdue them. Subsequently it became a place of retreat for the servants of the Nazim. Ruins of his abode still exist. Another Amla Kedar Rai, Built fortress at Garbari, and resided there. A Muhammedan of the name of Sultan cleared a part of this forest, brought lands under cultivation, and gave the tract his name.

In the year 722/723 B. S. two brother, Banku Singha and Anku Singha, Rajput of Gorakhpur in the north western Province, came on a visit to their relation, the Raja of Kharagpore. As the neighbouring chiefs, who had control of small tracts of country on the east of Kharagpore were at feud with each other, these young Rajputs fired by ambition, collected a band of upcountry men and with the aid of the Raja subdued these chiefs and took possession of their territories. Banku Singh, the elder, appropriated the tract north of Bansloee, and the younger Anku Singha retained a portion of the country near Handua. Having established their authority, they presented themselves before the Nawab of Murshidabad with valuable gifts and obtained recognition as Rajas of the territories subjugated by them. Banku Singha paid his tribute in forest produce, and was the founder of the Maheshpur Raj family. In later times the territory was extended to what is known as Sultanabad. The following are some of his successors :- Gandhrab Singh, Hansraj singh, Doman Singh, Golel Singha, and Darbar singh, each being succeeded by his son. Darbar Singh left two sons, Kishan Singh having died without issue, was succeeded by his brother Singha, who was brave and powerful. He died in

B. S. leaving two sons, Ratan singh and Garjan Singh, both dying without issue, the former in B. S. and the latter in B. S. The Raj passed into the hands of Gurjan Singh's widow,Rani Sarbeshwary. In the latter part of the Mohammedan rule the inhabitants were constantly harried by Maratha Lords on their way through Sultanabad to the richer plains of Bangal. A large number of the inhabitants being driven from their homes crossed the Ganges and **settled in Maldah**. The raja took precautions against the invaders and for concealment built subterranean rooms, the ruins of which still exists at Maheshpur.

B. S. settlement was made with Rani Sarbeshwary, but owing to her misconduct and oppression the estate was taken out of her hands and she was deported from Maheshpur. The estate was managed by Government Offical for 9 years and in 1199 B. S. Mahka, Singha, son of Raja Darbar Singha's daughter Ramanee, was appointed as zamindar of Sultanabad and the property restored to the family. In 1205 B. S. a new settlement was made with him, he died in 1209 B. S. without a male issue, but left a daughter who was married to one Dayal Singha of Kanoopore in Murshabad(=Murshidabad). Rani Maheshwary succeeded her husband Mahakum Singh and after her death in 1237 B. S. her daughter Rajmanee's son, Raghunath Singh succeeded her, he died in 1239 B. S., while still a minor. The property then devolved on his sister, Rani Janki Kumari Devi, who died in 1839 A. D. In 1241 B. S. Rani Janki Kumari married Babu Gopal Chandra singha, son of Manohar Singh of Oudh, their issue being three sons and a daughter, Kamal Kumari. The eldest son died young, the second son was Harendra Narayan and third Indra narayan. The daughter Kamal Kumari (married) to Janaki Prosad Singh of Lakshmipore. On the 18th of july, 1867 A. D. Gopal Chandra Singh in recognition of his many acts of public liberality, obtained the title of Raja Bahadur from Sir John Lawrence, Viceroy of India. Later on the raja received the title of Maharaja Bahgulpore, specially for his service during the famine in Bengal. He repaid Rs. 42,000/- the value of 19,500 maunds of rice which had been advanced by Government to his tenants during the famine. On the death of Maharaja Gopal Chandra Singha and his son Harendra Narayan, Maharani Jannki Kumari transferred (to) the estate to her son, Indra Narayan Singh. The debts with which the estate is now encumbered were contracted before his time.

In the beginning of this ceuntry, Santhals came and settled in the country and gradually cleared the forests. They formed community villages and entered into settlement with Zamindar. In 1856 they were driven into rebellion by the oppression of the money-lenders and such money–lenders were captured, put to death, their houses were pillaged and burnt and families massacred. On the suppression of the insurrection, the Santhals returned their homes. In latter they became discontented and the Government intervened and made asettlement between them and the landlords under Regulation III of 1872. "

❍❍❍

11. Ambar-Records

PAKUR RAJ

Collected by Dr. K. K. Datta, mentioned in old Zamindari Records.

" When the Mogul emperors were on the throne of Delhi, there broke out a plague in the province of Oudh **when about 1500 Brahmins left their home at Kanouj and settled in Tappa Kharagpur in the district of** Bhagalpur and Monghyr. **Thence they proceeded southwards and settled in Manbhoom.** Those who passed through the plain of Santhal Parganas, found the place in Occupation of the aborigines, i. e. ' Harees,Domes, Santhals, Dhangars and Angeers, etc. . As soon as they saw the soil very fertile, they got up a quarrel with them for the mastery of it and succeeded in driving aspect under the skilful management of the new-comers and numerous prosperous villages sprang up on all sides. **There was one leader of these settlers called Sulakhan Tewary.** He took possession of Paragauna Ambar without taking any Sanad from the then Emperor Akbar Sah of Delhi. It is stated that this gentleman was once called before the emperor for his having taken possession of the land and was imprisoned. He was then brought to the Darbar houses and the Emperor was very much pleased by his learning and rewarded him for the same with Sanad of the Pargana.

He was succeeded by his son Gopal Tewary, who is said to have been a very able proprietor. Raja Man Singha encamped in this Pargana during the time of this gentleman, while he was proceeding to conquer raja Pratapadditya of Jessore by the order of the Emperor. The guest was very much pleased by his behaviour and recommended for him in the Darbar.

Gopal Tewary Succeeded by his son Bhupal Tewary who lived a very short life leaving his son Prithipal Tewary, a minor, as his successor.

The emperor, as the result of the recommendation of Raja Man Singha, adorned this Prithipal Tewary with the title of the "Sahee of Ambar" as his father and grand father died before leaving this minor one, as their successor. He also kindly sent one of his Ujeer(=Vizir) to this place to manage the "Jaigir property Amber" during the minority of the Sahee, Prithipal Tewary.

Pargana Amber derives its name from the word "Ambari", which means mangoe gardens. It is stated that there were many such gardens in this Pargana and so it is so named. The Ujeer was very able manager and very pious gentleman. He called aborigines from the deep recess of the forest and returned some of their lands to them for cultivation and **ordered to settle them near the villages of the Brahmins and thus rendering and receiving help from each to each.** He acquired many new lands by the aid of these aborigines and made the villages much prosperous than as it was before. He used the system of temporary markets called "Hauts" in different villages on different days of the week and constructed villages roads from one to the other. He appointed one collector of rents to each village called **Mostagir** among the villagers and one officer to decide the disputes among these mostagirs. This circle officer was called Parganait. He engaged some of the aborigines as the " Estate Tirandaz" who used to fight always by their bows and arrows with the fierce animals of the forest such as lions, tigers, elephants, etc. And thus to drive them away and clear the jungles from their claws, while the others used to make the soil fit for cultivation. He thus made Sahee Prithipal Tewary, a master of a vast tract of land called Pargauna Amber and made his known as raja Prithipal Sahee when he attened his majority. This gentleman was called as Dewan Saheb of Pargauna Amber and afterwards as " Fakir Dawan Saheb" of Isakpur, a village in the said Pargauna – where he breathed his last. His tomb was erected there and is yet re......as a sacred place among the settler of Pargauna Amber and everyone pays a visit to it at the time of their ceremonies.

A genealogical table of the Rajas of Ambar is given below and one of them proceeded eastward and settled at Pakur and was know as " Raja of Pakur and the family is called as " Pakur Raj family".

Raja Prithipal Sahee
Raja Kirti Ch. Sahee (son).

↓	↓
Raja Profulla Sahee (son)	Raja Tej Ch. Sahee (son)
Died withott issue.	Raja Bhupati sahee (son)
	This Raja was dethroned by his father –in –law Ananta Prasad who afterwards succeeded him as Raja Bhupati Sahee who never returned from his Sanyasi life.

Raja Ananta Prasad Sahee

Ranee Chandanmayee Devi(his wife)

Raja Ajodhya Prasad Sahee (adopted son)

↓	↓
Raja Prithi Chandra Sahee	Raja Devi Prasad
Built many Deb mandirs Lakhraj lands to Brhamin settlers with him.	Sahee (son) Awarded Died without issue

Raja Krista Chandra Sahee
(son)
Died without issue and
Succeeded by his mother, Rani
Khema Sundari Devi, wife of
Raja Prithi Chandra Sahee.
(a very kind –hearted benevolent lady)

Raj Kuimari
Taranguni Devi daughter
married to Babu Gopilal
Pandey

Taresh Chandra
Panday
(Son)

Raja Sitesh Chandra
Panday
(Son)
This Raja Succeeded Rani
Khema Sundari Devi before her
Death and acquired the title of
Raja also from the British Government
Died 14/12/1901

Kulesh Chandra
Panday
(Son)

Here beigns the three branches of this Raj family. The line of the eldest son as Raj Taraf and of the third son as Chottotarf. A separate genealogical table of each Taraf is given below.

BARATARAF
Taresh Chandra Pandey
(Son of Gopilal Pandey)

Kumar Satyendra
Chandra pandey
Son
Died without issue
Leaving his wife
Surjyavati Devi

Kuar Pratapendra
Chandra pandey
son

Kumari Hemangini
devi
daughter
Married to Babu Bidya
Prasad Chowbey
Sudhangshu Sekhar
Chowbey
(Son)

Son

Daughter.

Son.

Kumar Benoyendra
Chandra Pandey.
(Son).

"Chachee"
Daughter

Daughter
Amarendra pandey

"Baboo"

By the first wife of his

By the second wife of his father Father

CHOTTOTARAF
Kulesh Chandra pandey

(Son of Gopila Pandey)

Kumar Gnanendra Ch.
Pandey (son)

Kumari Ushangini Devi
(daughter)
Married to Babu

Daughter (window)

Nripedra Chandra Pande (son)

Daughter

Eknath Chowbey

Promode Chowbey

Nirmal Chowbey

RAJ TARAF

Raja Sitesh Chandra pandey

(son of Gopala Pandey, but successor

Of Rani Khemasundari Devi during her life time by gift.)

Raj Kumari Sailangani Devi Daughter, Married to Pandey

(son) Kumar Kaildas Minority under of Wards and after majority died without issue on 8th August 1920, leaving his wife Pandey Rani Jyotirmayee Devi as successor

Raj Kumar Puspangini Devi, daughter, married to Babu Jwalla Prasad

Susil Pandey Died without Issue.

Subala Devi married to Pandey Bidhu Bhusan Panday

Son "Haboo"

(Daughter).

Rama Prasad Pandey

Kamala Prasad

This Raja Sitesh Chandra Pandey gifted certain property by the request of Rani Khema Sundari Devi during her life time to the sons of his other brothers as they have no right to the Raj being the great grandson of the said Rani according to Mitakhara law of the Hindu School and as they had no other means to support them.

This gifts were actually turned into the Pattain leases of which Pattus and Kabuliats were made according to law by the said Raja to Kumar Satyendra Chandra Pandey and Kumar Gyanendra Chandra Pandey.

"The merits of your character and disposition have long since been known to me.

I have now been informed by Captain Roughsedge that lately when a party of sepoys in the Company's service, commanded by Meer Roostum Ali Jemmadar, were for the most part over taken by sickness as they were passing throught your estate on their return from Nagpore to the Company's provinces, you immediately are hearing to their unhappy situation, with a degree of humanity and kindness which reflects the nighest honoer on your character, had them conducted in Doolics to your own house, and affording them every medical aid, treat them with the greatest care until they were sufficiently recovered to procced on their journey, when you provided them with conveyance to Chota Nagpoor, a distance of 150 Mile.

Your generous conduct on this occasion towards these soldiers and servants of the Company who were struggling with sickness and disease, and would for the most part have perished on their march but for your humane assistance, is equally creditable to the benevolence of your disposition and to your attachment to the British Government. It has impressed me with sentiments of the highest esteem and respect for your charcter, and entitles you to the lasting favour and regards of this Government.

In its affairs being of opinion that a clear perception of the past and passing events in Sirgooja will tend materially to facilitate the ultimate decision of the Government with regards to its further arrangements.

It appears to have been formely much more extensive that it is at present the ancient boundary of Sirgooja is said to have approached with in amile of the Fort of Sumbhulpoor, and the whole belonged to the Soobah Records relating to Chotanagpur and some border areas.

(Ed.) These Records give a full accounts of the Estate of Sultanbad (Amber) Pakur Raj.

Surendra Jha

ooo

Chapter-IX

1. Records related to the Santal Hul

Original Records about the Santhal Insurrection of 1855

The Santhal Insurrection of 1855 had its origin in the economic grievances of the Santhals inhabiting the tracts now include within the district of Santhal Paraganas, due to the oppressions and frauds committed on those simple –mind people by the merchants and money-lenders then flocking thither on the one side from the districts of Burdwan and Birbhum and on the other from Arrah, Chuprah, etc. The Santhal inhabitant of the place also attributed their hardships to the evil practies of the Naib suzawals or darogas : and they directed their attacks against the agents of the Company as well as against the non –Santhals. One daroga of the Company named Mahesh Dutt, stationed at Dighee Thana (latterly transferred to Borio) was brutally murdered with several followers by the Santhals near Panckethia; a bazar in the Rajmahal subdivision of the district of SanthalParaganas; another named Partabnarain of Kuruhrea Thana (near Mahagama) met a similar fate; and the whole district from Bhagalpur to Suri presented for sometime a scene of plunder and rapine causing immense loss and great distress for the common people.

This episode in the history of Bengal and Bihar has been so long referred to very briefly by writers like Marshman (1) Wheeler (2)Hunter (3) Lee-Warner (4) Sir H. Verney Lovett (5) and Buckland (6) Recently certain important original records have been discovered by me and utilised for a detailed and critical study of the subject.

The records are too long to be quoted here in extenso. I Dr. K. K. Datta am giving here only a short extract from each one of them. which will give some idea about their importance.

These records may be noted under six heads:-

(1) **Documents in English preserved in the record –room of the Divisional Commissioner of Bhagalpur,** These documents consist of (a) letters from the Commissioner of Bhagalpur, (b) letters to the Commissioner, (c) grants of rewards etc, to those who helped the Government in suppressing the insurrection. The following is an extract **Of a letter from the Commissioner of Bhagalpur to the Secretary to the Government of Bengal, dated 9th July, 1855:-** On the 4th instant the Offg. Magistrate of Bhagalpur received a report from the Daroga (otherwise called the Sazawal or Naib Sazawal) of ThannahDighee (the situation of the Thannah has been recently removed to Burrio in the centre of the Hills about 20 miles due west from Rajmahal) to the effect that a large body of Santals had assembled to the south and expressed their determination to seize the country. The report seemed so strange and unlikely that at first little credit was attached to it, but being repeated the next day, the offg. Magistrate Mr. H. E. Richardson and Mr. Pantel. Superintendent of the Damin Koh, lost no time in proceeding of Rajmahal where they reached on the evening of the 6th inst.

No further news of the disturbance reached this place till yesterday afternoon, when two reports were received ; one (dated 7th July) from the Thannah Mohurrier of Burrio, and the other (dated 5 A. M of 8th July)from the post office overseer at the same place stating that the Thannadar, a Mahajan, two Barkandazes and some chowkidars person in all)had been killed by the insurgents ; the intelligence was brought by a Brahmin daroga who had escaped wounded and two of the Daroga's own servants who were eyewitnesses of what had happened.

From more detailed reports subsequently received it appears that the Santals had collected from Beerbhum, Bancoora, Chotanagpur and Hazaribagh to the number of 6 or 7,000 for the purpose (it was rumoured) of avenging the punishment inflicted on their comrades concerned in the last year's Dacoities. These Dacoities were committed on the Bengalee Mahajans who had oppressed them, and they complained that their comrades had been punished while nothing had been done to punish the Mahajans whose exactions had compelled them to take the law into their own hands. Be this as it may, there was no doubt that the Santals had assembled in very large numbers; commenced raising taxes and declared their determination to take possession of the country and setup a Government of their own. The first demand they are said to have made of the Daroga was to compel every Bengalee in the place to pay a tax of five rupees; the next was that he should deliver up every Bangalee in to their hands. On his refusing to do so they first bound him and his companions and then knocked them on the head.

As I said before the news of the outrage reached me yesterday afternoon and I immediately requested the officer commanding the Hill Rangers (7) to dispatch a force to Rajemahal for the purpose of quelling the disturbance; the insurgents having given out that they intended to attack that place.

From information received this morning I have every reason to believe that the insurgents are moving in this direction as well as in that of Rajemahal having plundered several villagers between Burrio (Borio)and Colgong ; and that they are in fact within 20 miles of the latter place. I have therefore changed my former application and asked Major Burroughs in arranging for a detachment being sent to Rajemahal, to be careful to reserve a force sufficient for defence of this station if necessary.

I have also issued orders to the Hill Sirdars, to the Zamimdars of the adjacent Pergannahs and the neighbouringDarogas for aid in suppressing the insurrection. I have obtained the loan of a hundred muskets from Major Burroughs with the view of arming the town Police. This latter step is the more necessary as it has been given out by the Station will be attacked and the inhabitants have in consequence been afraid with panic.

As there is some fear of the Dawk between this place and Rajemahal being stopped I shall send a duplicate of this via Patna.

(Ed.) This document gives us an idea of the different sources for the reconstruction of the history of the santal Hul.

(2) **History of the Santhal Hool of 1855 by late BabuDigambarChakravarty of Pakur in the district of SanthalParganas, written towards the end of the 19th century**. The author has critically discussed the causes of the insurrection. In one pargraph he writes :- In this way the produce of the lands was always drained off, the poor people always remaining steeped in hopelessly heavy debts and no better than the slaves of their creditors throughout their life".

(3) **Manuscript No. 2096 preserved in the Ratan Library of Suri, Birbhum.** It is a contemporary Bengali ballad describing the activities of the Santhal insurgents towards Birbhum. From its concluding lines we know that it was composed in the year 1262 B. S. (1855 A. D) the very year of the insurrections. by Ray Krishnadas, an inhabitant of Kulkuri a village in the Birbhum district The author describes the condition of the panic-striken people of Nagore (once capital of Birbhum) when the Santhals entered there, in the following way:-"...The old men and women with sticks in their hands began to run away. The grey –bearded Muhammadan fakirs followed suit ; they exclaimed, " Oh God! how fierce are their arrows ; oh Satyapir ! save us in this calamity .... Then the Santhals with cheerful hearts entered the palace and cut off the heads of about 40 or 50 men"

(4) A **contemporary Bengali manuscript in prose** being the autobiography of a gentleman, **belonging to a Maratha family settled at Karun,** a village in the Deoghur subdivision of the district of Santhal Paraganas. We know from internal evidences in the text that the writer himself took part in suppressing the insurrection, and he gives a detailed description of the ravages commited by the Santhal insurgents all round and also within his village.

(5) A Bengali ballad giving many important details about the insurrection. It was composed during the end of the 19th century by Late BabuDhanakrishnaRuj, BazarChowdhry of Panckethia in the Rajmahal subdivision of the district of SanthalParaganas. A few sentences may be translated here :- "Different batches of uncivillisedSanthals went out plundering the forests and killing the people One batch surrounded the Hiranpur bazar, cut off a few men and plundered whatever they could get in cash or kind. They proceeded towards Pakur, plundered the house of the local Raja and took away pearls and jewels to their hearts content. They even proceeded to plunder the house of another Raja at Mahespur; and this news soon spread everywhere."

(6) Documents in English, Bengali, Hindi and Persian preserved in the record room of the Deputy Commissioner of SanthalParaganas. These include dispatches records of cases, etc.

(1) "From Mr. J Alen, the Commissioner of Chotanagpur, to William Grey Esquire, Secretary to the Government of Bengal. Fort William, dated Hazaribagh, 17th December, 1885 :- "I do myself the honour to report that I have made very careful enquiries, both public and private, at Hazaribagh regarding the statement made by the Santhal prisoner Ranjeet Manjee(RanjitMajhi) charging the Ex- Amir, Meer Abbas Ali Khan with being concerned in the Sontal rebellion."

(2) I have not been able to obtain evidence or information which leads me to believe or suspect that Meer Abbas Ali Khan has been guilty of any direct or indirect participation in the Sonthal insurrection.

(3) The Ameer like others of his race is passionately fond of the pleasures of the chase, and maintained, while he resided at Hazareebagh a large hunting Establishment. He had in his service many professional hunters of all castes, among whom was the Sonthal Manjee Urjoon who is mentioned in the statement of the Prisoner Runjeet Manjee as one of the originators of the Sonthal Disturbances.

(4). This Urjoon Manjee has been apprehended by my orders but unfortunately he effected his escape close to the Station of Hazareebagh from the persons sent by the Principal Assistant Commissioner to bring him in. I have offered a reward of 50 Rs. For him, and if the police exert themselves he ought to be reapprehended in a few days.

(5) The hunting parties of the Ameer, were conducted on a large scale according to the custom of his country, a thousand or sometimes as many as 2,000 Jungle beates were collected togeheron those occasions, a very large portion of these were Sonthals from the Ramgurh and Khurruckdeahhils who are almost all skillful hunters.

(6) Urjoon Manjee as a servant of the Ameer, was a person of some consequence among the Ramgurh Sonthals, his family reside in the Pulgunge Division Pergunnah Khurrckdeah (Kharakdiha –Giridih), and through them he had some influence also with the Khurruckceah Sonthals, for this reason he was employed by the Ameer to assemble the Sonthal beaters for his hunting expeditions. These Sonthals came not only from the Ramgurh and Khurruckdeath Pergunnahs, but sometimes on grand occasions from the neighbourhood of Deogarh(Deoghar) and from the villages of the Bhagalpur and Beerbhum Districts which are contiguous to the boundaries of the South West Frontier Jurisdiction.

(7) About the middle of April last (the 11th and 12th I think are the dates) the Ameer had a grand hunting party at Nurkundie (not Burokoonide as stated by RanjitManjee). There were I understand about 1500 beaters engaged on this occasion about two-third of whom were probably Sonthals. This evidently is the Shikar party referred to by the PrisonerSonthals. This evidently is the Shikar party referred to by the Prisoner RunjeetManjee, for I find that the Ameer had no other large shooting party in the month of April or about that time. The HazaribaghCutcherry being closed for the Churruck Poujah holidays the Ameer invited Mr. W. C. Spencer the officiating Principal Assistant and Dr. Kelly the civil Assistant Surgeon to join his party and both these Gentlemen were with the Ameer from the beginning to the end of the shooting excursion.

(8) If the Ameer had any treasonable intentions had he assembled those Sonthals with the view of instigation them to rebellion, it is not probable that these two Gentlemen would have been invited to his Camp, and had any communication of this kind been made to those Sonthals it is likely that either Mr. Sepencer or Dr. Kelly or some of their servants would have heard something about the matter.

(9) Urjoon Manjee does not bear a good character, he is a violent man addicted to drink. In February last the Ameer discovered that this Sonthal and one of his Scindian servants had been oppressing the Ryots of some of the villages which he used to frequent for shooting purposes and he sent them both to the Principal Assistant Commissioner at Hazareebaugh requesting that they might be punished ; on the 24th of March last Urjoon Manjee and Mehto were sentenced by the Principal Assistant Commissioner to 15 days imprisonment, and to a fine of 25 Rs. each or a further imprisonment of 15 days with labour which was commutable to a fine of 10 Rupees, Against this order the Defendants appealed to the Deputy Commissioner but their appeal was rejected and they were relased from Jail at the expiration of their sentence on the 24th of April, 1855.

(10) At the time therefore of the Nurkundee shooting party UrjoonManjee was a Prisoner in the Hazareebagh Jail. Under these circumstances it is in my opinion highly improbable that the Ameer should have taken these proceeding against his Sonthal servant and thus exicited his animosity, had he made or intended to make use of him as an instrument in any insurrectionary movement.

(11) I ought not to omit to mention that at these hunting parties the Defendants and servants of the Maharajah of Ramgurh were always present and generally the Ameer entrusted the payment of the Sonthal beaters to them if a conspiracy on a large scale was being hatched at any of these shooting parties the Ramgurh Rajah's people must have been cognisant of it and they are not likely to have concealed it from their Master. The Ramgurh Rajah has always shown himself to be a loyal and well conducted chief and I am satisfied that he would not in any way connived at a plot of this kind.

(12) Amongst the witnesses that I have examined at Hazareebagh, was a Sonthal named Purthee, a nephew of Urjoon Manjee; he was brought to me and I took his evidence before he had time to communicate with any one ; he is a simple country lad of about 19 or 20 years of age, and spoke out frankly as the Sonthals generally do when kindly spoken to and when they have nothing to fear or to conceal, he stated that in August and September 1854 about 10 Sonthals from a distant part of the country came to Urjoon's house in MouzaDurmiah Pergunnuh Jugaseer, the names of five of them were SedhooManjee, KanooManjee, SonahManjee, Sormah Manjee, and Urjoon Manjee ; the names of the five other he did not know. The strangers complained, that they had been obliged to abscond from their homes on account of the tyranny and oppression of the Mahajans, who under the pretence of having lent them money had plundered all their property. Urjoon Manjee offered to get his Master, Meer Abbas Ali Khan to interest himself in their favour, and he went or pretended to go to Hazareebagh to see the Ameer on the subject leaving the Sonthals at his house, he remained absent for 3 days, and on his return home told the stranger that he had brought a letter from the Ameer ordering their property to be given up to them.

(14) This is the only fact I have able to elicit which tends in any way to connect the Ameer with those who have been in rebellion, but I am bound to observe, that I have very little dependence upon anything that Urjoon Manjee may have told these stranger Sonthals for it is much more likely that he falsely stated that he brought an order from the Ameer than that Ameer should have given an order to persons whom he had never seen and over whom he had no influence or control.

(15) UrjoonManjee formerly resided at ChumeerKoh (or ChurneerKoh) in Pergunnuh Khurruckdeah (in Giridih district), his two brothers (KierooManjee and InteeManjee) and other members of his family are the inhabitants of that village, he is said to be distantly connected with Kanoo, Seedho, and Bhyrow the leaders of the Sonthal insurrection : he is just the sort of man with whom evil disposed persons would be likely to communicate if they wished to excite the Insurection, he is a determined and reckless man, he is not waiting in intelligence and has some influence with the Hazareebaugh Sonthals.

(16) After a careful enquiry I have arrived at the Conclusion, that Meer Abbas Ali Khan has not had anything to do with this insurrection.........

(17) I think it not improbable that Urjoon Manjee may have listened to the overtures of the Bhaugalpur and Beerbhoom rebels and that he may have made use of the Ameer's name to encourage them but it does not appear that he has been absent from his house and the neighbourhood since the insurrection commenced or has taken any active part in the Bhaugulpore and Beerbhoom disturbances".

Collected by Dr. K. K. Datta

ooo

2. EXTRACTS FROM THE DIARY OF R. I. RICHARDSON COLLECTOR, BIRBHUM: SEPTEMBER 1855.

(i) Dated 13th September, 1855

Reports from Afzulpore Thannah (In Kundiht Block, Jamtara), mention that the inhabitants of Baboopore Deolee and Kejoree have their villages which have not as yet, however been plundered by the Sonthals.

Sonthals have again looted 'Rajor' 4 miles from Nungolea thanah suspected to be the same men…

N. B. I have requested Co! Burney, to order Captn. Gott stationed with a detachment at Nungolea, to make a night march, and if possible surprise these Insurgents numbering about 600 men.

All quiet at Mohmud Bazar, spies had not returned. A detachment of sepoy ready to march if necessary, at a moment's notice from hence. .

The Daks to Rampore Haat, Nuggur Cong. Deoghur, have been put on an efficient footing by me they now arrive regulary with the exception of the last.

(ii) September 14th, 1855

Nothing new from Afzulpore, Doobrajpore & Nuggur.

Late last evening Co1 Burney at my request sent an expree to Captn. Gott Commanding at Nungolea, ordering that Officer to make a night march, attack the Sonthals at Rajor early this morning.

A report just in from Captn. Gott mentions that after 3 hours trial, he had been unable to get across the river More (N. B. very heavy rain fell during the night) last night. I sent a messenger off to Sergeant Gillon at Mohmud Bazar, directing him to start immediately with his Irregulars' & attack the Sonthals at

Deocha, where they were plundering grain. The result has not been reported yet, but the white flag is now flying at Mohmud Bazar, which means all well.

No reports have yet come in from Operbundha Sarhutt (Sarath) or Deoghur. The Sonthals are in great force at & about Rajbandh Palace Bare Battan.

(iii) September 15th, 1855 2 P. M

(N. B. The Dak leaves Sooree at past 2p. m)

Shree Mundle of Kooreempore, and Kanto Mundle of Fazilpore have been murdered by the Sonthal's in the village of Amjurra (on the boundary N. of Soory) whither they had gone to look for their cattle. This took place yesterday, a third man escaped and gave notice of what had occurred to the Nungolea Darogah. Sergeant Gillon has made an attempt to reach Deocha, but could not get (owing to the flood) across the Dwarka river will try again tonight.

The river More is much swollen consequently the Sonthals are stationary at Bora Bathen.

The Saruth Abkaree Darogah reports that all the abkars in the north of his jurisdiction have run away.

Mr. ward has not arrived yet the expected yesterday.

(Forwarded for the information of the secy. to the Govt. of Bengal.

(Sd-R. I. Richardson).

(iv) September 19th, 1855

No news of importance from Nugger Doobrajpore, Afzulpore. The Sonthals are in large number at Gae Bathan and Telobunnee 18 miles. N. of Sooree they are said to be erecting stockades, but this is doubtful. The Telobonee men are headed by a stronger, most likely, a Mannjee from the Damini Koah.

Captain Gott has made an excursion as far as Buddinathpore, but previous from Saruth & Opurbandah are most unsatisfactory. The Sonthals are evidently steadily advancing, looting every villages en route.

A detachment consisting of 100 men of the 56th N. I marched to Mohumaad Bazar this morning to relieve Sergeant Gillon's force which, when recruited will be sent up to strengthen Gurjori a large town 6 miles west of Nugger, on the Deoghur & Sooree Road. Supplies & good –Shelter will be forthcoming and the place is considered the healthiest in the neighbourhood. This force with another, about to be raised by Mr. Ward & sent to Surhut or Opurbundah will, it is to be hoped, prove sufficient to keep the Sonthals in check until more active separations can be untaken. Registrations being carried on by me several of the Manjies tendered their submission this morning.

The health of the Troops continues to be satisfactory weather very coo!.

The river More must be nearly fordable, so that the intentions of the Sontals in the North must soon become known.

(Received from Heralal Panday, Zemadar 56th Regiment N. I. . 21 wooden boxes said to contain small silver coins and copper Pyee to the value of Company's Rupees thirty thousand 30000 remitted to this Treasury by the Sub-Treasurer

sd /R. I. RICHARDSON.)

(V) SEPTEMBER 20TH, 1855

Birchunder a, village about 8 miles west of Nugger, has been looted.

The Sonthals have stopped the Dak running from Deoghur to Sooree. The police Zemadar at Nugger, reports that the Chandra Dawh Pharee has been shut up by the Sonthals, who have ill used the runners. Two Sonthals are daily withdrawing in number to the N. C. about Chamoosapara Telobunee where they have built 11 large houses in the former villages, where all their loot is said to be stored. It reported that they will make a stand if attacked.

A branch of a sual (=sal)Tree has just been sent in to me by the Nugger Police Zemadar who received it from Goluck Chowkeedar of Afzoolpore. This man states it was made over to him by Shiboo Gope Mudle of Champore, with the message that the Sonthals would shortly proceed to Sooree for the purpose of having a meeting with the authorities.

Shiboo Gope state he does not know who brought the branch but the messenger expressed a hope that the ryotts would not run from their villages on the morning from Mohamud Bazar, it will be recrited defended upto strength and armed with the Treasury Guard muskets which have been placed in the lands of the Armourer of the 56th N. I. for inspection. I hope to get this detachment of men very soon for they are much wanted in the direction of Garjari.

All quiet at Rampore Haut & Doobrajpore.

(VI) SEPTEMBER 21ST, 1855

It is reported that the Opurbundah Thanah has burnt, but the report requires confirmation.

The Sonthals are looting to their hearts' content in the Saruth & Opurbandah jurisdiction, no remedy however are adopted.

The Dak which left this for Deoghur last evening has been brought back, the runners stating that they could not get beyond Laopie 2 Miles this side Of Nugger. This however only the Magistrate's Zemindaree Dark. My own special dak from Nugger has arrived quite punctually and the Police Jemadar is still at Nugger.

A report has just come in that the Sonthals in very great numbers, are at Bindabone and that they have looted Bilkandu.

The Gomashta who gave notice of this at the Nungolea Thanah states that it is the intention of the Sonthals to attack

Sooree immediately. I do not put much confidence in his statement as this very man has several times given the alarm without cause & apparently only desires that the troops shall be sent to protect his master's Zemindaree. Due precautions, however have been taken, the march of Sergeant Gillon's detachment for Gurjee has been postponded & parties of his Burcondauze have been stationed to guard the Loard 3 or 4 miles down.

The officer commanding the Troops has likewise taken which measures as seemed fit to him to be required.

I hope to be able to report more fully tomorrow.

(Forwarded for the information of the Secy. To the Govt. of Bengal.

Sd/- R. I RICHARDSON)

OOO

EXTRACTS FROM LETTERS RELATING TO SANTAL REBELLION, FROM GOVERNMENT OF BENGAL

JULY 30- SEPTEMBER 28, 1855

3. Letter

From,

The Secretary to the Government of Bengal

To,

W. H. Elliott Esquire

Commissioner of Burdwan

Dated, Fort William the 30th July, 1855.

Major General Lloyd has been appointed to take command of the whole of the Troops operating against the Sonthals. General Lloyd has been directed by the supreme Government to proceed, in the first instance, to Rajmehal. He has been informed that the President in Council, considering it very desirable that prompt and speedy measure should be taken to put down the insurrection, has resolved upon placing the conduct of the operations entirely in his hand; and he has been requested to take immediate steps for dispersing and capturing the insurgents and for putting down the rebellion.

In communicating these orders to this Government, the President in Council has requested that the Lieutenant-Governor would instruct the Civil officers of the several Division to communicate with the Major General and to afford him every information and assistance in carrying into effect the line of operations he may decide upon.

In a subsequent communication, the President in Council has explained that it was not intended by the above quoted instructions to general Lloyd that the Military should act independently of the Civil power against our own subject but simply that the nature of the Military Operations necessary for dispersing and capturing the insurgents, and for putting down the rebellion, should be entirely in the hands of the Military commanders. It is stated also that the Civil Authorities have still power to act with the Civil means at their disposal and that the only charge intended to be made is in transferring the power each Civil officer had over the movements of the Troops to a Military of experience; operations necessary for quelling the insurrection. The President in Council considers it is added, that the Civil authorities should abstain from ordering out troops except in cases of sudden emergency, but that they should keep the Military officers, particularly the Officer in command in the district, fully informed on all points connected with the state of the country, and the movements of the rebels, and offer such suggestions as may occur to them connected with the general object in view.

Since General Loyd's appointment, it has also seemed desirable to the President in Council to appoint Colonel Bird, with the position of a Brigadier, to the special command of the Troops employed in the Berbhoom and Bancoorah Districts. This officer is instructed to take immediate measures, in concert with the Civil officer, for dispersing and capturing the insurgents wherever they may be, and for putting down the rebellion. He is informed that Mr. Loch at Munglepore and yourself at Sooree will afford him every information and assistance ; and he is requested to act in concert with Mr. Loch and yourself in carrying out line of operations necessary to suppress the insurrection.

The Lieutenant –Governor has only to add to the above instructions the expression of his earnest hope that you yourself and all the Civil officers subordinate to you will in every possible way, aid and promote the operations of the Troops. your attention should more particularly be directed to procuring efficient and trustworthy guides for the troops, and to providing them with carriage and supplies. Orders have some days since been issued to the Magistrates of all the surrounding districts, urging them to produce as many Elephants as possible, and forward them into Birbhum and Bhagalpur; and some have already been sent up direct form Calcutta. Also, as soon as it shall be devised at what places detachments of troops are to be posted. You should see that every exertion is made to afford good shelter both for officers and men; and especial care should be taken to provide, as early as possible charpoys or some elevated platforms for the sepoys to be upon.

You should likewise, if as may be possible, the medical arrangements as not yet efficiently organised that it upon yourself to see that the officer in command of every detached body of troops so furnished with a few simple medicine particularly Quinine, with brief instructions as to the quantities to be given.

The Lietunant Governor is desirous to receive reports from you of the progress of affairs as frequently as possible.

You will communicate the above orders to the several officers subordinate to you who are employed in the disturbed districts.

W. GREY
Secretary to the Govt. of Bengal.

OOO

4. Letters

From,

The Secretary to the Government of Bengal

To,

A. C. Bidwell Esqr

Date 6th August 1855, No. 1808,

The Govt. received from the Magistrate Of Bhagalpur a copy of documents which had been forwarded to the officer by Santhals. a translation of this document is enclosed and the Lt-Governor considers that having regard to the tenor of it, and also to the circumstance that the Santhals would appear more particularly from the accounts received from the Beerbhoom Districts already in a great measure to have abandoned active opposition to the Troops sent against them, you should take every means of publishing and proclaiming among them by written notices both in the Hindee and Bengallee languages, that the government will freely pardon all who may tender a speedy submission except those who shall be proved to have been the principal instigator and leaders of principally concerned in the perpetration of any murder. They shall be warned at the same time that against all who continue to offer resistance,that prompt and severe measures will be unhesitatingly adopted, while on the other hand, that as soon as complete submission is shown to the authority of Government, you will be prepared to receive and carefully enquire into all well ground complaints which they may have to prefer.

The Lieutenant Governor has observed in several of the reports, public and private, that have come before him since the troops have been in the field, mention of Santhal-village having been burnt in the course of active measures against the rebels.

This may sometimes have happened unavoidably and some time he has no doubt as in the case of Bugnadihee (Bhognadih) the chief position of the leading Santhals near Burhait(Bornet), of the destruction of which he entirely approves may have been done purposely With a view to striking terror and inflicting a summry and immediate punishment on leading rebels through their the property in a particular and important instance likely to make a striking impression on all the subordinate insurgents.

But it is necessary to keep in mind that the Laws have not been suspended and that a responsibility will attach to all acts of wanton and unnecessary severity and even were it otherwise, it can never, the Lieutenant – Governor believes, conduce to the early settlement of the present unhappy disturbances to make large bodies of armed men, our subjects homeless, houseless, desperate. A few served examples must be necessary and ought assuredly to be made, but you will not, the Lieutenant- Governor feels sure overstep yourself or allow to overstep the bounds of that true moderation and humanity which should distinguish all our dealings with our subjects, even the most perverse and misguided.

(True Extract) A. C. BIDWELL
Comr. on Spl. Deputation.

ooo

5. Letter

From,

The Secretary to the Govt. of Bengal

To,

R. l. Richardson Esqr.

Collector of Berbhoom.

Dated Fort William, 17th Septr., 1855.

With reference to your diary of the 14th instant the Lieutenant-Governor directs me to point out to you that in making requisitions to the Military to act offensively against the Santals, you are going beyond the strict line of your duty, and as it is possible that your requisitions might at some time or other interfere, with the places of Brigadier Bird and Mr. Ward, it is better, the Leiutt. Governor thinks that you should refain from addressing any dtrect requisitions to the Military officers in the Beerbhoom District. This will not of course prevent you from assisting the Military with the advice and information which

Your local position and knowledge enable you to give, in case the officer in Chief Command in your neighbourhood has a discretionary authority from Brigadier Bird to act offensively without previous reference to him, and should himself consider it desirable to do so.

W. GREY
Secy. to the Govt. of Bengal

ooo

6. Letter

From,

The Secretary to the Govt. of Bengal.

To,

J. R. Ward Esquire
On special duty at Raneegunge. (Raniganj)
Dated, Fort William the 21st Sept., 1855

With reference to the Extract from Mr. Richardson is Diary of the 19th Instant copied on the margin. I am directed to observe that, if the Manjees referred to by him are Leaders, which the Lieutenant – Governor is inclined to believe is the case, they are not included in the proclamation and ought not therefore to be allowed to escape all punishment by submission, you are requested to point this out to Mr. Richardson.

*Registratration is being carried on by me of Manjies who tendered their submission this morning.

W. GREY
Secretary to the Govt. of Bengal

(Copy forwarded to Mr. Richardson for his information and guidance. Sd/-J. R. WARD, Commr. on Special Duty)
Raneegunge, 23Sep, /55,

ooo

7. Letter

From,

The under Secretary to the Govt. of Bengal.

To,

R. I. Richardson Esqr.
Collector of Beerbhoom.
Dated, Fort William the 28th Sept., 1855

I am directed to acknowledge the receipt of your Diary dt the 26th instt, and in reply to state that the Lieutt. Governor approves of your having indented for muskets but he desires me to say that all indents on the arsenal should be sent through the Government. His Honour approves also of your endeavouring to raise the irregulars under Sergeant Gillons to100 Strong as well as of your proposal for securing the services of three or four hundred more men by the 1st of November, you are desired to report further upon the progress which you made in doing this and to state whether more in doing this more European Sergeants will be required to command the men ; and you will keep the Govt. punctually informed of the number of additional men that you entertain and at what cost. The number at present entertained under Sergeant Gillons is undersood to be as noted in the margin.

In reference to the accounts received by you of the doings at Operbundh the Lieutt, Governor requests that you will submit detailed and seprate report regarding them.

A copy of these orders will be furnished to Messrs, Bidwell and Ward to the letter of which you should report your proceedings in connection with the Selection of the men you have been authorized herein to procure.

A. W. RUSSELL
Under Secy. to the Govt. of Bengal

ooo

8. Letter

From,

R. I. RICHARDSON
Collr, of Beerbhoom.
Soory,
Septr, 12, 1855

To,

Colonel Burney
Commg. 56 N. I. Soory.

In Reply to your letter no. 155 of this day's date, I beg to state that I do not consider it absolutely necessary that at present a force should be sent from here to reinforce the party of Irregulars under Sergeant Gilion.

I have adopted measures by means of which information may be very rapidly obtained from Mahmud Bazar.

I shall be very careful to give you any & every information which I may receive & trust, you will keep two companies in readiness to make a tour in case of necessity....... .

9. Letter

From,

R. I. RICHARDSON
Collr, of Beerbhoom.
Soory,
September 13, 1855

To,

Colnel Burney

Commg. 56 N. I. Sorry

In today's report received from Thannah Nungoiea it is mentioned, that the Sonthals are at the village of Rajor. This village cannot be more than four or at the utmost five miles, from Nungolea and I should think Captn. Gott. With his detachment might surprise the Insurgents by making a night march & coming upon them early in the morning.

I apprehend these Sonthals are the same men who burnt Puriharpore, immediately after the departure of Captain Fooks detachment & it is essentially necessary that a servere example should be made of them, if possible.

ooo

10. Letter

From,

R. L. RICHARDSON

Collector of Beerbhoom.

Sooree,

September 21st/55

To,

Colonel Burney

Commanding at Sooree.

I have the honor to report for your information that I yesterday received from the Police Zemadar at Nugger, a Saul twig, sal leaves with 3 leaves upon it.

This twig had been sent to the Zemadar, from a person calling himself the Soobah Baboo with a request that he (the Jemadar) should forward it to the authorities at Sooree, whom he was shortly coming to see.

I have enquired among the Sonthal prisoners in the Jail, as to the meaning of this symbol, but they are either un-willing or unable to give any information in the matter, except that the three leaves express the intention of the sender to come at the third day. Under the above circumstances, I beg you will make whatever arrangements you may consider called for, I for my part, shall send no answer to the message, it being my intention to put Soobah in irons on his arrival.

The question as to whether he is about to come in peace – fully to submit, or to try his strength with us, must remain for the present, a matter of doubt.

(Received from the Sub-Treasurer at the Presidency the sum of company's Rupees thirty three thousand / costs 33,000/of small silver and Copper Pyce packed in 21 Boxes as follows;

25 DOCUMENTS

Eight anna Pieces	15,000 0
Four anna pieces	15,000 0
Copper Pyce	3,000 0
Total	33,000 0

The above treasure was examined before Lalla Rooplall Native Treasurer, and Gora Chand Dhur, Nittannund sen, and Ramharry Dutt Poddar of this Colloctorate.

R. I. RICHARDSON
Collr. Of Beerbhoom
Beerbhoom Collr's office
the 21st Septr., 1855

OOO

11. Letter

From,

R. I. RICHARDSON

Collr. of Beerbhoom
Soory September 27th /55.

To,

Colonel Burney
Commanding at Sorry.

In reply to your letter no. 10 of this day's forwarding dispatch from Major Membhard(returned herewith) I beg to state that Raneebehal is a village on the north side of the More River, distant from Mahmud Bazar 10 or 12 miles.

Major Membhard could not, I think, get to Raneebahal, without coming across the whole body of Santhals, collected at Bora Bothan Rangaloya.

My information is to the effect that a considerable number of Santhals are leaving Rangaloya for Raneebehal from whence they are going, it surmised, to Raneebehal, who will be back tomorrow, with fresh information.

ooo

12. Letter

From,

R. I. RICHARDSON
Collr, of Beerbhoom

To,

The Magistrate of Beerbhoom,
Soory,
Dated September 28th, 1855.

Every available man, belonging to Sergeant Gillon's force, being required to protect Nugger, I shall feel obliged by your Directing the Soory and Nungolea Darogahs to have the Ghats or fords on the More guarded by their Police.

Should you think it necessary to put on extra police, I will sanction the expenditure, the Commissioner having authorized me to do so.

ooo

13. Letter

From,

R. I. RICHARDSON
Collr, of Beerbhoom
September 28th/55.

To,

Col. Burney,
Commanding at Soory.

In consequence of reports received by me from various quarters I think it very advisable that a detachment should be sent to hold Doobrajpore.

The Santhals are said to be crossing the More at Raneebehal and I think it not unlikely that their purpose is to join the Operbundah rebels at or about Gurjore and strike southward for the purpose of escaping into the Bancoorah District. Doobrajpore is outside the jungle & contains an enormous amount of property, very many of the villagers from the North –western portion of the district having taken refuge there. Supplies & shelters for sepoys will be available on their arrival.

14. Letter

From,

R. I. RICHARDSON
Collr, of Beerbhom
Soory
September 29th /55

To,

Colonel Burney

Commanding at Soory.

I have honour to send in original a letter received by me yesterday from Mr. Ward.

He is anxious that Gurjore should be occupied by troops, and I consider the measure most expedient ; moreover the locality is as Mr. Ward observes, a very healthy one Sergeant Gillon stationed at Nugger reports that a very large body of Santhals are assembled at Tantiapore, a village on the Sidh Nulah north of Indurpohare, (which latter place you will find marked in the Zillah map) and that supplies for 10,000 men are being collected there. Tantipore is exactly north of Gurjore, distant about 7 miles so that if a strong detachment be pooled at the last mentioned place : and the Santhals may have of going southerly must be entirely frustrated.

With detachments at Gurjore, Nungolea Mahmud Bazar ; & Gillon's force at Nugger, I do not think the Santhals can do much, and if besides we hold Doobrajpore nothing more I am convinced can be done until the cold season commences.

The only drawback, is that Gurjore may, by this time exist only in name, I have however, sent out men to ascertain & I will, on their afford the necessary information.

(Be so good as to return Mr. Ward's letter when done with

Sd/ -R. I. RICHARDSON)

OOO

14 (A). Letter

From,

R. I. RICHARDSON)

To,

Colonel Burney

Commanding at Soory.

In order to clear up all doubts as to the existence or non – existence of the Santhal camp at Chamoapara & adjacent villages, I yesterday proceeded with Major Numbhard & Mr. Kerr, to within 2 miles of Chamoapara.

My spies have reported quite correctly. From beside a piece of ground we discovered huts innumerable, apparently newly built & which the villagers who accompanied us, declared to be the advanced post of the rebels, whose encampment extended at broken intervals for 3 miles, **up to Telobunnee, the residence head quarters of the Soobah.**

The road as far as we went was in very fair order & the jungle nothing at all in the vicinity of Chamoapara there appeared to be none Mumbhart, & Mr. Kerr state that between that village & Telobunnee amere bush wood jungle (intervenes).

As we proceeded we learnt but one story that the Santhals were daily packing up their loot, & retiring to the hills in anticipation of a cold weather campaign.

It is occur to me that an advantageous & decisive blow might by the force now quartered at & about Soory.

To cripple the resources of the rebels is to gain a great step as regards future operations but the blow must be struck speedily & secretly.

There are no dense jungles in the vicinity of the rebels" camp.

The country is high & dry I should say the climate just as pure as that of Soory.

Mr. Kerr of Muhmud bazaar volunteers to act as scout. He knows every inch of the country & his services would be invaluable.

I shall only be too happy to accompany the Troops in my capacity in which I can be of the least use.

OOO

15. Letter

From,

R. I. RICHARDSON
Collr,of Beerbhom
Soory
oct12th, 1855

To,

Colonel,
Commanding at Soory

Having been requested by the Lieutt. Governor of Bengal,to discontinue any connection with the Santhal Insurrection, in as much as may appertain to the suppression thereof, I beg to request the favour of your calling in future upon the Magistrate of the District, for any information you may require, regarding the Santhals. I have also to beg that you will direct the Quarter-master of the 36 Regt. N. I. to take charge of all elephants (the property of private individuals) now here for Government use. Commanding certificate of a Guard directed to proceed on Escort duty towards Soory, in charge of Muskets and ammunition for the use of Sert. Gillon's Irregulars.

Corps	*Strengh*	*Remarks*	*To what date paid*
60 Regt. N.1	1 Habildar 12 Sepoys	To be relieved on the banks of the River Adji	To 31 Aug.1855

Raneegunge — B. P. Parott, Capt.
12th October, 1855 — Major of Brigade

Received from Koomur Sing Havildar 63rd Regtt. N. 1. 10 Boxes said to contain mauskets & ammunition.

Soory — R. I. RICHARDSON
October 1855 — Collector

OOO

EXTRACTS FROM SOME IMPORTANT LETTERS ISSUED BY THE COMMISSIONER, SPECIAL COMMISSIONER AND OTHER OFFICERS DEPUTED IN CONNECTION WITH SANTAL REBELLION

15 (a). Letter

From,

The Commissioner of the Nuddea Dt.
On Special Deputation.

To,

The Magistrate of Bhagulpore
Dated Bhagulpore, 15th August, 1855.

I have the honor to annex extract paras 4 to 7 of a letter from the Secretary to the Government of Bengal to my address no. 1868, dated 6th August and to request your particular attention to the observations and instructions contained therein.

You will be good enough to promulgate amongst the Santhal population by every means in your power, copies of the enclosed proclamation and the name of every one appearing before you to make submission should be entered in a book exhibiting the following particulars.

Name/Father name:	Age/Place of Residence	Whether he admits having been engaged in any act of rebellion ,if so the particular	Remark

To all who tender their submission a certificate in the accompanying form should be given and the accompanying Mochoolka should be signed by them.

A. C. BDWELL
Comm. On special Deputation.

16 . Letter

From,

A. C. BDWELL

special Deputation.

To-V. GREY

Secy. To the Govt. of Bengal

PROCLAMATION

In as much as it appears that amongst the Santhals, who have risen in rebellion against the Government, Plundering and devastating the Country and Opposing the Troops, there are many who see the folly and iniquity of their proceedings & are desirous of being pardoned and resuming their former quiet life, notice is hereby given that the Government ever anxious for the welfare of its subjects, though led away by counsels of bad men, will freely pardon all Santhals who may within 10 days appear before any constituted authority (Hakim) and tender their submission always excepting those, who shall be proved to have been principal instigators and leaders of the insurrection, and those who shall be proved to have been principally concerned in the perpetration of any murder, as soon as complete submission is shewn, all well grounded complaints preferred by the Santhals will be fully enquired into. But on the other hand, all insurgents remaining in opposition to Government of the issue of this proclamation will be visited with the promptest and severest punishment.

No. 102

Commr's Office Burdwan Dn

Burdwan The 23rd August, 1855

17. Letter

From,

J. M. ELLIOTT

Offg. Commr.

To,

The Offg. Collector of Beerbhoom

I have directed the magistrate of Burdwan and joint Magistrate of Bankore to remit to you the salaries of the six sowars named in the margin who are stationed-

1. Chel Alee Khan
2. Meer Mazfer Khan
3. Emamjuma Khan
4. Asuk Meer Khan
5. Meer Ahur Alee
6. Sheekh Tofozul Hossen

At Sooree; and beg that you will see to its payment to them after deducting an advance of 10 Rupees each made by me to the 4 first sowars, and crediting the same to me in part repayment of the advance of 250 Rupees I obtained from you debitable to the Santhal Insurrection.

OOO

18. Letter

From,

J. M. ELLIOTT

Offg. Commr. of Revenue & Circuit

To,

The Offg. Collector of Beerbhoom

I have unfortunately mislaid, till today, your letter of the 14th instant no. 110, But as I have addressed you privately on its subject, the delay will not have caused any detriment to the Public service.

During my residence at Soory, all that I heard from you and saw of your management of supplies for the Troops convinced me of the propriety of the course you have adopted in obtaining Provision from Cutwa(Katwa) by advances from the Public Treasury, realisable on the sale of the supplies, and I can but repeat, what I told you verbally that I approved of your plan; indeed I myself got some supplies from Jamoo Kandee through the Collector of Moorshidabad, and felt sure that His Honor the Lieutenant-Government will relieve you of all responsibility in the matter.

As to Ata you could not have got any thing like requisite quantity in your own District. To get it elsewhere was a matter of necessity, as was the advance of Money for its purchase. Other supplies you might have obtained, though with great difficulty, by collection from various parts; but with a kind fore-thought for the inhabitants of Soory, and for the swarms of poor who have sought refuge there, you preferred a plan which removed all pretext on which the Soory Shop-keepers might have demanded famine prices. And should it be objected that the Regiment ought to be supplied by its own Moodies, I can bear you witness that its Commanding Officer admitted their utter inability to provide supplies. If I be not mistaken, they managed to raise 90 Rupees amongst them and he offered an advance of 50/- total 140 Rupees, or about 2 day's supply of provision to be brought from a distance of 4 day's journey.

You have been purchasing largely in the Cutwa market where supplies can be had in any quantity at reasonable prices, and retailing these supplies to the Troops at the Soory rates. You will doubtless at the end of each month find that what with cost of carriage by injury from Rain &. . your recipts have fallen some what short of your Expenditure; and I think you should as soon as possible after the close of each month, send me an exact Debit and

Credit Account, the result of which I will submit to Government and I doubt that the arrangements you have made will meet the approval. I believe they deserve and that the Lieutenat- Governor will authorise you to write off the losses incurred.

A copy of your letter and of the reply will be submitted for His Honor's consideration and orders.

OOO

19. Letter

From,

J. R. WANES
(on Spl. Duty)
(Camp. Deoghur, 21st August, 1855)

To,

The Collector of Beerbhoom
Raneegunge., 5th Sept., 1855.

I have acknowledge the receipt of your letter no. 130 of the 3rd inst. To the address of Mr. Elliott who forwarded it to me.

If you have enough copies of the proclamation, you had better distribute them to posted in as many village as possible or otherwise made public in any manner you may think best. I have not the means of getting a sufficient nos. of copies made here, but have such translations to be lithographed as desired by Govt.

I hope they will be up in a day or two. I shall then send you a number of copies.

Should any Santhals come in to you I would solicit the favour of registering their names and acting as per instructions which accompany. The forms of mochulkas and certificates will also be lithographed and copies supplied with the least practicable delay.

You would also oblige me by preparing the register required. I hope to relieve you of this duty as soon as I can make some satisfactory arrangement for putting the troops here and on the Grand Trunk road, after which I shall proceed to Sooree. Should I however be delayed and detained from Govt. but for the present I hope the present arrangement may hold but you will no doubt let me know should you experience any difficulty or should your duties prevent your giving the subject sufficient time or attention.

With regards to the Santhals your reports as collected at Rajbund Pollassee you will observe that oppressive measures are not be suspended against armed bodies and orders were yesterday issued to Major Nembhard to obtain if possible, ample information and should this turn out to be an armed body to attack and disperse them. Major Nembhard has also authority to use without further orders the troops at his command agst,. any armed assemblage and I hope he will not hesitate to act promptly agst. Any such bodies.

ooo

20. Letter

From,

H. W. B. Gordon, Ltt

Comdg. Detachment

To,

The Magistrate of Monghyr,

I have the honor to inform you of my arrival here this morning in command of a detachment strength as per margin.

I beg to annex an extract from Circular no. 299 dt. H. d. Quarters Dinapore Dn. On board the H. C. S. V. Jumna 7th August, 1855 regarding shelter being provided for the men and as the length of time the Detachment may be kept here is very uncertain, I would feel obliged by your issuing the necessary orders regarding it. There are at present six men suffering from fever and dysentery, and I much fear, if they are kept in Tents for any length of time the numbers will greatly increase.

The Commr. Of Bhagulpore kindly lent me five Elephants to bring on my ammunition and tents, but I am obliged to send them back to him again as he has to send them to some other quarter, in the event of my having to move from this I will find the greatest difficulty in doing so without them I would therefore, be much obliged if you could procure some 3 or 4 to me. I was directed to report my arrival here to you soon that account I ask you to assist me, if possible with Elephant.

*42 N. D. n(Lt) INFANTRY

1 Lieutenant, 1 Subadar, 1 Jemadar, 6 Havildars, 6 Naiks, 2 Buglers, 94 Sepoys,1 lascar, 1Bheestee;

HILL RANGERS

1 Lieutenant, 1 Subadar, 1 Jemadar, 3 Havildars, 5 Naiks, 2Drummers, 97 Sepoys, 1 lascar, 1 Bheestee,1 Native Doctor.

OOO

21. Letter

From,

J. R. Ward

Commissioner on Special Duty

To,

The Collector of Soory

Raneegunge, the 9th Sept., 1855

I have to thank you for demi official reports of 6th and 7th instant which reached me this morning.

There can be no doubt, that the Doomkah Santhals are determined to hold out, and all we can do is to prevent their espacing, for I hope that unless the proclamation has a very different effect to what I anticipate. Govt. will direct a sweep throught the jungles in the cold weather.

As regards the assemblages at Rajbond Polasee, I am inclined to think the Santhals there are not, whatwere, they may have been before, peaceably disposed. I would therefore ask you to communicate with Major Nembhard who has the Brigadier's authority to mark against any armed body of Santhals and if these Santhals are still Rajbond Polassee and it be not very clearly established either by a demonstration from themselves, or on other good information that their object is submission a Deatachment should in my opinion be marched against them. There may be good reason for not risking the health of the troops such as the nature of the country ; the shelter to be found, supplies to be procured, distance to be traversed and the like of which the military officer is to be judged but this the theory which I would, if possible put into practice. It is however, difficult from here to say how it should be acted on, and you will no doubt be guided by the information you receive, for you judge of the reliance to be placed thereon beter than I can, but I would on no account harass the troops unless satisfied of the emergency of the case.

The Burkundages may be sufficient at Mohamed Bazar, but if the place is not unhealtly, Brigadier Bird aggress(agrees) with me in thinking a Company of sepoys should hold the village, if an attack is intended. The Brigadier intends I believe, to write to Major Nembhard on this subject.

Would you oblige me by letting me know whether **Harmah Majhee of Seetasal** who I believe surrendered to Mr. Loch or to you has returned to Sooree. I hear he **was sent out to bring in other head men but was attacked by the rebels, his village destroyed, and property plundered,** he himself narrowly escaping because he had set such a bad example.

The lithographed translations of the proclamation have not yet been received.

22. Letter

(Camp: Raneegunge, 10th Sept., 1855)

B. PAROTT CAPTAIN

Major of Brigade

In consequence of a Communication received yesterday from R. Richardson Esqr, at Sooree reporting the assemblage of Sonthals in the neighbourhood of Mohamed Bazar and apprehending an attack in that quarter. I am direct desired by the Brigadier Commanding to call your particular attention to the circumstance and to request, you will not fail to employ the Troops and at your disposal should you consider the men under Sergeant Gillon insufficient for the protection of the above named Bazar.

I am further directed to add, that in the event of your obtaining reliable informations of the assemblage of armed Sonthals, alarming the inhabitants, and plunderidg villages in the neighbourhood of Sooree, you will attack and disperse any such band within reach, instructions the officer in Command to lose no time in returning to Cantonments when the necessity which caused the movement, ceases to exist.

OOO

23. Letter

Commer's Office, Burdwan Dn.

Burdwan, the 27th September, 1855

To,

The offg. Collector of Beerbhoom

During my recent deputation to Beerbhoom. I drew upon your Treasury for 3 sums of 1,00, 500 and 250 Rs. total Rs. 1750/-

OOO

24. Letter

SOME IMPORTANT LETTER AND REPORTS SENT BY THE DISTRICT AUTHORITIES OF BIRBHUM SEPTEMBER 13- DECEMBER 31, 1855

To,

Brigadier Bird
Commg, in the Beerbhom & Bancoorah
Soory, September 13th 1855

I beg to report for your information, that for the last few days, report of a very unfavourable nature have been received by me from the Darogah of Sarhut(Sarath Deoghar) and Opurbundah as also from member of the inhabitants residing in that part of the district.

The Sonthals are without doubt looting, burning & Mudering in all the villages, in the vicinity of Rukoha on the Boundary.

They have committed four murders in the villages of Katahur. Sgt. Gordon with 200 men is at Deoghur. Could not half this number be sent to Sarhut ? The measure would be productive of much good & Suruth is a much healthier place than Deoghur.

I trust you will give the subject your attention.

Sgt. Gordon being stationed within the Beerbhoom district I conclude he is under your orders.

R. I. RICHARDSON
Collr. Of Beerbhoom.

(P. S. There is good accommodation to be had at Saruth & plenty of Supplies. The Officer on Duty might live in the Moonsiffs Cutchery. Sd /-R. I. RICHARDSON,Collr.)

ooo

25. Letter

REPORT FROM THE MAGISTRATE OF BEERBHOOM TO THE COMMISSIONER OF BURDWAN DIVISION

DATED 24TH SEPTEMBER, 1855

During the past fornight, upwards of thirty villages have been plundered and burned by the insurgents in Thannah Operbundah and Nangoola. **The whole of the Country, from Lorojore, four miles west of Nuggur, to within a short distance of Deoghur, is in their hands.** The Dawks (mails) are stopped, and the inhabitants have deserted their villages, and fled. They are divided into two large bodies : one encamped at Raksadangal, ten milies north of the Operbandah Thannah in Zillah Bahgulpore; and also in Bhagulpore, but on the confines of Thannah Nagoolea, and their number average, as nearly as we can ascertain from 12,000 to 14,000 and are receiving augmentations from all quarters.

A party of about 3000 of the Raksadangal Santals, **led by Mooheea Kosnjola, Rama and Soondra Manjhees,** encamped near Operbandah on the afternoon of the 16th inst, and on the following day plundered and burnt the Thannah and village.

The **darogah and Burkundazes** remained at their post till the last moment; but seeing the overwhelming on their part must be **useless, they retreated, and the Darogah contrived to escape with great difficulty via Shanna and Afzulpore,** and arrived here on the 22nd with only the clothes on his back. He had heard some days before that the Santhals intended attacking the Thannah, and had sent all the records, etc. to Deoghur for security and also applied to the Officer commanding the detachment there for assistance; but the latter, owing to the distance and dense jungle en route, declined to send troops to his aid. On informing Mr. Ward of the circumstances, he told me that detachment of troops were to be sent forthwith from Raneeginge to Jumterra

(Jumtara) in Thannah Shanna, to Operbandah, and to Afzulpore, to be stationed there until the military force can take the field against the Santhals after the rains are over; and I have just heard that the detachment has arrived at the fomer place. Which will suffice for the protection of Thannah Shanna in the jurisdiction of which no plunder has yet been committed; but the Santhals are now assembling with the intention of joining the rebels. Until troops are stationed at Operbandah everthing must remain in the present state of anarchy and confusion ; but directly they arrive I shall send the Police back to the Thannah, and so the Dawk (mail) going again. At present it is impossible, **as Rama Manjhee, with 200 men, has taken up his position in the jungle near Haldigurh Hill**, and waylays and plunders everthing that attempts to pass that way. The absence of, a civil officer at Deoghur is greatly to be regretted at the present juncture, when his services would be of so much value; but I have already brought this to your notice in a former letter.

The gang of from 5000 to 7000 Santals, under **Seeroo Manjhee.** who had taken Sooleah Takoor at Teelabooney, have strengthened their position by earthworks, and dug tanks there. They have also made preparations for celebrating the Doorgah Pooja, for which purpose they have carried off and detained two Brahmins from one of the villages plundered by them in Thanna Nangoolea; and spies who came in yesterday say that they are only waiting for the Raksadangal gange to join them, before advancing to attack Soory; but I think it improbable that they will venture to attack the station under present circumstances. They sent us in what is called in their language a 'dahra' or 'Missive ' viz. a twig of the Sal tree leaves on it, each leaf signifying a day that is to elapse before their arrival a few days ago, which was brought by one of the Deoghur Dak runners whom they seized and sent back for the purpose.

The Colonel commanding has taken the precaution of stationing piquets(Pickets) at different points on the north and west side of the station,. Which would be most exposed in the event of an attack and I understand that Segt. Gillon and his Burkundazes, whom I placed at the disposal of the Special Commissioner when here at the latter's request, is to be sent to Nuggur, where the residents are in a state of great alarm, and many have deserted their houses.

OOO

26. Letter

To,

J. R. WARD Esqr.

Commissioner Raneegunge.

It is not my wish to pry into the kind of operation about to be undertaken by the Govt. with regards to the suppression of the Sonthal Insurrection, but I must request the favour of information upon one point, Viz, who is to be Commissariat Officer to the troops now here, & those perhaps about to come when an advance shall be made into the Jungles.

You are aware that for the last 3 months I have furnished supplies, but I am now winding up my account, owing to the Bunneahs in the town, being able to meet the present demand.

This last arrangement will do very well as long the troops remain on the station, but not so, when detachment go out into the Jungles.

I wish to know therefore, what arrangement shall be made ; if the Govt. intend that I shall continue the duty, some intimation ought to be conveyed to me of the probable number of men likely to be assembled at Soory for field service.

I submit that the means adopted by me of drawing supplies from a rather distant market Cutwais(Katwa) the best under existing circumstances ; it may cost the Govt. somewhat more; but by so doing, the distant markets are not impoverished and prices not raised to famine rates. There is little enough grain in the district owing to the rascally Sonthals, without causing a further drain.

In soliciting instructions. I beg most strongly to represent that I do not so with the hope of becoming Commissariat Officer. The work is laborious in the extreme, but I wish that something may be done, in time too, to supersede the custom of making the local Zemindars provide for all wants. when by so doing they oppress their ryots and raise the price of food into the bargain.

The probable number of men to be fed from Soory should be secretly furnished and I would send funds quickly to Cutwa & buy up before the Bunneah, received information and raised their prices all round.

R. I. RICHARDSON
Collector

ooo

27. Letter

To,

J. R. Ward ESq
Special Commissioner,

I beg to forward for perusal a letter just received by me, from Captain Ford, commanding at Deoghur, requesting me to send supplies for the use of his detachments, consisting of five companies.

It is not possible, for me, to comply with Captain Ford's request. Deoghur is distant 85 miles from Soory, and the communication has been intercepted by the Sonthals for more than a month past.

I cannot positively speak as to the remissness of the Ghatwals of the Police at Deoghur, is not procuring provisions and I am much inclined to believe that the fault does not rest with them, for the last six weeks the country around Deoghur has been altogether in the hands of the Sonthals and the collecting of supplies most difficult.

It must be borne in mind moreover that wheat and Dhal are not cereals indigenous to this district, and consequently supplies of the kind essentially requisite for up country men have to be procured from a distance.

On the whole, though many other officers besides Captain Ford, have complained in some instances, very strongly against the Ghatwals and Police, I must say, that throught out the district the Zemindars, ghatwals and Police, with few exceptions have done their best to meet the calls made upon them by me. They have had innumerable obstacles to contend against, many of them have lost their all, many have procured supplies but not received payment for the same, for weeks, some have run away altogether despatching of. . and some have met their fate at the hands of the Sonthals. It is not for me to suggest what ought to have been done. . time to secure

Supplies for the troop at Deoghur and its Vicinity, the mischief is now done, and I can afford no assistance whatever to Captain Ford ; Nearly all the detachment in the Beerbhoom District are furnished with supplies by me, either through the Zemindars & ca. . , or directly from my stores, the only exception being Deoghur, to which place as the Ghatwals have hitherto provided pass and the road in now closed. I am unable to send what is so much needed.

If the Government do not speedily make known their intentions as to how the Beerbhoom Field Force is to be supplied with provisions in the operations about to be taken against the Sonthals, there will be terrible oppression exercised upon the inhabitants of these of crisis like the present.

Soory

R. I. RICHARDSON
Collector

October 27th, 1855

ooo

28. Letter

To,

Major General Lloyd,

I reply to your letter no. 310, dt. 4th Decr. I have the honor to forward to you the Sonthal prisoners noted below:

1. Kanoo Soobha, 2. Chand Ray Manjhee, 3. Bhuro Manjhee, 4. Kamoo manjhee, 5. Durga manjhi, 6. Mota Manjhee. 7. Nemay Manjhee, 9. Rumabsa Manjhee, 10, Alhar Manjhee, 11. Hareedass Manjhee, 12. Morarea manjhee 13. Muttah Manjhee.

The four men, who apprehended the Santhals when they were attempting to effect their escape towards the Damodar also aecompany the prisoners.

I beg to transmit at the same time the papers of the Mofussil investigation made by the Operbandha Darogha and different articles of property which were found in the possession of the prisoners.

Among these will be seen the clasp belonging to the late lieutt. Toulmen which the prisoner Kanoo was wearing on his arm not at the time of his capture, also some books & papers belonging to other gentlemen I should wish that latter might be returned to this Court at the conclusion of the trial, so that I may be enabled if possible to find out the owners & restore the property. There are some other things left here such as clothes & a few rupees &.... But as they would form no evidence against the prisoners, I have detained them here pending the result of the Court martial.

R. THOMPSON
Zillah Beerbhoom

Dated 6th December, 1855

(P. S. I would further add that there will be found in the box here with sent some letters which were in the possession of Kanoo & are convincing proof against him.)

29. Letter

To,

The Hon'ble A. Eden
Asstt. Spl. Commissioner
Koomerabad.

With reference to an application made by Major General Lloyd to Govt. for the appointment of a special Judge to trial some Santhals prisoners who have been committed by be Civil authorities in the Camp for charge not cognizable by Court martial I have the honor to request you would supply me with information as how many of these cases are ready for disposal. I should be obliged at the same time if you would kindly give me the particulars as to the number of men in each case, on what charges they are committed & how many belong respectively to this districts –that of Bhagulpore.

R. THOMPSON
Offgr.

The 8th December, 1855.

OOO

30. Letter

To,

Brigadier Bird
Commanding in the Beerbhoom
And Bancoorah District
Sooree, December 9th 1855.

Scarcely a day now passes, but either Magistrate,or myself receive petitions from the Zemindars and Ghatwalls, in the North-western portion of the district, praying that some assistance may be given them, in furnishing supplies for the troops.

Petitions lately presented, state that the number of troops, is very considerable. You are aware that I have a large quantity of supplies in store, and that I am most anxious to relive the landholders from duties which they cannot efficienty perform : this however I am unable to do, owing to the road beyond Gurjori being stopped.

I can bush up any quantity of supplies, as far that place if you will instruct officer commanding Regiments, or Companys to have their elephants, at a certain place, on any fixed day. My principal object in undertaking Commissariate duties, was to prevent the necessity of the local Zemindars & Ghatwals being called upon for supplies, **it is in reality the poorer classes who suffer & from whom the grain is procured. Invariably without payment or any return being made by the Zemindars' subordinates.**

Under these circumstances, I trust you will see the necessity (if in your power) of indents being made upon me for what may be required.

ROBERT I. RICHARDSON
Collr. of Beerbhoom

OOO

31. Letter

To,

W. Grey Esqr. Secy. To the Government of Bengal
Fort William.

In continuation of my letter no. 542. dated 8th instant and in reply to your communication requesting me to state my opinion as to the necessity of deputing a special Judge to try these cases in Major General Loyd's camp, which were not congnizable by a Court martial,I have the honour to state that from a letter I have received from Mr. Eden the Astt. S/oecial Commissioner I ascertain that there are 33 prisoners camps awaiting trial on different charge of murder and other heinous crimes of these or prisoners in one case belong to the Beerbhoom District, the remainer to Bhagalpore –Mr. Eden further adds 10 or 12 prisoners captured by Mr. Ponet are daily expected and that their cases would only be disposed of by the Civil authorities. Even with this expect increase however, I cannot consider the deputation of a special officer in any way necessary. I believe the the whole of the prisoners are comprised in about 4 to 5 cases and the trial of these would occupy a judge with ordinary labour but while the expense and inconvenience which the me…

Would render necessary would hardly be justified by the in disposal of the cases.

I mentioned in my former letters that the Burkundages under Sergt. Jackson now stationed at Nugore about 14 milies from this,were especially retained by Krig (see letter dated 17th nov.) for the escort of prisoners or any other such duties as would save the troops this extra work. There are in this force besides Jemadar and Duffadars 66 men who for a long iime have been comparatively idle. Their only duty has been to guard the villages of Nugore but as the troops are now stationed on all sides for an advance of this position, there seems little use in keeping them at that port. I would beg to recommend that 30 of these men with 2 (Duffadars should be deputed to convey the Beerbhoom prisoners to this station where their trial would proceed.

In usual form as to the rest of His Honor the Secutt Goor should think fit to confer upon me the authority to try these cases, under the prisoners of Regul. Vii of 1822, it would in my opinion be a more expedient course than either sending the prisoners to such a distance as Bhagulpore or deputing a special Judge to conduct their trial in the Major Generals' Camp.

By two division of the prisoners the whole of these might be safely conveyed to Soory on one week, and though the Calendar of the commitment for this districts in the present month is very heavy I have little doubt that by the end of Jany, all these extra trials might be brought to a conclusion. At least in the choice of difficulties this course seems to me the most feasible.

RIVERS Thompson

Dated 11th December, 1855

OOO

32. Letter

To,

Frances Lowth, Esqr. Session Judge of Beerbhoom

I have the honor to acknowledge the receipt of your letter no. 185,dt,17th Decr. & beg in reply to submit the report called for therein.

The prisoner Juttoo Rae had been placed on the 29th Novr. last under the charge of Gujoo Singh Burkundaze I had given strict orders to the Darogah not to send him to labor away from the jail & accordingly on the day in question the prisoner had been employed in carrying the bags of rusuds which were being loaded on some Elephants to be forwarded to Major General Lloyds Camp. This work necessarily kept the prisoners with the precincts of the prison. It appears however that in the evening the Burkundaza Gujoo Sing contrary to all orders took the prisoner Ghutto Sing & four other to a neighbouring field for the purpose of allowing them to case themselves. While there the prisoner absconded and effected his escape. The Burkundaz must have been aware of the circumstances within a few minutes of its occurrence and had he given notice at once, escape would have been impossible as there was sufficient day light remaining to ensure the recapture of the prisoners before he could have gone beyond the limits of the station. Instead however of acting upto his duty, the Burkandazes resorted to the expedient of making over his four prisoners to 3 Burkandazes who were returning to the jail with some other convicts Gujoo Sing himself, making a pretence of being unwell, went off his home.

The Burkandazes arrived at the Jail and made over their own prisoners and the four they had received from Gujoo Sing to the guards who were on duty at the front gate. From the evidence of these Burkandazes it does not appear that the absence of one prisoner was detected by these guards – and in this lies their neglect or if as they assert they discover the circumstances, their misconduct appears in a worse light from their not reporting the matter at once either to the Jail Darogah or to myself, as I was standing at the time within a few wards of the Prison Walls.

Nothing appear to have been said about the matter till between 7 & 8 O'clock in the evening. There has been lately a strong ill feeling between the Darogah & his subordinates in the jail. arising from the fact of the Darogah having reported since my arrival here, many delinquencies in the conduct of the official who are under him & I have little doubt in concluding that it was in the hope of bringing their suspicion into some kind of disgrace that they withheld from him the information of the escape of the prisoner till all hopes of his immediate recapture had passed.

Notice of these events was given to me about 12 O,Clock neighbourhood in the chance of securing the prisoner before he has got off his fetters. The next morning, notices were sent throught out the District and to the Magistrates of the adjoining Zillahs. I further offered a reward of Rs. 50 for his apprehension and have sent an active and intelligent Burkandazes to the villages where the prisoner resided (situation in the Bahgalpore District) & hope that before long his recapture will be effected.

As regards the man through those gross neglect, amounting almost to connivance the prisoner succeeded in absconding, I have after a full enquiry into the matter, sentenced the Burkandaze Gujoo Sing to be imprisoned for 3 months and pay a fine of Rs.5 in lieu of labor.

The other guards named in the margin * who were on duty at the gate I have dismissed from Employ. I hope the punishment will be efficacious in suppressing such gross carelessness for the future, though I cannot conceal the fact that there is not only a great want of discipline throughout the jail management, but also that there exists a strong sympathy between the jail officials had the prisoners which is altogether to a strict control & restraint there under confinemet.

RIVERS THOMPSON
Offg. Magistrate
Zillah Beerbhoom

Dated 19th December, 1855

OOO

33.

To,

W. Grey. Esqr.
Secretary to the Govt. of Bengal.

I have the honor to bring the following circumstances to your notice.

Having been ordered by the Govt. to furnish supplies to the Forces employed against the Sonthals, I entered into arrangements as nothing was to be obtained in this district to get what I considered the necessary quantities from Cutwa a large market 44 miles from this.

I am guided in making my purchases, by a letter received by me from Captn. Macpherson, Asstt. Comissart, who at the request of General Lloyd acquainted me that among other supplies 2100 manuds of Atta would be required from the 24th of November to the 24th December for the Bhagulpur Force.

This Calcutta was made at the rate of I seer per day per fighiting man & in this I made my Calcutta for the Beerbhoom Force. Which was fully equal in number to that of the Bhagulpore and for whose want I was certain to have to provide as the Ghatwals and Zemindars had previously by petitions incessantly pouring in, advised me that they had nothing to do to feed troops. Nor could they under existing circumstances procure any.

I therefore commissioned Mr. Hewett the Deputy Magistrate of Catwa to buy me immediately, as the Bhagherutty(Bhagirathi) was shut and grain daily rising in price, 5,000 maunds of wheat.

To grind this quantity, I procured from Moorshedbad 100 Chukkee which according to the best information, would turn out fully 100 maunds of Atta per diem or something under the demand to be made upon me.

This Calcutta however was set at nought by the fact after trial that 20 seers was the utmost that could daily be turned out from each chukkee per diem.

In this emergency, I was obliged to indent upon the Dy. Magts. Of Cutwa " Atta and he sent me daily as much as he could get prepared.

On or about the 25th Novr. Captn. Macpherson indented upon me for 700 mds. Of atta or one third of the whole quantity. I could not comply with his demand but sent him 625 maunds. On or about the Ist Dec. he indented for 385 mannds more, I was only able to supply 100.

After the date last mentioned Captn. Macpherson, desisted from taking further supplies, and indeed onpassing through Soore, with General Loyd, returned a considerable quantity into my Godown. He also informed me that some of the Regiments in the jungles were well supplied.

I have ground down about 1000 mds. of my wheat but 4000 mds. Remain.

In times like the present, when the Military occupy every nook and cornor in this small place, room for storage was most difficult to obtain. The Magistrate however kindly gave me a pucca ward in his jail. In this I placed wheat.

Lately having occasion for the Ward the magistrate requested me to vacate it. On removing the bags of wheat, it was discovered that Weevil had attacked the grain to a considerable extent, measures were immediately taken up by me to try and remedy the evil & about 1500 mds. Will I hope be reseved tolerably intact. The remaining **2000 maunds have been thrown down loose on straw & mixed with husks, which I believe is the only remedy capable of being adopted.**

The business is a most unfortunate one, but quite unavoidable. Wheat I believe is now at famine prices at Cutwa there is none at Burdwan country is selling at 3 per maund & at Moorshidabad, Atta is only 15 seers per rupee, and much adulterated. I do not in this extremity known what to do the markets are empty, the shut & until next harvest, wheat will not be procurable. I doubt the likelihood of the Dy. Commissary General allowing Lt. Agilvie to receive wheat in the state about 2000 maunds are in & I therefore request the permission of His Honor the Lt. Governor of Bengal to be allowed to intihar the sale of the above quantity and then dispose of the same to the highest bidder as more damage ensues.

R. I. RICHARDSON
Collector
Sooree

Dated 31 Ist December, 1855

ooo

Collected from Dumka Records-Room

34. Letter

To,

H. Stainforth Esq.
Commissioner

Dated Doomkah 13th February, 1856.

Sir,

I have the honour to report you that I have received a private communication from Mr. W. C. Taylor Asst. Comm. in which he refers to certain subject connected with the Daminkoh, which I think it right to bring to your notice.

He reports that Santal villages have based out to Bengallies who are committing different acts of oppression & extortion, and he considers that unless the Bengallies are ousted, their conduct may lead to serious disturbance. He has requested instructions on the subject and I have informed him in reply that as you intend shortly to visit the Daminkoh he had better leave the question in abeyance, till you are enabled to decide upon the subjects by personal investigation. In the meantime I have directed to take every opportunity of giving employment to the Santal population by opening up a communication between his station & this place. The Government has, I believe, authorized him to draw upon the Moorshidabad Treasury for this purpose.

With reference to the oppression and extortions' Committed by the Zamindars and their Gomastas, Mr. Taylor desired to know whether he had any authority to punish the delinquents. I have instructed him as to the extent of his powers and urged him to put them in force against evil-doers who may be brought before him.

The Asst. Comm. has also applied to me for tents, elephants and stationery all are urgently required, not only by him but by every asst. in the Pergunnahs for the execution of duties, which to be satisfactorily carried out require continual movement & communications among the Santhal Pargamas.

I have the Sd. Mr. A. R.
Thompson Dy. Commissioner.

ooo

35. Letter

To,

H. Stainforth Esq.
Commissioner,
Dated Doomkah 20th February, 1856.

Sir,

In compliance with your instructions I have the honor to submit this report, conveying the Suggestions I would propose for a reorganization of the police establishment in the Santhal pergunnahs.

2. The chief difficulty we have to contend with in approaching the subject seems to me to be the diversity of race which exists thought the pergunnahs now brought under one control. Had we simply to deal with the Santal tribe, or had we even the Hill man and Santal only on our hands, there would be sufficient of similarly in their nature, habits and character, to enable us to form a system that would apply equally to both and of the success of which there could be no doubts as the case now stands however we have Santals and Bengallis, Paharees & Patans(Pathans) generally living separate but often intermingled in one part of the country and frequently in one village.

3. It seems to be decided on all hands that the present system of Thannahs and Darogahs must be at once abolished. Leaving out of the question, the general complaints brought against this form of establishment everything points to the conclusion that it is especially unadapted for the wild races with whom we have to deal. It seems also to be an object in view to bring these races themselves into employment as public servants and to use them as sub ordinals in the system for the suppression of crime and discovery and apprehension of offenders.

4. Mr. Eden proposes in the Commencement of his report (Para -3) to entrust the Mahjhees and certain power and to compel them under penalties to report the commission of all crime.

5. There is scarcely sufficient of definition in the proposal – For it does not appear what the powers are with which they should be invested –nor it is clear that Mahjhees of villages would accept the responsibility of duties, which would entail penalty without some kind to remuneration or salary for their services.

6. I have during my short incumbency in this office been making enquiries as to the nature of the office which the Manjhee of a Santal village holds, and I baru that in every village there is a Manjhee or chief selected generally by punch yet from amongst the community, who is chief among its occupants, responsible for the rent and bound to report the commission of all crime- the office descends from father to son, and in reward for these services, the Manjhee is entitled to certain amount of land (in proportion to the extent of the village in which he presides trace of all rent under the Manjhee I believe there is in most places another officer styled Parmanick whose duties in a subordinate position are of a similar character to the Manjhees. who also enjoy, without payment the possession of a few beeghas of Land in the village. I am told further that a Gorait exists in many villages employed I believe in communicating intelligence to the superior officials, who receives a salary of 4 Annas from every house at the end of the year.

7. Above the class just referred to (which constitutes the village police) another order of official exists who exercise control and supervision over 50,80. or 100 village. they are called Pergunnaits, are appointed either by the govt. officer or the zemindar as the case may be) and though especially of the revenue are responsible for the well-being of the villagers which are under them and for giving aid to the Thannah officials in all police duties. They receive annually as their due 1 Re from every village over which they exercise authority and have under them a Desh Manjhee, collecting the rents and forwarding intelligence to the Regular police.

8. If such be the case we have already organized to our hands, a system that may be formed, at least in villages comprising a Santal population into an efficient and numerous police – No community is without its head. no mouza a hamlet without some kind of chief whatever it's denomination and I have little doubt that if we recongnise this petition and by conciliation & and prompt attention to their wants shown an inclination to act for their benefit and welfare we shall obtain their co-operations in the suppression of crime & detection of evildoers.

9. I have said that for a Santal population such as establishment would for all that we require, be sufficient. Information as to crime is the chief object to be gained, enquiry and apprehension would be generally the work of the asstt. . or his sub- ordinates and with the large amount of European supervision that we shall be able to command, when the proposal number of assts have joined their appointments. I feel no doubt that with the existing, institutions of the Districts & by a right bestowal of Countenance & confidence we should obtain a force fully capable to cheek all crime of a heinous nature.

10. we have, however, a large Bengallee population to deal with for larger than those of the Santal tribe, who reside chiefly in those portions which have been detached from the Beerbhoom Zillah the greater wealth of these men, their deeper cunning, innate proneness to deceit would be obstacles to the success of such a scheme as I have suggested and therefore I would propose over and above the village establishment referred to them should be in each of the five division of the Santhal Pergunnahs two Joojders or Jhamadars (or call them what we like) whose headquarters should be fixed in some Central locality – but whose avocation should require them to be continually on the move throughout their jurisdiction-I would entrust to them no powers of investigation without orders from their superiors, beyond that prima facie sort of enquiry which would be absolutely requisite for the detection of criminals suspected quality neither I would

allow him to keep any record they should merely be employed as a check against Bengalee chicanery or attempts at concealment and with this object I would recommend the appointment of only up to countrymen.

11. In the Bengalee villages chowkeedars must still be retained – as watch they are useless, they must be made as serviceable as strict supervision with permit in conveying prompt and accurate information. It is conveying prompt and accurate information. It is indispensible that these men should receive regular payment – at present their poor pittance is not only very small and inadequate for subsistence, but in most cases many months in arrears.

12. The very small jurisdiction in which each Thanadars would have authority and the generally light natures of the work salary which would be required from them will not justify a greater salary than 24 Rs month for each nominee. Two peyadas on 5 a month would be all that I would ask as assts to these men.

13. It may be said that in advocating this organization of Thanadars and Burkandazes – I am reverting to that much abused system which it is the object in this new district to abolish entirely. I would urge in reply that had we only the Santals to consider. No. task would be easier or more likely to succeed. But amongst a Bengalee population something that will succeed as well as required and I can think of nothing that will succeed as well as the establishment of a system which will bring rapid information to the European officer & leave all investigations in his hands.

14. I would recommend, therefore that as soon as all the stations have been fixed & the assets with their sub-ordinates are at their posts, a register should be formed of all the Santhal villages, showing the names, amount of Land held by each Manjhee By summoning these men at different time to the headquarters of the sub-division – each assets would be enabled to explain by personal communication the services would be required from him as officers than a nearly reports of every important occurrence that took place in their respective villages & the detection of any

criminal caught in the act of committing an offence organist whom any suspicion of having perpetrated it rested. They should be also made to understand that connivance at concealment or any attempt to bush up proceedings would make them Liable not only to dismissal from their rights and office, but might entail punishment in jail as accessories in the offence committed.

15. The pergunaits may be similarly instructed and if we could establish a Fund from the chowkeedaree money for the better payment of this class & afford them the support which they would deserve from their position, I have little doubt of their cordial cooperation.

16. Over all would be the Thanahdar I have alluded to the expenses for such an establishment throughout the whole pergunnahs would amount to a little under Rs 400/ a month the saving by the abolition of about 10 Thannas would reach (I speak in round numbers) to 3,000 Rs per mensum.

17. With reference to the present police establishment I think all might be at once removed within the exception of the Darogahs & four Burkundazes, who would act in the same capacity as the Thanadars to whom I have alluded During the but weather & rainy season I would allow this force to continue not only because some inconvenience might arise from the two sudden introduction of any new system but also because the season during the next 5 months will be very inclement for outdoor work for Europeans and this we know & are to govern much uncertainty must exist in all our operations.

18. I have omitted much regarding the details on many points such as servicing processes summoning witnesses but I find from the short experience I have had of the work here that the plan is in use is well adapted for the people of the District. In petty cases when the plaintiff has first come to make his complaint and names, witnesses whom he wishes to have examined < I give him a perwannah on the Manjhee of the village where the witness resides, directions him to send into me the men that is required

should the plaintiff return without his witness & state that the man was unwilling to leave his home or made any other excuse. I would send a chuprasee of my own court to go to the village & bring in the witness. In nine cases, out of ten, I believe no further would be required but should any other delay arise, I would proceed myself or depute the assts to bring in the party.

19. I cannot conclude without making a few remarks on the course. I would propose for adoption towards the Ghatwals of the Beerbhoom district. I know from any tenure of office in that Zillah that the insurrection was absentees & never reside on their estates but allow the anything but satisfactory some are absentees& never reside on their estates but allow the arduous duties that belong to their office to be conducted entirely by agents who are most unscrupulous both as to the means they use & the measures they adopts many others who are residents take much more care for their personal advantage than for the right performance of the duties of their position. There is no. doubt whatever that the Ghatwals, who hold their estates solely on condition of services to Govt. By aiding in the maintenance of good order a security should be compelled under penalty of forfeiture of their lands to give the assistance & support which they are bound to afford. The remedy against all neglect is entirely in our own hands. I don't think that under the circumstances which have lately secured throughout the District and the position in which it is now placed we should hesitate on every occurrence of neglect to in force our rights by the resumption of their Mehals-Many of these estates I believe are largely in arrears.

20. I shall hope with strict supervision to effect much through the cooperation of zemindars and when all our stations and jurisdiction are arranged, the many Europeans Employed over a tract of country not very extensive will bring, I have little doubt success to our endeasours.

21. The general object in any opinion which we should keep in view in the willing co-operation of the people themselves & if

we succeed in that we shall in time is greater gainers, than under a police which worked by compulsion & in the degraded state of inferiors.

I have the Mr. A. R. Thompson Dy Comm.

OOO

36. Letter

No. 175

To,

The Secretary to the Gov. Of Bengal.
Dated Nya Doomkah 26th 1856

Sir,

With reference to my letter no. 101 dated 26r – reporting the capture of Gora Manjhee a Santal Sobah and of your reply no. 775 dated 1st instant conveying the sanction of Govt. for the payment of the reward of Rs-250 to the individual who captured him. I have now the honor to state for the information of his Honour the Leutt Governor that after careful investigation in the matter. I have come to the conclusion that the party had been apprehended was not the notorious Soubah Gora Thacoor but a man whose name is Borha manjhee who has been secured with the object of obtaining the reward that was sanctioned for the apprehension of the santal leader Gora manjhee. The first intimation I get up the Circulstance was in the course of the trial of the prisoner – I had recorded the man's confession & had forwarded it for the information of his Honour of the Lt. Governor. it was made to all appearances with perfect Voluntariness, but I regret that I allowed the presence of the Darogah who had brought in the prisoner & who was near me during his examination. When the case was resumed a few days after I assembled the jury to aid me in the investigation.

2. After the deposition of the plaintiff, who had spoken to having witnessed the murder of his own Father by the prisoner in court whom he called Gora Manjhee I asked the panchayet it they wished to put any questions to the plaintiff. One Cukun perganit said he did not accordingly asked. In this Gora Manjhee in Court. the prosecutor seemed taken by Supervise hesitated a little at first, but afterwards said in a blunt manner – " this is Gora Manjhee-" Two of the panchyet immediately get up & stated that the prisoner in fourth was not Gora Manjhee but one Burha Manjhi of Dakab and that they both knew the defend believe that the case had been must reward which had just been must severely ill – treated by the Darogah & his companions ever since he had been apprehended and that the presence of the Darogah in the court on the day of the trial had prevented his telling me the truck of the matter.

3. As the doubt rested only on the identity of the prisoner I determined to proceed with the case against him as if he were Gora Manjhee but to examine only at first those who knew the prisoner & could speak to his being the noted chief Gora Thacoor or otherwise.

4. The evidence of all has been recorded as given before me and I have little doubt in coming to the conclusion that the prisoner is not the Gora Manjhee of Settooa and fully believed that the case against him has arisen from interested motives of securing the money granted for the capture of the chief of that name.

5. Under the circumstance I directed the prisoner's release from confinement & as there appeared to me good grounds for believing that the Darogah had some shares in extorting a confession from the man & proceeded against that officer on a charge of Torture.

6. The case has just been brought to a conclusion, I can have little doubt but that violence of some kind must have been

employed against the Manjhee before he admitted himself to be a man noted for many acts of murders and plunder & who there is little doubt would be liable to the highest penalty if ever he was apprehended.

7. But I cannot find in the case reason for supposing that the Darogah personally contended any act of torture. I believe he was a super in the hands of the others It is in evidence that notice was brought to him of the residence of Gora Manjhee he proceeded & apprehended the man whom he had never seen before and the days after challenged him to my court.

8. The origination of the intelligence as to the where about of Gora Manjhee is one Kurrun Manjhee a Santhal, I recorded my opinion of him is the former cases. I have only to add that his examination in the present one though is lasted nearly an hour, produced only evasions and contradictions which it is impossible his any way to connect or understand. In both instances he committed perjury by most culpable contradictions & for theses he will be brought to trial and yet this man is the Foundation on which nearly the whole of the rest of the evidence is supported to establish the fact that the man is court is Gora Thacoor.

I (Beyond) have strong suspicion there in not sufficient is the case to punish the Darogah for the higher charge of Torture but I can form no high opinion of his capabilities as a police officer even if his own account be true namely that the apprehended the man on the representations of others & believed him fully to be Gora Manjhee.

10. I have, therefore, dismissed him from the service as incapable and unfit for duty. The four Burkandazes who accompanied him on the expedition are also to be removed from their posts in the None Thannah.

I have the Mr. A. Rivers Thompson.

ooo

37. Letter

No. 178

To,

The session Judge of Beerbhoom.

Dated Naya Doomkah 27th March 1856

Sir,

I have the honour to submit explanations called for your letter no. 107 dated 25th March referring to the cases committed by me to the sessions court at Beerbhoom is January last.

I would wish to add that, I write without any record of the case before me and beg the indulgence of the court for any omissions or deficiency in the explanation.

I have the honour

Sd. Rivers Thompson Dy. Com.

ooo

38. Letter

Govt & Ooduy Money & Neha Bhola and others

The facts are as stated in the Remarks of the Session Judge on the trial held before him.

The woman Oodry Moomy when sent in by the Jemadar who was conducting the enquiry made before me a confession which to all appearances was perfectly and & which after detailing her own participation in the robbery implicated the three other prisoners as principles, when the trial was brought to conclusion in my Court I found that beyond of the discovery of some brass vessels (identified by the pff) in the possession of the three defendants there was nothing else in the case to bring home be charged to them considering this to be scarcely sufficient for their convictions deeming that the guilt of the women compared with theirs was of every trifling nature. I tendered to her person on the condition of her making a full statement of her knowledge of the facts of the case.

The at first declined to accept the offer but I told her I would allow her 24 hour to consider the matter & on the next day she give the statement which coincided in all material points with the confession which she had before made.

Under the circumstances, I considered the conviction of the prisoners to be not in probable a therefore committed them to take their trial on the higher court.

I would beg leave to add that I was informed during the trial that many persons had been exerting their utmost to dissuade the woman from accepting the conditional pardon assuring that acquittal was certain if she refused be offer but I failed to ascertain how far this report was founded on truth in sessions court. The woman's son requested me to be allowed to visit mother in the Jail. I asked his reason and he stated that wished to tell his mother that it would be right for her to adhere to the confession and statement she had made before me. I need not add that I refused my consent to his application.

Sd. Mr. Thompson Dy. Com.

ooo

39. Letter

No. 179

To,

H. Stainforth Esq.

Commissioner in the Santhal Pergunnahs.

Dated Naya Doomkah, March 27th 1856

Sir,

I regret to inform you that 124 of the prisoners who brought down from Bhagalpore & was tried to convict to your Court escaped from confinement on the might of Monday last.

2. It appears that these placed within the compound allotted for them under the usual guard of Burkundazes belonging to Luitt. Jackson's force.

3rd. about 8 o'clock at night before to the moon had risen all the prisoners with the exemption of 6 rose in one body and scattering in different directions mad for the jungles which around on all sides.

The showers hearing the disturbances at once hastened to the spot and followed the fugitives the broken nature of the ground and the darkness prevented any great succap attending their labors.

For two hours search made throughout the neighborhood sawars were sent to Komrabad in which direction many of the sonthals had been flying to parties of the irregular secured the jungles in search of the fugitives'.

The result shows that out of 202 who were undergone on the evening in question 124 have been succeeded in effecting their escape of two remainder it was found that one had been killed by a bayonet thrust through his body and seventeen others have received wounds in the some instances of a severe nature.

There can be doubt that this movement was preceded amongst the prisoners who had that day been informed of the sentence which had been piped upon them. The statement of two men who have been recaptured show throughout the day they had been conversing in the subject and had agreed among themselves to make simultaneous rise and run for the jungles.

I most effect my opinion that I do not consider that any blame can stench to the guard who were on duty the space occupied by the prisoner is open and unprotected save by a slight on hedger which is constructed on their sides and was guarded on the fourth by the Burkandages. The prisoners were secured two & two by handcuffs and in some instances were fastened by ropes. These are the only Elytra means we popeyed for binding them.

Altogether, there were 301 prisoners under confinement on that day 99 men in separate shed and a separate guard and it was therefore impossible to detach a larger guard than the one placed near the 202.

Sd. A. R. Thomson.
Dy. Com. Dumka.

OOO

40. Letter

No. 220

To,

The Secretary to the Government of Bengal
Fort William
Dated Naya Doomka 7 April, 1856

Sir,

I have the honour to acknowledge the receipt of your letter no.

909 dated 2nd April I to state in reply that I consider that fears entertained regarding the great insecurity of that part of the country through which the railway passes, are very much exaggerated.

2. All reports that I receive both from the paths and nature officials in that guarder speak of an earnest desire on the part of the Sonthals to settle down quietly and resume their peaceable occupations.

3. A Statement showing the disposition of troops along the line of Railway or it's neighborhood will prove that anything liken attempt again to disturb the peace could be stayed & punished before any success could attend to outbreak.

4. Detachments of Rights are located at the following places 150 men at Pointe, 200 at Burhait, 100 at Pulsa, 50 at Colgong, 100 at Heranpuro, 150 at Sreecoond. 0

5. The Hill Rangers are at Bhagalpore and a party from the 42 L. I Monghyr a Detachment might be spared at Rajmehal but I believe that Brigadier in concurrence with law of the Santal Pergunnahs has determined on account of the Unhealthy(unnheathiness) of the place not to place troops him that a part of the country.

6. I for myself can entertain no fears of any repetitions of the outrages which the last year has witnessed anything approaching an organized movement among the Sonthal for evil purpose wants be known to us before it could be put into successful execution and I believe we have quite sufficient troops to crush arising before it gained any dangerous proportions.

7. There are now in our employ many Sonthals who act as spies in tracing out notorious offenders in the Late disturbances and who daily bring into Doomkah those whom they have succeeded in apprehending – The very circumstances of their own claps taking part against them acts most beneficially by proving to the Sonthals that they could attempt nothing against the authorities without it's being immediately deleted.

8. I beg to annex extracts from letters received from officers on duty through him of Railway which all intend to show that apprehensions regarding the Sonthals are grounded.

Sd. A. R. Thomson. Dy. com.

ooo

41. Letter

No. 247

To,

B. Wood Esq.
R. E. Ronald Esq.
Assistant commissioner.
Dated Nya Doomkah 14th April, 1856

Sir,

I have the honour to forward herewith for you information a list of the person that prisoners who have made their escape the guard this place and have not been yet recaptured.

A Reward of Rs101 /- for the apprehension of each of them has been sanctioned by commissioner.

I have the Sd. Rivers Thompson Dy. Com. (S. P)

List of Prisoners absconded from the guard at Nya Doomkah and are to be captured.

No.	*Name of Prisoners*	*Name of Prisoners Father*	*Residence*
1	Borhair Sonthal Subah	Shamoo	Moongyr Dangal
2	Sukur Manjee	Bhyroo	BIlcoppee
3	Sukur Manjee	Jeetoo	Bundero
4	Joyram Manjee	Lail	Chundenee
5	Bhadoo Manjee	Sobhun	Rajuldhee of Koomurdea
6	Chundoo Sonthal	Bhadoo	Do.
7	Kurron Dome	Munbode	Domeria
8	Gunesh Dome	Lulneer	Surrurra
9	Ruttu Pujhar	Jorawver	Chundra
10	Bahadoor Nyee	Muddun	Jurtab
11	Jeetoo Sonthal	Chandoo	Bhattooria
12	Joolhur Sonthal	Peetoo	Do
13	Luckun Sonthal	Koour	Do

14	Bhadoo Sonhal	Peetoo	Do
15	Doomun Sonthal	Meeria	Umbur
16	Bullia Sonthal	Sidhoo	
17	Bood Roy	Chand Roy	Katojah
18	Herma	Do.	
19	Gunee	Kuldap	
20	Beerau (Birum)	Doorga	Goideebar
21	Joomna	Hemra	
22	Goolia	Do	
23	Soorye	Goomer	
24	Ramjeer	Bughoo Nauth	
25	Soondra	Ram roce	Jubna
26	Chytun	Neemyee	
27	Neemaye	Kanoo	
28	Mudun	Nuraun	
29	Kangalee Cheegoo	Gundoore Nundo	Damnca
30	Jagroo	Nundo	Murkadee
31	Kundna	Bhoje Roy	Kumerdeea
32	Sham	Mohun	Hatdoobaor Sikatia
33	Chundoo Sonthal	Ram Manjee	Burramasea
34	Kishun	Mirya	Do
35	Kumul Nya	Magoo	Basjora
36	Poorna	Chytun	Buddea
37	Bhageerut	Oochul	Operbyar
38	Beesoo Sonthal	Ram dap	Lobatar
39	Bhadoo Sonthal	Chytun	Do
40	Sona	Mochun	Chugoonee
41	Deuur	Chumpye	Rngdih
42	Paroo	Rama	Domnadee
43	Mnpa	Megra	Tengardee
44	Dhanye	Bhoje	
45	Ching Roy	Do	
46	Boap nath	Nundoo	Hadooba
47	Dookia	Do	
48	Goonier	Mnoop	Gurdaha
49	Bullia	Mahu	

50	Tello	Do.	
51	Neemoo	Do.	
52	Jeeluck	Mohbul	Basjora
53	Kumra Sonthal	Byjoo	Jhunkpoor
54	Nanoo Pujhur	Nanoo	Kureua
55	Laloo Naya	Do	
56	Luffoo	Manik	
57	Bhaluck	Dilloo	
58	Bhechoo Nya	Manik	Kerrcou
59	Nunkoo Sonthal	Delloo	
60	Bhudu	Raghoo nath	Mutta
61	Thakoor	Doorga	
62	Mnbye	Kishuno	Gurchappaor kaktee
63	Lukun	Nal	Umber
64	Mungut	Do	
65	Teka	Randass	Domohance
66	Sookoo Sonthal	Kallo	
67	Kooer	Sona	Mutta
68	Gangoo	Dhanoo	
69	Bhugirut	Mudoo	
70	Rammoo	Reenshoo	Taree
71	Pusa or Poosa	Bhag Rai	
72	Ragoo	Jy singh	
73	Doorga	Jadoo	Goideebar
74	Doorga	Noona	do
75	Dulloogeree Nya	Boodhan	Byjoo Koora
76	Burrcor Rai	Lohana Rai	Bhuguanpoor
77	Feerungee Rai	Dhunee Rai	
78	Teka Sonthal	Kasoo	Sikatia
79	Nengoo	Sembhoo	
80	Goomda	Thakoora	Sikatia
81	Mnoop Cole	Tond Manjee	
82	Poorun Cole	Sham	
83	Therree	Jusmat	Dhunadee
84	Thurca	Do	Do
85	Moorra	Ram Shahee	Bhagmara

86	Poosa	Thumra	
87	Bhurrut	Bhaghut	Gurchamppa
88	Dasoo	Bhow Singh	Do
89	Doomka	Singra	
90	Mungut	Moora	
91	Dasoo	Toonoo	

ooo

42. Letter

No. 256

To,

The magistrate of the Midnapoor
Dated Nya Doomkah 19 April, 1856

Sir,

With reference to the accompanying copy of a letter from the under secretary to the Govt of Bengal no. 1290 dates 8 instant I have the honour to inform you that I have this day dispatched 81 eight one prisoners for safe custody in the Midnapoore Jail as per challans sent with the guard who accompanied them.

Sd. A. R. Thomson Dy. Com

List of Prisoners Senture -! Year with Labour in irons 7 years from 8 April. 56

Si. No.	*Name*	*Father Name*	*Residence*	*Age*
72	Deboo manjee	Purao	Mohodangal	30
73	Ruttu	Jooraun	Chundna	20
74	Tika	Ramdoss	Domohanee	20
75	Dulloo GereeNya	Bood hum	Byjookoom	20
76	Umfye	Kishun	Gurchuppa	20
77	Lukhun	Lall	Amber	16

78	Mungut	Do	Do	30
79	Bhurnt	Bhugmut	Gurchunmpa	40
80	Mungut	Moira	Do	20
81	Thakoora Manjee	Bag Roy	Sumul tolla	30

In this there are 1 to 81 prisoners, but 72 to 81 a were on rebellious charge.

ooo

43. Letter

No. 62

To,

J. Pontet Esquire,
Superintendent of Damin Koh Bhagalpore

Sir,

I examined your Suzwal stationed at Kurhureeah today and he reports to me that the petty traders residing in Delta of his Thannah oppress your Sonthals most disgracefully. He also informs me that there are 4 or 5 Mahojous (Mahajans) who advance money to the Sonthal and reyait from them 10 times the amount borrowed. On the former occasion I directed you to serve notices on all the Mahajans residing in the Dehat to remove to the Bazars and from the settlement made by the Souzwals it appears you have only notices on 3 of these Mohajans. I request you will serve notices on all of them and that in future you will insert a clause in the engagement entered into by the Sonthals who take farms to the effect they will not permit any traders of the plains to reside in their villages without your expend Sanction.

2 It appears also that you collect rent from these Mahajans not by entering into any engagements with them but according to your own idea as to their capabilities of paying rent.

I request a full explanation on the letter point also any papers that you may have in your office relating to Busorce Mahals within the Damin I Koh

Collector's office
Bhaugalpore
The 20 Oct., 1854

sd. E. F. Lantour
Offg. Collr

OOO

44. Letter

No. 29

To,

G. J Browne Esquire.
Commissioner of Revenue Bhagalpore.

Sir,

In reply your letter no. 456 and 722 dated 29th March and 30th April, 1855. I have the honour you to inform that no. measures have been taken to secure the right to Govt. of all mines, iron, Copper and coal –existing in this Zillah

2. There is a Coal mines at Iugutpore Tuppah Belputtah in the Ghatwali of Narain Singh which is worked (I believe) by the Messers Erskine there is also a copper mine in the neighborhood of Deoghar which is not worked but leased out to Mr. James Burnes.

3. The Collieries in the DaminIKoh, the property of the Govt. , you are aware let are to Messes Nelson and Co.

4. Iron exists in Tuppah Belputtah in large quantities, but no European capitalist has yet been come forward to work these mines.

Sd. Et. Lantour Collector. Bhag
7th May, 1855.

OOO

45. Letter

To,

James Pontent Esquire

Superintendent of Daminkoh, Bhagalpore,

Sir,

In reply to your Roobkary dated the 27th of April, I have the honour to inform you that the offg. Magistrate of Bhagalpore has appointed Mehomed Ushreuff to officiate as Naib Sujwal in the room of Mohesh Dutt and as that individual appears fully competent to carry out the duties of the office. I have confined him in appointment.

I beg to point out of you that you have no power to appoint individuals to officiate as Naib Sujwal such power is vested in the Magistrate.

Sd. E. F. Lantour Collector
Collector'Office,
Bhagalpore

30th April, 1855

ooo

46. Letter

To,

G. F. Brown Esquire

Commissioner of Revenue Bhagalpore

Sir,

In reply to your letter no. 192 dated the 14th instant I have the honour to inform you that the Naib Sujwals noted in the Margin have been examined by me and I have found them intelligent officers and quite equal to carry on the duties of a Tuhseeldar.

2. The Naib Sujwal at Dighee where Dutt and the Muharir have not yet been examined as I hesitated to call them away from their posts during the collection season directly Mr. Pontet has completed his collections these officers will be sent for and examined as you have ordered.

3. Purwannahs have been issued calling upon the Sujwals to furnish securities according to the Lease laid down by Mr. Potent.

Sd. E. F. Lantour Collector

ooo

47. Letter (Post-Hul Records)

No. 229

Report to be submitted quarterly by all the assistant commissioner on the subject noted below.

State of Roads and ferries

There are no ferries in this division. The roads, as is always the case have been much out up during the rains, but steps have already been taken to put them in a state of repair.

Conduct of officers of Police

Satisfactory on the whole the Darogahs of Deoghar and Oopurbundah have rendered good service in having with Santhal and others and under Mr. Sub assistant commissioner, J. A. Lyods, order successes in apprehending one of two notorious Paharias the Leader of a small gang of that caste. Who have infested he Fooljoorec Hills ever since the Santal troubles several of the miner members of the some gang have also been captured.

Santhals peaceful

Perfectly quiet and apparently contented a number of them are at present in attendance on the sub-assistant and prove of much assistance in fact one of their number called Hattie Manjee mainly contributed to the capture of the Pahariah Chief before mentioned.

Cultivation

There is an excellent crop of rice which promises well with seasonable rain the Bhusdge (=Bhadai)crop proved a complete failure owing to which I regret to state that there is great suffering among the poorer classes much more than was experienced at this season of the past year. The Bhudga crop is their chief support until the rice harvest and its almost total failure has entailed much want and misery.

Any remarkable increase or dimunition of crimes in what localities.

With the exception of two cases of murder now under investigation there has been no remarkable increase or diminution of crime during the past quarter. The pharaoh Band already once than alluded to committed several Dacoits in the neighborhood of the joolyoorce Hill but measures are at present being taken which will it is to be hoped result in the capture of this gang and the consequent peace of the country side.

Sd. R. E. Ronald
Deoghar Asst
Commissioner's office
The 2nd October, 1857

OOO

48. Letter

No. 3

Report to be submitted quarterly by the entire assistant commissioner's on the subject noted below.

1. State of Roads and Ferries having only taken charge of this office on the 28th December 57. I cannot give any satisfactory statement for the quarter.

The roads on the north of this by which I came are in a very bad state indeed.

Santals

Appears well to do and orderly Scarcely any of them appear in court. These only bring one case in which they are connected. I find them tractable as those in the Damin and willing to enlist in the Santhal Police Corps now forming some having come to me to have their names entered since my arrival here and more having Promised to come.

Sd/ Ni. G Baraddon
Assist. Commissioner.

OOO

49. Letter

No. 96

Report to be submitted quarter by all the assistant Commissioners on the subjects noted below:-

1. State of Roads and ferries

There are no ferries in this district the roads during the last quarter have been put into very tolerable condition outlay. But owing to the undulating nature of the country they are in any places very much cut up and the want of Bridges over the numerous ravines and Nullas make each road by no means continuants – the ghautwal for the most part put the road through their ghutwalis into decent repair without any trouble given – some have some so much compulsion and a few have not done so at all, but as their estates were attached until the 3rd March there is considerable excuse for these short comings.

The roads through the town of Deoghar which I found in a very bad state and which was impassable during the rains of former years. I have widened and repainted with Jail labour and it will be are the rains set in metaid – the want of this road was greatly felt.

Sonthals

The sonthals are very quiet and give no trouble – They have scarcely any cases in court and these few they are almost invariably on the right side not the lilted shade of illfeclings exists among them, they are all well disposed and whether it is to gain the santal police corps or to aid in the apprehension of criminals I always find them willing – in two signal instances I have received great assistance from them viz. in the apprehension of Delbert by Mater as mentioned above and in the information given by Kanoo Purgunait in a Dacoit case by which was ultimately discovered both offenders and property.

From this Division two hundred Santals have been enlisted in the new police corps and if necessary as many more could I have no doubt be procured.

The condition of the sonthals is much improved during the past year. They no longer exhibit such fearful instances of starvation and poverty as they did immediately after the insurrection and their home and cultivation have been resumed somewhat of their ancient prosperity.

The greatest inflictions with which the santhals have to contend is the form of pattah granted to them by the zamindars for their lands and Mouzahs – These Pattas are generally for a term not exceeding one year, the santals takes it and farmers I the most binding instrument imaginable, granting lands or Mouzhas in perpetuity. He goes on improving his tenure in the hope of repairing the gain himself. When on some untoward day the zamindar brings to a close the short paid pattas.........

Cultivation

The few crops at this season of the year have succeeded very much mustard, soorsa, Demised in very small quantities were all good. The genera,(=Maize) sugarcane and few kinds of Dhal (=Pulse) cultivated on a larger extent were and are all good. In one or two places, the paddy is produced this has answered very well. At present the great slaple of flood for the from in the " Moohooah" and this no very abundant. Last year this crop failed and is loss must have a secure flow to the people generally for the Moohooah is one of the natures the most prodigal gift. The flower really a fruit in its use drops from the tree and is eaten and made into a peril the fruit is gathered and eaten as Jurkari or made into oil and even the fares and used by the most needy as vegetable under every tree and the trees are scattered likely over the older country may be seen a grape of busy man women and children picking up the flowers which he think upon the ground.

Sd. N. G. Braddon.
Asst. Commissioner

ooo

50. Letter

No. 218

Report to be submitted quarter by all the assistant Commissioners on the subjects noted below:-

Santhals

The Santals as here to fare have been quiet and disposed except as off. , they scarcely ever appear in my court and then their cases are so moderate and just that the other party generally does what is required without allowing the investigations to become a very tedious one.

Twice during the present quarter I have reason to suppose that the Santals were not as subservient to orders as I could wish but in both instances I found them, on enquiry willing to obey as cheerfully as ever. The first occasion was when the Santhal attempted to have a day of Churruck. I had prior to this pounded the zamindars and influential men in the Division to use their best exertion to check this practice among the Hindoos and they had some so effectually and it appeared like setting my orders at naught when the sonthals made preparations for ceremony which the Hindus had foregone at my request, but I found that some of the Santal police have misapprehended an order I gave and that through them the impression had been spread that I had consented to a day's swinging. Timely information had given me of their intention and four trusty men of the Sonthal police whom I dispatched arrived on the ground in time to put a step to the proceeding before more than four men had swing.

The second occassion was when the Santhal collected in the large bodies in two places armed with bows and arrows and Lattices for shikar. On receiving information of this I ordered them to dispense and issued Parwannah to the Zamindars Pergunnaits to disarm them, one or two other Pergunnaits came to me and pleaded that the Santal must have arrows because it was one of their religious rites on the birth of a child to make an arrow in honour of it, but I put this argument aside by saying they need not have a bow to match and the deputation quite satisfied went away and assisted in the disarming. One Pergunnait Kanoo Manjee reports that he has collected about a thousand bows in his Elakha and I have received from others quarters 776 bows, 1160 arrows, 46 swords and 79 phursas all but the swords and a few phursas being taken from the santhals. It still continues.

Cultivation

In consequence of the rain off so long a time the dhan cultivation has been commenced very late in the season up to the end of May not shower had fallen to give the ryots a chance of plouhging and then it was so slight and partial as to be of mentioned. On the 16 instant the rain act was such from in that may be dated the general ploughing Hitherto the Ryots have only had employment in irregulating their sugar cane and Janara and inamsinfg their Dhan lands and to this want of occupation and the of the Mahajans to advance money in such an improvising season may be attributed the amount of crime reported.

The sugarcane and janara crops in the ground are very good having been kept alive by irrigation, but these bear a very small proportion to the number of cultivators and the peoples growing them through too well off to need advances from Mahajans are not efficiently well to do empty laborers.

The Bueeds which Mr. Grant I making on the Rohinee Estate.

Sd/ E. N. G. Braddon.
1st July, 1858

ooo

51 Letter

No. 266

From – E. N. G. Braddon
Assistant commissioner Deoghar

To,
Brown Wood Esq.
Assistant Commissioner Raj Mahal
Dated camp Sarath July 30th 1858.

Sir,

In reply to your letter no. 179 of the 15th inst. I have the honour to forward herewith Receipt in duplicate for the June pay of the 33 Santhals of your detachment.

The pay of the Santal Police force having been raised to 6 Rs. from the first of June. I have made the receipts out at that rate and request that you will be so good as to pay the additional 1 R each to them.

I beg to acknowledge the receipts of 2 stamps for 8 ans each, the amount due to Chalbul Sepoy.

If you required phursas and bows and arrows for your detachment I shall on your intimate the same forward them to you.

Sd/ E. N. G. Braddon.

ooo

52. Letter

No. 272

From:- E. N. G. Braddon.
Assistant Commissioner of the
Santal Parganas
To,
R. O. Keywood Esquire
Magistrate of Beerbhoom.
Dated Deoghar the 10th August, 1858.
Sir,

With the Sanction of the commissioner of the Santal Pergunnahs I have commenced employing the prisoners of the Deoghar Jail in manufactures.

From Bhagalpur and Monghyr the commissioner procured convicts acquainted with the manufacture of paper, sutiryees, Ehoth and wicken works and these have commenced their several calling with great success.

I am anxious that blankets and toweling should also be made in the Deoghar Jail an for this purpose have the honour to request that if you can spare them you will be kind enough to transfer a couple of prisoners acquainted with these manufactures to introduce them and instruct the prisoners here.

Sd. E. N. G. Braddon
Assit. Commissioner

OOO

53. Letter

No. 357

From,
E. N. G. Braddon Esqn.
Assistant commissioner santal pargans.
To,
W. G. Taylor
Asst. commissioner S. P Doomka
Dated camp Pathrole September 18-1858. (Pathrol near Sarath)
Sir,

In reply to your letter no. 357 of the 13 September 1858 requesting me to realize certain sums lent to the men of the Sonthal police force by Mahut Sah of Doomka, I have the honour to state that I am Unable to comply with your request.

The Sonthals received their pay regularly and need no Loan from Mahajans, this the Mahajun know but if the Mahajun protected in his exactions there will be no end to debt and the S. P corps and demoralization must occur.

I observe that the Mohajans in this instance have charged interest on Rs 4/-8 Annas and on Rupee\ -2 Annas and as the debtors state that these Loans were made up to than a month ago the interest exceeds 24%.

In my opinion it would be an advisable warning to Mohajans if this man Mohut Sah never receives his money at all.

I would be only the proper result of his notorious dealing, and I would suggest that he be told to recover his claim through the courts as in any way he legally can without any assistance.

N. B. - Interest rate -2 Annas per rupee .

Sd. E. N. G. Braddon

ooo

54. Letter

No. 211

From,

The Assistant commissioner Santal Pargans

To,

The Commissioner Santal Pargans Bhagalpoor.

Dated the 23rd October,1856

Sir,

I have the honour to inform you that I have this day committed Tibroo Santal alias @ Goppa Thakooran to your court on a charge of Rebellion attended with plunder.

1. The witness for the prosecution together with the prisoner can be attendance at your court on the 15th (Preplans) or any day after that day you may be pleased to first.

2. I have the honour to request you will have the goodness to intimate to me on what days the parties shall be directed to attend at your court.

3. I beg to bring your notice that there in another and a more serious charge against the prisoner Gopha Thakooran Pending in this court. The charge is Rebellion attempted with the willful Murder of five moosalman Mahanjans in the January last. " I regret to say I have not been able to get the evidence of the two Paharias, who gave the first information of this above murders to my predecessor Mr. W. G. Taylor. I have heard that Mr. Taylor at Dhooria called for the attendance of these two (2) witnesses at the sometime as myself and that they are now with him at Dhooria I further hear that Arjoon Manjhee the Gopha Thakooran's Jemadar has also been apprehended and taken to Mr. Taylor's as the crime charged took place in this Division and the chief or leader Tibroo Santal is now with me. I prpose addressing Mr. Taylor and request that he send to this court Arjoon Manjhee as likewise the 2 Pahari witnesses to this court.

4. A third prisoner by name Karan Santhal is also in my Hazat here, he confessed before Mr. Taylor in march last that he was one of the parties of Santhals under Gopha Thakooran at the murder of five Mahajaus ; but misfortunately Mr. Taylor failed to have his confession attested by witnesses – it is consequently he took any active hand in that murder he admits however before me having been present at such murders and saw the 5 men killed.

5. As it will be a difficult matter to convict the Gopha Thakooran of the murder of the Mahajans unless by the evidence of eye witnesses, I would solicit your orders as to the advisability of allowing Karan Santal, the prisoner, none here to be a witness for the prosecution – he is a men of now light among the Santals where as the Gopha among the Santals whereas the Gopha Thakooran and the Jamadar Arjoon Manjhee were the cause and mainspring of the 2nd Santhallce outbreak in November and December last.

6. Pending full enquiry into this more serious charge may I request you will be good enough not to pass any sentence in the prisoner Gopha Thakooran should you find on enquiry him guilty of the charge on which he is none committed to your court.

Sd. B. Wood

OOO

55. Letter

To,

The commissioner of Santal pergunnas Bhagalpore.

Sir,

I have the honour to forward you a statement of expenses incurred in giving employment to destitute Sonthals men and women & children from July to November 1856 as sanctioned under the orders of the govt. dated the 19h January 1856 and shall feel obliged by your passing the amount in order to enable me to adjust my meets.

2nd Of the 5,000/- sanctioned for the purpose of giving employment to destitute Sonthals, I have the honour to inform you that 2,500 were returned to the collector of Moorshedabad as not being required for the purpose granted of the unarming 2500/- Santals I have expended at and around the station at second during rains in giving employment to those who had not the means of gaining a livelihood elsewhere and 2099-11-3 remain in hand.

3rd- The Santhals being non- comparatively well off do not require assistance from Govt. except in a few individual cases and there I provide for by giving them daily labour at Buildings at RajMehal as there is still a large Balance Rs. 2099-11Annas-03 Paise, I would request your sanction to the disbursement of 1000/- for the leveling & filling up to holes and about the new station of Rajmahal and the remaining 1,099-11-3 for updating the High road passing the Rajmahal Bazar towards Bhagalpore which is at present in a very bad state and next to impossible in the rains as you are about visiting this station you will yourself pedicure how necessary both their works will be and I want to receive your sanction to the above disbursement on your arrival at RajMahal

N. B. Rs 400-4 Annas-9 Paise
Sd. Browne Woro

The 18th Feb 1857
Raj Mahal
No. 214

ooo

56. Letter

To,

The commissioner of S. P. Bhagalpore.

Sir,

I have the honour to inform you that I have this day committed this day **Gunnia Santhal to your court in a charge of Rebellion attended with plunder.**

2. The witness for the porsecution and the defence together with the prisoner can be in attendance on the 10 Proy. Or any day after that date you may be placed to fit.

3. I request you will have the goodness to intimate to me on what days to parties shall be directed to attend on your Court.

Sd. B. Wood
Assist. Commissioner
Raj Mahal 19th Sept., /57

ooo

57. Letter

From

The Deputy Commissioner of the Santal Parganas Naya Doomkoh

Sir,

I have the honour to bring your notice the meritorious conduct of Julio Manjee Sonthal of Jeer in this Dim. in the hope that the ngeal that he has deployed in the service of Cum. Amy meet with is following rewards.

2. This men at present as informer and receiving a salary of Rs 7/ =no per mensum has as you are aware been very successful in seizing and bringing in several notorious characters who took prominent parts in last years disturbances and only three years ago he with the apthee of his two men **Khayla and Mongulah** Manjee and 3 other Sonthals effected the capture of Kareeo Manjhee Soobha, a most notorious vagabond who had hither to constructed to escape the hands of Justice now with standing that several parties have been out in search of him.

3rd – In begning of May O ordered Jeetoo manjhee to proceed to Kurruckdeeah and offer his services to Mr. Tweedie …………… For the purpose of ended souring to bring some of & these santhal to justice who were lately disturbing the peace of that part of the country and the following is a short narrative of his conduct while these which I have taken down from his own dictation but which I should mention has been verified by Lt. Murray of the 42 no. I who was in command of the troops employted on the occasion about to be alluded to.

4th About the 12 of May Jeetoo Manjhee and his men were sent outlay Mr. Tweedie to ascertain where about the santals had assembled. He come upon them not for from Kurruckdiach and he remained among them four days when they were attacked by troops under the command of Lt Murray of the 42 N. I. It has been previously that in the event of an attack by the soldiers during his stay with the Sonthal young Jeetoo should hoist a cloth on a stick so that he might be known by the troops to be friend.

Sd. R. E.

ooo

58. Letter

No. 193

Quarterly Reports on the Deoghar or of the Sonthal Parganas ending June 30 1856

State of Roads and Ferries

The roads in this division have been completely neglected for the six years since the time of Mr. Dy Magistrate Vincent,. One road extending from Deoghar to Rohinee about three miles in length was made by me within the last quarter and is in good repair. These are no ferries in this Div.

Santhals

They are now quietly settling down in their old villages and busying themselves about the cultivation of their lands.

Return of Elephants furnished from the pergunnahs for the use of Government during the Santhal Insurrection.

Name of	*2*	*3*	*4*	*5*	*6*
owener	2 Elephans	Mahoots	Value fixed by c	From the date which return to	Date on which to the owner

Pooranan and Pandah of Deoghur	Tara Prasad	Cheer-ungee @ Lall mo-hamed	1700---------------	24th July1855	10th January 1856
Ditto	Hurihar Pershad	Peerbure	1800---------	6 Nov .1855	2600
Cork-Bassinath Singh Ghatwal of Talook Dewly	Lutchmn	Sheik		1 Dec	9th do.

1. The animal in Col 11 was paid by the captain of the 13th Regiment no. I
2. Ditto by 42nd Rest No. I
3. Do Do

Sd. R. E. Ronald
Asstt. Commissioner

ooo

Quarterly Reports on the Deoghar Division of the Sonthal Parganas ending September 30th 1856.

Santhals

They are perfectly quietly and busy with their crops their condition has much improved since the Indian corn and other Bawdy crops have been gathered in on the 16th instant they held their Kurna Poojah in my presence when everything passed off satisfactorily.

The proposal to hold the Poojah before me emanated from themselves as they stated that had it been performed in the interior of the Division they might have been accused by their neighbors' of assembling with some unlawful object in view.

Imp- In a letter no- 382 of G. U Yule commissioner Bhagalpur issued instructions and in his compliance R. ER. Ronald Ass. t com. Deoghar whole to him letter no. 339 a report regarding establishment of school at Deoghar.

OOO

No. 375

Quarterly Reports on the Deoghar Division of the sonthal Parganas ending 31st December 1856.

Sonthals

These people are perfectly quiet and living in all appearance I great contentment complaints against them are very rare indeed and their complains entirely consist of attemprsat exaction on the part of Mohajans and land holders, but which invariably meet with prompt recites.

Cultivation

The only land in cultivation at this time of the year is that on which the Dhan mustard and corn crops are standing the former crop is nearly all reapplied and the cutting of the latter has commenced upon. The Dhan has yielded none than an average return this season.

OOO

Chapter-X

BIDWELL'S REPORT

1. BENGAL JUDICIAL CONSULTATIONS

Letter dated 14th February, 1856, No. 157

(No. 827A From A. C. Bidwell, Esq. Late Special Commissioner for the Suppression of the Sonthal Insurrection To the Secretary to the Govt, of Bengal, Fort William, Dated Bhaugulpore, 10th December, 1855.)

Sir,

I have the honor to acknowledge the receipt of your letter No. 2777 dated 9th October last, directing me to report at any earliest convenience.

1st–The cause of the late Sonthal insurrection as far as I have yet been able to ascertain them.

2nd–The measures which I would recommend for putting an end to the insurrection to be carried into effect at the close of the rains.

3rd–The measures to be taken to prevent such rising for the future.

For the cause of the insurrections on naturally turns in the first instance to the manifestoes of the Insurgents as well as to the Statements of those of them who have been taken prisoners, and been put upon their trial.

The first manifesto which comes before us, which is the fullest and contains everything, that is set forth in any other, is the notice issued by Seedoo to the residents at Rajmahal, see Appendix A. The grievances therein referred to are **1st** a sort of complaint of excessive taxation implied in a prescribed reduction of rent to 1 Anna for each bullock plough and 2 Annas for each bufoalloe, and the country his to be taken away from the Sahibs on account of the prevalence of falsehood the negligence of the Sahibs, the extortion of the Mahajans the corruption of the Amlahs, and the oppression of the Police.

In Seedoo's examination before Mr. Eden he states that he and other had repeatedly complained of the oppression of the Mahajans to Mr. Pontet, but could get no redress. That these Mahajans take 5 Rupees interest for 1 Rupee lent and purchase their rice at unfair rates, and if they don't give it, pull their ears and beat them. That his rent has been raised, and that the Naib Sezawals who make the collections take 10 or 5 Rupees from each village for " Balance". That one of the Railway Sahibs carried off 2 Sonthal womwn, wounded a Sonthal man and killed another. For these reasons the Sonthals were dissatisfied and were pondering what was to be done, when a God descended, in the form of a cartwheel, and advised them to kill Pontet and the Mahajans and then they would have justice and a father and mother.

Peetoo Pergunnait:-, another prisoner, says the Mahajans oppress us dreadfully. They take our rice at unfair rates and charge exorbitant interest. We complain of this to Pontet, who gives a Perwannah on the Naib Sazawal to enquire into the case. The Naib Sazawal does nothing for us. If we don't pay the Mahajuns they seize our cows and cattle. We are willing to give 4 Annas interest in the Rupee but no more. The rent we pay is just, we have nothing to find fault with in that respect. We give it willingly. The Naib Sazawals take 3 Rupees "Expenses "from each village when they come to collect rent; but we give it willingly. If the Mahajuns are kept in order and punished, we have nothing to complain of.

Manick Sonthal another prisoner states that the outbreak occurred on account of the Mahajuns oppression. I suggest Singh of Nainsook lent him 4 Rupees and took 8 in payment. He complained to Mr. Pontent who gave him a Perwannah on Kalleepurshad Naib Sazawal to enquire into the case. But the Naib Sazawal did nothing.

Dullas Manjee Sonthal attributes the outbreak to the oppression of the Mahajun and that of the Sahibs of the Railway who committed great oppression at Seetapaharee. The Sahib (Mr. Thomas) the women of whose family were killed, used to commit very great oppression. He used to go out with a Mussaul at night and dishonour the women of the Sonthals, and carry off goats, fowls and kids by force. On one occasion he took a goat- a Sonthals endeavoured to get it from him and they were both pulling at it, on which the Sahib or a Burkundanzi who was with him, drew his sowrd and killed the Sonthal. A Sontal came to complain of this at Bhagulpore but got put into jail himself for his trouble (I have looked at the record of this case which certainly appears to have been very imperfectly prosecuted by the Magistrate of Bhaugulpore. The wounded Santhal, no one was killed, were set to the hospital which perhaps led to the supposition that they were sent to the jail. The offenders escaped punishment.)

Purtoo Purgunnait (since condemned to death for rebellion and murder) states that he was addressed by Seedoo and Kanoo, who told him that justice had arrived and that the hakims had erred in taking too much rent, and the Mahajans in taking too much interest, that 2 Annas were in future to be paid for a bullock plough and I pice in ten Rupees is to be the rate of interest.

The above exhibit the causes of the insurrection a gathered from the replies of the prisoner many more of whom answered to the same effect, while others replied that it was the " Thakours " order for them to rise which was warrant enough for them.

I have called upon the principal zamindars and gentlemen of the District, whose occupations have thrown them into collision with the Sonthals, for any information which they can afford as to the causes of the outbreak, and their replies are some more and more less in accordance with the views which I have been lead to adopt from other sources.

Captain Sherwill who was asked for his opinion on the subject by Mr. Browne in July last, states in reply that his survey duties in the years 1851 and following have led him much into intercourse with the Sonthals- that he took his family and lived amongst them unarmed, and fearless, visited nearly all their village, conversed with nearly every lead man, counted their houses, surveyed and mapped their country, obtained supplies, coolly-labour and every assistance, all of which was rendered with the greatest cheerfulness and willingness.

That he heard no complaints against any one during his stay with them, but was particularly struck with the barefaced capacity of the Mahajans and Merchants buying grain and produce of them. The Sonthal hatred and detestation of whom has been shown by the murder of every one of them that fell into their hands. After the outbreak, Captain Sherwill states that there were about 50 Bengally Traders at Burhait the captain of the Damun(Damin) and a number more at Burio an important town eleven miles north of it- that it was at these two places that the insurrection broke out. And he really believest that the oppression, exactions and gross capacity of these traders have in a great measure been the cause of the present lamentable outbreak –that religion has been mixed up with the rebellion in order to strengthen the hands of the rebel chiefs by acting upon the minds of the Sonthals for the Sonthal in his own way is a peculiarly religious man and when his ideas are assisted by the powerful Manooa (=Mahua) spirit and smoking Ganja (mauri guana) which two excitants are resorted to in all their religious dances and exercises, and freely used upon the present occasion, the Sonthal may be driven to acts of violence and desperation.

Captain Sherwill adds thatthe Sonthals in the Damunikoh are far better clothed, better fed have more cattle and better houses than those outside the Government boundary, and that wherever he has not fallen into the snares of the Bengally traders he is a happy and contented man. He has always heard Mr. Potet's name mentioned by them with respect and reverence, and he is satisfied that a high assessment has had no share in producing the present outbreak.

Mr. Charles Barnes a gentleman engaged in indigo-planting and agricultural pursuits for many years in his District and who has considerable knowledge of the Sonthal tribe has come to the conclusion that the origin of the outbreak is to be tracked to religious fanaticism alone. He does not believe that Sonthal has been oppressed by Zamindar, Police or Mahajan, because as a valuable ryot, particularly expert in clearing jungle, punctual in his payments though he will pay no undue cess not yield to forced labour, he is especially protected by the zamindars that they were a quiet peaceable set and were never seen at the Police Thannahs. That their assessment is so light they have seldom occasion to resort to the Mahajan and their dealings with them must therefore be limited. He believes that a few designing individuals of the tribe, taking advantage of the idea of a Divine revolution into their minds calling upon them to recover an imaginary kingdom once to rise to plunder villages and massacre all, except the lower castes. With the recovery of their kingdom the land rent was to be commuted to a tax on ploughs.

These orders tallied with their savage instincts and their innate love of bloodshed was apparent from the very commencement of the rising. They did not confine their cruelties to those who had injured or offended them – **but women and children beggars and travellers,** all shared the same fate. Many of the victims were bound had and foot, and deliberately sacrificed before an emblem of their Thakour with the same expressions as used by the Hindoos in their sacrifices of animals of Kallee. the universal answer given when remonstrate with being it is ' the Thakoor's order and must be obeyed. The poorest and quietest Sonthals committed as great atrocities as the Manjees and Pergunnaites who led them. That many were deceived there is no question, but it is equally evident that others were glad of the opportunity furnished by the orders of men in no better position of life than themselves, to commit these depredations.

Though I think that Mr. Barnes is, for want of the same information's that is before me, mistaken in his notion that the Sonthals had no complaint against the Mahajans, his view of the affair is deserving of great consideration as that of an intelligent observer long resident on the spot.

The **Rev. Mr. Droese,** whose avocations have taken him much among the Sonthals, says of them I have never anywhere in India, met with Nations of a disposition of track and kind. Their industry, their perseverance, their love of order, their inquisitiveness, their joviality are conspicuous to the most casual visitor what can have turned such a race into the furious savages they have shown themselves to be? He heard that their grievances are as follows that they are over taxed in having to pay a ruinous ground rent to Govt. but also in having to pay to Govt or to Govt. officials on the produce of trees standing on ground already taxed. that they complain of the encouragement given to Bengally Merchants to settle in Sonthal villages, and Mr. Droese has seen ' enough of these lying rascals to understand what a grievance their presence must be to a simple frank-hearted race,and mostly they complain of the rapacious villainous and merciless conduct of Hindoo and Mohamadan Darogah, appointed by Govt. to keep order in their villages.

The Sonthal is, he says, closely knit in brotherhood. 'Some twelve years ago, Mr. Droese learns, arrangements were made for uniting the whole of the Sonthals in one body –near the Damoodah (Damodar) lives a Sonthal chiefs of Chiefs whose name **is Morgo Rajah**-he is said to have been successful in making about 300 disciples within the last 12 years. **These are sworn men and fully instructed in all plans for uniting all the Sonthals in one brotherhood.** They are scattered among the Sonthals and continue to act under the instructions of their chief and continually refer to him for advice. From all I have heard I am inclined to believe that they are as secret, active and **obedient an agency as the Jesuits in the Romish Church.** "

Strong suspicions have been excited as to the complicity of one or more of the Ameers of Saiside(Sindh) in this insurrection. But I have not yet had to observe anything more than is in support of this view of Mr. Daroese.

Mr. I Grant,, a European Zemindar long resident in the District attributes the rising to a discontented feeling caused by the illegal exactions and oppressions of the Naib Sezawals, which afforded a favourable opportunity to desigining men like Seedoo and other, to work upon their feelings and led to the lamentable result which followed. **He does not consider the oppression of the Mahajans could have been the cause of the outbreak for the people of the surrounding Pergunnahs are also forced to submit to the same exactions which prevail wherever there are ryots to borrow and Mahajans to lend.**

Mr. I Grant was not aware of the circumstances of the Decoitees which took place in the year 1854, nor of numerous petitions presented by Sonthals to the different Courts complaining of the oppression of the Mahajans.

Baboo Girdharee Col., Govt. pleader and a zemindar in the District attributes the insurrection to the fanatic and credulous disposition of the tribe, which enabled afew of their number, notorious characters, impoverished by hard drinkings, to lead them into rebellion by giving out that the time of their kingdom was come. That God himself had revealed this to Seedoo, and that the Mandate was to kill and plunder all. Meeting a first with little check from the Govt. Troops on this side, they believed the dictum of their chiefs. Had troops been available when the outbreak occurred, thousands of lives and much valuable property would have been saved.

The agent of the Ranee Khema Soouduree of Packour attributes the rising to the oppression of the Mahajans and the unwarrantable conduct of some of the Railway employees who insulted their women and refused to pay the sonthals when employed on the railway works. This enabled Seedoo to assemble the whole body, in revolt through the stimulus of religious fanaticism.

The **Rajah Maheshpore** attributes the dissatisfaction of the Sonhals to the increase of land rent the extortions of the mahajans and the oppression of the Railway Managers, who forced them to hard labour and paid them very little. This dissatisfaction was fanned into aflame by the fraud of apprehended descent of the deity in the houses of Seedoo, who told them to take arms and drive the people out of the country.

Mr. Taylor a very intelligent engineer of the Railway Department who was stationed at Shreekond near which the outbreak commenced and who saw a great deal of the Sonthall tribe says;

"The Railway Officals Mr. Pontet, the police and the Mahajans have all in their turn been accused of causing the insurrection. From my position and good understanding with the Sonthals, I am fully certain that no cause of oppression on the part of Europeans employed on the Railway should have occurred –without my knowing something about it, and I don't believe any thing of the sort ever happened. It is my opinion that no case ever occurred of Sonthals being underpaid for work done, or one of their women being forcibly carried off by any of the Europeans employed on the line.'

Mr. Taylor states that very few sonthals could be induced to work on the line, not because they were underpaid or ill treated, but because they were generally so well off that they preferred drinking and dancing and amusing themselves. He has often heard the Sonthals speak of Mr. Pontet but never heard them say anything against him or complain of having to pay too much rent, in fact he always understood that they rent themselves by Panchayat and that Mr. Pontet took in fact whatever they chose to give.

Mr. Taylor's opinion of the cause of the outbreak is that the Sonthals from living such a lazy drunken life for some time past, had got into a very excited inflammable state and that the leader perceiving this and knowing that a great deal could be done before the arrival of Trops formed a plan to plunder the country and make off with the loot across the work upon their superstitions and impose upon them the story of the Takoor having given them the order to do so.

The above constitutes the opinion of such of the zemindars and gentlemen residents in the neighbourhood who have favoured me with them. I have next employed myself in looking over the correspondence regarding the Damun for the last ten years especially the reports of Mr. Pontet.

Before recording my own my own opinion as to the cause of the outbreak, I will give a short sketch of the administration of the Damunikoh for the last 20 years. This track which, as the Govt. is aware, embraces what are called the Rajmahal Hills and the lands skirting the same which were not included in the Decennials Settlement with the remainder of the District was declared to be Govt. property in the year 1823 and a special officer was for many years entertained to decide and demarcate the boundaries thereof. For several years the cultivable lands included in this tract were reserved for the years the cultivable lands included in this tract were reserved for the Hill people, but in the year 1827-31 1st October the Board supported Mr. ward's recommendation that other classes should be admitted to cultivate these lands; that the clearance of the forests if they left to the Hill people would never take place, were as the Sonthals race were largely employed by neighbouring reminders in bringing forest land into cultivation and no possible objection existed to employ them in the same way in the Damun.

The Govt. however replied that his Lordship in Council was unwilling to depart from the resolution which the Govt. had come to that the Damun lands should be exclusively reserved for the encouragement the Hill race in agriculture. Should the hill race disappoint these expectations it will then be at the option of Govt. to change their plan and look to other classes for the improvement of their lands.

No formal orders of Govt. repealing these instructions appear on record; but the Sonthals gradually located themselves on the Damun lands, and in 1830 the Govt, recognised their existence there by authorising the local authorities to protect them from any demand, beyond that which it is customary for them to pay, by taking a stipulation to that effect from the Hill grantees.

After repeated recommendations from the local authorities in favour of encouraging Sonthals to settle on these lands as the only means of clearing the jungle, the Govt. on the 21st November 1836 consented to the appointment of a special officer for the Superintendence of the Damunikoh; and the collector Mr. Dunbar, in his instructions to Mr. Pontet, who was nominated to the office, intimated to him that his duty was to use his best efforts to bring the culturable portion of the Damun lands under cultivation by means of the Sonthals, and that the sooner to effect this desirable object, he should not only afford protection to those already settled in the Damun, but also give every encouragement to fresh settlers upon the unoccupied lands.

The following notes of the revenue received on account of the Damun lands from the year 1837-38 to 1854-55 shows the result of this changes of system, from discouragement to encouragement of Sonthal settlers.

Yearwise Receipt of revenue from Damin-i-koh (From 1837-1855)

Year	*Amount*	*year*	*Amount*
1837/38	Rs. 6682	1846/47	Rs 36407
1838/39	7798	1847/48	39905
1839/40	10644	1848/49	40947
1840/41	20074	1849/50	43724

1841/42	20997	1850/51	47665
1842/43	22372	1851/52	50160
1843/44	25450	1852/53	51825
18344/45	28002	1853/54	53455
1845/46	32430	1854/55	58033

It has been the fashion to attribute this result to the 'admirable management ' of Mr. Pontet the Supt. But I confess that I took upon it as arising from causes independent of management that is to say to the policy of Govt. in encouraging instead of, as before, discouraging the settling of these Tribes, and to the attractive quality of the soil which is of the finest description. As the same time I hope, when I come to notice Mr. Pontet's qualifications as a public officer. I shall not be found to treat them with injustice.

Mr. Dunbar stated that there were, when he wrote, 427 villages inhabited by Sonthals and Bhooyans; (sic) that he thought the number of Santhals who might be induced by a very moderate degree of encouragement to settle was limited only but the extent of the lands, and that they are already themselves in large numbers without invitation. They are almost industrioes under their laboures with astonishing celerity. Mr. Dunbar adds that their produce was generally disposed of at a rate considerable lower than the market price of the day to the Mahajans or to dealers who come into the Damun for the purposes of purchasing grain.

From the time of his appointment to the date of the outbreak Mr. Pontet's management received the undeviating approbation of Collector, Commissioner and the Board. It seems, I fear,ungracious in me to say that looking at the avidity which the Sonthals already shown to settle in this tract, and their extremely tractable and straight forward character as ryuts, this high praise was a litle too hastily conceded.

Beside carefully going over the correspondence regarding the Damun for the last 10 years. I have looked into all the complains sent to me by the supt. Magistrate, Collector and Commissioner as comprising all presented to them by Sonthals for the last two years.

I cannot say that Mr. Pontet's reports impress me highly with his capacity as a public officer. At the same time there are obvious marks of sense and discretion in his account of his administration tours. I see not anywhere either in the correspondence or in petitions, of over assessment of the Sonthals. Mr. Pontet's demands indeed seem to be limited to what the Sonthal community decide was just and proper and they have always paid without demur or difficulty.

In the year 1851 Captain Sherwill ascertained by survey that the quantity of land under cultivation by Sonthals in the Damun was 162560 acres, equal to 491744 Beeghas, and as the govt. rent for the following year did not exceed Rs. 47555, we find the average rate of assessment imposed on land held by Sonthals in the Damun to be about one and a half anna per beeghah which considering the fine quality of much of the land in the Damun must be considered moderate in the extreme.

The system in force there is to give the uncleared land rent free for the first three years. A trifling rent is taken for the next three years according to what the Pergunaite may consider just, averaging from 3 to 10 rupees per village. The next lease is for five years when the rent to be paid is fixed by a Panchayat of Manjees, who have been holding villages for the last five years, and with my knowledge Mr. Ponet says, of the length breadth of the village under settlement as also the number of houses in it. I can generally judge if the assessment has been a fair one ' Mr. Ponet states elsewhere that he never takes from Sonthals a higher rate than 8 annas per bighas as estimated by him.

The Sonthals are said to object to pay their lands by the beegha though there are zemindarees in the districts in which this objection is overcome, and considerable credit I believe has been given to Mr. Pontet for ingenuity in the indirect means which he took to ascertaining the quantity contained in each holding, which was by getting them to erect a post in the centre of each village cultivation to serve as defining their boundaries, from which I obtained at the same time a rough calculation of the quantity of land. But the objection of the Sonthals is to paying by the Beegha, not I believe to the measurement of his. And at any rate a better plan than the rude one adopted by ?Mr. Pontet, of estimating the area of each village, would have been to go found it with the chain and prismatic compass with which he had been supplied, marking the boundaries as he went along and working out the area on paper.

The Collections are made through the Naib Sazawals once in the year and that at a time when Mr. Pontet himself is present in the Damun, ready to check any exaction on the part of these officers.

Mr. Pontet is satisfied that these men do not extort money from the Sonthals, but I am certainly disposed to coincide in the opinion generally prevalent here, that they do. Indeed from the insufficient manner in which Mr. Ponet has gone into the one or two cases of complaint against Naib Sazawals which are now before me. I am satisfied that he was not sufficiently on his guard to prevent it.

The Statement made by Peetoo Sonthals prisoner as quoted in the Margine, 1 I consider to be as near the truth as may be. And the return of Sonthals village in the Damun being given that 1218 the amount of illegal cess extorted by the Naib Sezawals will be about 8308. No. one had any experience of the difficulty of controlling native officer employed in Bengal in the collection of revenue will consider this as over estimated, and the names of several of the Naib Sazawals of the Damun are mentioned to me as having notoriously amassed large sums of money in the office.

1 The revenue we pay is just. We have nothing to find fault with in that we give it willingly. the Naib Sezawals take 6 Rupees from each village when they come to collect the rent, but we give that willingly. If the mahajans are kept in order and punished we have nothing to complain of.

As I said before I find no symptom of over taxation in any part of the correspondence. Mr. Ponet's mode of dealing with disputes was judicious, I had the parties before me face to face and settled the amount due by Punchait. ' But I find in his reports early notice of the sufferings of the Sonthals from the oppression of the Mahajans, which I think he might have done more to obviate. In 1847 (Nov. Ist) in advocating the extension of the provision of Regn. I of 1827 to the Sonthals, as well as the Hill men, which would give the Magistrate jurisdiction over Civil cases between Sonthals are left to carry on their suits before the Monnsiff's Courts, it is impossible that they can compete with the cleverness and chicanery of the people of the plains. '

I August 1848 he states This year villagers absconded in consequence of the oppression of the Mahajuns who had gained cases in the Moonsiff's Court from the ignorance of the Sonthals to defend them. I fully believe(what) he says' the whole cases (are) false-certainly as regards the amount used for; but in some instances I am sure the whole debt had been paid tenfold. These poor fellows from not being able to read or write, have no check whatever over the Bengally in marking off their payments, and as for the Bengally giving a receipt when paid in full, or returning the bonds, such a thing is never known. Mr. Pontet then suggests that if the provisions of Section III of Regn. I of 1827 cannot be made applicable to the Sonthals he should be authorised to appoint a Mookhtar in the Moonsiff's Court to defend cases against Sonthals.

In his report of the 22nd May 1849, Mr. Pontet says. "Received complaints against petty Mahajuns allowing their tattoos to graze on the ryuts corn reported the same to the Collector in the hope of his being able to punish the offending parties. "

In May 1851 he says' great complaint against the Mahajuns taking exorbitant interest, and using larger measures than those established by me in former years which I had settled with the consent of all parties. This oppression is a hardship, and with the trifling power I hold can scarcely be rectified. I can only in consequence merely summon the parties. This oppression is a hardship, and with the trifling power I hold can scarcely be rectified. I can only in consequence merely summon the parties and point it out, threatening them if they don't desist to turn out of the Damun.

In 1853 his report on the past season, he notices a number of petitions received against petty Mahajans who are always exacting an illegal interest from the ignorant Sonthal.

In his report of the 15th May 1854 Mr. Pontet notices complaints made of petty oppression on the part of servants of the Railroad employees taking fowls and kids at their own prices. The Mahajans have also causedsome injury to the settlers by carrying them into the Moonsiff's Courts and getting out attachments upon their cattle before the ryuts even hear of it.

In reporting to the Collector as to the causes of the Dacoitees of that year, Mr. Pontet wrote on the 5th July, 1854, when visiting the Damun this past season, the Sonthals have complained to me generally of the oppression committed by the Mahajans in exacting enormous interest, also in taking grain almost on their own terms. I often endeavoured to protect my ryuts when any glaring case is brought to my notice, but my notice, but when I return to my station in April, the Moonsiff's Court is set a going, and decrees are obtained exparte in most cases, when the unfortunate ryuts is sold up houses and cattle, and is thereby reduced to beggary after a legal fashion.

In his report of 28th May 1855 Mr. Pontet again revert to the oppressions of the Mahajuns and states that on examining their books we found that they steadily charged 50 percent interest on money lend-8 annass in the rupee, and that they had taken bonds on stamped paper including this illegal charge.

This is all that I find in the correspondence of the last 10 years bearing upon the point under consideration. viz the cause of the insurrection. I will now proceed to notice the petitions sent to me from the various offices of the Districts.

The petition to me by Mr. Pontet as those put in by Sonthals within the last two years are 24 and 67 in 1855. In the case of 1854 fiften are complaints regarding dispossession and non-payment of rent by ryute-(raiya) the remaining 9 refer to oppression alleged against Mahajans. In these cases the dispute was settled generally by bringing the parties face to face, and adjusting the matter on apparently equitable grounds >but although Mr. Pontet complains, in many of his letter of his limited power to protect the Sonthals against the Mahajans. I see that he exercises extraordinary powers, which if justifiable in one instance, might have been used by him other to the manifest advantage of the Sonthals for instance. on the report of the Naib Sezawal of Doomkah that Monzah Koolgattee is deserted by the ryuts owing to the Mahajuns having in My last caused the ryuts to pledge their cattle to him for debt Mr. Pontet often he says satisfying himself that the fact was associated ordered the Niab Sazawal to recover the Govt. revenue from the Mahajuns. The same order was also passed as regards the bukya balance due from the ryuts of Mouzah Konaidihee.

Again when Boodhun Roy Petitioned that Sectarm Mahajan has taken away 5 rupees worth of Teel from his ryuts and there by driven them from the place, leaving 5 rupees due from them to him, and desired that the Mahajuns might be called upon to pay it, was ordered accordingly 20th July 1854 that the Mahajamns should pay the balance of Govt. revenue due from petitioner, and of he has any claim on the ryuts he can recover it.

Of the 67 cases of 1855 upwards of one half are complaints of oppression against Mahajans. The Mahajans when sent for by Mr. Pontet, generally denied the charge, on which they were warned against oppressing the Sonthals on pain of being turned out of his Damun.

On one occasion Kanoo Manjee Pergunnaite and other complainted against Kishen Jenum Singh Naib Sezawal of

Doomkah representing that he extorts 6 rupees from each Mouzah on his own account- on the 7th November the complaint was by Mr. Pontet ordered to produce his witness in the Mofussil. But the complainant afterwards represented that the petition was got up by the acting Naib Sezawal and it was struck off. In this case by the Superintendent would have shown the truth of the complaint thuogh it is very probable that it was suggested by the acting Naib Sezawal.

Mr. Pontet frequently refers to the orders of Govt. prohibiting the settling of any others than Sonthals in the Damun, and on this ground threatening expulsion to Mahajans accused of oppression. I do not find any such order of Govt. on record : but it appears to me that if Mr. Pontet had actually expelled one or two notoriously oppressive Mahajans the act, if of questionable legality, would not have been more so than other of his acts, and would have been attended with the best efforts in checking the gross oppression which prevailed.

The Petition sent by the Collector are mostly, unimportant complaints regarding right to settlement petty boundary disputes. One however is a serious complaint brought by Samoo Manjee and 8 others against Mohesh Dutt, the Naib Sazawal of Digghee for extortion and oppression. That he takes from some ryuts 4 rupees from others, 5 from other r2. The petitioners particularly beg that the enquiry may be conducted by the collector himself. The Collector however sent it to Mr. Pontet for investigation who ordered it to be brought up in the Mofussil. Afterwards he ordered petitioners to be in attendance before him at Buchroogunge on the 20the and 21st instant.

When the petitioners are so brought before Mr. Pontet the Naib Sazawal had of course made matters smooth and the petitioners one and all denied that the complaints had been made by them. Mr. Pontet then sent the case to the collector in order that the instigators of the complaint might be punished. But on the collector enquiring he found good cause to make him consider the complaint a genuine one even if now denied and he struck the case off his file 19th of April 1854.

The Collector should in my opinion have gone into the case himself but when Mr. Pontet found it was transferred to him, he ought to have known that his only chance of eliciting the truth was to take up the case and sift it thoroughly, without a day's delay. he did not do this and of course the complaint was by cajolery and intimidation hushed up and denied.

Mr. Pontet states in his letter to me No. 130 dated 30th Sept as his grounds for believing that the exortion is not practised by the Naib Sazawals, that so few complaints were preferred of this kind but when men see that their complaints are not properly gone into by the authorities, they will not expose themselves to additional oppression by repeating them. Mr. Brown in his letter no. 1514 dated 15th October makes the same remark. viz that very few charge have been preferred against the Serawala and (torn –burnt).

OOO

2. SANTAL CIVIL RULES

Santal Civil Rules- With reference to the Provision of section 1. Clause (2) of the Santal Parganas Act, 1855(XXXVII of 1855) and section 27 of the Santal Parganas Justice Regulation, 1893 (V of 1893), the Governor of Bihar is pleased to issue the following direction for observance by officers appointed under section 2 of the declare that they shall come into force on the 1st January 1946. The directions should be known as The Santal Civil Rules.

CHAPTER 1

Appearance of parties :- Paties shall appear in person but such as are –(a) resident of other districts; (d) landlords for the purpose of rent suits and rent executions only); and (e) excused from personal appearance by the Court for good and sufficient Cause in any particular case to be recorded in writing ; may by permission appear through agents to be approved by the Court ; provided that such permission may, if the Court thinks fit, be withdrawn at any time; and that no agents fees shall be allowed as cost.

CHAPTER II

Institution of plaint :- (1) Plants shall be present in the Court of the Subdivisional Officer or of an officer authorized by the Subdivisional Officer to receive them.

(2) A plaint May be either verbal or written.

(3) A verbal plaint shall be recorded by the Court on presentation of a Court fee of the value requisite for the suit.

(4) A written plaint shall be written by –

(a) The plaintiff or one of his household

(b) a registered petition – writer or

(c) an approved Pleader or Mukhtear of the District Court, and shall be properly stamped, signed and verified by the plaintiff.

(3) Details to be given in the plaint

(1) The plaint shall contain

(a) The name, father's name, residence and occupation of each plaintiff and defendant where known ; and

(b) a brief statement of the claim, including its value estimated where the subject matter is land which is not saleable, in accordance with the first schedule.

(2) If the suit for rent, the number of the holding in the settlement jamabandi shall be given. If there has been no settlement the boundaries of the land shall be clearly given. If the suit is for land the settlement jamabandi shall be given, if possible. If the plaintiff is unable to give this information or if the land is situated in an area which has not been settled, the boundaries and the land shall be clearly given. If the land cannot be so described and the plaint is not accompanied by a plan of the land, the Court

shall order the plaintiff to deposit the mains, fees and have a plan prepared before issuing process against the defendant.

(3) the court receiving a plaint or the Court to which the plaint is transferred may, if it thinks fit, examine the plaintiff before issuing process, and if no cause of action is found, shall dismiss the suit.

(4) If the suit is dismissed under sub-rule (3), the plaintiff may appeal on paying the court –fee chargeable on a petition. 4. Court fees to be paid –

(1) Where the claim is not for loss of caste, defamation, abuse or assault the plaintiff, if he is satisfied the Court that he is, too poor to pay the proper court- fee, may be allowed to sue without payment of any such fee.

Provided that if it appears to the court that permission so to sue was obtained by fraud, the suit may be dismissed and the court-fee, may be not paid may be recovered from the plaintiff as if it were due under a decree against him.

(2) If a plaintiff who has been allowed to sue without payment of court fee wins the suit, the proper court-fee may be recovered from the defendant.

5. Filing of documents- If a plaint rests on, or is supported by document, these must be filed with it.

(6) After admission of plaint a date and place for appearance to be fixed, and summons to be issued – When the plaint is admitted, a date and place shall be fixed for the appearance of the defendant and the evidence of the plaintiff and his witness and summons shall be issued accordingly. The summons shall include a brief statement of the claim.

Provided that in suits brought by village headman against raiyats arrears of rent the original summons to the defendant shall require them to appear in court and make their payments or their defence.

7. Service of summons by the Plaintiff himself or through Court – The plaintiff may himself serve the summons on the

defendants or on payment of costs require it to be served by the Court. Service shall, if possible, be personal. Otherwise the summons shall be served on an adult male member of the defendants household or by attaching it to his house in presence of either the village headman or chaukidar, if any, and at least one other resident of the locality, both of whom shall be required to write or sign a report as to the manner or service

CHAPTER III

HEARING

8. Defendant to file written statement on the date of hearing. Orders to be passed- On the date fixed by the summons, the plaintiff, if he appears, and likewise the defendant, shall be examined by the Court, and the defendant may be allowed to file a written statement. If the merits of the case are disclosed by the examination of the plaintiff and the defendant and the inspection of the documents (if any) then orders may be passed forthwith.

9. (1) If further evidence is required, postponement to be allowed – If further evidence is required, the court shall proceed to examine the witness of the plaintiff, and the plaintiff shall not be entitled to claim a postponement in order to produce them. The defendant shall be entitled to one postponement for producing his witness. Further postponement shall not be granted to either party or ordered by the Court except for good and sufficient cause, and when a postponement is granted for the convenience of a party, he shall be required to pay the costs thereof and such costs shall not be costs in the case.

(2) Notice shall be given to the parties of every change in the date or place fixed for the trial of the suit.

10. Parties to be examined on oath or solemn affirmation – Parties and witness shall be examined on oath or solemn affirmation and the substance of their evidence shall be recorded by the Court.

11. (1) Summons to persons to give evidence – After institution of suits parties may obtain summons to person whose attendance is required either to give evidence or to produce documents. Such summons must be applied for in the case of the plaintiff on the date of the institution of the suit, and in the case of the defendant on the date on which he first appears.

(2) Issue of warrant to witness. Imposition of time- If on due service of summons a witness fails to attend the Court or to produce documents on the dates fixed, or having attended in response to summons departs without leave of the court before his discharge, the Court may, unless cause be shown on its satisfaction, issue a warrant either with or without bail for the arrest of such witness, and may impose a fine not exceeding Rs-50 to be realized by attachment and sale of his moveable property.

(3) Deposit of travelling allowance of witness – the Court may require the parties to deposit in advance the travelling expenses of witness and may refuse to summon a witness for reasons to be recorded in writing.

12. Dismissal of Suit - If neither party appears on the date fixed for the trial of the suit, the suit shall be dismissed. If the plaintiff only appears, the suit may be decreed ex-parte, provided always that the claim and service of summons and proved to the satisfaction of the Court. If the plaintiff does not appear but the defendants does, the suit may be dismissed for default, unless the defendant admits the claim or apart thereof in which case the court shall pass a decree against the defendant upon, and to the extent of such admission.

13 (1) Application for setting aside the order of dismissal within thirty days – If the suit in wholly or partially dismissed under rule 12, the plaintiff may within thirty days of the order of dismissal apply for an order to set aside the dismissal upon such term as to costs or otherwise as it thinks fit and shall appoint a day for proceeding with the suits.

(2) Fresh suit when to be instituted – the plaintiff may bring a fresh suit only where the first suit has been dismissed on the nonappearance of both parties.

14. Application to set aside an ex-parte decreed suit – If the suit is decreed ex-parte, the defendant may, on any date either within 30 days of the service of any process issued in execution or earlier apply to the Court for an order to set it aside, and if he satisfies the court that there was sufficient excuse for default, the court shall make an order setting aside the decree upon such terms as to costs as it thinks fit and shall appoint a date for proceeding with the suit.

15. Notice to be issued – No order setting aside the dismissal of a suit for default or an exparte decree shall be made without previous notice to the other side; provided that where the order of dismissal is passed before service of summons on the defendants no notice need be given to the defendant.

16. Appointment of a commission by the Court – the Court may issue a commission for the examination on interrogatories or other wise of a witness who-

(a) Resides outside the local limits of its jurisdiction; or

(b) Is a civil or military officer of Government and cannot in the opinion of the Court attend without detriment to the public service ; or

(c) Is exempted by the Court from attendance on account of sickness, infirmity or other sufficient reason to be recorded by the Court.

(17) Enquiry to be held by the Court itself or through commission – The Court may itself hold, or send a Commissioner to hold, a local enquiry, assessing costs as it may think fit. The Court may appoint one or more Commissioners to investigate cases of a complicated nature involving for instance for instance, tedious accounts, or the unraveling of pedigree or the setting of a boundary accounts. Costs incurred by the Government and recoveries shall be credited to the Government.

(18) Documents filed should be marked as exhibits – Documents tendered by a party in evidence in a suit shall be marked as exhibits with a letter or number and attached in serial order to a separate exhibit list, which shall form part of the records of the case. Documents not so admitted shall be returned to the parties, and a receipt for them shall be taken in the list of documents filed by the parties.

(19) (1) Demand of security from the defendant – Security may in the discretion of the Court, be demanded from the defendant during the progress of a suit; and, if it is not furnished on demand, the property of the defendant, which would be attachable in execution of a decree, may be attached under these rules to the extent necessary to make good the security.

(2) Where the Court is satisfied that the order for attachment was obtained by misrepresentation or false allegation, the court may award the defendant such compensation as it deems suitable.

(3) Property attached before judgment need not be re-attached in execution proceedings.

20. Issue of a temporary injunction restraining the alienation or wastage of the property in the suit – Where in any suit the court is satisfied that any property in the suit is in danger of being wasted damaged or alienated by any party to the suit, or wrongfully sold in execution of a decree, the court may in its discretion grant a temporary injunction to restrain such act.

21. Appointment of receiver – the Court may if necessary appoint a receiver to hold or administer any properly pending determination of the rights of the parties thereto. If it does so, it shall fix the remuneration of the receiver and define his powers and duties.

CHAPTER IV

ARBITRATION

(22) Cases to be referred to arbitration- (I) Cases may be referred to arbitration with the consent of both parties, each naming one and a third being named by the Court. Arbitration named by the parties must be acceptable to the Court.

(2) The arbitration named by the Court shall preside and shall be in charge of the papers connected with the case. The arbitration may hold the enquiry where they please and in their own way, and shall report their award within a time to be fixed by the Court, or ask for an extension thereof. The court may, for good and sufficient cause, withdraw the case at any time before the award.

(3) Nothing herein contained shall debar the parties to any suit from referring their differences to any person or persons mutually agreed upon by them.

23 Issue of summons at the request of arbitration – At the request of arbitration the court may issue a summon to any witness to appear before them.

24. **(1)**Award of arbitration: - The arbitration shall give their award in writing and they may be summoned to explain it. Any explanation so given shall be recorded and from part of the record.

(2) An Award, whether unanimous or not, shall not be confirmed if fraud is proved or it is on the face of it contrary to the statutory law or the record –of-rights. In such cases the Court shall proceed to hear and dispose of the suit itself.

(3) Where the award is unanimous the Court shall, save in the cases mentioned in sub-rule (2) confirm it. Where the award is not unanimous the Court may, if it disagrees with it on any ground other than those mentioned in sub-rule (2) refer it to the next superior Court which shall, after giving the parties an opportunity to be heard pass such decision on the case as it thinks fit.

(4) An award when confirmed shall have the effect of a decree of the Court.

(25) Costs of arbitration to be realized – Penalty to arbitration – The parties may be required to deposit the reasonable costs of arbitration. An arbitration who has neglected his duty or has fraudulently concealed any interest of his in the case shall be liable to a penalty not exceeding Rs 50 which may be recovered as if it were due under a decree against him, and shall on realization be credited to the headman's reward fund.

(26) Decision of tribal council to be confirmed by subdivisional Officer – in a dispute decided by a local tribal council consisting of a Parganait as president of the council or the party in whose favour the disputes has been decided by the council may apply to the Subdivisional officer having jurisdiction over the matter for confirmation of the council's award. the Sundivisional Officer shall then obtain a statement of the dispute from the Parganait together with the award and after hearing the parties and the council may either confirm the award or pass such orders as he thinks fit. Such an award when confirmed shall have the effect of a decree of a court. No court fee shall be payable on such applications. All such applications must be made within a period of one year from the date of the council's award.

CHAPTER V

JUDGMENT AND DECREE

27. Money decree to be recovered in installment – In suits for the recovery of money other than rent, the court may at the time of passing the decree order that the payment of the amount decreed shall be made in one or more installment.

28. Details to given in judgment and decree – The Judgment shall contain a concise statement of the case, the points for determination, the decision thereon and the decree shall issue unless the suit has been dismissed for default under rule 12. The

decree shall agree with the judgment, shall contain the number of the suit, the names and descriptions of the parties and particulars of the claim, shall specify clearly and relief granted or other determination of the suit and shall embody any order passed by the Court in the matter of costs.

29. (I) Suit for restoration to possession of proprietary rights of tenants, rights transferred as security for money advanced as loan –(I) In a suit instituted for being restored to possession of proprietary rights of tenants, rights transferred as security for money advanced as loan, either on the ground of the expiry of the term for which the property had been transferred or on valid tender and payment of all outstanding dues, the court shall after due hearing and examination of the accounts pass such order as it thinks necessary in the circumstances of the cases, provided that no court shall entertain such a suit unless the right to transfer has been recorded in the record of rights and then only to the extent to which such right is so recorded, and is permitted by any enactment for the time being in force.

(2) Attachment of tenants, holding – Tenants holding of which the right of transfer had been recorded in the record of rights may be attached either before or after decree or sold in execution but only to the extent to which such right or transfer is so recorded and I permitted by any enactment for the time being in force. Before such rights are put to sale, the Court may pass an order allowing the judgment –debtor such time as it thinks proper to pay the decrial amount. If payment is not made by the date fixed, the court may pass an order for the sale of the tenant's rights but the sale must have the prior sanction of the Deputy Commissioner. The Court may in its discretion order the sale of such portion of the tenants' rights as will satisfy the decree inclusive of costs of an interest, if any.

(30) (I) The cost of the suit and interest after decree shall be a discretion of the Court and when costs are disallowed the court shall state the reason for it,

(2) Fees of pleaders or mukhtear – No pleader's or mukhtear fees shall be allowed as costs except only in cases where pleader's or mukhtear are entitled to appear as of right. The fees in such cases shall be based on the valuation of the suit and shall be assessed a not more than 2 ½ percent on such valuation subject to a minimum of Rs. 2

(31) Compensation for false claim- If the court finds in any suit that the claim or defence is false or vexatious to the knowledge of the party by whom it has been put forward, it may make an order for payment by the party by whom such claim or defence has been put forward to the other party of costs by way of compensation not exceeding RS. 5.

CHAPTER VI

WITHDRAWL AND COMPROMISE OF SUITS

(32) Withdrawal OF Suits – AT any time after institution of a suit the plaintiff may withdraw his suit or abandon part of his claim. If he withdraws the suit without permission of the Court, he shall be precluded from instituting a fresh suit in respect of the same subject matter or part of the claim.

(33). Compromise of Suits – At any stage of the suit, the parties may apply to the Court to pass a decree in accordance with the terms of a compromise, and a decree shall be passed accordingly provided that the terms are lawful (and) appear to the Court to be fair and equitable.

CHAPTER- VII

EXECUTION

(**34**) Execution of decrees – All question arising between the parties to the suit in which the decree was passed or their representatives, and relating to the execution, discharge or satisfaction of the decree shall be determined by the Court executing the decree and not by a separate suit.

(35) Imprisonment for debt at the cost of the decree –holder – There shall be no imprisonment for debt, but the Court, with the sanction of the Deputy Commissioner, may commit to civil jail at the cost of the decree – holder, as for contempt, a fraudulent male debtor of full age, who can but will not pay, may release him at any time, and may recommit him; and it may likewise imprison any judgment debtor who disobeys a decree ordering him to do or abstain from doing a certain act. The limit of imprisonment in such cases shall be three months, and imprisonment shall cease on payment of the amount due under, or on compliance with the decree. All imprisonment under this rule shall be simple.

36(1) Payment of a decree money not exceeding Rs. 25 – When a decree is given for an amount not exceeding Rs. 25 the court shall fix a date for the payment of the decretal amount by the judgment debtors to decree- holder in the presence of the court. If the judgment debtor does not appear does not pay the full amount on the date fixed and the decree-holder appears, the court may at once order attachment on the verbal application of the decree-holder and on receipt of the requisite process-fees.

(2) Decree to be executed on the written application of the decree-holder – Save as otherwise provided by any law for the time being in force, all other decrees are to executed on the written application of the decree-holder and a first application for execution must be accompanied by a certified copy of the decree.

(37) (i) Period of execution of a decree - Execution of a decree shall be taken out within a year, and if the decree is not satisfied execution may again be taken out at any time so long as a suit remains in force ; provided that, if there is a return of no effects to three successive orders of attachment decree shall become void unless the court execution it is satisfied that the judgment –debtor is fraudulently concealing property within its jurisdiction. If more than a year has elapsed since the date of the last application for execution, no action shall taken until the judgment debtor has been served with a notice calling on him to show cause against it.

(ii) Limitation of an installment decree- In the case of an installment decree the period of limitation shall be calculated from the date on which each installment is due for payment.

(38) Decree becomes void at the end of three years- a decree shall ordinarily become void, except as regarding pending proceedings, at the end of three years from the date of the decree, or where an appeal has been filed, from the date of the appellate decree:-

Provided that-

(a) Proviso in a suit for money valued at more than Rs. 50 the decree may on the application of both parties made at any time within three months of the date of the decree be continued in force for not more than six years in order to admit of payment by easy installments.

(b) Where a decree permits payment by installments or after a period of grace, the limitation of three years will commence from the date of the first default or from the conclusion of the period of grace allowed under the decree.

(c) Where a decree permitting payment by instalments contains a provision that on default of payment of any installment on due date the whole amount will fall due, the decree –holder may waive the penal provision and take execution of each installment as it falls due, but once he has exercised his option of realizing all the installment in default in one lump sum, he cannot relax it and limitation shall run from the date of the first default and the period of three years shall count from the date of such default.

39. Transfer of a decree for execution in another district – A decree transferred for execution from another district shall be executed under these rules, if passed in a suit valued at not more than Rs. 500 : and all previous proceedings shall be deemed to

have been regular, if the court transferring the decree certifies that satisfaction thereof has not been obtained by execution within its jurisdiction or where the decree has been executed in part, certifies the extent to which satisfaction has been obtained and what part of the decree remains unexecuted and also furnishes a certificate setting forth the value of the suit in which the decree was passed. Similar certificate shall be given in the case of decrees transferred for execution to other districts.

40. Attachment and sale of money and other properties of judgment debtor – Subject to the following exceptions, money and all property of a judgment- debtor which he is himself competent to transfer, may be attached and sold in execution of a decree namely:-

(a) Executions - The necessary wearing apparel, cooking vessels and bedding of judgment –debtor, his wife and children.

(b) The tools of an artisan and, where the judgment –debtor is an agriculturist, his implements of husbandry, seed grain, plough – cattle up to two pairs, and the food grain required by his family till the next harvest.

(c) The materials of kutcha houses and other building's belonging to and occupied by an agriculturist.

(d) The nets and one boat of a fisherman and one cart and pair of bullocks or buffaloes of a carter.

(e) The wage of a laborer or domestic servant;

(f) The stipends, gratuities, pensions, salaries, pay, allowances and Provided Fund deposits exempted by section 60 clauses (g), (i), (j),(k) and(o) of the code of civil Procedure.

(g) Crops on the field or on the threshing, unless the decree is for rent due on a raiyat s holding, in which case such crops may be attached, but only to the extent necessary to cover the rent payable for one year and the cost of attachment.

(h) Books of accounts

(i) Any right of personal service.

41. Attachment of movable property – In a first application for execution the movable property to be attached need not be specified but his shall be done in every subsequent application. The court may direct that movable property shall be attached before execution is taken out against immovable property.

42. (1) List of property to be attached and their sale – When execution is taken out against movable property the decree- holder or his representative accompanied by a peon or with an order on the headman and chukidar of village, shall proceed to attach the defendant's property in the presence of the defendant himself, if notified by beat of drums. A list of the property attached shall be prepared by or under the supervision of the head of the village, and a copy there of shall be given to the defendant or the representative at the time of the attachment, together with a notice that the sale of the property will be held date and at the places which have fixed by the Court as specified in the order of attachment. The date shall be so as to allow 15 days at least between the attachment and sale. The place may be the defendants village, or the nearest market place or the Sub divisional Court –house. the court may, if it thinks fit postpone fixing the day and place of sale until a return of the attachment has been made to it.

(2) Notice of sales to be affixed – In the absence of the defendant or his representative the list and the notice of sale be affixed to some conspicuous part of the house or homestead occupied by the defendant; or if the defendant has no house or homestead in the village or within two miles of it, in some conspicuous place in the village.

43. Entry in the house of judgment deflor- No person shall for the purpose of attachment enter a house after sunset and

before sunrise or break open any outer door, unless such house is in the occupation of the judgment debtor and he refuses or in any way prevents access thereto. But having entered he may break any inner door after giving the female occupants (if any) a reasonable opportunity to retire.

Explanation – A shop godown is not house within the meaning of this rule.

(44) (1)Attached property to be put in charge of a headman, etc. - Attached property shall be put in charge of headman, choukidar or substantial villager who shall give a receipt there for and produce the property in good order when required.

(2) Compensation for failure to produce the attached properly by the Custodian – If the Custodian fails to produce the attached property before the Court on the due date he shall be liable to pay compensation amounting to the value of the attached property such compensation shall be recovered from him as if it were a decree against him.

(3) Attached property to be brought to the court if no one be willing to take its custody – If no person can be found willing to take custody of the properties so attached the attaching peon will bring the property to the Court at once at the decree-holder's expense. In the event of the decree-holder failing to provide the necessary funds the attachment shall be withdrawn.

(4) Disposal of perishable goods – Perishable goods shall be disposed of at once on attachment.

45. (i) Sale of movable property – Every sale of movable property shall be held at the place and date fixed. The court or any person deputed by it shall preside at the sale.

(2) Allowance to auctioner of the sale takes place in the mufassil –Where the sale takes place in the mufassil an allowance not exceeding one anna in the rupee of sale-proceeds shall be granted to the auctioner but the aggregate of this allowance shall not exceed what may be considered a fair remuneration for his

trouble. Where the sale takes place at the Court house no such allowance shall be made.

(3) List of articles sold- A list of the articles sold, their prices and the purchaser's names shall be made and filed with the papers of the case.

46. Making of a return to the Court by the decree-holder- If the attaching decree holder does not make a return to the court by the date fixed, or if he does not report to the Court by the date fixed, the result of the sale in the mufassil satisfaction of the decree shall be entered.

47. Notice to be published for attachment of immovable property- Immovable property shall be attached by the publication of notices on or near the property and at the Sub-divisional Court houses, that the property is under attachment ; and if it revenue –paying land a copy thereof shall be sent to the Deputy Commissioner to be affixed at his Court house. On such publication any private transfer contrary to such attachment shall be void as against all claims enforceable under the attachment.

48. Notice to be published of the sale of immovable properly – Notice of sale of immovable properly shall be published in the same way as notice of attachment. Every such sale takes place in open Court not less than three weeks after the publication of the notices on or near the property. Attachment and sale notices may, if court thinks fit be issued simultaneously.

49. Notice of sale to contain details about the property to be sold and also about time and place of sale – Every notice of sale of immovable property shall state the time and place of sale and shall specify as fairly and accurately as possible:-

(A) The property to be sold

(B) The revenue assessed upon it, if it is land or an interest in land, paying revenue to Government

(C) Any encumbrance to which it is liable

(D) The amount for the recovery of which the sale is ordered and,

(E) Every other matter which the Court considers it material for the purchaser to know in order to judge the nature and value of the property.

50. Sale to be held auction- Every sale shall be held by auction and an upset price may be fixed by the court. No bid less than the upset price "(if any) shall be accepted without the order of the Court in the case of movable property the highest bidder shall, on his bid being accepted deposit the price on the say of sale; and in the case of immovable property he shall deposit one fourth of the price on the day sale and the balance within 14days.

51. Resale of property – If the highest bidder fails to make the deposit required by rule 50, the property shall be put to re-sale and, if the amount bid at the re-sale be less than the defaulters' bid the difference between the prices obtained at the first and second sales plus the costs of the re-sale shall be recoverable from the defaulter, as if it were due under a decree against him.

52. Decree-holder not to bid at the except with the permission of the court – The decree-holder shall in no case bid at a sale except without permission of the Court.

53. Setting aside of the sale (1) Any person owing the property or holding an interest therein by virtue of a title acquired before the sale, may, within 3 days from the date of sale apply to have the sale set aside on his depositing in Court.

(a) For payment to the purchaser a sum equal to 5 percent of the purchase money, and

(b) For payment to the decree-holder, the amount specified in the proclamation of sale as that for the recovery of which the sale was ordered, less any amount which may since the date of such proclamation of sale have been received by the decree-holder.

(2) Where a person applies under rule 54 to set aside sale he shall not unless he withdraws his application be entitled to make or prosecute an application under this rule.

(3) Nothing in this rule shall relieve the judgment –debtor from any liability he may be under in respect of costs and interest not convered by the proclamation of sale.

(4) If the sale is set aside the purchase money will be refunded to the purchaser.

54. Application for setting aside sale on the ground of fraud :- Where any immovable property has been sold in execution of a decree, the decree–holder or any persons entitled to a share in a ratable distribution of assets or whose interest are affected by the sale may apply to the Court to set aside the sale on the ground of material irregularity or fraud in publishing or conducting it.

Provided that such application must be made within 30 day of the sale; or in the case of fraud, within 3 days of the date on which the fraud became known to the applicant.

Provided further that no sale shall be set aside on the ground of irregularity or fraud unless the Court is satisfied that the applicant has suffered substantial injury thereby.

55. A sale certificated to be given to the purchaser after confirmation of the sale- when the sale of immovable property has been confirmed by the court a sale certificate shall be given to the purchaser in respect of such property.

56. Delivery of possession of the property sold-Delivery of possession of the property under a decree or after sale shall, if the property is moveable, be made by actual delivery of the same and, if it is immoveable and in occupancy of the judgment –debtor, by putting the purchaser or any person whom he may appoint to receive delivery on his behalf in possession of the property and if need be by removing any person who refuses to vacate the same, and if it is in the occupancy of a tenant or other person entitled to occupy the same by beat of drum on or near the property proclaiming to the occupant that the interest of the judgment –debtor has been transferred to the purchaser.

57. Satisfaction of the decree out of the sale- proceeds- After deduction of the reasonable costs of the sale the balance of the sale proceeds shall be applied in satisfaction of the decree, including cost and the excess (if any) shall be paid to the judgment –debtor.

58. Drawal of money by the decree-holder – The decree holder may draw the money due to him as follows:-

(a) if the property sold was moveable, immediately on conclusion of the sale or.

(b) if the property was immovable, after thirty days have expired and all objections (if any) have been decided.

59. Claim of a third party to the attachment and release of the property – Where a claim is preferred to any property or any objection is made by third party to the attachment thereof, the court shall investigate the claim or objection and if it satisfied that at the date of decree or attachment the property was in possession of the claimant or objector on his own account and not on account of the judgment –debtor the Court shall make an order releasing the property from attachment.

2. Stay of further proceedings after filing of objections- Where a claim or objection is made before the issue or proclamation of sale the court in its discretion may stay further proceedings and where it is made after publication of sale proclamation it shall postpone confirmation of sale until the claim or objection is decided.

3. If the claim or objection is allowed, then such sum as the court thinks proper, not exceeding the value of the property released, shall be deduced from the amount due under the decree and awarded to the claimant or objector as costs or compensation. If the claim is disallowed, then the decree-holder may be awarded against the claimant judgment –debtor or both such costs as may seen to the Court reasonable and equitable.

OOO

Chapter XI

S.No. 01. Chota Nagapur Recoreds

To,

The Principal Assistant to the Commissioner of Hazaribagh.

Sir,

1. In reply to your letter No. 584 dated the 3rd November, annexing copy letter No. 478 from the Commissioner of Chota Nagpur, dated 10th November, I have the honour to state that I do not think it would be advisable just now to set at large the Santals under surveillance at Hazaribagh.

2. I have no positive proof of the Santhal population of this district being in communication with the insurgents of Bheerbhoom and Bhagalpur, but the general impressions, both of the Zamindars and myself is, that the whole Santal Tribe are thus affected, and only wait for an opportunity to you those now in open rebellions.

These people inhabit localities usually close to jungle, adjacent to mountains streams, and apart from other natives, so that little of their natives are shown and since this rebellious other sects of natives seem to have a dread of them consequently little, or no communication and their misdeeds are unknown.

Burhee

The Magistrate' office

The 13th November 1853

I have the honour to be sir

Your most obedient servant

(Sd). Illegible

Comissioner, Hazaribagh.

S.No. 02.

From,

Commissioner of Chota Nagpore.

To,

Captain E. Sissmore
Offg. Principal Assistant Commissioner, Hazaribagh.
Dated. The Chotanagpore the 1st November, 1855.

Sir,

With reference to your letter No. 562, dated the 29th Ultimo, I have the honour to inform you that the nine Santhals now under surveillance at Hazaribagh may be released as soon as you and the deputy Magistrate at Burhee consider that they can be set at large with safety.

2 I wish to know whether the Santhals who came to Sirampore some time ago are still in Pergunnah Khurruckdeah, and if so, perhaps you will have the kindness to infrom me how they have conducted themselves since they have been in your Division.

2. Be so good as to ascertain from the deputy Magistrate at Burhee whether there is reason to believe that these fugitive Santhals have been in communication with the insurgent Santhals of Bhagalpore and Beerbhoom since they came into Khurruckdeah.

I have the honour to be
sir
Your most obedient servant
(Sd). Illegible
Commisssioner of Chota Nagpur

OOO

S.No. 03.

From,
The Secretary to the Govt. of Bengal.

To,
The Commissioner of Chotanagpur.
Dated, Fort Willion, the 10th November, 1855.

Sir,

I have the forward for your information six copies of a proclamation issued under this date declaring Martial Law in the disturbed districts.

I have & ca.
(sd) W. Grey,
Secretary to the Govt. of Bengal
(True copy)
(sd)Illegib
Offg. Uncood Assistant to the Commr.

ooo

Proclamation of Martial Law By the lt. Governor of Beugal

By the Lieutenant Governor of Bengal

The 10th November,1855.

Whereas certain persons of the tribe of Santhals and others, inhabitants of the Rajmahal Hills, of the Damin-i-koh, and of certain Pergunnahs in the district of Bhaugulpore, Moorshedbad and Beerbhoom and owing Allegiance to the British Government, are, and for some time post have been, in open Rebellion against the authority of the Government and whereas soon after the first outbreak of the said Rebellion, a Proclamation was issued offering a free pardon to all who should come in and submit within a period of ten days, except ring-leaders and persons convicted of murder, notwithstanding which act of clemency, the great body of the murder, notwithstanding which act of clemency, the great body of the rebels have not availed themselves of the offer of mercy thus held out, but continue in Rebellion wherefore it has become necessary for the speedy and effectual suppression of this Rebellion that advantage should be taken of the season to commence systematic military operations against the Rebels, for which purpose, it is expedient that Martial Law should be declared and that the functions of the ordinary Criminal Courts of Judicature should be partially suspended in the said districts.

It is hereby proclaimed and notified, that the Lieutenant Governor of Bengal, in the exercise of the authority given to him by Regulation X. of 1804 and with the assent and concurrence of the President in Council, does hereby establish Martial Law in the following District, that is to say:-

So much of the district of Bhaugulpore as lies on the right bank of the River Ganges.

So much of the District of Moorshedbad as lies on the right bank of the river Bhagirutee.

The District of Beerbhoom.

And that the said Lieutant Governor does also suspend the function of the ordinary Criminal Courts of Judicature within the Districts above described with respect to all persons, Santals and others. Owing Allegiance to the British Government, in consequence of their either having been born or being resident within its Territories and under its protection, who after the date of this proclamation and within the districts above described, shall be taken in arms in open hostility to the said Government, or shall be taken in the act of opposing by force of Arms the authority of the same, or shall be taken in the actual commission of any overt act of Rebellion against the State.

And that the said Lieutenant Governor does also hereby direct that all persons, Santhals and others, owing Allegiance to the British Government, who after the date of this Proclamation shall be taken as aforesaid, shall be tried by court Martial and it is hereby notified that any person convicted of any of the said crimes by the sentence of such Court will be liable, under Section 3, Regulation V. 1804, to the immediate punishment of death.

By order of the Lieutenant Governor of Bengal

W. Grey.

Calcutta November, 10th, 1855,

Thos, Jones," Calcutta Gazette"office
Secretary to the Govt. of Bengal.

OOO

4. Letter

No. 588

From,

The Commissioner of Chotanagpur

To,

Captain E. Sissmore
Officating Principal Assistant Commissioner, Hazaribagh.
Dated Camp –Prouleah the 3rd January, 1856.

Sir,

With reference to my letter No. 478 dated the 1st of November last. I have the honour to acquaint you, that I see no necessity for any further detention of the nine Santhal Manjhees now under surveillance at Hazaribagh.

2. From the inquiries which I made whilst I was in Khuruckdehah. I am dispose to believe that the Santhals who entered that Pergunnah in the month of August had been engaged in the insurrection, and they appear to have been in connection with the rebels after they took refuge in your Division.

3. These nine Santhals ought, I think to be sent to the Magistrate of the District to which they belong with instructions to release and send them to their provided they are not charged with any criminal offence in their own District.

I have the Honour to be
Sir,
Your most obedient servant. (sd)Illegible.

Commissioner of Chota nagpur

OOO

5. Letter

No. 89

Message received by Eletric Telegraph.
From Chuttra via Burhee,4th October, 9 a. m.
From Major English.
To Calcutta
To General Mansfield.

I came upon the Ramghur Mutineers at nine o'cock this morning, encamped on the West side of the town after the enemy, their guns are capture and their whole camp. We have taken four guns and wagons complete, ten elephants and much ammunition. Our loss is server, thirty-six of Her Majesty's 53rd and six of the Sikhs killed and wounded, all officers are safe, the men and officers behaved nobly.

Calcutta E. T. Office,
(sd) L. E. W. O'Brien
3R Assist. in charge
4th October, 1857, 9 P. M.

Secretary to the Government of India, Army Department

OOO

6. Letter

No. 152

Message received by Eletric Telegraph.
From Chuttra via Burhee,7th October, 8-30a. m.

From Major English.
To Calcutta
To General Mansfield.

I have moved my camp to the east of the Town on affine open plain. Major Simpson buried seventy seven of the enemy yesterday, and reports that above one hundred are lying wounded in the jungle and that the mutineers have dispersed. Two Susbadars were brought in yesterday mutineers have dispersed. Two Subadars were rough in yesterday and hanged this morning. For thesake of the wounded I shall return to Hazaribagh by easy march. The road is through Jungles in many places and my party very weak to escort the line of the Wounded, carts, guns and wagons. One hundred men would be great assistance, the guns will have to be dragged across many swamps and the road is very difficult; send me without delay Hospital bedding and clothing for thirty men, hospital comforts and two casks of Rum. Some treasure has been given over to Major Simpson.

(sd)L. E. W. O'Brien
ProHead Assistant in charge
Calcutta, E. T. Office,
7th October, 1857

OOO

7. Letter

No. 83.07

Message received by Electric Telegraph.

From,

Sherghatty, Saturday,
3rd October, 9-23 a.m.
From Lieutt. Stanton.
To Calcutta
To Secretary to the Government of India.

Following message received from Major English at Chuttra. I had a severe engagement yesterday with the Ramgragh Battalion, defeated them, taken four guns complete and forty five cartloads of ammunition. I have had forty five men killed and wounded, and am not strong enough to escort what I have through the Jungles surrounding me. Filled as they are with disbanded sepiys, and plunderers I take upon myself you to send me one hundred men if possible. Telegraph to Calcutta when you have done so. With reference to the above I have only twenty five Sikhs here. Shall I detain a detachment of Europeans and march on Chuttra to assist in bringing in the ammunition.

(sd) L. E. W. O. Brien,
3rd Assist, in Charge

Calcutta
Electric Telegraph Office,
The 4th of October, 1857.
Despd. 8-25

OOO

8. Letter

From,

The Commissioner of Chota nagapur.

To,

Captain E. Sissmore.
Offg. Prinl. Assistant Commissioner. Hazaribagh.
Dated : Camp Chyebassa, the 15th January, 1858.

Sir,

1. This day I have had the honour to receive your letter No. II date the 8th instant with enclosures and beg to infrom you

in reply, that I approve of the measures you have adopted towards the Santhals in pergannas Juggerssurpur. Rampoor, Singhpore and Tisree who are reported to be manufacturing arms and otherwise showing indications of disaffection.

2. There is probably much exaggeration in the statements of the petitioners, but it is desirable to obtain without delay as much credible information as possible regarding the proceedings of the Santhals in the Ramgurh Hills. I have therefore to request that you will immediately send some confidential and intelligent Native Officer to the Pergunnahs above mentioned to make inquiries into this matter. If it be true that those Santhals are making preparations to disturb the peace, you will have the goodness to proceed yourself forth-with to that part of the country with a Military Force sufficient to prevent the outbreak.
3. You are requested to institute very searching inquiry into the conduct of the Ammer's Department Hadgre Ishak, and he should not be permitted to return to the Mofussil till he has thoroughly cleared himself of these imputations.
4. Mohun Sonthal and Joyram Manjee should be immediately apprehended and kept under surveillance till they can be permitted to go at large without risk to the peace of the country.
5. Proclamation should be issued forthwith in the Pergunnahs above mentioned prohibiting, till further orders all blacksmiths and other from manufacturing arrows and other weapons of War of every description without the express permission of the authorities, and any wilful disobedience of this proclamation should be promptly and everely punised.
6. I have issued orders to the Maha Rajah of Ramngurh to affored the necessary aid and have called upon the service – Jagheirdars of the Ramgurh Estate to place at Rajah's disposal the quota of armed men which according to the terms of their respective engagements they are bound to maintain.

I have the honour to be
Sir,
Your most obedient servant.
(sd) Illegible
Commissioner of Chotanagpore.

ooo

Chapter XII

1. W. W. Hunter – Statistical Report of Bengal Santal Parganas-

CASTES- The following is a list of the principal Hindu castes in the Santal Pargunas, arranged as far as possible in order of precedence, showing the occupation of each caste. the number are taken **from the Census Repot of 1872:-** (1) **Brahman, members of the priesthoods;** many of them are also landholders, a d other are employed as ministerial officers by Government, and in a variety of respectable operations by private persons, number in (1872), **29,330**. (2) Rajput, the second or warrior case in the ancient Sanskrit social organization. At the present day, they are employed in various occupation**, 33,337** (3) Ghatwal, guardians of the hill passes **14,181** (4) Baidya hereditary physicians, but at the present day many of them have abandoned their employment and be taken them. selves to various respectable pursuits, **349**. (5) Bhat, herealds and genealogists, **757 c (6)** Kayasth, writers and clerk in Government and Private employ, and also engaged in other capacities, **5940.** (7) Babhan, employed in military service or as private guards, some of them are agriculturists, **102**. (8) Marwari, merchants and traders**. 1556**. (9) Agarwala, merchants and traders, **721**. (10) Gandhabanik, spice sellers, **4255.** (11) Bania, traders, **41**. The following nine (**12-20)** are the sub-divisionof the Bania caste:- (12) Barnawar, 357; (13) Changharia, **106**. (14) Kaparia,280. (15) Kasarwani, **52.** (16)

Kolapuri, **4** (17) Nauniyar, **394**. (18) Rauniyar, **134.** (19) Rabi. **36;** and(20) Sinduria, **125**. (21) Aguri, cultivators, 52. (22) Barui and Tambuli, betel sellers, **7320**. (23) Mali, gardeners and flower seller, **1262**. (24) Sadgop, cultivators, **1109.** (25) Napit of Hajjam, barbers, **12,338.** (26) Lohar or Kamar, blacksmiths, **14,870**. (27) Kumhar, potters **14,765.** (28) Thathera and Kansari, braziers, **402**. (29) Sankhari, workers of shell bracelets, **181.** (30) Teli, oil presser and sellers, **27,954.** (31) Chasa, cultivators, **6982.** (32) Goala cowherds and milkmen, **74,529**. (33) Kaibartta, agriculturists**, 2994**. (34) Kanai, cultivators, 610. (35) Kurmi, shopkeepers and agriculturists, **9777.** (36) Koeri, sweetmeat makers and cultivators, **9351.** (37) Kurar, cultivators, **2457,** (38) Nagar, agriculturists**, 211** (39) Net, cultivators, 433. They are supposed to be Nets who have given their nomadic mode of life and settled down to agriculture**, 429**. (42) Halwai, sweetmeat makers, **8524.** (43) Kandu, preparers and sellers of parched rice, **2121.** (44) Subarnabanik, goldsmiths and jewelers, **6865**. (45) Vaishnav, followers of Chaitanya a religious reformer in Nadiya who lived in the beginning of the sixteenth century, **6400.** (46) Gareri, apastoral tribe**, 112**. (47) **Gujar, 9**; a pastoral tribe of North–Western India. The nine Gujars recorded in the Census of the Santal Parganas were probably travelers. (48) Sunri or Suri, spirit seller, **18,242**. (49) Tanti, weavers, **4656**. (50) Barhi carpenters, **3456**. (51) Bautiri, ornament makers, **6**. (52) Laheri, lac-workers, **11.** (55) Sikalgir, cutler, **9** (56) Sonar, goldsmiths **3752**. (57) Behara, palanquin bearers and personal servants, **956**. (58) Kahar, palanquin bearers, **11,962**. (59) Dhanuk, personal servants, **12,429.** (60) Dhobi, washer men, **10,497**. (61) Jogi weavers, **3493**. (60) Dhobi, washermen, **10,497**. (61) Jogi weavers, **3493**. (62) Kapali, weaver, **42**. (63) Chapwal, weavers, **1089**. (64) Dhunia, weavers, **9** (65) Julaha, weavers, **698**. (66) Beldar, labourers, **683.** (67) Chundari, lime-burners, **298.** (68) Deohari, labourers, **18**. (69) Ekuar, labourers, **79**. (70) Kadar, labourers, **47**. (71) Kora, diggers, **2211.** (72) mareya, labourers **884,** (73) Matiyal, day labourers, 10. (74) Nuniya, makers of salt petre. **847.** (75) Pairagh, labourers, 1850. (76) Kandara, seller of fish and vegetables, **159**. (77) Metiya, fish sellers, **12**. (78) Pundari, seller of fish and vegetable, **23**. (79) Pura, fish, sellers, 136 (80) Jalia, fishermen and boatmen, **1147.** (81) Malla, fishermen and boatmen, 1865. (82) Kewat-Keut, finshmermen and boatmen, **1212**. (83) Gonrhi, fishermen, **895.** (84) Muriari, fishermen, **4.** (85) Naiya, boatmen, **40**. (86) Patni, boatmen, **744.** (87) Pod, fishermen, **39**. (88) Tier, fishermen and boatmen, **28367** (89) Surahia, fishermen, **855.** (90) Bajakar, drummers, **38.** (91) Baiti, dancers and singers, **310.** (92) Kan, singers, **8**. (93) Jadupeti, musicians**, 225**. (94) Khelta, dancers and beggars, **116**. (95) Kasbi, prostitutes, 4. A number of semi-Hinduised aboriginal classes, now ranked as very low castes in the Hindu social system, closes the list. These classes, are the following (96) Bargdi, **3507.** (97) Bahelia, **185.** (98) Bari, **118.** (99) Bauri **14,979.** (100) Chandal, **537.** (101) Chamar, **23,460.** (102) Bediya, **143.** (103) Bhuiya, **81,548**. (104) Bind, **2934**. (105) Chain, **17,576)** (106) Dom, **29,465.** (107) Dosadh, **8122.** (108) Gangaunta, **4.** (109) Hari, **6383.** (110) Karora**, 1958.** (111) Karanga, **1214.** (112) Khaira, **1172**. (1132) Koch, **3268**. (114) Labna, **17(115)** Mahili, **9521**. (116) Markande, **3044.** (117) Mukeri, **89.** (118) Musahar, **10,353.** (119) Paliya, **352**. (120) Pasi, **1716** (121) Rajwar**, 5080;** and (122) Mihtar**, 470.**

Carstairs' note on Settlement (Mcpherson)

The main object of the settlement was to settle. Accuracy was not as important as finality. It had to be carried out cheaply, for, in the first place, the government was bearing the expenses, and in the second, the rates of rent were too low to justify the cost of a detailed survey.

A survey involved a warm of surveyors and blackmail. The Santals, moreover, were opposed to a survey. No such thing had yet been ventured on, even in the Damin. For all these reasons, it was thought better to make an honest guess, at the risk of being wrong (indeed some of the guesses were wild), and stick to it, then to involve everyone in great expense, cause great delay, and incur much odium in the attempt to ascertain the exact truth by a survey.......

The records of rights were conclusive proof of any fact stated in it. There was for each village a separate record, of which a copy was given to the landlord, and another to the head of the village. For every village ren't-roll was ordered to be prepared, distributing among the tenants the lump-rent fixed by the Settlement Officer. For this purpose. The law required that the village panchayat (assembly) should be appointed ... In a great many villages of Godda (Subdivision) the plan broke down owing to the refusal of the villagers to serve in the panchayats. Mr Frederick Grant, the Sub divisional Officer, was accordingly deputed to frame rent-rolls for those villages.

Many years after, the settlement expert of the government was in Dumka (the headquarters of Santal Parganas) in connection with a revision of this first settlement ... For a long time he would not believe that there were no survey records of the settlement;... and in despair he asked if there was not still in the district someone connected with the settlement who could give information on the point. No one, he was told but Mr. Grant. So Mr Grant was consulted.

Mr. Grant: "Not exactly, but I framed rent-rolls. "

Expert: "And there were papers?"

Mr Grant:" Yes. "

Expert:" At last I have something tangible! Where are the papers?'

Mr Grant:" There are none now. "

Expert: “Why, what did you do with them?”

Mr. Grant:” I burned them all “

Expert:” Burned them? 1 Monstrous ! what on earth made you do such a thing so outrageous?”

Mr. Grant:” My orders were to do nothing to discredit the settlement, and my figures came out so different from the settlement figures that I burned them to save the credit of the settlement. ”

Clearly, in the interests of finality, this was the right thing to do.

Cited from the book of R. Carstairs entitled "The little world of an Indian District officer" London 1912.

Chapter-XIII

List of Santal Parganas
FREEDOM FIGHTERS
Early Revolutionaries

1. Basu, Mani
2. Basu, Usha
3. Basu Kalidas, Calcatta
4. Biswas Baidyanath, S/o- Durga Charan Biswas, clerk D. C. office, Dumka
5. Banerjee, Narendra Nath
6. Bakshi, Nani Gopal, Dumka
7. Bakshi, Gyanendra, Dumka
8. Banerjee, Govind, Dumka
9. Chakravarty, Prafulla
10. Chakravarty, Naren
11. Choudhry, Sayendra

12. Choudhry, Jyoti Pd.
13. Deuskar, Sakharam Ganesh, Karon, Jamtara
14. Dutt, Ullaskar, Calcutta
15. Devi, Sharanlata, M/O –Aurbindo Ghosh, Raydih, Rohini (Deoghar)
16. Dutta, Pratibha, Dumka
17. Dutta Haridas (his real name was Atul Chandra Nag), Dumka
18. Ghosh Aurbindo
19. Ghosh, Barindra, grandson, of- Rajnarayan Bose, Rohini (Deoghar)
20. Ganguly, Bipin, Dumka
21. Himmatsingka, Prabhu Dayal, Dumka
22. Haldar, Rasraj, clerk D. C. office, Dumka
23. Mukherjee, Anukul, Calcutta
24. Mitra, Bhav Bhusan
25. Mitra, Rajendra Narayan, Clerk D. C. office, Dumka
26. Mitra, Shrish Chandra, Calcutta
27. Sarkar, Sudhir Kumar
28. Sen, Sushil
29. Sen, Shailendra Nath
30. Sarkar, Surendra Nath, Dumka

Participants of Non-Cooperation Movement

1. Babu, Shyam Charan
2. Barar, Lokhan
3. Dey, Pramath Nath
4. Day, Prafulla Nath

5. Das, Narsingh
6. Jha, Binodanand
7. Jha, Buddihnath "Kairav"
8. Jha, Shivram
9. Lal, Rai Hari Prasad
10. Mandal, Sukhardi
11. Marwari Ramjas
12. Roy, Sashi Bhusan
13. Ray, Pramath Nath
14. Sen, Prafulla Chandra
15. Swami, Darshananand
16. Singh, Gorakh Prasad
17. Sharma, Muchkund
18. Sinha, Pramath nath
19. Singh, Roop
20. Sah, Jairam
21. Sah, Ramjanaki
22. Sah, Raghunath
23. Sah, Mangal
24. Sah, Mahavir
25. Sah, Manbodh
26. Saraf, Rameshwar Lal

Participants of Civil –Disobedience Movement

1. Babu, Raghu
2. Bhattacharya, Satyakali
3. Devi, Sadhna
4. Devi, Sharda

5. Dey, Pramath Nath
6. Devi, Saraswati
7. Hembrom, Sangram
8. Jha, Binodanand
9. Jha, Buddinath "kairav"
10. Jha, Barruchi
11. Jha, Dayanath
12. Jha, Radhika
13. Jha, Tarini
14. Kejriwal, Motilal
15. Lal, Jugal Narain
16. Mishra, Dwarikanath
17. Marandi, Ratu
18. Murmu, Raghu
19. Murmu, Jairam
20. Mukherjee, Lambodar
21. Mandal, Gopinath
22. Mishra, Dwarika Prasad
23. Mishra, Sujadhar
24. Mandal, Banarasi Prasad
25. Paharia, Kartik Singh
26. Paharia, Surya Singh
27. Paharia, Guhia singh
28. Purve, Chandrajit
29. Paharia, Surya Singh
30. Paharia, Radha
31. Paharia, Chandu

32. Pahari, Maisa
33. Paharia, Ram
34. Paharia, Resha
35. Paharia, Pandara
36. Rai, Shashi Bhusan
37. Singh, Vikku
38. Singh, Parmeshwar
39. Saraf, Rameshwar Lal
40. Surya, Sipahi
41. Sahay, Krishna Ballabh

Activists of Forward Bloc

1. Bose, Ashok Kumar
2. Bose, Shyama Prasad
3. Hembram, Lal
4. Hembram, Lagu
5. Mukherjee, Lambodar
6. Mukherjee, Usha rani
7. Mishra, Sarvanand
8. Murmu, Sukhu
9. Murmu, Paika
10. Murmu, Bhikhu
11. Manjhi, Alakhi
12. Roy, Amal (Dr.)
13. Tudu, Chandrai

Activists of Individual Satyagrah (1940-41)

	Name	Place
1.	Bhattacharaya, Satyakali	Jamtara
2.	Dalmia, Gauri Shankar	Deoghar
3.	Dokania, Brijlal	
4.	Hussain, Ulfat	
5.	Jha, Binodanand	Deoghar
6.	Jha Buddinath "Kairav"	Godda (Sanour)
7.	Jaiswal, Hari Prasad	
8.	Jha, Ratneshwar	Godda (Maheshpur)
9.	Kisku, Bhim	
10.	Kejriwal, Motilal -	Deoghar
11.	Kejriwal Mahadevi -	Deoghar
12.	Mishra, Ayodhya Prasad	
13.	Mishra, Yadav Chandra	
14.	Mishra, Bholanath	
15.	Mahto, Roopnath	
16.	Marik, Laljee	
17.	Nonia, Devchand	
18.	Paharia, Maisa	Sahibganj Damin
19.	Panday, Kripanath	Pakur
20.	Paharia, Gandolal	Damin-I- Koh
21.	Rajhans, Bhgwan Dutt	
22.	Ray, Bigu	
23.	Ray, Narsingh Prasad	
24.	Ray, Chando Prasad	
25.	Sah, Shrikrishna Prasad	
26.	Singh, Janki Prasad	

27. Singh, Kashi Prasad
28. Singh, Girjanandan
29. Thakur, Neelkanth

Those who were not arrested during the Individual Satyagrah (1940-41) but actively propagated the message of Congress-

1. Gopalnan K. , Kerala—Worked from Dumka
2. Hembrom Lal, Saraidaha, Shikaripada (Dumka)
3. Hembrom, Bariar, Saraidaha, Shikaripada (Dumka)
4. Jha, Ratneshwar, Maheshpur, Godda
5. Jha, Barruchi, Maheshpur, Godda
6. Jha, Suddhadev " Utpal" Maheshpur, Godda
7. Jha, Rudra Narayan, Dubrajpur, Godda
8. Jha, Devendra (Headmaster) Maheshpur Highschool, Godda
9. Jha, Kedarnath (Headmaster) Motia Highschool, Godda
10. Jajwarai, Ramraj, Deoghar
11. Jha, Mahendra Pd. , Pakaria, Godda
12. Jha Ram Pd. , Sanour, Godda
13. Jha, Tej Narayan, Lakhanpahari, Godda
14. Jha, Vijay Chandra, Maheshpur, Godda
15. Jha, Vijay Krishna, Amlo, Godda
16. Kejriwal, Motilal, Jasidih, Deoghar
17. Mandal, Jagdish Narayan, Buxra, Godda
18. Mishra Jaikant, Pratapur, Mahagama, Godda
19. Mishra, Sujadhar, Samukitta, Meharma, Godda
20. Mandal, Anirudha, Korka, Godda
21. Manjhi, Nandkishor, Hilawai, Godda

22. Mishra, Dwarika Pd. Sahibganj (Maheshpur Raj)
23. Mukherjee, Lambodar, Dumka
24. Mishra, Nityanand, Baratand, Jarmundi(Dumka)
25. Purve, Chandrajit, Purvedih, Poraiyahat (Godda)
26. Pathak, Sagar Mohan, Dumaria, Godda
27. Pandey, Bhuwaneshwar, Rohini, Deoghar
28. Pandey Satyanarayan, Sundmara, Godda
29. Patnaik Prafulla Chandra, Barapali, Sambalpur, Orissa
30. Singh, Parmeshwer, Panjwara, Banka
31. Singh, Ugra Mohan, Godda
32. Singh, Singheshwar
33. Sah, Ram Pd.
34. Sah, Srikrishna Pd, Mohanpur, Deoghar
35. Thakur, Prayagdutt, Lukluki, Godda

The above list is not exhaustive. Many others were engaged in the propagation of the message of the Congress.

List of the activists of Quit India Movement

1. Agrawal, Ganesh Pd. Sahibganj
2. Awasthi, Nageshwar, Deoghar
3. Agrawal, Devi Pd. Sahibganj
4. Arya, Baijnath Pd. Godda
5. Bose Ashok Kumar (Dr.), Dumka
6. Bhattacharya Satyakali, Mihijam
7. Baski Dhana, Latavar (Dumka)
8. Bhagat Jagarnath, Pakuria (Pakur)
9. Baskey Jata, Farhara
10. Besra, Singhrai, Kalikadar

11. Bose, Purnendu, Dumka
12. Baliyase, Shambhunath, Deoghar
13. Baliyase, Shiv Shankar, Deoghar
14. Banerjee, Umapati, Deoghar
15. Bhagat, Ramjanam, Godda
16. Bhagat, Ramjanam, Godda
17. Bhagat, Kedar, Sarauni, Godda
18. Bhagat, Suryanarayan, Sarauni, Godda
19. Bhagat, Chigar, Godda
20. Bhandari, Mundar, Sarba, Godda
21. Bhandari, Ram Pd. , Sarba, Godda
22. Bhagat, Birdeo Narayan, Kauri Ranbahniyar
23. Bhandari, Sunder, Godda
24. Bhandari, Lalji, Sarba, Godda
25. Bhagat, Nandkishor, Raghunathpur
26. Brahma, Pratap Narayan, Mahagama
27. Banwar, Dukhan, Devpahar
28. Bhagat, Sunder, Maheshpur (Pakur)
29. Barei, Ram Neresh, Sahibganj
30. Banerjee, Jagdish, Jamtara
31. Bhattachrya, Sunil Kumar
32. Bhui, Kisto, Jamtara
33. Babu, Mauni, Koeridih, Deoghar (Martyr)
34. Baskey, Jata, Amarpur, Ramgarh (Martyr)
35. Besra, Jeths, Singatand, Barharwa (Martyr)
36. Baskey, Bhima @ Langra Baskey
37. Chhabaria, Sitaram, Deoghar

38. Choudhary, Jailal, Nawadih
39. Choudhary, Suryanarayan, Motia, Godda
40. Choudhary, Deep Narayan, Motia, Godda
41. Choudhry, Ugralal, Godda
42. Choudhry, Jyotish Chandra, Mahagama
43. Choudhry, Ramavatar, Sahibganj
44. Choudhry, Ramshankar, Sahibganj
45. Choudhry, Bhagwan, Sahibganj

45.A. Choudhry, Randas, Sahibganj

46. Darve, Kalicharan, Sijua
47. Das, Balgovind, Deoghar
48. Dey, Madhusudan, Deoghar
49. Das, Vijay Kant, Godda
50. Das, Sahdeo, Godda
51. Das, Gajadhar, Godda
52. Das, Jageshwar, Mohani (Godda)
53. Dhangar Madhusudan, Jalboi, Lakarapahari (Martyr)
54. Dhobi, Guhia, Sahibganj
55. Dutt, Amlya Ratan
56. Dalmia, Gouri Shankar, Deoghar
57. Devi, Jambubati, Barapali, Sambalpur (Orissa)
58. Devi, Prema, Mohanpur, Deoghar
59. Gutgutia, Hari Ram, Deoghar
60. Goswami, Manmath Nath, Deoghar
61. Giri, Hariahar, Deoghar
62. Ghosh, Laxmi Narayan (Dr.), Palasi
63. Gope, Chunnilal

64. Gupta, Harihar Pd. Sahibganj
65. Gond, Sitaram, sahibganj
66. Gope, Titu, Jamtara
67. Grihi Kartik, Sindrijola, Godda(Martyr)
68. Himmatsingka, Ramjivan, Dumka
69. Hembrom, Lal, Pipra, Dumka
70. Hansdak, Konka, Sundraphalam (Dumka)
71. Hembrom, Lal, Saraidaha (Dumka)
72. Hansdak, Munshi, Patras (Dumka)
73. Hembram, Lagu, Palasi (Dumka)
74. Hembrom, Dhan, Ramkhuri (Dumka)
75. Hembrom, Prabhu
76. Hembrom, Baso, Mohulpahari, Pakur
77. Hansdak, Munshi
78. Hansdak, Prithivi
79. Hembrom, Bhado, Farhara
80. Hembrom, Thakur, Gadideoli
81. Hansdak, Pradhan, Amro
82. Hembrom, Rajam, Jordiha
83. Hembrom, Sunder, Amro
84. Hansdak, Bhudai, Kenchua (Martyr)
85. Hansdak, Kalidas, Kenchua
86. Hansdak, Munshi, Godda
87. Hembrom, Bhado, Saraidaha, Dumka (Martyr)
88. Hansdak, Konka, Sundraphalam, Shikaripara (Martyr)
89. Hembrom, Lagu, Palasi, Ranga Masalia (Martyr)
90. Hembrom Sundar, Nawadih (Martyr)

91. Hansdak, Kalidas, Amarpur, Ramgarh (Martyr)
92. Hansdak, Bhudai, Lakhanpur, Durgapur (Martyr)
93. Hembrom, Rajam, Jordiha, Ramgarh (Martyr)
94. Hansdak, Jitu, Busko, Dumka (Martyr)
95. Hansdak, Ragda, Lakhanpur, Pakur (Martyr)
96. Hembrom, Khaju, Durgapur, Pakur (Martyr)
97. Hansdak, Chand, Rakshi, Durgapur, Pakur (Martyr)
98. Hembrom, Bhagat, Rakshi, Durgapur, Pakur (Martyr)
99. Hansdak Ragda, Talbari, Durgapur, Pakur (Martyr)
100. Hembrom, Salkhu, Damakar, Godda (Martyr)
101. Hembrom, Lal, Pipra, Telo, Godda (Martyr)
102. Hembrom, Lapsa, Narayanpur, Karmatand, Godda (Martyr)
103. Jha, Buddihnath "Kairav", Sanour, Godda
104. Jajwarai, Ramraj, Deoghar
105. Jha, Hargouri, Deoghar
106. Jha, Chamaklal, Deoghar
107. Jha, Binodanand, Deoghar
108. Jha, Dashrath, Dumka
109. Jha, Kapileshwer, Dumka
110. Jha, Chhedi Pd. , Deoghar
111. Jha, Shivram, Deoghar
112. Jha, Laxmikant, Deoghar
113. Jha, Naresh, Sarath
114. Jaiswal, Hari Prasad, Deoghar
115. Jha, Sarveswar, Deoghar
116. Jha, Chalbal, Deoghar

117. Jha, Laxmishwar, Deoghar
118. Jha, Ratneshwar, Godda (Maheshpur)
119. Jha, Akleshwar, Deoghar
120. Jha, Suresh, Deoghar
121. Jha, Mahesh, Deoghar
122. Jha, Kamlakant, Godda
123. Jha, Kamleshwar, Godda
124. Jha, Mahendra Pd. (Pakaria), Godda
125. Jha, Ram Pd. Godda (Sanour)
126. Jha, Niranjan, Godda
127. Jha, Yudhisthir, (Baisarhi), Godda
128. Jha, Abhiram, Godda (Madhaiya)
129. Jha, Barruchi, Godda (Maheshpur)
130. Jha, Kedarnath, Godda (Motia)
131. Jha Vijay krishna, Godda (Amlo)
132. Jha, Karu, Basantpur, Godda
133. Jha, Maheshwar Prasad, (Lukluki), Godda
134. Jha, Sachchidanand Baisarhi, Godda
135. Jha, Devendra, Head Master, High School Maheshpur, Godda
136. Jha, Tej Narayan, (Maheshpur), Godda
137. Jha Vijay Chandra, (Maheshpur), Godda
138. Jha, Chiranjivi, Godda (Maheshpur)
139. Jha Chhotelal, Godda (Maheshpur)
140. Jha, Saputlal, Godda (Maheshpur)
141. Jha, Mahanand, Godda (Maheshpur)
142. Jha, Jatesh, Godda (Maheshpur)

143. Jha, Krishna Murari, Godda
144. Jha, Bhagwat "Azad", Kasba, Godda
145. Jha, Udit Narayan, Godda (Maheshpur)
146. Jha, Visnhu Kant, Deoghar
147. Jha, Arjun, Derma, Godda
148. Jha, Vijay Krishan, Amlo, Godda
149. Jha, Chandra Mani, Banarchua (Godda)
150. Jha, Kameshwar, Kasba
151. Jha Tripurendra, Kasba
152. Jha, Baikunth Pd. Mahagama
153. Jha, Nageshwar
154. Jain, Ratan lal
155. Kejriwal, Motilal, Jasidih
156. Kisku, Chhotu, Putkabra (Dumka)
157. Kisku, Barsha, Kashidih, Phulopani
158. Kisku, Durga, kashidih, Phulopani
159. Kumar, Darbari, Kashidih
160. Kumar, Dadhibal, Ghordand
161. Kol Katki, Lela Dhawatand (Dumka)
162. Kumar Lagan
163. Kasera Asharfilal, Deoghar (Martyr)
164. Khaware Trigunanand, Deoghar (Martyr)
165. Krean Parasmani, Deoghar
166. Kapri, Keshar, Deoghar
167. Kalicharan, Karamatand
168. Karmkar, Maniram, Hathigarh (Borio)
169. Kalwar, Narsingh, Sahibganj

170. Kurmi, Shivlal, Sahibganj
171. Kisku, Rengda, Kashidih, Phulopanui (Martyr)
172. Koeri, Manraj, Jogia Talab, Sahibganj (Martyr)
173. Kisku, Singra, Patra, Durgapur, Pakur (Martyr)
174. Layak, Bhudeo, Nakti
175. Layak, Anmani, Delipathar
176. Lal, Umesh, Deoghar
177. Lal, Vaidyanath, Deoghar
178. Lal, Brij
179. Lal, Baijnath, Deoghar
180. Lohar, Raghunandan, Sahibganj
181. Mishra, Panchanan, Deoghar
182. Mishar, Nityanand, Baratand, Jarmundi Dumka
183. Murmu, Mangal, Karmatand (Dumka)
184. Murmu, Ragda, Dharampur, Rajbandh (Dumka)
185. Murmu, Paika
186. Murmu, Bhikhu, Saraidaha (Dumka)
187. Murmu, Shiru, Ramkhuri (Dumka)
188. Murmu Ragda, Madara (Dumka)
189. Mukherjee, Lambodar, Dumka
190. Mishra, Sarvanand, Dumka
191. Marandi, Pagan, Dumka
192. Murmu, Bharat, Jamtara
193. Murmu, Lodga, Khijurdanga
194. Murmu, Champa, Pathra
195. Murmu, Suphal, Venaduti, Dumka
196. Marandi, Mangal, Mohulpahari, Dumka

197. Murmu, Suraiya, Pathria
198. Manjhi, Alkhi, Bhatania
199. Maraia, Darbari, Phulopani
200. Murmu, Barka, Ghati
201. Maraia, Diwan, Lilatari (Dumka)
202. Manjhi, Darogi, Shaltala
203. Manjhi, Dukhan, Lilatari (Dumka)
204. Murmu, Haridas, Karikadar
205. Murmu, Jetha, Thanpur
206. Marandi, Kanhu
207. Murmu, Luna, Mohulbana (Dumka)
208. Murmu, Pandu, Kashidih
209. Murmu, Somai, Gadideoli (Dumka)
210. Marandi, Saheba, Gardi
211. Murmu, Rupa, Kashidih
212. Murmu, Nuna, Mohulbana
213. Manjhi, Gulabi, Kusumdih
214. Mishra, Mahendra Pd. Deoghar
215. Mishra, Bhupnarayan, Deoghar
216. Mandal, Gopinath, Deoghar
217. Mandal, Kishori, Ghormara
218. Mandal, Umacharan, Ghormara
219. Mandal, Kunjbihari, Ghormara
220. Mandal, Ritlal, Deoghar
221. Mirdhaien, Viraji, Ghormara
222. Modi, Randev, Deoghar
223. Modi, Chhotelal, Rohini (Deoghar)

224. Mishra, Ayodhya Pd. , Deoghar
225. Mishra, Yadav Chandra, Deoghar
226. Modi, Vidyacharan, Deoghar
227. Mishra, Surendra, Lohardih
228. Mahato, Mangru, Manigarhi
229. Mahato, Birju, Sarwan
230. Mahato, Shanichar, Sarwan
231. Mandal, Pugari, Sarwan
232. Mahato, Mandu, Sarwan
233. Modi, Mahadeo, Deoghar
234. Murmu, Chandra, Tilaitand, Kathikund
235. Mishra, Mangalanand, Deoghar
236. Malviya, Kashninath, Katoria (Deoghar) (now Banka)
237. Mishra, Surendra, Deoghar
238. Mahto, Dukh Haran, Godda
239. Mandal, Gopeshwar, Deoghar
240. Mandal, Firangi, Deoghar
241. Mukherjee, Vimal, Deoghar
242. Mandal, Jagdish, Godda
243. Markandey, Firangy, Godda
244. Mistry, Premlal, Godda
245. Mandal, Shivcharan, Godda
246. Mishra, Ramji, Godda
247. Mandal, Mukund, Chorbad, Godda
248. Murmu, Mohan, Godda
249. Murmu, Chhotka, Godda
250. Murmu, Kisto, Godda

251. Mahto, Bhusan, Pipra, Godda
252. Mishra, Jichhu, Sonarchak, Godda
253. Mahto, Roopnarayan, Dhorichak
254. Mandal, Anirudh, Korka, Godda
255. Manjhi, Nandkishor Hilawai, Godda
256. Md. Musarraf, Mahgama
257. Mandal, Ramcharitra, Sarba, Godda
258. Marwari, Mangilal, Belbayan, Godda
259. Mandal, Ramcharitra, Buxra, Godda
260. Marwari, Onkarmal, Belbayan, Godda
261. Mandal, Banarasi Pd. , Godda
262. Murmu, Parcha, Godda
263. Mandal, Vishwanah, Buxra, Godda
264. Mandal, Rajkumar, Buxra, Godda
265. Mishra, Sujadhar, Samukitta, Godda
266. Mandal, Chandra Mohan, Fasia, Godda
267. Mandal, Surya Mohan, Fasia, Godda
268. Mahto, Devu, Nonbatta
269. Marwari, Nandlal, Belbathan, Godda
270. Mandal, Doman, Ramla
271. Mandal, Basudeo, Kurmichak
272. Mandal, Mahavir, Dumaria
273. Mandal, Kalanand, Poraiyahat
274. Mandal, Rameshwar, Hanuwara
275. Mishra, Bholanath, Pratappur, Godda
276. Mishra, Abhimanyu, Kasba
277. Mishra, Jabarlal, Godda

278. Marandi, Rattu, Khijuria
279. Murmu, Jaiarma
280. Murmu, Raghu
281. Murmu Tutu, Kaldah
282. Murmu Lodga, Maheshpur (Pakur)
283. Mishra Dwarika Pd. Sahibganj (Maheshpur Raj)
284. Mandal Chhedi, Sahibganj
285. Marwari Vanshidhar
286. Mahto Ganpat, Karmatand
287. Mandal Dukh Haran, Godda
288. Modi Vidya Charan, Manjhiladih, Sarwan (Martyr)
289. Murmu Mangal, Karmatand, Masanjore (Martyr)
290. Murmu Shiru, Ramkhuri, Kumrabad (Martyr)
291. Marandi Sundar, Sarsaria, Maharo (Martyr)
292. Murmu Nuna, Mohulbana (Martyr)
293. Manjhi Gulabi, Kusumdih, Dumka (Martyr)
294. Murmu Haridas, Amarpur, Ramgarh (Martyr)
295. Murmu Mangal, Ghati Narayanpur (Martyr)
296. Murmu Dheba, Kashidih, Phulopani (Martyr)
297. Murmu Kanhu, Garak, Dudhua (Martyr)
298. Murmu Narayan, Dumaria, Barharwa (Martyr)
299. Murmu Baju, Dumaria, Barharwa (Martyr)
300. Marandi Chandra, Singatand, Barharwa (Martyr)
301. Murmu Mohan, Lakhanpur, Durgapur (Martyr)
302. Mohli Lakiram, Durgapur, Pakur (Martyr)
303. Marandi Rattu, Khijuria, Rajmahal (Martyr)
304. Murmu Jhupru, Damakar Godda (Martyr)

305. Murmu Mohan Sagar, Chandna, Godda (Martyr)
306. Murmu Bhado, Pathardaha, Pakur
307. Murmu S. D. , Mihijam
308. Nag Haru, Sarwan
309. Newagi Laduram, Godda
310. Pandey Kedarnath, Ballampur
311. Prasad Radha Krishna, Deoghar
312. Patnaik Prafulla Chandra Barapali, Sambalpur (Orissa)
313. Pandey Satyanarayan, Sundmara, Godda
314. Pathak Sahdev, Deoghar
315. Pujari Ranglal, Deoghar
316. Pandit Harkhu, Banka
317. Pandey Jagdish, Deoghar
318. Pandey Gajanan, Chanan
319. Pandey Mathura Pd. , Chanan
320. Patralekh Nilai, Deoghar
321. Pathak Sagar Mohan, Dumaria (Godda)
322. Purve Nandkishore, Godda
323. Paharia Ganga Singh, Rajmahal
324. Roy Sashi Bhusan, Deoghar
325. Ray Ram Nishan, Manjhiaindih, Dumka
326. Rai Shukdev
327. Ray Angrej, Nankheta
328. Ray Dashrath, Delipathar
329. Ray Ganga, Paharpur
330. Ray Kishun, Delipathar
331. Ray Shukdev, Pandua

332. Ray Touji, Harhar
333. Ray Keshav, Kusumdih
334. Ray Bideshi, Pandu (Martyr)
335. Ray Nagdi Pd. , Sarwan (Deoghar)
336. Ray Kalicharan, Deoghar
337. Ray Aklu, Deoghar
338. Ray Vishwanath, Pandeydih
339. Ray Lakhi, Pandeydih
340. Ray Harkohan, Kenkhapra
341. Ray Chandreswari, Deoghar
342. Ray Nevani, Chitrapoka
343. Ray Kailcharan, Latasare
344. Ray Chandreswari, Raidih
345. Ray Jwala Pd.
346. Ray Saryu Pd. Deoghar
347. Ray Hemraj, Deoghar
348. Ray Birenchi, Deoghar
349. Ray Makhan, Benidih
350. Ray Jagdish, Deoghar
351. Ray Jawahar, Deoghar
352. Ray Kapileswar, Deoghar
353. Ray Harmohan, Deoghar
354. Ray Darogi, Deoghar
355. Ray Chando Pd. , Deoghar
356. Ray Devendra Pd. , Deoghar
357. Ray Rooplal, Deoghar
358. Ray Bigu, Deoghar

359. Ray Darpan, Deoghar
360. Ray Panchu, Deoghar
361. Ray Hargori Pd. , Deoghar
362. Ray Sahdev, Deoghar
363. Ray Sevaram, Deoghar
364. Ray Gajadhar, Deoghar
365. Ray Devendra, Deoghar
366. Ray Tikait, Deoghar
367. Ray Jaleshwar, Deoghar
368. Ray Pancham, Deoghar
369. Ray Shobhi, Deoghar
370. Ray Chhatradhari, Deoghar
371. Ray Gangadhar, Deoghar
372. Ray Prahlad, Deoghar
373. Ray Varda Pd. , Godda
374. Ram Gadadhar, Godda
375. Ray Shridhar, Godda
376. Raut Bhuwaneshwar, Birnia, Poraiyahat
377. Ramtatpa, Birnia, Poraiyahat
378. Ramdas Gangadhar, Godda
379. Ramdas Bhairav, Godda
380. Ram Ambika Pd. , Lorhi
381. Ram Shiv Narayan, Amour
382. Ram Bhikahari, Mahaur
383. Ram Mahadeo, Godda
384. Ray Ramanand, Jamtara
385. Raut Yadu, Jamtara

386. Raut Najju, Mohanpur, Deoghar (Martyr)
387. Ray Vidhu Bhushan, Amarpur, Jasidih (Martyr)
388. Raut Ayodhya, Rohini, Deoghar (Martyr)
389. Ray Bideshi, Siltha, Ramgarh (Martyr)
390. Singhania Nathmal, Deoghar
391. Sharma Badrinath, Deoghar
392. Sah Srikrishna pd. , Mohanpur, Deoghar
393. Singh Jagdish Pd. , Sikitia
394. Singh Awdhesh Pd.
395. Sharma Aagar, Dumka
396. Soren Lapsa, Palasi (Dumka)
397. Soren Khela, Palasi (Dumka)
398. Soren Bajun
399. Soren Matla, Pathardaha, Pakur
400. Soren Ram
401. Soren Bhattu, Kashidih, Phulopani
402. Soren Rasik, Kashidih, Phulopani
403. Soren Durga, Lagla, Nawadih
404. Soren Dipti, Nawadih
405. Saraf Rameshwar Lal, Sarwan (Deoghar)
406. Singh Ganga, Deoghar
407. Shastri Haridev, (Deoghar)
408. Singh Baleshwar Pd. , (Deoghar)
409. Sah Baijnath, (Deoghar)
410. Singh Bhairavnath Deoghar
411. Singh Janki Pd. , Sabaijore
412. Singh Bholanath, Deoghar

413. Sah Badri Pd. , Sarwan
414. Singh Abha, Deoghar
415. Shastri Ramnarayan, Deoghar
416. Singh Purusartha, Deoghar
417. Sah Shiv Sharan, Deoghar
418. Singh Ayodhya, Deoghar
419. Singh Parmanand, Deoghar
420. Singh Raghuvir, Chitrapoka
421. Singh Umesh Pd. , Dumka
422. Singh Anandi, Kevankathi
423. Singh Ram, Kevankathi
424. Singh Yamuna, Kevankathi
425. Sharma Anant, Deoghar
426. Singh Rameshwar, Deoghar
427. Singh Vikramaditya, Deoghar
428. Sah Bhagwan, Deoghar
429. Sah Ramjivan, Deoghar
430. Sah Chhotelal, Bagdat
431. Sonar Nathmal, Deoghar
432. Sah Sundar, Deoghar
433. Singh Ramcharitra Vidyarthi, Deoghar
434. Singh Kashinath, Deoghar
435. Singh Baleswar, Deoghar
436. Singh Hemraj Pd., Deoghar
437. Singh Yatindranath, Deoghar
438. Singh Kameshwar Pd., Deoghar
439. Singh Awadhesh Pd., Deoghar

440. Singh Raj Narayan, Deoghar
441. Singh Kalevar, Deoghar
442. Singh Indra Narayan, Deoghar
443. Singh Yadav Pd., Deoghar
444. Singh Banke Bihari, Deoghar
445. Singh Dineshwar Pd., Deoghar
446. Singh Shanti, Deoghar
447. Singh Indra, Deoghar
448. Singh Jitendranath, Deoghar
449. Singh Jagdamba, Deoghar
450. Singh Dwarika Pd., Deoghar
451. Singh Vakil Pd., Godda
452. Singh Durga Pd., Godda
453. Singh Parmeshwari, Godda
454. Sah Kedarnath, Godda
455. Sah Ganesh Pd., Godda
456. Sah Ramkishor, Godda
457. Sonar Prahlad, Godda
458. Singh Viswanath, Godda
459. Soren Viswanath, Godda
460. Soren Ganga, Godda
461. Sao Santoshi, Birnia, Poraiyahat
462. Singh Chandar, Deoghar
463. Sharma Ramadhikari, Deoghar
464. Singh Singheshwar, Godda
465. Sah Ram Pd., Godda
466. Singh Indradev, Godda

467. Singh Mittu, Rangania, Godda
468. Singh Laro, Rangania, Godda
469. Singh Parsuram, Godda
470. Sah Charan, Patna
471. Sah Narsingh, Ramla
472. Sah Shaligram, Sondiha
473. Singh Nageshwar, Khirondhi
474. Sheikh Kudrat, Godda
475. Sheikh Mushrali, Godda
476. Santalia Jagdish Pd., Mahagama
477. Singh Jagdish Pd., Rajmahal
478. Singh Hareshwar Pd., Rajmahal
479. Sah Nand Kishor
480. Soren Bajun, Chhota Kendua
481. Singh Fani Bhushan, Maheshpur (Pakur)
482. Singh Niranjan, Maheshpur (Pakur)
483. Sah Ramji, Sahibganj
484. Singh Bhup Narayan, Sahibganj
485. Sonar Chunnilal, Sahibganj
486. Sah Bishweshwar, Jamtara
487. Sah Kanhai Pd., Jamtara
488. Sah Shiv Pd., Jamtara
489. Singh Devi, Ghati Narayanpur
490. Sah Kali Pd., Jamtara
491. Sen Bamapada, Jamtara
492. Sen Kisto, Jamtara
493. Singh Madhav, Mahtodih, Deoghar (Martyr)

494. Soren Shiva, Talwa Pakuria (Martyr)
495. Soren Nuna, Latvidha, Rajbandh, Shikaripara (Martyr)
496. Soren Manjhi, Singatand, Barharwa (Martyr)
497. Soren Chaitanya, Albari, Durgapur, Pakur (Martyr)
498. Soren Ragda, Vrindavan, Tin Pahar (Martyr)
499. Soren Somay, Kathaldih, Godda (Martyr)
500. Soren Dugga, Mangalgarh, Boarijore Godda (Martyr)
501. Soren lakhan, Bhagwanpur, Telo, Godda (Martyr)
502. Thakur Shaligram
503. Tibrewala Sedmal
504. Tudu Baiman, Beseriam, Dhanbasa
505. Tudu Gurma, Kushpahari, Barmasia (Dumka)
506. Tudu Tumu, Pathra (Dumka)
507. Tudu Chhandrai, Dhakajal (Dumka)
508. Tudu Khudu, Nargitola
509. Tiwari Shambhunath, Devinagar (Pakur)
510. Tiwari Vachaspati, Devinagar (Pakur)
511. Tiwari Kapildev
512. Tiwari Balmiki, Devinagar (Pakur)
513. Tudu Khepa, Mohulbana (Dumka)
514. Tudu Ludhu, Amro
515. Tiwari Bhagwa, Godda
516. Thakur Prayagdutt, Lukluki, Godda
517. Tiwari Ramdeo, Pathargama, Godda
518. Tiwari Sinhasan, Godda
519. Thakur Rasiklal, Bhalsumia, Godda
520. Thakur Gadadhar, Basantpur, Godda

521. Tudu Dularchand, Boarijore, Godda
522. Tandon Jagannath, Chaura
523. Thakur Krishna Mohan, Banarchua
524. Tibrewala Giridhari Lal, Mahagama
525. Tiwari Laljit, Khatni
526. Thakur Umacharan, Sundmara, Godda
527. Thakur Neelkanth, Pakso, Godda
528. Tudu Khudu, Maheshpur (Pakur)
529. Teli Baijnath, Sahibganj
530. Tudu Shyam, Bishanpur, Amrapara(Martyr)
531. Tudu Baiman, Bisarim, Shikaripara (Martyr)
532. Tudu Gurma, Kushpahari, Shikaripara (Martyr)
533. Tudu Churka, Asanbani, Dumka (Martyr)
534. Tudu Luthu, Amro, Dumka (Martyr)
535. Tudu Baijnath, Dumaria, Barharwa (Martyr)
536. Tudu Ragda, Virajpur, Durgapur (Martyr)
537. Tudu Chandrai, Bara Pipra, Telo, Godda (Martyr)
538. Thakur Shaligram
539. Tibrewala Sedmal
540. Tudu Baiman, Beseriam, Dhanbasa
541. Tudu Gurma, Khushpahari, Barmasia (Dumka)
542. Tudu Tumu, Pathra (Dumka)
543. Tudu Chaandrai, Dhakajal (Dumka)
544. Tudu Khudu, Nargitola
545. Tiwari Shambhunah, Devinagar (Pakur)
546. Tiwari Vachaspati, Devinagar (Pakur)
547. Tiwari Kapildev

548. Tiwari Balmiki, Devinagar (Pakur)
549. Tudu Khepa, Mohulbana (Dumka)
550. Tudu Ludhu, Amro
551. Tiwari Bhagat, Godda
552. Thakur Prayagdut, Lukluki, Godda
553. Tiwari Ramdeo, Pathargama, Godda
554. Tiwari Sinhasan, Godda
555. Thakur Rasiklal, Bhalsumia, Godda
556. Thakur Gadadhar, Basantpur
557. Tudu Dularchand, Boarijore, Godda
558. Tandon Jagannath, Chaura
559. Thakur Krishna Mohan, Banarchua
560. Tibrewala Giridhari Lal, Mahagama
561. Tiwari Laljit, Khatni
562. Thakur Umacharan, Sundmara, Godda
563. Thakur Neelkanth, Pakso
564. Tudu Khudu, Maheshpur (Pakur)
565. Teli Baijnath, Sahibganj
566. Tudu Shyam, Bihanpur, Amrapara (Martyr)
567. Tudu Baiman, Bisarim, Shikaripara (Martyr)
568. Tudu Gurma, Kushpahari, Shikaripara (Martyr)
569. Tudu Churka, Asanbani, Dumka (Martyr)
570. Tudu Luthu, Amro, Dumka (Martyr)
571. Tudu Baijnath, Dumaria, Barharwa (Martyr)
572. Tudu Ragda, Virajpur, Durgapur (Martyr)
573. Tudu Chandrai, Bara Pipra, Telo, Godda (Martyr)
574. Upadhyay Viswanath, Dumka

575. Vaid Haldhar, Buxra, Godda

576. Vaid Sahdeo, Godda

577. Vidyarthi Sudhir Chandra, Karmatand

578. Yadav Mishry, Godda

579. Yadav Jayanti Pd. , Pathargama

Note- The list is not exhaustive. Innumberable persons participated in the Quit India Movement & propagated the message of Independence.

OOO

Chapter-XIV

The List of (Martyrs)

1. **Baskey Jata :-** Jata Baskey, the son of Sri Jarya Baskey was born at Amro under Amarpaur Circle, block. Ramgarth Dumka. He was Injured in the Police firing on 17th February 1943 when he was guarding on the down steps of the hill where the freedom fighters of "Lathi Pahar" struggle had camped. Severely injured Jata was brought back to home for herbal treatment where he died on 27th Feb 1943.

2. **Baba Mouni:** - A very handsome saintly person came to Dumka 2 or 3 months ago during the August revolution of 1942 Started. He was supposed to live earlier near Koeridih under Deoghar district. He lived in a vacant garage of Mr. Grant British force was called in Dumka to quell the revolt in September 1942. Mauni Babas dead body drenched in blood was found near the garage. He was brutally killed by the British force.

3. **Baskey Benjivan:-** Baskey Benjivan, the son of Sri K. K. Baskey, was born at the village Kumari under Sanal Parganas. He was the Lieutenant of the reinforcement group of Indian National Army. He was killed by the British Army.
4. **Baskey Bhima:** - Bhima Baskey alias Langra Baskey was the son of Sri Ramna Baskey. He was born at Narayanpur under the district Jamtara. He fell ill in undertrial situation. He died of illness in Dumka jail in September leaving two sons namely Ramna Champa and daughter.
5. **Dhandar Madhusadan:** - A Resident of the village Jalboi, Po. - Lakrapahari died in Dumka jail in the age of forty year. He left behind his widow Mandari Devi & two young daughters.
6. **Hansda Bhudai:-** S/o Sri Kaildas Hansda Resident of village – Kenchua (Santal Parganas) actively Participated in the Quit India Movements, Bhudai Hansda. Was arrested along with his father and sent to the Munger Reformatory jail for five years. His health started deteriorating there. The Jail Officer sent him back to Dumka Jail where met a premature death on 26th May 1944.
7. **Hansda Chand:-** Chand Hansda was born at the village Rakshi under Durgapur Bunglow. He was arrested on 9th May 1943 and sent to Rajmahal jail for his active involvement in the Quit India Movement. Police along with the Parganaits looted and burnt his house. He left on 14th Jan. 1944 in Dumka at the age of only thirty five years.
8. **Hansda Kaildas:-** Kaildas Hansda, the resident of Kenchua under the circle Amarpur (Santal Parganas) was arrested along with his minor son in the course of Quit India Movement. His health deteriorated vastly due to inhuman treatment of police in jail. Police released him from jail. He died shortly after his release.

9. **Hansda Konka:-** Konka Hansda belonged to the village Sundraphalam under Shikaripara block under Dumka district. His father's name was Tala Hansda. He succumbed to Police firing during the Rajbandh Palasi picketing. On 5th September 1942. He was only 20 years old when he slept forever.

10. **Hansda Jitu:** - Jitu was the resident the village Busko under Amarpur circle. He was arrested during the Quit India Movement. He died of dysentery in Buxar jail at the age of 28 leaving behind his wife and a daughter named Duli Hansda.

11. **Hansda Ragda:** - Ragda Hansda S/o Rasik Hansda was a native of the village Talbari under Durgapur Bunglow. He was Safa Hor. He died in Rajmahal jail due to police atrocity leaving behind his wife and two sons.

12. **Hembrom Bhagat:-** A staunch Safa Hor Bhagat Hembrom S/o Anup Hembrom was native of the village Rakshi was arrested on 9 May 1943 due to his struggle in Quit India Movement and convicted for a period of three years imprisonment. He fell a prey to Police atrocities inside the jail and died on 2 May 1944.

13. **Hembrom Bajun:-** Baijun Hembrom S/o Ledha Hembrom, the native of Pattarbara was arrested due to active participation in picketening during Quit India Movement and sent to jail, where he died in December 1942.

14. **Hembrom Lal:-** Lal Hembrom was a native of the village Bara Pipra under. Telo banglo of the subdivision Godda. He was arrested for his leading activities of Forward Bloc in the Bhagalpur central jail. Uprising look place in the jail on 4 September 1942. He was killed in the police firing in the jail.

15. **Hembrom Lapsa:-** Lapsa Hembrom S/o Sugda hembrom was a native of the village Narayanpur under Karmatand

Bunglow under Godda subdivision. The S. D. O., Godda along with some paraganaits and armed forces encircled the village at night and arrested Lapsa Hembrom along with other villagers. Langra Baskey, Kandana Hembrom, Doma Baskey and others. The S. D. O. got the village looted by the armed forces. Lapsa Hembrom was kept under trial in jail for many months. Ultimately the atrocities tok away his life in Dumka jail. When he died, he was of 45.

16. **Hembrom Bhado:-** Bhado Hembrom was born to Sri Fagu Hembrom and Mrs. Noha Marandi. He hailed from the village Saraidaha under the Barmasia Circle, block-Shikaripara under Dumka district. Since he belongs to a very pious and religious Safa Hor family he inherited the same quality. He was a very prestigious person of the area; He is accredited to have worked for prohibition and social reforms. He worked equally in social as well as political field. He was elected the member of District committee on the congress ticket. When Quit India Movement started, he instinctively jumped into it. On 5th September 1942 British forces reached Saraidaha to know where about of his son Lal Hembrom and trembled the aged person, but he refused to divulge the facts resulting in his arrest. He was convicted for four years rigorous imprisonment and sent to Bhagalpur Central Jail, where he died on 7th September 1943. He left behind two sons Lal Hembrom and Bariar Hembrom, who later become MLA.

17. **Hembrom Lagu:-** Lagu Hembrom, S/o Paru Hembrom hailed from the village Palasi under P. S. Ranga Masalia, under Dumka subdivision. He was arrested for picketing liqnor shops. He was kept under trial for six month and later convicted for a one year's rigorous imprisionment. He died in September 1943 a day after his realease from prison.

18. **Hembrom Salkhu:** - Salkhu Hembrom S/o Ondrope Hembrom was a native of the village Damakar under Bokrabandh Damin Bunglow. Salkhu Hembrom Jumped into the Quit India Movement due to the inspiration of Prafulla Chandra Patnaik. He was arrested for burnring liquor shops and attacking government building in August 1942 and sent to the Godda jail where he died after a couple of days due to illness.

19. **Hembrom Sundar:-** Sundar Hembrom, S/o Sardar Hembrom was a native of Nawadih village under the Amarpur Circle. He was arrested for his hectic activities in the Quit India Movement and the "Lathi Pahar "struggle and sent to Buxar jail, where he died at the age of only 34.

20. **Hembrom Rajam:-** Rajam Hembrom, S/o Durga Hembrom was born in the village Jordiha under P. S. Ramgarh. He was convicted for a terms of 5 years in connection with the "Lathi Pahar" struggle. He died of dysentery in Dumka jail on 8 August 1943 leaving behind eight members in the family. His son was Babaram Hembrom.

21. **Hembrom Khaju:-** Khaju Hembrom S/o Laghu Hembrom was the resident of the village Pattra. Khaju Hembrom's brother Daro Hembrom was a chowkidar. He turned a traitor and got his brother arrested by the Police Khaju was sent to the Dumka Jail where he died. It is really tragic to note that when he was in the jail, his wife and son died leaving two unmarried daughters in precarious conditions in the hand of Daro Hembrom, who illegally occupied his entire property.

22. **Hansda Ragda:-** Ragda Hansda, S/o Salkhu Hansda was a resident of the village Lakhanpur under Durgapur Bunglow. He was a Saphahor and involved actively in Quit India Movemnt. His Wife Rani Soren was mentally retarded and

the house was taken care of by his son in law John Kisku. He was arrested in August 1942 and sent to Dumka Jail, Where he died. The Police assisted by the Christian parganaits looted his houses and damaged everything in the houses.

23. Grihi Kartik:- Kartik Grihi S/o Surya Grihi was the resident of Sindarijola, under Godda subdivision. He belonged to the Mal Pahariya tribe. He had been working for Congress for a long time. He was arrested for burning the Alubera Bunglow during the Quit India Movement. The Police looted and burst his houses and left his family as beggar. He died in prison in Pakur jail after nine months of illness on 23rd Mrch 1943.

24. Kisku Rengha:- Rengha Kisku S/0 Uday Kisku was a resident of Kashidih Phulopani. He was an active worker of Quit India Movemn. He was arrested and convicted for six monhs imprisonment. He was sent to Dumka jail where he died at 50 leaving behind a son Munshi Kisku a daughter.

25. Khaware Trigunanand:- Trigunanand Khaware, S/o Thakur Prasad Khaware belonged to Maithil Brahmin family of Deoghar. He was a Panda by profession. His was a prestigious family with influence on the Panda society. He favoured the removal of social disabilities from the Panda society. He gave his room for the Congress office at Deoghar during the Salt Satyagrah in 1930 His brother Gaya Prasad Khaware was a freedom fighter, and was sent to jail for many times. During the course of Quit India Movement on 26 August, 1942, a bullet hit a minor Bengali boy named Purnendu Bose drenched in blood fell on the ground, Trigunand Khaware immediately rushed to the boy to take him. The next moment another bullet hit the thigh of Khaware and passed though it Khaware was rushed to Dumka hospital where he succumbed to the injury and died on 8 Sepetmber 1942.

26. **Kisku Singrai :-** Singrai Kisku, S/o Dhanai Kisku was a resident of the village Patra under the Durgapur Damin Bunglow. He dedicatedly worked in the struggle against the British rule in 1942. The brave son of mother India Singrai Kisku, who was a Safa Hor, was arrested in May 1942 and sent to Rajmahal jail, where he died in December 1942.

27. **Koeri Manraj:-** Manraj Koeri alias Dhela Koeri was resident of the village Jogia Talab under P. S. - Sahibhanj Mirja Chowki. He became a victim of Tomy's indiscriminate firing on the people assembled at hatia, the casual village market at Sherwani near Pirpainti railway station.

28. **Kasera Ashrfilal:-** Ashrfilal Kasera S/o Koko Sah was the resident of Deoghar. He was a Shopkeeper and a vaishya by caste. He was interested in wrestling since his child. He was a member of the "Mahabir dal" in Deoghar. He succumbed to the Police firing during the agitation in Deoghar on 26th August 1942 at 10 o'clock at night leaving behind the widow Bhagwati Sahuaine under the care of his elder brother Banarasilal Sah.

29. **Mahto Ganpat:-** Ganpat Mahto, S/o Mangru Mahto was a native of Karmatand under Jamtara subdivision. He was attracted to congress during the Non-cooperation Movement and kept actively working since then he was jailed in 1922 and 1932. Ramcharitra "Vidyarthi" gave him the nickname of "Jamvant". He was jailed twice in the Quit India Movement. He refused to go back to home till "Swaraj" was achieved. He was arrested in 1944 and sent to Deoghar Jail where he fell ill. He was shifted to Deoghar Hospial where he died. The police seized his property at his native village worth Rs. 500/- during the period he evaded arrest and auctioned the same for Rs. 150/- His last rites were performed at the Shaheed Ashram, Deoghar.

30. **Manjhi Gulabi:-** Gulabi Manjhi the naïve of the village Kusumdih under Amarpur circle of the Dumka subdivision, was arrested by the Police in suspicion and sent to Dumka jail as an under trial prisoner. His health started deteriorating due to Police torture in jail as a result of which he died in Dumka jail in 1942 at the age of 24. He left behind his wife. He actively partieipated in the Quit India Movement left behind his wife. He participated actively in Quit India Movement. He belonged to Khetauri caste. The Police looted his house and land took away his belonging kitchen tool, grains & cattles.

31. **Marandi Chandra:-** Chandra Marandi S/o Basu Marandi was resident of the village Shingatarn under Bunglow Range. He actively took part in Quit India Movement and was taken into custody. He was sent to Rajmahal jail where he died on 25th March 1944 at the age of 42. He left behind him four daughters and two sons namely Mangal Marandi and Jitu Marandi.

32. **Marandi Kanhu:-** Kanhu Marandi was a resident of the village Garak under Dudhu Talak under P. S. - Ramgarh. He was convicted for Five years rigourous imprisonment for his active involvement in "Lathi Pahar" Struggle and sent to Buxar jail where he died at the age of only 36 leaving behind his widow and a son named Gopin Marandi in Precarious economic conditions.

33. **Marandi Ratthu:-** Ratthu Marandi S/o Sitaram Marandi hailed from the village Khijuriya under the Banjhi Damin bunglow. He was a staunch religious Hindu as well as a Gandhian. He worked with the Congress since the days of Non-cooparation Movemnet in 1921. He worked under the leadership of Prafull Chandra Patnaik. He was arrested in 1942 and sent to Rajmahal jail, where 176 prisoners had been kept

in the space of 35 prisoners. The inhuman treatment, lack of minimum facilities in jail took away the life of Rattu Marandi on 14th January 1944. The same day saw the death of another freedom fighter from Rakshi Chand Hansda. Rattu Marandi had no son. His brother's name was Bhairav Marandi.

34. **Marandi Sundar:-** Sundar Marandi S/o Barandi Marandi was the resident of the village Sarsaria five miles west to Dumka near Maharo. He participated in Quit India Movement. Actually he worked in Babu Ramjeevan Himmatsingka's transport office. In the evening he was on the way back to home that he was sighted by the British force and they fired on Sundar Marandi near the village Belapur. He was griviously injured and died after a while. His son's name also was Barandi Marandi. He left behind him awidow and amny children.

35. **Modi Vidyacharan:-** Vidyacharan Modi was born in the year 1917. He was the son of Raghunath Modi and resident of Maliyahiladih under P. S. Sarwan in Deoghar subdistrict Modi entered into the Congress in 1930 and took part in Civil Disobedience and Quit India Movement. For this he was jailed four to five times. Taking active part in Quit India Movemnt he captured the Sarawan Police station and hoisted national flag there. He was arrested in this connection and sent to the Deoghar jail, where he died of ill-health caused due to mismanagement and inhuman treatment in 1943.

36. **Mohli Lakhiram:-** Lakhiram Mohli, S/o Faudi Ram Mohli was the native of the village Patra. He participated in the Quit India Movement and was arrested and sent to the Dumka jail when he died a premature death at the age of 35 leaving a son of 10 years and the widow Mrs. Neelmani Mohli behind.

37. **Murmu Baju:-** Baju Murmu was the resident of the village Dumaria. He took active part in the Quit India Movement

and evaded arrest for a long time. But on May 1943 he was arrested and sent to the Bhagalpur Central Jail, where he died in prison.

38. **Murmu Haridas:-** Haridas Murmu the resident of karikadar under the Amarpur circle under P. S. Ramgarth took very active part in Quit Movement he was arrested and convicted for five years rigorous imprisonment in connection with the "Lathi Pahar" Struggle. He was sent to the Buxar Jail, where suffering Police torture and atrocities, he died at the age of 35.

39. **Murmu Jhupru**:- Jhupru Murmu S/o Gopal Murmu was the resident of Damakar under Bokrobandh Damin Bunglow in Godda subdivision was arrested for his activities in the Quit India Movement. He was arrested and kept in the Godda Jail, where he caught somatic infection due to the inhuman condition and lack of basic requirements in the jail and consequently he died on 25th November 1943. When he died, he was barely of 32. When Jupru was in prison, his wife left his house out of poverty and went to Assam to work in tea garden leaving a minor daughter who was taken care of by the brother in law.

40. **Murmu Mangal:-** Mangal Murmu was born at the village Narayanpur situated near the hilly village Lathi Pahar, where famous struggle look place. Mangal was arrested for his activities in the Quit India Movement in the jail. He died shortly after he reached his home after release. He left behind a minor son Pradhan Murmu.

41. **Murmu Mangal:-** Mangal Murmu was the resident of Karmatand under the Massanjore Circle under Dumka subdivision. He took active part in picketing at Rajbandh-Palasi in course of the Quit India Movement Mangal Murmu was heavily injured in Police firing on the way to jail after arrest he died in the way to Dumka jail.

42. **Murmu Mohan:-** Mohan Murmu S/o Karan Murmu was the resident of Lakhanpur. At the age of 30 years, he was arrested in course of Quit India Movement in which participated actively. He was arrested hin May 1943. He died in Rajmahal jail due to Police excesses. The Parganaites with the help of Damin police looted his houses and tortured his family so much so that his family members fled from their native village only to return after years. Mohan Murmu left behind him a widow Ramni Hansda and two children Kayan and Suraj.

43. **Murmu Narayan:-** Narayan Murmu S/o Binod Murmu was the resident of Dumaria a village 12 miles away from Barharwa. He was arrested along with his brother Lakhi Ram Murmu on 9 May 1943 after the arrest, Narayan Murmu was convicted and sent to the Bhagalpur Central Jail where he died of cholera on 18 February 1944. The Police and Parganates looted his belongings worth thousands. The family became extremely poor after the Police loot.

44. **Murmu Nuna :-** Murmu Nuna S/o Sri Lal Murmu was the resident of Mahubana under P. S. - Jarmundi of Dumka subdivision. He took active part in " Lathi Pahar " struggle. He was arrested and convicted for a term of five years rigorous imprisonment. Due to excessive bad condition in the Dumka jail and police atrocity; He fell ill and died in Prison on 16 March 1944.

45. **Murmu Pandu:-** Pandu Murmu S/o Ani Murmu was the resident of Kashidih took very active part in the "Lathi Pahar". He was arrested and sent to the Buxar jail when he died in prison due to Police excesses. He died at the youg age of 30. Leaving behind an orphan daughter named Shani Murmu who used to live with her maternal uncle.

46. **Murmu Shiru:-** Shiru Murmu S/o Baro Murmu was the resident of the village Ramkhari, P. o- Kumrabad, P. S- Ranga Masalia. He was arrested and convicted for aterm of one year's rigorous imprision for Picketing and burning liqor shops. He

died in custody in Dumka jail due to police torture resulting in deteriortation of health.

47. **Murmu Dheba:-** Dheba Murmu of Kashidih, Fulopani was arrested in course of the Quit India Movement along with his father Khel Murmu and brother Churu Murmu. Though Churu Murmu was released but Dheba Murmu died in captivity due to police torture. He died on 2 August 1943 leaving behind a minor son named Mangal Murmu when Dhoba died he was only 25 years old.

48. **Mandal Kalanand:-** Kalanand Mandal who belonged to the village Dande, Kalanand Mandal was Khadi loving and attracted to congress. On the fateful day 11th August, 1942 he fell a prey to military firing and died after a couple of days.

49. **MirdhaineViraji:-** Viraji Mirdhaine, d/o Phulchand Mirdha was born of Behanga under P. S- Sarwan. She was married to Saudagar Mirdha S/o Harihar Mirdha of Ghormara. The freedom activists were breaking the bridge near Ghormara. The British force came and fired on Viraji Mirdhaine, who was quite ignorant of the things. She was simply a house wife. She died on the spot.

50. **Pahariya Badal Singh:-** Badal Singh Pahariya, S/o Bisan Pahariya resident of the village Paharpur under Bokrabandh Bunglow got himself recruited to the team of freedom fighters of Quit India Movement. Prafulla Chandra Patnaik refused to recruit him into the team for he was the only son of his widow mother Meghi Paharin, but was too much stubborn and he became a part of the team. He actively took part in the struggle of Quit India Movement and was arrested and sent to Godda jail, where he died in captaivity.

51. **Pahariya Doman:-** Doman Pahariya the resident of Sindrijola village under Bookrabandh Damin Bunglow of Godda subdivision fought bravely and was jailed for his

activities in Quit India Movement. After the release from the Godda jail his lands were occupied and he was tortured by the Parganaites. One day he was found killed beneath the tree shade.

52. **Pahariya Doman (Bara):-** Bara Doman Pahariya S/o Haria Pahariya was the resident of Telipara under the Bokrabandh Bunglow of Godda subdivision. He belonged to the Kumrabhag Pahariya tribe. He was arrested and convicted for a term of four year's rigorous imprisonment for burning liquor shops and breaking the bridge. He was kept in the Dumka jail where after a Prolonged illness he died in prison leaving behind him a widow wife and four children. His eledest son is Sonia Pahariya. The economy of his family was very poor.

53. **Pahariya Dharma (Chhota):- Chhota** Dharma Pahariya S/o Kalaya Pahariya was the native of Goradih Chapribhita village under the Bokrabandh Damin Banglo under Godda subdivision. He was arrested for his active participation in Quit India Movement and sent to Dumka jail where he died in prison. The atrocity and inhuman treatment by the Police took away his life. He left behind him the only loving daughter, who lived with her uncle after her father's death.

54. **Pahariya Ganga Singh:-** Ganga Singh Pahariya S/o Sharma Paharia was the resident of the village Deopahar under the Borio Bunglow. He was a brave fighter of the Quit India Movement. He was arrested and sent to Rajmahal jail, where prisioners were kept like cattles much beyond the capacity of jail. He seriously fell ill due to Police atrocities inside the jail. After repeated request of the Congress leader the Dy. Commissioner W. G. Archer initially passed the comment 'let' the dogs die'. But later he ordered his release from the jail. After 36 hours of release from the jail Ganga Singh Paharia died.

55. **Pathak Sahdeo:-** Sahdeo Pathak S/o Suryanarayan Pahak was the native of Badia near Jasidih under Deoghar subdivision. He was born in a Brahmin family in 1921. Despite the poor economic condition of the family he jumped into the Quit India Movement in 1942. He was arrested and convicted for three years rigorous imprisonment. He was kept at Bhagalpur Central Jail, where he died unmarried at the age of 24.

56. **Ray Bideshi:-** Bideshi Ray S/o Bihari Ray was the resident of the village Pandua under the Siltha circle under P. S. Ramgarh. A warrant was issued by the police against the elder brother of Biheshi Ray whose name was Shukdeo Ray but Bideshi Ray surrendered to Police as Shukdeo Ray. Bideshi Ray was conviceted for five years rigorous imprisonment and sent to Dumka jail where he breathed his last on 25 June 1943.

57. **Raut Ayodhya:-** Ayodhya Raut S/o Yadu Raut was the resident of the village Rohini under Deoghar subdivision was caught on suspicion by the police. Jitan Raut of the same village was arrested along with him. Ayodhya was sent to Dumka jail as under trial prisoner where he died on 25th May 1943 at the age of 16 years.

58. **Raut Najju:-** Najju Raut S/o Fauji Raut was the native of Chakrama village under P. S. Mohanpur under Deoghar subdivision Najju Raut was born in 1904. He started taking part in the movement since 1938. He was arrested in September 1942 along with his friends. He was sent to Dumka jail as an under trial prisoner. He suffered from dysentery. Though requests were made to the concerned jail authorities for treatment, but it went unheeded resulting in Najju's death.

59. **Ray Vidhu Bhushan:-** Vidhu Bhushan Ray the resident of the village Amarpur near Jasidih under Deoghar subdivision was arrested during the Quit India Movement for keeping arms, when the police torched his house at Amarpur, Vidhu

Bhushan Ray was not at home but after the lapse of eight months, he was arrested and sent to Deoghar jail. He died of illness, shortly after his release from the jail.

60. **Singh Madhav:-** Madhav Singh S/o Kato Singh was the resident of Mahtodih, a small village situated on the side of Deoghar- Sarath road. He was arrested for his active involvement in the Sarwan grain godown loot during the Quit India Movement. He was kept as an undertrial prisioner and later shifted to Dumka jail, where he died on 17 March 1943 at the age of 44. the Police looted his house giving immense economic losses to his family.

61. **Soren Durga:-** Durga Soren was born in a Santal Family at the village Mangalgarh, also known as Bhagra under the Boarijore Bunglow. Durga Soren was known in his area famously as Dugga Baba. He got himself recruited to the team of Prafulla Chandra Patnaik in the age of 65. He died fighting at the village Rakshi, which is situated near Barhet. He left behind him seven sons.

62. **Soren Chaitanya:-** Chaitanya Soren S/o Dubai Soren was the native of the village Talbari under Durgapur Damin Bunglow. His active Participation in Quit India Movement brought him into the Bhagalpur Central Jail. He fell seriously ill of police excesses inside the jail. He died shorty after release from the jail.

63. **Soren Durga:-** Durga Soren S/o Sundar Soren was born at Mahgalgarh. He was very active in Quit India Movement. He was killed in action during a clash with police at the village Rakshi, when picketing was going on. He died on the spot in the police firing on 6th Novemeber, 1942.

64. **Soren Ragda :-** Ragda Soren S/o Kail Soren was born at Virdaban village under the Damin bungalow near Tin Pahar station. He belonged to Safa Hor. He was asked to preach Gandhian views in the far flung areas. He was arrested during the Quit India Movement and sent to Rajmahal Jail where he

was kept as an under trial prisoner for a long time. He died in the Rajmahal jail, which actually had turned into the death cell at the age of 30 years.

65. **Soren Lakhan:-** Lakhan Soren resident Bhagwanpur village under the Telo Damin Bunglow. He participated actively in Quit India Movement. He was arrested by the Christian Parganate and convicted for imprisonment to Godda jail where he died in a mysterious condition. Even the news of his death was not informed to anyone. He left behind him the widow wife. Baraki Murmu and three sons namely. Son Soren, Mangal Soren and Jeso Soren.

66. **Soren Manjhi:- Manjhi** Soren S/o Man Singh Soren was the resident of Shingatarh village. Manjhi Participated actively in the Quit India Movement in the Damin area. He was a staunch Safa Hor and a very religious person. He was rewarded with arrest and being sent to Rajmahal jail, where he died due to the inexpressible bad conditions in the jail. He left a widow wife, a son and a niece.

67. **Soren Nuna:-** Nuna Soren S/o Arjun Soren was the resident of son the village Latvidha under Rajbandha area under Shikaripara block. He was arrested for burning liquor shops at Asanbani and convicted for two and half year rigorous imprisonment. He was sent to Bhagalpur jail, where he died in Novemeber 1943. He left behind his two daughters. Nuna Soren was the guru of Safa Hor of his area.

68. **Soren Shiva:-** Shiva Soren S/o Jolha Soren was the native of the village Talba under P. S. - Pakuria under Pakur subdivision. He jumped into the Quit India Movement at the age of 65. He was arrested in December 1942 for burning liquor shops at Pakuria. He was convicted for six months imprisonment 8 March 1943 and sent to Patna Camp Jail, where he died on 5 April 1943. His son Munshi Soren was the member of District Congress Working Committee.

69. **Soren Somay:-** Somay Soren S/o Haddi Soren was the resident of the village Kathaldih under Bokrabandh Bunglow Somay was a Santal. He worked in Congress in the Quit India Movement and was Jailed. He died in the Dumka Jail on 19 May 1943 at the age of 45. His father Haddi Soren was a teacher of a night school (Ratri Pathshala).

70. **Tudu Baijnath**:- Baijnath Tudu S/o Dharma Tudu was the resident the village Dumaria. His house was looted by the Police due to which his family became very poor. Baijnath took active part in the freedom struggle during the Quit India Movement. he wås arrested and sent to the infamous Rajmahal Jail. Where he died of Cholora.

71. **Tudu Baiman:-** Baiman Tudu S/o Haridas Tudu was the resident of the vIllage Bisariyam under Dhanwasa circle under P. S. Shikaripara. he died in the Police firing at Rajbandh Palasi during the Picketing on 5 September, 1942. Where he died he was of 50. He left behind him three unmarried daughters, two sons and a widow wife.

72. **Tudu Churka:-** Churka Tudu, the native the Tudu Murga tola of the village Asanbani was an old worker of the Congress his hand was broken by a liquor seller by wielding canes on him, while he was staging a sit-in-demonstration before the shop. He later joined the Forward Bloc and jumped into the August revolution of 1942. He was convicted for four years imprisonment and sent to Dumka jail, where died due to the prevailing bad conditions and adminstration's apathy on 15th February 1943.

73. **Tudu Gurma:-** Gurma Tudu S/o Chhotka Tudu was the resident Shikaripara. He died on spot in a Police firing at Rajbandh Palasi during picketing carried out by Congress activists. He died at the age of 50. He left behind him a widow wife, three sons and a daughter.

74. **Tudu Luthu:-** Luthu Tudu S/o Mangal Tudu was born at the village Amro. He was convicted for five years rigorous Punishment and kept in the Dumka Jail. He was killed in the Dumka jail and his dead body was disposed off without any information to her inmates. He was single. When he died his parents were alive.

75. **Tudu Ragda:-** Ragda Tudu S/o Kavale Tudu was the resident at the village Virajpur under Durgapur Damin Bunglow. He was a safaHor. He was arrested and convicted for rigorous imprisonment, where he died due to police torture and atrocity.

76. **Tudu Shyam:-** Shyam Tudu S/o Baso Tudu was the resident of the village Bisanpur under Alubera Bunglow near Amrapara of Pakar subdivision. He was arrested along with his friends Gande Mal Paharia, Babulal Maraiya and Kartik Grihi for burning the Alubera Bunglow. He was convicted on 15th march 1943 for a term of three years imprisonment and a fine of Rs. 50/-. His house was seized by police for auction for not submitting the fine. He was sent to Patna Camp jail where he died in prison.

77. **Tudu Chandray:-** Chandray Tudu S/o Kanan Tudu was the resident of the village Pipra under Telo Bunglow. Chandray started working for congress since 1936. Later he joined the Forward Bloc. He was jailed for refusing to pay revenues to Government officials. He was sent to the Bhagalpur Central Jail when he died leaving behind him an aged mother, a widow wife and three sons. His eldest son's name was Barun Tudu aged 12 years.

Note- The list is not exhaustive. Many persons may have died fighting the British colonial rule and have passed into oblivion but they could not be specified.